love & Classics

Grace
Livingston Hill

COLLECTION NO. 4

FOUR COMPLETE NOVELS

Including a novel by Isabella Alden,
aunt to Grace Livingston Hill

Grace Livingston Hill Collection #4

Grace Livingston Hill (1865–1947) remains popular more than fifty years after her death. She wrote dozens of books that carry her unique style for combining Christian faith with tasteful and exciting romance.

Isabella Alden (1841–1930), an aunt of Grace Livingston Hill, was a gifted storyteller and prolific author as well, often using her writing to teach lessons espoused by her husband, Gustavus R. Alden, a minister. She also helped her niece Grace get started in her career as a bestselling inspirational novelist.

The Finding of Jasper Holt, Grace Livingston Hill

A train ride West ends in disaster when the train crashes on a bridge. Jean Grayson, a passenger is rescued by Jasper Holt and brought to Hawk Valley. But the townspeople regard Jasper as a renegade and warn Jean about him. Should she heed their warning or follow her heart, which tells her Jasper Holt is a very different sort of man?

The Mystery of Mary, Grace Livingston Hill

After disembarking from a train, Tryon Dunham makes the short walk to a line of waiting cabs near the station. In the darkness a young woman pleads for his help. Tryon suddenly finds his life intertwined with the life of the girl, who is called simply "Mary." But who is she, and what does she have to do with the ominous newspaper stories?

Phoebe Deane, Grace Livingston Hill

Forced to live as a poor relation with her half brother and his sharp-tongued wife, Phoebe Deane passes the lonely years through hard work and occasional walks in the country. A chance encounter brings her into acquaintance with Nathaniel Graham, a young man training to be a lawyer in New York. He opens up the fascinating world of current events and intellectual pursuits to Phoebe and, through his kindness, wins a place in her heart. But a neighboring farmer, Hiram Green, has set his eye on Phoebe and won't take no for an answer. Part 2 of the *Miranda* trilogy.

Diverse Women, Isabella Alden with Mrs. C. M. Livingston

Isabella Alden and her sister Marcia, mother of Grace Livingston Hill, teamed up to write this collection of short stories. The authors introduce us to such different women as a pastor's wife who disdains her husband's role and leaves him when he makes commands; a young bride who discovers another way to make buckwheat cakes besides the way her mother made them; a young woman with enough faith to start a new home; and a newly widowed mother who must move from one of her adult children's home to the next, until she at last finds peace.

Grace Livingston Hill

COLLECTION NO. 4

FOUR COMPLETE NOVELS
Updated for today's reader

BARBOUR
PUBLISHING, INC.
Uhrichsville, Ohio

Edited and updated for today's reader by Deborah Cole and Angela Kiesling.

© MCMXCIX by R. L. Munce Publishing Co., Inc.

ISBN 1-57748-508-4

Published by Barbour Publishing, Inc., P.O. Box 719, Uhrichsville, Ohio 44683
http://www.barbourbooks.com

 Member of the
Evangelical Christian
Publishers Association

Printed in the United States of America

The Finding
of Jasper Holt

Chapter 1

S lowly the train rumbled out of the station, gathering speed with every moment and leaving behind the friendly faces on the platform.

The girl who had just entered the car looked in dismay at the rough-looking crowd that surrounded her. It was the last long stretch of her journey now, out on the plains and across the desert, and the porter of the sleeper car had refused to let her enter the Pullman coach without a Pullman ticket. Of course it would be all right when the conductor came, but suppose her brother-in-law forgot to telegraph for the reservation and she should have to spend the night in this car?

She slipped into the only vacant seat and sat anxiously awaiting the conductor, who was nowhere in sight.

For the most part the people about her were rough, stolid-looking men with hard, brown faces. Here and there a woman huddled wearily into a corner of a seat, trying to sleep. Nearly all of them were commonplace folk, and their very ordinariness brought her some measure of assurance. Yet she shuddered at the thought of spending her night huddled in a seat like the other women, with all those men free to gaze on her as she slept.

She glanced across the aisle where the seat was turned over and two men faced each other, an old man and a young one. The old man sat just across from her, his coarse, stubbly face turned boldly toward her. He had crafty little eyes that intruded with their merest glance and a repulsive atmosphere of cunning that made his face seem utterly evil. She shrank further into her seat and looked about to see if there might not be another vacant seat where she would be out of his range.

Her eyes suddenly met the eyes of his companion, who faced her—the young man in the turned-over seat—and she wondered how she could have failed to notice him before. Something about his face gave her confidence in him at once. Perhaps it was the splendid gray eyes that gazed at her so respectfully, or the firm chin and almost stern lines of the handsome lip and brow. She saw a strength and beauty in his face such as one seldom sees blended in a man, which marked him at once as being different from others. There was nothing weak or womanish about him, in spite of his perfect features. The fine golden-brown hair that rippled back from his forehead like a halo gave the impression of curling out of mischief rather than from the owner's wish.

He was tall and lean and wiry yet seemed to possess great strength and fine training. If it hadn't been for an abnormal gravity about his mouth, she would have judged him to be a mere boy. But he had an air of maturity that puzzled her.

His gray eyes met hers kindly, as if he knew her anxious thoughts and wanted to let her know she was safe, that he would see that she was safe. With an almost startled feeling she met his eyes a second time, as if to be sure she hadn't been mistaken, and then settled back into her seat, somehow comforted. Almost immediately his eyes had withdrawn from her face as if he would not intrude. He was looking now at the dreadful old man, silently rebuking him for his interest in her. The old man wriggled around uneasily in his seat and turned his eyes away to look out the window, the hate in his face getting the uppermost as he cast a furtive glance at the younger man and then turned back to the window.

They were a curious pair; the younger man appeared to be the keeper of the older one. The girl wondered how they came to be traveling together; they seemed so alien to each other. It was obvious the younger man had some power over the other, and this fact gave the girl comfort.

To these two men the entrance of the lovely girl into the monotony of the journey was a refreshment. Even the old man, Scathlin, whose low type of life received only fleshly impressions and who had grown up from his tainted babyhood without honor for any woman, felt the fineness of her nature, the rareness of her modest beauty as she came near.

To Jasper Holt she was the startling revelation of some pure dream of his childhood, the reality of which he had come to doubt. His knowledge of the world told him that probably she was frail and human and selfish like all the rest if one came to know her. But for the sake of what she seemed to be he was glad of the vision and would protect her at all costs because she was a woman and ought to be perfect.

Nevertheless, as he looked again at the profile turned now toward her window and studied the sweet outline of the firm chin and pleasant lips, the gentle contour of cheek and lash and brow, the luminous eyes that were glowing at the stain of sunset against the gloomy gray of the sky, he could only feel that here was something different. It was something he had been hoping and searching for all his life, but never finding.

She was slight and exquisitely fashioned, dressed in a simple dark blue material. Sheer white rolled-back collar and cuffs set off the white throat and the small gloved hands; the dark blue hat with its graceful tilt and simple garnishing seemed the loveliest setting for the beautiful face framed in soft dark hair. Her face was pure, free from self-consciousness and pride; yet she looked as if she knew her own mind and could stand like a rock for a principle. There was also a determined uplift to her chin that showed a spirit of her own and a fleeting dimple that promised a merry appreciation of humor if one knew her well enough. The whole dainty person was good to look upon, and Holt kept the vision within his consciousness while he covered Scathlin with his gaze.

He loathed his task of watching Scathlin, and somehow the sight of the girl had made it even more distasteful. For almost two weeks now he had been at it, day and night. He had not let the man out of his sight for one moment since he had found him in Pittsburgh two days after the theft of his wallet containing valuable papers, land grants, water rights and other documents relating to his silver mines.

Holt had suspected the old man at once when the wallet was missing, partly because Scathlin had been seen twice in conversation with Harrington, who was Holt's sworn enemy. Harrington was doing all he could to ruin his prospects and dispute his rights to the water power which made working his mines possible. He also suspected Scathlin because he had dismissed the man from his employment only a few days prior to the wallet's disappearance.

He had trailed Scathlin to Pittsburgh, where he found him in the station restaurant eating a comfortable breakfast. The old rascal turned white under his tan and stubble and dropped his knife and fork loudly on the marble of the counter at the appearance of his former employer. But the cunning in his face had come at once to the front, and he welcomed Holt as if it were the most pleasant thing in the world to see him.

It was Holt's way not to settle the matter right then by turning the old man over to the police on suspicion, but rather to attach himself to Scathlin and find out exactly where those papers were—and who had paid him to steal the wallet. He was wary enough to know that Scathlin might have already disposed of the wallet, and he wished if possible to find out what he'd done with the papers and make him produce them or tell their whereabouts.

Harrington was superintendent of large mine interests in Hawk Valley, located near Holt's veins of silver and owned by an Eastern syndicate. Holt knew that capital and cunning might do a great deal to cripple his interests if they once got him in their power. Therefore he had shadowed Scathlin day and night all these days. On pretense of wanting company for a pleasure trip, he had gone wherever Scathlin professed to be going, giving him no opportunity even to telegraph any of the other conspirators for money or instructions. He watched him every waking second.

It hadn't been a pleasant task. Scathlin was a foul-mouthed, foul-souled companion for any man, and his personal habits were anything but attractive. Time and again Holt had almost turned from his task with disgust, resolved to let his rights go rather than be tied to the creature another hour. Yet he had stuck to him. And now, after these many days of cunning and craftiness, of repeated attempts by Scathlin to escape, the old man had come to the end of his money and his wits and was compelled to accept the escort and financial aid of Holt back to the place from which he had started. He dared not do anything else. This he did both on his own account and for the sake of his employers, who would not hesitate to leave him in the lurch to save themselves and who had warned him above all things not to let Holt suspect his mission with those papers to the Eastern syndicate.

Besides, there was always the hope that he might yet escape and make his way back in time to present those papers to the man Harrington said would pay him a big reward for bringing them. Harrington and his men couldn't have done it without suspicion, but the plan was that Scathlin should profess to have found something valuable to the syndicate and be willing to sell it at a good price.

It was no wonder Scathlin's eyes had a hunted look, and his face under its stubby growth was almost pitifully desperate as he looked at the young girl's fresh face. For the moment he forgot his misery, gloating over her beauty, while Holt seemed to be engaged with the sunset view. But Holt caught the gleam in his victim's eye, and his heart burned hotly within him. He could have crushed him like vermin and felt no remorse. All the man in him roused to resent the evil look.

"Scathlin!" His tone was cutting with command, and the old man turned cringing and met the steely glance of his captor. Then, impatient and trembling with anger, he looked out the window, the crimson wrath surging up his leathery neck.

The girl, half aware of what had been going on, turned and took it all in. Her eyes, growing large with horror, met Holt's gaze, saw it change and soften reassuringly, as if he were holding at bay a loathsome bloodhound and wished her to understand she need not fear. The girl, with one fleeting look of gratitude toward the young man, turned back again to her window as if nothing had happened. In fact, no onlooker would have suspected that anything at all had happened, and yet really a little drama had been enacted, and all the actors understood it as thoroughly as if it had been spoken.

The dusk dropped down, and the train sped on over the plains.

And now the sunset stains grew deeper and blended into gold and crimson and lifted the gray into clear opal spaces of luminous beauty, spreading the panoply of color far along the horizon of the plain. It was a thing to make one look in awe. Something of its calm and strength crept into the girl's expression as she watched it, and once she turned to see if Holt was watching too. But he was sitting facing the other way and could see only the fading trails of glory in the sky as it sped away from his gaze, though he had caught the reflection of wonder from her face and averted his own eyes as if from too holy a sight.

Scathlin was not enjoying the view. He was looking furtively on every side to see if there could be a good place where he might risk throwing out that cursed wallet and hope ever to find it again. If only there would be a station— or he could risk dropping it out the window near some water tank or something. But the plain slid by, a level monotony, broken only by the colors of the setting sun.

Scathlin grew more and more desperate. They were nearing Hawk Valley. The morning would bring them within range of Holt's men—that band of trained outlaws who were as relentless in their justice as they were careless of their lives. No mercy was to be expected from their hands if he fell among them. He shivered as the shaft of a tall bare tree, dead and stark, stood out in the distance against the clear gold of the sunset line. It was on such a tree he had seen a cattle thief hang as he rode by once just at nightfall. It might easily be his fate before another sunset. If he could not get away in the night, all chance of escape before they reached Hawk Valley was gone, for he knew Jasper Holt's men were set at intervals along the way, sentinels ready to head him off. And what treatment could he expect from either Jasper Holt or his men with that incriminating wallet in his pocket?

He had been a fool to take up with Harrington's offer. Money or no money, it wasn't worth the risk. He was getting to be an old man and not so ready to face death as when his blood was hot and his hand steady. He didn't even have any weapons of defense, thanks to his grim captor, who had disarmed him while he slept on the first night of their journey together. There had never been any open recognition of the fact between them, save that one glance as Scathlin put his hand to the pocket where it had been and was not. Holt's clear gray eyes had met his unflinchingly in acknowledgment. That had been all, but Scathlin knew then that he could only to evade Holt and get away if possible. He would stand no chance in an open conflict, and his captor was untiringly vigilant.

He glanced again at the stern face opposite him, wondering what would be the fate to which he was surely hastening. State prison? Or would they take the law into their own hands? He knew what that might mean only too well. How he would like to spring at that slim brown throat opposite him and throttle the life from the young fellow. Only a kid, and yet he had withstood many and had power to crush Scathlin in spite of all his boasted cunning. The look of a serpent crept into the old man's gleaming eyes as he noticed the quick glance his companion cast at the girl across the aisle; his own eyes followed, filled with hate. Yes, he would like to drive his fingers into the girl's white throat before the eyes of her gallant defender if only he had Holt helpless! But instead, here he was, helpless himself. He must find a way to escape before morning or else get rid of the wallet in some safe way. Surely Holt would be off his guard sometimes for a little space. He had scarcely slept a wink in four days; how could he endure it much longer?

Scathlin's cogitations were cut short by the entrance of the conductor at last, and he turned to watch the girl as she spoke to him.

"I was to have a section reserved for me," she said. "My brother-in-law, Mr. James Harrington of Hawk Valley, arranged for it and telegraphed me that it was all right. See—I have the telegram. But the porter said I must come in here until I saw you because I had no ticket for the Pullman."

She held out the yellow envelope, and the conductor looked at it.

"Your brother's name is Harrington? You're going to Hawk Valley?" He looked at her sharply. "Just wait a few minutes till I go through the next car, and then I'll see to it. It ought to be all right."

He bustled on his way, and the girl sat back again to wait.

At the name "Harrington" Scathlin had turned with a start and looked toward the girl; but even in the act he caught the narrow gleam of Holt's half-closed eyes and, remembering, turned back again to his window while his thoughts went pounding into new channels. He had made a mistake, of course, to let Holt see that he had heard, so he kept his eyes toward the window until it grew quite dark. But he had a plan at last. In another minute he stood to his feet, yawning, and declared his intention of getting a drink of water from the cooler at the other end of the car.

"Good idea!" said Holt, rising and following his captive down the aisle lazily.

Scathlin reached for the cooler first and took his drink, while Holt stood waiting for the cup and let Scathlin go back to his seat alone, apparently not noticing him. Scathlin settled back in his seat with one eye on Holt and the other on the girl.

Holt stood drinking in a leisurely way, apparently interested in looking through the glass of the door into the next car though he was fully aware that Scathlin was fumbling in the inner pocket of his flannel shirt. He lingered, hoping the old man would do something which would make him more certain of what he already suspected, and saw Scathlin finally draw forth a small dark object that looked like his own leather wallet. Anxious to see what Scathlin's next move would be, he remained standing, still apparently looking through the car door, though not a move of Scathlin's was lost on him.

To his amazement he suddenly saw Scathlin bend forward and pick up something from the car floor, then lean toward the girl in the opposite seat and put the object in her lap as he spoke to her. Had the man picked up something the girl had dropped, or was he—? Preposterous! The fellow wouldn't dare, with a strange girl. She smiled and looked down at the thing in her lap and seemed to be thanking him. She had probably dropped her handkerchief or pocketbook, and Scathlin had picked it up. Holt sauntered back to his seat and found Scathlin fumbling with his shoelace. He studied him narrowly and fancied he detected a look of cunning satisfaction on the stubbly old face, yet he was puzzled to know what caused it. Had the scoundrel dared to give those papers to the girl when he stood in full view? If he had, Holt's hands were pretty well tied and he had two to watch instead of one. He didn't like the idea of shadowing this beautiful young woman.

The conductor returned and spoke to the girl.

"Well, your berth's reserved for you all right, but it was in the name of Harrington. It's section seven in the next car. This your baggage? Come this way, and I'll show you."

The girl followed the conductor with a hesitating glance toward Scathlin, who was engaged with his shoe. Holt noticed she held her handbag clasped tightly. When she was gone, the night settled down unpleasantly about them and Scathlin, apparently worn out, snored as he hadn't dared to do for a week. But Holt sat up and studied his problem. He couldn't afford to take any chances on sleep that night; moreover, his heart was in a tumult. This girl was coming to Hawk Valley to visit the Harringtons. She was a sister of Mrs. Harrington, the handsomest and most influential woman in the valley. Would he ever see the girl? Sometimes, from afar perhaps—and a bitter look swept over his face.

Scathlin slept on, his coarse lower jaw dropped down and all his unpleasant features relaxed. Holt noticed there was no longer that furtive grasp of one hand upon his breast which had been since their journey began. Scathlin's hands were lying idly by his side, and the old man was enjoying a well-earned rest, his heavily shod feet sprawled out under Holt's seat.

The night droned on; the train sped on its way through the darkness, and still Holt sat wide awake and thinking.

Chapter 2

Jean Grayson followed the conductor into the sleeper with a sense of deep relief. She had been frightened since the rough old creature across the aisle landed a worn-looking wallet in her lap and asked if he hadn't heard her say she was going to Mr. Harrington at Hawk Valley. And would she be so good as to give that case of important papers to him and not let anyone else know she had it?

She accepted the trust because she didn't know what else to do; after all, it seemed a simple enough request. The man had explained that he had to go off in another direction at the next stop and could not deliver the goods himself, and it was most important that it get to her brother-in-law at once. There didn't seem to be any good reason why she should refuse, and yet it had frightened her. She didn't know what to do with the dirty wallet. She hated to put it in her new handbag, and she restrained from a shrinking sniff as she hastily put it out of sight.

She had sat looking out of the darkened window with her heart in a tumult as the tall young man with the fine eyes came back to his seat. What had he to do with the old fellow? Could he be his son? No, never! But did he know about the important papers? Could he have put the old man up to giving them to her so that, under some pretense or other, he himself might speak to her? She dared not look his way lest he should presume upon the old man's speaking.

Yet, when she arose to follow the conductor and gave one swift glance toward the opposite seat, she saw a respectful pair of gray eyes looking at her, with nothing presumptuous in them, and she instantly felt there was no need to fear the young man. He might be dressed like a cowboy, but he had eyes like a gentleman.

Jean was tired, for she had come on a long journey, stopping a day on the way with relatives who had taken her sightseeing and kept her going every minute. She was glad to creep into her berth as soon as the porter had made it up.

After some hesitation she took the leather case out of her handbag and wrapped it in a leaf from a magazine she had brought with her. She couldn't bear to have the thing in with all her nice fresh handkerchiefs and dainty little articles. She had an impulse to throw it away or lose it; and then her conscience reproached her loudly for so dishonorable a thought. The papers might be valuable, of course, and in that case her brother-in-law would have just cause to blame her if she didn't bring them.

As she settled herself to sleep and drew around her the folds of the silk Pullman robe that had been her mother's parting surprise, loving thoughts of those she had left behind filled her mind. All the tender words, looks and acts of loving sacrifice came flocking to be recognized, until unbidden tears filled her eyes. The silken robe was an extravagance, she knew, and would be paid for by many a denial on the part of her father and mother, but it represented their great love for her. A thought of what they would have felt about her being accosted by that rough man and asked to carry that package for him troubled her. Yet what else could she do but accept it?

Her father? Yes, her father would undoubtedly approve of her taking the package. Her father was one who never thought of himself when anything in the shape of duty demanded attention, and he had brought her up with the same feeling. Anyway, now that she had taken it and agreed to deliver it, she could only keep her word, and it was, after all, quite reasonable. Why should it bother her so?

Nevertheless, it mingled with her dreaming thoughts as she drifted off to sleep, and a kind of assurance regarding it came as she remembered the steady, clear eyes of the younger man. The monotonous hum of the rushing train only lulled her into deeper slumber.

Suddenly, there came a grinding, grating shriek as of strong metal hard pressed and about to give way. A crash, a jolt, then terrible confusion. The very foundations of the earth seemed shaken, with the cars climbing through the air then pitching, writhing, tossing and at last settling uncertainly in strange positions, while the night was filled with horrid sounds too varied to analyze. Cries of women and children. Groans of men in agony. Breaking glass and splintering timbers. Rending of metal in discordant clang. And below, rising menacingly, came the crackle of fire that knows its opportunity and power; the desperate clamor of those who have discovered it; and the mad, brave shouts of those who would attempt to conquer it.

Jean Grayson awoke in bewilderment. For a moment the noise seemed a part of her dream; her strange, huddled position on the wood at the foot of her berth, a figment of her imagination. But almost at once the cold breath from the broken window brought her to her senses. An accident! It had come then! The thing her mother had feared and tried to provide against. She was in a railroad accident all alone and out in the wilds of the West! It was characteristic of Jean that, when she realized her plight, she thought first of how her mother would take the news and not of how she herself would bear the experience or whether it meant life or death to her. That she must get out of danger and let her mother know of her safety was her instant impulse, and from that moment her senses were on the alert for every detail.

Her mother's horror of railroad accidents made the possibilities of her present position as plain to her as if she had lived the whole experience before. She seemed to comprehend in a flash just what had happened and the position the car was in at the time. The flickering glare outside showed jagged glass in the window frame and scattered gleaming fragments all about her. She must move carefully not to be cut by them. Fire! That was the next thing she took in. That meant that her only hope of life was to get out at once.

Cautiously she looked out the window to get a better idea of things, and her heart stood still with the horror of it all. For one terrible second she forgot her mother's fears and felt her own choking terror at what was before her. Then her courage rose and steadied her nerves. She resolved not to die if there were any possible way out of it, and terror relaxed its hold upon her at sight of her courage.

With determination she held her eyes to take in the situation in detail. She must know everything, see everything, if she were to save herself, for she comprehended readily enough that as things were it was every person for himself. No one was going to risk his life to hunt her up and drag her forth from the pile of cars.

The train had been crossing a river when the crash came. There was water down below, black and terrifying in the glare of flame that leaped like a great tongue among the ruins just ahead. She couldn't tell if the cause of the accident had been a broken bridge and knew little about such things to judge. The cars were piled one upon another in wild confusion, and the Pullman in which she rode was standing on its forward end almost upright. The engine was overturned, and fire crept upward and threatened the whole mass. Below, the great black stretch of water reflected the sight, making doubly terrible every feature.

Jean drew back and attempted to look out into the car, but the curtains were jammed tight by some heavy object which had fallen against them, and she could get no idea of the situation on that side. When she at last succeeded in pulling the curtain away enough to look, she saw only a dark precipice below, with writhing forms and jumbled shapes. No one seemed to have thought of any way of escape for the passengers or to be trying to get them out before it was too late. The shouts and cries that came from below had no authority among them. The only hope of escape was through the broken window and down into that abyss of water and fire below.

Jean drew back and felt carefully around for her shoes. She couldn't take much with her and must work rapidly. The shoes and little handbag were almost under her, and she drew on the shoes, fastening a button or two. She hesitated a second with her hand on the precious bag. All her money, her trunk check and her little bits of jewelry were in it. She must save them if she could. Those papers that had been entrusted to her were there also. Quickly she stuffed the bag inside her garments and fastened it there with a large safety pin she took from the berth curtain.

She gave one frightened look out the window and then began slowly to creep through, feet first. It was a dangerous and painful task, as there was much glass still adhering firmly to the window frame. She had to draw back at first and hunt up her hairbrush to break away the sharp edges and make the opening large enough.

It seemed an hour, though in reality it was only a moment or two, before she finally get out of the window. But she clung, suspended, both arms still inside the berth, with her body hanging over the abyss of black depths mingled with flames.

Dark shapes were moving about down there; dark, moaning creatures were dropping with sickening splashes into the water. She dared not look to see if they rose. Her head grew light, and she felt her fingers slipping. Her strength wouldn't hold her long, and she was almost on the point of trying to creep back inside the berth when a long cry, mingled with moans and screams of women and children, arose from below. She saw a great sheet of fire leap up and lick the lower end of the car to which she clung. She could feel the heat of it where she was, and except for the slight inclination of the car it would have been between her and the water.

With a low moan of horror she closed her eyes and let herself drop. Down, down, she felt herself falling, through eons of time and space, and knew that she was wondering how her mother would bear it when she heard. Then came the shock of the water, and darkness closed over her in a smothering chill.

Chapter 3

She came up again gasping, choking, aware of the shouts and the noise, of the struggling figures and dropping objects; aware that she was only one more in the way and might better have stayed where she was. She struck out feebly, but something fell on her head, something soft like a pillow perhaps, but enough to put her underwater again, and she felt that this was the end.

When she caught her breath again, a strong arm was pulling her away from the crowd and noise. Things were in the way, people and heavy objects, but she was being steered through them all, out of the labyrinth of horror and into dark, still waters.

There followed a long stretch of toiling through the water, when her breath came in gasps and her heart seemed pounding her very life away as she ploughed through the blackness, making a brave effort to keep up with the strong, steady strokes beside her. She kept on, unconscious of anything save that she must keep going, till finally even that dim impulse flickered out and the water flowed about her very soul, softly, dreamily, possessingly. Yet still she was drawn on and on through the blackness to a distant shore.

He dragged her up on the bank at last, the man who had saved her and brought her with him at the expense of his own almost-exhausted strength. He was gasping and all but finished himself when he dropped beside her among the tall reeds that sheltered them from the night. For a few moments they lay quiet, passive—the girl unconscious, the man panting for breath and unable as yet to think what to do next.

In a moment, however, the chill of the night roused the man, and he shivered and sat up. Whoever it was that he had saved—a woman—her long hair and trammeling garments had already told him that—she would die if she lay long in that condition. What could he do?

He shivered again and got up, shaking off the water. His strength reasserted itself, and his breath was steady now. He was surprised that even a swim like that, encumbered as he was with heavy clothing and shoes, and bearing another helpless creature, should have knocked him out so completely. Then he reflected that he had lost much sleep during the past few days; still, that was not enough to make him feel so worthless. He shook himself again and stretched his muscles, as he used to do on the football field in his boyhood days after a knockout, when he heard the call back into the game. If ever there was a call to come back into the game it was now, for this woman would die if he didn't do something at once.

The night was wild and chill. Across the river, farther away than he dreamed they had come, the sky glowed amber with the fire. The current must have carried them downstream as they crossed. He had thought to go back and help save others so soon as he had this one safe, but the way was far and this woman was apparently helpless, perhaps unconscious, or at least exhausted. If she lay here in her wet garments she would die from the cold. He must get her to her feet and keep her warm somehow.

Stooping, he lifted her light weight and bore her farther up the bank into the woods, then laid her down on the ground and knelt to listen to her heart. It was beating weakly. If only he had fire or stimulant or both! Perhaps a house was nearby. He would carry her a little way and see. So he picked her up again, holding her close to keep her warm, and struggled on through the thick undergrowth in the darkness.

The young strength of the man seemed to revive with the necessity, and he carried the woman a long distance before, with the warmth of his body and the motion of the going, the girl came to her senses.

For the first instant of her waking her soul seemed to stand still with horror. Where was she, and who was carrying her? What would happen to her? Would she ever see her home and friends again? The questions rushed madly through her mind and almost paralyzed her thoughts for an instant. Then memory reasserted itself. All the facts of the disaster came back. She knew that whoever was carrying her must have saved her out of kindness. She knew that he must have had to swim alone during at least part of the way through the water, for she could distinctly remember now the horror of being unable to keep up any longer. Then there was something else, a kindly, strong, impersonal clasp that made her unafraid. After a minute she signified her ability to walk, and he set her down at once yet held her arm and put his own about her for support.

"If you can walk it will keep you warm," he said briefly, and with no apology for his arm about her he hurried her on. It was all she could do to keep up with his pace, and when her feet faltered he seemed almost to lift her from the ground as he strode on.

"We must keep going," he said again, as if he had no more breath to waste in words.

On and on they went, but still they didn't come to any human habitation. Finally, when he saw she could go no farther, he made her sit down in a sheltered place behind some trees. Later, when she was almost asleep, she knew her head was resting against his shoulder. Once in the night she awoke and saw a fire blazing near her; she was warm and comparatively dry. No one was in sight, but she heard a step not far away and the crackling of breaking branches. She didn't wonder how the fire came. She slept again.

It was in the early dawn that she awoke sharply as if she had been called. Stretching her stiff limbs, she looked wildly about her, aware of the night that had passed and her strange isolation with an unknown man.

He lay upon the ground at the other side of the fire, which had been piled high with wood and was burning brightly. His strong, fine figure was stretched wearily at full length, the brown curly hair tumbled back from his bronzed face, which in spite of its soil and grime showed a manly beauty. The utter relaxation of his body made him seem like a boy.

The girl looked and wondered, then turned away to remember. He must have had to swim with her quite a distance and drag her to land after she ceased to help herself. And he must have carried her a long journey. He had held her up when she walked beside him and had sat against a tree and made her lean against him part of the time while she slept. Then how did he get that fire? Some mystery known to woodcraft, no doubt. She glanced at herself with the thick brown coat tucked carefully about her. She touched it softly, almost reverently, with her fingertips. It was dry! He had contrived to dry it and put it about her!

She looked over at the man again. He wore a brown flannel shirt and heavy trousers like the coat. He must have been cold himself without his coat while she slept in comfort. And he had stayed awake all night to keep the fire going to dry her things and keep her warm!

Tears stood in her eyes as her glance lingered on the boyish face. She pictured writing to her mother what he was like, this strong man like an angel who had saved her. Then she shuddered at the thought of the wreck and all she had gone through. What would have been her fate if he hadn't put his arm beneath her when she was sinking?

Presently, as the dawn crept higher up in the sky and lit the world with rose and golden light, she stole shyly from her couch under the tree and, stepping softly, came to where he was and tucked the coat carefully about him as he lay, one cheek pillowed on his arm. Her hand brushed lightly against his hair, and she marveled at its softness. His skin, too, had that clear ruddy glow of perfect health, even beneath the grime of the night. She looked down on him with wonder and a great gratitude that seemed almost to overwhelm her. Perhaps all women felt so toward men who had saved their lives, but Jean Grayson had never before seen a man who seemed half as strong and great and good as this young man looked to her now in the early light of morning, asleep on the ground.

She slipped away quietly without waking him and stood a moment looking about her, wondering where she was. What state was this? She couldn't even be sure of that. Then she looked down at herself.

She wore the long black Pullman robe of soft silk, sadly draggled now and torn in two or three places. How beautiful and fine it had been but a few short hours ago. And her other pretty clothes that had been bought at the cost of such family sacrifice? Were they all gone? Would her trunk burn up? Or had it gone on ahead of her when she had stopped to visit her friends and so escaped destruction? But she dismissed the thought as unworthy of one who had just escaped with her life. What were clothes beside life?

Her hair was the worst of all, but she could put that right. Her handbag! She put her hand to her breast to be sure it was there safe. Yes, it was still fastened to her clothing, though the pin had torn away and there was only a small hold of the cloth still in it. She pulled it out and examined it, seated behind a tree away from the fire and the sleeping man. Yes, the bag was safe, and its contents, but its beauty was gone, for the thin leather finish was blistered and peeling from the inner lining. The things inside were all there, even the strange man's leather case, wrapped in a wet pulp of paper. She took the paper off and threw it from her; then, realizing how few worldly goods she now possessed, she reached and spread the paper out to dry. It would be needed, of course.

Her small store of money was safe, as well as her bits of pins and her watch, the little timepiece ticking bravely on as if it were alive and still trying to be cheerful under adverse circumstances.

Jean took out her combs and hairpins, which she had stowed in the pocket of her handbag that they might be easily found in the morning, and felt rich indeed to have them.

With the aid of the combs she presently had her hair soft and shining in its accustomed coils and fluffy masses. Her hair was of the kind that tries to curl in spite of floods and winds, and it fluffed its prettiest with the first rays of the sun glinting over it.

The handbag held, among other things, a needle and both black and white thread. With their aid Jean mended the tears in her robe and managed to make herself look presentable. Then, wrapping the damp paper again about the leather case, she bestowed it with a shrug of dislike in the disfigured bag once more and went in search of water to wash off the stains of the night.

Her hands were badly scratched, and one had been bleeding. She remembered the glass and wondered now how she had escaped with as few scratches as she had.

But she couldn't find water within sight of the fire and dared not go farther lest she get lost. She found, however, a dense growth of bushes bearing great luscious berries, and though they weren't like any berries she was familiar with, she decided they were probably edible and gathered her hands full. Then, coming softly back near the fire, she looked around for a suitable place for the breakfast table. The sleeper had not awakened. She found a great flat rock near where he lay that would do well. Here she laid her berries on a dish of green leaves, one on each side, for plates.

Then, remembering something, she opened her handbag again.

The day before, when her cousins had taken her sightseeing, they treated her to an ice cream soda, served with a tiny envelope of wax paper containing three small wafer crackers. She had put hers in the bag, saying she would eat them on the train when she was hungry, and one cousin had added her envelope as well. She hadn't thought of them when she opened it before, but now she hurried to bring them out. Of course they would be spoiled. But no—the envelopes were still about them, and though somewhat damp they had retained their shape and looked very good.

She set them out, three on each leaf-plate, and hurried back to the bush to get more berries.

Either the soft feet as they stepped lightly through the grass or a stick falling into the ashes of the fire disturbed the sleeper, for he awoke suddenly and looked about him.

The girl was gone! That was his first thought.

The look of boyishness fell away from him in a flash, and he rose to his feet and gazed about him anxiously, as if he feared danger near. Then his eyes fell on the flat rock with its mimic banquet spread forth. A flood of wonder swept into his face, and a great tenderness, such as no one of his friends or foes ever dreamed would be hidden away anywhere in his nature. He had never played dolls on a rock with some little girl, with moss and acorns for carpet and dishes, but the "playhouse" spirit was there in his heart and leaped at once into consciousness. A table for two! The woman had provided a meal even in the wilderness.

Something stirred in Jasper Holt's heart that he hadn't known was there, a longing for companionship in his life and home; the table set for two and some-one to care! He had never felt its need before, and he didn't call it by that name now—he merely experienced a strangely beautiful thrill at the new possibilities that life suddenly revealed to him, something higher and better and infinitely sweeter than any of the ambitions and ideals he had hitherto entertained.

He was still standing, gazing in wonder at the table, when the quick crackling of a twig made known her return.

Chapter 4

She stood for an instant, framed in the opening of the trees, her eyes bright, her lips parted, her cheeks pink with the exertion of picking the berries.

"Oh, good morning!" she said before he could think what to say. "I hope I didn't waken you. I'm sure you needed to sleep longer."

His eyes glowed with admiration, and he marveled that she had refreshed herself with so little at her command.

"How about you?" he said. "You didn't need any sleep at all, I suppose. You were just about all in last night and no mistake."

"Yes, I guess I was," she said, "and I'm afraid I gave you a lot of trouble, not being able to walk when I should. I can never thank you enough. You saved my life, of course! I never would have reached shore—"

"Forget it," he said with a smile. "It was nothing."

"And you had to carry me a long distance. I can remember a long time when I know I wasn't walking. You must be worn out!"

"Why, you're not heavy," he said amusedly, eyeing her slender frame. "I could carry you a good deal farther than that and not play out. I'm glad to see you look so rested this morning. I didn't expect it after what you went through. I see you have your nerve with you. It was a pretty nervy thing you did, you know, that stunt of dropping out of the window. I had just gotten myself further down and climbed on shore to see if there was anything I could do for anyone, when I saw you drop, and I thought you were gone for sure. There were rocks and timbers all around there and heavy things falling."

"And so you came and rescued me!" she said with a look of gratitude that brought a flush to his tanned face.

"Oh, I just floated over that way to see if I could pick up anybody. I couldn't tell who I was fishing out when I took hold of you."

"Well, I–I can't thank you enough now," she said, a glisten of tears in her eyes. "I know what you did was wonderful."

"Oh, forget it!" he said again, laughing lightly. "It was bad enough all around, and we were lucky to get off as we did. But we aren't out of the woods yet. We'd better let bygones be bygones for the present anyway. Don't you want to sit down?"

Jean dropped down beside the rock with her berries and leaned over to arrange them with the rest.

"These ought to be washed," she said as she arranged them on the leaf-plate in the center, "but I couldn't find any water."

"Water won't be so hard to find, but we haven't anything to put it in," he said.

"And besides, we shouldn't to mind a little dirt after all we've been through. I doubt if the berries I usually get are washed anyway. But if I had anything to carry it in, I'd find some water. I haven't even a hat."

"Why, I had a little drinking cup, but I don't remember whether it's in my bag or not," she said. "Perhaps I put it in the suitcase, though I think I left it in my bag."

She laid down the last berries, and, wiping the stains from her fingers on the grass, she opened the bag which she had slipped through the belt of her robe and hung at her side. It was rather full, and when it was opened the leather wallet, wrapped in its damp paper, fell out on the ground. The paper came unfolded, revealing what it contained.

The young man stooped gravely, a dark flush rising to his cheeks, and picked it up. He didn't look startled or surprised, and she noticed nothing strange in his manner as he handed it to her. Afterward she wondered at that.

The cup wasn't there, but the two little wax paper envelopes might hold water. She held them out to him, and, looking up, their eyes met.

"Why, you are the man who sat opposite me in the day coach," she said in pleased surprise. "I didn't recognize you before without your hat on. But I remember thinking when I went to the other car that you had a face that one need not be afraid of. I was a little frightened by the old man who sat with you—he spoke to me—but when I saw you I wasn't afraid anymore. Mother says I'm always going by my intuitions, but I think this time you've proved them true. I knew you were a person to be trusted."

He looked at her wonderingly, a strange expression of wistfulness crossing his face.

"People don't often feel that way about me," he said in a strange, low tone that seemed to hide a good deal more behind the words than was said. "I guess you're the first person who has trusted me in a long time."

"Oh," she said, looking at him seriously, "I guess you don't know, or else—" she paused as if in doubt whether to finish the sentence.

"Or else what, please?" he asked with a compelling gaze.

"I was going to say, or else they don't know you. But that sounds rather bold for a stranger to say when I've only known you a few hours. But I've had an opportunity to prove what I thought about you was true. Perhaps it's that you don't always let people see the nice things in you the way you have had to let me because of my need."

"Well, that's a new way of painting my character, I must say. I rather like it myself, but I doubt if anybody would recognize it for me. I wouldn't mind being that way, believe me, and I thank you for sizing me up in that style. I'll think it over, but I'm afraid you've got your characters mixed and I'm not in your line at all. I'm glad you think so, though. Now I'll see what I can do about water."

He took the two envelopes as if they had been cut-glass goblets and walked away into the woods. In a few minutes he returned with them dripping, his own face ruddy with recent washing and his curls still damp and dark above his forehead.

"Would you like to wash your face?" he asked as he held out the cup for her to drink. "Never mind the berries—they are all right as they are. I'll show you the water and then come back to guard the food. We don't know what wild creature may find our table and clear out with all of it."

"Oh, would they do that?" laughed Jean. "Wouldn't that be funny?"

"It might not be so funny if we don't strike a ranch pretty soon," said Holt, looking serious. "We need all that breakfast to help us on our way after the night we've spent."

"I won't wash my face until after breakfast," said Jean, coming back to the rock and seating herself by one of the leaf-plates. "Sit down, please, and eat, for we aren't running any risks on this trip. I want to get to a telegraph office and send word to my mother and father. They'll hear about the accident and be terribly frightened about me. You won't mind my eating with unwashed hands, will you?"

"I should worry!" declared Holt, seating himself on the other side of the rock.

"These crackers are a little limp," said Jean, "but it was the best I could do considering they were submerged for a long time."

"They're great," said Holt, sampling one. "But how did you happen to have them?"

She told him of her visit the day before and how she had saved them.

"They're all you have!" said Holt suddenly. "You may need the rest of them before we're through. Put these away and keep them till you need them. I'll just eat the berries. I'm used to going without for a long time."

"Wasn't your life the only one you had when you risked it to save me?" asked Jean, looking at him earnestly. "You'll get half of all there is, or I won't have any."

He looked at her with the glow of appreciation growing in his eyes. He never had seen a girl like this.

"You're a good fellow," he said at last. "I guess we're partners then."

He held out his hand as he would have done to a man, and the girl, with a quick appreciation of his words, laid her small berry-stained hand in his.

"Thank you," she said. "That rather puts us on an equality, doesn't it? But I'm not so foolish as to think we really are. I know it's only a very little bit that I can do on this expedition. You do all the big, grand, hard things. But you mustn't deny me the chance to do the little things I can do; and sharing, or even going without sometimes, belongs to my part. I haven't forgotten yet that you saved my life."

He looked at the little hand wonderingly and held it gently in his own, with just a slight, wistful closing of his strong fingers around it, then let it go as though he were afraid he might crush it.

"I can tell you one thing," he said. "You're some improvement on the last partner I had."

Jean gave him a swift, relieved look. "That horrid old man?"

He nodded but searched her face keenly, as if he would make sure of something. He seemed satisfied, however, with the frank look in her clear eyes and said no more. Perhaps he hoped she would confide in him—or perhaps he liked her all the better that she did not.

They ate their meager breakfast hungrily, yet lingered over it. The morning seemed to each as an exquisite treasure of time loaned to them for this once, and a charm fell upon them that neither quite understood. They were only conscious of joy in being alive and having each other. The experiences of the night and the unusual surroundings did away with all conventionalities and feelings of embarrassment they would otherwise have had in their strange plight. Their laughter mingled and rang out among the trees.

He led her down to the stream to wash while he made a basket of leaves, pinned together with stems, and filled it full of berries.

"We may need them for dinner," he remarked as he went back to the bushes.

Jean washed out her handkerchief and filled it also with berries. Thus provided with a lunch, they started on their way.

After coming out of the woods they climbed first to the highest point of ground near them and surveyed the landscape in every direction, but nothing more serene on a summer morning could be found anywhere than was before them. There was no sign of disaster or wreck. The soft, green hills on every side hid the secret of its location, and the world lay spread before them without a hint of ravage or distress. There was no way to tell direction except by the sun; and where the wreck had been it was impossible even to speculate, for they couldn't tell how they had come in the darkness.

This gave a new aspect to their situation. Holt had been thinking during the night that if they could work their way back to the wreck they would probably reach home more quickly, for surely by this time a relief train must have come. But now he saw it was useless to consider that any longer. They must press on till they came to a house, where possibly they could procure horses and certainly information as to their whereabouts. There was a reason why he wished to get back to the world as quickly as possible; yet something taught him to be glad that necessity had given him this day with this girl.

He looked down almost tenderly at the bright, trusting face that smiled up at him. He had a sudden comprehending glimpse of what it must be to such a girl to be dropped down into a strange world, far from home and protection, in company with a man about whom she knew nothing.

"Tough luck," he said, answering the look in her eyes. "But don't worry—

we'll get out sooner or later."

"I'm not worrying," she said. "But I was wishing we knew how to send a wireless to my father. I wonder if someday they won't perfect the system so that people can send messages from anywhere without any instruments."

"That would be great," said Holt thoughtfully. "I'd send one this minute to the nearest inhabited point for two good saddle horses. Can you ride?"

"A little. I've never had much opportunity. Father used to keep a horse, but when we moved to our present home he had to give it up. There wasn't really any need for it. But I'm to ride while I'm visiting my sister. That is, if we ever get there."

"Oh, we'll get there all right," said Holt, taking his bearings and deciding which way to strike out. "You're Mrs. Harrington's sister, aren't you?"

"Why, yes, how did you know that?" said the girl. "You know my sister then?" This was almost equivalent to an introduction, and she knew her mother would be particular about that.

"I heard you tell the conductor," he said. "Shall we start? We've got a good journey to travel judging by the look of things. This way," and he led her down the slope out into the open where they could see where they were going.

"But you wouldn't have remembered all this time if you hadn't known who she was," she flashed back, smiling. "How pleased Eleanor will be when she knows one of her own friends took care of me and saved my life."

Holt's face darkened suddenly, and he didn't answer at once. When he did his voice was cold and hard like a sudden storm on a sunny day.

"I don't think she'd exactly call me her friend."

His eyes were narrowed, and his chin was set with a haughty lift.

"Well, acquaintance, then," said Jean brightly. "Eleanor is a lot older than you, of course. She was married and went away from home when I was just a tiny girl. I haven't seen her all these years, and of course she's changed a great deal."

"Yes, I suppose you'd call us acquainted," answered Jasper, still in that strange, hard voice.

Jean felt it intuitively but talked on, feeling her way to surer ground.

"I wonder if my sister has ever mentioned you in her letters," she said. "She tells me about all the people."

"Possibly!" The sharpness of his tone could have cut ice.

Then he added quietly, "My name is Holt, Jasper Holt."

He watched her with wide, challenging eyes, but although there was a puzzled look in her face, the name evidently told her nothing.

"Jasper! What a beautiful name! I always thought that was the most beautiful word. The walls of the heavenly city are built of jasper, you know."

"No, I didn't know," he said slowly. This truly was a new kind of girl—more like a citizen of that heavenly city she spoke of with such assurance than like a mortal girl. His face softened as he looked at her and saw the morning shining in her eyes. His haughtiness fell away, and all the goodness and native purity that were hidden in his soul came out and sat upon his face. The people who thought they knew Jasper Holt would not have recognized him thus, walking beside the girl and looking down upon her as one looks upon the face of an angel.

Chapter 5

He helped her over rough places and up the steep climbs. Hand in hand they ran down the slopes like two children, their laughter ringing out, forgetting the recent dangers through which they had passed—forgetting, too, perilous possibilities before them. It was enough that the day was fresh, with the sun shining and their strength renewed, and they were together.

They ate their berries before the heat of the noon was fully come and hurried on. But Holt could see that his companion was growing weary, for more and more she faltered and leaned heavily on him up the hills. Then he found a quiet resting place under some trees and bade her sleep; and while she slept he hovered not far away.

He found a pool, and with due patience he at last secured enough fish to make a meal. Then he accomplished a fire once more and cooked the fish, so that when she awoke dinner was spread under a tree—broiled fish, with clear water from the brook to drink.

Holt was in a hurry to get on, for he was growing uneasy about the direction they were taking. It seemed as if they were off the regular line of habitation and travel. Was it possible he had turned too much to the north and was set to enter the desert at the most remote and lonely part, where they might travel for days without meeting anyone?

He changed the direction slightly, and they started on again, the young man watching the sun anxiously from time to time. And now he kept the girl's arm, touching her elbow lightly to be ready with help when it was needed. Often he drew her arm within his own and fairly lifted her over hard places; and so they came to higher ground and looked out before them once more. The sun was lower now and growing redder as it went down with premonition of the night. He could see that she looked anxiously about on all sides whenever they came to the higher ground and knew she was thinking of her mother.

At last they reached another slight elevation. He looked to the west and to his relief saw a small house with horses and cattle moving about in the fields. He showed it to her, and her eyes lighted with joy.

"Oh, that's so good! I was worried, for I know I'm a burden. You would have gone the distance twice if you'd been alone."

His hand pulled her arm more reverently close.

"I'm glad I wasn't alone," he said. "And I'm glad you weren't alone."

She looked up to meet his eyes, and there leaped from each to the other a wonderful realization of the beauty of their companionship.

"Yes, I'm glad I wasn't alone," she said with deep feeling. "Oh, it would have been dreadful! And this has been—beautiful," she finished, wondering at herself for speaking so freely. Then each was suddenly silent at the thought that the free companionship of the day was almost at an end. They were coming to the world of convention and form again, where words and actions were weighed and motives questioned. There had been nothing of that here, for necessity and common peril had blotted them out of existence for the time, and it had been blessed. Now the thought came to both: Would they ever see one another again and be friends?

The way wound down into a ravine, and the heavy growth of trees shadowed the path. It was rough, and he guided her tenderly, as one might guide a beloved little child. She felt his care in every step she took, and her heart responded gratefully to his gentleness. Her own father could not have been more thoughtful, and there was nothing familiar or presuming in his touch.

In the valley they came to the back of a stream, deep and turbulent; and, standing upon its brink, looking either way, they saw no possible ford. How deep it was they couldn't guess, but there was plainly a strong current.

Holt stood a moment, surveying the barrier to their progress, walked a few steps up the bank and down, and looked up at the westering sky. Then he walked out into the stream.

The girl on the bank caught her breath but said nothing. Must they swim across? Was there no other way? She watched Holt standing, strong and manly, in the middle of the stream, the water above his waist. Presently, when he had gone more than halfway across, he turned and came back to her.

She was white with excitement, but her lips were set and her eyes were bright with the intention of doing his bidding.

"I'm sorry. There's no other way, and we must hurry, for the sun is getting low. We should reach that house before dark."

He stooped and gathered her in his arms, lifting her shoulders high, and stalked out into the stream before she knew what he was doing.

"Oh, please, I can walk as well as you," she pleaded.

"Put your arms around my neck, please," he commanded and waded in, holding her high and dry above the water.

She obeyed instantly, in trust and shy wonder, and the water rose about them but did not touch her.

Once, when they were in the middle of the stream, Holt's foot slipped, and for an instant it seemed as though he would lose his balance. But he lifted her higher and almost instantly recovered himself. In a moment more they had crossed the stream, and he set her down upon the bank and shook the water from his garments. She looked down at herself. Not a shred of her garments was wet, while he was drenched almost to his armpits.

"You're soaked!" she exclaimed, conscience-stricken.

"You wouldn't expect me to keep dry in all that, would you?" he asked, with his eyes dancing.

They laughed like two children, and a frightened chipmunk ran chattering away in the trees.

"Are you all right?" he asked. "Are you perfectly dry?" His voice was husky with emotion and his eyes tender.

"Of course I'm dry," she answered, as if half ashamed of the fact. "Why wouldn't I be when I'm treated like a baby? It seems to me you didn't quite keep to the terms of our partnership."

"This was one of the big things," he said, "only I didn't want you to know it. To tell you the truth, I didn't know whether that stream was fordable or not. And, besides, I knew that if you got your clothes wet again it would hinder you in walking. Come, we must make that house before dark. I'm hungry, aren't you? And we're pretty sure to find bacon and corn bread at least. How does that sound?"

"Good!" she cried, laughing, and took the hand that was held out to her. Together they went on over the rough ground toward supper and rest.

But the way was longer than they thought, and Holt hadn't calculated on the slow steps of the girl, who was unused to such long tramps and going without adequate food. The sun went down, and the darkness was upon them before they were anywhere near the little house.

Once Jean stumbled and almost fell, and a sound like a sob came from her throat as she clutched at his arm to save herself. It was then he picked her up like a tired child and carried her over the rough ground, until she protested so vigorously that he was forced to set her down and both stopped to rest. For, indeed, Holt's own strength was somewhat spent by this time, though he showed no outward sign of fatigue, having been trained in a school that endures till it drops.

By this time they felt as if they had known each other for years, for there is nothing like a common peril and a common need to make souls know one another and to bring out the true selfishness or unselfishness of each character. Because these two had been absolutely forgetful of self, each felt for the other an extraordinary attraction and reverence.

As they sat silently under the stars, resting, it came to their minds how far from strangers they now seemed, and yet how little they knew about each other's lives. And they felt they did not need to know because of what each had been to the other during the night and the day that were passed.

When they started on their way again arm in arm, they walked silently for a time.

I cannot be mistaken, thought Jean. *He is fine and noble—all that a man should be. He looks as if he had never done anything wrong yet is strong enough to kill the devil if he would.*

By this time there was a light in the window of the house in the distance, and it guided them to its door, where three great dogs greeted them from afar and disputed their entrance.

The house was not very large—only three rooms. A man and his wife and some hired hands huddled around a kerosene light, the men smoking and playing cards, the wife knitting silently in the rear.

They looked up curiously to hear the stranger's story, incredulous. They hadn't heard of any railroad accident. They lived twenty miles from the railroad and went to town only once a fortnight.

"This your wife?" questioned the householder.

Jean's face flamed scarlet as a new embarrassment faced her. She hadn't thought of proprieties until now. Of course they existed even in the wilderness.

Holt explained haughtily.

"Hmm," said the man, still incredulous. "Any more in your party? Wal, my woman'll take keer your woman fer t'night, an' in the mornin' we ken talk business. Yas, I've got horses, but I need 'em." The man looked sharp from one to the other of the men.

Jean looked at Holt and thought how far above these people he seemed as he stood by the door in his wet, bedraggled clothing, with the bearing of a young king.

"Oh, I can pay for the horses and see that they are returned, too, if that's what's the matter." And he pulled out a roll of bills and threw several carelessly on the table.

"Wal, that alters the case," said the man, "of course, fer a consideration—"

"Can we get some supper?" asked Holt, cutting him short. "We've had very little to eat all day, and this lady is tired and hungry."

The man's wife bustled forward.

"Fer the land sake!" she exclaimed. "Hungry this time o' night? We ain't got much ready, but there was some corn bread and po'k lef' from supper, ef they'll do. The men is powah'ful eatahs."

She set out the best her house afforded, eyeing Jean's tattered silk robe enviously between trips to the cupboard. The men went on with their card game, and Jean and Holt ate in silence. The girl was beginning to dread the night and to wish for the silence of the starlit world and the protection of her strong, true friend. She didn't like the look of the men who fumbled the dirty cards and cast bold glances in her direction.

She was even more frightened when she learned the arrangements that were to be made for the night. She was assigned to a bunk in a small closetlike room opening from the big room in which they were all sitting—which appeared to be kitchen, parlor and dining room combined, and was to be, for that night at least, sleeping room for Holt and the other men.

Holt managed to get opportunity to whisper to her as the men were disputing over their game while the housewife retired to the guest chamber to "red up."

"Don't you worry," he reassured her. "I'll bunk across in front of your door. You can sleep and trust me."

She flashed up at him a bright, weary smile that sent a thrill of joy through him and made him feel that nothing in all life could be better than to defend this girl who trusted him.

In the early morning Jean awoke to the smell of cooking ham and the sizzle of frying eggs on the other side of her thin partition.

She had a little money carefully sewed inside her clothing. It was to have done for her whole Western trip and bought gifts for the dear ones at home before her return. Now she realized it was her fortune. She made a bargain with the woman for a khaki skirt and blouse, of doubtful cut and shabby mien, but whole and clean. For these she gave two dollars and the remains of the once-treasured, but now tattered and travel-stained, silk robe she wore. And so it was as a Western girl, in riding skirt and blouse, that she emerged from the little closet. So exquisitely did her face and golden-brown hair set them off that they took on a style and beauty entirely out of their nature; and their former owner stared in wonder and sighed with envy as she beheld. It had not been the silken garment that made this girl a queen, but her own beauty of countenance and regal bearing. For here were her own old clothes worn like a royal robe, making the stranger lovely as the morning.

Holt looked at the girl in startled wonder when she appeared, so sweet in her traveling garb, ready for the next stage of her journey, and trembled with joy at the day that was before him. All the while he knew the end of the journey would bring sadness and parting. He wanted to knock down the men, who stared insolently, offering audible comments on her complexion and bearing that made the swift, frightened color come to her cheeks. He ate his breakfast in silence, sitting between Jean and one of the men and shielding her as far as possible from any need of conversation save with her hostess, who waited on them all and hovered round her young guest's chair with offers of molasses and mush.

"Any need fer a clergyman?" asked the ugliest of the three men, leaning forward across the table, a large piece of ham aloft on his fork. He gave a wink at the others, and they laughed coarsely.

"Yas, you could git the elder by goin' about ten mile out o' yer way," added another and then devoted himself audibly to his thick cup of muddy coffee.

Holt ignored these remarks and asked questions of his host about the crops and the exact location of the house with regard to railroads, wondering meanwhile if Jean understood their rough jokes and hoping she did not.

If she did she was serene about it all and smiled her sweetest on the hostess, making her heart glad at the parting by the gift of a pair of cheap, but pretty, cuff pins that had been fastened on the front of her traveling robe.

So they mounted and rode away, Jean like the queen of a girl that she was and her companion no less noble in his bearing. The joy they felt in the day and each other was only equaled by their own shyness in speaking of it.

Chapter 6

They talked about many things that morning as they rode toward Hawk Valley. Holt felt no anxiety now about reaching there by night, for he knew exactly where he was and how to get there. He had bargained with one of the men for firearms, and he could shoot enough to keep them from hunger even if they were delayed. He had matches in his pocket and an old cowboy hat on his head, and he felt rested and fit for the journey. For the first half of the way, at least, he could give himself up to the bliss of a companionship such as he had never known in the whole of his young life. Reverence and adoration were in his glance as he looked at the girl, and a wistful sadness grew as the day lingered toward evening.

They rode first straight down to the telegraph station, which was about fifteen miles from the settler's cabin, and sent telegrams from the forlorn little office set alone in the middle of the prairie—one to Jean's father and mother back home and one to her sister, Eleanor Harrington, in Hawk Valley.

The first message was:

> *Don't worry about accident. Am safe and well and shall reach Hawk Valley tonight.*
>
> *Jean*

The second Holt worded for himself, for he had left the girl outside the station on her horse. She had asked him to be sure and tell her sister he was with her so she wouldn't worry, but the message he sent was:

> *Safe and well and on my way to you with a friend who will look out for me. Expect to reach Hawk Valley tonight.*
>
> *Jean*

Inquiry concerning the accident brought little information. The wreck had been on the "other road," and the agent said he hadn't heard much. He didn't know whether many lives were lost or not.

They rode on their way in happy conversation. Jean was led to tell of her home life. Not that Holt questioned her, but she seemed to love to talk of home and describe her family, her friends, the church where her father preached, the companions of her girlhood, school life and the church work to which she had been devoting herself. A wistful look came into his eyes as he thought what his life might have been if someone had cared for him and trusted in him that way, or if he had a sister like this girl.

Suddenly, in the middle of the afternoon, the girl looked up and asked, "Will your mother worry? Did you send her a telegram too?"

He looked at her.

"My mother?" he said in a strange, cold voice. "My mother never worries about me. She isn't that kind. I doubt if she even knows where I am these days. I've been West for a long time. Father died, and Mother married again since I left home. I don't suppose she would even hear of the accident. There's no one to care where I am." The bitterness in his voice and a hardness on his handsome features cast a pall over the beauty of the afternoon for Jean.

"Oh," she said earnestly. "Oh, don't say that! I'm sure someone cares."

He looked so noble and good to her, and her heart went out to him in his loneliness. In that moment she knew that she cared with all her heart and would always care. It was strange and wonderful, but she felt she would always care.

He looked at her with wonder again and a yearning he could not hide.

"I believe you would care."

She smiled through a sudden mist of tears.

"Yes, I would care; I couldn't help it," she said. "You have done so much for me, you know, and I—know you so well."

She hesitated. "I don't see how anybody who belonged to you could help caring." Her cheeks grew rosy with the effort to say what she meant without seeming unmaidenly.

His brow darkened.

"Belonged!" he spat out. "Belonged! Yes, that's it. I don't belong! I don't belong anywhere!"

His voice was so different and so harsh that it almost frightened her. She watched him, half afraid as he brought his horse to a sudden stop and looked about him. Then he changed the subject abruptly.

"This is a good place to camp for supper and rest," he said, as if he had quite forgotten what they had been saying.

He swung down from the saddle, hobbled his horse and came around to her side to help her dismount. He stood a moment looking tenderly into her eyes, and she looked back at him trustingly, with the worshipful homage a woman's eyes can hold for the man who has won her tenderest thoughts. She didn't know she was looking that way. She would have been filled with confusion if she had. It was unconscious, and the man knew so and treasured her look the more for that.

"I believe you do care now," he said in a soft voice.

Before she could answer or think to be embarrassed, he lifted her from the saddle and put her on the ground.

He hobbled her horse, unstrapped the pack of provisions and went off to gather firewood, but when he returned she was sitting where he had put her under the tree, her face buried in her hands, her slender form motionless.

He stood for a moment and watched her, then came over and knelt down beside her. And, taking her hands gently from her face, he looked into the dewy depths of her sweet eyes.

"Don't," he pleaded. "Let's have supper now, and then we'll talk it all out. Will you come and help me make a fire?"

Something in his strong, tender glance helped her rise to his call. She let him help her to her feet, and, casting aside the shyness that had fallen over her like a misty veil, she ran here and there, gathering sticks and helping make the fire blaze.

Holt shot a couple of rabbits and put them to roast before the fire. Jean set herself to toast the soggy corn bread and make it more palatable. Their laughter rang out again and again as they prepared their simple meal. They were like two children playing house. No one looking on would have seen any difference in their demeanor from what it had been all day. It was only when Holt was out in the open, shooting rabbits, that he allowed the sadness and gloom to settle upon his young face.

When supper was eaten and the fire flickering low in the dying light of sunset, Holt came and sat down beside the girl, and again a great silence fell between them.

Holt had planned their homecoming to be in the dark. For the girl's sake he would not have witnesses to their arrival. This thoughtfulness sprang from finer feelings than the people of Hawk Valley dreamed he possessed. There remained only a little over an hour's ride now to reach Hawk Valley, and Holt did not mean for them to get there before nine o'clock at the earliest.

He sat quietly, his strong hands folded across his raised knees, his back against a tree, looking off into the distance. He seemed a great deal older now, with that grave, sad expression. Jean stole a glance at him now and then as she plucked at the vegetation about her, and she wondered why this appalling silence had so suddenly fallen upon them.

The man's voice broke the stillness in a low tone. "There's something I must tell you."

The very air seemed waiting to hear what he would say. The girl scarcely breathed.

"It wouldn't have been the square thing for me to tell you I loved you if I had been the only one who cared. But we've been through all this together, and it's as if we had known each other for years—and—you care too! I can see it in your eyes. I'm not worthy of it, but you care, and it's up to me to help you stop it. It would be an easier job, perhaps, if I were used to being trusted, but it's an honest fact that you're the first respectable person that has really trusted me since I can remember, and it comes hard."

His voice broke. A sob swelled in the girl's throat, too, and her hand stole out and touched his arm reassuringly and withdrew as if to say, "I will bear my part of this trouble, whatever it is. Please don't suffer more than your own part."

He turned at that, and the cloud on his face cleared and brightened into a smile that seemed to enfold her in his glance of tenderness. Yet he lifted not a finger to touch her.

"I love you! How I love you!" he said in a lingering tone, as if the words must be treasured.

"I never knew there was a girl like you. I loved you at once as soon as I saw you in the train, but I knew, of course, you were not for me. I'm not fit for you. I'm not in your class at all, and I wouldn't have dreamed of anything but worshipping you, even after these days together—only you care! You trust me! That broke me all up! I'd give anything in this world if I could keep that and take it to the end and die with it, to remember that look in your eyes when you said you trusted me. If you weren't going where they know all about me and will tell you, I'd never have opened my mouth. I'd have stolen this one little bit of trust and kept it for my own; for down in my heart I know it isn't wrong. I know you may trust me. I'd give my life to keep that trust."

He was looking straight into her clear eyes as he talked, and his own eyes showed his strong, true spirit at its best. The appeal in his voice went to the girl's heart. With a growing uneasiness she had listened to his words, and she felt she could bear no more. The tears rushed to her eyes, and she put up her hands to cover her face.

"Please. Tell me quick!" she breathed softly.

Thrilled with the wonder of her tears and longing to comfort her, he put out his hand awkwardly and laid it on her bowed head, bending over her as he might have done to a child in trouble.

"There's nothing for you to feel bad about," he said. "I'm bearing this circumstance. I just wanted to tell you myself that I'm not what you think me. I'm not bad, really, the way I might be, but I've not been good, and I'm not a gentleman—not the kind you're used to. Nobody thinks I'm worth anything at all. Your people hate me and would think it a good thing if somebody killed me. You see how it is that I can't be like other men who love you. I cannot ask you to marry me; for after you've heard what your family will say about me you won't look at me yourself—and I don't blame you. It's all my own fault, I suppose. I can see it now, though I never thought so till I looked in your eyes on the train. If I had known a girl like you was coming my way I'd have made things different—I'd have been ready. And now it's too late. I'm not worthy of you."

He took his hand from her head and dropped back against the tree again, a bitter expression on his face.

"Oh, don't," she pleaded softly. "Please don't look like that. Won't you tell me what you have done that makes them all feel so about you?"

A silence passed between them for a moment while the twilight grew with the coming out of a pale, young moon. So in the holy of the evening he came to his confession, face-to-face with his sins, before the pure eyes of the girl he loved.

Chapter 7

The stars were large and vivid above them, like tapers of tall angels bent to light a soul's confession up to God.

The beautiful silence that brooded over the plain was broken now and again by distant calls of some wild creature, but that only emphasized the stillness and the privacy of the night.

Jasper Holt broke the silence at last.

"I was never as bad as they thought I was," he said in a broken voice. "They laid a lot of things at my door that I never thought of doing—some things I would have scorned to do. I suppose it was my fault they thought I did them. I let them think so. I grew to glory in their thinking so and sometimes helped it on just for the pleasure of feeling that they, through their injustice, were more in the wrong than I was. I suppose I had no right to do that. I see now that for your sake I should have kept my record clear." He lifted his gray eyes to her face for one swift look.

"It was none of their business what I did, though, and my theory always has been to do as I pleased so long as I lived up to my creed. For I had a creed, a kind of religion, if you want to call it that. Put into a single word, perhaps nine-tenths of my creed is independence. What people thought of me didn't come into my scheme of life. I thought it a slavery to bow to public opinion and gloried in my freedom. It seemed a false principle without cause or reason.

"I never reckoned on your coming. I thought I was living my life just for myself. I can see now that underneath all the falseness of the world's conventionalities there runs some good reason, and there may be circumstances where some of the things they insist upon are right—even necessary. This is one. I never considered anything like this. I couldn't see any reason why I should ever need to care what people thought of me or go out of my way to make them think well of me. I always relied on something else to get what I wanted, and so far it hasn't failed. They'll tell you that. They'll let you know I haven't been powerless because some men hated me. They've hated me but they've also feared me."

The girl turned her eyes to look at him, studying the fine outline of features against the starlit background of the sky. She could see the power in his face; power with gentleness was what she had seen when she first looked at him. But hate? Fear? How could men so misjudge him? What was there about him to fear?

He read her thought.

"You don't see how that could be," he said sadly. "I don't look that way to you now. But wait till you hear them talk. You'll get another viewpoint. You'll see me with their eyes—"

"Don't!" she said with a sob in her voice, putting up her hands as if to defend herself from his words.

"I won't blame you," he said, bending toward her. "It won't be your fault. It's almost inevitable. You belong with them and not with me, and you can't help seeing me that way when you get with them. It's a part of my miserable folly. It's my punishment. I have no right to make you think I'm better than they believe. It will be easier for you to forget me if you believe what they do."

"I will never believe as they do!" said the girl vehemently. "I will never listen to their opinion! You may have sinned; you may have done a lot of things you ought not to have done. But you're not bad! I know you're not! And I know I can trust you. I shall always trust you no matter what anybody says, no matter how things look. I know you are good and true! I know you!"

She put out her hands toward him. There was something glorious in the sparkle of her eyes. He took her hands reverently.

"You dear!" he breathed tenderly. "You wonderful woman!"

Her hands trembled in his, but she sat up proudly as if she were defying the world in his defense.

"Now tell me the rest," she said. "Tell it all! And then I shall believe just what you tell me, nothing more. If they tell me other things I'll know they are false. I won't be afraid when you tell me what you've done because you're here and I can look into your eyes and know you are sorry; so tell me the worst. But you needn't ever think I shall listen to them."

So, with her small hands in his and her eyes bright, looking straight into his, he told her. All the foolishness, the stubbornness and independence. All the fight against convention and law. His gambling and wild, rough living. His friendship with men who were outlaws and sinners. His revolutionary methods of dealing with those who did not do as he thought they should or who tried to interfere with him. His summary punishment of those who stirred his soul to wrath. He told it in low tones, searching out each confession of his heart as though he would make a clean sweep of it and lifting his eyes bravely each time to meet the pain he couldn't help seeing in hers. It was his real judgment, his first sense of shame and sorrow and repentance.

And when it was told he bowed his head in silence for a moment, still holding her hands, as though there yet remained something more to say. At last he spoke.

"There's one thing," he said, and he lifted his head with a sigh. "Yes. Two things I might say that I suppose you'll be glad to hear. I haven't been a drinking man. I doubt if many of your friends will believe that, for I'm often in the saloons and with men who drink. I haven't noised it abroad that I don't drink, and only those who have been with me a good deal understand it. I simply don't drink because I don't want to. I saw what it did to men when I first came out here. I knew I needed my brains for what I wanted to do, and I didn't like the idea of surrendering them for a few hours' carousing and putting myself out of my own control. So I just determined I wouldn't drink, and I didn't. But your brother-in-law and sister won't believe that. My reputation is understood to be of the worst, and drinking is a matter of course when one is hard and wild as they think I am.

"There's another thing too. I've kept away from women. Some of them hurt me too much when I was a kid and when I grew a little older, and so I decided against them all. That's kept me clean. I can look you in the eyes and not be ashamed. I didn't do it because I had any idea there would ever be one like you in my world. I did it because the kind of thing some men liked turned me sick to think of. This is probably another thing your people won't believe. They've heard otherwise of me. And perhaps they've had some reason from their standpoint. I haven't always tried to make things look right. I didn't care. It wasn't their business.

"A girl came to the valley once with a traveling show. She was down on her luck and just about ready to give up and take her own life. I helped her out a bit, paid for her at the hotel a few days till she got rested and sent her on her way to her father in Missouri. But you ought to have heard the rumpus the town raised! That added to my savory reputation, you see. Well, I'm no saint, but I've kept clean! So there you have the worst of me—and the best—but it's bad enough. Your father wouldn't stand for me a minute, and I guess he's right. As for your sister! Why, if Harrington knew I was out here alone with you he'd bring a posse of men and shoot me on the spot for daring to bring you home. He would. He feels just that way about me."

"I shall change all that," said Jean with a thrill in her voice. "I shall tell them that was only a kind of rough outside you wore—a mask that hid your inner feelings. I shall make them understand they haven't known the real man you are at all."

"You cannot do that, little girl," said the man, gently leaning toward her. "It would be best for you not to try. I tell you, you don't know in the least what the feeling is against me."

"But you'll help show them too," said Jean, wide-eyed with sorrow. "You won't go on doing those things. You'll make them see—for my sake if not for your own, you'll let them see how wonderful you are! How fine you have been to me! You'll not let them go on thinking. You'll change it all?"

Her voice choked off in a sob, and for a moment she dropped her face down on his hands that held hers. The man thrilled and trembled with her touch, and it was then he felt the most crucial moment of his punishment.

He sat white and silent for a moment, longing to gather her into his arms and comfort her, to crush her to him; but he would not. The nobleness in him held her sacred because he knew he was unworthy. Then he spoke in a low, grave tone, and his voice had a hollow sound.

"I'll change, of course," he said. "I couldn't do otherwise. Did you think I could go on that way after having known you? I never could do any of the things again that I know you wouldn't like. I couldn't, now that you've trusted me. I wouldn't want to. You've made everything seem different. If it'll please you I'll promise anything you like. But of course I know that doesn't matter so far as your ever having anything to do with me is concerned. Nothing I can do can make people forget what they think I am. They would feel it a disgrace for you to speak to me. They'd think you had gone to perdition if you had anything to do with me. I'm not fit for you. I know it, and there's an end of it, but I'll spend the rest of my life trying to make myself what I ought to have been, if that will comfort you any."

The girl's hands clung now with almost a painful clasp, and tears ran down her face.

"Don't! Don't!" he pleaded. "Don't take it so. I'm not worth it, really I'm not. You'll find it out when you get to your sister's and hear her talk and. . .forget. . .about. . .this—"

His voice broke, and he lifted his face, white with sudden realization of what that would mean to him. "Oh! What a fool I've been!"

"Listen!" Jean said, and he wondered at her quietness. "*I* shall never forget. Never! Nothing that anybody can say will ever make me think as they do of you. I know you—and you have saved my life."

He stirred impatiently and almost roughly tried to draw his hands away.

"Don't talk of gratitude," he said huskily.

"No," she said, taking his hands again and laying her own within them as before. He accepted them as if they were a sacred trust, folding his reverently about them.

"I'm not talking of gratitude," she said, her voice tense with feeling. "You saved my life, and I know what you are and what you have done for me. Nothing can ever change that, not even what you've done in the past. I know you, I trust you, and I—I love you!"

Her voice was low and sweet as she said this, and she didn't lift her eyes. The young man felt her fingers tremble within his own strong grasp, and he looked down at the slender wrists and thrilled with awe at her words. It humbled him, shamed him, with a pain that was a solemn joy. And he had nothing to say. What gracious influence had been at work in his behalf that a miracle so great should have been wrought in a pure girl's heart for him, an outlaw— a careless, selfish, wild man who had hitherto lived as he pleased, caring for nobody, and nobody caring for him. He had held his head high and gone his independent way. He had held the creed that the whole world was against him, and his chief aim in life should be to circumvent and annoy that world. Knowledge he had, and a certain amount of worldly wisdom learned in a hard school; but love, care, tenderness and trust had never been given to him even in his babyhood. No wonder he was confounded at the sudden treasure thrust upon him.

"I'm only a very young girl," Jean's voice went on. "I know you're right that I mustn't do anything to distress my father and mother. They love me very much, and I love them. You and I will go our separate ways if we must, but nobody can stop me from trusting you. It is right I should. I owe it to you for what you have done for me—and my love I couldn't help giving you. I know you are going to be right and true forever."

His eyes held depths of sincerity as he lifted them to her pleading ones.

"I promise you."

"And I promise you I will trust you always," she said, and thus their covenant was made.

For a long moment they sat with clasping hands, unaware of the beauty of the evening, aware only of their own two suffering spirits that had found and lost each other and learned the consequences of sin. They didn't seem to need words, for each knew what was in the other's heart.

He raised her at last to her feet and, bending low, whispered, "Thank you."

He stood a moment hesitating, then gave her hands one quick pressure again and turned away.

"I was going to ask something," he said, "but I guess that isn't square."

And she stood pondering what it might have been.

Silently he helped her on the pony, and without words they rode away into the moonlight.

There were tears in the girl's eyes when she lifted them at last and asked, "And won't I see you at all? Won't you ever come to the house?"

"I'm afraid not," Holt said sadly.

After that they talked in tones that people use when they are about to go apart on a long journey and may never meet again. Monosyllables, half-finished sentences, of which each knew the beginning or the ending without the words. This was their conversation.

They came at last to the brow of a hill where below them at a gentle slope Hawk Valley lay, its lights twinkling among the velvety shadows of the night. In the clear moonlight it seemed so near, so sudden, as it lay just below them. Jean knew without being told that the parting of their ways had come. By common consent they checked their horses and made them stand side by side. Holt put out his hand and laid it on hers.

"Don't!" he said huskily. "I won't disappoint you. No matter what anybody tells you, always remember that. I won't disappoint you! You needn't think I've forgotten or changed. I won't forget the only good thing that ever came into my life. You can trust me!"

"I know," she replied softly. "I know I can trust you. And I've been thinking. There's no reason why you couldn't come to see me. I don't care what anybody thinks. You saved my life! I'm not ashamed of you. I have the right to ask you to call and to receive you. My father would approve of that, I'm sure."

"You're wonderful!" he exclaimed. "You're not like any other girl I ever saw. But it wouldn't do. Your father might stand for it, but your brother-in-law never would. He hates me like poison, not so much because of my reputation as because I've stood in the way of some of his plans. He would kick me out like a dog if I darkened his doors. You'll understand when you hear them talk. It would be just as well if you didn't say anything about me. It won't be necessary for them to know who brought you home; just say a man who was on the train."

Jean straightened up in her saddle and grasped his hand.

"Indeed I'll tell them who brought me out of death and just what I think of him. They shall know all you've done for me. Do you think I would keep still about it? I couldn't. It would be disloyalty. It would be cowardly!"

He watched her kindling face and flashing eyes in the moonlight and stored the picture away in his memory.

"Darling!" he breathed reverently, as if the words were drawn from his lips in spite of all resolution. Then, raising his voice a trifle and lifting his head to the night sky, he said, "I never knew a girl could be like this! What a fool I have been!"

The words ended almost in a groan, and for answer the girl drew nearer to him and laid her other hand gently upon his.

Lights flashed below them in the village, and voices rose. A coarse laugh rang out and a child's cry; some people talked in an open doorway in another place and called good night. Then a door slammed and other lights twinkled—just the commonplace noises of life jarring in to break a moment of tremendous import in the lives of these two. The time had come to go down to their valley, and they knew it. With one lingering handclasp they started on down to the village.

Holt selected the shadowed ways and quieter approach to the Harrington home, and the two rode silently until they came to the house.

Chapter 8

H olt checked the horses and, dismounting, stood beside Jean in the shadow of a great tree by the roadside. Within ten feet of them the light from a wide window streamed out upon the grass in front of a pleasant house built in bungalow style, with broad porches and vine-clad approaches. Hammocks and easy rockers were dimly visible, with a brighter hint of glow and warmth inside the swaying curtains of the window where a piano was sounding pleasantly. A man and a woman sat on either side of a table under a shaded reading lamp. A boy's voice called down the stairs, and the little girl at the piano stopped playing and answered him, then tinkled on with her music.

All this the two under the tree saw and heard without sensing it. They were looking into one another's eyes in the semidarkness, realizing that across that streak of light was separation for them, perhaps forever.

Jean put her hands timidly on Holt's shoulders. "I've been thinking what it was you wanted to ask of me," she said. She waited, and Holt looked at her wistfully.

"I have no right," he said. "It wouldn't be square."

The girl's eyes looked steadily into his.

"Was it—" she stopped, her heart beating fast. "Was it this?"

She leaned forward and kissed him softly on the forehead just where the curls waved away, and her lips were like a benediction that seemed to bring forgiveness and a purging away of the past.

With a bowed head he stood, then quietly said, "You have understood, and I thank you. I had no right to ask, but I can never forget or be false to that."

He stooped and pressed his lips gently to her hands, then lifted her down quickly as if he couldn't bear to make the sorrow of the parting longer. Together they went forward across the patch of light, up the path and the wide low steps to the porch.

Holt knocked once on the door, not loudly, but there was in the sound a menace that made Jean shudder as she heard it. She reached out her hand to his. Holt pressed her fingers in a clasp that almost hurt her and then, dropping her hand, stepped back into the shadow of the vines as the tinkling piano stopped.

The door was flung wide, and in the stream of light Mr. and Mrs. Harrington stood looking eagerly out into the darkness, with a little girl of twelve in a white dress peering around her mother and a boy of five struggling to get into the center of the family group. Jean stood alone in the light on the porch, with Holt in the shadow at her side.

"I have brought Miss Grayson," said Holt in a grave, almost challenging, tone from his dark position just outside the stream of light.

But the people in the doorway whose eyes had come from the lighted room saw only the figure of the girl standing in the brightness.

"Oh, Jean! My little sister! You've come at last!" cried Mrs. Harrington, rushing forward to clasp her in her arms and draw her inside the door. In the confusion of the greetings the girl's escort was quite forgotten for the moment.

Within the doorway at last they looked about for him and found no one.

"Why, who came with you, child? Where is he?" asked her brother-in-law. "We must ask him in and hear all about your adventures." He stepped out on the porch and looked down the path in the moonlight but saw no one.

"Yes, please ask him in," pleaded Jean. "He has been so wonderful! He saved my life. If it hadn't been for him I wouldn't be here." And she hurried to the door and peered out into the darkness.

"Of course," said her sister, going to the door to look. "How thoughtless of us not to have welcomed him at once, but we were so overwhelmed to have you at last, after all the anxiety—you can't think how terrible it's been. Which way did he go? James, look down that road. He can't be far away. What was his name, Jean? Can't you call after him?"

"He must be over there." Jean pointed toward the great tree where the horses had stood but a moment before. "We dismounted just under that tree. He can't have gone far with two horses, so soon." She hurried across the grass to the tree, but there was no sign of horse or man in the serene moonlight.

"Call, James!" commanded Mrs. Harrington, and her husband obeyed, but no answering call came back, except the echoes of his voice.

"What did you say his name was, Jean?" asked the puzzled woman, walking slowly back to the steps. "It seems very strange he could get away so soon. Where was he going? Did he live near here? We ought to put him up for the night, of course. It's mortifying for him to disappear like this when he's been so good to you. He must have gone to find rest and food for his horses and himself. I'll send the servant out to look him up. He'll surely find him. What did he look like? What did you say his name was?"

Jean, slowly climbing the steps to the porch and comprehending that Holt's disappearance had been intentional, answered in a strange voice that tried to be natural: "Holt, his name was Holt, Jasper Holt."

Her voice lingered on the words as if she would glorify the man by merely speaking his name and elevate him in their eyes to the place he occupied in her heart.

"Holt!" exclaimed her brother-in-law. "Not Jasper Holt! Impossible! There must be some mistake."

"It couldn't have been Jasper Holt, of course," said his wife. "He isn't capable of saving anybody's life, much less a relative of ours, Jean, dear. It must have been someone else. Are you sure about the name?"

"Quite sure!" said Jean, her whole frame trembling.

"Perhaps it was his father," suggested Eleanor, looking at her husband. "Have you ever heard that Jasper Holt had a father living, James? How old a man was he, Jean?"

"He was a young man, Eleanor, tall and handsome, and very brave and strong." Jean lifted her eyes to meet her sister's smiling doubt and raised her chin with an attitude of defiance.

"Listen, Eleanor. He was wonderful. I dropped from the window of the burning sleeper into a river, and something struck me on the head when I rose and tried to swim."

"You poor, dear little girl!" exclaimed Eleanor, reaching out to clasp her sister again, but Jean held her gently back and went on with her eager tale.

"He caught me and dragged me along, helping me as far as I could go, and when I couldn't swim any longer he brought me a long distance himself to land and carried me a great ways through the woods. He built a fire, dried his own coat and put it over me while I slept. He took care of me just as our own father might have done; found food, water and a house where we slept the first night and got horses. He has been splendid to me all day."

"Well, he can't be our Jasper Holt, dearie—it's impossible. He isn't a bit like that."

"Yes," said Jean, looking bravely at her sister. "Yes, Eleanor, it is your Jasper Holt. He told me you didn't like him, but I'm sure you don't know what he really is, or you couldn't possibly think ill of him. Oh, Eleanor!" Suddenly Jean's courage gave way in a flood of tears, and she threw herself in her sister's arms.

"You poor girl! You're worn out, and we're letting you stand here and talk when you ought to be in bed this minute," said her sister, folding her in loving arms. "Never mind now, dear. You just forget it till tomorrow. It was an awful experience for you to go through all alone with a strange man, and you need a lot of rest before you can tell us about it. Come now. James will send the man out to hunt for your escort, and you needn't worry anymore. We shall find out there's some mistake. I'm sure the Jasper Holt we know would never turn out of his way to save anybody's life—he'd much rather kill someone—unless he had some evil purpose in it. It's possibly someone who has used his name for fun or something.

"Come now, Jean. Take off your hat. Why, child, where did you get this ridiculous rig you have on? It's good it wasn't daylight when you arrived. It was thoughtful of your escort to bring you in the dark. Your trunk arrived yesterday. Come up to your room and wash while I have your supper put on the table. I've kept it nice and hot, for I knew you would be hungry."

Jean lifted up her head and wiped the tears away.

"I'd like to tell you just a little first, if you please," she said. "It's no use whatever for you to try to find Mr. Holt. He won't come back, I'm sure. I suppose he meant to slip away. He told me before he got here that you wouldn't want him. He didn't want me to mention him at all, but I had to tell you how fine he has been."

Mrs. Harrington and her husband stood looking at one another aghast, while Jean, her hair disheveled, her face glowing with eagerness, sketched the peril through which she had come and the faithfulness and care of her protector. More than one glance of incredulity passed between husband and wife as the girl went on with her story; and yet, as she came to her final sentences, they perceived that her protector must have been the Jasper Holt they knew and despised.

"I guess it was Holt all right!" said Harrington with an ominous frown. "And he did well to disappear like the coward he is. He knew he isn't wanted around here."

"Coward?" exclaimed Jean. "Coward! Jasper Holt is no coward! You don't know him!" Her eyes flashed fire.

Eleanor tried to smile at her sister. "Never mind tonight, dear," she said soothingly. "He's evidently appeared to you as an angel of light. He is handsome, I must admit—in a kind of dashing, dreadful way—and of course anyone who saved you would be under a kind of glamor just now. I'm sure we're grateful to him for not letting you drown. It's quite the unexpected. But, really, when it comes to bringing you home, you're quite attractive, you know, and I've no doubt he thought it would be pleasant to have a little flirtation with a pretty girl. Besides, I think he rather enjoyed putting James under an obligation to him. I hope he will know enough not to presume upon this for further acquaintance. He has been most unpleasant, not to say criminal, in a business way—but never mind now, Jean. We'll talk about it more tomorrow. Wait until you hear what everybody says about him, and then you'll see we aren't prejudiced. We don't blame you for being grateful. Be as grateful as you like. But don't have anything more to do with him! Come now. This is the way to your room. Let me help you unfasten this ridiculous frock. Where did you say you got it? I know you never had this in your wardrobe when you started from home and Mother—"

Mrs. Harrington chattered on, giving the girl time to recover her calmness, for she saw that she was terribly excited. Jean choked back the hot tears that welled to her eyes and went about freshening up.

A few minutes later, attired in one of her own cool muslins, she was seated in the dining room with an admiring audience about her, asking questions about home, the journey and the cousins she had visited on the way. The children hung about her eagerly, patting her shyly and watching her every move with shining eyes. Almost, for a little while, the girl forgot the perils through which she had passed and the man of whom she must not speak.

When supper was finished the children were sent to bed, and Jean suddenly remembered the leather case she had been charged to convey to her brother-in-law.

"Oh, James," she said, "I've a package for you. 'Very important papers,' the strange old man who gave it to me said they were. He was going to get off at the next station, he said—he had been telegraphed for or something—and he heard me tell the conductor that you had telegraphed for a berth for me, so he asked if I would give you these papers at once. If he knows about the accident, he's worrying about his precious bundle by this time, I suspect. Wait, I'll get it. It's upstairs in my bag."

Jean hurried up to her room and had a little trouble finding the bag, which she finally discovered under a trunk tray. The sight of the little wax paper cups and her own damp wad of a handkerchief she and Holt had both used for a towel that afternoon when they washed their hands at a spring struck a pang to her heart. The dampness of the bag made it difficult to get the bundle out, and giving it an impatient jerk she turned the whole thing upside down on the table that stood by the bedside. The bundle rolled to the floor, opening as it fell, and let out the papers it held. Jean stooped and gathered them up, remembering the uncouth old man who had given it to her, and was rather surprised that the papers themselves looked clean and were evenly folded. She hurried down to the bright living room, holding them out to Mr. Harrington, and was startled at the look on his face as he saw what she gave him.

"You needn't be afraid—it's not a ghost," she laughed as she put the damp package in his hand. "It's rather dilapidated, but it's all there. I did the best I could with it, but it was submerged for a long time, and I had no opportunity to dry it."

Harrington said nothing, but his face turned suddenly white and his hand shook as he turned back the limp leather and looked at the folded papers inside. She saw by his expression that he knew what it was.

"Are they so very important?" she asked.

"Pretty important," he said, opening the papers one at a time and half turning away from her as if he didn't wish her to see them.

"I'm glad I saved them then," she said. "I came near throwing them away when I dropped out of that window. The old man was so dirty I couldn't bear to have anything he had handled. Well, good night."

She turned away, feeling that he wished to be alone with the papers, but he looked up and called her back.

"Wait, Jean. What kind of a man gave them to you?"

She told him in detail.

"Did you let anyone see this case?" he asked sharply.

"No," said Jean and then remembered. "Well, not exactly. It fell out of my bag once, and the paper I had wrapped it in fell off. But there was no one by but

Mr. Holt, and he didn't notice it in the least."

"Are you sure?" questioned her brother-in-law, his expression growing tense with anxiety. "How near was he?"

"He was standing close by, not three feet away, and he stooped and picked up the case and handed it back to me without saying a word," said Jean, a hint of indignation in her tone that warned him he had gone far enough in his inquiries.

"Well, never mind," he said, turning away. "It's all right, of course. They are very important papers relating to some business my company is carrying on, and Holt has been making a good deal of trouble for us. I'd rather he didn't know about them."

Jean was vexed, she scarcely knew why, and stood for an instant, hesitating. Should she say more or go immediately upstairs? It was very strange for James to act that way, as if it were her fault. And it was most unreasonable and unjust for him to feel that way about Jasper Holt. Her soul revolted against it.

Harrington looked up, annoyed, as if he would be rid of the girl; then, realizing the look of wonder on her face, he tried to control his expression and smile.

"Well, good night, Jean. Don't let this trouble you. I'm deeply grateful you were so faithful to guard the papers through all your experiences. Rest well, and don't think any more about it."

So dismissed, the girl turned slowly and mounted the stairs, but as she glanced back she saw him fluttering the papers over as if he were counting them two or three times. As she reached the landing she heard him summon a servant and send him in haste for someone named Garrett.

"Tell him he must come at once—it is important, urgent business," was the message sent. Then she closed her door and went about her preparations for the night, but her mind was strangely disturbed.

Chapter 9

E leanor Harrington came presently to the door and tapped.

"You're not asleep yet, are you, Jean?" she called. "James just wanted me to ask if there was any possibility that some of those papers were lost on the way? Did they fall, or did anything happen where one might have slipped out? He thinks two of the most important ones are missing."

"Not while they were in my possession, Eleanor," said Jean, feeling a return of her annoyance at her brother's manner. She opened the door and stood framed in the doorway, looking adorable in her pale blue kimono, with her hair tumbling over her shoulders. The elder sister hugged her and kissed her affectionately.

"How tired you look. Get to bed quickly. It was a shame to trouble you any more about those horrid papers. There, good night, dear! This is positively my last appearance," and she closed the door and went downstairs.

Five minutes later Jean turned to put out the light and saw, lying on the floor on the further side of the bedstand, a slip of paper folded once across, about the size of the wallet she had given her brother-in-law. She pounced on it and took it nearer the light. It looked more like an old letter that might have slipped from her trunk tray than a business paper.

As she opened the paper the name of Jasper Holt caught her eye, and her interest was at once enlisted. How did a paper bearing that name come to be in the guest chamber of her brother's house? It couldn't possibly have come through her. Nothing of his could have caught in her garments, for there was no place for anything to catch and no way his possessions could get into her bag. It couldn't, of course, be the missing paper from the wallet, since it bore his hated name. Yet her brother had spoken of disagreeable business relations. Would this paper, perhaps, explain to her the animosity that had sprung up between the two men? She felt she had the right to know. She glanced quickly down the page.

It was a simple contract, the grant of certain water rights to Jasper Holt in consideration of payment received. To any who could read, it was obvious that the paper must be the private property of Jasper Holt. How did it land here in the house of his enemy?

She read the lines over many times until she knew them thoroughly. Slowly there grew in her heart a conviction that something was wrong somewhere. Her first impulse, to call her sister and consult her, she couldn't bring herself to follow. It seemed that here was something she must think out for herself.

However and whatever her brother and sister felt, she owed a loyalty to Jasper Holt. She might not do a wrong, even inadvertently, to the one who had saved her life and cared for her so tenderly. If he were here she would have put the paper into his hands and asked him what to do about it. She had promised to trust him, and she felt such great confidence in him that she was convinced he would send the paper back to Harrington if it belonged to the latter.

But Holt was not here, and the problem of the future was still shrouded in difficulty. Would she ever see him to consult? Was this, perhaps, one of the missing papers James wanted, and why didn't she trust James to give it back to Holt as quickly as she would have trusted Holt to give it to James? The question brought a furrow to her brow. Did she distrust her brother-in-law just a little bit? Had she always done so without knowing it? Or was it just a prejudice because he seemed not quite so fine in his nature as her beloved sister? Besides, James was prejudiced against Holt. It might be hard for him to be generous and true under those circumstances. Yet her heart rebuked her for the thought.

She stood holding the bit of paper for a long time and finally put out the light and went and sat by the open window, trying to clear her thoughts and understand what she ought to do.

Out on the lawn the shadows were dark under the great tree where she and Jasper Holt had said good-bye. She thrilled again as she remembered.

The stars were clear and friendly as though they, too, remembered. The long stream of light still marked the divide between the shadows and the path to the house, for the lamps burned brightly downstairs, though all seemed quiet. Jean had heard Eleanor come upstairs again and tiptoe softly by her door as if fearing to wake her. She felt almost guilty sitting there in the dark awake.

The day had been long and full of excitement, and the night wrapped softly about the young girl. With the paper still held tightly in her hand, her head dropped back against the chair, and she was asleep.

It might have been an hour later that she awoke, the gruff voice of a man startling her into consciousness once more.

"That you, Jim? What's the matter? It's fierce when somebody's having the time of his life to have to turn and run at a moment's call. What's up? Something pretty stiff or you never would have sent that message. If I find it's any nonsense and squeamishness I'll—"

"Shh."

The voice suddenly changed into a gruff whisper. Jean realized that the man James had sent for was there. Then she addressed herself to the problem again, and the voices in low mumble, gradually rising to distinguishable sentences now and then, continued under her window.

She was not conscious of hearing them until she was startled into sharp attention by a name.

"I tell you if Jasper Holt gets onto this in time it will mean state's prison at least for us. It looks bad." It was Harrington's voice that spoke.

"I don't see it that way," said the stranger. "Holt hasn't got onto it, and Holt won't get onto it. You say the girl said he handed her back the wallet and never said a word. Don't you know Holt would never have let his own valuable private papers out of his hand if he suspected in the least that he held them? You know Holt better than that. Ten to one he was so taken with the girl that he never noticed the wallet; and why would he think she had his wallet anyway? I think it was pretty rare of old Scathlin to think of giving the papers to her. It threw Holt entirely off the track for good. Now what we want to do is to get hold of Blount. He's the whole show up there in New York, anyway. I'll just wire him to come on at once and talk it over, and we'll get to work and cut off the water supply while little Jasper's training his roses and wondering what has become of his perfectly good deeds to his perfectly good silver mine."

"But one of the missing papers is the grant of water rights. If that were here we might talk—"

Jean sat up suddenly, and her arm hit against the hairbrush which, in her excitement of preparing for bed, she had laid down on the windowsill. The hairbrush fell with a sharp noise on the polished floor just over the edge of the rug, and the two men in the vine-draped porch below started fiercely and looked up, the stranger with an oath.

"What's that?"

"Oh, nothing, I guess," said Harrington, his own voice a trifle strained. "Probably my wife has gone in to tuck up the baby and dropped something. Oh, you needn't worry. My sister-in-law was fast asleep hours ago. Her light went out just after I came out here to watch for you, and there hasn't been a sound overhead since. She was worn to a frazzle."

"Where is her room? This window up here?"

"No, just next, but she's asleep, I'm sure."

Harrington rose and stepped off the porch, walked out on the lawn and looked up. Jean, huddled back against her chair, could see his face as he surveyed the windows and then, reassured, came back to the porch.

"It's all right," he said in a low tone, "but maybe we'd better go to the other end of the porch. I was afraid of waking up the baby over there, and the rascal is a difficult problem when he wakes in the night."

"Well, talk lower anyway," said the stranger. "What did you say the other missing paper was? You have the list of them all, haven't you?"

"Yes, copies. I wish we'd sent the copies instead of the originals. Only Scathlin's story about finding them wouldn't have worked then. The other lost paper is the claim, with the location of the ore—most important. Strange that those two, the ones on which the others all hinge, are gone! I can't understand. Do you suppose Scathlin has something up his sleeve? Maybe he kept only those two and means to get these later—but what object could he have?"

The two men were silent for a moment while they thought.

At last Garrett spoke. "What do you suppose Holt was doing on that train—the same train as Scathlin? Holt didn't leave home till Scathlin had been on his way nearly two days. When was the last we heard from Scathlin?"

"Pittsburgh. A telegram. He'd just arrived," answered Harrington.

"What day was that? Could Holt have reached Pittsburgh before Scathlin got away? He's sharp, you know. Do you have the telegram?"

"It's inside," said Harrington. "Just step in." And the two men went into the house. Jean could hear their low, troubled voices rumbling on, but she couldn't hear any more words, and she sat shivering over what she had heard.

Scathlin! Scathlin! Why was that word so familiar? Scathlin! Ah! She had heard it from the lips of Holt himself, before she went into the sleeper. It was what he had called the old man.

Was this wrong, this involuntary eavesdropping? She didn't mean to listen, had never thought there might be anything said that she would understand or that they would care if she did hear, until the whole revelation was in her possession. Then she was too much frightened to stir or think what she ought to do. Wasn't it right, perhaps, that she should have heard; and, yet, what could she do? It was all too evident that Jasper Holt was about to be cheated in some way. That remark about his private papers was unmistakable. And the paper in her hand that had to do with water rights was his also. Water rights were sacred things in the West. The loss of them had often been the cause of whole fortunes lost as well, and the little bit of paper that proved his right was in her trembling hand to bestow where she would!

It was plain that if she should go down now and give it to those two men, she would be most welcome. But she was sure it would not be right for them to have it. They had admitted enough to make her feel that there was some plot against Holt. Suddenly all her latent dislike of her brother-in-law, which had lain dormant through the years because there was nothing to rouse it, sprang into being. Her decision was made. She must somehow get that paper to Jasper Holt and as soon as possible. She mustn't let her brother know she had it. If she were mistaken about this, Jasper Holt would be true and tell her so and return the paper. She felt as sure of him as if she had known him all her life. But there could be no mistake. It must be his. The men had practically said as much.

It made her shiver to think how dreadful all this was. Brought up to the strictest integrity, it seemed terrible that one in their own family should swerve from it; there must be some other explanation to the talk she heard. Things in the business world were odd, and a lot of shady things were done under the name of righteousness. Maybe James thought he was doing good service to cut Jasper Holt out of his water right somehow; and maybe, in some unexplainable way, he was justified. And yet—what did they mean about the location of the silver mine? If she had never known and loved Jasper Holt, and trusted him, she would have gone down and put the whole thing in James's hands and gone to bed thinking no more about it. But now her whole soul was roused to do the right thing toward her friend, who seemed to be in the right in this case at least.

It occurred to her how easily she might wash her hands of the whole matter by dropping that bit of paper out the window and letting it be found or not, as the case might be. How easy to live sometimes if one had no conscience to reckon with!

It seemed a long time that she sat by the open window, afraid to stir lest the men downstairs should hear her move. But at last the two men came out on the porch again, the guest apparently about to take his leave. His voice had lost its easy assurance.

"It looks bad," he said, "very bad! It looks as if Scathlin bungled things. If Holt suspects we have anything to do with it, why, our fish is dished. I guess there's nothing else to do but send him back those papers, saying that a stranger put them into your sister's hands to bring to you, and you know nothing about them, but seeing his name among them you suppose they must be his. You could add a word about being grateful for his care of the girl or something of the sort to make it look natural."

"But that throws all the responsibility on me," said Harrington angrily. "And it looks mighty funny to have those two important papers gone. These are no use to anybody without those."

"Of course, but you're not supposed to know that, and he can't do anything but bluster. Anyhow, as far as I see, it's your only chance, and you'll have to do it mighty quick or that won't do any good. I wouldn't keep them a day."

"I shall do nothing of the kind!" snarled Harrington. "I would rather destroy them than play into his hand that way. I'm not in a position to throw suspicion on myself that way."

"Do as you please," said the guest scornfully. "That's my advice. I wash my hands of it. If you want to hang on to a lost cause for the sake of pride, you'll have to do it without me. I know when to quit."

"But suppose Scathlin returns in a few days with Blount."

"Scathlin won't return with Blount. You can take my word for that. Either Scathlin's dead or he's sold those other two papers to Holt and given away our secrets into the bargain. You may depend on it. If Scathlin was all right he'd have telegraphed at intervals as he was ordered. There's some reason why he quit telegraphing at Pittsburgh."

Garrett departed noisily, and after a few minutes of pacing up and down the porch, Harrington went in, put out the lights and came upstairs.

Jean crept softly into bed, still grasping the paper close to her breast. Weary and troubled, she soon fell asleep.

Later, when the moon had died and only the luminous mist in the east proclaimed the dawn at hand, a rider came quietly down the road, his horse stepping as if with padded feet, and stopped before the house.

The rider dismounted silently in the darkness and with noiseless tread came and laid something down at the door, then mounted and slipped away into the mist again.

Chapter 10

Down the long, silent road beyond the sleeping town the rider passed, out to the plains. His horse knew the trail well, was rested and glad to be used. He stepped away into the gray dawning carrying his beloved master with willing feet. There was no need to hurry him. He seemed to know as if by instinct just how fast to travel to arrive at the junction in time for the early morning train. It was not the first time he had journeyed thus at that hour.

The rider sat his horse with weariness in his aspect and in profound thoughtfulness.

Now and then he bent his head and laid his lips on the cool fragrance of a bud stuck carelessly into his buttonhole, its branch and thorns and leaves still attached as if it might have been plucked from the vine by hasty impulse. Later, when the day came up and houses were in sight, he tore it from its stem and wrapped it in his handkerchief to hide away in his pocket.

The stars were paling when he started. They slipped one by one into the oblivion of a background of light as he rode, but before they left him they spoke many things to his sad, determined soul. Sometimes it almost seemed to him that a girl rode at his side and understood his thoughts.

The young face lost its boyishness and grew grave and haggard with suffering. Then he laid his lips on the cool flower petals and heard again the voice of the girl like music in his soul: "I will trust you always, no matter what anybody says!"

It thrilled him and gave him courage, so that when morning burst upon the plain and he came in sight of the straggling houses surrounding the junction, he lifted up his face to the golden morning sky and breathed aloud the words: "O God! Help me to keep my vow to her, always, even to the end of my life! Help me to be what she believes me to be! Help me to be worthy of her trust!"

With these words upon his lips and the memory of her kiss upon his brow, he went forward into the new day and the new life that was before him. His duty today was by no means a pleasant one, and it might be long and hard, but he must do it in a different way from how he would have done it three days before. Today he was a different creature. He had seen himself as he was before God, and henceforth all things were become new.

He was in time to make all his arrangements to leave the horse before the train arrived. He had chosen to travel across country to the junction rather than take the train at his home station, partly to avoid publicity and partly to save time, for there was no train from Hawk Valley early enough to connect with this Eastern express, which stopped at the junction. Passengers from Hawk Valley wishing to catch this train would be forced to leave the evening before and put up at the junction tavern, a most unpleasant experience for any traveler. Jasper Holt preferred traveling on horseback at all times to riding on the railroad, but every minute counted now in the errand he was on his way to perform.

All morning, while the train glided over the level plain, his mind ran through his recent experience; going back to the moment when the girl entered his vision and looked at him with that clear, direct gaze that trusted him; thinking over every detail of his finding her in the peril; the miracle that he and not some other should have found and saved her; recalling every incident of the beautiful, wearisome way by which they had gone home together; and the wonder of the girl's faith in him, her love for him—his love for her.

Anyone watching the absorbed, silent man sitting alone, his head dropped back against the seat, his hat drawn down over his eyes, would have judged him for a much older man than he was, so maturing had life thus far been to him.

And now the task set before him was to find Scathlin—if indeed he were still alive—or some evidence that he was dead, and to know beyond question what became of those papers and just how far Harrington was responsible for the theft.

He loathed his task yet felt compelled by some inner urging to finish it. Almost his soul revolted to the extent of giving up the case and letting his enemies triumph over him. What was his silver mine to him now since he had found her—and lost her forever? Why not let his property go and leave Hawk Valley forever, where his reputation had undone him in his greatest opportunity? Why not go to some new land where he was unknown and start all over again?

But his soul was too strong and true for that. He must face his mistakes in the place where he had made them and undo, if possible, some of the harm he had done. It was right that he should find his papers and make good his claim. It was a part of the true living he had set himself from this time forth. He had promised to let people see that he was trustworthy, and this was the first step. If Harrington and his men got their way, he would be branded as a thief and a liar again and the old reputation only fixed the firmer.

Toward evening the train passed the scene of the disaster, and the long rays of the sun rested over the river and valley where peril and death had brooded. A temporary way had been made for the tracks, all signs of death and disaster swept out of sight by the wrecking train, and the tide of travel was already rolling calmly on again. A swarm of workmen, like ants carrying grains of sand over a wall, were at work on the broken bridge, and the passing traveler got no hint of fire and fear and sudden death. Even the trainmen answered gruffly, in brief sentences, when questioned about the wreck, turning it off lightly as a small thing, until they heard that here was one of the almost-victims of the accident. Then they looked sharply a second time and stole back to talk in low tones with guarded sentences about where the blame should lie. But no one knew much about the details. The conductor said the victims, those who had been saved, were taken to the nearest city and distributed among the hospitals. That was all.

So on to the nearest city Jasper Holt went, arriving shortly after sundown, and began his search among the hospitals after visiting the railroad office and gathering all the information they could give him.

Three days and two nights Jasper Holt searched, in hospitals and morgues and even private homes. Wherever he could learn of a person who had been through the accident, he went to see if they held any clue to the man he sought, but not a hint did he find.

It was reasonable to suppose that Scathlin had lost his life in the fire or the river and to feel that further search was unnecessary. But Holt, standing at the window of his hotel room and looking out on the busy streets toward evening of the third day, could not feel it so. More and more it became necessary to find that man or be sure of his death.

To look any longer in the city was absurd. He had already covered every clue he could find, and the railroad authorities were growing weary of this assiduous young man with the firm jaw and the blue-gray eyes of steel who steadily demanded the missing man. They offered to send him back to the scene of the accident with a man to help him and authority to search the river and vicinity. This offer he finally accepted and the next morning was on his way back.

The last time Holt saw Scathlin he had not really seen him at all.

They had both been sleeping—Scathlin with the relaxation of one who no longer needs to be on the alert, Holt with half his senses on guard—when the crash came. Splintering glass and a rush of cold air brought Holt to himself. The car was turned on end and sinking down with creak and groan; and the two men were thrown together for a moment into the aisle, clinging to the arms of the seats. Holt had heard Scathlin's terrible oaths. They sounded now like a challenge to the Almighty. The younger man had reached out a hand in the darkness to strike the other and shouted, "Cut that out!" But the profanity continued, and Scathlin struck him a blow across his eyes that bewildered him for a second and made the confusion more terrible. Then he had been aware of Scathlin scrambling up over the arm of the seat to the window, about to climb out. The red glow from outside flared up and showed Scathlin's bulk against the night, his head and shoulders already out the window.

It was then he realized that Scathlin was escaping from him and he must not let him get away. Even in such a situation he remembered his long quest and, pulling himself up by force, caught Scathlin by the foot. Suddenly he remembered the curious actions of Scathlin the day before and his fumbling with his shoestrings afterward. The shoe Holt held in his firm grip was laced and tied in a hard knot, but Holt's knife was ready, and he cut the string in several places. Scathlin did not stay for shoes. He left his footgear readily in his pursuer's hands and made good his escape, but Holt, forgetful of his peril for the moment, searched in the shoe and found a folded paper.

It was too dark to tell if the paper was one of those he sought. He put it safely in his pocket for further investigation, felt in the shoe once more to make sure there was not another and then climbed out the window after Scathlin. But when he dropped into the melee below he could not see Scathlin anywhere. There were some rocks far below, and down there he thought he saw a white face as he first looked from the window, when the fire broke out with a flare. But after he dropped and found himself in the water, he couldn't locate the rocks again, and while he searched he heard another victim drop and sink and rise again, and he went to her rescue. So Scathlin had his wish and escaped from the train before they reached Hawk Valley.

Holt and his assistant searched the scene of the wreck until the young man was convinced that further search was useless and sent the man back to the city. Then he dropped down to the riverbank and talked with one or two men on the wrecking crew while they waited for the construction train to come and bear them back to their camp. Here for the first time he got a clue. They had found a man down on the rocks with a broken leg a whole day after the others had been taken to the city hospital. Some bushes had hidden him, and no one had noticed him till they heard him groaning and cursing. A man who said he had a shack "up a piece" took him in his wagon. He promised to get a doctor to fix the man up. The man himself had begged them to shoot him. He was almost out of his head with suffering. Their vague description tallied with Scathlin's rough appearance, and Holt became convinced he had found his man.

Making the best he could out of their indefinite directions, Holt started off in search of the shack.

He found Scathlin before nightfall, lying alone and moaning with pain and fever in the deserted shack. The owner had gone away at dawn on business, promising a speedy return, but had not come back, and Scathlin, his broken bone set rudely by an unskilled hand, lay suffering torments. When Holt pushed the door open and looked in, he started up with a yell, his eyes protruding in fear. He thought Holt was dead in the fire of the wreck and his spirit had come to demand account.

It was only when Holt laid his hand on the dirty brow and spoke in a voice of quiet command that Scathlin settled back, the terror still in his eyes, and consented to be still. He gradually realized Holt was there in the flesh and not for retribution. He hadn't succeeded in escaping his captor. He never could do that. That was plain. So cunning and contemptible was the creature that when he was assured of the fact that Holt would not strike him when he was down, he set about to take advantage of it. It was as if he had found a spot of honor wherein Holt was vulnerable, and there upon his bed of pain, in his loathsome helplessness, he attacked that one pregnable spot of Holt's fortress. Day and night he moaned and fretted. Hour after hour he demanded this and that, whining like a baby and cursing like a demon by turns.

The owner did not return. Holt was there alone with Scathlin for many days, nursing him as tenderly as a woman might have done; bearing with his varying moods; washing him, feeding him, cooling his hot forehead. Only once did Scathlin lapse from his role of pampered patient and beg with terror and abject humility in his eyes and voice, and that was the day when Holt declared his intention of going after a doctor. Scathlin was sure Holt meant to desert him, and he cried like a baby, swore like a madman, and then pleaded and promised contritely. But it was all to no avail, and Holt left him for a few hours and went for a doctor. Scathlin's cries and curses followed him as far as he could hear, and something like pity came into his heart for the wicked old criminal.

When he returned four hours later with a gruff but kindly doctor, the cunning look came back into the old man's beady eyes, and the bristly jaw grew stubborn and selfish again. He saw that Holt's honor still held, and he meant to get the worth of his money out of him.

The doctor came every few days after that, and Scathlin improved rapidly, growing more arrogant every day.

Holt went about silently for the most part, nursing the patient, cooking his meals. There was something about his stern face even in his gentleness that sometimes shamed Scathlin and silenced him for a while. It was as if his mind was far away on higher things, and Scathlin's petty torments did not reach up into the heights where he lived.

Once, when he was getting better and sitting up, Scathlin attempted a story so vile that the devil himself must have originated it. He laughed as he told it, hoping to break the stern sadness of Holt's face. But Holt looked at him with a kind of pity for a second, and then the sternness grew terrible.

"Scathlin, cut that out, you beast!" he said and left the cabin for the open air.

Holt struggled with himself to stick to his job. There was no longer the necessity that brought him. The papers, the rest of them, wherever they were, were surely not here. He had gone over every inch of Scathlin's clothes and possessions, and there was no place where he could possibly have hidden them about the shack that Holt hadn't looked. He watched Scathlin by night and by day when he didn't know he was being watched, and he was convinced that Scathlin was no longer protecting any of his papers. The one he had taken from the toe of Scathlin's shoe had proved to be his own and most important. What Scathlin had done with the rest he wasn't sure, but he had probably given some of them to Jean with the wallet—which he had, of course, recognized when he picked it up and handed it to her. It was also possible the man who owned the shack had, by some means, been wheedled into taking the papers back to Harrington. Every circumstance made his speedy return to Hawk Valley advisable, and yet here he was chained to this peevish old man who, when he was done with him, would, if he could, stab him in the back.

And so as the days at last came when the patient could walk about a little, the beady old eyes took on new cunning. When Holt urged that they return home, Scathlin's eyes filled with fear, and he whined and begged for just a little more time. For once more the vision of the stark tree against the sky, the swinging body, the retreating backs of Holt's strong men, haunted Scathlin's memory.

One day when Holt went to procure a wagon and some other necessities for the journey, he returned to find the old man gone.

At first it seemed only a relief from a disagreeable task, and he would have let him go. But that inner sense of needing to finish a job made him go out and search. He knew the weak leg could not carry the man far, and he felt too that he must keep hold of Scathlin and take him back to face what he would find awaiting him in Hawk Valley, whether of good or ill. He might need the old man for a witness.

And so he drew him from his crouching shelter, spoke to him firmly and made a pact with him, for he recognized his fear. That night saw the two again on their way to Hawk Valley. Scathlin was to have shelter and food, and work when he was able, but in return he must abide by certain rules. Relieved and cunning still, Scathlin promised eagerly, with many mental reservations. So the pilgrimage at last was ended, and Holt was going back—back where the girl he loved was staying, the girl he loved but might not see.

Chapter 11

There had been no fuss made over Jasper Holt when he was born. They handed him an honored name from some fierce old warrior of a forebear, relegated him to a fourth-story back nursery with a trained nurse and left him to himself.

His mother paused long enough before returning to her interrupted social career to look him over, declare that he had nice eyes and she believed his hair was going to curl; then she was swallowed up in the world from which she had reluctantly stepped aside. She had little use for a son except to dress him in velvets and Lord Fauntleroy collars and make of him a toy to amuse her guests. Until he reached that stage she saw very little of him.

Of his stern father he saw less. He was immersed in business. He was rich, but what of that? He had to make more riches to keep the social whirl fed.

The baby had a face and form worth noticing, even in his first days. The great blue eyes that had attracted his mother's flitting attention could be gray sometimes and held depths of light and wisdom that fairly startled his practical nurse. He had the brow of a philosopher, and gold hair rippled around the fine little head like a halo. The old warrior-namesake must have bestowed upon him that firm chin beneath the cupid's bow of the lips, and surely an angel had lent him that smile!

But as he grew older there came into his eyes a wistfulness that was almost pathetic at times. He was an affectionate child, quite embarrassing his cold, reserved nurse with his demonstrations, but winning the devotion of all who had to serve him.

He was not a good boy in the conventional sense of the word. He sweetly had his own way in everything from the time he could walk and talk. He would neither eat what he did not like nor wear what he did not fancy. He did not take kindly to his mother's velvets and curls and lace collars. He always disappeared when made ready for a dress parade. He would fight any bully on the back street who undertook to cheat the little lame newsboy, and he was always trying to take the part of some weak dog or child. He could run down the street with the swiftness of a swallow, his pockets full of sharp stones, and hit every electric light in the block as he ran. And he was forever taking the blame for all the broken windows and looted garden plots in the neighborhood.

During his boyhood days, his acquaintance with his father was limited to severe interviews in which stern threats and scathing reprimands mingled with a galling sarcasm. It was as his clear eyes looked steadily into the angry steel ones of the man that his young face hardened, his chin took a firm set, and the light in his face was deadened by a stab of pain. He was growing wise and losing faith in the love he had taken for granted in both father and mother. To compensate, he lived mostly on the street and companioned with boys of the rougher class. No one but his nurse knew it, and she only seldom. She was only too glad to have the time off duty.

When they discovered a childish plot in the neighborhood to mob the president of a defaulting bank in which the hardworking parents of some of his playmates had lost their all, Jasper was taken hold of by the law as leader of the whole enterprise. Proudly he took the blame, exonerating the other boys and declaring himself instigator of the affair.

His father paid a heavy fine to hush it up and took his son in charge. Jasper received his merciless whipping like a gentleman. But when it was over he lifted reproachful eyes, steadied his quivering chin and said: "But all the same, Father, I think I was right! That man had been stealing those poor people's money!"

The father looked at the son with the unbroken will and swore. He took away the cheap little firearms that the boy had purchased with his allowance for himself and the other boys, and he declared the allowance would cease until the boy owned to his fault and came to his senses.

Jasper went up to his room and thought. Then he went out and consulted with a newsboy friend, and presently he was established on a paper route of his own. For several weeks he sold papers till he had enough money to replace his lost revolver. Satisfied, he retired from business for the time, but this was not his first business venture, and his father began to discover that the threat of taking away the allowance had no effect on his determined son.

Yet in spite of his bravery and strength, in spite of his high purposes and anarchistic tendencies, there was in the boy's nature a great wealth of love and a desire to be loved. He was, in his younger days, forever throwing his arms about his beautiful mother's neck and kissing her, to her great disgust and the severe detriment of her complexion. Thus rejected, he gradually became shy about showing his affection, and the lines of loneliness and yearning grew deeper about the young mouth.

It was the time he ran away that made him sure no one cared for him.

Jasper had been up before the paternal tribunal for some trivial offense, and his word had not been taken in explanation, against the word of his younger brother—who for some reason was the beloved darling of his mother.

Perry Holt had effeminate features like his mother's and had been petted and spoiled from the moment his whimsical mother first saw him. If there was any trouble, Perry was usually at the bottom of it, and Jasper was blamed for it, because Jasper was "so wild" and "always getting into trouble and doing what he ought not to do." That was the way his mother put it. And so she had ordered Jasper to his father's den for a reprimand for something Perry had done, and Jasper's word was doubted.

He took his punishment silently and went to his room, where he lay motionless, staring into the darkness. If he had been a girl, he might have sobbed, so hurt was his soul; but being Jasper he held back the stinging tears that burned his eyes and stared hard into the dark. At midnight, when the servants were asleep, he arose and stole softly from the house before his mother and father had returned from some social function they were attending.

He stayed away three days, companioning with waifs who had no homes, and then his homesick heart brought him back again with longing to see his mother. He reached the house at early dusk and found his mother and Perry getting into the car to ride to the station, where they were to meet his father and take a pleasure trip to Washington for a few days. They had not even missed him and were going off without knowing where he was! His mother looked at him with disgust and told him to go into the house and wash his face. Then the car whirled off and left him gazing after his dream of what a mother ought to be.

After that Jasper never expected anything more from his mother or his family. He began to see that life was meant to be a lonely job and it "was up to him" how it turned out. He seemed to grow up and be wise beyond his years in those few seconds that he stood gazing after the car vanishing in the dusk.

When it was discovered that he was spending most of his time on the street in the company of newsboys and workingmen's sons, he was fitted out expensively and sent away to boarding school, where he began a lively career. Those who understood him adored him, but they were few and were mostly confined to small boys and the working class. The little boys in the school followed him like flies after molasses and obeyed him abjectly. The teachers dreaded and feared and hated him, with the exception now and then of a woman who had a fine instinct and saw the yearning for love in his eyes.

From school to school he went, out of one scrape into another, yet no one stopped to inquire what it was all about or discover that almost every trouble he got into was for the sake of someone else, for some real principle. That his efforts at reform were against the rules of the school, and could therefore but fail, made no difference to him. He went right on setting things right as far as he could and then taking the consequences. He saw the futility of his efforts and sometimes clenched his fists and thought of the future when he should be able to "lick" those unfair teachers who couldn't see that they were letting some fellows go scot-free who were more to blame than the ones they punished. Someday he would be bigger than they, and then he would back up his protests with a strength that could not be denied. And so he went on fighting bullies who were bigger than he was and who did not hesitate to put the whole story in a good light for themselves. He always took the consequences in such a way that when he left a school the principal had a feeling that, after all, the boy had gotten the better of him, for there had been the look of a conqueror in Jasper's eye as he parted from him at the station.

Somehow he got through his preparatory studies and was allowed to pass on. It surely was not from any great scholastic attainments, for he never bothered to learn lessons he didn't care for nor recite them after he had learned them, and examinations meant nothing at all to him. If he chose to take one he did so. If he did not choose to take an examination he calmly sat through the allotted time intent upon his own thoughts and handed in no paper at the close. His teachers raved and ranted. They punished and threatened. But Jasper went calmly on and did as he pleased. And strange to say, in all that checkered career, only two teachers understood the boy's soul and could lead him like a lamb by a mere smile or word to do the hardest tasks. For those two he slaved, not because he saw any reason in their demands always, but because he desired to please them, for they had proved themselves what he called "square."

Nevertheless, he acquired through it all a marvelous and varied amount of knowledge. Nothing escaped him. He never forgot anything he heard, and the classes through which he sat, perpetrating many of his jokes on the teachers, all left their impression upon him. What he heard the other students recite, that he knew. If one began to quote a line of poetry which had been studied in English class, he would promptly finish it and, when he chose, tell much about the author. His teachers would have been amazed if they could have heard him. And often when another fellow took a high rank in the class in mathematics, it had been Jasper who showed him how to work the problems—problems he had not taken the trouble to work out for himself.

"Why should I?" he once answered a troublesome principal who was admonishing him about preparing his lessons. "I get what I need out of them, and that's all that's necessary, isn't it? It's my education, isn't it? My teacher isn't getting anything out of my writing out all that junk, is he? It isn't doing him any good. Why should I take the trouble?"

And this was his hopeless attitude whenever he had to deal with teachers he did not reverence.

In college he was much the same; only it didn't matter there so much. There were more men, and he was less under authority. It was expected that he should have some independence. Yet even here he was mixed up in a great many of the troubles. Finally, in his third year, his college career came to a sudden ending in the midst of a disgrace that was not his own but which he took upon his shoulders to save another youth who had a widowed mother dependent upon him and must get through college before he could support her. Jasper's mother, by that time an attractive widow, was so outraged by her son's behavior—she never knew, of course, that he himself had not been at fault—that she drove him from his home in scorn and contempt.

Hurt to the heart, the boy obeyed; too proud to explain; knowing she would be only angrier if she knew the truth; knowing she had no mother heart in her for him nor ever had.

He went straight to the great, wide, free West and roamed for a year from one place to another, still expecting someday to return when his mother would feel differently. Then he saw in the papers the notice of her marriage to a man he had never liked, and so he settled down on the claim he had already taken and built up around his young, lonely life something which he called home.

Gradually the outcasts of society were drawn to him for help in dire need and peril from the law. And always he had sympathy for any who were without the pale of the respectable world, even though in no other way could he feel anything congenial toward them. His home came to be a refuge for sinners, and because their crimes were many and his hearth was wide, their sins were fastened to him in name if not in deed—as when a child he bore the blame for others and himself grew strong.

He built them rude dwellings on his land, and some he chose to be his trusted ones. One by one he tested them and found them true to him and to his few simple principles of life. Sternly he ruled them, and greatly did they love and reverence their boy leader and were proud to follow him. If one of them transgressed again, he was dealt with justly; and once a body swayed and hung stark against the sky for a deed of shame. It was this memory that Scathlin held and feared, although it happened long before he came to take refuge from some petty deed of his. Scathlin never entered the closer brotherhood of men who guarded Holt's own private quarters. His place had been upon the outer edge of things. He was not trusted—never had been—and knew he was not trustworthy. So he dreaded going back to those relentless men who, if they found out he had robbed their leader of valuable property and betrayed him into the hands of an enemy who looked with hungry eyes at his rich silver mine and abundant water supply, would stop at nothing till justice had been done. But by that same honor that made men love and serve him, Scathlin knew Holt had not yet told his men about his loss of the wallet or whom he suspected.

This was Jasper Holt, and this his story up to the time he met Jean and laid his roses at her threshold.

Chapter 12

It was late when Jean awoke. The household had been quiet on her account, and breakfast was delayed. She came down white with her vigil, but sweet and smiling otherwise.

The morning brought clear vision, and she was sure now that the paper in her possession must be given to Holt and no other. She was settled on the matter and would await her opportunity. This decided, her mind was at peace, and she entered the dining room with a smile of greeting for everyone.

Late as it was, the master of the house had not yet appeared, and the family stood about waiting for him. But as Jean entered, the servant came in from an opposite door with his arms full of roses and stood before her.

Such roses! Jean had never seen such wealth of beauty. They all exclaimed in wonder over them. Their fragrance filled the room like a burst of incense. The servant laid them in her arms as though he were offering her a crown and scepter.

"How wonderful!" murmured the girl, receiving them. "Where did they come from? Are they mine? Do they grow here?"

"I found them at the door, miss," said the man. "There's only a card with your name."

"Why, how strange!" said Mrs. Harrington, stepping forward to inspect the card. "Who could have sent them? I told a number of the young men about your coming, and they're eager to see you; but it's strange that whoever sent these beautiful roses shouldn't have given his name. They're wonderfully rare. Somebody must have squandered his month's earnings on them. They couldn't have been bought around here. I suppose they came from some florist a long way off."

The discreet servant narrowed his eyes and turned away suddenly as he saw his master enter.

"Just look here, James, what beautiful roses someone has sent Jean! Wasn't that lovely of him, whoever he is? They were at the door when John opened it this morning, and no name on them. Who do you suppose could have sent them? Stockton Holmes or Gartney Fowler or even Captain Wetherill, perhaps?"

But the master of the house glanced sharply at the roses, and a frown came between his brows.

"There's only one place around here where roses like that grow," he announced ominously.

His wife looked at him with a frightened expression.

"You don't mean—?"

"Yes," said Harrington. "They're Holt's Golden Sunset!"

Silence filled the room as the husband and wife looked at each other. Then Mrs. Harrington turned to her sister, who stood behind her with an exquisite flush on her cheeks and a soft, burning light of battle in her eyes.

"Jean, did you know where they came from?" her sister asked, almost haughtily.

But Jean's lovely face showed no sign of intimidation as she raised it from the roses in her arms.

"I thought perhaps Mr. Holt sent them," she said simply. "He told me about his roses. But excuse me just a minute till I put them in water. I won't keep you waiting."

When Jean returned after laying her roses tenderly in the washbowl in her room and bending to touch her lips to their petals, there was no look on her face as if anything unusual had passed. She began at once to give her sister a message from their mother, tactfully ignoring the flowers and their donor. But Harrington's set look did not relax during the entire meal.

After breakfast there was the whole place to be seen: the garden, the horses, the rabbits, the lawn-tennis court—the only one in town—where the young officers from the fort came down to play sometimes.

The children came out of their shyness and adopted their new relative ecstatically. They drew her down on the garden seat and plied her with questions, and they chattered away, feeling her hair, touching her cheek softly now and then, playing with the ribbons at her throat.

"Papa's awfully angry that Jasper Holt brought you home," confided Betty. "I heard him tell Mama he'd rather have lost fifty thousand dollars than for it to happen."

The color stole into Jean's cheeks, and a flash came into her eyes, but she tried to control herself. She didn't want to discuss the matter with the children, and yet she felt she must be true to the man who had saved her life.

"Mr. Holt was very kind to me, Betty," she said quietly. "I'm sorry he isn't a friend of your papa's. If he hadn't taken care of me I would probably have drowned, and I'm sure I never would have gotten safely here. He was wonderful!"

"Jasper Holt's a bad, wicked man," said Jamie, looking at her with round eyes and a frown that was a very good imitation of his father's. "He–he–he hanged a man once! On a tree! Yes, he did! Tied a string around his neck and hung him up hard till he died! Nicky Deens told me that. My mama don't know he told me. Nicky said not to tell. But Nicky Deens saw the tree once when he went riding with his papa out to the desert, and he heard the men tell all about it. They didn't know he heard it, but he did."

"I don't think much of a little boy who tells you not to tell your mother things," said Jean in a choking voice. "I don't believe I shall like Nicky Deens."

"Oh, you will," said Jamie in distress for his friend. "He can ride a horse just like his papa." Jamie launched into a description of the prowess of Nicky Deens.

But Jean, although she tried to smile, wasn't listening. Her heart was in a tumult, and her eyes were full of fire and indignation. Jasper had told her about that man who hung on the tree. She knew the whole story with all its circumstances, and she knew that Nicky Deens had heard a false account of the affair. Suddenly she turned on her astonished young nephew.

"Jamie," she said, looking earnestly into his big, blue eyes, "Jamie, I want to tell you something. That story you heard about Mr. Holt is not true. He is not a bad man. People don't know. He is good and kind, and he has been Auntie Jean's friend. It isn't right or fair for you to listen to stories about him. Little boys like Nicky Deens don't know about things always, and maybe they don't mean to tell what isn't true. But if you love Auntie Jean and believe she tells you what is true, you won't let anybody say bad things anymore about Mr. Holt. It isn't necessary for you to talk about it all if your papa doesn't like Mr. Holt, but you don't need to listen to unpleasant things about him. People haven't understood Mr. Holt, or they would not have talked that way."

Jamie looked at her with round, wondering eyes, and his paternal frown grew. He didn't like to have his thrilling story spoiled by being told it wasn't true, but then, this new aunt had pretty eyes and a good smile. Besides, she had promised to tell him a story.

"Aw right, I won't!" he finally said, with mental reservation, and sighed to relinquish this choice bit of gossip, even during the period of his aunt's stay.

It was a relief to Jean that her sister came just then and sent the children off to play, sitting down for a real visit about home and their dear ones.

Finally there came a pause in their conversation about home, and the two sisters looked at each other contentedly, glad to be together again after the long separation.

"Jean, dear," said Eleanor, "I hope you're going to have a lovely time while you're here. I've told every man in the region about you, and they are dying to call on you. I don't know how many have tried to bribe me to let them be first. There are no end of charming young fellows here. The post being so near brings some of them, you know, and they love to come over to our house and get a real home meal and a glimpse of something like what they are used to. There's Charlie Evans—you'll like him, I know. He's quite serious—thought of studying for the ministry at one time, but I understand he got to be rather skeptical and gave it up. You'll be just the one to do a little missionary work on him. You have great talents in that direction, I remember. Mother has been telling me what wonders you've worked in your Sunday school class at the mission.

"And there's Freeman Thorne," she went on. "He's grave and serious enough to suit your most solemn mood, and there are scores of others. You'll have flowers and invitations, more than you can attend to, pretty soon. We've lots of plans made already to help you have a good time. But I want to give you a little warning, dear." A kind of constraint came into her voice. "Don't speak about Jasper Holt unless you have to, and then the very briefest word. He isn't in good repute at all—indeed, he isn't! I understand how grateful you feel, of course. You weren't in a position to judge what kind of a fellow he was. I don't suppose one's manners would show up very badly in the woods when two people had been drowning and barely escaped with their lives. People don't think of manners at such a time—"

"Eleanor, he was a perfect gentleman," put in Jean indignantly. "There were lots of chances to show unrefinement, and he was a perfect gentleman every time. You don't understand, Eleanor."

"Well, now, dear, you'll have to trust me a little. I know just what he is, a bad man—a really bad man. Papa wouldn't have your name mixed up with his for anything in the world. I know you can't be convinced just now, because you've come through an unusual experience together, and I'm sure I'm glad if he was half decent—it wasn't to be expected—though it's what I've always claimed, that a really nice girl always has the upper hand of a man, even a bad man, and he dare not be rude to her. Then, of course, it was quite thoughtful of him to leave those roses the way he did and go away without any message. I'll give him credit for that. But it was most unfortunate that he should have been the one to save you! Papa would not at all approve of your having anything more to do with him whatever."

"That is just what he said," said Jean quietly.

"What he said!" exclaimed her sister. "Really! Then he does realize a little what people think of him. Well, that is a commendable attitude, of course, and if you think it necessary, you might write a formal little note and thank him for bringing you home. But make him understand that he is not to presume—or, if you prefer, I might do it for you. On second thought I think Mama would prefer that I—"

"It is not in the least necessary, Eleanor. I have thanked Mr. Holt already, and he understands perfectly that it would not be agreeable to you to have him come here. You said you had sewing to do. Don't you want me to help you with something? I'd love to."

There was a dignity in the set of the head and the firm curve of the lip that made Mrs. Harrington survey her young sister with wonder and silence as they arose and went toward the house. The way Jean had set aside the topic of Holt was masterly. Mrs. Harrington had not said nearly all she meant to say on the subject again. She looked at Jean uneasily from time to time as they sat together in the house or went about from room to room, flying from one topic to another as people will do who have been long separated. Three distinct times she attempted to give an extended dissertation on the evil deeds and reputation of Jasper Holt, and each time the subject was summarily closed, quietly set aside by Jean as if she had no interest whatever in the young man. It gave the woman an uncanny feeling and actually disturbed her, so that she was threatened with one of her nervous headaches. After lunch, having had to confess to her husband that she'd made no headway in enlightening her sister with regard to his enemy, she retired to her darkened room to sleep. Jean, glad of escape, fled to her roses.

Broodingly, as a mother would touch her little child while it sleeps, Jean hovered over the flowers. The door was locked safe from intrusion, and the children had been sent to a neighbor's that the house might be quiet. She drew the little table near the great window chair and placed the bowl of roses upon it.

They filled the bowl, lying heavy-headed in great sheaves over its rim on their cool, luscious leaves, those leaves of that peculiar green touched with burnt sienna on tips and veins, that speak of a high state of cultivation and rare stock. She laid her cheek against the cool yellow of the flowers, then her lips, then her closed eyelids, while she let her thoughts rove back to the time when their giver had been at her side; the words he had spoken, the way he looked, the sound of his voice, and the firm clasp of his hand. It all rushed over her in a tumult of joy and sorrow. This was the man she knew, so kind, so tender, so strong, so true; and that other was the one they thought he was! She could never feel that way about him no matter what people told her, for she had seen what they had not. If they had been in her place they might have understood. She would, of course, respect their wishes and not do anything to trouble those who loved her, but she would trust him always.

And now there stirred in her mind the remembrance of that paper, the disposition of which she must decide at once. How should she get it to him? It would not do to send for him. He could not, probably would not, come if she did. Even a little which did not explain too much would be a difficult thing to manage, at least until she knew the way to the post office and could mail it herself. If it were carried by a servant or a member of the family it might be subject to inspection. Yet the paper ought to go to him at once. Still, of course, in her keeping it was at least out of his enemies' hands, if enemies they were, these dear people of her own family. Oh, why were things at once so bitter and so sweet in this hard, bright world?

She buried her face in the roses again and let their sweetness rush over her. As she did so a slight rustling sound startled her, and when she lifted up her face and then pressed it close again she heard it once more. Curious, with a wild fleeting hope, she sat up and began to touch the buds and blossoms softly, searching with her fingers. Yes, there it was, that sound of crackling paper!

She folded back the petals of the largest bud, and there, laid deftly inside like another flower-leaf, she found a tiny bit of folded paper. She took it out and opened it, for it was very thin and folded close, and there was writing, small and fine, but distinctly clear.

*I have to go away. For how long I don't know. I shall not forget
my promise. You may trust me. I hope you have a happy time.*

Tears welled in her eyes as she read the brief message over and over again.
Bright drops fell upon the roses and stood like dewdrops.

She searched the other blossoms carefully, but there were no more messages, and she had known there would not be. He would not think it "square"
to write more of the things that were in his heart, and she loved him the more
for his sense of honor toward her.

Then she remembered the water contract.

Now what should she do with the paper? She could not give it to him while
he was away. It might await his return and be lost if she trusted it to the mail.
She must wait for a few days and see if he came back; and meantime she would
listen and watch as far as it lay in her power, that no harm came near his rights.
If worst came to worst she would confide in her father. He was wise, and he
would understand. He would feel as she did about this matter if he knew all.
The difficulty would be to make him know all through the medium of a mere
letter. But for the present she would wait.

A sense of desolation settled down upon her when she realized that Jasper
Holt was gone away; yet she was at peace about it. At least she need not always
be fearing lest her relatives should be unpleasant to him or that embarrassing
circumstances might arise where she would be obliged to choose between her
sense of loyalty to him and her sense of loyalty to her relatives, in whose home
she was a guest. But for a little time she put away these thoughts and let her
heart dwell on the fact that he had sent these glorious roses with their secret
message. Finally she lay down for a rest and slept, with one great yellow bud
nestled against her cheek.

Chapter 13

The days which followed fulfilled all of Mrs. Harrington's prophecies. One round of pleasure succeeded another. The days were filled with picnics and rides and the evenings with merrymakings of all descriptions at the houses in the region round about Hawk Valley. Many young officers and others were eager to teach the sweet young stranger from the East to ride. Horses especially trained and gentled for her use were brought as offerings to her, and flowers from near and far were sent to her. There was no opportunity for her to become lonely as the summer days sped by.

Yet through it all Jean moved lovely and serene as a summer morning.

"She acts as if she had been in society for years," complained Eleanor to her husband. "Nothing moves her out of her quiet dignity. She doesn't gush or become enthusiastic at anybody. The sky and the flowers and the children please her more than all the adulation she receives. One would almost judge her engaged already. I wonder if there is a sweetheart at home we don't know about. I must write and ask Mama. I can't make it out. I thought Captain Hawthorne would surely make an impression. He has such charming manners and is so deferential to women. But she looked at him today with that sweet faraway expression, exactly as she might have looked at her grandfather. Of course it made him desperately determined to get her attention, but she never seemed to know or care. One would almost think it was a studied pose to get as many at her feet as possible, if one didn't know Jean better."

"Did you ever think that perhaps her thoughts are with that scoundrel Holt?" her husband asked.

"Nonsense!" said his wife sharply. "She never mentions him. She's forgotten all about him. I think she was extremely annoyed at our making so much of his bringing her home."

"Well, don't you be too sure. I wonder where he is. I'll be willing to bet he's up to some mischief."

"Don't worry," said his wife. "I'm only too glad he's taken himself away. I hope he'll keep hidden until Jean is safely home again so we won't be annoyed."

"I hope he'll come back and let us see what he's up to," growled her husband as she left the room.

And at last one day, shortly before Jean was to return to her father's house, Holt came back.

With him appeared Scathlin, riding into town daily, side by side with the younger man, on one of Holt's horses—looking older, with a sheepish expression and a shifty eye that failed to meet a man's gaze. It was rumored that Holt had found him with a broken leg, nursed him into strength again and brought him home. Those who knew Scathlin felt that Holt's power over him was more than that of gratitude.

It happened that Jean was riding with the captain one morning when they came down to the post office together, and the glad smile with which she greeted Holt was followed by a frightened expression as she recognized Scathlin. Her escort was so astonished at having to lift his hat to Holt that he failed to notice her startled glance.

No one could have told by Holt's grave bow that he was meeting the one of all the earth to him. Only the light in his eyes told of his joy in seeing her once more and reassured the girl as she glanced from Scathlin back to his own face. It was Captain Hawthorne's annoyed drawl that recalled her to the present out of the whirl of joy that the sight of Holt brought.

"Where in the world did you ever meet that scoundrel that he should presume to speak to you?"

A flush of indignation rose to her cheeks, her chin tilted just the slightest bit haughtily, and her eyes held a dangerous light in them.

"Excuse me, Captain Hawthorne, Mr. Holt is my friend. He did me the greatest service one can do for another. He saved my life."

"I beg your pardon, Miss Grayson. I didn't mean to offend you. That alters the case, of course. One is always grateful for one's life and may thank even a dog. You can afford to be generous sometimes, but have a care! You don't know Holt. It's the only good thing I ever heard of him, that he saved your life. I wish it had been my privilege instead of his."

"Thank you, Captain Hawthorne," Jean said icily, "but you misunderstand me. I am not speaking to Mr. Holt because I am grateful or generous, but because I honor and trust him as a friend."

"You don't know him, Miss Grayson. He isn't a man anyone trusts."

"It is you who doesn't know him, Captain Hawthorne. I know him better than you, and I trust him entirely. During our terrible experience together at the time of the wreck I had ample opportunity to test Mr. Holt, and I found him a gentleman and a true friend in every trying situation."

And now Jean's tone was unmistakable, and the alarmed captain, who had congratulated himself that he was making pretty good headway with the fair lady, made hasty apologies.

"I beg your pardon, of course," he said humbly. "I'm sure I'm glad to hear that he behaved decently. To tell you the truth, I don't know much personally about Holt. I've only taken what others say, and I've always thought his reckless appearance bore out their insinuations. Forgive me if I have annoyed you, and try to forget what I've said. This day is perfect, and the road is particularly fine. Shall we try a gallop?"

Jean was glad of the relief from conversation and kept her horse on a wild gait most of the way; for her mind was in a tumult. How was she to get that paper to Holt, and what should she say in explanation of its being in her possession? The question had been much in her mind during Holt's absence, and she had been unable to decide just what she should do when he returned, but now it must be decided at once, for there ought to be no delay about the paper. The sinister look in Scathlin's faded blue eyes as he looked at her made her afraid to keep it in her possession any longer.

The ride at last was ended. It had not been a very great success from the captain's point of view, and he went away dejected, while Jean hurried to her room and tried to plan what to do. The sight of Scathlin worried her. If the old man knew what papers the wallet had contained, he probably knew the significance of each. The conversation she'd overheard seemed to include him in the plot against Holt. Of course, since he had returned, he would seek out the other two men and explain why he had sent the wallet; and perhaps he had the other missing paper himself, the one that contained valuable information about the location of ore. It was even possible that he knew already that she, his unwilling messenger, had the water contract. He must have known it was in the wallet when he gave it to her, and it would be entirely natural for him to think she had taken it out. Something in the gleam of his eye as he looked at her had made her tremble. She longed to fly straight to Holt and give him the paper openly, but it was a matter that could not be handled openly, and she was not a diplomat.

Finally, after careful thought and much writing and tearing up of what she had written, she framed a brief note to Holt.

On the morning she mailed it, Scathlin happened to be in the village.

Holt had gone away very early in the morning, on a matter of business, leaving word that he might not return until the next day, and Scathlin felt like a prisoner let out of jail. It was his first opportunity to go about without Holt's eyes upon him. True, he was under oath to do and not to do certain things, with penalty of judgment which he knew would not be light. Yet his natural cunning found many ways to carry on his schemes without violating the letter of his contract with Holt. He knew Holt had brought him there as a witness against his enemies in the case of the stolen papers—he knew this, though Holt had said no word of it to him—and he knew that Holt would watch him closely, that he probably had him under espionage even during this brief absence; yet he longed to outwit his keeper and get the better of him. If it only had not been for the loss of that water contract his way would have been plain.

He had already managed an interview with Harrington and learned the facts without revealing all the facts in his own possession. He professed to Harrington that all the original papers were in the wallet when he gave it to the girl and that it had been his only hope of saving them from Holt. That Holt had managed to save the girl and bring her home only proved that he was as hard to get away from as the devil himself. This explanation Scathlin devised while he listened to Harrington's story, secretly realizing, with bitterness, his own blunder in leaving the water contract in the wallet. His excuse was that he had no time to take out another paper and secrete it safely before Holt saw him.

Night and day Scathlin worried over that water contract, coming always back to the conclusion that Holt must have it or know where it was. He had searched every available hiding place in Holt's house for it but failed as yet to discover it. When they met Jean riding, the old man had noted carefully the expression on his companion's face as he touched his hat to her and the lighting up of the girl's face. His keen eyes searched and found an idea.

Therefore, that first morning of his freedom from Holt, when he sat on the curbstone with one of the men from the Divide, talking over the latest cattle stealing, his eye took in with keen interest the figure of Jean coming down the street accompanied by her little niece, a bundle of letters in her hand to be mailed. He watched her furtively as she passed him, though she did not see him, and as soon as she was inside the post office door he got up and followed her, professing that he had an errand.

He watched her slipping her letters one by one into the post box and kept his eye on her as she turned and went out again.

He made a small purchase at the counter on the other side of the post office room and went out. But an hour later, when he returned that way, the postmaster leaned from his window and called him.

"Hey, there, Scathlin. Goin' up home? Here's a letter fer Holt."

Scathlin, wary as any fox, concealed the start he almost gave and turned with indifference.

" 'Spose I might's well take it," he said and receiving the letter went on his way toward home.

The way was long and bright and hot, and Scathlin was not feeling up to a hard walk yet after his weeks in bed but he managed it, and as he walked he studied the letter.

It was dainty and white, the writing unmistakably feminine, and mailed in Hawk Valley. Scathlin's imagination stirred within him, and he was almost sure he needed to know what was in that letter. He held it up to the light, but nothing was revealed. He tried to pry open a corner of the flap that was not closely sealed and squint in, but not a glimpse of writing was visible. He went home, laid it on the desk in Holt's office and sat down to watch it and think. Then, just before the return for dinner of the other two men who were about the place, he quietly put it in his pocket. He preferred to think about that letter a while longer before anyone else saw it. When they came in, Scathlin had the fire glowing and a fine steam ascending from the teakettle, an unusual attention on his part toward other members of the group, unless he was pressed to service.

But Scathlin had exhausted his capacity for work with putting on the teakettle, for he sat dreamily meditating in a chair tilted back against the wall, his feet on the rounds, a straw in his mouth, and his eyes narrow and gleaming.

"Dear friend: I have something that I am sure belongs to you. Is it safe for me to send it to you through the mail? I think it must be valuable. Please let me know quickly, for I am going home in a few days."

Those were the magic words the steam had revealed to Scathlin and on which he meditated with his eyes half closed while his companions scornfully cooked the corn bread and bacon and cursed him for being a lazy good-for-nothing. He continued his meditations unmoved until the men had eaten and were gone on their way. When they were out of sight he arose with alacrity and prepared a hasty meal, keeping his eye on the clock. He ate hurriedly, cleaned and loaded a pistol which he took from a hiding place behind a loose brick of the chimney, and went out the back door toward the woods.

About the same time Jean Grayson mounted the pony that had been set aside for her to use while in Hawk Valley and started out for her daily call on an old lady who had taken a great fancy to her, because of her likeness to a daughter long since dead. She was fond of the sweet old lady and found her quiet little home a refuge from the round of society that sometimes became almost oppressive at her sister's house. She had discovered that she could avoid certain annoyingly frequent callers by being thus absent a little while, and especially during the last two weeks she made this pleasant pilgrimage almost every day. Perhaps a part of the pleasantness of the trip was the fact that the road lay back of Holt's land, and his house, though almost a mile from where she had to pass, was plainly visible at one high point on the road as it stood boldly against the sky, its wide verandahs shrouded in rose vines.

Jean never ventured on the road that led past the house itself, for it was off the general highway. But she had often longed to see the spot where he lived at closer range.

As she rode along she mused about the letter she had written and whether that had been the right way and the only thing to do about getting the paper into the hands of its owner.

As she reached the high point in the road she looked as usual off toward the rose-vined dwelling, half hoping to see a sign of the master of the house. But the vines lay shimmering in the sun of the warm midday, and nothing seemed stirring about the place. She walked the pony slowly along until the house was out of sight, and the road entered the shady quiet where wooded land on either side hid the glare of the afternoon. Just beyond the woods a few rods away was the home of the old lady. It was early yet, and Jean lingered.

She had gone perhaps fifty feet into the shadow of the wooded road when suddenly, out from behind a great tree with stocky brushwood growth around it, slunk forth Scathlin, close to the pony, and laid hands upon the bridle.

"I beg pardon, miss, but Mr. Holt sent me with a message," lied Scathlin, shifting his eyes hastily from the clear ones that looked in horror upon him.

Jean's heart beat wildly, not reassured by his words.

"He said would you please give me the paper you had for him. It would be safer for me to get it, as no one would suspect."

A great doubt seized Jean's soul. Holt had not sent this man. Holt could never trust such a man as this. But if he did trust him, she did not.

"Did Mr. Holt send me a letter?" Jean looked keenly into the cunning old face.

"Mr. Holt had to go away in a hurry, and so he sent me," said Scathlin glibly. "He didn't have no time to write letters. He said you knowed me; that you'd seen me with him, an' you'd know 'twas all right."

"Tell Mr. Holt, please," said Jean, making up her mind hurriedly, "that there is nothing and no message I can give to anyone. I wish to speak with him. If that is not possible we will have to let the matter pass."

She drew the rein and signaled to her pony to go on, but Scathlin jerked the bridle sharply.

"Not much, you don't go on," he threatened, "not till I get that paper. I was sent here to get it, and I mean to have it. You can't try any of your pretty little tricks on me. I want that paper, and I mean to have it. Ef I can't get it one way I kin another!"

His voice and eyes were ominous, and Jean, so frightened that her throat trembled, could scarcely control her lips to speak.

"Of what paper are you speaking?"

"That there paper you wrote about in the letter. You know well enough what I mean. You've got it about you now. I know you dassent go off and leave it to home, where that fine brother-in-law of yours could find it. Come, are you going to fork it over, or do you want me to search you for it? I'll find it quick enough."

Chapter 14

Jean turned white with fear but kept her head raised. She whipped up her pony and tried to get away, but the strong hand held the bridle and the little beast could only rear, almost throwing her. Moreover, a gleaming pistol shone into Jean's terrified eyes, and Scathlin in gloating voice spoke low.

"On, no, my pretty, you don't try any of your little tricks on me. You've stolen a paper I give you to give your brother-in-law, an' I mean to have it without any further nonsense. Hand it over!" And he grasped her roughly by the arm.

"Help! Mr. Holt! Jasper!" she screamed.

Something was stuffed into her mouth, and the barrel of the pistol gleamed between her eyes. She could feel the cold steel against her flesh. The earth seemed reeling beneath her, and her senses were going from her.

"Now, my pretty, I'll just he'p myself to that paper." Scathlin's voice was malevolent, his eyes gleaming.

Like the cold length of a serpent coiling around her soul, the meaning of his words slid about her consciousness. She felt she was sinking out of the world of knowledge into a blackness where she could not protect herself.

Then quickly, sharply, a voice brought her back to consciousness.

"Drop that pistol! Let go of that lady! Now, march!"

It was Holt's voice, low, merciless, commanding, and a revolver was in his hand.

Scathlin fell away like water, turning deadly white and cringing. The day of his judgment had come swiftly, and there was no escape. He knew that look in Holt's eye. He had sinned away his last probation. Holt would never trust him again. There wasn't even time to destroy the letter he had wanted to keep and give to Harrington as evidence against the girl.

"March!" said Holt again, and the revolver came uncomfortably near Scathlin's temple. He marched.

"Go straight to the house and wait there till I come," commanded Holt as Scathlin backed away. "If you attempt to escape I'll turn the bloodhounds loose after you."

Scathlin turned a shade paler. He had had experience with one of those bloodhounds. He had no desire to meet the whole pack. He hastened his footsteps.

Jean sat with wild eyes watching, her hand on her heart.

"You didn't send him for the paper, did you?" she demanded eagerly. "I knew you would never have sent him."

"Send for the paper—what paper?" asked Holt in wonder. "I never sent him for anything."

"Then how did he know what was in my letter to you?"

"Letter? What letter? I never received a letter from you."

"Then he must have opened it and read it. Oh, he will show it to my brother-in-law!"

But Holt's voice rang out clearly before her sentence was fairly finished: "Halt! Scathlin!"

Scathlin had almost reached the turning at the edge of the woods, but he paused instantly.

"Come back here."

Scathlin came, cringing and white with fear. When he was within ten yards of the two, Holt spoke again, and all the time the sinister weapon kept guard in his hand, aimed straight at Scathlin.

"Give me my letter."

"W—what l—let—tt—ter?" chattered Scathlin.

"The letter you have in your pocket. Take it out instantly and drop it on the ground, or I shall fire," said Holt sternly.

"Well, put down that gun," whimpered Scathlin, fumbling nervously in his inside pocket. "You make me n–n–nervous!"

"Be quick! Drop that letter!" said Holt, still holding the revolver.

Scathlin took out the letter and dropped it on the ground, but his eyes gleamed hatred at the girl in one look of wrath as he turned and stumbled back again.

Holt, still holding the revolver and watching the retreating man, advanced and picked up the letter. When Scathlin was out of sight he read it, then turned with softened eyes to the girl who had meantime secured the paper from its hiding place pinned inside her blouse. She held it out to him, her hand still trembling.

Holt took the paper but gathered the little hand into his tenderly and, stooping, kissed it.

"To think you have been through all this for me." There was awe in his voice. "To think you trusted me instead of your own people!"

For an instant they looked into each other's eyes. Then Holt's horse, trained to stand and await his master's will, whinnied softly.

"We mustn't stand here," said Holt, looking up sharply. "Someone might come. I'll take you on to Mrs. Foster's and then go back and see that Scathlin is where he can do no further harm. How long will you wish to be there? Can you stay an hour and then ride back? I'll be waiting just in the shadow of the woods and see you to the edge of town where you'll be safe. Please don't ride out of town alone again."

"But I won't be afraid to go back," protested Jean. "You need not take all the trouble. Now that you have the paper I won't be afraid."

"Trouble!" said Holt, looking at her with eyes that adored. "You know it is no trouble. But what is this paper that has made so much disturbance?" He had mounted his horse and was riding by her side now. He unfolded the paper, but it needed only a glance to show him what it was.

"How did you happen to have it?" he asked, looking at her startled. "Have you the others?"

"No," she said, a cloud of trouble coming into her eyes. "I had them, I suppose, but I didn't know they were yours. I had the wallet, with them in it. That man gave them to me on the train before the wreck. You picked the wallet up once when it fell—don't you remember? Didn't you know they were yours?"

"Yes," said Holt. "I knew. At least I supposed I knew."

"Why didn't you tell me?"

"I didn't want to mix you up in the trouble," he said, looking at her tenderly. "And, besides, I knew they were safe in your possession for the present."

"But they weren't. I didn't know they were yours, and I gave them to my brother-in-law."

"I knew you would, of course. But I was pretty sure I could stop any harm he would do before he could do it. The only thing I was troubled about was this paper. I didn't think Scathlin was fool enough to leave all the papers in the wallet. I was pretty sure he had kept this and one other himself and only sent the rest back to throw me off the track and make me think he had sent all of them. He knew I saw him give you the wallet, and he meant I should see. He thought I would stop watching him and give my attention to you, but I knew Scathlin better than that. I kept my eye on him. But how did you happen to have this one paper?"

"I'm not sure," said Jean. "When I came back to my room after giving my brother-in-law the wallet, I found this on my floor. It may have fallen when I dumped the things out of my bag. The wallet fell apart, and all the papers went out on the table, but I thought I picked up every one. Then when I came back to my room I found this on the floor just as I was about to turn out the light. Later I overheard a conversation in which this paper and another were described as missing. The other was something to do with a mine."

"Yes, I have it," said Holt.

"You have it? Oh, I am so glad! Then they can't trouble your claim, can they? I suppose that was what they meant; I'm not very much of a businessperson. But how did you get it? They said it was in the wallet."

"It was," said Holt, "till Scathlin took it out. I think he intended taking this also and leaving only the other paper with you, which were utterly valueless without these two. But he had to work quickly while I was at the other end of the car, and he blundered. I got it out of Scathlin's shoe, just after the accident occurred and before I left the car we were in. We had a struggle in the dark, but I secured my paper before he flung me off and crawled out the window. After that, I lost sight of him. I was hunting for him in the water when I found you. I didn't know who you were till I drew you up on the bank. But I never dreamed you had this paper. I thought, of course, it was still with Scathlin. That's why I was away so long, hunting him. I thought once I'd lost him completely, but I finally got on his track. I was sure he knew where this paper was, and I didn't dare to lose him. I brought him home to watch him, and I've kept him in sight all day today. He thought I was away from home for two days, but I've been in hiding. I had him watched when he went to town, and I knew he came home. If he had had this paper he would have gone straight to your brother-in-law. A field glass and a whistle will do a good deal to keep track of a man. When he stole out of the house toward the woods, I knew something was happening and signaled my men. They're waiting now. They'll look after Scathlin till I get back."

He raised a tiny whistle to his lips and blew a long, silvery blast, followed by two more, and in a moment two answers came back from slightly different directions.

They had come now to the open road, and Holt drew his horse to one side. Mrs. Foster's home was but a stone's throw away, and she was sitting on the porch in her reclining chair.

"I'll be here when you're ready to go home," said Holt, looking at her tenderly. Then, touching his hat, he wheeled his horse and was out of sight in a twinkling.

The next hour was always a blur in Jean's memory. Somehow she drew her senses together and dismounted at her friend's door, going through the formalities of meeting and adjusting herself to the occasion. But not for an instant did her subconsciousness cease to rehearse the events just passed. Her whole body quivered again with the fear that swept over her at sight of Scathlin; she shrank once more from his touch as the full realization of her escape was made known to her; and Holt's look and voice thrilled her as nothing had ever done in her life. How could they say he wasn't good when he was like that? She had seen the soul of him looking out of his wonderful eyes, and she knew. But how had it come about that others had not seen also? Oh, if they could just get a glimpse of the true man, they would never again feel as they did about him.

She recognized fully the separation between them, and it brought a constriction of tears in her throat. But in her heart was a glad glow that he cared for her, and for the time it seemed enough to fill her with deep joy. She was going to see him again in a few minutes. She had had no words to tell him of the infinite relief his appearing brought; everything had happened so quickly. But it seemed as if a lifetime would be too brief to voice her gratitude for her deliverance. She shivered as she remembered the look on Scathlin's face when he took hold of her.

"Why, you're not cold, are you, dearie, on this warm day?" said Mrs. Foster. "I believe they are letting you do too much, with all their parties and things. You look white. You'd better come down and stay with me a week and get rested up."

Jean's laugh rang silverly.

"Oh, no, I'm not cold, Mrs. Foster. I'm just glad over something. It's very nice of you to ask me to visit you, and I would be delighted. I'm going home next week, and I'm afraid Eleanor wouldn't want to spare me when the time is so short."

"Going home next week!" exclaimed the old lady in dismay. "Why, I thought you were going to stay till Christmas."

"So I was, but Father had to go to New York to a convention. He's been made a delegate, and it's a splendid thing for him. He hasn't had an outing in a long time. He needs it, and we couldn't leave Mother alone, you know. Mother is an invalid. So of course I'm going home a little sooner. But I've had a beautiful time here, and maybe I can come again sometime."

All the time Jean was talking, her real self was thinking how wonderful it had been that it was Holt who saved her again and not just some passing stranger.

The hour was over at last, and Jean mounted her pony and bade her friend good-bye. But when she rode into the shadow of the woods and saw Holt on his shining black horse waiting quietly beside the road for her, a great shyness overcame her, and she knew she would never be able to put into words the great thoughts of her heart. Perhaps it was as well; for he would understand, and words were not necessary for them. There could not be much said without saying too much.

After all, they said very little. The way was short till they came to the edge of town, though they walked their horses as slowly as possible. But there were looks and glances of the soul, trustful, grateful, worshipful; and each felt the blessedness of these few minutes alone together.

Holt told her briefly of Scathlin. She need fear him no more. He would not be abroad to trouble her during the rest of her stay. His eyes more than his words informed her how he regretted the brevity of that stay. His eyes told her also that Scathlin's judgment would be tempered with mercy and righteousness.

There was one question she wished to ask him. She hesitated long but finally risked it.

"You will enter the tournament?" she asked, lifting her eyes full of pleading that his answer would be yes. "You know about it, of course? You know they're giving me a tournament before I go home?"

He bowed gravely.

"Yes, I know. You'll like it. It's one of the most interesting affairs they have in town. I'm glad you'll see it."

She saw he was evading her question.

"You will enter?" she asked again anxiously.

He searched her face keenly.

"You want me to?"

"I do, very much," she said, and the rich color in her cheeks told him how much she wanted it.

"Your friends won't like it," he said.

"But the tournament is given for me, and I shall like it," she said with spirit. "I'm sure you can ride."

"I can ride a little," he said indifferently.

"Then you will enter?"

"If you really wish it."

"I certainly wish it," she said.

Then suddenly out from the woods rode two men. Fine, tall, sturdy fellows they were, perhaps ten or more years older than Holt, but with strong faces, keen eyes and muscles that looked like iron.

They saluted Holt as if he were their military officer, and one rode close to him and said a few words in a low tone. Holt nodded gravely, his fine, boyish face taking on maturer lines as he gave attention to the message and uttered his brief directions, unintelligible to the girl, who looked on in bewilderment at this new phase of the young man's character.

The second rider had halted at a respectful distance, without a glance in her direction, and waited as a trained servant should do. Devotion to Holt and absolute obedience were in the attitude of both.

The interview occupied scarcely a minute; then the two men wheeled, saluted and rode away once more into the woods.

"A little trouble at the mine," Holt explained, in answer to her questioning glance. "It'll be all right now, since I have this paper again. We haven't dared to exercise our water privileges as we should and have been moving under difficulties, but now that I have the grant there will be no further trouble. I'll take care it's put where no one can steal it again."

"Oh, I'm so glad," breathed Jean. "But who are they?"she added, pointing after the two riders who were just disappearing behind the trees.

"My men," said Holt. "I have fifty-four of them, fine fellows every one."

"Your men?" questioned Jean in surprise.

"They work for me—in the mine and around the place. I've picked them up here and there. That big fellow that waited—I took him down from a tree where they'd hung him up for stealing a horse. He's the one I told you of—I thought he was dead, but there he is! He wouldn't take a pin now that belonged to anyone else. He's the straightest fellow on the place. The other one was almost gone with fever when I met up with him. We've nursed each other twice apiece since then. There are others I'd like you to know if things weren't as they are. You'd see the good in them, I'm sure. You seem to understand."

Jean's eyes were alight as she watched him.

"They know you!" she exclaimed. "They've seen the real you, and they trust you! I saw it in their eyes."

"Maybe," he said, returning her look. "They'd fight for me anytime I asked it, and they'd die for me if it came to that."

"Greater love hath no man than this, that a man lay down his life for his friends." The words seemed to come of themselves from the girl's lips as she watched the man in wonder and admiration.

"You took a mighty slim chance on yours for me about an hour ago." Holt's eyes spoke volumes. "Why didn't you give him the paper? It was by far the safest thing for you to do. Didn't you know that?"

"Yes," said the girl, her soft lips setting in a firm line and her chin taking the tilt that gave her face its strength and fineness. "But the paper was yours, and I was sure it was valuable. I didn't trust him."

"And you trust me yet, in spite of all the things I know you must have heard about me?"

"I trust you forever!"

Her eyes were clear and steady, and her voice was sweet with a ring of triumph in it as she made the declaration.

For a moment they looked at one another with a light of deep gladness shining from their eyes. Then the man bowed his head gravely and, reaching over, took her hand in a strong, quick clasp.

"You shall never have cause to lose that trust," he murmured and, turning, rode back into the woods and left her to go on alone through the town.

Chapter 15

When Jean reached the Harrington home she found a group of girls on the porch waiting for her, who chattered and laughed and took possession of her. They were planning an all-day trip on horseback with lunches and all sorts of interesting things, and Jean must help them. They gave her no chance to speak but told her all in chorus, until she could scarcely make out what it was about. She smiled and agreed, but half the time she didn't know what they were saying, for something still and beautiful within her soul was claiming her attention, something that seemed too high and holy to be affected by any of these foolish little things. Yet she smiled and agreed, and they all thought her charming and went on making their plans.

They made out their list of men who were to be invited. She heard the names read and took no account of whom they had selected for her escort. What did it matter? *His* name was not among them. She heard their talk about their horses.

"Robin Hood has gone lame," declared one girl pettishly. "Isn't that a shame? Father says it's my fault, but I know better. He's going to get me a new horse pretty soon when he can find one to suit him. I know just the one I want, coal-black and shines like satin. He can go like the wind and take a river as if he had wings. I'm dead in love with him. I'm just dying to ride him, but his owner won't sell him. Isn't that mean? He belongs to Jasper Holt. Father has offered him a fabulous price, but he won't sell him at any price, he says. I think he's perfectly horrid. Of course he only does it just to be disagreeable because he thinks I want the horse. That man makes me tired!"

A soft color rose to Jean's cheeks, and she looked up as if a challenge to defend her friend had been flung to her.

"Perhaps he's fond of the horse," she said gently, as she glanced around on all those scornful young faces.

"He, fond of anything! Oh, my dear! You don't know him!" declared one of the girls.

"He never was fond of anything in his life," laughed another. "Why, he's the cruelest thing! You don't know, Jean."

"Men grow very fond of horses," said Jean, holding her head high, "and their horses grow fond of them. A horse loves one who is kind to him."

She was remembering the proud arch of Jasper Holt's black as he rode beside her in the woods but a short half hour before.

Her words were met by a shout of merriment, and a boisterous young voice with a sneer in it pierced above the laughter.

"Kind to them! Jasper Holt was never kind to anything in his life! My dear, you simply don't know him."

"But I do know him!" said Jean, rising from her rocker and standing slim and straight against the vine-covered pillar of the porch. "I know him better than you all, and I know he is kind. He was kind and splendid to me. No man could have done more. I am sorry you feel that way about him. It isn't right! He is my friend!"

She had spoken! She always meant to, ever since she came. But there had been little opportunity without being deliberately disagreeable and dragging the subject in. Perhaps Eleanor had warned her callers not to mention Jasper Holt, for they usually seemed to avoid speaking of him. But she had always felt the time would come when she could speak and let them all know what she thought about him, and now it had come and she had spoken. Her heart beat wildly, her cheeks were rosy, and her eyes shone, but she stood unabashed and faced them all.

A sudden silence fell upon the little group, and they exchanged furtive glances of understanding as if a mutual agreement sealed their lips to things they might say if she were not with them.

"Oh, well, of course you're grateful," said one girl in a conciliatory tone. "One couldn't help being grateful under such circumstances. But he would have been a brute not to have pulled you out of the water and showed you the way to Hawk Valley."

"Perhaps he wants his black to ride in the tournament," said another girl mischievously, hoping to lift the cloud that had fallen over them all. "He has audacity enough for anything, though he has never seemed to care for anything going on in the town. Of course he has never been encouraged to."

"He wouldn't dare!" said another with flashing eyes.

"Why wouldn't he dare?" asked Jean, turning steady eyes to the haughty young speaker.

"Because it wouldn't be tolerated," declared the girl.

"I have seen him dare greater things than that," said Jean with a faraway look in her eyes.

The girls looked at her a minute in silence and wonder, exchanged quick glances that said, "She doesn't know," and changed the subject. They liked Jean too well, and she was too popular among the men for them to risk angering her, so they chattered on about what they would have in the boxed lunch and who should bring what. But Jean, with that faraway look still in her eyes, said no more.

They chattered and giggled to the end of their time at last and took themselves away. But it was the dinner hour, and Harrington was coming up the walk with two men who were to be their guests for dinner. There was just time for Jean to change her riding habit for a dinner dress and hurry down again—no chance for the rest and quiet thoughts that cried out to have their way.

The evening was filled with callers, as every evening had been since she came that was not taken up by some entertainment or invitation. It seemed a wearisome time to Jean, who longed for her quiet room and her own thoughts. She watched the men who were talking to her, trying to please her; saw that they were good to look upon, cultured and refined; saw that any one of them would be a good friend to her if she would let him. And yet, when she considered it, there was not one who came up to the standard of the man who had saved her life. She tried to look at the matter from their standpoint and understand why it was that she could not like any of them as she liked him; why they all seemed rather tedious in their conversation. And the thought came to her that it was because she had first known him, and he was so much larger and finer a man in every way than they.

She had no more thought than at the beginning that she would ever see more of Holt. The future showed no bright hope that they might come together. He had said it would not do, and she trusted him. Whatever he willed concerning their friendship she bowed to, for she trusted him utterly. But something vivid and both strong and gentle in him made all others vapid beside him.

She roused herself to be pleasant and entertaining, but her heart was not in it. Her sister, noticing as the evening went on that she looked white and tired, finally managed to send their guests away. And indeed, there had been moments when all the laughter seemed far away to her, and she had only seen the evil face of Scathlin and heard his voice demanding the paper and threatening to find it for himself. Once she had shivered visibly as if she were chilly, and the captain hastened to pick up a gauze scarf and throw it around her shoulders, while Freeman Thorne pulled down the window.

But when they were all gone, Eleanor was not at peace about her sister, and she came in presently to perch on the bed and question her.

"Is anything troubling you, Jean?" she asked anxiously. "You seemed so white and tired tonight."

"Nothing at all, dearest," said Jean brightly. "What a big responsibility I am to you! You mustn't worry about me; I've had a lovely visit. But I get a little tired of talking to so many people sometimes and having to say the same things over to all those men."

"You odd child!" said her sister, looking at her curiously. "Almost any girl would be proud to have so many admirers, and you take them as a matter of course and don't seem to care a bit for any of them."

She studied the fair face of the girl keenly for any trace of self-consciousness, but Jean's smile was as placid as ever.

"They're all nice, Eleanor," said the girl wearily, "but they do grow a little tiresome—all day long some of them, and every day. I wouldn't mind if you and I had a day or two now and then just to ourselves."

"Well, you certainly are hopeless!" said her sister. "Tell me, child—is there someone at home you've given your heart to?"

"Oh, no!" said Jean, laughing at the thought. "Who would there be? You know all the boys, and there isn't one I could care for."

"Well, I didn't know but that new bank cashier—"

"Tom Lloyd? Why, he's engaged to Bella Harkness. Did no one tell you? Besides, he's years older than I am."

"Well, there's that oldest Shafton boy. Mother wrote he had come home from college and started in business. They're a good family, Jean."

"Jimmy Shafton? Oh, Eleanor! You ought to see him. He's the biggest snob. I suppose he's nice enough, but I don't like him, that's all. He has a weak chin, and somehow I don't trust him. Now, Eleanor, you funny little matchmaker, just give me up as a hopeless case. You can't marry me off yet a while, and you'll have to make up your mind to it. I'm going home where I belong to take care of Mother and teach my Sunday school class. But I've had a glorious time while I was here, and I shall enjoy thinking it over a lot when I get home."

Eleanor was baffled but persistent.

"Don't you like the captain?" she asked.

"Yes, a lot. He's going to take me on a ride through the canyon tomorrow. Will you go along? He promised to ask you."

"Well, probably he didn't want me," said Eleanor significantly.

"Well, I do," said Jean. "I told him I wouldn't go without you."

"Why, yes, I suppose I could take Betty on her pony."

"Do," said Jean. "I love to ride with Betty, and then you can talk to the captain when I get tired."

"You funny little girl! Well, don't you like Freeman Thorne?"

"Of course," said Jean. "He's going to bring me some Indian arrowheads to give to my boys at home."

Eleanor sat back and surveyed her inscrutable litter sister. There was one more question she wanted to ask, but somehow she didn't dare, because she hated to see that look of hurt dignity come into Jean's eyes whenever she spoke of Jasper Holt. But there lingered in her heart just a little uneasiness about the handsome outlaw whose part the girl had so loyally taken on her arrival and about whom her lips had remained so significantly sealed ever since. Yet, despite her uneasiness, she went to her room with the question unasked, and Jean locked her door and turned out her light with a sigh of relief that at last she was alone.

Down on her knees beside the open window she knelt, her arms on the window seat, her face raised to the stars. There was a kind of triumph in her face, for though she knew that great sadness was coming, yet over all the excitement of the day, the terror of peril and escape, there was a great exultation. For just this one night at least she must exult in the thought of Jasper Holt and his second saving of her life; she must rejoice in his love and the fact that she could trust him. Memory brought back every glance of his true eyes, every word and gesture, every movement and attitude of the perfect body. He seemed so much stronger and finer and nobler in every way than all the others.

What a pity he must rest under their disapproval. How dreadful they couldn't know him as he really was—that she must presently go on her lonely way home and see no more of him, know no more of him—perhaps never on this earth again. He had it in him to be true to this terrible separation because he thought it ought to be, and she was proud of him for it, but her heart already ached in anticipation of the sorrow that was in store for her.

With a sob she put her head down on the windowsill and prayed softly, "Dear God, take care of him, and help people to know him. Help him to be true always, and let others find it out and be ashamed of the way they have treated him. Bless him and keep him—my dear friend!"

Then, with one lingering look away to where the stars shone quietly above his dwelling as above hers, she went to sleep.

Chapter 16

T he tournament was set for the day before Jean started home.
It was to be a great event, the biggest thing the town of Hawk Valley could devise for its most honored guests. It was an all-day affair, with contests and games of every kind, races and matches and a big procession with everyone wearing the most fantastic garments the resources of the town afforded.

The climax of the program would be late in the afternoon when the feats of riding were performed and the prizes and wreaths given out to the victors.

The highest honor had been allotted to Jean, for she had been selected to give out the prizes and crown the victor of the final riding contest.

It had been the custom in other similar contests that a lady so honored should ride once around the running track in company with the victor and share with him the triumph of the occasion. Great was the eagerness of all the young men to win this privilege, for Jean's delicate beauty and sweet, gentle ways had made her most popular, and everyone was striving for the privilege of riding with her and being crowned by her hand. There had been much merriment about it, much betting and chaffing, much practicing of horsemanship, much boasting; and many a gallant gentleman besought her to wear his flowers on the gala day, that he might stand the better chance of winning.

But Jean smiled upon them all and would promise none. She took it all as a beautiful piece of pleasantry in her honor, though sometime she was secretly distressed at the earnestness with which many of her admirers pressed their suit. They were splendid fellows, all of them, and it was hard to be refusing and disappointing them all the time. Hard, too, it was to disappoint her sister Eleanor, who was an enthusiastic matchmaker and felt real chagrin that her beloved sister should go back home from all that adulation still unattached. Eleanor would have liked nothing better than to have Jean marry and settle out near her. Then the father and mother would eventually come, of course, and the family would be reunited. It was most aggravating to her that Jean remained so unimpressionable.

The day before the tournament great boxes of flowers began to arrive for Jean, embarrassing her with their profusion and costliness. Orchids and lilies, gardenias and roses of rare varieties, carnations, jessamine, even delicate wildflowers and wonderful poppies. Each admirer had spent much thought and care on his offering, hoping to have it chosen for wearing upon the great occasion, and each had tried to have his flowers unusual and noticeable enough to draw her choice away from all others. With each box came a card or note or sometimes letter bearing the name and earnest plea of the giver, three even offering themselves with their flowers.

Jean stood among her blossoms, her cheeks vying with the roses, her eyes as starry as the lilies, distressed and touched but not quite pleased. It was terrible to her that she seemed to have wrought such havoc in the hearts of men.

Eleanor and the children hovered excitedly around, far more pleased than Jean over the honors that were heaped upon her. Eleanor talked about the merits of the different flowers and the reasons why each should be worn in preference to the others.

"There were the captain's orchids—so expensive, poor fellow—and he so handsome!" Eleanor always ended with the captain, where she had begun. It was plain that Eleanor favored the captain most.

Jean stood and touched the flowers tenderly, compassionately, as she might have looked at and touched something very beautiful that did not belong to her. It seemed a big responsibility to have all these lovely blossoms with all they represented, and as she filled each vase and jar and bowl to overflowing, her eyes grew more and more troubled. Somehow it seemed wrong for her to have all these perishing beauties, knowing that the lasting treasure they were here to plead for their donors was not hers to give.

"Which flowers are you going to wear, Jean?" asked Eleanor that night as they went upstairs together after tucking all the blossoms away under damp papers. "You know you'll have to decide in the morning, and there really aren't any more to come in, unless Mr. Frazer sends some. Everybody, literally every man in the region who could have a shadow of right to do so, has sent you some. It shows how popular you are! I don't believe any girl that ever came here before was so well treated and so universally admired. It's wonderful, Jean. You quiet, sweet child—you've got them all under your thumb! I never would have suspected it of you."

Jean smiled wearily. She was tired, and her sister's idea of triumph was not hers. It savored too much of counting the scalps of those she had slain. She didn't want to have men at her feet to be turned away. She looked at life more seriously than just a game where she was to win all, no matter who lost.

She turned away with a gentle good night, and Eleanor's eyes followed her.

"You know, you might wear one of each and satisfy them all," she suggested.

Jean smiled and shuddered inwardly. The scalps again! A display of them!

"Never!" she murmured.

"Well, what are you going to do?" Her sister was out of patience with her dallying.

"I'll sleep on it," she said brightly. "Aren't you tired, dear?"

And Eleanor had to let it go at that.

Young Frazer sent his flowers in the morning: wonderful violets, blue as the sky over Hawk Valley. And more roses came from several men at a distance who had not been reckoned upon. But Eleanor was not told of the roses the servant found on the doorstep when he went to sweep the porch early in the morning— the roses with the dew upon them and the golden ruby of sunset in their hearts.

They were not wrapped or in a box or accompanied by a card; nor was there even any name on them. They simply lay on the doorstep and made their mute appeal of fragrance. And the manservant, who, like all the other men in Hawk Valley, had surrendered to the gentle, beautiful girl, understood and carried them straight up to her door without telling anyone. He knew from whom they came, and he knew, by the starry look in her eyes when the other roses like them had come, that she would know.

She gathered them into her arms and thanked him. Her problem was solved, and she could go down to breakfast with a light heart.

"Have you decided which flowers to wear, Jean?" her sister asked sharply the minute she came into the room.

"Yes," said the girl with a smile, "but it's a secret. I'm not going to tell. You will see them when I wear them."

Eleanor looked anxiously at the bright face with the firm lips and sighed. She knew she would have to wait.

Jean was to go on her pony to the scene of the day's festivities that she might be ready for the triumphal ride at the end. The captain had begged the privilege of accompanying her, being confident he should both see his costly orchids adorning her and win the right to ride home by her side, triumphant. It seemed to him that it would be but a short way to the other heights he hoped to attain.

He arrived at the house on the minute appointed, but Jean, usually punctual, kept him waiting. The Harringtons were all packed in their motorcar. They kept calling impatiently.

"We'll be late, Jean, and James has to see about the signals and put up some more ribbons. You know he's marshal of the day."

"Go on," called Jean from her window. "I'm just fastening on my flowers. I'll be there in a minute. Don't wait; we'll catch you."

They heard her footsteps flying down the stairs, and Harrington started the car.

"Wait, James—I must see what flowers she chose."

"Nonsense!" said her husband, sending the car shooting forward at a pace. "You can wait till she gets there. What difference does it make anyway?"

"Why, if she doesn't take the right ones I can send her back," said Eleanor, twisting her neck to see her sister, who was just mounting her pony.

"The right ones? You don't know which ones you want her to wear yourself; you've said so a dozen times this morning," laughed her husband.

"Well, I know, but there are some quite impossible ones, you know, and Jean is so unconventional. It would be just like her to wear John Beard's poppies because she felt sorry for him on account of his lameness. She always was that way. Mama let her choose a canary when she was little, and she chose a poor little faded thing that wouldn't sing a note, because she said it wasn't pretty like the others and would enjoy a nice cage."

"Well, I guess you'll have to let her choose her own husband, anyway. She's got to live with him, and she's got a big will of her own."

"I know," said Eleanor, sighing. "I shall be relieved when she gets safely married. Mama is so shut in that she doesn't realize how unworldly Jean is. But, James, I do wish you'd slow up a little. I must see those flowers. Betty, dear, can you tell what Aunt Jean is wearing?"

The little girl craned her neck.

"I think they're just roses, Mama," said Betty indifferently.

"Roses? Are you sure, child? Aren't they orchids? The poor captain! But there were multitudes of roses. I wonder whose they are."

They had turned into the main street now. Banners were flying, and a band played martial music. The question of the flowers must become a side issue, for there were numberless little things to be decided, and Mrs. Harrington was consulted many times before she finally mounted the grandstand and took her seat among the prominent people of the place. She looked with satisfaction to see Jean ascending the steps followed by the handsome captain, whose dejected face still showed his disappointment about the orchids. For the moment she was too much taken up with the captain to look closely at the wonderful roses Jean wore. Then suddenly she turned her attention to them. Where had she seen roses like that? Who could have sent them?

Then she remembered. Roses yellow as gold and with a heart of ruby! Holt's Golden Sunset! She could hear her husband's sharp voice repeating the hateful name. Was it possible that Holt had had the audacity to send Jean roses on this day, when all eyes would be turned to the girl? And Jean, knowing how they felt about him, had dared to wear them!

Her cheeks grew red, and her eyes flashed. She looked daggers at the girl and then, realizing that the captain could see her, tried to control her face. Even now Jean was moving away to the seat on the right, the seat of honor for the lady who was to present the prizes.

"Jean, wait! I must speak to you," she called.

Jean, two chairs away, leaned over, smiling. Perhaps she knew what was coming, because her lips had that firm little twist as her question said "What is it?" indicated courage to stick to a decision.

Eleanor leaned over the two chairs, speaking low and vehemently.

"Jean, take those flowers off and give them to me at once! I'll send the man back for the orchids. People will just think you've forgotten your flowers. Quick, give them to me."

Jean drew back with dignity and laid her hand protectingly over the flowers on her breast.

"I'm sorry, Eleanor," she said. "I can't do what you ask. These are the flowers I intend to wear. Captain Wetherill understands me perfectly. I told him beforehand not to send me flowers."

And she turned away.

"But, Jean," cried her sister frantically, "you simply must not wear those roses! Send the man back for any others, but don't wear those. You don't understand! Everybody will know those are Jasper Holt's roses. People will think it very strange. Why, he isn't even here. It isn't respectable for you to have anything to do with him."

Jean looked her sister straight in the eyes.

"I understand perfectly, Eleanor," she said softly, for a group of people were coming in and taking the seats around them. "I cannot and will not wear any of those other flowers."

"Then take them off entirely and don't wear any," said Eleanor, the vexed tears coming into her eyes.

"I'm sorry, Eleanor, but I must wear them," Jean said and went almost sadly to her seat. She hated to hurt her sister, but the wearing of these flowers had become to her a sacred duty and privilege. She knew that to Holt, if he should see her, it would be a symbol of her trust in him. If he did not come to the tournament, at least she would have the satisfaction of knowing in her heart that she had been loyal to him, in the only way vouchsafed her—that of wearing his flowers before them all.

Eleanor settled back, defeated, in her chair, two red spots glowing on her cheeks and angry flashes in her eyes. She was mortified beyond expression. That her young sister, who had the adulation of the whole county poured at her feet, should choose to wear the favor of a man whom nobody recognized or favored filled her with rage. What would James say when he found her sister was wearing his enemy's flowers? Well, it was James's fault anyway, for if he had kept the car waiting a minute she would have discovered Jean's folly in time to stop it. If she had seen those yellow roses glowing on her sister's gown before she mounted her pony, they would never have come to the tournament— no, not if she had to detain Jean forcibly at home for the day and tell people she was suddenly taken ill! This came of bringing the girl up in a purely domestic and religious atmosphere and not teaching her a little worldly wisdom. Well, she would tell James it was his fault; that would be some satisfaction. Yes, and she would tell Jean just what she thought of her headstrong folly, too, when she got her home.

The waves of angry color had not yet ceased to flow over Eleanor's handsome face when the Thornes bustled in and took the next seats. Mrs. Thorne was a large, imposing person and had much to say of her son's admiration for Jean.

"So simple and sweet in that white dress with those beautiful yellow roses! Freeman wouldn't tell me what flowers he sent her. I wonder if they can be his. I never saw any like them around here, did you? The boy is completely gone about her. I suspect he spent a fabulous sum on the flowers. He sent to

Kansas City for them."

Eleanor began to take heart. If Mrs. Thorne didn't know whose roses Jean wore, perhaps the other women didn't either. Women didn't visit Jasper Holt's home, and men didn't notice those things much.

She settled back relieved and allowed herself to think how well Jean was looking and how devoted the captain seemed in spite of his floral setback. Perhaps, after all, he would only be the more keen that Jean was not in a hurry to land him. Was she, after all, a little deeper than they thought, and did she plan her campaign with a view to making her admirers all the more eager? Eleanor Harrington never had been able to comprehend a nature higher than her own.

Chapter 17

Into the midst of Eleanor's troubled thoughts came the herald, a boy from a neighboring ranch who rode on a white pony with fluttering blue ribbons for reins, and blew three sharp blasts on a silver bugle, the signal for the opening of the sports. Eleanor Harrington whispered a few words to Betty and helped her slip quietly out of the seat into the aisle, then settled back, relieved. She had sent a message to Jean not to tell anyone whose flowers she wore, and Jean looked up and smiled brightly across the heads of the people between them, nodding her consent.

Betty came back to her seat, pleased to have been the center of all eyes for a moment, and her mother patted her hand and reflected that, after all, it was wise in Jean not to wear any of her special admirers' flowers, for then they could none of them be angry with her. And if it should come out that she wore Holt's roses, a little judicious hint of "gratitude" and "sense of duty" toward one who had saved her life would only add charm to the lovely character of the girl. As Holt was not present, what harm could come of it?

The day's sports went forward briskly. Each feature of the program had been put into separate and capable hands, and each vied with the other to make his or her stunt the best of all. There were children's games, marches and dances. There were folk dances, speeches, contests and races of all sorts, each highly entertaining in its way. And there was the great picnic dinner when the entire company adjourned to the edge of the woods, where tables had been prepared and the good things of the town had been set forth to tempt the appetite. Everybody was hungry, and everybody laughed and talked.

Eleanor had a vague hope that she might induce Jean to send home at noon for some other flowers on the plea that the ones she wore were faded. But Jean was surrounded by a company of young people, and there was no opportunity to speak to her. Harrington, too, who might have taken the matter in hand, had been summoned to the grounds to perfect some arrangement for the afternoon, so there was nothing to be done.

When the bugle blew for the afternoon program to begin, Harrington was beside his wife, his work done, ready to enjoy the best part of things without any more responsibility. But Eleanor, knowing well his moods, thought it unwise to tell him about the flowers for the present. It was too late now to change, and James would simply be furious; it was best to save that stroke about its being his fault until another time when she needed to convince him of something else.

The children had finished their entertainment in the morning, and the remainder of the program was to be by the men.

When the first set of riders came out in line, one among their number the crowd didn't at first recognize—a man with bright, curly hair and fine bearing, dressed in white flannels and riding a jet-black horse. Everywhere among the seats could be heard the murmur "Who is he?" But no one answered.

Harrington raised his field glass and looked, then dropped his hand with an exclamation of dismay. Eleanor, watching her husband's face, reached for the glass, looked a moment, then she too dropped the glass in her lap and gave her attention to controlling her countenance. No one must suspect what a bitter drop in the day's cup of pleasure this was to them.

Harrington sat, grimly reflecting that he might have prevented this possibility if he had framed the entrance qualifications aright. But Holt had been away indefinitely when the tournament was planned, and he hadn't thought of him. Now it was too late to do a thing, and there were reasons that made it unwise for him to show displeasure or unfriendliness to Holt, lest suspicion of a worse character fall upon Harrington.

For the remainder of the afternoon life to Eleanor Harrington became a matter of self-control. Now and then she managed to glance furtively at her husband and wonder why he hadn't flown into a rage. But she was wise enough to say nothing, knowing that, since he didn't, there must be a reason. Nevertheless, she mentally resolved to give her young sister a piece of her mind on their return home; and for the first time since the date of Jean's early departure had been set, she was reconciled to it. What made matters so much worse was that Jasper Holt looked distractingly handsome in those unaccustomed white flannels, wearing them as though he had grown up in them and sitting his mount like a young god. There wasn't a man of the whole lineup who seemed so thoroughly a part of his horse as Holt, and every line of his head and body, every easy movement he made was beautiful. Of course Jean was taken with his looks. Girls were such fools—that is, girls who had no worldly wisdom.

Up on the grandstand a group of girls looked and exclaimed and whispered together, "Do you suppose Jean knew all the time he was going to enter? Do you suppose maybe she's in love with him? Really? Wouldn't that be exciting! But of course it couldn't ever amount to anything but a little romance. And she looks so innocent. I don't believe she knew, after all." And so they speculated.

Jean had known him the first moment he appeared on the scene, and her heart stood still as if this were the moment for which she had waited all her life. He was here, and how splendid he looked! He fairly took her breath away. There wasn't a man among them, no matter what he wore, who could match him for looks. Her heart swelled with joy beneath his roses. This was her moment to rejoice. Tomorrow she was going away, and she might not see him anymore, but today it was right that she should have this beautiful sight of him to carry away with her. So she watched, her eyes shining and her cheeks glowing warmly.

There was no question but that he was the rider of them all. His horse skimmed the hurdles as though they had been mere imaginary lines and flew over the highest bar like a swallow in the air. He sat the black creature with ease and grace, and from the start all eyes followed his every move. The crowd forgot for the time its prejudice and sat in absorbed admiration of his skill and courage.

They all knew him as a daring rider, for often women held their breath to see him go tearing through the street on some wild beast of a horse whose mad flight seemed uncanny. But the incomparable riding he did now was beyond all he had ever done for them before. They watched and glowed and applauded, and the heart of the girl he loved swelled with pride so that tears of joy came into her eyes and blinded her from seeing him. She was glad that everyone was watching him, and no one would be looking at her. She didn't know that her sister had the field glass focused straight on her and was studying her closely. Eleanor looked, and her heart sank in dismay. She began to rejoice that Jean was going tomorrow; in fact, the afternoon could not come to a close too soon for her now.

The final race, the hardest of them all, in which the obstacles were many and the skill required was great, was at its climax. Holt had kept easily abreast, often ahead of all the others, and the next to the last round was almost finished. People leaned forward in their seats, then rose upon their feet, shouting and cheering and waving their hands. Jean, with the others, leaned over the front rail of the grandstand, waving her handkerchief excitedly; the bit of sheer linen slipped from her fingers and fluttered to the ground. Quick as a flash, Holt spurred ahead and, wheeling in a circle in front of the judges' stand, he leaned and picked up the bit of linen from the ground, wheeled shortly again and handed it to its owner. Then he was off like a flash down the track on the last round but a quarter of the way behind the rest, his wonderful advantage lost.

It was a pretty bit of gallantry; a skillful trick of horsemanship, but, oh, the pity of it to lose the race for a handkerchief! The crowd could hardly forgive him. Who cared about all the rest? They were but secondary now even though he had fallen behind. What madness and folly when the handkerchief could have waited, or was he doing it to be smart? The crowd was angry at their sudden loss and began to think how just like Jasper Holt it was to trifle with them so, when suddenly they sat up and took notice. Holt had passed the last two riders and was running neck and neck with the third, and now he passed the fourth from the end.

There were but two more to pass. Still, the others were nearly to the three-quarter line, and the foremost was Captain Wetherill on his powerful roan mare. He was riding hard and meant to win. There was a bitter, haughty look upon his face. His triumph would by spoiled by all that gallery play that had preceded it, though it was plain he felt the victory easy now. Would Holt attempt to pass him? It seemed impossible, yet on he came, his black skimming like a swallow on the outside of the ring, gaining every second, and the rider with his easy, nonchalant air sitting as if the victory were a matter of indifference to him. The crowd stood up and shouted a deafening roar, and Jean stood with them, holding her breath in wonder and excitement. The man who rode second was only a few paces ahead when his horse suddenly swerved outward, staggered and fell, carrying the rider down with him straight in Holt's track, coming on at his terrible pace.

The shouting hushed as the crowd waited for the catastrophe that seemed inevitable. Then, before they were fully aware of the danger, the black horse had leaped over the sudden obstacle and was racing neck and neck with the captain's horse and gaining every step.

Only fifty yards remained.

Breathlessly the crowd stood and watched as the two riders sped forward. Would he make it? Would it be possible after all the hindrances for him to compass that?

The captain was on his mettle now, spurring his horse to its utmost, but still the black kept easily with him. Like two moats in the sunshine set to swim in unison, the racers looked to the excited crowd as they skimmed along together.

Jean clutched the rail in front of her, her eyes blinded once more by sudden tears of excitement, her heart thumping wildly.

Suddenly, the black seemed to take on new speed.

A gasp from the crowd, a breath of satisfaction, and then through her tears Jean saw the black horse leap ahead of his rival and clear the line with a lead of fully ten feet.

Chapter 18

For a moment there was silence, as if the crowd could not grasp the import of the feat just witnessed; as if senses had not yet registered results in human brains. Then a great shout arose, gathering force as it swept along. They stamped, they cheered, they yelled, and they waved wild, excited hands with handkerchiefs, umbrellas, canes—anything that was in them. They prolonged the sound until it was deafening. And there didn't seem to be one in the whole crowd who remembered that the man they shouted for had been for years despised by them all.

No one noticed Jean, her face wreathed in smiles. She stood on her railed platform, one hand upon her breast to still its excitement, the other hand wiping away her foolish tears which she hoped to get rid of before anybody had time to notice them. It was all so wonderful to have her beloved recognized in this way. To be sure, it was only an athletic feat, not recognition of his sterling worth that the crowd was giving him in this ovation. She wasn't deceived. She knew it didn't mean any change on their part, no difference in the circumstances that divided them; but it was something great to her to have even his riding recognized thus.

The cheering continued for several minutes.

Holt dismounted, halting his horse for a moment, and stood facing the shouting mob. Then with a slight, dignified bow he turned away and walked toward the fallen rider.

Already a doctor had been called, and a crowd was gathering. Holt dispersed them with a wave of his hand and, kneeling beside the injured man, began ministering to him with a skillful touch, regardless of the shouting throng who cheered this new action yet more madly.

A delegation came in haste to bring the hero to the judges' stand where Jean, with shining eyes, stood waiting with the wreath in her hand to crown him. But he paid not the slightest attention to them. Instead he raised a silver whistle to his lips and blew a keen blast, that even in their excitement startled the crowd and made them remember the tales connected with that whistle and the deeds it had summoned men to do.

Two men jumped down instantly from the front seat of the grandstand and were at his side before the echo of the whistle died away. Jean saw them and knew them for the men who had ridden out of the woods the day Scathlin attacked her. They were his special bodyguards, tried and true. He sent them off with a word, and in a moment they were back with a hastily improvised stretcher and, lifting the injured man from the ground, bore him away to the tent that had been set up for use of the ladies. Holt would have followed but for the detaining committee, who laid hands upon him now and insisted that he was holding up the whole performance and had no right to spoil the day and keep the lady waiting. Even then Holt might have resisted had they not made mention of the lady, and he looked up and caught her eye and wistful smile, for he had no mind to be further in the public eye—he had ridden for Jean only.

He took off his hat to her and came forward, and the action touched off the crowd again in a hoarser cry of excitement than before. Someone even ventured to bring his name into the cry: "Holt! Holt! Holt! Hurrah!"

Holt lifted up his head proudly at that and went forward, not as a man goes who is ashamed before his fellowmen. His bearing was of one who dares to face others, a "gentleman, unafraid." The shout died down in hushed surprise and then rose on a higher wave that had in it something of the honor and respect his bearing demanded. And so he came and knelt before her.

In all that wild company only Eleanor Harrington sat unmoved.

"What are they shouting again for?" she asked her husband. "Isn't this thing almost over? I'm tired."

"They are calling Holt to come to the stand and receive his prize," said Harrington under his breath, as if it were a bitter thing for him to see.

"How annoying!" said Eleanor, rising to look. "And I suppose Jean will have to present it. If I had foreseen any such thing as this I would have forbidden her to take such a prominent position. I think they have made altogether too much fuss over that creature already. It was an impertinence in him to come today, and he knew it. I wonder you didn't take steps to have him put out at the start, James. But there is one thing—Jean must not ride around the track with him. I simply will not have it! You must go down there quickly and tell her not to. Forbid it! Tell her to say she is sick or anything; only she must not ride with him. Quick! Go, James, or it will be too late! She won't have sense enough herself. It will be just like her to think she must; she is so afraid of hurting people's feelings. See, she is standing up with the wreath in her hands. Why don't you go?"

"Hush!" said Harrington, drawing his wife down into her seat again and speaking in a low tone. "Hush! Somebody will hear you. Don't you see she's got to go now? Don't you understand that public opinion will demand it? She'd be a fool to turn back now; she must go the whole show. Besides, I can't afford to get his ill will, and if she didn't go with him Holt would know I had prevented her."

"You can't *afford!*" said his wife angrily. "You can't *afford!*" And she raised her voice in astonishment. "What do you mean? I thought you told me only a few days ago that you had him where he couldn't do you any more harm?"

"Hush, Eleanor! Haven't you any sense at all? This is no place to discuss business matters. Don't say another word. Things have changed. I had a message from Scathlin. It's all up! Don't mention the matter to Jean; let her ride with him if she likes. I've got to make friends with him somehow, or I'm in a bad hole."

Eleanor's face would have been a sight for the neighbors if they hadn't been too busy shouting to notice.

"Well, I think things have come to a pretty pass if my sister's reputation has to be sacrificed for business," she retorted.

The furious look her husband gave her silenced her, however, and she sat back, struggling to master her own feelings and understand what her husband had meant.

Dazed and indignant she beheld what was going on at the judges' stand.

Jasper Holt was kneeling almost reverently before the girl he had twice saved from death, his bright head bowed, and she, with her eyes starry bright, bent and laid the laurel wreath upon his brow.

The crowd hushed its sound while the little ceremony was performed and then shouted aloud again while Jasper Holt arose and helped the lady down the steps and to her saddle. Mounting, he rode beside her, bowing gravely to the line of other contestants over whom he had won his victory. These, in spite of their chagrin, bowed and smiled back graciously, for they would not have the lady know how bitter was their defeat. And so together rode the two amid the storm of cheers, out into the arena and around the track.

Holt did not presume upon the occasion to show his intimacy with the girl beside him. Instead he rode with respectful mien, save for one grave, understanding smile at the start, by which she knew how much he hated all this publicity and would have slipped away without it but for her sake. As if their every thought and word could be understood, they rode with downcast eyes and silent lips, and there was nothing in the whole journey around the course that could offend the watching, mortified sister.

Not until they were almost back to the judges' stand did Holt even glance her way, and then he spoke quite low: "You are going on the morning train?"

She bowed assent because she could not speak. A rush of tears was in her throat at thought of leaving.

"I shall see you again to say good-bye," he said and gave her one look and a smile that filled her with joy. Then he left her at the judges' stand with a low bow and rode out of the arena alone, a long, appreciative shout following him out of sight.

Jean, her heart too full for words, watched him, then turned to face her host of admirers, who, making the best of their disappointment, clustered around her saying pleasant things.

The madness of the crowd over the late hero died down with his disappearance from the arena. Habit and prejudice held sway once more. Men laughed over their recent frenzy and said: "Well, that certainly was great riding. It takes a daredevil to do the impossible. Of course, we know Holt can ride. Still, I didn't really think he could do as well as that."

By the time they were back in their homes they had recovered their sanity enough to agree with their wives that it was a great piece of impudence for him to ride in and take all the honors away from the men who had worked so hard to make the affair a success. Yet in their hearts all felt again the thrill of excitement as they thought of those last fifty yards of the race and secretly rejoiced that, impudence or not, Holt had entered the lists.

"You poor little girl," gushed Mrs. Thorne over Jean. "It certainly was a shame that you couldn't have had a more respectable escort in your ride around the track. Of course he looked very well and all that. And he really behaved much better than I would have expected of him, quite modest. But, still, it was a great disappointment that some of your friends couldn't have shared the honor with you. Freeman, I know, will be terribly down about not winning."

"Thank you, Mrs. Thorne," said Jean. "I'm sorry your son had to be disappointed, but of course everyone couldn't win, although they all did well. But, after all, Mr. Holt is one of my friends, in fact, my first friend in Hawk Valley, because he saved my life in the wreck when I was on my way here. I really felt it quite an honor to ride with him today."

She turned pleasantly to greet the wife of one of the officers from the fort and left Mrs. Thorne to gasp and roll her eyes in astonishment. "Of course she doesn't know him; she doesn't understand," said the poor woman in an aside to Eleanor, who came up just then. "And perhaps it's just as well she shouldn't, as she's going home so soon. Poor Freeman! I don't know what he'll do. He's completely gone over her!"

Then all those fluttering girls came around Jean and began to talk at once. "Oh, wasn't he simply great! And isn't he handsome in those togs? Isn't it a shame he has to be so wicked? And such a woman hater? I declare I thought he was going to refuse to ride around with you. And, oh, Jean, you sly thing! You knew he was going to enter when you talked about it the other day, didn't you?"

They chattered and buzzed, and the young men came presently and bore them away one at a time. It was the captain who at last, by his very persistence, won the right to ride back to the house by Jean's side. Poor captain! His last ride, and that glorious smile in her eyes, but not for him.

She was gentle with him when he tried again to persuade her to accept his love. She told him with a wistful sigh that happiness was not in getting what we wanted but in knowing things were real and true and fine. She said she would always think of him as her friend, and she hoped he would forget that he had wanted anything else. And she thanked him for his beautiful orchids so sweetly that she left a warm glow in his heart, despite his double defeat.

Later, as she knelt before her window seat and looked out into the starry night and over toward the cottage where the Golden Sunset roses grew, she forgot all the petty things that had been bothering her all day and just let herself be glad for a little while. Then she bowed her head and prayed: "Dear Father, I thank You for letting them see so much. Please, someday, let them all know him as he really is. Bless him and keep him. I trust him with You, dear Lord."

And when she fell asleep at last, weary from the long day, against her pillow under her cheek lay soft petals of the golden roses, and their fragrance mingled with her dreams and brought a smile to her lips.

Chapter 19

Jean awakened in the early morning and lay still, thinking she was to see Jasper once more before she left. She would have some glance to carry with her on the way. She would have the beautiful day that was past to put with their other experiences together and keep, and she would have that good-bye. It was the knowledge that he promised to see her again that brought a smile to her lips when she remembered this was her last day in Hawk Valley, perhaps forever.

There were not many minutes for such happy thoughts. Her trunk was packed, except for a few little things, but they must be put in. And the children were already clamoring for her to come downstairs—they could not spare her any longer on this, her last morning.

Before she was ready to go down, people began to come to the house to say good-bye and attend her to the station, and when she was finally ready she had gathered quite an escort; so that her going through the street seemed like a tri-umphal procession, a fit continuation of the festivities of the day before.

Eleanor was proud and pleased and weeping all in one, and there was laughing and chatter and many invitations for her to return.

More flowers had arrived this morning, and there were boxes of candy and books for her to read on the way. Just before she left the house Eleanor brought to her more orchids from the captain and begged her to wear them just this one last time, but she was already wearing a glorious mass of fresh Golden Sunset roses that she had saved for this purpose. Eleanor tried to make her take them off, but Harrington interfered unexpectedly.

"What do you do that for?" he said. "It's all right if she wants to wear them. People will sort of expect it. It's a piece of her triumph of yesterday. It won't do her any harm."

Jean looked up surprised, caught an uneasy glance in his eye and read his mean, cringing soul. He would sacrifice her readily to his worst enemy if it suited his needs, and she had always felt it—now she knew it. He colored under her glance and tried to affect an elderly air of cosseting her, but Jean was not deceived.

The train was twenty minutes late. A renewal of yesterday's merriment filled the station while they waited. Jean was enthroned on a pile of packing cases with her flowers about her and her admirers at her feet. But though her eyes searched the landscape in every direction, from her vantage point she could see Holt nowhere. And when the train at last was sighted, a mere speck down the track, she felt her heart sinking in dismay. He had promised to come! It seemed as though she couldn't go without that last look from his eyes, the covenant for the lonely future.

She tried to smile and say all the bright things that were expected of her, but she couldn't keep her eyes away from the road that led to Holt's house. When the train finally pulled out amid the waving multitude of friends and the shouting of last messages and fond good-byes, the tears sprang into her eyes unbidden and dimmed the faces of those on the platform into a great blur.

"Well, I'm glad she's safely off," sighed Eleanor, climbing into the car beside the children. "And I must say that man behaved pretty well not to come down to the train. I didn't think he had that much sense!"

But her husband answered not a word. He drove his car in grim silence. He was wishing Holt had come and wondered if his absence portended evil for him.

The travelers on the Eastern express watched with delight the beautiful girl surrounded by her bank of flowers that had come to brighten the monotony of their long trip. They wondered where she was going and if she had left a sweet-heart behind, for she wiped the tears away furtively and kept her head turned, looking out the window at the landscape.

Captain Wetherill had assumed the care of putting Jean on the train and had turned over a seat, giving her plenty of room to pile the flowers in the empty seat. She seemed like a young queen in her garden, with roses and lilies and violets all about her; but at none of them did she look. Her lips were touching the petals of the golden rose on her breast, and her thoughts were with its giver. His fine bearing as he skimmed the ground on his black steed, the touch of his soft, bright hair as she laid the wreath on his brow, the look of homage in his eyes as he raised her hand and led her to her horse, the thrill of his voice when he promised to see her again to say good-bye; and then the leaden fact that he had not come! Over and over she went the round and always came back to that, with a choke in her throat and tears in her eyes. Excuse after excuse for his not coming were conjured in her mind and rejected, and vague fear for his safety mingled with them too. But the fact remained—he had not—and now she would see him no more.

She tried again and again to gather herself together and finally succeeded in mastering the tears so that there was only a bright hint of them in her eyes. But the sense of sadness and something dear, unfinished and now impossible pervaded her thoughts.

Fifty miles from Hawk Valley the train came to a halt at a tiny flag station, and a young man entered, tall, handsome, wearing a dark blue suit and a soft Panama hat—a perfect gentleman in every detail, with a light in his eyes and a smile of welcome on his lips.

Jean did not look up until he was almost beside her seat, and then her heart leaped when she saw that it was Holt.

With a soft little cry she hustled the flowers that lay on the seat beside her into the opposite one and made room for him. The car looked and was satisfied. Her sweetheart had not been left behind after all, and he was good to look upon. All was as it should be. They settled back to watch the look on the two young faces. And there were no unkind critics here, for none of them had ever heard of Jasper Holt.

In the still dark of the evening before, Holt had ridden forth in the opposite direction from that he intended to take. Skirting the town in a wide trail, he had taken his way across country to the little flag station, where he left his horse to be cared for until he should return.

Very quietly they sat together, after the first wonderful greetings, and talked. There was over them the sadness of a coming separation which each felt might be forever, and they spoke no word of hope that it might be otherwise. The day before them was a precious treasure they meant to have and keep for life. Many things they learned in that brief time, of each other's hopes, longings and desires. Quietly Holt drew from her many thoughts of her own pure heart wherewith to build his ideal for the future.

Once he looked at the great bank of flowers before him and then down at the golden roses on her gown. They did not need to talk much about such things, for their eyes could say it all, and Holt read thoughts quickly and spoke the language of a glance to perfection. The words he felt he hadn't a right to speak she might read in his face if she chose.

And she chose.

Once, as the afternoon drew to a close, he said suddenly, "Harrington sent the papers back to me last evening."

Jean looked up startled, questioning, and met amusement in Holt's eyes.

"He didn't dare keep them. He professes that he sent them the minute he knew I was at home and that he has been much disturbed by their presence in his house for fear I misunderstood his possession of them"

A little cloud of apprehension came into Jean's eyes.

"Don't be afraid to trust me," Holt said, with gentleness in his eyes. "I'm not going to make any trouble for your sister. You know that."

A great light of joy came into her face, and the tears that had caused her so much annoyance earlier in the day came rushing back.

It was in the late afternoon that they reached the city where Jean was to change to the sleeper.

Holt gathered up the flowers to take with her, but she put up a protesting hand.

"Oh, please, I don't want any but these," she said and laid her hand tenderly over the golden roses on her breast.

A look of love and appreciation came into Holt's eyes, and he dropped the flowers quite happily to gather up her suitcase and umbrella.

"Let the brakeman take them home to his wife then," he said, smiling.

He left her at last in the sleeper, and as he stood beside the train until it moved out of the station, their eyes made promises of trust and loyalty long after their lips were forced to remain silent.

Jean didn't weep when she saw the last glimpse of his splendid figure on the dim station platform. She had entered upon her desert, but she had the light of his look to shine in her heart, and her courage rose. No tears should break her down now. She was content. He would be true, and she would trust him always, even if she never saw him again.

Just what the future would hold for her she didn't care to think. This strange vow she had made with a man she couldn't hope to marry with her parents' consent, and whom she would not marry without, she had made on trust, and on trust she would keep it.

She didn't mean to trouble her family with the story. They had been far away and couldn't understand. She would trust and live her life and know that somewhere, somehow, he was being true also.

Most unpractical but ideal. Her sister Eleanor would have said it was foolish and secretly hope, of course, that now when she saw no more of him she would get over it very soon. But Jean was not made like that. She knew the heartache that was before her and, knowing, dared to rejoice in it.

Chapter 20

Three days later Jasper Holt rode into Hawk Valley from a westerly direction, serious and silent, with a light of purpose in his eyes and a new dignity about him. Harrington, meeting him in trepidation, was surprised and not a little disturbed by the steady look of understanding that accompanied the grave bow he gave him.

The tournament had accomplished one thing in Holt's favor, for many men meeting him now acknowledged his presence by a formal greeting who had formerly ignored him or treated him with contempt. A few men even went so far as to try to talk with him in a friendly way when they met him in the post office, though perhaps there was the least bit of condescension about their manner. But Jasper Holt held on his reserved way, mingling little with any except his chosen few and presuming not at all on his popularity from the tournament. That incident was closed, and he wished it to be as far as they were concerned. The greetings of his fellowmen he answered coolly, briefly, and was gone. Would-be friends found little encouragement in any advances they made. A recognition won by mere physical skill was not what he desired. His pride lay not in that direction. Certain things he intended to do, but they would take time. Meanwhile he went on his independent way, and men saw little of him.

Time passed on, and Jean's languishing suitors recovered from their various heartbreaks. Other maidens visited Hawk Valley and were feasted and feted and cherished with flowers and tournaments; but Jasper Holt came no more to dispute their victories. He kept on his quiet, steady way and gained their respect every day.

Not a word passed between Holt and the girl in the East whom he loved. Eleanor never mentioned him in her letters, although her conscience hurt her now and then that she did not; for she was an honest woman and liked to give even the devil his due. Moreover, Harrington, after a period of restlessness and unstrung nerves, appeared to have settled down to the fact that his enemy was not going to bring him to justice and had developed a most extraordinary way of saying pleasant things about him now and then. He even suggested once that Eleanor include him in a dinner they were giving for business purposes, but his wife promptly vetoed the idea. Even for business purposes she would not lay aside her principles, she said, and shut her lips in a firm line that reminded Harrington of her younger sister.

Jean had not expected letters from Holt and so had nothing to be disappointed about; but sometimes when her sister's letters came she read eagerly, hoping for some little word that would tell her how he was faring. After they were read she would invariably sit looking wistfully out the window. Her father and mother noticed it and wondered if she had left her heart behind with any of the many admirers of whom Eleanor had written. They talked it over at dusk sometimes when they were alone and looked ahead to the years when their girl would be without them.

"I'd like her to find a strong, noble man," said her father. "I cannot bear to think of her treading her years alone. And yet there are very few men of that kind," he said and sighed.

"Perhaps we ought to send her back to Eleanor's for another visit," suggested her mother. "We called her home so soon before her visit was done, you know. It may be that someone was there. It may be she would like to go."

But when they suggested it to Jean, although her face lit up, she shook her head.

"No, Mother, dear," she said firmly. "I'm going to stay with you. I'm not going off there again to get my head turned."

And from that purpose they could not turn her, although they tried more than once. And so they settled back relieved and happy that she was content to stay with them.

Nevertheless, she cried her heart out that night with longing, yet she knew it was better that she should stay.

A year and more passed with Jean continuing on her quiet way in the home and church. It was not an unhappy place to be. The manse in which they lived was beautiful, built of stone with pretty rooms and many windows, the rooms all cheerful and light. The people of the church loved Jean as they loved her father and mother, and she was welcome everywhere in all the merrymakings. She had a large Sunday school class in the church and another in a mission in the lower part of town, and her boys were the most devoted followers.

Neither was she without admirers, for all the young men in the church and neighborhood were her friends, and she was as popular at home as she had been in the West. The little manse reception room was never for long unadorned with flowers of some kind that had been sent to her, and she was never without an escort to anything she cared to attend. Yet, although she had a pleasant circle of friends and seemed to enjoy their company, she never was deeply interested in any of them. And one by one those who had tried their fortune at her hand went sadly away and seldom came anymore.

Jean seemed happy. She spent much time with her music and her books, when she was not actually busy about the house or in the parish helping her father. But she was growing thin, and the wistful look was ever in her eyes now. Her mother watched her anxiously and petted her more every day, and her father sighed and wished he could afford to take her off on a foreign trip for a little while. Jean only smiled and went on her way, doing each day the duty that came next.

Sometimes the longing to hear from Holt grew intolerable. Sometimes she almost yielded to her mother's suggestion that she pay Eleanor another visit, but something always held her back. What was she waiting for? A sign from Holt? No, that would probably never come. He had said he was unworthy, and he would not of himself cross her path again. But she couldn't go after him. He might have forgotten, yet she believed in her heart he had not. Her faith in him glowed bright as ever. Even when her common sense got to work and told her he was only human and by this time the incident of their days together was a thing of the past to him, still she didn't believe he had forgotten. She believed he was doing just what he had promised to do, and she must stay here and trust him. At least, if he had forgotten, she would rather never know.

So she lived her life and struggled with her heartache, and when the pain was too much she knelt and prayed for the one she loved. Then, at last, one day there came a great, fat letter from Eleanor, addressed to Jean. Most of Eleanor's letters were addressed to their mother, so when Jean took this one from the post office she caught her breath and her heart beat a trifle faster than usual. What could Eleanor have to say to make such a thick letter, and why was it sent to her instead of to Mother? Perhaps she was worried about Mother, or perhaps she wanted to tell some trouble to her and not worry their parents. But always when a letter came from her sister, she felt there was that blessed chance that perhaps she might say some little word about Holt, just to let her know he was alive. It was foolish, of course, because she never had done so, and yet hope is a subtle thing and often abides without reason for its hiding and springs forth at the least encouragement.

Jean did not open her letter at the post office. Her hand was trembling too much. She didn't wish to have anyone watch her while she read that letter, for she had a feeling her face might tell its secrets when she was off guard, reading. So she held the letter with a firm grip and walked down the leaf-strewn street, trying to remain calm and remember that this was probably just a commonplace letter about everyday affairs, and she must not be disappointed or expect anything great.

She didn't open the letter until she was safe on the vine-covered porch at home, sitting in the hammock where she wouldn't be disturbed. Some strange power held her from taking it to her mother and sharing its first reading with her as she usually did any letters she received, especially one of Eleanor's. Afterward, she wondered at this; she wondered too as she remembered how cold her hand had been and how it trembled when she tried to open the envelope with her hatpin.

She was so agitated, so sure by this time that something was the matter, that as she took the folded sheets from the envelope she closed her eyes and breathed a quick petition: "Oh, dear Father, make me strong for whatever it is."

Then she unfolded the thick sheets and read the letter.

Chapter 21

Dear little Sister,

  I have a strange task before me, to tell you of the fineness and greatness and goodness of a man I once told you was not good enough to save your life. I feel as if I must ask your forgiveness and his. You were keener-sighted than we were, and we are ashamed!

  Jean, what will you say when I tell you that Jasper Holt lies in our guest chamber, your old room—dying, I'm afraid? And that we have him to thank that our precious baby did not die a horrible death?

  Let me go back and tell you the whole story.

  After you went away James had the most extraordinary change of mind about Jasper Holt. He just turned right around and began to talk in his favor, even wanted me to invite him to dinner once. It was some business, of course, that he thought he could help him in; but he really got to liking him a little, I could see. I suppose it was that tournament and his riding so well; though I never could understand why men make so much of sports. But after it happened you didn't hear nearly so many people talking against Jasper Holt. I think, too, your being so good as to ride around the track with him had something to do with it. People saw you weren't ashamed, and they had a good look at him and saw the possibilities. They say he was asked, yes, even begged, to come to the next tournament and ride, but he wouldn't do it. He hasn't appeared that way since you left. He just went about his business gravely, and everybody began to have a lot of respect for him.

  They say he has done a lot of good to those men he has living on his place, and they simply worship him. Somebody told James that there wasn't one of them but would give his life for him any day. Well, that's something, of course. Strange we never heard about it before. Why, people used to be actually afraid of him and his men. But he has been doing some splendid things here lately.

  When Mr. Whateley died, just before the harvest, and Mrs. Whateley was left to look after her five little children, he took his full force of men over to her place and harvested everything and fixed up things a great deal better than they were ever fixed up before, for Mr. Whateley wasn't much of a manager.

  And when Lucy Whitcorn was lost for three days he organized his men and went out and searched till he found her. They took hold of hands and marched across the countryside, through the wheat fields, over every spot so they couldn't miss her. And her grandmother just

*put her arms around Jasper Holt's neck and cried and kissed him
when he brought Lucy back asleep in his arms.*

*But the greatest thing was when he made the raid on the saloons.
You remember Slosson's and The Three Geese? They used to have terrible carouses there. Slosson built a concert room over his saloon and
advertised—had balls and dinners there—and The Three Geese got
a moving picture show over their place. Between them they made a
pretty fair imitation of the bottomless pit in Hawk Valley for a while.
People got together and talked about it and said something ought to
be done to stop it, and Sallie White even started a petition about it
and got some people to sign, but it was never near election and no
one dared do much.*

*Then one night when things were at their height, and there had
been a shooting or two, we heard the silver whistle of Jasper Holt's
men, and the whole cavalcade cantered by on horseback. They went
like a streak on their dark horses, and they rode straight up to The
Three Geese and dismounted. Before anybody knew what was happening they had marched into the barroom and the concert hall and taken
possession. They handcuffed everybody in the place and bound them,
men and women, and then set to work and emptied out all the liquor
and turned the big fire hose into every room till there wasn't a smell of
whiskey left, and it was cleaner than it ever was since it was built.
They went to Slosson's and did the same thing. Slosson, and Craven of
The Three Geese, they put into jail, and some of the others who had
been most criminal, and they cleaned the whole place out. Jasper Holt
took some of the prisoners to his own house and kept them there till he
reformed them, and he has been keeping an eye on them right along
ever since.*

*Of course after that people rallied around him and were only too
glad to be counted in with him. They all admired his nerve, and they
saw he could make things go, so they turned to work, and last month
they made him mayor of the town, and he has reformed everything in
the place. Now that's the preface, and I ought to have told you long
ago, little sister, but I suppose I was ashamed to, after all I had said.*

*But now I'm coming to the real story, the one that makes me feel
like sobbing, and I have to stop writing and go and kiss my baby
before I can go on.*

*This morning (it seems a week ago) I sat at my desk writing my
paper for the next club meeting. Baby was out in the yard in his white
rompers and his little white hat, with his new red cart that James
brought him from Chicago on his last trip. The window was open, and
I could see him gathering leaves and carrying them in his cart to the*

sidewalk, where he dumped them in a pile at the edge of the road. I had been having a terrible search for a word in the dictionary, and when I looked up again I saw Baby standing out in the middle of the road working away with all his might to back up his cart, the way he saw the big carts do, and dump his leaves on the outside of the pile. I didn't think much about it, because there are no teams around in the early morning usually, and the autos, the few we have in town, don't come on this street much.

But just as I was beginning to write again I heard a horrible roaring sound and horse's feet flying down the street. Something gripped my throat with fear, and I could scarcely get out of my chair. I could see the baby standing perfectly still, looking at something coming toward him. His little red wagon was standing on end, the red paint gleaming in the sun. Then I heard that roar again, and I called to Jamie to come in quickly, but he didn't seem to know what to do. He took hold of the handle of his cart and seemed to be worried for fear it would be run over. He tried to hurry with it onto the sidewalk, but being on end it wouldn't work quickly. On came that terrible roar! I don't know how I got out on the porch, but there I was, watching a great, angry bull bearing down straight upon the baby. I screamed and tried to run down the steps, but I was so frightened my knees just sank under me, and I was in a heap on the steps struggling to get up, and my baby standing still, not ten feet from that snorting, fiery creature, with its horns lowered at him.

I shut my eyes—it was so terrible, like a nightmare, when you can't do a thing. I thought I was going to faint, and I tried to call James, though I knew he wasn't at home. Then a wonderful thing happened. A horse was flying down the street from the opposite direction, straight at the bull, but Baby was between. I hadn't time to think before the man on the horse swung over from his saddle, gathered up the baby, and dashed sideways out of the bull's way. It was Jasper Holt, and he picked up Jamie just as he did your handkerchief that day at the tournament. The poor little dear held onto his red cart handle till he was up in the saddle, hindering the horse's movements, of course, and it dangled for a minute right in front of the bull's eyes, who charged at it viciously. Then the weight of the cart wrenched it from Jamie's hand, and it fell clattering under the horse's feet. But the bull turned and made for the horse, who dashed back and forth from side to side, dodging those awful horns as if he were a human being and knew how to reason.

Jasper Holt tried to get near the fence to drop the baby over, but every time he came close the bull was in the way. It all took only a second of time, of course, but it seemed hours. I could only scream, but the bull roared so loud that I couldn't be heard. Then the black horse plunged right over the bull and started down the street. But the bull turned and caught him in the thigh with his horns and tore a great gash—oh, Jean, I can't describe it all! The horse stumbled on bravely for a few paces, but you could see he hadn't a chance with the bull anymore, for he was crippled, and Jasper Holt saw it too.

By that time some men had come with guns, and that splendid fellow, with the horse staggering under him and the bull charging straight at him, held the baby up in the air and told the men to shoot. It meant a terrible risk to him, of course, because he was in the line of fire. But there was nothing else to do. They shot as carefully as they could, and in a minute or two the bull gave one awful roar and lurched back. The horse sank, too, and someone took the baby. It is all confusion in my mind. I don't really know what happened—only that after I got Jamie in my arms and hugged him till he cried, I looked up and saw them bringing Jasper Holt in at the gate. His eyes were shut, and one arm hung at his side. They said he had been shot but had held up the baby till the bull was out of the fight.

I made them take him to your room, and someone brought the doctor almost at once. It was a serious thing; I could see from the first. They wouldn't let me in the room. I telephoned for James and put the baby to sleep. But just as I laid him down in his crib the doctor came and said Jasper Holt wanted to see me.

Jean, I didn't think a few minutes could make a difference like that in a great, big, strong man. He lay there so still I thought he was dead at first. Under all his fine tan he was white as a ghost, with his head all done up in bandages and his beautiful hair clotted with blood—one of the shots plowed deep into the scalp, it seems. He opened his eyes—what wonderful eyes he has!—and looked at me as if he were pinning his last hope upon me, and he smiled faintly. One could see it was a great effort for him to speak.

"Will you tell your sister I've kept my promise?" he said, slowly and distinctly.

When I told him I would, his eyes lighted up, as if the sun were shining behind them, and then they fell shut, and I think he must have fainted again. I tried to tell him how grateful I was to him for saving my baby's life, but his eyelids never even quivered. Then the doctor drew me away and said it wasn't any use to talk, that he couldn't hear me, so I came away, but I couldn't do a thing but just hover around the door till James came. Then he went in and found out how things were. It seems the bull gored him—they call it a "scratch," but by *their faces I know it's a pretty serious scratch.*

Three shots entered his body, one a deep scalp wound, one in his shoulder and one in his arm. They've been probing the wound and having some kind of an operation. They don't know whether he will pull through or not. They say the only thing that is in his favor is his splendid health. The men are talking now about his fine clean life. It seems he never drank or did a lot of things people took for granted he did. Oh, Jean, I can't stand it if he doesn't get well so I can thank him for saving my baby!

Jean, I know now why you looked that way when you said I did not know Jasper Holt—the fine, true, strong, brave, tender—

But tears blinded Jean's eyes, and she could read no more. For a moment she bent her head and sobbed behind the vines. But only for a moment. A frenzy of fear seized her. He was dying perhaps, and he needed her!

She lifted her head with sudden resolve and hastily read the closing sentences of the letter. Then, gathering up the scattered sheets, she hurried in to her father.

Chapter 22

Father!" said Jean, closing the study door and standing guard in front of it lest her mother enter suddenly and be frightened at what she was saying. "Father, I must go to Hawk Valley at once—today! No, it isn't Eleanor. Father, it's the man who saved my life! He is dying, and he needs me. I know he wants me. I love him, Father, and he loves me! He didn't think you would like him, and so we never said anything about it—but now he's dying and I must go!"

The look in her eyes and the tilt of her chin were her father's own when he felt he must fulfill some high calling and would not be denied. He knew at a glance that it was useless to try to stop her. Besides, he had all confidence in her.

"I see," he said with instant comprehension of what the wistfulness of her face had meant all these months. "How soon can you be ready? There's a train at six, I think."

"I will be ready, Father," she said.

He folded her close and kissed her. "Courage, daughter! Trust in our Father's tenderness."

"Thank you so much for understanding," she said, lifting her eyes to his face.

"You will want me to go with you, daughter?" he asked, trying to think how it would be possible.

"No, Father, you couldn't. You have that funeral tomorrow, and they need you," she answered, drying her tears. "And it wouldn't do to leave Mother. No, I can go alone perfectly well. Here is Eleanor's letter. Read it with Mother. That will explain a good deal. I will tell you more on the way to the station. He is the one who won the laurel wreath at the tournament. I told you a little about him—"

"Yes, I know. I understand! Now go quickly, and I will explain to your mother about it. You haven't much time. Don't try to pack more than a suitcase. We can send your trunk on after you."

It was in the sunset gloaming that she arrived in Hawk Valley, and the gold of the sky lay behind the hills, ruby lined, like the gold of Jasper Holt's roses, whose sweet withered leaves lay stored among her linen in her bureau drawer at home.

Her sister and brother-in-law met her at the station, for a telegram had heralded her coming. Quietly, with hushed voices, they met her; for death waited beside the couch in the guest room of their home, and they guessed how it must be between these two.

"He seems to be sleeping his life away," said Eleanor, folding a cloak about

Jean. "They can't rouse him. He seems content to go. He doesn't want to live. It is strange with one so strong and so young—"

The light of battle came into the younger sister's eyes, but she said nothing.

"Better come and get something to eat first," said Eleanor when they reached the house, but Jean shook her head and fled up the stairs.

There couldn't have been anything quieter than the way she opened the door and slipped into that room. Her very garments seemed to cling and hush about her as she walked. But he opened his eyes at once. A strange, wondering look came into them as she crossed the room and knelt beside him with a smile. Then she bowed her head and laid her lips upon his.

The doctors and nurse who stood by were as nothing. There were just these two in the universe, and all else was hushed.

She moved about his room or sat close behind his couch. She was there when he woke in the night and looked at her, murmuring very low, "Are you real or a dream?"

"I'm real, dear. I will not go away," she breathed and laid her soft lips on his again. This time his own responded feebly.

In the morning the doctors said there was hope, though they confessed afterward that recovery began with his first sight of Jean's face.

Jean scarcely left his side day or night and seemed tireless. Often she slept on a low stool beside the bed, with her head against his pillow. One bright morning he awoke to find her sleeping so and laid his weak hand softly upon her head. She opened her eyes, met his smile and knew that he was better.

"A life for a life," he said softly. "Dear, you must go to your bed and rest. I will get well now. You are killing yourself."

But her smile shone forth radiantly.

"I couldn't rest away from you," she said, giving him a dazzling look. "I'm not going to leave you anymore, ever!" Then she paused and looked shyly up again. "Unless, unless—you've changed your mind and don't want me. In that case I'll go back home as soon as you are able to be out."

"Oh, my dear!" he said softly and drew her down to his breast with his one good arm. "Do you mean it? Not leave me again ever? Are you willing to be my wife? Can you really trust me now?"

"I've always trusted you," she said, nestling her face against his cheek. "I trusted you the first time I saw you."

"But your people, Jean?"

"My people all love and honor you," said Jean with shining eyes. "They think you are magnificent! They cannot say enough about you. Eleanor would bow down and kiss your feet, and my father and mother know all about you and have sent me to you willingly. But, Jasper, listen, if everyone on this wide world were against you, even my dear people, I should marry you anyway and stay with you! I couldn't live any longer without you!"

He looked into her eyes and drank in her trust and loveliness and beautiful self-surrender as if it had been a life-giving draught. Then he laid his hand upon her hair and pressed her closer to him.

"Oh, you wonderful woman!" he said.

It didn't take Jasper Holt long to get well after that. Hope and joy shone in his eyes so that his face was dazzling to look upon. Those who came into his room walked softly, filled with awe that a man who had come and gone among them for years and been held in contempt could have within him a soul so great and noble as to shine like that in his face.

Jean's father and mother came West for a visit about that time, for Jean wrote that there was no use expecting her to return now. And when Jean's father and her beloved met and stood hand in hand, looking into one another's eyes, each felt entirely satisfied.

Of course all this could not go on without the town knowing something of the state of things, for everybody came to find out how the hero was getting on. And Jasper Holt's men, as they came and went in grave concern, were beset with questions. When Jean arrived, then her parents, the town opened eyes of understanding and nodded gravely, thinking it was well.

So when it was announced that a wedding would take place no one was surprised. Indeed, Jean's girlfriends had been embroidering wedding gifts for a week before it was whispered officially that they would be needed.

Once more the Harrington house was smothered in flowers for Jean. Gifts came from far and near, from all her old admirers who were now also Holt's admirers. But the flowers that Jean carried in her arms when she came down the stairs, white-clad and smiling, to meet her bridegroom, were great Golden Sunset roses, gathered by Holt's faithful men for her. And among the guests were all those men, fifty-four of them, standing grim and embarrassed outside the door to watch their leader stand among the flowers and take his beautiful girl-bride by the hand.

It was sunset again, gold and ruby sunset, when they went home to his house after the wedding supper.

The sky was broad and translucent gold behind the rose-wreathed cottage when Jean saw it for the first time. The roses hung in wealth about the doorway, and the men stood double-ranked on each side of the path. They had decked the house for her coming, those rough men who loved her husband, with boughs of sweet-smelling branches and had heaped up blazing logs in the big stone fireplace and swept the floor all clean and fresh.

There alone at last together in their own home they stood with ruby and golden light from the sunset mingling with the soft flicker of firelight and looked into each other's eyes and knew that their heavenly Father had been good to them.

The Mystery
of Mary

Chapter 1

He paused on the platform and glanced at his watch. The train he had just arrived on was late. It hurried away from the station and was swallowed up in the blackness of the tunnel, as if it knew its own shortcomings and wished to make up for them.

It was five minutes before six. He had a dinner engagement at seven, and it was yet some distance to his home, where he must change quickly if he were to arrive on time.

The stairway was long and thronged with people. A shortcut led down along the tracks under the bridge and up the grassy embankment. It would bring him a whole block nearer home, and a line of cabs waited at the corner just above the bridge. It was against the rules to walk beside the tracks—there was a large sign to that effect in front of him—but it would save five minutes. He scanned the platform hastily to see if any officials were in sight, then bolted down the darkening tracks.

Under the center of the bridge a noise of soft, hurrying footsteps behind him caught his attention, and a woman's voice broke upon his startled senses.

"Please don't stop or look around," it said, and the owner caught up with him now in the shadow. "But will you kindly let me walk beside you for a moment, till you can show me how to get out of this dreadful place? I'm very much frightened, and I'm afraid I'll be followed. Will you tell me where I can go to hide?"

After an astonished pause he obeyed her and kept on, making room for her to walk beside him, while he took the place next to the tracks. He was aware, too, of the low rumble of a train, coming from the mouth of the tunnel.

His companion had gasped for breath but began again in a tone of apology: "I saw you were a gentleman, and I didn't know what to do. I thought you would help me to get somewhere quickly."

Just then the fiery eye of the oncoming train burst from the tunnel ahead. Instinctively, the young man caught his companion's arm and drew her forward to the embankment beyond the bridge, holding her, startled and trembling, as the screaming train tore past them.

The black smoke from the tunnel rolled in a thick cloud about them, stifling them. The girl, dazed with the roar and blinded by the smoke, could only cling to her protector. For an instant they felt as if they were about to be drawn into the awful power of the rushing monster. Then it had passed, and a rush of silence followed, as if they were suddenly plunged into a vacuum. Gradually the noises of the world began again—the rumble of a trolley car on the bridge, the "honk-honk" of an automobile, the cry of the newsboy. Slowly their breath and their senses came back.

The man's first thought was to get out of the cut before another train should come. He grasped his companion's arm and started up the steep embankment, realizing as he did so that the wrist he held was slender and that the sleeve which covered it was made of the finest cloth.

They struggled up, scarcely pausing for breath. The steps at the side of the bridge, made for the convenience of railroad hands, were out of the question, for they were at a dizzying height and hung unevenly over the yawning pit where trains shot constantly back and forth.

As they emerged from the dark, the man saw that his companion was a beautiful young woman and wore a light cloth dress, with neither hat nor gloves.

At the top of the embankment they paused, and the girl, with her hand at her throat, looked backward with a shudder. She seemed like a young bird that could scarcely tell which way to fly.

Without an instant's hesitation, the young man raised his hand and hailed a four-wheeler across the street.

"Come this way, quick!" he urged, helping her in. He gave the driver his home address and stepped in after her. Then, turning, he faced his companion and was suddenly keenly aware of the strange situation in which he had placed himself.

"Can you tell me what is the matter and where you would like to go?" he asked.

The girl had scarcely recovered breath from the long climb and the fright, and she answered him in broken phrases.

"No, I can't tell you what is the matter." She paused and looked at him with a sudden comprehension of what he might be thinking about her. "But there is nothing. . .that is. . .I have done nothing wrong." She paused again and looked up with clear eyes that, he felt, could hide no guile.

"Of course," he murmured with decision and then wondered why he felt so sure about it.

"Thank you," she said. "I don't know where to go. I never was in this city before. If you will kindly tell me how to get somewhere, I suppose to a railroad station. . .and yet. . .no, I have no money, and—" Then with a sudden little gesture of dismay she cried, "And I have no hat!"

The young man felt a strong desire to shield this girl so unexpectedly thrown on his mercy. Yet vague fears hovered about the margin of his judgment. Perhaps she was a thief or an adventuress. It might be wise to let her get out of the odd situation she appeared to be in as best she could. Yet even as the thought flashed through his mind he seemed to hear an echo of her words, "I saw you were a gentleman," and felt incapable of betraying her trust in him.

The girl was speaking again. "But I must not trouble you anymore. You have been very kind to get me out of that dreadful place. If you will just stop the carriage and let me out, I'm sure I can take care of myself."

"I couldn't think of letting you get out here alone. If you're in danger, I'll help you." The warmth of his own words startled him. He knew he ought to be more cautious with a stranger, but impetuously he threw caution to the wind. "If you would just tell me a little bit about it, so that I would know what I ought to do for you—"

"Oh, I mustn't tell you! I couldn't!" said the girl, her hand fluttering up to her heart as if to control its wild beating. "I'm sorry to have involved you for a moment in this. Please let me out here. I'm not frightened, now that I've gotten away from that terrible tunnel. I was afraid I might have to go in there alone, for I didn't see any way to get up the bank, and I couldn't go back."

"I'm glad I happened to be there," said the young man. "It would have been dangerous for you to enter that tunnel. It runs an entire block. You would probably have been killed."

The girl shut her eyes and pressed her fingers to them. In the light of the street lamps, he saw that she was very white and jewels were flashing from the rings on her fingers. It was apparent that she was a lady of wealth and refinement. What could have brought her to this pass?

The carriage came to a sudden stop, and, looking out, he saw they had reached his home. A new alarm seized him as the girl moved as if to get out. His dignified mother and fastidious sister were probably not in, but if by any chance they had not left the house, what would they think if they saw a strange, hatless young woman descend from the carriage with him? Moreover, what would the butler think?

"Excuse me," he said, "but there are reasons why I don't want you to get out of the carriage just here. Suppose you sit still until I come out. I have a dinner engagement and must make a few changes in my dress, but it will take me only a few minutes. You're in no danger, and I'll take you to some place of safety. I'll try to think what to do while I'm gone. On no account get out of the carriage. It would make the driver suspicious, you know. If you are really being followed, he will let no one disturb you in the carriage, of course. Don't distress yourself. I'll hurry. Can you give me the address of any friend I might phone or telegraph?"

She shook her head, and a glitter of tears shone in her eyes as she replied, "No, I know of no one in this city who could help me."

"I'll help you then," he said with sudden resolve in a tone that would be a comfort to any woman in distress.

His tone and the look of respectful kindliness he gave her kept the girl in the carriage until his return, although in her sudden distrust of the world, she thought more than once of attempting to slip away. Yet, without money, and in a costume which could only lay her open to suspicion, what could she do? Where was she to go?

As the young man let himself into his home with his latchkey, he heard the butler's well-trained voice answering the telephone.

"Yes, ma'am, this is Mrs. Dunham's residence. . . . No, ma'am, she is not at home. . . . No, ma'am, Miss Dunham is out also. . . . Mr. Dunham? Just wait a moment, please. I think Mr. Dunham has just come in. Who shall I say wishes to speak to him? . . . Mrs. Parker Bowman? . . . Yes, ma'am; just wait a minute, please. I'll call Mr. Dunham."

The young man frowned. Another interruption. And Mrs. Bowman! It was at her house that he was to dine. What could the woman want? Surely it wasn't so late that she was looking him up. But perhaps something had happened and she was calling off her dinner. What luck if she was! Then he would be free to attend to the problem of the young woman whom Providence had suddenly thrust upon his care.

He took the receiver, resolved to get out of going to the dinner if it were possible.

"Good evening, Mrs. Bowman."

"Oh, is that you, Mr. Dunham? How relieved I am! I'm in a bit of difficulty about my dinner and called up to see if your sister could help me out. Miss Mayo has failed me. Her sister has had an accident, and she can't leave her. She has just phoned me, and I don't know what to do. Isn't Cornelia at home? Couldn't you persuade her to come and help me out? She would have been invited in Miss Mayo's place if she hadn't told me she expected to go to Boston this week. But she changed her plans, didn't she? Isn't she where you could reach her by phone and beg her to come and help me out? You see, it's a very particular dinner, and I've made all my arrangements."

"Well, now, that's too bad, Mrs. Bowman," began the young man, thinking he saw a way out of both their difficulties. "I'm sorry Cornelia isn't here. I'm sure she would do anything in her power to help you. But she and Mother were to dine in Chestnut Hill tonight, and they must have left the house half an hour ago. I'm afraid she's out of the question. Suppose you leave me out? You won't have any trouble then except to take two plates off the table. And you would have even couples!

"You see," he hastened to add, "you see, Mrs. Bowman, I'm in somewhat of a predicament myself. My train was late, and as I left the station I happened to meet a young woman—a friend. She is temporarily separated from her friends and is a stranger in the city. In fact, I'm the only acquaintance or friend she has, and I feel under obligation to see her to her hotel and look up trains for her. She leaves the city tonight."

"Now, look here, Tryon Dunham, you're not going to leave me in the lurch for any young woman," replied the lady. "I don't care how old an acquaintance she is! You simply bring her along. She'll make up my number and relieve me wonderfully. No, don't say a word. Just tell her that she needn't stand on ceremony. Your mother and I are too old friends for that. Any friend of yours is a friend of mine, and my house is open to her. She won't mind. These girls who have traveled a great deal learn to step over the little formalities of calls and introductions. Tell her I'll call on her afterward, if she'll only remain in town long enough, or I'll come and take dinner with her when I happen to be in her city.

"I suppose she's just returned from abroad—they all have—or else she's just going," she continued. "And if she hasn't learned to accept things as she finds them, she probably will soon. Tell her what a plight I'm in and that it will be a real blessing to me if she'll come. Besides—I didn't mean to tell you; I meant it to be a surprise, but I may as well tell you now—Judge Blackwell will be here, too, with his wife, and I especially want you to meet him. I've been trying to get you two together for a long time."

"Ah!" breathed the young man with interest. "Judge Blackwell! I've wanted to meet him."

"Well, he has heard about you, too, and I think he wants to meet you. Did you know he was thinking of taking a partner into his office? He has always refused—but that's another story, and I haven't time to talk. You ought to be on your way here now. Tell your friend I will bless her forever for helping me out, and I won't take no for an answer. You said she'd just returned from abroad, didn't you? Of course she's musical. You must make her give us some music. She will, won't she? I was depending on Miss Mayo for that this evening."

"Well, you might be able to persuade her," murmured the distracted young man as he struggled with one hand to untie his necktie and unfasten his collar and mentally calculated how long it would take him to get into his dress suit.

"Yes, of course. You'd better not speak of it—it might make her decline. And don't let her stop to make any changes in her dress. Everybody will understand when I tell them she's just arrived—didn't you say?—from the other side, and we caught her on the wing. There's someone coming now. Do for pity's sake hurry, Tryon, for my cook is terribly cross when I hold up a dinner too long. Good-bye. Oh, by the way, what did you say her name was?"

"Oh!" He had almost succeeded in releasing his collar and was about to hang up the receiver when this new difficulty confronted him.

"Oh, yes, of course, her name—I had almost forgotten," he went on wildly to make time as he searched about in his mind for a name, any name, that might help him. The telephone book lay open at the Rs. He pounced upon it and took the first name that caught his eye.

"Yes. . .why, Remington, Miss Remington."

"Remington!" came the delighted scream over the phone. "Not Carolyn Remington? That would be too good luck!"

"No," he said distractedly. "No, not Carolyn. I. . .ah. . .I think Mary—Mary Remington."

"Oh, I'm afraid I haven't met her, but never mind. Do hurry up, Tryon. It's five minutes till seven. Where did you say she lives?" But the receiver was hung up with a click, and the young man tore up the steps to his room three at a bound.

Dunham's mind was by no means at rest. He felt that he had done a tremendously daring thing, though when he came to think of it, he hadn't suggested it himself; and he didn't quite see how he could get out of it either. For how was he to have time to help the girl if he didn't take her with him?

Various plans floated through his head. He might bring her into the house and make some sort of an explanation to the servants, but what would the explanation be? He couldn't tell them the truth about her, and how would he explain the matter to his mother and sister? They might return before he did and would be sure to ask innumerable questions.

And the girl—would she go with him? If not, what should he do with her? And about her dress? Was it such as his "friend" could wear to one of Mrs. Parker Bowman's exclusive dinners? To his memory, it seemed quiet and refined. Perhaps that was all she required for a woman who was traveling. There it was again! But he hadn't said she was traveling nor that she had just returned from abroad nor that she was a musician. How could he answer such questions about an utter stranger, and yet how could he not answer them under the circumstances?

And she wore no hat or cloak. That would be a strange way to arrive at a dinner. How could she accept? He was settling his coat into place when a little bulge attracted his attention to an inside pocket. Impatiently he pulled out a pair of long gloves. They were his sister's, and he now remembered she had given them to him to carry the night before on the way home from a reception; she had removed them because it was raining. He looked at them with a sudden inspiration. Of course! Why hadn't he thought of that?

He hurried into his sister's room to make a selection of a few necessities for the emergency—only to have his assurance desert him at the threshold. The room was immaculate, with no feminine finery lying about. Cornelia Dunham's maid was well-trained. The only article that seemed out of place was a hatbox on a chair near the door. It bore the name of a fashionable milliner, and across the lid was penciled in Cornelia's large, angular hand, "To be returned to Madame Dollard's." He caught up the box and strode over to the closet. There was no time to lose, and this box doubtless contained a hat of some kind. If it had been called for, no further inquiry would be made about the matter. He could call at Madame's and settle the bill without his sister's knowledge.

He poked back into the closet and discovered several wraps and evening cloaks of elaborate style, but the thought came to him that perhaps one of these would be recognized as Cornelia's. He closed the door hurriedly and went down to a large closet under the stairs, from which he presently emerged with his mother's new black raincoat. He patted his coat pocket to be sure he had the gloves, seized his hat and hurried back to the carriage, the hatbox in one hand and his mother's raincoat dragging behind him. His only anxiety was to get out before the butler saw him.

As he closed the door, there flashed over him the sudden possibility that the girl had gone. Well, perhaps that would be the best thing that could happen and would save him a lot of trouble. Yet, to his amazement, he found that the thought filled him with a sense of disappointment. He didn't want her to be gone. He peered anxiously into the carriage and was relieved to find her still there, huddled into the shadow, her eyes looking large and frightened. She was trembling, and it required all her strength to keep him from noticing it. She was half afraid of the man, now that she had waited for him. Perhaps he was not a gentleman after all.

Chapter 2

I 'm afraid I've been a long time," he said as he closed the door of the carriage, after giving Mrs. Parker Bowman's address to the driver. In the uncertain light of the distant street lamp, the girl looked small and appealing. He felt a strong desire to lift her burdens and carry them on his own broad shoulders.

"I've brought some things that I thought might help," he said. "Would you like to put on this coat? It may not be just what you would have selected, but it was the best I could find that would not be recognized. The air is growing chilly."

He shook out the coat and threw it around her.

"Oh, thank you," she murmured gratefully, slipping her arms into the sleeves.

"And this box has some kind of a hat, I hope," he went on. "I ought to have looked, but there really wasn't time." He unknotted the strings and produced a large picture hat with long black plumes. He was relieved to find it black. While he untied the strings, there had been a growing uneasiness lest the hat be one of those wild combinations of colors that Cornelia frequently purchased and called "artistic."

The girl received the hat with a grateful relief.

"And now," he said, as he pulled out the gloves and laid them in her lap, "we're invited out to dinner."

"Invited out to dinner!" gasped the girl.

"Yes. It's rather a providential thing to have happened, I think. The telephone was ringing as I opened the door, and Mrs. Parker Bowman, to whose house I was invited, was asking for my sister to fill the place of an absent guest. My sister is away, and I tried to beg off. I told her I had accidentally met—I hope you will pardon me—I called you a friend."

"Oh," she said. "That was kind of you."

"I said you were a stranger in town, and as I was your only acquaintance, I felt I should show you the courtesy of taking you to a hotel and helping to get you off on the night train. I asked her to excuse me, as that would give her an even number. But it seems she had invited someone especially to meet me and was distressed not to have her full quota of guests, so she sent you a most cordial invitation to come to her at once, promising to take dinner with you sometime if you would help her out now.

"Somehow she gathered from my talk that you were traveling, had just returned from abroad and were temporarily separated from your friends," he continued. "She is also sure that you're musical and means to ask you to help her out in that way this evening. I told her I wasn't sure whether you could be persuaded or not, and she mercifully refrained from asking whether you sang or played. I tell you all this so that you'll be prepared for anything. Of course I didn't tell her all these things. I merely kept still when she inferred them. Your name, by the way, is Miss Remington—Mary Remington. She was elated for a moment when she thought you might be Carolyn Remington—whoever she may be. I suppose she'll speak of it. The name was the first one my eye lit upon in the telephone book. If you object to bearing it for the evening, it's easy to see how a name could be misunderstood over the phone. But perhaps you'd better give me a few pointers, for I've never tried acting a part and can't be sure how well I shall do it."

The girl had been silent from astonishment while the man talked.

"But I cannot possibly go there to dinner," she gasped, her hand going to her throat again as if to pluck away the delicate lace about it and give more room for breathing. "I must get away somewhere at once. I cannot trouble you in this way. I've already imposed upon your kindness. With this hat and coat and gloves, I'll be able to manage quite well, and I thank you so much! I'll return them to you as soon as possible."

The cab began to go slowly, and Tryon Dunham noticed that another carriage, just ahead of theirs, was stopping before Mrs. Bowman's house. There was no time for halting decision.

"My friend," he said earnestly, "I cannot leave you alone, and I don't see a better way than for you to go in here with me for a little while, till I'm free to go with you. No one can follow you here or suspect that you have gone out to dinner at a stranger's house. Believe me, it's the very safest thing you could do. This is the house. Will you go in with me? If not, I must tell the driver to take us somewhere else."

"But what will she think of me," she said in trepidation, "and how can I do such a thing as to steal into a woman's house to a dinner in this way? Besides, I'm not dressed for a formal occasion."

The carriage had stopped in front of the door now, and the driver was getting down from his seat.

"Indeed, she will think nothing about it," Dunham assured her, "except to be glad she has the right number of guests. Her dinners are delightful affairs usually, and you have nothing to do but talk about impersonal matters for a little while and be entertaining. She was most insistent that you take no thought about the matter of dress. She said it would be perfectly understood that you were travelling and that the invitation was unexpected. You can say that your trunk hasn't come or has gone on ahead. Will you come?"

The driver opened the carriage door.

In an instant the girl assumed the self-contained manner she had worn when she first spoke to him. She stepped quietly from the carriage and only answered in a low voice, "I suppose I'd better, if you wish it."

Dunham paused for a moment to give the driver a direction about carrying the great pasteboard box to his club. This idea had come as a sudden inspiration. He hadn't thought of the necessity of getting rid of the box before.

"If it becomes necessary, where shall I say you are going this evening?" he asked in a low tone as they turned to go up the steps. She summoned a faint smile.

"When people have been traveling abroad and are stopping over in this city, they often go on to Washington, do they not?" she asked shyly.

He smiled in response and noted with pleasure that the black hat was intensely becoming. She wasn't ill-dressed for the part she had to play, for the black silk raincoat gave the touch of the traveler to her costume.

The door swung open before they could say another word, and the young man remembered that he must introduce his new friend. As there was no further opportunity to ask her about her name, he must trust to luck.

The girl obeyed the motion of the servant and slipped up to the dressing room as if she were a frequent guest in the house, but it was in some trepidation that Tryon Dunham removed his overcoat and arranged his necktie. He had caught a glimpse of the assembled company and knew that Mr. Bowman was growing impatient for his dinner. His heart almost failed him now that the girl was out of sight. What if she didn't prove to be accustomed to society, after all, and showed it? How embarrassing that would be! He had seen her only in a half light as yet. How had he dared?

But it was too late now, for she was coming from the dressing room, and Mrs. Bowman was approaching them with outstretched hands and a welcome in her face.

"My dear Miss Remington, it is so good of you to help me out! I can see by the first glance that it is going to be a privilege to know you. I can't thank you enough for waiving formalities."

"It was very lovely of you to ask me," said the girl with perfect composure, "a stranger—"

"Don't speak of it, my dear. Mr. Dunham's friends are not strangers, I assure you. Tryon, didn't you tell her how long we've known each other? I shall feel quite hurt if you have never mentioned me to her. Now, come, for my cook is in the last stages of despair over the dinner. Miss Remington, how do you manage to look so fresh and lovely after a long sea voyage? You must tell me your secret."

The young man looked down at the girl and saw that her dress was in perfect taste for the occasion and also that she was very young and beautiful. He was watching her with a kind of proprietary pride as she moved forward to be introduced to the other guests, when he saw her sweep one quick glance about the room and for just an instant hesitate and draw back. Her face grew white; then, with a supreme effort, she controlled her feelings and went through her part with perfect ease.

When Judge Blackwell was introduced to the girl, he looked at her with what seemed to Dunham to be more than a passing interest. But the keen eyes were almost immediately transferred to his own face, and the young man had no further time to watch his protégée, as dinner was announced.

Miss Remington was seated next to Dunham at the table, with the judge on her other side. The young man was pleased with the arrangement and sat furtively studying the delicate shape of her face, the sweep of her dark lashes and the ripple of her brown hair as he tried to converse easily with her, as an old friend might.

At length the judge turned to the girl and said, "Miss Remington, you remind me strongly of a young woman who was in my office this afternoon."

The color flickered out of the girl's face, leaving even her lips white, but she lifted her dark eyes bravely to the kind blue ones and with sweet dignity baffled the questioned recognition in his look.

"Yes, you are so much like her that I would think you were—her sister perhaps?—if it weren't for the name," Judge Blackwell went on. "She was a most interesting and beautiful young lady." The old gentleman bestowed upon the girl a look that was like a benediction.

"Excuse me for speaking of it, but her dress was something soft and beautiful like yours and seemed to suit her face. I was deeply interested in her, although until this afternoon she was a stranger. She came to me for a small matter of business, and after it was attended to, and before she received the papers, she disappeared! She had removed her hat and gloves, as she was obliged to wait some time for certain matters to be looked up, and these she left behind her. The hat is covered with long, handsome plumes the color of rich cream in coffee."

Dunham glanced down at the cloth of the girl's gown and was startled to find the same rich cream-coffee tint in its silky folds; yet she did not show by so much as a flicker of an eyelash that she was passing under the keenest inspection. She toyed with the salted almonds beside her plate and held the heavy silver fork as firmly as if she were talking about the discovery of the North Pole.

Her voice was steady and natural as she asked, "How could she disappear?"

"Well, that is more than I can understand. There were three doors in the room where she sat, one opening into the inner office where I was at work, and two opening into a hall, one on the side and the other on the end opposite the freight elevator. We searched the entire building without finding a clue, and I am deeply troubled."

"Why would she want to disappear?" The question was asked with as much interest as a stranger would be likely to show.

"I cannot imagine," said the old man. "She came to me of her own free will on a matter of business. Immediately after her disappearance, two well-dressed men entered my office and inquired for her. One had an intellectual head but looked hard and cruel; the other was very handsome—and disagreeable. When he couldn't find the young lady, he laid claim to her hat, but I had it locked away. How could I know that man was her friend or relative? I intend to keep that hat until the young woman herself claims it. I haven't had anything happen that has so upset me in years."

"You don't think any harm has come to her?" questioned the girl.

"I cannot think what harm could, and yet—it is very strange. She was about the age of my dear daughter when she died, and I cannot get her out of my mind. When you first appeared in the doorway you gave me quite a start. I thought you were she. If I can find any trace of her, I mean to investigate this matter. I have a feeling that girl needs a friend."

"I am sure she would be very happy to have a friend like you," said the girl.

"Thank you," said he warmly. "That is most kind of you. But perhaps she has found a better friend by this time. I hope so."

"Or one as kind," she suggested in a low voice.

The conversation then became general, and the girl didn't look up for several seconds. But the young man on her right, who hadn't missed a word of the previous tête-à-tête, could not give attention to the story Mrs. Blackwell was telling, for pondering what he had heard.

The ladies now left the table, and though this was the time Dunham had counted on for an acquaintance with the great judge who might hold a future career in his power, he wished that he might follow them to the other room. He felt confident in his new friend's ability to play her part to the end, but he wanted to watch her, to study her and understand her, if perchance he might solve the mystery that was ever growing more intense about her.

As she left the room, his eyes followed her. His hostess, in passing behind his chair, whispered, "I don't wonder you feel so about her. She is lovely. But please don't begrudge her to us for a few minutes. I promise you shall have her afterward."

Then, without any warning and utterly against his will, this young man of much experience and self-control blushed furiously and was glad when the door closed behind Mrs. Bowman.

Miss Remington walked into the drawing room with a steady step, but her heart beat wildly. Her real ordeal had now come. She cast about in her mind for subjects of conversation that would forestall unsafe topics and intuitively sought the protection of the judge's wife. But she saw her hostess making straight for the little Chippendale chair beside her.

"My dear, it is too lovely," she began. "So opportune! Do tell me how long you have known Tryon?"

The girl caught her breath and gathered her wits together. She looked up shyly into the pleasantly curious eyes of Mrs. Bowman, and a faint gleam of mischief came into her face.

"Why—" Her hesitation seemed only natural, and Mrs. Bowman decided there must be something very special between these two. "Why, not so very long, Mrs. Bowman—not as long as you have known him." She finished with a smile which Mrs. Bowman found charming.

"Oh, you sly child!" she exclaimed, playfully tapping the round cheek with her fan. "Did you meet him when he was abroad this summer?"

"Oh, no, indeed!" said the girl, laughing now in spite of herself. "Oh, no; it was after his return."

"Then it must have been in the Adirondacks," Mrs. Bowman went on. "Were you at—"

But the girl interrupted her. She couldn't afford to discuss the Adirondacks, and the sight of the grand piano across the room gave her an idea.

"Mr. Dunham told me you would like me to play something for you, as your musician friend has failed you. I shall be very glad to, if it will help you any. What do you care for? Something serious or something light? Are you fond of Chopin, Beethoven or something more modern?"

Scenting a possible musical prodigy and desiring to give her guests a treat, Mrs. Bowman exclaimed, "Oh, how lovely of you! I hardly dared to ask, as Tryon was uncertain whether you would be willing. Suppose you give us something serious now, and later, when the men join us, we'll have the brighter music. Make your own choice, though I'm very fond of Chopin, of course."

Without another word the girl moved quietly over to the piano and took her seat. For just a moment her fingers caressed the keys, as if they were old friends and she were having an understanding with them. Then she began a Chopin nocturne. Her hands were deft, and she brought out a belllike tone from the instrument that made the company of women realize the player was mistress of her art. Her graceful figure and lovely head, with its simple ripples and waves of hair, were more noticeable than ever as she sat there, controlling the exquisite harmonies.

Even Mrs. Blackwell stopped fanning and looked interested. Then she whispered to Mrs. Bowman: "A very sweet young girl. That's a pretty piece she's playing."

Mrs. Blackwell was sweet and commonplace and old-fashioned. Mrs. Parker Bowman sat up with a pink glow in her cheeks and a light in her eyes. She began to plan how she might keep this acquisition and exploit her among her friends. It was her delight to bring out new features in her entertainments.

"We shall simply keep you playing until you drop from weariness," she announced when the last sobbing, soothing chord had died away; the other ladies whispered their approval.

The girl smiled and moved into a Chopin valse, under cover of which those who cared to could talk in low tones. Afterward, the musician dashed into the brilliant movement of a Beethoven sonata.

It was just as she was beginning Rubinstein's exquisite tone portrait, *Kamennoi-Ostrow,* that the gentlemen came in.

Tryon Dunham had had his much-desired talk with the famous judge, but it hadn't been about law. They had been drawn together by mutual consent, each discovering that the other was watching the young stranger as she left the dining room.

"She is charming," said the old man, smiling into the face of the younger. "Is she an intimate friend?"

"I–I hope so," stammered Dunham. "That is, I should like to have her consider me so."

"Ah!" said the old man, looking deep into the other's eyes with a kind smile, as if he were recalling pleasant experiences of his own. "You are a fortunate fellow. I hope you may succeed in making her think so. Do you know, she interests me more than most women, and in some way I cannot disconnect her with an occurrence that happened in my office this afternoon."

The young man showed a deep interest in the matter, and the judge told the story again, this time in more detail.

They drew a little apart from the rest of the men. The host, who had been warned by his wife to give young Dunham an opportunity to talk with the judge, saw that her plans were succeeding admirably.

When the music began in the other room, the judge paused a moment to listen and then went on with his story.

"There is a freight elevator just opposite the left door of my office, and somehow I can't help but think it had something to do with the girl's disappearance, although the door was closed and the elevator was down on the cellar floor all the time, as nearly as I can find out."

The young man asked eager questions, sensing that the story might in some way explain the mystery of the young woman in the other room.

"Suppose you stop in the office tomorrow," said the judge. "Perhaps you'll get a glimpse of her and then bear me out in the statement that she's like your friend. By the way, who is making such exquisite music? Suppose we go and investigate. Mr. Bowman, will you excuse us if we follow the ladies? We are anxious to hear the music at closer range."

The other men rose and followed.

The girl did not pause or look up as they came in, but played on, while the company listened with a rapt, wondering look. She was playing with a skill that could not fail to command attention.

Tryon Dunham, standing just behind the judge, was transfixed with amazement. That this delicate girl could bring forth such an entrancing volume of sound from the instrument was a great surprise. That she was so exquisite an artist filled him with an intoxicating elation—it was as though she belonged to him.

At last she played Liszt's "Hungarian Rhapsody," her slender hands taking the tremendous chords and octave runs with a precision that seemed inspired. The final crash came in a shower of liquid sound, and she turned to look at him, her one friend in that company of strangers.

He could see that she had been playing under a heavy strain. Her face looked weary and flushed, and her eyes were brilliant with feverish excitement. Those eyes seemed to be pleading with him now to set her free from the kind scrutiny of those good-hearted, curious strangers. They gathered about her in delight, pouring their questions and praises upon her.

"Where did you study? With some great master, I am sure. Tell us all about yourself. We are dying to know!"

Tryon Dunham interrupted the disquieting questions by drawing his watch from his pocket with apparent hasty remembrance and a well-feigned exclamation of dismay.

"I'm sorry, Mrs. Bowman. It is too bad to interrupt this delightful evening," he apologized, "but I'm afraid if Miss Remington feels that she must take the next train, we'll have to make all possible speed. Miss Remington, can you get your wraps? Our carriage is probably at the door now."

With a look of relief, yet keeping up her part of dismay over the lateness of the hour, the girl sprang to her feet and hurried away to get her wraps, in spite of her protesting hostess. Mrs. Bowman was held at bay with sweet expressions of gratitude for the pleasant entertainment. The great black picture hat was settled becomingly on the small head, the black cloak thrown over her dress, and the gloves fitted on hurriedly to hide the fact that they were too large.

"And whom did you say you studied with?" asked the keen hostess, determined to be able to tell how great a guest she had harbored for the evening.

"Oh, is Mr. Dunham calling me, Mrs. Bowman? You will excuse me for hurrying off, won't you? And it has been so lovely of you to ask me—perfectly delightful to find friends this way when I was a stranger."

She hurried toward the stairway and down the broad steps, and the hostess had no choice but to follow her.

The other guests crowded out into the hall to bid them good-bye and to tell the girl how much they had enjoyed the music. Mrs. Blackwell insisted upon kissing the smooth cheek of the young musician and whispered in her ear: "You play very nicely, my dear. I should like to hear you again sometime."

The kindness in her tone almost brought a rush of tears to the eyes of the weary, anxious girl.

Chapter 3

D unham hurried her off amid the good-byes of the company, and in a moment more they were shut into the semidarkness of the four-wheeler and whisked away from the curb.

As soon as the door was shut, the girl began to tremble.

"Oh, we ought not to have done that!" she exclaimed. "They were so very kind. It was dreadful to impose upon them. But you weren't to blame. It was my fault. It was very kind of you."

"We didn't impose upon them," he said. "You are my friend, and that was all we claimed. For the rest, you have certainly made good. Your wonderful music! How I wish I might hear more of it sometime!"

The carriage paused to let a trolley pass, and a strong arc light beat in upon the two. A passing stranger peered curiously at them, and the girl shrank back in fear. It was momentary, but the minds of the two were brought back to the immediate necessities of the occasion.

"Now what may I do for you?" asked Dunham in a quiet, businesslike tone, as if it were his privilege and right to do all that was to be done. "Have you thought where you would like to go?"

"I haven't been able to do much thinking. It required all my wits to act with the present. But I know I must not be any further trouble to you. You have done more already than anyone could expect. If you can have the carriage stop in some quiet, out-of-the-way street where I won't be noticed, I'll get out and relieve you. If I hadn't been so frightened at first, I would have had more sense than to burden you this way. I hope someday I shall be able to repay your kindness, though I fear it is too great ever to repay."

"Please don't talk in that way," he said. "It has been a pleasure to do the little that I've done, and you have more than repaid it by the delight you've given me and my friends. I couldn't think of leaving you until you're out of your trouble, and if you will only give me a little hint of how to help, I'll do my utmost for you. Are you quite sure you were followed? Don't you think you could trust me enough to tell me a little more about the matter?"

She shuddered visibly.

"Forgive me," he murmured. "I see it distresses you. Of course it is unpleasant to confide in a stranger. I won't ask you to tell me. I will try to think for you. Suppose we go to the station and get you a ticket to somewhere. Have you any preference? You can trust me not to tell anyone where you've gone, can't you ?" There was a kind of rebuke in his tone, and her eyes, as she lifted them to his face, were full of tears.

"Oh, I do trust you!" she cried, distressed. "You mustn't think that, but—

you don't understand."

"Forgive me," he said again, holding out his hand in appeal. She laid her little gloved hand in his for an instant.

"You are so kind," she murmured, as if it were the only thing she could think of. Then she added suddenly, "But I can't buy a ticket. I have no money with me, and I—"

"Don't think of that for an instant. I will gladly supply your need. A little loan shouldn't distress you."

"But I don't know when I shall be able to repay it," she faltered, "unless—" She hastily drew off her glove and slipped a glittering ring from her finger. "Unless you will let this pay for it. I don't like to trouble you so, but the stone is worth a good deal."

"Indeed," he protested, "I couldn't think of taking your ring. Let me do this. It is such a small thing. I shall never miss it. Let it rest until you are out of your trouble, at least."

"Please!" she insisted, holding out the ring. "I shall get right out of this carriage unless you do."

"But perhaps someone gave you the ring, and you are attached to it."

"My father," she answered briefly, "and he would want me to use it this way." She pressed the ring into his hand almost impatiently.

His fingers closed over the jewel. Somehow it thrilled him to hold the little thing, still warm from her fingers. He had forgotten that she was a stranger. His mind was filled with the thought of how best to help her.

"I'll keep it until you want it again," he said kindly.

"You needn't do that, for I won't claim it," she declared. "You are at liberty to sell it. I know it's worth a good deal."

"I'll certainly keep it until I'm sure you don't want it yourself," he repeated. "Now let's talk about this journey of yours. We are almost at the station. Have you any preference as to where you go? Have you friends to whom you could go?"

She shook her head.

"There are trains to New York every hour almost."

"Oh, no!" she gasped in a frightened tone.

"And to Washington often."

"I'd rather not go to Washington," she said.

"Pittsburgh, Chicago?" he hazarded.

"Chicago will do," she asserted with relief.

Then the carriage stopped before the great station, ablaze with light and thronged with people. Policemen strolled about, and trolley cars twinkled in every direction. The girl shrank back into the shadows of the carriage for an instant, as if she feared to come out from the sheltering darkness.

"Don't feel nervous," he said in a low tone. "I'll see that no one harms you.

Just walk into the station as if you were my friend. You are, you know, a friend of long standing, for we have been to a dinner together. I might be escorting you home from a concert. No one will notice us. Besides, that hat and coat are disguise enough."

He hurried her through the station and up to the ladies' waiting room, where he found a quiet corner and a large rocking chair from which she might look out the window upon the evening street and yet be thoroughly screened from all intruding glances.

He was gone fifteen minutes. The girl sat quietly in her chair, yet alert, every nerve strained. At any moment the mass of faces might reveal one she dreaded to see, or a detective might place his hand on her shoulder with a quiet "Come with me."

When Dunham came back, the nervous start she gave showed him how tense she was. He studied her face under the great hat and noted the dark shadows beneath her eyes. He felt that he must do something to relieve her. It was unbearable to him that this young girl should be adrift—friendless—and apparently a victim to some terrible fear.

Drawing up a chair beside her, he began talking about her ticket.

"You must remember I was utterly at your mercy," she smiled sadly. "I simply had to let you help me."

"I should be glad to pay double for the pleasure you've given me in allowing me to help you," he said.

At that moment a boy in blue uniform planted a leather suitcase at his feet and said, "Here you are, Mr. Dunham. Had a fierce time findin' you. Thought you said you'd be by the elevator door."

"So I did," confessed the young man. "I didn't think you had time to get down yet. Well, you found me anyhow, Harkness."

The boy took the silver coin given him, touched his hat and sauntered off.

"You see," explained Dunham, "it wasn't exactly the thing for you to be traveling without a bit of baggage. I thought it might help them trace you if you really were being followed. So I took the liberty of phoning over to the clubhouse and telling the boy to bring down the suitcase I left there yesterday. I don't know what's in it. I had the man pack it and send it down to me, thinking I might stay all night at the club. Then I went home after all and forgot to take it along. It probably hasn't anything very appropriate for a lady, but there may be a hairbrush and some soap and handkerchiefs. Anyhow, if you'll accept it, it'll be something for you to hitch onto. One feels a little lost even for a single night without a rag to call one's own except a Pullman towel. I thought it might give you the appearance of a regular traveler, you know, and not a runaway."

He tried to make her laugh about it, but her face was serious as she looked up at him.

"I think this is the kindest and most thoughtful thing you have done yet," she said. "I don't see how I can ever thank you."

"Don't try," he returned. "There's your train being called. We'd better go and make you comfortable. You're beginning to be very tired, I can see."

She didn't deny it but rose to follow him, scanning the waiting room with one quick, frightened look. A porter at the gate seized the suitcase and led them to the Pullman.

The girl found herself established in the little drawing room compartment, and her eyes gave him thanks again. She knew the seclusion and the opportunity to lock the compartment door would give her relief from the constant fear that an unwelcome face might at any moment appear beside her.

"The conductor on this train is an old acquaintance of mine," he explained as the official came through the car. "I have taken this trip with him a number of times. Just sit down a minute. I'm going to ask him to look out for you and see that no one annoys you."

The burly official looked over his glasses at the sweet face under the big black hat, while Tryon Dunham said, "She's a friend of mine. I hope you'll be good to her."

In answer, he nodded grim assent which was nevertheless comforting. Then the young man walked through the train to interview the porter and the newsboy and in every way arrange for a pleasant journey for the girl who three hours before had been unknown to him. As he went, he reflected that he would rather enjoy being the conductor himself just for that night. He felt a strange reluctance to give up the oversight of the young woman, who was about to pass out of his world as quickly as she had entered it.

When he returned he found the shades closely drawn and the girl sitting in the corner of the section, where she could not be seen from the aisle, but where she could watch in the mirror the approach of anyone. She welcomed him with a smile but instantly urged him to leave the train, lest he be carried away.

He laughed and told her there was plenty of time. Even after the train had given its preliminary shudder, he lingered to tell her she must be sure to let him know by telegraph if she needed any further help. At last he swung himself from the platform after the train was in full motion.

Immediately he remembered he hadn't given her any money. How could he have forgotten? And there was the North Side Station yet to be passed before she would be out of danger. Why hadn't he remained on the train until she was past that stop and then returned on the next train from the little flag station a few miles ahead?

The swiftly moving cars asked the question as the long train flew by him. The last car was almost past when he made a daring dash and flung himself headlong upon the platform, to the horror of several trainmen who stood on the adjoining tracks.

"Whoa!" said one, shaking his head. "What does that dude think he's made of, anyway? Like to got his head busted that time, fer sure."

The brakeman, coming out of the car door with his lantern, dragged him to his feet, brushed him off and scolded him vigorously. The young man hurried through the car, oblivious to the harangue and happy only to feel the floor jolting beneath his feet, a sign that he was safely on board.

He found the girl sitting where he had left her, only she had flung up the shade of the window next to her and was gazing with wide eyes into the flying darkness. He touched her gently on the shoulder, and she turned with a cry.

"Oh, I thought you had fallen under the train!" she gasped. "It was going so fast! But you didn't get off, after all, did you? Now what can you do? It's too bad, and all on my account."

"Yes, I got off," he said, sitting down opposite her and pulling his tie straight. "I got off, but it wasn't altogether satisfactory, and so I got on again. There wasn't much time for getting on gracefully, but you'll have to excuse it. The fact is, I couldn't bear to leave you alone just yet. I couldn't rest until I knew you had passed the North Side Station. Besides, I forgot to give you any money."

"Oh, but you mustn't!" she protested.

"Please don't say that," he said eagerly. "I can get off later and take the down train, you know. I couldn't let you go right out of my existence this way without knowing more about you."

"Oh!" she gasped, turning a little white about the lips and drawing closer into her corner.

"Don't feel that way," he said. "I'm not going to bother you. You couldn't think that of me, surely. But isn't it only fair that you should show me a little consideration? Just give me an address or something, where I could let you know if I heard of anything that concerned you. Of course, it isn't likely I shall, but it seems to me you might at least let me know you are safe."

"I will promise you that," she said. "You know I'm going to send you back these things." She touched the cloak and hat. "You might need them to keep you from having to explain their absence."

The moments flew by. They passed the North Side Station and were nearing the flag station. After that there would be no more stops until past midnight. The young man knew he must get off.

"I almost have a mind to go on to Chicago and see that you are safely located," he said. "It seems too terrible to set you adrift in the world this way."

"Indeed, you must not," said the young woman with a gentle dignity. "Have you stopped to think what people—what your mother, for instance— would think of me if she ever knew I had permitted such a thing? You know you must not. Please don't speak of it again."

"I can't help feeling that I ought to take care of you," he said, only half convinced.

"But I cannot permit it," she said firmly, lifting her trustful eyes to smile at him.

"Will you promise to let me know if you need anything?"

"No, I'm afraid I can't promise even that," she said, "because, while you have been a true friend to me, the immediate and awful necessity is, I hope, past."

"You will at least take this," he said, drawing from his pocket a small leather purse and putting into it all the money his pockets contained. "I saw you had no pocketbook, and I ventured to get this one in the drugstore below the station. Will you accept it from me? I have your ring, you know, and when you take the ring back you may, if you wish, return the purse. You'll need it to carry your ticket. And I've put in the change. It wouldn't do for you to be entirely without money. I'm sorry it isn't more. There are only nine dollars and seventy-five cents left. Do you think that will see you through? If there had been any place downtown here where I could cash a check at this time of night, I would have made it more."

He looked at her anxiously as he handed over the pocketbook. It seemed a ridiculously small sum with which to begin a journey alone, especially for a young woman of her refinement. On the other hand, his friends would probably say he was a fool for having hazarded so much upon an unknown woman who was perhaps an adventuress. But he had thrown discretion to the winds and was undeniably interested in his new acquaintance.

"How thoughtful you are!" said the girl. "It would have been most embarrassing not to have a place to put my ticket, nor any money. This seems a fortune after being penniless." She smiled ruefully. "Are you sure you haven't reduced yourself to that condition? Have you saved enough to get you back home?"

"Oh, I have my mileage book with me," he said. It pleased him absurdly that she had not declined the pocketbook.

"Thank you so much. I shall return the price of the ticket and this money as soon as possible," she said.

"You mustn't think of that," he protested. "You know I have your ring. That is far more valuable than anything I have given you."

"Oh, but you said you were going to keep the ring, so that won't pay for this. I want to be sure that you lose nothing."

He suddenly became aware that the train was whistling and the conductor was motioning him to go.

"But you haven't told me your name," he cried in dismay.

"You have named me," she answered, smiling. "I am Mary Remington."

"But that isn't your real name."

"You may call me Mary if you like," she said. "Now go, please, quick! I'm afraid you'll get hurt."

"You'll remember that I'm your friend?"

"Yes, thank you. Hurry, please!"

The train paused long enough for him to step in front of her window and wave his hat in salute. Then she passed on into the night, and only two twinkling lights, like diminishing red berries, marked the progress of the train until it disappeared in the cut. Nothing was left but the hollow echoes of its going, which the hills gave back.

Chapter 4

Dunham listened as long as his ear could catch the sound, then a strange desolation settled upon him. How was it that a few short hours ago he had known nothing, cared nothing, about this stranger? And now her going left him bereft. It was foolish, of course—just highly wrought nerves over this extraordinary occurrence. Life had heretofore run in such smooth, conventional grooves, and now to be plunged suddenly into romance and mystery unbalanced him for the time.

Tomorrow, most likely, he would readjust to sane living and perhaps call himself a fool for his unusual interest in this chance acquaintance. But at this moment, when the memory of her face lingered with him, when her bravery and fear were both so fresh in his mind, and the sound of her music was still in his brain, he could not without a pang turn back again to life which contained no solution to her mystery, no hope of another vision of her face.

The little station behind him was closed, though a light over the desk shone brightly through its front window and the telegraph sounder was clicking busily. The operator had gone over the hill with an important telegram, leaving the station door locked. The platform was windy and cheerless, with a view of a murky swamp. Frogs croaked out a late fall concert. A cricket in a crack of the platform chirped now and then, and off beyond the swamp, in the edge of the wood, a screech owl hooted.

Turning impatiently from the darkness, Dunham sought the bright window and found a newspaper lying inside it. He could read the large headline of a column—no more, for the paper was upside down. It read:

MYSTERIOUS DISAPPEARANCE OF
YOUNG AND PRETTY WOMAN

His heart stood still, then went thudding on in dull, horrid blows. Vainly he tried to read further. He followed every visible word of that paper to discover its date and origin, but the date was blocked by a cluster of handbills lying across the top. He felt like dashing his hand through the glass but reflected that the act might cause him to be locked up in some miserable country jail. He tried the window and gave the door another vicious shake, but all to no purpose. Finally he turned on his heel and walked up and down for an hour, tramping the length of the shaky platform, back and forth, till the train rumbled up.

As he took his seat in the car he saw the agent come running up the platform with a lighted lantern on his arm and a package of letters, which he handed to the brakeman; but there was no time to beg the newspaper from him. Dunham's mind continued to dwell upon the headline. He resented the adjective "pretty." Why should any reporter dare to apply that word to a truly lovely woman? It seemed so superficial, so belittling. But then, of course, this headline did not apply to his new friend. It was some other poor creature, someone to whom perhaps the word "pretty" applied; someone who was not really beautiful.

At the first stop a man in front got out, leaving a newspaper in the seat. With eager hands Dunham leaned forward and grasped it, searching its columns in vain for the tantalizing headline. But there were others equally intriguing. This paper announced the disappearance of a young actress who was suspected of poisoning her husband. When last seen, she was boarding a train en route to Washington. She had not arrived there, however, so far as could be discovered. It was supposed that she was in the vicinity of Philadelphia or Baltimore. The story added a few incriminating details concerning her relationship with her dead husband and a brief sketch of her sensational life. The paragraph closed with the statement that she was an accomplished musician.

The young man frowned and, opening his window, flung the scandalous sheet to the breeze. He determined to forget what he had read, yet the lines kept coming before his eyes.

When he reached the city he went to the newsstand in the station and procured a copy of every paper on sale. Then, instead of hurrying home, he found a seat in a secluded corner and examined his purchases.

In large letters on the front page of a New York paper blazed:

> HOUSE ROBBED OF JEWELS
> WORTH TEN THOUSAND DOLLARS
> BY BEAUTIFUL YOUNG ADVENTURESS
> MASQUERADING AS A PARLOR MAID

He ran his eye down the column and gathered that she was still at large, though the entire police force of New York was on her track. He turned to another paper, only to be met by the words:

> ESCAPE OF YOUNG LUNATIC

and underneath:

> Prison walls could not confine Miss Nancy Lee, who last week threw a lighted lamp at her mother, setting fire to the house, and then attempted suicide. The young woman seems to have recovered her senses and professes to know nothing of what happened, but the physicians say she is liable to another attack of insanity and deem it safe to keep her confined. She escaped during the night, leaving no clue to her

whereabouts. How she managed to open the window through which she left the asylum is still a mystery.

In disgust he flung the paper from him and took up another.

FOUL PLAY SUSPECTED!
BEAUTIFUL YOUNG HEIRESS MISSING

His soul turned sick within him. He looked up and saw a little procession of late revelers rushing out to the last suburban train, the girls leaving a trail of perfume. One of the men was a city friend of his. Dunham half envied him his unperturbed mind. To be sure, he would not get back to the city till three in the morning, but he would have no visions of robberies and young lunatics and fearful maidens unjustly pursued, to mar his rest.

Dunham buttoned his coat and turned up his collar as he started out into the street, for the night had turned cold. As he walked, his blood pumped vigorously in his veins, dispelling the horrors of the evening papers. In their place came pleasant memories of the evening at Mrs. Bowman's and of their ride and talk together. He began to hope that her dark days would pass and he might find her again and know her better.

His brief night's sleep was cut short by a sharp knock at his door the next morning. He awoke with a confused idea of being on a sleeper car and wondered if he had time enough to dress, but his sister's voice quickly crushed the illusion.

"Tryon, aren't you almost ready to come down to breakfast? Do hurry, please. I've something awfully important to ask you about."

His sister's tone told him there was need for haste if he wanted to keep in her good graces, so he dressed quickly and went down to find his household in a state of subdued excitement.

"I'm just as worried as I can be," declared his mother. "I want to consult you, Tryon. I have put such implicit confidence in Nora, and I cannot bear to accuse her unjustly, but I've missed a number of little things lately. There was my gold link bag—"

"Mother, you know you said you were sure you left that at the Century Club."

"Don't interrupt, Cornelia. Of course it is possible I left it at the club, but I think now that I didn't have it with me at all. Then there's my opal ring. To be sure, it isn't worth a great deal, but one who will take little things will take large ones."

"What's the matter, Mother? Has Nora been appropriating property not her own?" her son asked.

"I'm very much afraid she has, Tryon. What would you do about it? It is so unpleasant to charge a person with stealing. It is such a vulgar thing to steal. Somehow I thought Nora was more refined."

"Why, I suppose there's nothing to do but charge her with it, is there? Are you quite sure it's gone? What is it, anyway? A ring, did you say?"

"No, it's a hat," said Cornelia shortly. "A sixty-dollar hat. I wish I'd kept it now, and then she wouldn't have dared. It had two beautiful willow ostrich plumes on it, but Mother didn't think it was becoming. She wanted some color on it instead of all black. I left it in my room and charged Nora to see that the man got it when he called, and now the man comes and says he wants the hat, and it's gone! Nora insists that when she last saw it, it was in my room. But of course that's absurd, for there was nobody else to take it but Thompson, and he's been in the family for so long."

"Nonsense!" said her brother sharply, dropping his knife in his plate with a clatter that made the young woman jump. "Cornelia, I'm ashamed of you, thinking that poor, innocent girl has stolen your hat. Why, she wouldn't steal a pin, I'm sure. You can tell she's honest by looking into her eyes. Girls with blue eyes like that don't lie and steal."

"Really!" Cornelia remarked haughtily. "You seem to know a great deal about her eyes. You may feel differently when I find the hat in her possession."

"Cornelia," interrupted Tryon, quite beside himself, "don't think of such a thing as speaking to that poor girl about the hat. I know she hasn't stolen it. The hat will probably be found, and then how will you feel?"

"But I tell you the hat cannot be found!" said his exasperated sister. "And I shall have to pay for a hat that I can never wear."

"Mother, I appeal to you," he said. "Don't allow Cornelia to speak of the hat to the girl. I wouldn't have such an injustice done in our house. The hat will turn up soon if you just go about the matter calmly. You'll find it quite naturally and unexpectedly, perhaps. Anyway, if you don't, I'll pay for the hat rather than have the girl suspected."

"But, Tryon," protested his mother, "if she isn't honest, you know we wouldn't want her about."

"Honest, Mother? She's as honest as the day is long. I am certain of that."

The mother rose reluctantly.

"Well, we might let it go another day," she consented. Then, looking up at the sky, she added, "I wonder if it's going to rain. I have a Reciprocity meeting today, and I'm a delegate to some little unheard-of place. It usually rains when one goes into the country, I've noticed."

She went into the hall and soon returned with a distressed look on her face.

"Tryon, I'm afraid you're wrong," she said. "Now my raincoat is missing. My new raincoat! I hung it up in the hall closet with my own hands, after it came from the store. I really think something ought to be done."

"There! I hope you see!" snapped Cornelia. "I think it's high time something was done. I shall phone for a detective at once!"

"Cornelia, you'll do nothing of the kind," her brother protested, now thoroughly aroused. "I'll agree to pay for the hat and the raincoat if they are not found before a fortnight passes, but I won't let you ruin that poor girl's reputation. I insist, Mother, that you put a stop to such rash proceedings. I'll make myself personally responsible for the girl's honesty."

"Well, of course, Tryon, if you wish it," said his mother hesitantly.

"I certainly do wish it, Mother. I shall take it as personal if anything is done in this matter without consulting me. Remember, Cornelia, I won't have any trifling. A girl's reputation is certainly worth more than several hats and raincoats, and I know she has not taken them."

He walked from the dining room and from the house in angry dignity, to the astonishment of his mother and sister. Consulting him about household matters was merely a form, for he almost never interfered. The two women looked at each other in bewilderment.

"Mother," said Cornelia, "you don't suppose he's fallen in love with Nora, do you? Why, she's Irish and freckled! And Tryon has always been so fastidious."

"Cornelia! How dare you suggest such a thing? Tryon is a Dunham. Whatever else a Dunham may or may not do, he never does anything low or unrefined."

The small, prim mother looked quite regal in her aristocratic rage.

"But, Mother, one reads such dreadful things in the papers now. Of course Tryon would never marry anyone like that, but—"

"Cornelia!" Her mother's voice had almost reached a scream. "I forbid you to mention the subject again. I cannot think where you learned to voice such thoughts."

"Well, my goodness, Mother, I don't mean anything, only I do wish I had my hat. I always did like all black. I can't imagine what ails Try."

Tryon Dunham made his way to his office much disturbed in mind. With the dawn of morning had come that stern common sense which told him he was a fool for taking up with a strange young woman on the street, who was evidently fleeing from justice. He had deceived not only his close friends by palming her off as a fit companion for them, but his mother and sister as well. He had practically stolen their garments and had squandered more than fifty dollars of his own money. And what did he have to show for all this? The memory of a sweet face, the lingering beauty of her voice when she bade him good-bye and a diamond ring. The cool morning light presented the news that the ring was probably valueless and that he was a fool.

Ah, the ring! A sudden warm thrill shot through him, and his hand searched his vest pocket, where he had hastily put the jewel before leaving his room. That was something tangible. He could at least know what it was worth and so make sure whether he had been deceived. No, that would not be fair either, for her father might have made her think it was valuable, or he might have been taken in himself, if he were not a judge of jewels.

Dunham walked down the street, too perplexed to remember his usual trolley. He slipped the ring on his finger and let it catch the morning sunlight, now shining broad and clear in spite of the hovering rain clouds in the distance. The sun illumined the diamond brilliantly, causing it to break into a million fires of dazzling light. The stone seemed to be of unusual purity, but he would step into the diamond shop as he passed and make sure. He had a friend there who could tell him all about it. His step quickened, and he covered the distance in a short time.

After the morning greeting, he handed over the ring.

"This belongs to a friend of mine," he said, trying to look unconcerned. "I'd like to know if the stone is genuine and about what it is worth."

His friend took the ring and examined it with a curious little instrument for the eye, presently emerging with a respectful look on his face.

"Your friend is fortunate to have such a beautiful stone. It is unusually clear and white and exquisitely cut. I'd say it was worth at least—" He paused and then named a sum which startled Dunham.

He took the jewel back with a kind of awe. Where had this mysterious girl acquired such a ring, which she had tossed to him as a trifle? He went on to his office more perplexed than ever. Suspicions of all sorts crowded into his mind, but for every thought that shadowed the reputation of the lady, there came into his mind her clear eyes and cast out all doubts. Finally, after a bad hour of trying to work, he slipped the ring on his little finger, determined to wear it and thus prove to himself his belief in her, at least until he had absolute proof against her. Then he took up his hat and went out, deciding to accept Judge Blackwell's invitation to visit his office.

He found a cordial reception, and the judge talked business with him. His proposals hinted at bringing about some of the young man's deepest wishes; and yet as he left the building he was thinking more about the mysterious stranger who had disappeared from the judge's office the day before than about the wonderful career that may lay before him.

They had not talked much about her. The judge had brought out her hat— a beautiful velvet one with exquisite plumes—her gloves, a costly leather purse and a fine hemstitched handkerchief, and as he put them away on a closet shelf, he said no trace of her had yet been found.

On his way toward his own office, Dunham pondered the remarkable coincidence which made him the possessor of two parts of the same mystery—for he had no doubt that the hat belonged to his new friend.

Meantime, the girl who was speeding along toward Chicago could not forget about him, for all about her were reminders of him. The conductor took charge of her ticket, telling her in his gruff way what time they would arrive in the city. The porter was solicitous about her comfort; the newsboy brought the latest magazines and a box of chocolates and laid them on the seat beside her with a smile of admiration. The suitcase lay on the seat opposite; the reflection of her face in the window, as she gazed into the inky darkness outside, was crowned by the hat he had provided. And when she moved, the silken rustle of the raincoat reminded her of his kindness and forethought. She put her head back and closed her eyes and for an instant wondered what it would mean if the man she was fleeing from had been such as this one.

Presently she opened the suitcase, hesitantly, as if she were intruding upon another's possessions.

There were a dress suit and a change of linen, handkerchiefs, neckties, a pair of gloves, a black silk muffler, a bathrobe and the usual silver-mounted brushes, combs and other toiletry articles. She looked them over in a businesslike way, trying to see how she could make use of them. Removing her hat, she covered it with the silk muffler, to protect it from dust. Then she took off her dress and wrapped herself in the soft bathrobe wondering as she did so at her willingness to put on a stranger's garments. Somehow, in her brief acquaintance with this man, he had impressed her with his own pleasantness, so that there was a kind of pleasure in using his things, as if they belonged to a valued friend.

She touched the electric button that controlled the lights in the compartment and lay down in the darkness to think out her problem of the new life that lay before her.

Chapter 5

B eginning with the moment when she first realized her danger and the necessity to flee, she lived over in her mind every instant, her nerves straining as if she were experiencing it all once more. The horror of it! But finally, worn with excitement, she sank into a deep sleep.

At last she woke from a terrible dream in which the hand of her pursuer was upon her, and her rescuer was off in the dark distance. With that strange insistence which torments the victim of nightmares, she was obliged to lie still and imagine it again and again, until the face and voice of the young man grew very real in the darkness, and she longed for the comfort of his presence once more.

At length she shook off these pursuing thoughts and roused herself to plan her future.

The first necessity, she decided, was to change her appearance so that if news of her escape had been telegraphed, she might evade notice. To that end, she arose and arranged her hair as she had never worn it before—in two braids wound closely about her head. It was neat and appropriate to the vocation she had decided upon, and it changed her appearance more than any other thing she could have done. All the soft fullness of hair that had framed her face was drawn tightly back, and the smooth bands gave her the severity of a saint in some old picture. She pinned up her gown until it didn't show below the long black coat and folded a white linen handkerchief about her throat over the delicate lace. Then she looked dubiously at the hat.

With a girl's instinct, her first thought went to the borrowed hat. A fine mist was slanting down, blurring the view out of the window until nothing was visible but dull gray shadows that flew by. She suddenly remembered the suitcase, opened it and took out the folded black hat. It was mannish, of course, but girls often wore such hats.

As she surveyed herself in the long mirror of her door, color stole into her cheeks. Yet the costume was neither unbecoming nor unusual. She looked like a simple schoolgirl or a young businesswoman going to her day's work.

She looked at the fashionable proportions of the other hat with concern. How could she protect it? She did not for a moment think of abandoning it, for it was her earnest desire to return it at once, unharmed, to its kind donor.

She summoned the newsboy and purchased three thick newspapers. From these, with the aid of a few pins, she made a large package for the hat. To be sure, it did not look like a hat when it was done, but that was all the better. The feathers were held up and packed softly about with bits of paper crushed together to make a springy cushion, and the whole was built out and then covered over with paper. She reflected that girls who wore their hair wound about their heads and covered by plain felt hats would not be unlikely to carry large newspaper-wrapped packages through the city streets.

She decided to go bare-handed and put the white kid gloves in the suitcase, but she took off her beautiful rings and hid them safely inside her dress.

When the porter came to announce that her breakfast was waiting in the dining car, he looked at her with a start, but she answered his look with a pleasant, "Good morning. You see I'm fixed for a damp day."

"Yes, miss," he said deferentially. "It's a nasty day outside. I 'spect Chicago'll be mighty wet. De wind's off de lake, and de rain's comin' from all ways 'twoncet."

She sacrificed one of her precious quarters to get rid of the attentive porter and started off with a brisk step down the long platform to the station. It was her plan to get out of the neighborhood as quickly as possible, so she followed the stream of people who, instead of going into the waiting room, veered off to the street door and out into the great, wet, noisy world.

With the same reasoning, she followed a group of people into a car, which presently brought her into a neighborhood of large stores, as she had hoped it would. She recognized the name on one of the stores as being of worldwide reputation.

An experienced shopper, she went straight to the millinery department and arranged to have the hat boxed and sent to the address Dunham had given her. Her gentle voice and handsome raincoat proclaimed her a lady and commanded respectful attention. As she walked away, she had an odd feeling of having communicated with her one friend and preserver.

It had cost less to send the hat than she had feared, yet her stock of money was very small. She must have some kind of a dress, and a wrap, that she might be disguised, but what could she buy and still have something left over for food? There was no telling how long it would be before she could replenish her purse. Life must be reduced to its lowest terms. True, she had jewelry which might be sold, but that would scarcely be safe, for if she were watched she might easily be identified by it. What did the very poor do who were yet respectable?

The ready-made coats and skirts were beyond her means, even those that had been marked down. With a hopeless feeling, she walked aimlessly between the tables of goods. The suitcase was as heavy as lead, so she put it on the floor to rest her aching arms. Lifting her eyes, she saw a sign over a table: Linen Skirts, 75 cents and $1.00.

Here was a ray of hope. She turned eagerly to examine them. Piles of somber skirts, blue and black and tan. They were stout and coarse and not of the latest cut, but what did it matter? She decided on a seventy-five-cent black one. It seemed pitiful to have to economize over twenty-five cents, yet she was glad to have gotten for that price any skirt that would do. A dim memory of what she'd read about ten-cent lodging houses, where human beings were herded like cattle, hovered over her.

Growing wise with experience, she discovered that she could get a black sateen shirtwaist for fifty cents. Galoshes and a cotton umbrella took another dollar and a half. She must save at least a dollar to send back the suitcase by express.

A bargain table of woolen jackets, golf vests and old-fashioned blouse sweaters, selling off at a dollar apiece, solved the problem of a wrap. She selected a dark blouse of an ugly, purply blue, but thick and warm. Then she asked a pleasant-faced saleswoman if there were anyplace near where she could slip on a walking skirt she had just bought to save her other skirt from the muddy streets. She was ushered into a little fitting room nearby. It was only about four feet square, with one chair and a tiny table, but it looked like a palace to the girl in her need. As she fastened the door and looked at the bare walls that reached only a foot or so above her head, she wished that such a refuge might be her own somewhere in the great, wide, fearful world.

She slipped off her silk-lined cloth garments and put on the stiff sateen waist and the coarse black shirt. She surveyed herself and was not displeased. But there was a striking lack of collar and belt. She sought out a black necktie and pinned it about her waist and then, with a protesting frown, tore a strip from the edge of one of the hem-stitched handkerchiefs and folded it in about her neck in a turnover collar. The result was quite startling and unfamiliar. The gown, the hair, the hat and the neat collar gave her the look of a young nurse-maid or upper servant.

On the whole, the disguise could not have been better. She added the blue woolen blouse and felt certain that even her most intimate friends would not recognize her. She folded the raincoat and placed it in the suitcase, then with dismay remembered that she had nothing in which to put her own cloth dress, except the few paper wrappings that had come with her simple purchases. Vainly she tried to reduce the dress to a bundle that would be covered by the papers. It was of no use. She looked down at the suitcase. There was room for the dress in there, but she wanted to send Mr. Dunham's property back at once. She might leave the dress in the store, but some detective with an accurate description of the dress might be watching, find it and trace her. Besides, she shrank from leaving her garments about in public places. If there had been a bridge near at hand where she might throw the dress into a dark river unobserved, she would have done it. But whatever she chose to do with it must be done at once. Her destiny must be settled before sundown. She folded the dress smoothly and laid it in the suitcase, under the raincoat.

She sat down at a writing desk in the waiting room and wrote: "I am safe, and I thank you." Then she paused an instant and with nervous haste wrote

"Mary" underneath. She opened the suitcase and pinned the paper to the lapel of the evening coat. Only three dollars and sixty-seven cents were left in her pocketbook after paying the expressage on the suitcase.

She wondered whether she might not have done wrong in sending her dress back in the suitcase, but what else could she have done? If she had bought a box in which to put it, she would have had to carry it with her. At any rate, it was too late now, and she felt sure the young man would understand. She hoped it would not inconvenience him to get rid of it. Surely he could give it to some charitable organization without much trouble.

At her first waking, in the early gray hours of the morning, she had looked her predicament calmly in the face. It was entirely likely that it would continue indefinitely—perhaps throughout her whole life. She could see no way of help for herself. Time might, perhaps, give her a friend who would assist her, but for now she must hide and find a way to earn a living.

She had gone over the list of her own accomplishments. Her musical attainments were out of the question. Her skill as a musician was so great, and so well-known by her enemy, that she would probably be traced by it at once. As she remembered the hour spent at Mrs. Bowman's piano, she shuddered to realize that it might have been her undoing had her enemy happened to pass by the house, with a suspicion that she was inside. She would never dare to seek a position as accompanist, and she knew how futile it would be to attempt to teach music in an unknown city, among strangers. She might starve to death before a single pupil appeared. Besides, that too would put her in a position where she would be more easily found. The same arguments held true for the positions of teacher or governess, although she was thoroughly competent to perform the duties of either.

She determined to change her station entirely, at least for the present. She would have chosen to do something in a quiet hired room somewhere, sewing or decorating or something of the sort, but that too would be hopelessly out of her reach without friends to aid her. A servant's place in someone's home was the only thing possible that presented itself. She could not cook or do general housework, but she thought she could fill the place of waitress.

With a brave face but a shrinking heart, she stepped into a drugstore and looked up in the directory the addresses of several employment agencies.

Chapter 6

It was half past eleven when she stepped into the first agency on her list, and business was in full tide.

While she stood by the door the eyes of a dozen women fastened upon her with keen scrutiny. The color stole into her cheeks. As the proprietress of the office began to question her, she felt her courage failing.

"You wish a position?" The woman had a nose like a hawk and eyes that held no sympathy. "What do you want? General housework?"

"I should like a position as waitress," she said.

The hawk nose went up contemptuously.

"Better take general housework. There are too many waitresses already."

"I understand the work of waitress, but I've never done general housework," she answered with the voice of a gentlewoman, which somehow angered the hawk, who had trained herself to get the advantage over people and keep it or else know the reason why.

"Very well, do as you please, of course. But you bite your own nose off. Let me see your references."

The girl was ready for this.

"I'm sorry, but I can't give you any. I've lived only in one home, where I had entire charge of the table and dining room, and that home was broken up when the people went abroad three years ago. I could show you letters written by the mistress of that home if I had my trunk here, but it is in another city, and I don't know when I shall be able to send for it."

"No references!" screamed the hawk. "Ladies, here is a girl who has no references. Do any of you want to venture?" The contemptuous laugh that followed had the effect of a warning to every woman in the room. "And this girl scorns general housework and presumes to dictate for a place as a waitress."

"I want a waitress badly," said a troubled woman in a subdued whisper, "but I really wouldn't dare take a girl without references. She might be a thief, you know, and then—really, she doesn't look as if she's used to houses like mine. I must have a neat, stylish-looking girl. No self-respecting waitress nowadays would go out in the street dressed like that."

All the eyes in the room seemed to bore through the poor girl as she stood trembling, humiliated, her cheeks burning, while tears threatened to spring to her eyes. She held her head proudly and turned away with dignity.

"But, if you care to try," called out the hawk, "you can register at the desk and leave two dollars. If in the meantime you can think of anybody who'll give us a reference, we'll look it up. But we never guarantee girls without references."

The tears were too near the surface now for her even to acknowledge this information. She went out of the office, and immediately two women got up and hurried after her.

One was flabby, large and overdressed, with a pasty complexion and eyes like a fish. She caught up with the girl and took her by the shoulder just as she reached the top of the stairs that led down to the street.

The other was a small, timid woman with anxiety and indecision written all over her. When she saw who had stopped the girl, she lingered behind in the hall and pretended there was something wrong with the braid on her skirt. While she lingered she listened.

"Wait a minute, miss," said the large woman. "You needn't feel bad about having references. Everybody isn't so particular. You come with me, and I'll put you in the way of earning more than you can ever get as a waitress. You weren't cut out for work, anyway, with that face and voice. I've been watching you. You were meant for a lady. You need to be dressed up, and you'll be a real pretty girl—"

As she talked, she drew nearer and now leaned over and whispered so that the timid woman could not hear.

But the girl stepped back with sudden anger and flashing eyes, shaking off the bejeweled hand that grasped her shoulder.

"Don't you dare speak to me!" she said in a loud, clear voice. "Don't you dare touch me! You are a wicked woman! If you touch me again, I will go in there and tell all those women how you have insulted me!"

"Oh, well, if you're a saint, starve!" hissed the woman.

"I would rather starve ten thousand times than take help from you," said the girl, and her clear eyes seemed to burn into the woman's evil face. She turned and slid away.

Down the stairs fled the girl, her head up in pride and horror, her eyes still flashing. And down the stairs after her sped the small, anxious woman, panting and breathless, determined to keep her in sight till she could decide whether it was safe to take a girl without a character reference—yet who had just shown a bit of her character unaware.

Two blocks from the employment office the girl paused to realize that she was walking without any destination. She stood trembling, not sure whether she had the courage to enter another office.

The little woman paused, too, eyeing the girl cautiously, then began in an eager voice: "I've been following you."

The girl started, a cold chill of fear coming over her. Was this woman a detective?

"I heard what that awful woman said to you, and I saw how you acted. You must be a good girl, or you wouldn't have talked to her that way. I suppose I'm doing a dangerous thing, but I can't help it. I believe you're all right, and I'm going to try you, if you'll take general housework. I need somebody right away, for I'm going to have a dinner party tomorrow night, and my girl left me this morning."

The kind tone in the midst of her troubles brought tears to the girl's eyes.

"Oh, thank you!" she said as she brushed the tears away. "I'm a stranger here, and I've never before been among strangers in this way. I'd like to come and work for you, but I couldn't do general housework, I'm sure. I never did it, and I wouldn't know how."

"Can't you cook a little? I could teach you my ways."

"I don't know the least thing about cooking. I never cooked a thing in my life."

"What a pity! What was your mother thinking about? Every girl ought to be brought up to know a little about cooking, even if she does have some other employment."

"My mother has been dead a good many years." The tears brimmed over now, but the girl tried to smile. "I could help you with your dinner party. That is, I know all about setting the tables and arranging the flowers and favors. I could paint the place cards too—I've done it many a time. And I could wait on the table. But I couldn't cook even an oyster."

"Oh, place cards!" said the woman, her eyes brightening. "I wish I could have them. They cost so much to buy. I might have my washerwoman come and help with the cooking. She cooks pretty well, and I could help her beforehand, but she couldn't wait on table to save her life. I wonder if you know much about menus. Could you help me fix out the courses and say what you think I ought to have, or don't you know about that? You see, I have this very particular company coming, and I want to have things nice. I don't know them very well. My husband has business relations with them and wants them invited, and of all times for Betty to leave this was the worst!"

"I should like to help you," said the girl, "but I must find somewhere to stay before night, and if I find a place I must take it. I just came to the city this morning and have nowhere to stay overnight."

A troubled look flitted across the woman's face for a moment, but her desire got the better of her.

"I suppose my husband would think I was crazy to do it," she said aloud, "but I just can't help trusting you. Suppose you come and stay with me today and tomorrow and help me out with this dinner party, and you can stay overnight at my house and sleep in the cook's room. If I like your work, I'll give you a recommendation as waitress. You can't get a good place anywhere without it, not from the offices, I'm sure. A recommendation ought to be worth a couple of day's work to you. I'd pay you something besides, but I really can't afford it, for the washerwoman charges a dollar and a half a day when she goes out to cook. But if you get your board and lodging, a reference ought to pay you."

"You are very kind," said the girl. "I shall be glad to do that."

"When will you come? Can you go with me now, or have you got to go after your things?"

"I haven't any things but these," she said simply, "and perhaps you won't think I am fine enough for your dinner party. I have a little money. I could buy a white apron. My trunk is a good many miles away, and I was in desperate straits and had to leave it."

Hmm. A stepmother, probably, thought the kind little woman. *Poor child! She doesn't look as if she's used to roughing it. If I could only hold onto her and train her, she might be a treasure, but there's no telling what John will say. I won't tell him anything about her, if I can help it, till the dinner is over.*

Aloud she said, "Oh, that won't be necessary. I've got a white apron I'll lend you—perhaps I'll give it to you if you do your work well. Then we can fix up some kind of a waitress's cap out of a lace-edged handkerchief, and you'll look fine. I'd rather do that and have you come right along home with me, for everything is at sixes and sevens. Betty went off without washing the breakfast dishes. You can wash dishes, anyway."

"Why, I can try," said the girl.

And so they got into a car and were taken away into a pretty suburb. The woman, whose name was Mrs. Hall, lived in a common little house filled with imitation oriental rugs and cheap furniture.

The two went to work at once, bringing order out of the confusion that reigned in the tiny kitchen. In the afternoon the would-be waitress sat down with a box of watercolors to paint dinner cards, and as her skillful brush brought into being dainty landscapes, lovely flowers and little brown birds, she pondered the strangeness of her lot.

The table the next night was laid with exquisite care, the scant supply of flowers having been used to the best advantage and everything showing the touch of a skilled hand. The long hours Mrs. Hall had spent poring over the household department of fashion magazines helped her recognize that in her new maid she had what she called "the real thing." She sighed when the guest of honor, Mrs. Rhinehart, spoke of the deftness and pleasant appearance of her hostess's waitress.

"Yes," Mrs. Hall said, swelling with pride, "she is a treasure. I only wish I could keep her."

"She's going to get married, I suppose. They all do when they're good," sympathized the guest.

"No, but she simply won't do cooking, and I really haven't work enough for two servants in this little house."

The guest sat up and took notice.

"You don't mean to tell me you're going to let a girl like that slip through your fingers? I wish I had known about her. I've spent three days in employment offices. Is there any chance for me, do you think?"

The little woman launched into a voluble account of the new maid's virtues until the other woman was ready to hire her on the spot. The result of it all was that "Mary" was summoned to an interview with Mrs. Rhinehart in the dining room and engaged at four dollars a week, with every other Sunday afternoon and every other Thursday off, and her uniforms furnished.

The next morning Mr. Hall gave her a dollar bill and told her he appreciated the help she'd given them and wanted to pay her something for it.

She thanked him graciously and took the money with a kind of awe. Her first earnings! It seemed so strange to think she had really earned some money, she who had always had all she wanted without lifting a finger.

She went to a store and bought a hairbrush and a few little necessities, with a fifty-cent straw purse in which to put them. Thus, with her modest baggage, she entered the home of Mrs. Rhinehart and ascended to a tiny room on the fourth floor, furnished with a cot, a washstand, a cracked mirror and one chair. Mrs. Rhinehart had planned that the waitress should room with the cook, but the girl insisted that she must have a room alone, no matter how small, and they had compromised on this unused, ill-furnished spot.

As she took off the felt hat, she wondered what its owner would think if he could see her now, and she brushed a fleck of dust gently from the felt, as if in apology for its humble surroundings. Then she smoothed her hair, put on the apron Mrs. Hall had given her and descended to her new duties as maid in a fashionable home.

Chapter 7

Three days later Tryon Dunham entered the office of Judge Blackwell by appointment. After the business was completed, the judge said with a smile, "Well, our mystery is solved. The little girl is all safe. She telephoned me just after you left the other day and sent her maid after her hat. It seems that while she stood by the window, looking down into the street, she saw an automobile containing some of her friends. It stopped at the next building. Wanting to speak with a girlfriend who was seated in the auto, she hurried out to the elevator, hoping to catch them. The elevator boy who took her downstairs went off duty immediately, which accounts for our not finding any trace of her, and he was kept at home by illness the next morning. The young woman caught her friends, and they insisted that she get in and ride to the station with one of them who was leaving the city at once. They loaned her a veil and a wrap and promised to bring her right back for her papers and other possessions, but the train was late, and when they returned the building was closed. The two men who called for her were her brother and a friend of his, it seems. I must say they were not so attractive as she is. But, the mystery is solved, and I got well laughed at by my wife for my fears."

But the young man stood silent, puzzling how all this could be if the hat belonged to the girl he knew as "Mary." When he left the judge's office, he went to his club, determined to have a little quiet in which to think it over.

Matters at home had not been going well. An ominous cloud hung over the breakfast table. The bill for the hat had arrived from Madame Dollard's, and Cornelia laid it by his plate with an exaggerated gesture. Even his mother had looked at him with a glance that spoke volumes as she remarked that she would need a new raincoat before another storm came.

A distinct coolness existed between Tryon Dunham and his mother and sister ever since the morning when the loss of the hat and raincoat was announced. Or did it date from the evening of that day when both mother and sister noticed the beautiful ring he wore? They exclaimed over the flash of the diamond and its rare brilliancy, and Cornelia became quite disagreeable when he refused to take it off for her to examine. He had replied to his mother's question by saying that the ring belonged to a friend. He knew his mother was hurt by the answer, but what more could he do at present? True, he might have taken the ring off and prevented further comment, but it had come to mean loyalty to and belief in the girl whom he had so strangely been permitted to help.

He made his way in deep perplexity to his club and sat down in a far corner to meditate. He was annoyed when the office boy appeared to tell him some packages awaited him in the office.

"Bring them to me here, Henry," he said.

The boy hustled away and soon came back bearing two hatboxes—one of them in a crate—and the heavy leather suitcase.

With a start of surprise, Dunham sat up in his chair.

"Henry, those things ought not to come in here." He glanced about anxiously and was relieved to find only one old gentleman was in the room and he was asleep. "Suppose we go up to a private room with them. Take them out to the elevator, and I'll come in a moment."

"All right, sah," the boy replied.

"And, Henry, suppose you remove that crate from the box. Then it won't be so heavy to carry."

The young man hurried out to the elevator, and he and Henry made a quick ascent to a private room. He gave the boy a generous tip and was left in quiet to examine his property.

As he fumbled with the strings of the first box his heart beat wildly, and he felt the blood mounting to his face. Was he about to solve the mystery surrounding the girl in whom his interest had now grown so deep that he could scarcely get her out of his mind?

But the box was empty, save for some crumpled white tissue paper. He took up the cover in perplexity and saw his own name written by him. Then he remembered. This was the box he had sent down to the club by the cabman, to get it out of his way. He felt disappointed and turned quickly to the other box and cut the cord. This time he found the great black hat, beautiful and unhurt in spite of its journey to Chicago. The reputation of his mother's maid was saved. But was there no word from the beautiful stranger? He searched hurriedly through the wrappings, pulled out the hat and turned the box upside down, but nothing else appeared. Then he went to the suitcase. Yes, there was the raincoat. He took it out triumphantly, for now his mother could say nothing. Moreover, his trust in the fair stranger was justified. He had done well to believe in her. He began to take out the other garments, curious to see what had been there for her use.

A long, golden brown hair nestling on the collar of the bathrobe gleamed in a chance ray of sunlight. He looked at it reverently and laid the garment down, that it might not be disturbed. As he lifted the coat, he saw the little note pinned to the lapel and seized it. Surely this would tell him something!

But, no, there was only the message that she had arrived safely and her thanks. She signed her name "Mary." She had told him he might call her that. Could it be that it was her real name?

He pondered the delicate writing, thinking how like her it seemed, then put the note in an inner pocket and lifted out the evening clothes. It was then that he touched the silk-lined cloth of her dress and drew back as if he had ventured upon something sacred. Awed, he gazed at it, and then with gentle fingers lifted it and laid it upon his knee. Her dress! The one she had worn to the dinner with him! What did it all mean? Why was it here, and where was she?

He spread it out across his lap and looked at it as if it hid her presence. He touched the lace and delicate garniture about the waist. What did its presence here mean? Did it bear some message? He searched carefully but found nothing further. Had she reached a place of safety where she did not need the dress? No, for in that case, why would she have sent it to him? Had she been desperate perhaps and—? No, he would not think such things of her.

Gradually, as he looked, the dress told its own story, as she thought it would—how she had been obliged to put on a disguise, and this was the only way to hide her own dress. He felt a great pleasure in the fact that she trusted him with it. Perhaps there hadn't been time to make further explanation. But if she needed a disguise, she was still in danger! Oh, why hadn't she given him some clue? He dropped his head on his hand in troubled thoughts.

A faint perfume of violets stole upon his senses from the dress lying across his knee. He laid his cheek against it, breathing in the perfume. But he put it down quickly, looking quite foolish, and reminded himself that the girl was still a stranger and might belong to another.

Then he thought again of the story the judge had told him and of his own first conviction that the two young women were identical. Could that be? Why couldn't he discover who the other girl was and get someone to introduce him? He resolved to interview the judge about it at their next meeting. In the meantime, he must wait and hope for further word from Mary. Surely she would write him again and claim her ring perhaps. And, as she had been so thoughtful about returning the hat and coat, she would probably return the money he had loaned her. At least he would hear from her in that way. There was nothing to do but wait.

There was the immediate problem of how he should restore his sister's hat and his mother's coat to their places, unsuspected.

With a sigh, he folded up the cloth dress, wrapped it in folds of tissue paper from the empty hatbox and placed it in his suitcase. Then he transferred the hat to its original box, rang the bell and ordered the boy to care for the box and suitcase until he called for them.

During the afternoon he ventured to the judge's office about some unimportant detail of the business they were transacting. As he was leaving he said, "By the way, who was the young woman who gave you such a fright by her sudden disappearance? You never told me her name. Is she one of my acquaintances, I wonder?"

"Oh, her name is Mary Weston," said the judge, smiling. "I don't believe you know her, for she was from California and was visiting here only for a few days. She sailed for Europe the next day."

That closed the incident and, so far as the mystery was concerned, only added perplexity to it.

Dunham purposely remained downtown and had a clerk telephone home for him, saying he had gone out of the city and would not be home until late, so they need not wait up. Then he took a twenty-mile trolley ride into the suburbs and back, to make good his word, and all the way he kept turning over and over the mystery of the beautiful young woman. Surely he had been crazy to let her drift out into the world alone and practically penniless. The dress had told its tale. He saw, of course, that if she were afraid of detection, she must have been forced to buy other clothing, and how could she have bought it with only nine dollars and seventy-five cents?

He should have found some way to cash a check and supply her with what she needed. It was terrible! True, she had those other beautiful rings, but would she dare to sell them? Perhaps, though, she had found someone else as ready as he had been to help her. But, to his surprise, that thought was distasteful to him. During his long, cold ride in solitude he discovered that the thing he wanted most in life was to find the girl again and take care of her.

Of course he reasoned with himself from one end of the trolley line to the other and called himself all kinds of a fool, but it was no use. Underneath all the reasoning, he knew he was glad he had found her once, and he determined to find her again and unravel the mystery.

A little after midnight he arrived at the clubhouse, secured his suitcase and the hatbox, and took a cab to his home. He left the vehicle at the corner, lest the sound of it waken his mother or sister.

He let himself silently into the house with his latchkey and tiptoed up to his room. The light was burning low. He put the hatbox in the farthest corner of his closet, then took out the raincoat and, slipping off his shoes, went softly down to the hall closet.

In utter darkness he felt around and finally hung the coat on a hook under another long cloak, then gently released the hanging loop and let the garment slip down in an inconspicuous heap on the floor. He stole upstairs as guiltily as if he had been a naughty boy stealing sugar. When he reached his room, he turned up his light and, pulling out the hatbox, surveyed it thoughtfully. This was still a problem. How should he dispose of the hat so that its discovery would cast no further suspicion upon the maid? How would it do to place the hat in the hall closet, back among the coats? No, it might excite suspicion to find them together. Could he put it in his own closet and profess to have found it there? No, for that might lead to unpleasant questioning and perhaps involve the servants again. If he could only put it back where he had found it! But Cornelia, of course, would know it had not been there in her room all week. It would be better to wait until the coast was clear and hide it in Cornelia's closet, where it might have been put by mistake and forgotten. It was going to be hard to explain, but that was the best plan he could evolve.

He took the hat out and held it in his hand, looking at it from different angles and trying to remember just how the girl had looked out at him from under its drooping plumes. Then with a sigh he laid it in its box again and went to bed.

The morning brought clearer thought, and when the summons to breakfast pealed through the hall he took the box boldly in his hand and descended to the dining room, where he presented the hat to his astonished sister.

"I'm afraid I am the criminal, Cornelia," he said in his pleasantest manner. "I'm sorry I can't explain just how this thing got on my closet shelf. I must have put it there myself through some unaccountable mix-up. It's too bad I couldn't have found it before and saved you a lot of worry. But you are one hat the richer for it, for I paid the bill yesterday. Please accept it with my compliments."

Cornelia exclaimed with delight over the recovered hat.

"But how in the world could it have gotten into your closet, Tryon? It was impossible. I left it in my room, I know I did, for I spoke to Nora about it before I left. How do you account for it?"

"Oh, I don't attempt to account for it," he said with a wave of his hand. "I've been so taken up with other things this past week, I may have done almost anything. By the way, Mother, I'm sure you'll be glad to hear that Judge Blackwell has made me a most generous offer of business relations and that I have decided to accept it."

Amid the exclamations over this bit of news, the hat was forgotten for a time, and when the mother and sister finally reverted to it, he broke in upon their questions with a suggestion.

"Mother, I suggest that you make a thorough search for your raincoat. I'm sure that you must have overlooked it. Such things often happen. We were so excited the morning Cornelia missed the hat that I suppose no one looked thoroughly."

"But that's impossible, Tryon," said his mother. "I had that closet searched most carefully."

"Nevertheless, Mother, please me by looking again. That closet is dark, and I would suggest a light."

"Of course, if you wish it," she said stiffly. "You might look yourself."

"I'm afraid I don't have time this morning," he professed. "But suppose you look in your own closets, too, Mother. I'm sure you'll find it somewhere. It couldn't get out of the house of itself, and Nora is no thief. This idea is preposterous. Please have it attended to carefully today. Good-bye. I have to hurry downtown, and I can't tell just what time I shall get back this evening. Phone me if you find the coat anywhere. If you don't find it, I'll buy you another one this afternoon."

"I shall not find the raincoat," said his mother sternly, "but of course I want to satisfy you. I know it's not in this house."

He left hastily, for he didn't care to be present when the raincoat was found.

"There's something strange about this," said Mrs. Dunham as she emerged from the hall closet holding her lost raincoat at arm's length. "You don't suppose your brother could be playing some kind of joke on us, do you? I never did understand jokes."

"Of course not," said Cornelia, with a sniff. "It's my opinion that Nora knows all about the matter, and Tryon has been helping her out with a few suggestions."

"Now, Cornelia, what do you mean by that? You surely don't suppose your brother would try to deceive us—his mother and sister?"

"I didn't say that, Mother," answered Cornelia, with her head in the air. "You've got your raincoat back, but you'd better watch the rest of your wardrobe. I don't intend to let Nora have free range in my room anymore."

Chapter 8

Meantime, the girl in Chicago brought to her task a disciplined mind, a fine artistic taste, a delicate but healthy body and a pair of willing, if unskilled, hands. To her surprise, she discovered that the work for which she had so often given orders was beyond her strength. Try as she would, she could not wash and iron table napkins and delicate embroidered linen pieces in the way she knew they should be done. Willpower can accomplish a good deal, but it can't always make up for ignorance, and the girl who had mastered difficult subjects in college and astonished music masters in the Old World with her talent found that she could not wash a window even to her own satisfaction, much less to that of her new mistress.

That these tasks were expected of her was a surprise. Yet with her ready adaptability and good sense, she saw that if she was to be a success in this new field she must be ready for any emergency. Nevertheless, as the weary days succeeded each other into weeks, she found that while her skill in table-setting and waiting was much prized, it was more than offset by her discrepancies in other lines. And so it came about that with mutual consent she and Mrs. Rhinehart parted company.

This time, with her reference, she did not find it so hard to get another place, and, after trying several, she learned to demand certain things, which put her finally into a home where her ability was appreciated and she was not required to do things in which she was unskilled.

She was growing more secure in her new life now and less afraid to venture into the streets lest someone should be on the watch for her. But night after night, as she climbed to her cheerless room and crept onto her uncomfortable bed, she shrank from all that life could now hold out to her. She felt imprisoned in a narrow round of toil, with no escape and no one to know or care. And who knew but that any day an enemy might trace her?

Then the son of the house came home from college in disgrace and began to make advances to her, until her case seemed almost desperate. She dreaded to make another change, for in some ways her work was not so hard as it had been in other places, and her wages were better. But from day to day she felt she could scarcely bear the hourly annoyances. The other servants, too, were not only uncompanionable but deeply jealous of her, resenting her gentle breeding, her careful speech, her dainty personal ways, her room to herself, her loyalty to her mistress.

Sometimes in the cold and darkness of the night vigils she would remember the man who had helped her and promised to be her friend and begged her to let him know if she ever needed help. Her heart cried out for sympathy and counsel. In her dreams she saw him coming to her across wide-stretching plains, hastening toward her, but she always awoke before he reached her.

Chapter 9

About this time the firm of Blackwell, Hanover & Dunham had a difficult case to work out which involved the gathering of evidence from Chicago. With pleasure Judge Blackwell accepted the eager proposal from the junior partner that he should go out and attend to it.

As Tryon Dunham entered the sleeper and placed his suitcase beside him on the seat, he remembered the night when he had taken this train with the girl who now occupied a great part of his thoughts. He had begun to feel that if he could ever hope to shake off his anxiety and get back to a normal state of mind, he must find her and unravel the mystery about her. If she were safe and had friends, perhaps he would be able to put her out of his thoughts, but if she were not safe—. He did not quite finish the sentence even in his thoughts, but his heart beat quicker, and he knew that if she needed him he was ready to help her, even at the sacrifice of his life.

All during the journey he planned a campaign for finding her. He knew in his heart that this was the real mission for which he had come to Chicago, although he intended to perform the other business thoroughly.

Upon his arrival in Chicago, he inserted a number of advertisements in the daily papers:

If M.R. is in Chicago, will she kindly communicate with T. Dunham, General Delivery? Important.

Mrs. Bowman's friend has something of importance to say to the lady who dined with her October 8th. Kindly send address to T.D., Box 7 Inter-Ocean office.

"Mary," let me know where and when I can speak with you about a matter of importance.—Tryon D., Record-Herald L.

These and others appeared in the papers, but when he began to get communications from all sorts of poor creatures—every one demanding money—and found himself running wild-goose chases after different Marys and M.R.s, he abandoned all hope of personal columns in the newspapers. Then he began a systematic search for music teachers and musicians, for it seemed to him that this would be her natural way of earning her living.

In the course of his search he came upon many objects of pity, and his heart was stirred with the sorrow and misery of the human race as it had never been stirred in all his life. Many a soul was helped and strengthened because of this brief contact with him. But always, as he saw new miseries, he was troubled over what might have become of her—"Mary."

Whenever he looked upon the face of a young woman, no matter how pinched and worn with poverty, he dreaded lest she might have come to this pass and be in actual need. As these thoughts went on day by day, he came to feel that she was his by a God-given right—his to find, his to care for. If she was in peril, he must save her. If she had done wrong—but this he could never believe. Her face was too pure and lovely for that. So the burden of her weighed upon his heart while he went about the business of gathering evidence link by link in the law case that had brought him to Chicago.

Dunham had set apart working hours, and he seemed to labor with double vigor because of the other task he had set for himself. When at last he finished the legal business and might go home, he lingered yet another day, and then another, devoting himself with almost feverish activity to the search for his unknown friend.

On the evening of the third day after his law work was finished, he walked toward the hotel where he was staying, obliged at last to face the fact that his search had been in vain.

He had almost reached the hotel when he met a business acquaintance, who welcomed him warmly, for Judge Blackwell's legal firm was known far and wide and commanded respect.

"Well, well!" said the older man. "Is this you, Dunham? I thought you were booked from home two days ago. Suppose you come home to dinner with me. I've a matter I'd like to talk over with you before you leave. I shall count this a most fortunate meeting if you will."

Catching at any straw that would keep him longer in Chicago, Dunham accepted the invitation. Just as the cab door was flung open in front of the businessman's handsome house, two men passed slowly by, and he heard a voice in broadest Irish: "She goes by th' name of Mary, ye says? All roight, sorr. I'll keep a sharp lookout."

Tryon Dunham turned and caught a glimpse of silver changing hands. One man was slight and fashionably dressed, and the light cast from a neighboring window showed his face to be dark and handsome. The other was short and stout and clad in a faded Prince Albert coat that bagged at the shoulders and elbows. He wore rubbers over his shoes, and his footsteps sounded like those of a heavy dog. The two passed around the corner, and Dunham and his host entered the house.

Soon they were seated at a well-appointed table where an elaborate dinner was served. The talk was of pleasant things, but the guest's mind was troubled and constantly kept hearing that sentence: "She goes by the name of Mary."

Then, suddenly, he looked up and met her eyes!

She was standing just back of her mistress's chair, with a quiet, watchful attitude, but her eyes had been unconsciously upon the guest, until he looked up and caught her glance.

She turned away, but the color rose in her cheeks, and she knew that he was watching her.

Her look startled him. He had never thought of looking for her in a menial position, and at first he noticed only the likeness of her for whom he was searching. But he watched her furtively until he became more and more startled with the resemblance.

She did not look at him again, but he noticed that her cheeks were scarlet and that the long lashes drooped as if she were trying to hide her eyes. She went now and again from the room on her silent, deft errands, bringing and taking dishes, filling the glasses with ice water, seeming to know at a glance just what was needed. Whenever she went from the room he tried to persuade himself that it was not she and then became impatient for her to return that he might convince himself that it was. He felt a helpless rage at the son of the house for the familiar way in which he said, "Mary, fill my glass," and he could not keep from frowning.

He was startled, too, at the similarity of names. Mary! The men on the street had used that name! Could it be that her enemy had tracked her? Perhaps he, Dunham, had appeared just in time to help her. His brain scarcely heard the questions with which his host was plying him, and his replies were vague and monosyllabic. At last he broke in upon the conversation.

"Excuse me, but I wonder if I may interrupt you for a moment. I have thought of something I ought to attend to at once. I wonder if the waitress would be kind enough to send a phone message for me. I'm afraid it will be too late if I wait."

"Why, certainly," said the host. "Would you like to go to the phone yourself, or can I attend to it for you? Please make yourself at home."

Already the young man was writing a line or two on a card he took from his pocket, and he handed it to the waitress, who at his question had moved silently behind his chair to do his bidding.

"Just call up that number, please, and give the message below. They will understand, and then you will write down their answer?"

He handed her the pencil and turned again to his dessert, saying with a relieved air, "Thank you. I'm sorry for the interruption. Now will you finish that story?"

He pretended that his entire attention was devoted to his host, but in reality he was listening to the click of the telephone and the low, gentle voice in an adjoining room. It came after only a moment's pause, and he wondered at the calmness with which the usual formula of the telephone was carried on. He could not hear what she said, but his ears were alert to the pause, just long enough for a few words to be written, and then to her footsteps coming quietly back.

His heart was beating wildly. It seemed to him that his host must see the strained look on his face, but he tried to fasten his interest upon the conversation and keep calm.

He had applied the test. There was no number on the card, and he knew that if the girl were not the one for whom he searched, she would return for an explanation.

If you are Mary Remington, tell me where and when I can talk with you. Immediately important to us both!

His fingers trembled as he took the card from the silver tray which she held out to him demurely. He picked it up and read the delicate writing—hers —the same that had expressed her thanks and told of her safe arrival in Chicago. He could scarcely refrain from leaping from his chair and shouting aloud in gladness.

The message she had written was simple. No stranger reading it would have thought twice about it:

Y.W.C.A building, small parlor, three tomorrow.

He knew the massive building, for he had passed it many times, never supposing it could have any interest for him. Now suddenly his heart warmed to the great organization of Christian women who had established these havens for homeless ones in the heart of the great cities.

He looked up at the girl as she passed the coffee on the other side of the table, but not a flicker of an eyelash showed she recognized him. She went through her duties and withdrew from the room, but, though they lingered long over the coffee, she did not return. When they went into the other room, his interest in the family grew less and less. The daughter of the house sat down at the piano, after leading him up to ask her to sing, and chirped through several sentimental songs, tinkling out a shallow accompaniment with her plump, manicured fingers. His soul revolted at the thought that she should be here entertaining the company, while that other one whose music would have thrilled them all stayed humbly in the kitchen, doing some menial task.

He took his leave early in the evening and hurried back to his hotel. As he crossed the street to hail a cab, he thought he saw a short, baggy figure shambling along in the shadow on the other side, looking up at the house.

He had professed to have business to attend to, but when he reached his room he could do nothing but sit down and think. That he had found her filled him with a deeper joy than any he had ever known before. That he had found her in such a position deepened the mystery and filled him with a nameless dread. Then out of the shadow of his thoughts shuffled the baggy man, and he could not rest but took his hat and walked out again into the city night, walking on and on until he again reached the house where he had dined.

He passed in front of the building and found lights still burning everywhere. Down the side street he saw brightly lit windows in the servants' quarters and heard loud laughter emanating from them. Was she in there, enduring such company? No, for there high in the fourth story gleamed a little light, and a shadow moved about across the curtain. Something told him it was her room. He paced back and forth until the light went out, and then reverently, with lifted hat, he turned and found his way back to the main avenue and a car line. As he passed the area gate a bright light shot out from the back door. There was a peal of laughter, an Irish good night, and a short man in baggy coat and rubbers shuffled out and slipped noiselessly down to the back street.

Chapter 10

Dunham slept very little that night. His soul hovered between joy and anxiety. He was almost inclined to send her word about the man he had seen lingering about the place, and yet perhaps it was foolish. He had doubtless been to call on the cook, and there might be no connection whatever between what Dunham had heard and seen and the lonely girl.

The next day, the girl made herself neat and trim with the few materials she had at hand. Her own fine garments that had lain carefully wrapped and hidden ever since she went into service were brought forth, and the coarse ones with which she had provided herself against suspicion were laid aside. If anyone came into her room while she was gone, he would find no fine French embroidery to tell tales. Also, she wished to feel as much like herself as possible, and she never could quite feel that in her cheap outfit. True, she had no finer outer garments than a cheap black flannel skirt and coat which she had bought with the first money she could spare, but they were warm. She had not bought a hat and had nothing to wear on her head but the black felt that belonged to the man she was going to meet. She looked at herself in the tiny mirror and wondered if the young man would understand and forgive? It was all she had, anyway, and there would be no time to go to the store and buy another before the appointed hour, for the family had brought unexpected company to a late lunch and kept her far beyond her hour for going out.

She looked down at her shabby shoes, their delicate kid now cracked and worn. Her hands were covered by a pair of cheap black silk gloves. It was the first time she had noticed these things so keenly, but now it seemed to her most embarrassing to go thus to meet the man who had helped her.

She gathered her little hoard of money to take with her and cast one look back over the cheerless room, with a great longing to bid it farewell forever and go back to the world where she belonged. Yet she realized it was a quiet refuge from the world that she must hereafter face. She closed her door, went down the stairs, and out into the street, like any other servant on her afternoon out, walking away to meet whatever crisis might arise. She had not dared to speculate much about the subject of the coming interview. It was likely he wanted to inquire about her comfort and perhaps offer material aid. She would not accept it, of course, but it would be a comfort to know that someone cared.

She longed for this interview, just because he had been kind and belonged to the world from which she had come. He would keep her secret. He had true eyes. She didn't notice the soft, padded feet that came wobbling down the street after her, and she only drew a little further out toward the curb when a bleary-eyed, red face peered into hers as she stood waiting for the car. She didn't notice the shabby man who boarded the car after she was seated.

Tryon Dunham stood in the great stone doorway watching the passing throng. He saw the girl at once as she got out of the car, but he didn't notice the man in the baggy coat who lumbered after her and watched with wondering scrutiny as Dunham came forward, lifted his hat and took her hand respectfully. Here was an element he didn't understand. He stood staring, puzzled, as they disappeared into the great building; then he planted himself in a convenient place to watch until his charge should come out again. This was perhaps a gentleman who had come to engage her to work for him. She might be thinking of changing her place. He must be on the alert.

Dunham placed two chairs in the far corner of the inner parlor, where they were alone, except for an occasional passer through the hall. He put the girl into the most comfortable one and then went to draw down the shade to shut a sharp ray of afternoon sunlight from her eyes. She sat there and looked down at her shabby shoes, her cheap gloves and her coarse garments and honored him for the honor he was giving her in this attire. She had learned by sharp experience that such respect to one in her station was not common. As he came back, he stood a moment looking down at her. She saw his eye rest with recognition upon the hat she wore, and her pale cheeks turned pink.

"I don't know what you will think of my keeping this," she said shyly, putting her hand to the hat. "But it seemed really necessary at the time, and I haven't dared spend the money for a new one yet. I thought perhaps you would forgive me and let me pay you for it sometime later."

"Don't speak of it," he said in a low voice. "I'm so glad you could use it at all. It would have been a comfort to me if I had known where it was. I hadn't even missed it, because at this time of year I have very little use for it. It's my traveling hat."

He looked at her again as though the sight of her was good to him, and his gaze made her forget the words she had planned to say.

"I'm so glad I found you!" he went on. "You haven't been out of my thoughts since I left you that night on the train. I've blamed myself over and over again for having gone then. I should have found some way to stand by you. I haven't had one easy moment since I saw you last."

His tone was so intense that she couldn't interrupt him; she could only sit and listen in wonder to the low-spoken torrent of feeling he expressed. She tried to protest, but the look in his face stopped her. He went on with an earnestness that would not be turned aside from its purpose.

"I came to Chicago so I might search for you. I couldn't stand the suspense any longer. I've been looking for you in every way I could think of, without openly searching, for that I dared not do lest I might jeopardize your safety. I was almost in despair when I went to dine with Mr. Phillips last evening. I felt I couldn't go home without knowing at least that you were safe, and now that

I've found you, I can't leave you until I know at least that you have no further need for help."

She summoned her courage now and spoke in a voice full of feeling: "Oh, you mustn't feel that way. You helped me just when I didn't know what to do and put me in the way of helping myself. I shall never cease to thank you for your kindness to an utter stranger. And now I'm doing very well." She tried to smile, but the tears came unbidden instead.

"You poor child!" His tone was full of something deeper than compassion, and his eyes spoke volumes. "Do you suppose I think you are doing well when I see you wearing the garb of a menial and working for people to whom you are far superior—people who by all the rights of education and refinement ought to be in the kitchen serving you?"

"It was the safest thing I could do, and really the only thing I could get to do at once," she tried to explain. "I'm doing it better every day."

"I have no doubt. You can be an artist at serving as well as anything else, if you try. But now that is all over. I'm going to take care of you. There is no use in protesting. If I may not do it in one way, I will in another. There is one question I must ask first, and I hope you will trust me enough to answer it. Is there any other—any other man who has the right to care for you and is unable or unwilling to do it?"

She looked up at him, her large eyes still shining with tears, and shuddered slightly.

"Oh, no!" she said. "Oh, no, I thank God there is not! My dear uncle has been dead for four years, and there has never been anyone else who cared since Father died."

He looked at her, a great light coming into his face; but she didn't understand and turned her head to hide the tears.

"Then I'm going to tell you something," he said, his tone growing lower, yet clear enough for her to hear every word.

A tall, oldish girl with a discontented upper lip stalked through the hall, glanced in at the door and sniffed significantly, but they didn't see her. A short, baggy-coated man outside hovered anxiously around the building and passed the very window of that room, but the shade opposite them was down, and they didn't know.

The low, pleasant voice went on: "I have come to care a great deal for you since I first saw you, and I want you to give me the right to care for you always and protect you against the whole world."

She looked up, wonderingly.

"What do you mean?"

"I mean that I love you, and I want to make you my wife. Then I can defy the whole world if need be and put you where you ought to be."

"Oh!" she gasped.

"Wait, please," he pleaded, laying his hand gently on hers. "Don't say anything until I have finished. I know this will be startling to you. You've been brought up to feel that such things must be more deliberately done. I don't want you to feel that this is the only way I can help you, either. If you aren't willing to be my wife, I will find some other plan. But this is the best way, if it isn't too hard on you, for I love you as I never dreamed I could love a woman. The only question is whether you can put up with me until I can teach you to love me a little."

She lifted her eyes to his face.

"Oh, it isn't that," she stammered, her cheeks flushing. "It isn't that at all. But you know nothing about me. If you knew, you would very likely think as others do and—"

"Then don't tell me anything about yourself if it will trouble you. I don't care what others think. If you have poisoned a husband, I should know that he needed poisoning, and anyway I should love you and stand by you."

"I haven't done anything wrong," she said gravely.

"Then if you have done nothing wrong, we'll prove it to the world, or, if we can't prove it, we will fly to some desert island and live there in peace and love. That's the way I feel about you. I know you're good and true and lovely! Anyone might as well try to prove to me you were crazy as that you had done wrong in any way."

Her face grew pale.

"Well, suppose I was crazy?"

"Then I would take you and cherish you and try to cure you, and if that couldn't be done, I'd help you to bear it."

"Oh, you are wonderful!" she breathed, the light of a great love growing in her eyes.

The bare, prosaic walls stood stolidly about them, indifferent to the drama that was being wrought within the walls. The whirl and hum of the city without, the grime and soil of the city within, were alike forgotten by the two as their hearts united in a great passion.

"Do you think you could learn to love me?" said the man's voice.

"I love you now," said the girl's low voice. "I think I have loved you from the beginning, though I never dared to think of it in that way. But it wouldn't be right for me to become your wife when you know practically nothing about me."

"Have you forgotten that you know nothing about me?"

"Oh, I do know something about you," she said shyly. "Remember that I have dined with your friends. I couldn't help seeing that they were good people, especially that delightful old man, the judge. He looked startlingly like my dear father. I saw how they all honored and loved you. And then what you have done for me, and the way you treated a defenseless stranger, were equal to years of mere acquaintance. I feel that I know a great deal about you."

He smiled. "Thank you," he said, "but I haven't forgotten that something more is due you than that slight knowledge of me, and before I came out here I went to the pastor of the church I've always attended and asked him to write me a letter. He is so widely known that I felt it would be an introduction for me."

He laid an open letter in her lap. Glancing down, she saw that it was signed by one of the best-known pulpit orators in the land and spoke in highest terms of the young man, whom it named as "my well-loved friend."

"It is also your right to know I've always tried to live a pure and honorable life. I've never told any woman but you that I loved her—except an elderly cousin with whom I thought I was in love when I was nineteen. She cured me of it by laughing at me, and I've kept my heart ever since."

She raised her eyes from reading the letter.

"You have all these, and I have nothing." She spread out her hands help-lessly. "It must seem strange to you that I am in this situation. It does to me. It's awful."

She put her hands over her eyes and shuddered.

"It is to save you from it all that I've come." He leaned over and spoke tenderly, "Darling!"

"Oh, wait!" She caught her breath as if it hurt her and put out her hand to stop him. "Wait! You must not say anymore until I've told you all about it. Perhaps when I've told you, you'll think about me as others do, and I'll have to run from you."

"Can't you trust me?" he reproached her.

"Oh, yes, I can trust you, but you may no longer trust me and that I cannot bear."

"I promise you solemnly that I will believe every word you say."

"Ah, but you will think I don't know and that it is your duty to give me into the hands of my enemies."

"That I most solemnly vow I will never do," he said earnestly. "You need not fear to tell me anything. But, listen, tell me this one thing: In the eyes of God, is there any reason—physical, mental, or spiritual—why you should not become my wife?"

She looked him clearly in the eyes.

"None at all."

"Then I am satisfied to take you without hearing your story until afterward."

"But I'm not satisfied. If I'm to see distrust come into your eyes, it must be now, not afterward."

"Then tell it quickly."

He put out his hand and took hers firmly into his own, as if to help her in her story.

Chapter 11

My father died when I was a young girl. We didn't have much money, and my mother's older brother took us to his home to live. My mother was his youngest sister, and he loved her more than anyone else living. There was another sister, a half sister, much older than my mother, and she had one son. He was a sulky, handsome boy with a selfish, cruel nature. He seemed to be happy only when he was tormenting someone. He used to come to Uncle's to visit when I was there, and he delighted in annoying me. He stretched barbed wire where he knew I was going to pass in the dark, to throw me down and tear my clothes. He threw a handful of burrs in my hair, and once he led me into a hornet's nest.

"After we went to live at my uncle's, Richard was not there so much. He had displeased my uncle, and he sent him away to school; but at vacation times he came again and kept the house in discomfort. He seemed always to have a special spite against me. Once he broke a rare Dresden vase that Uncle prized and told him I had done it.

"Mother didn't live long after Father died, and after she was gone I had no one to stand between me and Richard. Sometimes I had to tell my uncle, but more often I tried to bear it because I knew Richard was already a great distress to him.

"At last Richard was expelled from college, and Uncle was so angry with him that he told him he would do nothing more for him. He must go to work. Richard's father and mother had little money, and there were other children to support. Richard threatened me with all sorts of awful things if I didn't coax Uncle to take him back into his good graces again. I told him I wouldn't say a word to Uncle. He was very angry and swore at me. When I tried to leave the room he locked the door and wouldn't let me go until I screamed for help. Then he almost choked me, but when he heard Uncle coming he jumped out of the window.

"The next day he forged a check in my uncle's name and tried to throw suspicion on me, but he was discovered, and my uncle disinherited him. Uncle had intended to educate Richard and start him well in life, but now he would have nothing further to do with him. It seemed to work upon my uncle's health, all the disgrace to the family name, although no one ever thought of my uncle in connection with blame. As he paid Richard's debts, it wasn't known what the boy had done, except by the banker, who was a personal friend.

"We went abroad then, and everywhere Uncle amused himself by putting me under the best music masters and giving me all possible advantages in languages, literature and art. Three years ago he died at Carlsbad, and after his death I went back to my music studies, following his wishes in the matter and staying with a dear old lady in Vienna who had been kind to us when we were there before.

"As soon as my uncle's death was known at home, Richard wrote the most pathetic letter to me, professing deep contrition and saying he could never forgive himself for having quarreled with his dear uncle. He had a sad tale of how the business he had started had failed and left him with debts. If he had only a few hundred dollars, he could go on with it and pay off everything. He said I had inherited all that would have been his if he had done right, and he recognized the justice of it but begged that I would lend him a small sum until he could get on his feet, when he would repay me

"I had little faith in his reformation but felt as if I could not refuse him when I was enjoying what might have been his, so I sent him all the money I had at hand. As I was not yet of age, I could not control all the property, but my allowance was liberal. Richard continued to send me letters telling of his changed life and finally asked me to marry him. I declined emphatically, but he continued to write for money, always ending with a statement of his undying affection. In disgust, I at last offered to send him a certain sum of money regularly if he would stop writing to me. I succeeded in reducing our correspondence to a check account.

"This has been going on for three years, except he has constantly asked for larger sums. Whenever I would say I couldn't spare more, he would tell me how much he cared for me and how hard it was for him to be separated from me. I began to feel desperate about him and made up my mind that when I received the inheritance I would ask the lawyers to make some arrangement with him so that I should no longer be annoyed.

"It was necessary for me to return to America when I came of age, in order to sign certain papers and take full charge of the property. Richard knew this.

"He wrote telling me of a dear friend of his mother's who was soon to pass through Vienna and who by some misfortune had been deprived of a position as companion and chaperone to a young girl who was traveling. He suggested that she be my traveling companion on the voyage. He knew I wouldn't want to travel alone, and he sent her address and all sorts of credentials, with a message from his mother that she would feel perfectly safe about me if I went in this woman's guardianship.

"I really did need a traveling companion, of course, having failed to get my dear old lady to undertake the voyage, so I thought it could do no harm. I went to see her and found her pretty and frail and sad. She made a piteous appeal to me, and though I was not greatly taken with her, I decided she would do as well as anyone for a companion.

"She didn't bother me during the voyage but fluttered about and was quite popular on board, especially with a tall, disagreeable man with a cruel jaw and small eyes, who always made me feel as if he would gloat over anyone in his power. I found out he was a physician, a specialist in mental diseases, so Mrs. Chambray told me. And she talked a great deal about his skill and insight into such maladies.

"At New York my cousin Richard met us and literally took possession of us. Without my knowledge, the cruel-looking doctor was included in the party. I did not discover it until we were on the train, bound, as I supposed, for my old home just beyond Buffalo. It was some time since I had been in New York, and I didn't notice much which way we were going. The fact was, every plan was anticipated, and I was told that all arrangements had been made. Mrs. Chambray began to treat me like a little child and say, 'You see, we are going to take good care of you, dear, so don't worry about a thing.'

"I had taken the drawing room compartment, not so much because I had a headache, as I told them, but because I wanted to get away from their company. My cousin's marked devotion became painful to me. Then, too, the attentions and constant watchfulness of the doctor became most distasteful.

"We had been sitting on the observation platform, and it was late in the afternoon when I said I was going to lie down, and the two men got up to go into the smoker. In spite of my protests, Mrs. Chambray insisted upon following me in, to see that I was perfectly comfortable. She fussed around me, covering me up and offering smelling salts and eau de cologne for my head. I let her fuss, thinking that was the quickest way to get rid of her. I closed my eyes, and she said she would go out to the observation platform.

"I lay still for a while, thinking about her and how much I wanted to get rid of her. She acted as if she had been engaged to stay with me forever, and it suddenly became very plain to me that I ought to have a talk with her and tell her that I wouldn't need her services after this journey was over. It might make a difference to her if she knew it at once, and perhaps now would be as good a time to talk as any, for she was probably alone out on the platform.

"I got up and made a few little changes in my dress, for it would soon be time to go into the dining car. Then I went out to the observation platform, but she wasn't there. The chairs were all empty, so I chose the one next to the railing, away from the car door, and sat down to wait for her, thinking she would soon be back.

"We were going very fast, through a pretty bit of country. It was dusky and restful out there, so I leaned back and closed my eyes. Presently I heard voices approaching, above the rumble of the train, and, peeping around the doorway, I saw Mrs. Chambray, Richard and the doctor coming from the other car. I kept quiet, hoping they wouldn't come out, and they didn't. They settled down near the door and ordered the porter to put up a table for them to play cards.

"The train began to slow down and finally came to a halt for a long time on a sidetrack, waiting for another train to pass. I heard Richard ask where I was. Mrs. Chambray said laughingly that I was safely asleep. Then, before I realized it, they began to talk about me. There were no other passengers in the car. Richard asked Mrs. Chambray if she thought I had any suspicion that I was not on the right train, and she said, 'Not the slightest.' Then, by degrees, I heard them describe the most diabolical plot.

"I discovered that we were on the way to Philadelphia and would then proceed to a place near Washington, where the doctor had a private insane asylum in which I would be shut up. They were going to administer some drug that would make me unconscious when I was taken off the train. If they could not get me to take it for the headache I had talked about, Mrs. Chambray was to manage to get it into my food or give it to me when asleep. Mrs. Chambray, it seems, had not known the entire plot before leaving Europe, and this was their first chance of telling her. They thought I was safely in my compartment, asleep, and she had gone into the other car to give the signal as soon as she thought it safe to do so.

"They had arranged every detail. Richard had been using as models the letters I had written him for the last three years. He had constructed a set of love letters from me to him, in perfect imitation of my handwriting. They compared the letters and read snatches of the sentences aloud. The letters referred constantly to our being married as soon as I returned from abroad, and some of them spoke of the money as belonging to us both and that now it would come to its own without any further trouble.

"They even contrived a marriage certificate, which, from what they said, must have been made out without names, with Mrs. Chambray and the doctor signed as witnesses. They were going to use this as evidence that Richard was my husband and had the right to administer my estate during the time I was incapable. They had even arranged that a young woman who was hopelessly insane should take my place when the executors of the estate came to see me, if they took the trouble to do that. As it was some years since either of them had seen me, they could easily have been deceived. And for their help Mrs. Chambray and the doctor were to receive a handsome sum.

"I could scarcely believe my ears at first. I thought I must be mistaken, that they couldn't be talking about me. But my name was mentioned again and again, and as each link in the horrible plot was made plain to me, my terror grew so great that I was on the verge of rushing into the car and calling for the conductor and porter to help me. But something held me still, and I heard Richard say that he had just informed the trainmen that I was insane and that they need not be surprised if I had to be restrained. He had told them I was harmless, but he had no doubt that the conductor had whispered it to our fellow passengers in the car, which explained their prolonged absence in the smoker. Then they all laughed, and it seemed to me that the cover to the bottomless pit was open and I was falling in.

"I sat still, hardly daring to breathe. Then I began to go over the story bit by bit and to put together little things that had happened since we landed and even before I left Vienna. And I saw that I was caught in a trap. It would be no use to appeal to anyone, for no one would believe me. I looked wildly out at the ground and had desperate thoughts of climbing over the rail and jumping from the train. Death would be better than what I would soon have to face. My persecutors even described how they had deceived my friends at home by sending telegrams of my mental condition. There would be no hope of appealing to them for help. The only witnesses to my sanity were far away in Vienna, and how could I reach them if I were in Richard's power?

"I watched the names of the stations as they flew by, but it gradually grew dark, and I could hardly make them out. I thought one looked like the name of a Philadelphia suburb, but I couldn't be sure. I was freezing with horror and cold but didn't dare move, lest I attract their attention.

"We began to rush past rows of houses, and I knew we were approaching a city. Then suddenly the train slowed down and stopped, with very little warning, as if it intended to halt only a second and then hurry on.

"There was a platform on one side of the train, but we were out beyond the car shed, for our train was long. I couldn't climb over the rail to the platform, for I was sitting on the side away from the station and would have to pass the car door to do so. I would surely be seen.

"On the other side were a great many tracks separated by strong picket fences as high as the car platform and close to the trains, and they reached as far as I could see in either direction. I had no time to think, and there was nothing I could do but climb over the rail and get across those tracks and fences somehow.

"My hands were so cold and trembling that I could scarcely hold onto the rail as I jumped over. I can't remember how I got across. Twice I had to cling to a fence while an express train rushed by, and the shock and noise almost stunned me. It was a miracle I wasn't killed, but I didn't think of that until afterward. I was conscious only of the train I had left standing by the station. I glanced back once and thought I saw Richard come to the door of the car. Then I stumbled on blindly. I don't remember anymore until I found myself hurrying along that dark passage under the bridge and saw you just ahead. I was afraid to speak to you, but I didn't know what else to do, and you were so good to me—!" Her voice broke in a sob.

All the while he had held her hand firmly. She forgot that anyone might be watching; he didn't care. The tall girl with the discontented upper lip went to the matron and told her she thought the man and woman in the parlor should be made to go. She believed the man was trying to coax the girl to do something she didn't want to do. The matron started on a voyage of discovery up the hall and down again, with penetrating glances into the room, but the two didn't see her.

"Oh, my poor dear girl!" breathed the man. "And you have passed through all this awful experience alone! Why didn't you tell me about it? I could have helped you; I'm a lawyer."

"I thought you would be on your guard at once and watch for evidences of my insanity. I thought perhaps you would believe it true and feel it necessary to return me to my friends. I might have been tempted to do that, perhaps, if any-one had come to me with such a story."

"One couldn't do that after seeing and talking with you," he replied. "I never could have believed it. Surely no reputable physician would lend his influence to put you in an asylum, yet I know such things have been done. Your cousin must be a desperate character. I shall not feel safe until you belong to me. I saw two men hanging about Mr. Phillips's house last evening. They were looking up at the windows and talking about keeping a close watch on some-one named Mary. One of the men was tall and slight and handsome, with dark hair and eyes; the other was Irish and wore a coat too large for him, and rub-bers. I went back later in the evening, and the Irishman was hovering about the house."

The girl looked up with frightened eyes and grasped the arms of her chair.

"Will you go with me now to a church not far away, where a friend of mine is a pastor, and be married? Then we can defy all the cousins in creation. Can't you trust me?" he pleaded.

"Oh, yes, but—"

"Is it that you don't love me?"

"No," she said, and her eyes drooped shyly. "It seems strange that I dare to say it to you when I've known you so little." She lifted her eyes, full of a won-derful light, and she was beautiful to him, poorly dressed though she was. The smooth braids around her shapely head, covered by the soft felt hat, seemed more beautiful to him than all the elaborate headdresses of modern times.

"Where is the 'but' then, dear? Shall we go now?"

"How can I go in this dress?" She looked down at her shabby shoes, rough black dress and cheap gloves in dismay.

"You needn't. Your own dress is out in the office in my suitcase. I brought it with me, thinking you might need it—hoping you might, I mean." He smiled. "I've kept it near me—partly because I wanted the comfort of it and partly because I was afraid someone else might find it and desecrate our secret with their commonplace wondering."

At that moment the matron of the building stepped up to the absorbed couple, resolved to do her duty. He lips were pursed to their thinnest, and dis-pleasure showed in the lines of her face.

The young man arose and asked in a grave tone, "Excuse me, but can you tell me whether this lady can get a room here to rest for a short time while I go out and attend to a matter of business?"

The matron noticed his refined face and true eyes, and she accepted with good grace the ten-dollar bill he handed to her.

"We charge only fifty cents a night for a room," she said, glancing at the humble garments of the man's companion. She thought the girl must be a poor dependent or a country relative.

"That's all right," he said. "Just let the change help the good work along."

That altered the atmosphere distinctly. The matron smiled and retired to snub the girl with the discontented upper lip. Then she sent the elevator boy to carry the girl's suitcase. As the matron came back to the office, a man in a baggy coat hustled out the open door into the street, having first cast a keen, furtive glance that searched every corner of the place.

"Now," said Dunham, as the matron disappeared, "you can go up to your room and get ready, and I'll look after a few little matters. I called on my friend, the minister, this morning, and I've looked up the legal part of this affair. I can make sure everything is all right in a few minutes. Is there anything you want me to do for you?"

"No," she answered. "But I'm afraid I ought not to let you do this. You scarcely know me."

"Now, dear, no more of that. We have no time to lose. How long will it take you to get dressed? Will half an hour do? It's getting late."

"Oh, it won't take long." She caught her breath with gladness. Her companion's voice was so strong and comforting, his face so filled with a wonderful love, that she felt dazed with the sudden joy of it all.

The elevator boy appeared in the doorway with the familiar suitcase.

"Don't be afraid, dear heart," whispered the young man as he attended her to the elevator. "I'll be back again soon, and then we shall be together!"

It was a large front room to which the boy took her. The ten-dollar bill had proven effective. It was not a "fifty-cents-a-night" room. Someone—some guest or kind patron—had put a small illuminated text upon the wall in a neat frame. It met her eye as she entered: "Rejoice and be glad." Just a common little picture card it was, with a phrase that had become trite to many, yet it seemed to be a message to her. Her heart leaped to obey. She went to the window to catch a glimpse of the man who would soon be her husband, but he wasn't there, and the hurrying people reminded her that she must hasten.

Across the street a slouching figure in a baggy coat looked up and caught her glance. She trembled and drew back out of the sunshine, remembering what Dunham had told her about the Irishman of the night before. With a quick instinct, she drew down the shade and locked the door.

Chapter 12

The rubbered feet across the way hurried into a cigar store, where the man had a good view of the Y.W.C.A. building. He flung down some change and demanded the use of the telephone. Then, with one eye on the opposite doorway, he called up a number and delivered his message.

"Oi've treed me bird. She's in a room all roight at the Y.W.C.A. place, fer I seed her at the winder. She come with a foine gintlemin, but he's gahn now, an' she's loike to stay a spell. You'd best come at once. . . . All roight. Hurry up!"

He hung up the telephone receiver and hurried back to his post in front of the big entrance. Meanwhile the bride-elect upstairs was putting on her own beautiful garments once more and arranging the waves of lovely hair in their old accustomed way.

Tryon Dunham's plans were well laid. He first called up his friend the minister and told him to be ready, then a florist not far from the church, then a large department store where he had spent some time that morning.

"Is that Mr. Hunter, head of the fur department? Mr. Hunter, this is Mr. Dunham. You remember our conversation this morning? Kindly send the coat and hat I selected to the Y.W.C.A. building at once. Yes, just send them to the office. You remember it was to be C.O.D., and I showed you my certified check this morning. It's all right, is it? How long will it take you to get it there? . . . All right. Have the boy wait if I'm not there. Good-bye."

His next move was to order a carriage and have it stop at the florist's on the way. That done, he consulted his watch. Seventeen minutes of his precious half hour were gone. With nervous haste he went into a telephone booth and called up his own home long-distance.

To his relief, his mother answered.

"Is that you, Mother? This is Tyron. Are you all well? That's good. Yes, I'm in Chicago but will soon be home. Mother, I've something to tell you that may startle you, though there is nothing to make you sad. You've known something was on my mind for some time." He paused for the murmur of assent.

He knew how his mother must look right now, even though he couldn't see her—that set look of being ready for anything. He wanted to spare her as much as possible, so he hurried on, "You remember speaking to me about the ring I wore?"

"Tryon! Are you engaged?" There was a sharp anxiety in the tone as it came through the hundreds of miles of space.

"One better, Mother. I'm just about to be married."

"What have you done? Don't forget the honorable name you bear!"

"No, Mother, I don't forget. She's fine and beautiful and sweet. You will love her, and our world will fall at her feet."

"But who is she? You must remember that love is very blind. Tryon, you must come home at once. I shall die if you disgrace us all. Don't do anything to spoil our lives. I know it's something dreadful, or you wouldn't do it in such haste."

"Nothing of the kind, Mother. Can't you trust me? Let me explain. She's alone, and legal circumstances that would take too long for me to explain over the phone have made it necessary to give her my immediate protection. We are going at once to Edwin Twinell's church, and he will marry us. It's all arranged, but I felt that you ought to be told beforehand. We shall probably take the night express for home. Tell Cornelia I shall expect congratulations telegraphed to the hotel here inside of two hours."

"But, Tryon, what will our friends think? It is most extraordinary! How can you manage about announcements?"

"Bother the red tape, Mother! What difference does that make? Put it in the society column if you want to."

"But, Tryon, we don't want to be conspicuous!"

"Well, Mother, I'm not going to put off my wedding at the last minute for a matter of some bits of pasteboard. I'll do any reasonable thing to please you, but not that."

"Couldn't you get a chaperone for her and bring her on to me? Then we could plan the wedding at our leisure."

"Impossible, Mother. In the first place, she never would consent. Really, I can't talk anymore about it. I must go at once, or I'll be late. Tell me you'll love her for my sake, until you love her for her own."

"Tryon, you always were unreasonable. Suppose you have the cards engraved at once, and I'll telegraph our list to the engraver if you'll give me his address. If you prefer, you can get them engraved and sent out from there. That will keep tongues still."

"All right, I'll do it. I'll have the engraver telegraph his address to you within two hours. Have your list ready. And, Mother, don't worry. She's all right. You couldn't have chosen better yourself. Say you will love her, Mother, dear."

"Oh, I suppose I'll try," she sighed disconsolately. "But I never thought you would be married in such a way. Why, you haven't even told me who she is."

"She's all right, Mother—good family and all. I really must hurry—"

"But what is her name, Tryon?"

"Mother, I really must go. Ask Mrs. Parker Bowman what she thinks of her. Good-bye! Cheer up; it'll be all right."

"But, Tryon, her name—"

The receiver was hung up with a click, and Dunham looked at his watch nervously. In two minutes his half hour would be up, yet he must let Judge Blackwell know. Perhaps he could still catch him in the office. He sometimes stayed downtown late. Dunham rang up the office. The judge was still there, and in a moment his cheery voice came on the line.

"Hello!"

"Hello, Judge! Is that you? . . . This is Dunham. . .Chicago. Yes, the business is all done, and I'm ready to come home, but I want to give you a bit of news. Do you remember the young woman who dined with us at Mrs. Bowman's and played the piano so well? . . . Yes, the night I met you. . . Well, you half guessed that night how it was with us, I think. And now she is here, and we are to be married at once, before I return. I'm just about to go to the church, but I wanted your blessing first."

"Blessings and congratulations to you both!" came the hearty voice over the phone. "Tell her she shall be taken into the firm at once as chief consultant on condition that she plays for me whenever I ask her."

The young man smiled as he again hung up the receiver. The future was full of bright possibilities. He hurried into the street, forgetful of engravers. The half hour was up and one minute over.

The girl had slipped into her own garments once more with a relief. Had it all been an ugly dream, this life she had been living for the past few months? And now she was going back to rest and peace and real life. No, not going back, but going forward. The color came into her beautiful face at the thought of the one who, though not knowing her, yet had loved her enough to take her as she was and lift her out of her trouble. It was like the most romantic of fairy tales, this unexpected lover and the joy that had come to her.

A knock at the door brought her back to realities again. Her heart throbbed wildly. Had he come back to her already? Or had her enemy found her out at last?

Tryon Dunham hurried up the steps of the Y.W.C.A. building, nearly knocking over a man in rubbers who was lurking in the entrance. The young man had seen a boy in uniform, laden with two enormous boxes, run up the steps as he turned the last corner. Hastily writing a few lines on one of his cards and slipping it into the largest box, he sent them both up to the girl's room. Then he sauntered to the door to see if the carriage had come. It was there. He glanced inside to see if his orders about the flowers had been fulfilled and spoke a few words of direction to the driver. Turning back to the door, he found the small, red eyes of the Irishman fixed upon him. Something in the slouch of the figure reminded Dunham strongly now of the man he had noticed the night before, and as he went back into the building he looked the man over well and determined to watch him.

As he sat in the office waiting, twice he saw the bleary eyes of the man pressed to the glass panes in the front door and as suddenly withdrawn. It irritated him, and finally he strode to the door and asked the man if he were looking for someone.

"Just waitin' fer me sweetheart," said the man with a cringing attitude.

"She has a room in here, an' I saw her go in a while back."

"Well, you'd better move on. They don't care to have people hanging around here."

The man slunk away with a vindictive glance, and Tryon Dunham went back to the office, more perturbed at the little incident than he could understand.

Upstairs the girl had dared to open her door and was relieved to find the elevator boy there with two boxes.

"The gentleman's below, an' he says he'll wait, an' he sent these up," he said, depositing his burden and hurrying away.

She locked the door once more, for somehow a great fear stole over her now that she was again dressed in her own garments and could easily be recognized.

She opened the large box and read the card lying on the top.

> *These are my wedding gifts to you, dear. Put them on and come as soon as possible to the one who loves you better than anything else in life.*
>
> *Tryon*

Her eyes shone brightly and her cheeks grew rosy as she lifted out from the tissue paper wrappings a long, rich coat of Alaska seal with exquisite brocade lining. She put it on and stood a moment looking at herself in the glass. She felt like one who for a long time had lost her identity and suddenly had it back again. Such garments were ordinary comforts of her former life. She had not been warm enough in the coarse black coat.

The other box contained a beautiful fur hat to match the coat. In shape and general appearance it was like the hat he had borrowed for her use in the fall. She smiled as she set it upon her head and then laughed outright as she remembered her shabby silk gloves. Never mind. She could take them off when she reached the church.

She packed the little black dress into the suitcase, folded the felt hat on the top and, putting on her gloves, hurried down to the one who waited for her.

The matron had gone upstairs to the linen closet and left the girl with the discontented upper lip in charge in the office. The latter watched the elegant lady in the rich furs come down the hall from the elevator and wondered who she was and why she had been upstairs. *Probably to visit some poor protégée,* she thought. The girl caught the love-light in the eyes of Tryon Dunham as he rose to meet his bride, and she recognized him as the same man who had been in close conversation with the cheaply dressed girl in the parlor an hour before. She sneered as she wondered what the fine lady in furs would think if she knew about the other girl. Then they went out to the carriage, past the baggy-coated man, who shrank back behind a stone column and watched them.

As Dunham shut the door, he looked back just in time to see a slight man with dark eyes and hair hurry up and touch the Irishman on the shoulder. The latter pointed toward their carriage.

"See!" said Dunham. "I believe those are the men who were hovering around the house last night."

The girl leaned forward to look and then drew back with an exclamation of horror as the carriage started.

"That man is my cousin Richard!" she cried.

"Are you sure?" he asked, and a look of determination settled onto his face.

"Perfectly," she answered, looking out again. "Do you suppose he has seen me?"

"I suppose he has, but we'll soon turn the tables." He leaned out and spoke a word to the driver, who drew up around the next corner in front of a telephone pay station.

"Come with me for just a minute, dear. I'll telephone to a detective bureau where they know me and have that man watched. He is unsafe to have at large." He helped her out and drew her arm firmly within his own. "Don't be afraid anymore. I'll take care of you."

He telephoned a careful description of the two men and their whereabouts, and before he hung up the receiver a man was dispatched for the Y.W.C.A. building.

Dunham put the girl tenderly into the carriage, and to divert her attention he opened the box of flowers and put a great sheaf of white roses and lilies-of-the-valley into her gloved hands. Then, taking her in his arms for the first time, he kissed her. He noticed the shabby gloves and, putting his hand in his breast pocket, drew out the white gloves she had worn before, saying, "See! I've carried them with me ever since you sent them back! My sister never asked for them. I kept them for your sake."

The color had come back into her cheeks by the time they reached the church, and he thought her a beautiful bride as he led her into the dim aisle. Someone up in the choir loft was playing the wedding march, and the minister's wife and young daughter sat waiting to witness the ceremony.

The minister met them at the door with a welcoming smile and handshake and led them forward. As the music hushed for the words of the ceremony, he leaned forward to the young man and whispered, "I neglected to ask you her name, Tryon."

"Oh, yes." The young man paused in his dilemma and looked for an instant at the sweet face of the girl beside him. But he couldn't let his friend see that he didn't know the name of his wife-to-be, and with quick thought he answered, "Mary."

The ceremony proceeded, and the minister's voice sounded out solemnly in the empty church: "Do you, Tryon, take this woman whom you hold by the hand to be your lawful wedded wife?"

The young man's fingers held the timid hand of the girl firmly as he answered, "I do."

"Do you, Mary, take this man?" came the next question, and the girl looked up with clear eyes and said, "I do."

Then the minister's wife, who knew and prized Tryon Dunham's friendship, said to herself, *It's all right. She loves him.*

When the solemn words were spoken that bound them together for life, and they were once more out in the carriage, Tryon said, "Do you know you haven't told me your real name yet?"

She laughed happily as the carriage started on its way and answered, "Why, it is Mary!"

As they rounded the first corner beyond the church, two breathless individuals hurried up from the other direction. One was short and baggy, and the sole of one rubber boot flopped as he struggled to keep up with the brisk strides of the other man, who was slim and angry. They had been detained by an altercation with the matron of the Y.W.C.A. building and puzzled by the story of a plainly dressed girl who had taken the room and the fine lady who had left the building with a gentleman. Finally, it had been settled by the elevator boy, who declared the two women to be one and the same.

A moment later a man riding a motorcycle rounded the corner and puffed placidly along near the two. He appeared to be looking at the numbers on the other side of the street, but he heard every word they said as they caught sight of the disappearing carriage and hurried after it. He had been standing in the entrance of the Y.W.C.A. building, apparently a careless observer, while the elevator boy gave his evidence.

The motorcycle shot ahead, passed the carriage and cast a keen glance at the occupants. Then it rounded the block and came almost up to the two pursuers again.

When the carriage stopped at the side entrance of a hotel, the man on the motorcycle was ahead of the pursuers and discovered it first, long enough to see the two get out and go up the marble steps. The carriage was driving away when the thin man came in sight, with the baggy man struggling along half a block behind, his padded feet sounding like a St. Bernard dog in bedroom slippers.

The pursuers had one glimpse of their prey as the elevator shot upward. They managed to evade the hotel authorities and get up the wide staircase without observation. By keeping on the alert, they discovered that the elevator had stopped at the second floor, so the people they were tracking must have apartments there. Lurking in the shadowy parts of the hall, they watched and soon saw Dunham come out of a room and hurry to the elevator. He had remembered his promise to his mother about the engravers. As soon as he was gone they presented themselves boldly at the door.

Filled with joy and feeling entirely safe now in the protection of her husband, Mary Dunham opened the door. She supposed, of course, it was the bellboy with a pitcher of ice water, for which she had just rung.

"Ah, here you are at last, my pretty cousin!" It was the voice of Richard, with all the stored-up wrath of his long-baffled search.

At that moment the man from the motorcycle stepped softly up the top stair and slid unseen into the shadows of the hall.

For an instant Mary thought she was going to faint, and in one swift flash of horror she saw herself overpowered and carried into hiding before her husband could return. But she controlled herself and faced her tormentor with unflinching gaze. Though her strength had deserted her at first, every faculty was now collected. As if nothing unusual were happening, she put out her trembling fingers and pressed them over the electric button on the wall. Then with new strength coming from the certainty that someone would soon come to her aid, she opened her lips to speak.

"What are you doing here, Richard?"

"I've come after you, my lady. A nice chase you've given me, but you shall pay for it now."

The cruelty in his face eclipsed any lines of beauty that might have been there. The girl's heart froze within her as she looked once more into those eyes which had always seemed to her like sword-points.

"I shall never go anywhere with you," she answered steadily.

He seized her wrist roughly, twisting it as he had when he tormented her in their childhood days. None of them saw the stranger who stepped quietly down the hall toward them.

"Will you go peaceably, or shall I have to gag and bind you?" Richard hissed. "Choose quickly. I'm in no mood to trifle with you any longer."

Although he hurt her wrist cruelly, she threw herself back from him and with her other hand pressed still harder against the electric button. The bell was ringing furiously down in the office, but the walls were thick and the halls lofty. It could not be heard above.

"Catch that other hand, Mike," commanded Richard, "and stuff this in her mouth while I tie her hands behind her back."

Mary screamed.

The man in the shadow stepped up behind them and asked in a low voice, "What does this all mean?"

The two men, startled, dropped the girl's hands for an instant. Then Richard, white with anger at this interference, answered insolently: "It means that this girl's an escaped lunatic, and we're sent to take her back. She's dangerous, so you'd better keep out of the way."

Mary's voice, clear and penetrating, rang through the halls: "Tryon, Tryon! Come quick! Help! Help!"

As if in answer to her call, the elevator shot up to the second floor, and

Tryon Dunham stepped out in time to see the two men snatch Mary's hands again and attempt to bind them behind her back.

In an instant he had seized Richard by the collar and landed him on the hall carpet, while a well-directed blow sent the flabby Irishman sprawling at the feet of the detective, who sat on him and pinioned his arms behind his back.

"How dare you lay a finger on this lady!" said Tryon Dunham as he stepped to the side of his wife and put a strong arm about her, where she stood white and frightened in the doorway.

No one had noticed that the bellboy had come to the head of the stairs and received a quiet order from the detective.

In sudden fear, the discomfited Richard arose and attempted to bluff the stranger.

"Indeed, sir, you wholly misunderstand the situation," he said to Dunham, with an air of injured innocence, "though perhaps you can scarcely be blamed. This girl is an escaped lunatic. We've been searching for her for days and have just traced her. It is our business to take her back at once. Her friends are in great distress about her. Moreover, she is dangerous and a menace to every guest in this house. She has several times attempted murder—"

"Stop!" roared Dunham in a voice of righteous anger. "She is my wife. And you are her cousin. I know all about your plot to shut her up in an insane asylum and steal her fortune. I have found you sooner than I expected, and I intend to see that the law takes its full course with you."

Two policemen arrived on the scene, with a number of eager bellboys and porters in their wake, ready to take part in the excitement.

Richard had turned deadly white at the words, "She is my wife!" It was the death knell of his hopes of securing the fortune for which he had plotted. When he turned and saw impending retribution in the form of the two stalwart policemen, a look of cunning came into his face, and he turned to flee up the staircase.

"Not much, you don't," said a bellboy, flinging himself in the way and tripping up the scoundrel in his flight.

The policemen had him handcuffed in an instant. The Irishman now began to protest that he was but an innocent tool, hired to help discover the whereabouts of an escaped lunatic, as he supposed. He was walked off to the patrol wagon without further ceremony.

It was all over in a few minutes. The elevator carried off the detective, the policemen and their two prisoners. The door closed behind Dunham and his bride, and the curious guests who had peered out, alarmed by the uproar, saw nothing but a few bellboys standing in the hall, describing to one another the scene as they had witnessed it.

Dunham drew the trembling girl into his arms and tried to soothe her. The tears rained down her white cheeks as she lay her head on his chest, and he kissed them away.

"Oh!" she sobbed, shuddering. "If you hadn't come! It was terrible, terrible! I believe he would have killed me rather than let me go again."

Gradually his tender ministrations calmed her, but she turned troubled eyes to his face.

"You don't know yet that I am all I say. You have nothing to prove it. Of course, when I can get to my guardians, and with your help perhaps make them understand, you will know. But I don't see how you can trust me till then."

For answer he brought his hand up in front of her face and turned the flashing diamond—her diamond—so that its glory caught the single ray of the setting sun that filtered into the hotel window.

"See, darling," he said. "It's your ring. I've worn it ever since as an outward sign that I trusted you."

"You are taking me on trust, though, in spite of all you say. And it is beautiful."

He laid his lips upon hers. "Yes," he said. "It is beautiful, and it is best."

It was very still in the room for a moment while she nestled close to him, and his eyes drank in the sweetness of her face.

"See," he said, taking a tiny velvet case from his pocket and touching the spring that opened it. "I amused myself finding a mate to your stone. I thought perhaps you would let me wear your ring always, while you wear mine."

He lifted the jewel from its white velvet bed and showed her the inscription inside: "Mary, from Tryon." Then he slipped it on her finger to guard the wedding ring he had given her at the church. He bent and kissed her again, and their eyes met like other jewels, in which gleamed the glory of their love and trust.

Phoebe Deane

Chapter 1

The night was hot and dark, for the moon rose late. The perfume of the petunia bed hung heavy in the air, and the katydids and crickets kept up a symphony in the orchard close to the house. Its music floated in at the open window and called to the girl as she sat in the darkened upper room rocking Emmeline's baby to sleep in the wooden cradle.

She had washed the supper dishes. The tea towels hung smoothly on the line in the woodshed, the milk pans stood in a shining row ready for the early milking, and the kitchen, swept and dark, had settled into its nightly repose. The day had been long and full of hard work, but now as soon as the baby slept Phoebe would be free for a while before bedtime.

Unconsciously her foot tapped faster on the rocker in her impatience to be out, and the baby stirred and opened his eyes, murmuring sleepily, "Pee-bee, up-e-knee! Pee-bee, up-e-knee!" Interpreted, it was a demand to be taken up on Phoebe's knee.

But Phoebe toned her rocking into a sleepy motion, and the long lashes drooped again on the little cheeks. At last the baby was asleep.

Phoebe slowed the rocking until she could hear the soft regular breathing. Then she rose from her chair and tiptoed from the room.

As she reached the door the baby heaved a long, deep sigh, and Phoebe paused, her heart standing still for an instant lest the baby would waken and demand to be taken up. How many times had she just reached the door, on other hot summer nights, and been greeted by a loud cry which immediately brought Emmeline to the foot of the stairs, with "I declare, Phoebe Deane! Can't you keep that poor child from crying all night?" And Phoebe would be in for an hour or two of singing and rocking and amusing the fretful baby.

But the baby slept on, and Phoebe stepped over the creaking floorboards and down the stairs lightly, scarcely daring to breathe. She slipped past the sitting room door.

Albert, her half brother, was in the sitting room. She could see his outline through the window—his long, thin, kindly face bent over the village paper he'd brought home before supper. Emmeline sat over by the table close to the candle, her sharp features intent on the hole in Johnny's stocking.

Hiram Green, the neighbor whose farm adjoined Albert Deane's on the side next to the village, sat opposite the hall door, his lank form in a splint-bottomed chair tilted back against the wall. His slouch hat was drawn down over his eyes, and his hands were in his pockets. He often sat with Albert in the evening. Sometimes Emmeline called Phoebe in and gave her some darning or mending, and then Phoebe had to listen to Hiram Green's dull talk. To escape it, she'd slip out to the orchard after her work was done. But she couldn't always elude Emmeline's vigilance, for she seemed determined that Phoebe not have a moment to herself.

Phoebe wore a thin white dress. Those thin white dresses she insisted on wearing in the afternoons were one of Emmeline's grievances—so uneconomical and foolish; they'd wear out sometime. Emmeline felt Phoebe should keep her mother's dresses till she married and so save Albert from spending so much on her. Emmeline had a very poor opinion of Phoebe's dead mother; her dress was too fine to belong to a sensible woman, Emmeline thought.

Like some winged creature Phoebe flashed across the path of light that fell from the door and into the orchard. She loved the night with its sounds, scents and velvet darkness, with depths for hiding. Soon the summer would be gone, the branches would be bare against the snow's whiteness, and her solitude and dreaming would be over until the spring again. She cherished every moment of the summer like rich gold.

She loved to sit on the fence separating the orchard from the meadow and wonder what the crickets were saying to each other—whether they talked about their fellows the way people were picked to pieces at the sewing bees. That was how they used to talk about young Mrs. Spafford. Nobody was safe from gossip—for they said Mrs. Spafford belonged to the old Schuyler family. When she came as a bride to the town, how cruel and babbling tongues were!

The girl seated herself in her usual place, leaning against the high crotch of the two upright rails supporting that section of fence. The sky was powdered with stars, the fragrance of the pasture fanned her cheek, and the tree toads joined in the nightly chorus. She heard a crackle of the apple branches, and Hiram Green stepped heavily out from the shadows and stood beside her.

Phoebe had never liked Hiram Green since the day she saw him shove his wife out of his way and say to her, "Aw, shut up, can't you? Women are forever talking about what they don't understand!"

She'd watched the faint color flicker into the wife's pale face and then flicker out again as she tried to laugh his roughness off in front of Phoebe, but the girl had never forgotten it. She was only a little girl then, almost a stranger in town, for her mother had just died and she'd come to live with the half brother who'd been married so long she scarcely knew him. Hiram Green hadn't noticed the young girl then and treated his wife as if no one were present. But Phoebe remembered. She grew to know and love the sad wife, to watch her gentle, patient ways with her boisterous children. And her heart always filled with indignation over the coarse man's rude ways with his wife.

Hiram Green's wife had been dead a year. Phoebe was with her for a week before she died. She had watched the stolid husband without a shadow of anxiety in his eyes tell the neighbors Annie would "be all right in a few days. It was her own fault, anyway, that she got sick. She *would* drive over to see her mother when she wasn't able." He neglected to state she was making preserves and jelly especially for him and prepared dinner for twelve men who were harvesting for a week. He also failed to state she only went to see her mother once in six months, and it was her only holiday.

When Annie died he blamed her as always and hinted that he guessed now she was sorry she hadn't listened to him and been content at home. As if any kind of heaven wouldn't be better than Hiram Green's house.

But Phoebe had stood beside the dying woman as her life flickered out and heard her say, "I ain't sorry to go, Phoebe, for I'm tired. I'd rather rest through eternity than do anything else. I don't think Hiram'll miss me much, and the children ain't like me. They never took after me—only the baby that died. Maybe the baby that died'll want me."

Hiram's only expression of regret was, "It's going to be mighty unhandy, her dying just now. Harvesting ain't over yet, and the meadow lot should be cut before it rains, or the hull thing'll be lost."

Phoebe felt a fierce delight in the fact that everything had to stop for Annie. Whether Hiram would or not, for decency's sake, the work must stop, and the forms of respect must be gone through even though his heart wasn't in it. The rain came, too, to honor Annie—and before the meadow lot was cut.

The funeral over, the farmwork went on with doubled vigor, and Phoebe overheard Hiram tell Albert that "burying Annie had been mighty expensive on account of that thunderstorm coming so soon—it spoiled the whole south meadow; and it was just like Annie to upset everything. If she had only been a little more careful and not gone off to her mother's on pleasure, she might have kept up a little longer till harvest was over."

Phoebe had just come into the sitting room with her sewing when Hiram said that, and she looked indignantly at her brother to see if he wouldn't give Hiram a rebuke. But he only leaned back against the wall and said, "Such things are to be expected in the natural course of life."

Phoebe turned her chair so she wouldn't have to look at Hiram. She despised him. She wished she knew how to show him what a despicable creature he was, but as she was only a young girl she could do nothing but turn her back. She never knew that all that evening Hiram Green watched the back of her shining head, its waves of bright hair bound about with a ribbon and conforming to the beautiful shape of her head. He studied the shapely shoulders and graceful movements of the girl as she patiently mended with her slender fingers.

He remembered that Annie had been "pretty" when he married her, and he could see the good points in the girl Phoebe, even though she sat with her indignant shoulders toward him. In fact, the very sauciness of those shoulders, as the winter went by, attracted him more and more. Annie had never dared be saucy or indifferent. Annie had loved him from the first and had let him know it too soon and too often. It was a new experience to have someone indifferent to him.

He rather liked it, knowing as he did that he always got his own way when he was ready for it.

As the winter went by, Hiram spent more and more evenings with the Deanes, and Phoebe spent more and more of her evenings with Johnny, or the cradle, or in her own room—anything to get away from the unwelcome companionship. Then Emmeline had objected to the extravagance of an extra candle. Emmeline was "thrifty" and could see no sense in a girl wasting a candle when one light would do for all, so the days went by for Phoebe full of hard work and constant companionship, and the evenings with no leisure and no seclusion. Phoebe had longed for the spring to come, when she might get out into the night alone and take long deep breaths that were all her own, for it seemed that even her breathing was ordered and supervised.

But through it all it never once entered Phoebe's head that Hiram was turning his thoughts toward her. So when he came and stood beside her in the darkness he startled her merely because he was something she disliked, and she shrank from him as one would shrink from a snake in the grass.

"Phoebe," he said, putting out his hand to where he supposed her hands would be in the darkness, "ain't it about time you and me was comin' to an understandin'?"

Phoebe slid off the fence and backed away in the darkness. Her heart froze for fear of what might be coming, and she felt she mustn't run away but stay and face whatever it was.

"Whatever do you mean?" said Phoebe, her voice full of antagonism.

"Mean?" said Hiram, sidling after her. "I mean it's time we set up a partnership. I've waited long enough. I need somebody to look after the children. You suit me pretty well, and I guess you'd be well enough fixed with me."

Hiram's air of assurance made Phoebe speechless with horror and indignation.

Taking her silence as a favorable indication, Hiram drew near her and once more tried to find her hands in the darkness.

"I've always liked you, Phoebe," he said. "Don't you like me?"

"No, no, no!" Phoebe almost screamed, snatching her hands away. "Don't ever dare to think such a thing again!"

Then she turned and vanished in the dark like a wraith of mist, leaving the crestfallen Hiram alone, feeling very foolish and not a little astonished. He hadn't expected his suit to be met quite this way.

"Phoebe, is that you?" called Emmeline as she lifted her sharp eyes to peer into the darkness of the entry. "Albert, I wonder if Hiram went the wrong way and missed her?"

But Phoebe was up in her room before Emmeline decided whether she heard anything or not, and Albert went on reading his paper.

Phoebe sat alone in her little kitchen chamber, with the button on the door fastened. She kept very still so Emmeline might not know she was there. Every time she thought of the hateful sound of his voice as he made his cold-blooded proposition, the fierce anger boiled within her. Great waves of hate surged through her soul for the man who had treated one woman so that she was glad to die and now wanted to take her life and crush it out.

Finally she heard Albert and Emmeline shutting up the house for the night. Hiram didn't come back, as she feared he might.

He started to come, then thought better of it and felt his way through the orchard to the other fence and climbed over it into the road. He felt a little dazed and wanted to think things over and adjust himself to Phoebe's point of view. He felt a half resentment toward the Deanes for Phoebe's action, as if the rebuff had been their fault somehow. They should have prepared her better. They understood the situation fully.

They'd often had an interchange of remarks on the subject, and Albert had responded by a nod and a wink. It was tacitly understood that it would be a good thing to have the farms join and keep them "all in the family." Emmeline, too, had often given some practical hints about Phoebe's capabilities as a housewife and mother to his wild little children.

Then he began to wonder if perhaps after all Phoebe wasn't just flirting with him. Surely she couldn't refuse him in earnest. His farm was as pretty as any in the county, and everyone knew he had money in the bank. Surely Phoebe was only being coy for a time. Perhaps it was natural for a girl to be a little shy. It was a way they had, and if it pleased them to hold off a little, why, it showed they'd be all the more sensible afterward. Maybe it was a good thing Phoebe wasn't ready to fall into his arms the minute he asked her. Then she wouldn't always be clinging to him and sobbing in that maddening way Annie had.

By the time he reached home he was pretty well satisfied with himself. As he closed the kitchen door he reflected that perhaps he might fix things up a bit in the house in view of a new mistress. That would probably please Phoebe, and he certainly did need a wife. Then Hiram went to bed and slept soundly.

Emmeline came to Phoebe's door before she went to bed, calling softly, "Phoebe, are you in there?" and tapping on the door two or three times. When no answer came, Emmeline lifted the latch and tried to open the door, but when she found it resisted her, she turned away.

"I s'pose she's sound asleep," she said to Albert in a fretful tone, "but I don't see what call she has to fasten her door every night. It looks so unsociable, as if she was afraid we weren't to be trusted. I wonder you don't speak to her about it."

But Albert only yawned good-naturedly and said, "I don't see how it hurts you any."

"It hurts my self-respect," Emmeline said in an injured tone, as she shut her own door with a click.

Far into the night Phoebe sat looking out the window on the world she loved but couldn't enjoy anymore. The storm of rage and shame and hatred had passed, leaving her weak and miserable and lonely. She put her head down on the windowsill and cried out softly, "Oh, Mother! If only you were here tonight! You'd take me away where I'd never see his hateful face again."

The symphony of the night wailed on about her, as if echoing her cry in throbbing chords, growing fainter as the moon rose, until a sudden hush fell. Then, softly, the music changed into the night's lullaby. All the world slept, and Phoebe slept too.

Chapter 2

Phoebe was late coming downstairs the next morning. Emmeline was already in the kitchen rattling the pots and pans significantly. Emmeline always did that when Phoebe was late, and the degree of her displeasure could be plainly heard.

She looked up sharply as Phoebe entered the room. Dark circles showed under Phoebe's eyes, but otherwise her spirits had arisen with the morning light. She felt only scorn now for Hiram Green and was ready to protect herself. She went straight to her work without a word. Emmeline had long ago expressed herself with regard to the "Good morning" with which the child Phoebe used to greet her when she came down in the morning. Emmeline said it was "a foolish waste of time, and only stuck-up folks use it. It was right along with dressing up at home with no one to see you and curling your hair." And she looked at Phoebe's waves, while her own stood straight as a die.

They worked in silence. The bacon was spluttering to the eggs, and Phoebe was taking up the mush when Emmeline asked, "Didn't Hiram find you last night?" She cast one of her sidelong gazes at the girl as if she'd look through her.

Phoebe started and dropped the spoon back into the mush. She sensed something in Emmeline's tone, then understood at once. The family had been aware of Hiram's intention! Her eyes flashed, and she turned abruptly back to the kettle and went on with her work.

"Yes," she answered inscrutably, which only irritated Emmeline more.

"Well, I didn't hear you come in," she complained. "You must have been out a long time."

"I wasn't out five minutes in all."

"You don't say!" said Emmeline. "I thought you said Hiram found you."

Phoebe put the cover on the dish of mush and set it on the table before she deigned any reply. Then she came over and stood beside Emmeline calmly and spoke in a cool, clear voice.

"Emmeline, did Hiram Green tell you what he was coming out to the orchard for last night?"

"For mercy's sake, Phoebe, don't put on heroics! I'm not blind. One couldn't very well help seeing what Hiram Green wants. Did you think you were the only member of the family with eyes?"

When Emmeline looked up at Phoebe's face, she saw it was white as marble, and her beautiful eyes shone like two stars.

"Emmeline, did you and Albert know what Hiram Green wanted of me, and did you let him come out there to find me after you knew that?"

Her voice was calm and low. Emmeline was awed by it for a moment. She laid down the bread knife and stood and stared. Small and dainty, Phoebe had features cut like a cameo, with a childlike expression when her face was in repose. Emmeline thought her too frail-looking and pale. But for the moment the delicate girl was transformed. Her face shone with a light of righteous anger, and her eyes blazed dark with feeling.

"Phoebe! Now don't!" said Emmeline in a conciliatory tone. "What if I did know? Was that any sin? You must remember your brother and I are looking to your best interests, and Hiram is considered a real fine ketch."

Slowly the fire went out of Phoebe's eyes, and in its place came ice that seemed to pierce Emmeline till she felt like shrinking away.

"You're the strangest girl I ever saw," said Emmeline. "What's the matter with you? Didn't you ever expect to have any beaux?"

Phoebe shivered as if a north blast had struck her at that last word.

"Did you mean, then," she said coldly, "that you thought I'd ever be willing to marry Hiram Green? Did you and Albert talk it over and think that?"

Emmeline found it hard to answer the question, put in a tone which seemed to imply a great offense.

"Well, I'd like to know why you shouldn't marry him!" declared Emmeline. "There's plenty of girls would be glad to get him."

Emmeline glanced out the window and saw Albert and the hired man coming to breakfast. It was time the children were down. Alma came lagging into the kitchen, asking to have her dress buttoned, and Johnny and Bertie scuffled in the rooms overhead. Emmeline was about to dismiss the subject, but Phoebe stepped between her and the little girl and placed her hands on Emmeline's stout, rounding shoulders, looking her straight in the eyes.

"Emmeline, how can you possibly be so unkind as to think such a thing for me when you know how Annie suffered?"

"Oh, fiddlesticks!" said Emmeline, shoving the girl away roughly. "Annie was a milk-and-water baby who wanted to be coddled. The right woman could wind Hiram Green around her finger. You're a little fool if you think about that. Annie's dead and gone, and you've no need to trouble with her. Come, put the things on the table while I button Alma. I'm sure there never was as silly a girl as you are. Anybody'd think you were a princess in disguise instead of a poor orphan dependent on her brother, and he only a *half* at that!" Emmeline slammed the kitchen door and called to the two little boys in a loud, harsh tone.

The crimson rose in Phoebe's cheeks till it covered her face and threatened to bring tears to her eyes. Her soul seemed wrenched from its moorings at the cruel reminder of her dependence upon this coarse woman and her husband. She felt as if she must leave the house at once and never return; only she had no place to go.

Albert appeared at the kitchen door with the hired man behind him, and the sense of duty made her turn to her work, that blessed refuge for those who are turned out of their Eden for a time. She hurried to take up the breakfast while the two men washed their faces at the pump.

"Hello, Phoebe," called Albert as he turned to surrender his place at the comb and mirror. "I say, Phoebe, you're looking like a rose this morning. What makes your cheeks so red? Anybody been kissing you this early?"

This pleasantry was intended as a joke. Albert had never said anything like that to her before. Phoebe guessed that Emmeline had been putting ideas about her and Hiram into his head. It almost brought tears to hear Albert speak like this; he was always so kind to her and treated her as if she were still almost a child. She hated jokes of this sort, and it was all the worse because of Alma and the hired man standing there. Alma grinned knowingly. Henry Williams, the son of a neighboring farmer who had hired himself out for the season, turned and stared admiringly at Phoebe.

"Say, Phoebe," put in Henry, "you do look real pretty this morning. I never noticed before how handsome your eyes were. What's that you said about kissing, Albert? I wouldn't mind taking the job, if it's going. How about it, Phoebe?"

Jesting of this sort was common in the neighborhood, but Phoebe had never joined in it, and she always looked upon it as unrefined. Now that it was directed toward her, and she realized it trifled with the most sacred and personal relations of life, it filled her with horror.

"Please don't, Albert!" she said in a low voice. "Don't! I don't like it."

Alma saw with wonder that there were tears in Aunt Phoebe's eyes and gloated over it. That would be something to remember and tell. Aunt Phoebe usually kept her emotions to herself with the door shut too tight for anyone to peep in.

"No?" said Albert, perplexed. "Well, 'course I won't if you don't like it. I was only telling you how bright and pretty you looked and making you know how nice it was to have you around. Sit down, child, and let's have breakfast. Where's your mother, Alma?"

Emmeline entered with a flushed face and a couple of small boys held firmly by the shoulders.

Somewhat comforted by Albert's assurance, Phoebe finished her work and sat down at the table. But every time she raised her eyes she found a battalion of other eyes staring at her.

Emmeline glanced at her in puzzled annoyance that her well-planned matchmaking wasn't running as smoothly as expected. Albert studied her in the astonishing discovery that the thin, sad little half sister he'd brought into his home, who had seemed so lifeless and colorless and unlike the other girls of the neighborhood, had suddenly become beautiful and was almost a woman.

The worst pair of eyes belonged to Henry Williams, bold and intimate, who sat directly opposite her. He seemed to feel that the way had been opened for him by Albert's words and only awaited his opportunity to enter in. He'd admired

Phoebe ever since he came there early in the spring, and he wondered that no one seemed to think her of much account. But somehow her quiet dignity always kept him at a distance. But now he felt he was justified in being more free with her.

"Did you hear that singing school was going to open early this fall, Phoebe?" he asked, after clearing his throat.

"No," Phoebe said without looking up.

That rather disappointed him, for it had taken him a long time to think up that subject, and it was too much to have it disposed of so quickly, without even a glimpse of her eyes.

"Do you usually 'tend?" he asked again after a pause.

"No," Phoebe said again, her eyes still down.

"Phoebe didn't go because there wasn't anyone for her to come home with before, Hank, but I guess there'll be plenty now," said Emmeline with a meaningful laugh.

"Yes," Phoebe said, looking up calmly. "Hester McVane and Polly said they were going this winter. If I decide to go I'm going with them. Emmeline, if you're going to dry those apples today, I'd better begin them. Excuse me, please."

"You haven't eaten any breakfast, Aunt Phoebe! Ma, Aunt Phoebe never touched a bite!" announced Alma.

"I'm not hungry this morning," Phoebe said as she escaped from the room, having baffled the gaze of the man and the child and wrested the dart from her sister-in-law's arrow.

It was hard on the man, for he'd decided to ask Phoebe if she'd go to singing school with him. He sought her out in the woodshed where she sat, and he gave his invitation, but she only made her fingers fly faster around the apple she was peeling.

"Thank you, but it won't be necessary for you to go with me if I decide to go." Then she arose hastily, exclaiming, "Emmeline, did you call me? I'm coming," and vanished into the kitchen.

The hired man looked after her wistfully.

Phoebe was not a weeping girl. Ever since her mother died she'd lived a life of self-repression, hiding her inmost feelings from the world, for her world since then hadn't proved to be a sympathetic one. She quickly perceived that no one in this new atmosphere would understand her sensitive nature.

Refinements and culture had been hers that these new relatives didn't know or understand. She looked at Albert wistfully sometimes, for she felt if it weren't for Emmeline she might in time make him understand and change a little in some ways. But Emmeline resented any suggestions she made to Albert. Emmeline resented almost everything about Phoebe. She had resented her coming in the first place. Albert was grown up and living away from home when his father married Phoebe's mother, a delicate, refined woman, far different from him. Emmeline felt that Albert had no call to take the child in at all when she wasn't a "real relation." Besides, Emmeline had an older sister of her own who would have been glad to come and live with them and help with the work. But of course there was no room or excuse for her with Phoebe there, and they couldn't afford to have them both, although Albert was ready to take in any stray chick or child that came along.

But in spite of her nature this morning Phoebe had much to do to keep from crying. If not for her work she would have felt desperate. As it was she kept steadily at it. The apples fairly flew out of their skins into the pan, and Emmeline, glancing into the back shed and noting the set of the forbidding young shoulders and the fast-diminishing pile of apples on the floor, decided it best not to disturb her. She was anxious to have those apples off her mind. And with Phoebe in that mood she knew it would be done before she could possibly get around to help. There was time enough for remarks later.

The old stone sundial by the side door shadowed the hour of eleven when Emmeline came into the shed with a knife and sat down to help. She looked at Phoebe sharply as she seated herself. She intended to have it out with the girl.

Phoebe didn't help her begin. Her fingers flew faster than ever, though they ached with the motion. With set lips she went on with her work, though she longed to fling the apple away and run out to the fields for a long deep breath.

Emmeline pared two whole apples before she began. She eyed Phoebe furtively several times, but the girl might have been a sphinx. This was what Emmeline couldn't stand, this distant, proud silence that wouldn't mix with other folk. She longed to break through it by force and reduce the pride to dust. It would do her heart good to see Phoebe humbled for once, she often told herself.

"Phoebe, I don't see what you find to dislike so in Hiram Green," she began. "He's a good man. He always attends church on Sunday."

"I would respect him more if he was a good man in his home on weekdays. Anybody can be good once a week before people. A man needs to be good at home in his family."

"Well, now, he pervides well for his family. Look at his comfortable home and his farm. There isn't a finer in this county. He has his name up all around this region for the fine stock he raises. You can't find a barn like his anywhere. It's the biggest and most expensive in this town."

"He certainly has a fine barn," said Phoebe, "but I don't suppose he expects his family to live in it. He takes better care of his stock than he does of his family. Look at the house—"

Emmeline marveled at the scorn in Phoebe's voice. She was brought up to think a barn one of the most important features of one's possessions.

"It's a miserable affair. Low and ugly and with two steps between the kitchen and the shed, enough to kill one who does the work. He should have built Annie a pleasant home up on that lovely little knoll of maples, where she could have seen out and down the road and had a little company now and then. She might be alive today if she had one-half the care and attention Hiram gave the stock!" Phoebe's words were bitter and vehement.

"It sounds dreadful silly for a girl your age to be talking like that. You don't know anything about Annie, and if I was you I wouldn't think about her. As for the barn, I'd think a wife would be proud to have her husband's barn the nicest one in the county. I declare you do have the strangest notions!"

Nevertheless, she determined she'd give Hiram a hint about the house.

Phoebe didn't reply. She was peeling the last apple, and as soon as it lay with the rest she shoved back her chair and left the shed. Emmeline felt she'd failed again to make any impression on her sister-in-law. It maddened her to have a girl like that around, who thought everything beneath her and criticized the customs of the entire neighborhood. She was an annoyance and a reproach. Emmeline felt she'd like to get rid of her if it could be done in a legitimate way.

At dinner, Henry Williams looked at Phoebe and asked if she'd made the pie. Phoebe said she had.

"It tastes like you, nice and sweet," he declared gallantly.

At this remark, Albert laughed, and Alma leaned forward to look into her aunt's flaming face.

"Betsy Green says she thinks her pa is going to get her a new ma," Alma said when the laugh subsided. "And Betsy says she bets she knows who 'tis, too!"

"You shut up!" Emmeline hissed, giving Alma a dig under the table.

But Phoebe hastily pushed back her chair and fled from the table.

A moment of uncomfortable silence ensued after Phoebe left the room. Emmeline felt that things had gone too far. Albert asked what was the matter with Phoebe, but instead of answering him Emmeline yanked Alma from the table and out into the woodshed, where a whispered scolding was administered, followed by a switching.

Alma returned to the table chastened outwardly but inwardly vowing vengeance on her aunt. She determined to get even with Aunt Phoebe even if another switching happened.

Phoebe didn't come downstairs again that afternoon. Emmeline hesitated about sending for her and finally decided to wait until she came. The unwilling Alma was pressed into service to dry the dishes, and the long, sunny afternoon dragged drowsily on, while Phoebe lay on her bed up in her kitchen chamber and wondered why so many tortures were coming to her all at once.

Chapter 3

Hiram Green kept his word to himself and didn't go to see Phoebe for two evenings. Emmeline wondered what in the world Phoebe had said to him to keep him away when he seemed so anxious to get her. But the third evening he arrived promptly, attired with unusual care, and asked Emmeline if he might see Phoebe alone.

Phoebe had finished her work in the kitchen and gone up to rock the baby to sleep. Emmeline swept the younger children out of the sitting room and called Albert sharply to help her with something in the kitchen, sending Alma up with a carefully worded message to Phoebe. Emmeline was relieved to see Hiram again. She knew by his face that he meant business this time, and she hoped to see Phoebe conquered at once.

When Phoebe came down to the sitting room, she explained quietly as she entered, "I couldn't come sooner. Alma woke the baby again."

Hiram, mollified by the gentle tone of explanation, arose, answering, "Oh, that's all right. I'm glad to see you now you're here," and reached out with the evident intention of taking both her hands in his.

Phoebe looked up in horror, knowing Alma stood behind the crack of the door and watched it all with wicked joy.

"I beg your pardon, Mr. Green. I thought Emmeline was in here. She sent for me. Excuse me— I must find her."

"Oh, that's all right!" said Hiram, putting out his hand and shutting the door sharply in Alma's impudent face. "She don't expect you—Emmeline don't. She sent for you to see me. I asked her could I see you alone. She understands all about us—Emmeline does. She won't come in here for a while. She knows I want to talk to you."

Cold chills crept down Phoebe's back and froze her heart. Had the horror returned with redoubled vigor and with her family behind it? Where was Albert? Wouldn't he help her? Then she realized she must help herself and at once, for it was evident Hiram Green meant to press his suit energetically. He was coming toward her with his hateful, confident smile. He stood between her and the door. Besides, what good would it do to run away? She had tried that once, and it didn't work. She must speak to him and end the matter. She summoned all her dignity and courage and backed over to the other side of the room, where a single chair stood.

"Won't you sit down, Mr. Green?" she said.

"Why, yes, I will. Let's sit right here together," he said, sitting down at one end of the couch and making room for her. "Come, you sit here beside me, Phoebe, and then we can talk better. It's more sociable."

Phoebe sat down on the chair opposite him.

"I would rather sit here, Mr. Green," she said.

"Well, of course, if you'd rather," he said. "But it seems to be kind of unsociable. And I wish you wouldn't 'mister' me anymore. Can't you call me Hiram?"

"I would rather not."

"That sounds real unfriendly," Hiram said in a tone that suggested he wouldn't be trifled with much longer.

"Did you wish to speak to me, Mr. Green?" said Phoebe, her clear eyes looking at him steadily over the candlelight.

"Well, yes," he said, straightening up and hitching a chair around to the side nearer to her. "I thought we better talk that matter over a little that I mentioned to you several nights ago."

"I don't think that's necessary, Mr. Green," answered Phoebe. "I thought I made you understand that was impossible."

"Oh, I didn't take account of what you said that night," said Hiram. "I saw you was sort of upset, not expecting me out there in the dark, so I thought I better come round again after you had plenty chance to think over what I said."

"I couldn't say anything different if I thought it over for a thousand years," declared Phoebe. Hiram Green was not thin-skinned; it was just as well to tell the truth and be done with it.

But the fellow wasn't daunted. He admired Phoebe all the more for her vehemence, for here was a prize worth winning.

"Aw, git out!" said Hiram pleasantly. "That ain't the way to talk. 'Course you're young yet and ain't had much experience, but you certainly had time enough to consider the matter all this year I been comin' to see you."

Phoebe rose to her feet.

"Coming to see me!" she gasped. "You don't come to see me!"

"Now, Phoebe. You needn't pertend you didn't know I was comin' to see you. Who did you s'pose I was comin' to see then?"

"I supposed you were coming to see Albert," said Phoebe.

"Albert! You s'posed I was comin' to see Albert every night! Aw, yes, you did a whole lot! Phoebe, you're a sly one. You must of thought I was gettin' fond of Albert!"

"I didn't think anything about it," said Phoebe haughtily, "and you may be sure, Mr. Green, if I had dreamed of such a thing I would have told you it was useless."

Something in her tone and matter ruffled Hiram Green's self-assurance. Up to this minute he'd persuaded himself that Phoebe was only acting coy. Was it possible she didn't care for his attentions and really wished to dismiss him? Hiram couldn't credit such a thought. Yet the firm set of her lips bewildered him.

"What on earth makes you keep sayin' that?" he asked in an irritated tone.

"What's your reason for not wantin' to marry me?"

"There are so many reasons I wouldn't know where to begin," said the girl. Had he heard her right?

"What reasons?" he growled, frowning. He began to feel that Phoebe was trifling with him. He'd make her understand he wouldn't endure much of that.

Phoebe looked troubled. She wished he wouldn't insist on further talk, but she was too honest—too angry—not to tell the exact truth.

"The first and greatest reason is that I do not love you and never could," she said, looking him straight in the eyes.

"Shucks!" said Hiram, laughing. "I don't mind that a mite. In fact, I think it's an advantage. Folks mostly get over it when they do feel that sentimental kind of way. It don't last but a few weeks, anyhow, and it's better to begin on a practical basis, I think. That was the trouble with Annie. She was so blamed sentimental she hadn't time to get dinner. I think you an' I'd get along much better. You're practical and a good worker. We could manage things real prosperous over to the farm—"

Phoebe arose quickly and interrupted him.

"Mr. Green, you must please stop talking this way. It is horrible! I don't want to listen to any more of it."

"You set down, Phoebe," commanded Hiram. "I've got some things to tell you. It ain't worth yer while to act foolish. I mean business. I want to get married. It's high time there was somebody to see to things at home, but I can wait a little while if you're wantin' to get ready more. Only don't be long about it. As I said, I don't mind about the love part. That'll come all right. And you remember, Phoebe, there's plenty of girls around here that would be glad to marry me if they got the chance."

"Then, by all means, let them marry you!" said Phoebe, steadying her trembling limbs for flight. "I shall never, never marry you! Good night, Mr. Green."

She swept out the door and was gone before he fully took it in. The latch clicked behind her, and he could hear the soft stir of her garments on the stairs. He heard the button on her door creak and turn. He went after her as far as the door, but the stairway was quiet and dark. He could hear Albert and Emmeline in the kitchen. He stood a moment, puzzled, going over the conversation and trying to make it all out.

What mistake had he made? He had failed, that was certain. It was a new experience and one that angered him, but somehow the anger was blunted by the memory of the look in the girl's eyes, the dainty movement of her hands, the set of her shapely head. He didn't know he was fascinated by her beauty; he only knew that a dogged determination to have her for his own was settling down upon him.

Albert and Emmeline were talking in low tones in the kitchen when the door was flung open and Hiram Green stepped in, his brow dark.

"I can't make her out!" he muttered as he flung himself into a kitchen chair. "She's for all the world like a wild colt. When you think you have her she gives you the slip and is off further away than when you begun.

"What's the matter with her anyway?" Hiram growled, turning to Emmeline, as though she were responsible for all of womankind. "Is there anybody else? She ain't got in with Hank Williams, has she?"

"She won't look at him," Emmeline said. "He tried to get her to go to singin' school with him today, but she shut him off short. What reason did she give you?"

"She spoke about not havin' proper affection," he said, "but if I was dead sure that was the hull trouble I think I could fix her up. I'd like to get things settled 'fore winter comes on. I can't afford to waste time like this."

"I think I know what's the matter with her," said Emmeline. "She isn't such a fool as to give up a good chance in life for reasons of affection, though it is mighty high-soundin' to say so. But there's somethin' back of it all. I shouldn't wonder, Hiram, if she's tryin' you to see if you want her enough to fix things handy the way she'd like 'em."

"What do you mean?" Hiram asked, gruffly, showing sudden interest. "Has she spoke of anything to you?"

"Well, she did let on that your house was a bit unpleasant, and she seemed to think the barn had the best location. She spoke about the knoll being a good place for a house."

Hiram brightened.

"You don't say! When did she say that?"

"Just today," Emmeline answered.

"Well, if that's the hitch, why didn't she say so? She didn't seem shy."

"Mebbe she was waitin' for you to ask her what she wanted."

"Well, she didn't wait long. She lit out before I had a chance to half talk things over."

"She's young yet, you know," said Emmeline in a soothing tone. "Young folks take odd notions. I shouldn't wonder but she hates to go to that house and live way back from the road that way. She ain't much more than a child in some things—though she's first-class when it comes to work."

"Well," said Hiram, "I been thinkin' the house needed fixin' up some. I don't know as I should object to buildin' all new. The old house would come in handy fer the men. Bill would like to have his ma and keep house right well. It would help me out in one way, fer Bill is gettin' uneasy, and I'd rather spare any man I've got than Bill—he works so steady and good. You might mention to Phoebe, if you like, that I'm thinkin' of buildin' a new house. Say I'd thought of the knoll for a location. Think that might ease her up a little?"

"I'll see what can be done," said Emmeline matter-of-factly.

The atmosphere in the kitchen brightened as if extra candles had been brought in. Satisfied, Hiram lit his pipe, tilted his chair back in his accustomed way and entered into a brisk discussion of politics while Emmeline busied herself with kitchen work.

Emmeline mentally rehearsed the line of argument with which she intended to ply Phoebe the next day. She felt triumphant. Not every matchmaker would have had the grit to tell Hiram just what was wanted. Surely Phoebe would listen now.

Up in her kitchen chamber, Phoebe sat with burning cheeks, looking wildly into the darkness. She didn't hear the nightly symphony outside. She was thinking of what she had been through and wondered if she'd finally freed herself from the hateful attentions of Hiram Green. Would he take her answer as final or not? She thought not, judging from his nature. He was one of those men who never gave up what they'd set themselves to get, be it sunny pasture, young heifer or pretty wife. She shuddered at the thought of many more encounters such as the one she'd passed through tonight. It was all dreadful to her.

She wondered what her life would be like if her mother were alive—a quiet little home, of course, plain and sweet and cozy, with plenty of hard work, but always someone to sympathize. Her frail mother hadn't been able to stand the rough world and hard work, but she had left behind her a memory of gentleness and refinement that couldn't be crushed out of her young daughter's heart, no matter how much she came in contact with the coarse, rude world.

Often, in her silent meditations, the girl would take her mother into her thoughts and tell her all that had happened that day. But tonight she felt that were her mother here, she couldn't bear to tell her of the horrid experience she'd endured. She knew instinctively that her mother, if alive, would shrink with horror from the thought of her child being united to a man like Hiram Green.

Tonight she needed some close, tangible help, someone all-wise and powerful; someone who could tell what God meant her life to be and make her sure she was right in her fierce recoil from what life seemed to be offering. She felt sure she was right, yet she wanted another to say so also, to take her part against the world that was troubling her.

Her young pride rose and bore her up. She must tell nobody but God. And so she knelt timidly down and poured out her wounded spirit in a prayer. She had always prayed but never felt it meant anything to her until tonight. When she arose, not knowing what she'd asked, or if indeed she'd asked anything for herself, she yet felt stronger to face her life, which somehow stretched out ahead in monotonous torture.

Meanwhile, the man who desired to have her, and the woman who desired to have him have her, formed their plans for a campaign against her.

Chapter 4

It was the first day of October and Phoebe's birthday. The sun shone clear and high, and the sky overhead was a dazzling blue. Off in the distance a blue haze lay softly over the horizon, mingling the crimsons and golds of the autumn foliage with the fading greens. It was a perfect day, and Phoebe was out enjoying it.

She walked with a purpose, as though it did her good to push the road back under her impatient feet. She wasn't walking toward the village but out into the open country, past the farm, where presently the road turned and skirted a maple grove. But she didn't pause here, though she loved the crimson maple leaves that carpeted the ground. On she went, as though her only object was to get away.

A farm wagon approached. She strained her eyes ahead to see who was driving. What if it happened to be Hank and he stopped to talk! She wished she'd worn her sunbonnet so she might hide in its depths, but her departure had been too sudden for that. She'd simply untied her apron and flung it from her as she started. Even now she didn't know whether it hung on the chair where she'd been sitting shelling dried beans or whether it adorned the rosebush by the kitchen door. She hadn't looked back to see.

No one knew it was her birthday, or, if they knew, they hadn't remembered. Perhaps that made it harder to stay and shell beans and bear Emmeline's talk.

Matters had been going on in much the way they'd gone all summer—at least outwardly. Hiram Green still spent the evenings talking with Albert while Emmeline darned stockings and Phoebe escaped upstairs when she could and sewed with her back to the guest when she couldn't. Phoebe had taken diligent care that Hiram should have no more tête-à-têtes with her, even at the expense of having to spend many evenings in her dark room when all outdoors beckoned her with the lovely sounds of the dying summer. Grimly and silently she went through the days of work.

Emmeline, since the morning she attempted to discuss Hiram's proposed new house and found Phoebe unresponsive, had held her peace. Not that she was by any means vanquished, but, having made so little headway in talking to the girl, she concluded it would be well to let her alone a while. In fact, Albert had advised that line of action in his kind way, and Emmeline shut her lips and went around with an air of offended dignity. She spoke disagreeably whenever it was necessary to speak at all to Phoebe, and whenever the girl came downstairs in anything other than her working garments Emmeline showed her disapproval in unspeakable volumes.

Phoebe went about her daily routine without noticing, much as a bird might whose plumage was being criticized. She couldn't help putting herself in dainty array, even though the materials at hand might be only a hairbrush and a bit of ribbon. Her hair was always waving about her lovely face, and a tiny rim of white collar outlined the throat, even in her homespun morning gown. It was all hateful to Emmeline—"impudent," she called it, in speaking to herself. She had tried the phrase once in a confidence to Albert, but somehow he hadn't understood. He almost resented it. He said he thought Phoebe always looked "real neat and pretty," and he "liked to see her around." This had fired Emmeline's jealousy, although she wouldn't have owned it. Albert made so many remarks of this sort that Emmeline felt they'd spoil his sister and make her unbearable to live with.

But Emmeline continued to meditate upon Phoebe's "impudent" attire until the afternoon of her birthday, when the thoughts culminated in words.

Phoebe had gone upstairs after the dinner work was finished and come down arrayed in a gown Emmeline had never seen. It was of soft buff merino, trimmed with narrow lines of brown velvet ribbon, and a bit of the same velvet around the throat held a small gold locket that nestled in the white hollow of Phoebe's neck as if it loved to be there. The brown hair was dressed in its usual way except for a knot of brown velvet. It was a simple girlish costume, and Phoebe wore it with the same easy grace she wore her homespun, which made it doubly annoying for Emmeline.

Years ago when Phoebe had come to live with them she brought with her some boxes and trunks and a few pieces of furniture for her own room. They were things of her mother's which she wished to keep. Emmeline had gone over the collection with ruthless hand and critical tongue, casting out what she considered useless, laying aside what she considered unfit for present use and freely commenting upon all she saw. Phoebe, fresh from her mother's grave, had stood by in stony silence, holding back the angry tears that tried to get their way. But when Emmeline had reached the large trunk and demanded the key, Phoebe had quietly cropped the string that held it round her neck inside her dress, where it lay cold against her heart.

"You needn't open that, Emmeline. It holds my mother's dresses that she put away for me when I grow up."

"Nonsense!" Emmeline answered sharply. "I think I'm the best judge of whether it needs to be opened or not. Give me the key at once. I'm not going to have things in my house that I don't know anything about. I've got to see they're packed away from moths."

Phoebe's lips had trembled, but she continued to talk steadily. "It's not necessary, Emmeline. My mother packed them all away carefully in lavender and rosemary for me. She didn't wish them opened till I got ready to open them myself. I don't want them opened."

Emmeline had been very angry at that and told the little girl she wouldn't have any such talk around her. She demanded the key at once.

But Phoebe said, "I've told you it's not necessary. These are my things, and I will not have any more of them opened, and I will not give you the key."

That was open rebellion, and Emmeline carried her to Albert. Albert had looked at the pitiful little face with its pleading eyes—and sided with Phoebe. He said Phoebe was right, the things were hers, and he didn't see why Emmeline wanted to open them. From that hour Emmeline barely tolerated her little half sister-in-law, and the enmity between them had never grown less. Little did Phoebe know, whenever she wore one of the dresses from that unopened trunk, how she roused her sister-in-law's wrath.

The trunk had been stored in the closet in Phoebe's room, and the key had never left its resting place against her heart, night or day. Sometimes Phoebe unlocked it in the still hours of the early summer mornings when no one else was stirring, and she looked lovingly at the garments folded within. It was there she kept the daguerreotype of her beloved mother. Her father she couldn't remember, since he died when she was only a year old. In the depths of the trunk lay several large packages labeled: "For my dear daughter Phoebe Deane on her eighteenth birthday."

For several days before her birthday Phoebe had felt an undertone of excitement. It was almost time to open the box which had been packed more than eight years ago by her mother's hand. Phoebe didn't know what was in the box, but she knew it was something her mother put there for her. It contained her mother's thought for her grown-up daughter. It was like a voice from the grave. It thrilled her to think of it.

On her birthday morning she awakened with the light and applied the little black key to the keyhole. Her fingers trembled as she turned the lock and opened the lid. She wanted this sacred gift all to herself now, this moment when her soul would touch again the soul of the lost mother.

Carefully she lifted out the treasures in the trunk until she reached the box, then drew it forth. She placed the other things back, closed the trunk and locked it. She took the box to her bed and untied it. Her heart beat so fast she felt as if she'd been running. She lifted the cover. There lay the buff merino in all its beauty, complete with the brown knot for the hair and the locket which had been her mother's at eighteen. And there on the top lay a letter in her mother's handwriting. Ah! This was what she had hoped for—a real word from her mother that could guide her in this grown-up life that was so lonely and different from the life she had lived with her mother.

She hugged the letter to her heart and cried over it.

But the house was beginning to stir, and Phoebe knew she would be expected in the kitchen before long, so she dried her tears and read her letter.

Before she was half done the clatter in the kitchen had begun, and Emmeline's strident voice called up the stairway: "Phoebe! Phoebe! Are you going to stay up there all day?"

Phoebe cast a wistful look at the rest of her letter, patted the soft folds of her merino tenderly, swept it out of sight into her closet and answered Emmeline, "Yes, I'm coming!" Not even the interruption could dim her pleasure on this day.

It didn't take long to dress, and with the letter tucked in with the key against her heart she hurried down, only to meet Emmeline's frowning words and be ordered around like a child.

The morning passed away happily in spite of Emmeline and hard work. Words from her mother's hastily read letter floated back to her. She longed to pull it out and read it once more. But there was no time.

After dinner, however, as soon as she finished the dishes and while Emmeline was looking after something in the woodshed, she slipped away upstairs. She'd decided she would put on her new dress, for it had been her mother's wish in the letter, and go down to the village and call on Mrs. Spafford. She felt she had a right to a little time to herself on her birthday, and she meant to slip away without Emmeline seeing, if she could. With the letter safely hidden she hurried down.

But her conscience wouldn't let her go out the front door as she'd planned. It seemed a mean, sneaking thing to do on her birthday. She would be open and frank. She would step into the kitchen and tell Emmeline she was going out for the afternoon. So, though much against her own desire, she went.

And there sat Emmeline with a large basket of dried beans to be shelled and put away for the winter. Phoebe stood aghast and hesitated.

"Well, really!" said Emmeline, looking up severely at the apparition in buff that stood in the doorway. "Are you going to play the fine lady while I shell beans? It occurs to me that's rather taking a high hand for one who's dependent on her relatives for every mouthful she eats. That's gratitude, that is. But I take notice you eat the beans—oh, yes! The beans Albert provides and I shell, while you gallivant round in party clothes."

The hateful speech brought a flush to Phoebe's cheeks.

"Emmeline," she broke in, "you know I didn't know you wanted those beans shelled today. I would have done them this morning if you'd said so."

"You didn't know," sniffed Emmeline. "You knew the beans was to shell, and you knew this was the first chance to do it. Now you wash your white hands and dress up, no matter what the folks that keeps you have to do. That wasn't the way *I* was brought up. I didn't have a fine lady mother like yours. My mother taught me *gratitude*."

Phoebe reflected on the long hard days of work she'd done for Emmeline without a word of praise or thanks, work as hard or harder than any wage earner in the same position would have been expected to do. She had earned her board and more, and she knew it. She made her clothes from the material her mother had left for her. She hadn't cost Albert a cent in that way. Nevertheless, her conscience hurt her because of the late hour of her coming down that morning. With one desperate glance at the size of the bean basket and a rapid calculation of how long it would take her to finish them, she seized her clean apron that hung behind the door and enveloped herself in it.

"I've wanted to go for a long time, but if those beans have to be done this afternoon I can do them first."

She spoke calmly and went at the beans with determined fingers.

Emmeline sniffed.

"You're a pretty figure shellin' beans in that rig. I s'pose that's one of your ma's outfits, but if she had any sense at all she wouldn't want you to put it on. It ain't fit for ordinary life. It might do to have your picture took in or go to a weddin', but you do look like a fool in it now. Besides, if it's worth anything, an' it looks like there was good stuff in it, you'll spoil it shellin' beans."

Phoebe shelled away feverishly and said not a word. Emmeline surveyed her angrily. Her wrath verged on the boiling point, and she felt the time had come to let it boil.

"I think the time has come to have an understandin'," said Emmeline, raising her voice harshly. "If you won't talk to me, Albert'll have to tend to you, but I'm the proper one to speak, and I'm goin' to do it. I won't have this sort of thing goin' on in my house. It's a disgrace. I'd like to know what you mean, treatin' Hiram Green this way? He's a respectable man, and you've no call to keep him danglin' after you forever. People'll talk about you, and I won't have it!"

Phoebe raised astonished eyes to her sister-in-law's agitated face.

"I don't know what you mean, Emmeline. I have nothing whatever to do with Hiram Green. I can't prevent him from coming to my brother's house. I wish I could, for it's most unpleasant to have him around continually."

The cool words angered Emmeline even more.

"You don't know what I mean!" mocked Emmeline. "No, of course not. You don't know who he comes here to see. You think, I suppose, he comes to see Albert and me. Well, you're not so much of a little fool as you want to pretend. You know well enough Hiram Green is just waitin' round on your whims, and I say it's high time you stopped this nonsense, keepin' a respectable man danglin' after you forever just to show off your power over him, and when all the time he needs a housekeeper and his children are runnin' wild. You'll get your pay, miss, when you do marry him. Those young ones will be so wild you'll never get 'em tamed. I think it's time for you to speak, for I tell you plainly it ain't likely another such chance'll come your way ever, and I don't suppose you want to be a hanger-on all your life on people that can't afford to keep you."

Phoebe's fingers still shelled beans rapidly, but her eyes were on Emmeline's angry face.

"I thought I told you," she said, her voice steady, "that I would never marry Hiram Green. Nothing and nobody on earth could make me marry him. I despise him. You know perfectly well that the things you're saying are wrong. It isn't my fault he comes here. I don't want him to come, and he knows it. I have told him I will never marry him. Nothing he could do would make any difference."

"You're a little fool to let such a chance go!" screamed Emmeline. "If he wasn't entirely daft about you he'd give you up at once. Well, what are you intendin' to do then? Answer me that! Are you layin' out to live on Albert the rest of your life? It's best to know what to expect and be prepared. Answer me!"

Phoebe dropped her eyes to hide the sudden tears that threatened to overwhelm her calm.

"I don't know." The girl tried to say it quietly, but the angry woman snatched the words from her lips and tossed them back.

"You don't know! You don't know! Well, you better know! I can tell you right now that there's goin' to be a new order of things. If you stay here any longer you've got to do as I say. You're not goin' on your high-and-mighty way doin' as you please an hour longer. And to begin with you can march upstairs and take off that ridiculous rig of your foolish mother's—"

Phoebe shoved the kitchen chair back with a sharp noise on the bare floor and stood up, her face white with anger.

"Emmeline," she said, and her voice was low and controlled, but it reminded Emmeline of the first low rumbling of a storm. "Emmeline, don't you dare to speak my mother's name in that way! I will not listen to you!"

Phoebe cast her apron from her and went out through the kitchen door, into the golden October afternoon, away from the cruel tongue, the endless beans—and the sorrow of her life.

The sunlight lingered on the buff merino, as though it had come out to meet it, and she flitted breathlessly down the way, she didn't know where, only to get out and away. All the air was filled with golden haze, and Phoebe, in her golden, sunlit garments, seemed a part of it.

Chapter 5

Phoebe felt desperate as she fled along the road, pursued by the thought of her sister-in-law's angry words.

To have such awful words spoken to her and on her birthday! To feel so cornered and badgered, and to have no home where one was welcome, save that hateful alternative of going to Hiram Green's house! Oh, why did one have to live when life had become a torture?

She had gone a long distance before her mind cleared enough to think where she was going. The sight of a distant red farmhouse made her pause in her wild walk. If she went on she'd be seen from the well-watched windows of that red house, and the two women who lived there were noted for their curiosity and their ability to impart news.

In sudden panic Phoebe climbed a fence and struck out across the field toward Chestnut Ridge, a small hill rising to the left of the village. There she might hope to be alone a little while and think it out and perhaps creep close to her mother once more through the letter. She hurried over the rough stubble of the field, gathering her buff garments in her hand to hold them from any detaining briars.

Breathless, at last she reached the hill and found a log where she sat down to read her letter.

My dear little grown-up girl,

This is your eighteenth birthday, and I've thought so much about you and how you will be when you're a young woman, that I want to be with you a little while on your birthday and let you know how very much I love you. I can't look forward into your life and see how it will be with you. I don't know whether you'll have had sad years or bright ones between the time when I said good-bye to you and now when you are reading this. I had to leave you in God's care, and I know you'll be taken care of, whatever comes.

If there have been trials, somehow, Phoebe, they must have been good for you. Someday you will learn why, and sometime there will be a way out. Never forget that. God has His brightness ready somewhere for you if you are true to Him and brave. I'm afraid there will have been trials, perhaps very heavy ones, for you were always such a sensitive little soul, and you're going among people who may not understand.

In thinking about your life I've been afraid you would be tempted because of unhappiness to take some rash, impulsive step before God is ready to show you His plan for your life. I would like to give you a little warning through the years and tell you to be careful.

You have entered young womanhood and will perhaps be asked to give your life into the keeping of some man. If I were going to live I would try to train you through the years for this great crisis in your life. But when it comes, remember that I've thought about you and longed for you to find another soul who will love you better than himself, and whom you can love better than you love anything else in the world, and who will be noble in every way.

Dear child, hear your mother's voice, and don't take anything less. It won't matter so much if he is poor, if only he loves you better than himself and is worthy of your love. Never marry anyone for a home or a chance to have your own way or freedom from good honest work. There will be no happiness in it. Trust your mother, for she knows. Do not marry anyone to whom you cannot look up and give honor next to God. Unless you can marry such a man it is better not to marry at all, believe me. I say it lovingly, for I've seen much sorrow and want to protect you.

And now, my sweet child, if when you read this anything has come into your life to make you unhappy, just try to lay it all down for a little while and feel your mother's love about you. See, I have made this bright sunny dress for you, every stitch set with love, and I want you to wear it on your birthday to remind you of me. It is yellow, because that's the glory color, the color of the sunshine I've always loved so much. I want you to think of me in a bright, happy way, as in a glory of happiness waiting for you; not as dead and lying in the grave. Think of my love for you as a joy, and not a lost one either, for I'm sure that where I'm going I shall love you just the same, and more.

I'm very tired and must not write anymore, for there's much to do before I can feel ready to go and leave you. But as I write this birthday letter for you I am praying that God will bring some brightness into your life, the beginning of some great joy, on this your eighteenth birthday, that shall be His blessing and my birthday gift to you. I put a kiss here where I write my name and give you with it more love than you can ever understand.

Your Mother

Tears ran down onto her hands as she held the letter, and when it was finished she put her head on her lap and cried as she hadn't cried since her mother died.

The sunlight sifted down between the yellowed chestnut leaves, sprinkling gold on the golden hem of her gown and glinting on her shining hair. The brown nuts dropped now and then about her, reverently, as if they wouldn't disturb her if they could help it, and the fat gray squirrels silently regarded her, pausing in their work of gathering the winter's store, then whisked noiselessly away.

Phoebe didn't sob aloud. Her grief was deeper than that. Her soul cried out to one who was far away and yet who seemed so near to her that nothing else mattered for the time.

Would her mother have been just as sure her life would all come out right if she had known the real facts? Would she have given the same advice? She thought it over, washing the anger away in her tears. Yes, she felt sure her mother could not have written more truly than she had done. She would have had her say no to Hiram, just as she had done, and exhorted her to be patient with Emmeline and to trust that brightness would come sometime.

She thought of her mother's prayer for her and almost smiled through her tears to think how impossible that would be. But the day wasn't done—perhaps there might be some little pleasant thing yet that she might consider a blessing and her mother's gift. She would look and wait for it, and perhaps it would come.

Then, quite suddenly, she knew she was not alone.

A young man stood in the shadow of the tallest chestnut tree, regarding her with troubled gaze, his hat in his hand.

He was tall, well-formed, and his face was fine and handsome. His dark brown eyes looked like the shadowed depths of a quiet woodland stream. His heavy dark hair was tossed back from a white forehead that hadn't been exposed to the summer sun of the hayfield, and the hand that held the hat was white and smooth also. His graceful aspect reminded Phoebe of David Spafford, who seemed to her the ideal of a gentleman. If it hadn't been for his eyes and the hint of a smile on his lips, Phoebe would have been afraid of him as she lifted shy eyes to the intruder's face.

"I beg your pardon," he said. "I didn't mean to intrude, but some young people are coming up the hill. They'll be here in a moment, and I thought perhaps you wouldn't care to meet them. You seem to be in trouble."

"Oh, thank you!" said Phoebe, rising in sudden panic and dropping her mother's letter at her feet. She stooped to pick it up, but the young man reached it first, and their fingers met for one brief instant over the letter. In her confusion Phoebe didn't know what to say but "thank you" and then felt like a parrot repeating the same phrase.

Voices floated up the hill now, and the girl turned to flee, but there seemed nowhere to go for hiding except a dense growth of mountain laurel that still stood green and shining amid the autumn brown. She looked for a way around it, but the young man caught her thought and, reaching forward with a quick motion, parted the strong branches and made a way for her.

"Here, jump right in there! Nobody will see you. Hurry—they're almost here!" he whispered.

The girl sprang quickly on the log, pausing an instant to gather her golden garments about her, and then fluttered into the green hiding place and settled down like a drift of yellow leaves.

The laurel swung back into place, nodding as if it understood the secret. The young man stooped, and she saw him take a letter from his pocket and put it down behind the log that lay across her hiding place.

Up the hillside came a troop of young people. Phoebe couldn't see them, for the growth of laurel was very dense, but she could hear their voices.

"Oh, Janet Bristol, how fast you go! I'm all out of breath. Why do you hurry so? The nuts will keep till we get there, and we have all afternoon before us."

"Go as slow as you like, Caroline," said a sweet, imperious voice. "When I start anywhere I like to get there. I wonder where Nathaniel can be. It's been five minutes since he went out of sight, and he promised to hail us at once and tell us the best way to go."

"Oh, Nathaniel isn't lost," said another girl's voice crossly. "He'll take care of himself likely. Don't hurry so, Janet. Maria is all out of breath."

"Hello! Nathaniel! Nathaniel Graham, where are you!" called a chorus of male voices.

Then from a few paces in front of the laurel hiding place came the voice Phoebe had heard but a moment before.

"Aye, aye, sir! That way!" it called. "There are plenty of nuts up there!"

He stood with his back toward her hiding place and pointed farther up the hill. Then, laughing, scrambling over slippery leaves, the company of young people frolicked past, and Phoebe was left, undiscovered.

She stooped a little to look at the letter the young man had left and read the address, "Nathaniel Graham, Esq.," written in a fine hand.

The girl studied the name till every turn of the pen was engraved on her mind, the fine clearness of the small letters, the bold downward stroke in the capitals. It was unusual writing of an unusual name, and Phoebe felt it belonged to an unusual man.

As she waited and listened to the happy jingle of voices, the barren loneliness of her own life came over her and brought a rush of tears. Why was she here in hiding from those girls and boys who should have been her companions? Why did she shrink from meeting Janet Bristol, the sweetly haughty beauty of the village? Why was she never invited to their teas and their berry and nut gatherings? She saw them in church, and that was all. They never seemed to see her. True, she hadn't been brought up from childhood among them, but she'd lived there long enough to have known them intimately if her life hadn't always been so full of care.

Janet Bristol had gone away to school for several years and was only at home in summer, when Phoebe's life was full of farm work—cooking for the field hands and the harvesters. But Maria Finch and Caroline Penfield had gone to school with Phoebe. She felt a bitterness that they were enjoying such good times and she was not. They weren't to blame, perhaps, for she'd always avoided them, keeping to herself and her studies in school and hurrying home at Emmeline's strict command. They'd never attracted her as had the tall, fair Janet. Yet she would never likely know Janet Bristol or come any nearer to her than she was now, hidden behind God's screen of laurel on the hillside.

The young man with the beautiful face and kind ways would forget her and leave her to scramble out of her hiding place as best she could while he helped Janet Bristol over the stile and carried her basket of nuts home for her. He wouldn't cross her path again. Nevertheless, she was glad he'd met her this once, and she could know there was one so kind and noble in the world.

She would stay here till they were all out of hearing, then creep out and steal away as she'd come. Her sad life and its annoyances, forgotten for the moment, settled down upon her, but with this change. They now seemed possible to bear. She could go back to Albert's house and work her way twice over. She could doff the golden garments and take up her daily toil and bear Emmeline's hateful insinuations. She could even bear Hank's disagreeable attentions and Hiram Green's hateful presence. But never again would she be troubled with the thought that perhaps she ought to accept the home Hiram Green offered her. Never! For now she had seen a man who looked at her as she felt sure God meant a man to look at a woman, with honor and respect and deference.

All at once she knew her mother's prayer had been answered and that something beautiful had come into her life. It wouldn't stay and grow as her mother had hoped. This stranger could be nothing to her, but the memory of his helpfulness and the smile of sympathy that lighted his eyes would remain with her always.

Meanwhile, under the chestnut trees but a few yards away, the baskets were being filled rapidly. Nathaniel Graham helped each girl impartially. The laughing and joking went on, but Nathaniel said little. Phoebe watched them and felt that the young man would soon pilot them farther away. She could hear bits of their talk.

"What's the matter with Nathaniel?" said Caroline Penfield. "He's hardly said a word since we started. What deep subject is your massive mind engaged upon, young man?"

"Oh, Nate is thinking about Texas," said Daniel Westgate flippantly. "He has no thoughts or words for anything but setting Texas free. We'll hear of him joining the volunteers to help them fight Mexico the next thing. I wouldn't be one bit surprised."

"Don't, Daniel," said Janet Bristol. "Nathaniel has far more sense than that."

"I should hope so!" echoed Maria Finch. "Nathaniel isn't a hotheaded fanatic."

"Don't you be too sure!" Daniel called back. "If you'd heard the fine heroics he was getting off to David Spafford yesterday, you wouldn't be surprised at anything. Speak up, Nate, and tell them whether you're going or not."

"Perhaps," said Nathaniel, lifting pleasant eyes of amusement toward the group.

"Nonsense!" said Janet sharply. "As if he'd think of such a thing! Daniel, you should be ashamed to spoil the lovely afternoon with talk of politics. Come, let's move on to that next clump of trees. See, it's just loaded, and the nuts are falling with every breath of wind."

The company picked up their baskets and began to move out of sight, but Nathaniel stood still thoughtfully and felt in his pockets, until Phoebe could see none of the others. Then she heard him call in a pleasant voice, "Janet, I've dropped a letter. It can't be far away. Go on without me for a moment. I'll be with you right away."

"Oh, Nathaniel!" came Janet's vexed tones. "Can't you let it go? Was it important? Shall we come and help you find it?"

"No, Janet, thank you. I know just where I dropped it, and I'll be with you again before you've missed me. Keep right on."

Then he turned swiftly and came back to the laurel before the startled Phoebe could realize he was coming.

She sprang up with the instinct of fleeing from him, but the laurel caught her hair. Down came the soft, shining brown waves in lovely disorder about the flushed face and rippling far below the waist of the buff dress. A strand here and there clung to the laurel and made a fine veil of spun gold before her face. Thus she stood abashed, with her hair unbound before the stranger and her face in beautiful confusion.

The young man had gazed on many maidens' hair with entire indifference. In his boyhood he'd even dared to attach a paper kite to the yellow braids of a girl who sat in front of him in school, and he laughed with the rest at recess as the kite lifted the astonished victim's yellow plaits high in the air and she cried out angrily. He'd watched his cousin Janet brush and plait and curl her abundant locks into the various changing fashions—and criticized the effect freely. He had once untied a hard knot in a bonnet string in a mass of golden curls without a thrill. Why then did he feel such awe as he approached in deep embarrassment to offer his assistance? Why did his fingers tremble as he laid them upon a strand of hair that had tangled itself in the laurel? Why did it bring a fine ecstasy into his being as the wind blew it across his face? Did all hair have that delicate, indescribable perfume about it?

When he had set her free from the entangling bushes, he marveled at the dexterity with which she reduced the flying hair to order and imprisoned it meekly. It seemed like magic.

Then, before she had time to spring out of her covert, he took her hands and helped her to the top of the log and then to the ground. She liked him for the way he did it, so different from the way the other men she knew would have done it. She shuddered to think if it had been Hank or Hiram Green.

"Come this way. It's nearer to the road," he said, parting the branches at his right to let her pass.

When she had gone a few steps, she saw that the crossroad lay not far below them.

"But you've forgotten your letter," she turned to say as they came out of the woods and began to descend the hill. "And I can get out quite well now. You've been very kind—"

"I'll get the letter presently," he said with a smile. "Just let me help you over the fence. I want to ask your pardon for my intrusion. I didn't see you at first—the woods were so quiet—and you looked so much like the yellow leaves that lay all about—" His eyes cast an admiring glance at the buff merino.

"Oh, it wasn't an intrusion," she exclaimed, her cheeks growing warm, "and I'm so grateful to you for telling me they were coming. I wouldn't have liked to be found there." She looked up shyly. "Thank you very much."

He saw that her eyes were beautiful, with ripples of laughter and shadows of sorrow in their glance. He experienced a deep satisfaction that his first impression of her face was verified, and he stood looking down upon her as if she were something he was proud to have discovered and rescued from an unpleasant fate.

Phoebe felt a warm glow breaking over her in the kindness of his look.

"Don't thank me," he said. "I felt like a criminal, intruding upon your trouble."

"But you mustn't feel that way. It was only that I'd been reading a letter from my mother, and it made me feel so lonely that I cried."

"That's trouble enough," he said with quick sympathy. "Is your mother away from home, or are you?"

"My mother is dead. She's been gone a good many years," she said. "She wrote this letter long ago for me to read today, and I came away here by myself to read it."

He helped her over the rail fence that separated the field from the road, and they stood, she on the road side and he on the field side of the fence, as they talked. Neither of them saw a farm wagon coming down the road over the brow of the hill, a mere speck against the autumn sky when they came out of the woods.

The young man's face kindled as he answered. "Thank you for telling me. Now I understand. My mother has been gone a long time too. I wish she'd written me a letter to read today."

Then, as if he knew he mustn't stay longer, he lifted his hat, smiled and walked quickly up the hill. Phoebe sped down the road, not noticing the glories of the day, not thinking so much of her own troubles, but marveling at what had happened and living it all over once more in her imagination. She knew without thinking that a wagon rumbled nearer and nearer, but she gave it no heed.

When he reached the edge of the wood, Nathaniel Graham turned and looked back down the road, saw the girl in her yellow garments and watched her intently. The driver of the farm wagon, now almost opposite him, watched glumly from behind his bags of wheat, sneered under his breath at the young man's fine attire and half guessed who he was. He wondered who the girl was who kept tryst so far from any houses, and with a last glance at the man vanishing into the woods he whipped up his team, resolved to find out.

Chapter 6

Nathaniel Graham went to pick up the letter he'd left behind the log, but as he did so his eye caught something brown lying on the ground among the laurel. He reached out and took it. It was a small bow of brown velvet and seemed strangely a part of the girl who had been there but a few moments before. His fingers closed about the soft little thing. For a moment he pondered whether to go after her and give it to her. Then farther up the hill he heard voices calling him, so he tucked it into his inner pocket. He liked to think he had that bit of velvet himself, and perhaps it wasn't of much value to the owner. It might at least make another opportunity of seeing her. And so he passed on up the hill with something besides the freedom of Texas to think about.

Meanwhile, the load of wheat chased down the road after Phoebe, and its driver, in no pleasant mood because he'd been all the way to Albany with his wheat and was unable to sell it, studied the graceful figure ahead of him and wondered what was so strangely familiar about it.

Phoebe had just reached the high road and paused to think which way she would go when the wagon overtook her. Turning a face bright with pleasure and momentary forgetfulness, she met the countenance of Hiram Green! She caught at the fence to steady herself. One hand flew to her heart, and with frightened eyes she sought the way by which she'd come, hoping to catch sight of her new-found protector. But the hillside lay unresponsive in the late sunshine, and not a soul was to be seen. Nathaniel Graham had just picked up his cousin Janet's basket.

"Well, I swow!" said Hiram Green, pulling his horse up sharply. "If it ain't *you* tricked out that way, away off here!" Then slowly his little pig eyes traveled to the lonely hillside, gathered up an idea, came back to the girl's guilty face and narrowed to slits. He brought his thin lips together with satisfaction. He felt that at last he had a hold upon the girl, but he could wait and use it to his best advantage.

She never dreamed he'd seen the young man with her and was only frightened of being alone in an unfrequented spot with him. In an instant her courage came to her aid, and she steadied her voice to reply.

"Oh, is that you, Mr. Green? You almost frightened me. I was taking a walk and didn't expect to see anyone I knew. This is the Albany road, isn't it? Have you been to Albany?"

Her unusually friendly tone threw the man off his guard for a moment. He couldn't resist the charm of having her speak so pleasantly to him.

"Yes, been to Albany on business," he responded. "Won't you get up and ride? 'Tain't a very pretty seat, but I guess it's clean and comfortable. Sorry I ain't got the carryall. You're a long piece from home."

"Oh, thank you, Mr. Green," she said. "I'm sure the seat would be very comfortable, but I'm out taking a walk this beautiful afternoon, and I'm enjoying every minute of it. I'd much rather walk. Besides, I'm not going directly home. I may stop at Granny McVane's and perhaps another place before I get home. Thank you for the invitation."

Without waiting for a reply she flew lightly in front of the horses and sped up the road toward the old red farmhouse. It wasn't the direction she would have chosen, but there was no time to do anything else. She dared not look behind lest she was being pursued.

Hiram Green, left alone after his attempt at gallantry, looked after the flying maiden with venom in his eyes. His mouth hardened once more into its cruel lines, and he took up the reins again and said to his horses, "G' long there," pointing his remark with a stinging cut of the whip.

When Phoebe neared the old red house, she noted with relief that the shades were drawn down and a general air of not-at-home-ness pervaded the place. She went on by the house and turned down another crossroad that led to a second road going into the village. On this road, just on the border of the town, lived Granny McVane with her silent old husband. She was a sweet old lady whom care and disappointment hadn't hardened, but only made more humble and patient.

Phoebe had come there on occasional errands, and her kindness had won the girl's heart. From Granny McVane's it would be only a short run home across the fields, and she'd escape meeting any more prying eyes. She wasn't accustomed to calling on the neighbors without an errand, but the idea came to her now to stop and ask how Granny's rheumatism was and wish her a good day. If she seemed glad to see her, she might tell her it was her birthday and this was the dress her mother had made. She longed to confide in someone.

As she walked along the country road, she began to think of home and the black looks she would get from Emmeline. But the day was good yet, though a chill had crept into the air that made her cheeks tingle. The sun was dropping low now, and the rays glowed deeper.

She reached the door of Granny McVane's cottage and knocked. The old lady, in her white ruffled cap with its black band and a soft kerchief folded across her bosom, opened the upper half of the door. Seeing Phoebe, she opened the lower door too and invited her in most warmly. She made her sit down and looked her over with delight, the old eyes glowing with pleasure at sight of the visitor.

Phoebe told her about the dress, her birthday, her mother's letter and her walk. Then Granny McVane urged her to take tea with her, for her husband was off to Albany on business and wouldn't be back that night.

The cat winked cordially from the hearth, the pot of mush sputtered sleepily over the fire, and the old lady's face was so wistful that Phoebe put off her thought of home and the supper she should be getting this minute. She decided to stay just this once, as it was her birthday. Yes, for one short hour more she'd have what her day offered her of joy. Then she'd go back to her duty and cherish the memory of her pleasure.

Precisely at five o'clock the little round table was drawn out from the wall and its leaves put up. The old woman laid a snow-white homespun cloth upon it, followed by lovely blue dishes of quaint designs.

It was a delicious meal, and Phoebe ate it with the appetite gained in her long walk. After it was over she bade Granny McVane good-bye, kissed her for the beautiful ending to her birthday and hurried guiltily across the fields to the farmhouse she called home.

The family had just sat down to supper when Phoebe opened the door and came in. She had hoped this ceremony would be over, for the usual hour for supper was half past five, but Emmeline had waited longer than usual, thinking Phoebe would surely come back to help. Emmeline had been angry, astonished and bewildered all afternoon. She hadn't decided what to do about the way her young sister-in-law acted. But now that she was home, after staying away till the work was done, Emmeline's wrath kindled anew. She stood at the hearth taking up the second pan of johnnycake when the girl came in. And when she saw Phoebe looking cheerful, Emmeline set her lips in haughty disapproval.

Alma, with her mouth full of fried potatoes, stopped her fork midway with another supply and stared. The little boys chorused in unison: "Hullo, Aunt Phoebe! Where'd ye get the clo'es!" Hank, who was helping himself to a slice of bread, turned around and gazed in awed embarrassment. Only Albert looked pleased, his chair tipped back and a look of real welcome on his face.

"Well, now, Phoebe, I'm real glad you've got back. I was getting uneasy about you, off so long. It isn't like you to stay away from your meals. My, but you do look pretty in that rig! What took you, anyway? Where've you been?"

She wouldn't have told the others for the world, but somehow Albert's pleasant tones and kind eyes unsealed her lips.

"I've just been for a walk in the woods this afternoon, and I stopped a few minutes to see Granny McVane. She made me stay to tea with her. I didn't mean to stay so late."

"That sounds very sweet, I'm sure," broke in Emmeline's sharp voice, "but she forgets she left me with all her work to do on top of my own."

Phoebe's cheeks flushed.

"I'm sorry I didn't get back in time to help get supper," she said, looking straight at Albert as if explaining to him alone. "But it was my birthday, and I thought I might take a little time to myself."

"Your birthday! To be sure you can. You don't go out half enough. Emmeline, you wouldn't want her to work all day on her birthday, of course. Sit down, child, and have some more supper. This is real good johnnycake. You should have told us before that you had a birthday comin', and then we might have celebrated. Eh, Hank? What do you say?"

"I say yes," said Hank, endeavoring to regain his usual composure.

"Other people have birthdays, too, and I don't see much fuss made over them," sniffed Emmeline, flinging the tea towel up to its nail with an impatient movement.

"Thank you, Albert," said Phoebe. "I don't care for any more supper. I'll go up and change my dress and be ready to wash the dishes."

She headed toward the door, but Albert detained her.

"Wait, Phoebe! You come here and sit down. I've got something to tell you. I'd clean forgot about the birthday myself, but now I remember all right. Let's see—you're eighteen today, aren't you? I thought so."

Hank lifted bold, admiring eyes to her face, and the girl, standing patiently behind her chair at the table waiting for her brother to finish, felt as if she'd like to extinguish him for a little while till the conference was over.

"Well, now, child, I've got a surprise for you. You're eighteen and of age, so you've got a right to know it."

"Wouldn't it be better for you to tell me by and by when the work is done?" pleaded Phoebe, casting a glance about on the wide-eyed audience.

"No," said Albert. "It isn't a secret, leastways not from any that's here. You needn't look so scared, child. It's only that there's a little money coming to you, about five or six hundred dollars. It's a nice tidy little sum for a girl of eighteen with good prospects. You certainly deserve it, for you've been a good girl ever since you came to live with us. Your mother wanted me to keep the money for you till you was eighteen, and then she said you would know how to use it and be more likely to need it."

"Say, Aunt Phoebe," broke in Alma, tilting her nose to its most inquisitive point, "does Hiram Green know you got a birthday?"

"Shut up!" said Emmeline, applying the palm of her hand in a stinging slap to her daughter's cheek.

"Now, Emmeline, don't be so severe with the child! She doesn't realize how impertinent she is. Alma, you mustn't talk like that to Aunt Phoebe." Then, with a wink, he said in an aside to Hank, "It does beat all how keen children will be sometimes."

Phoebe, with scarlet cheeks, felt as if she could bear no more. "Thank you, Albert," she said in a trembling voice. "Now if you'll excuse me I'll change my dress."

"Wait a minute, child. That's a mighty pretty dress you've got on. Look pretty as a peach in it. Let's have a look at you. Where'd you get it? Make it yourself?"

"Mother made it for me to wear today," said Phoebe in a low voice.

Then she vanished into the hall, leaving an impression of victory behind her and a sense of embarrassment among the family.

"There'll be no livin' with her now," snapped Emmeline over the teacups. "I'm sure I thought you had better sense. You never told me there was any money left for her, or I'd've advised you about it. I'm sure we've spent for her, and if there's anything left her it belongs to you. Here she's had a good home and paid not a cent for it. If she had any spirit of right she wouldn't touch a cent of that money!"

"Now look here, Emmeline," said Albert in his conciliatory tone. "You don't quite understand this matter. Not having known about it before, of course, you couldn't judge rightly. And it was her ma's request that I not tell anybody. Besides, I don't see why it should affect you any. The money was hers, and we'd nothing to do with it. As for her home here, she's been very welcome, and I'm sure she's earned her way. She's a good worker, Phoebe is."

"That's so, she is," said Hank. "I don't know a girl in the county can beat her workin'."

"I don't know as anybody asked your opinion, Hank Williams. I'm able to judge work a little myself, and if she works well, who taught her? She'd never done a stroke when she came here, and nobody thinks of the hard time I've had breakin' her in and puttin' up with her mistakes when she was young."

"Now, Emmeline, don't go and get excited," said Albert. "You know we ain't letting go a mite of what you've done. Only it's fair to the girl to say she's earned her way."

"Hmm!" said Emmeline. "That depends on who's the judge!"

"Won't Aunt Phoebe do any more work now she's got some money, Ma?" broke in Alma, panicked about what might be in store for her.

"Haven't I told you to keep still, Alma?" reproved her mother. "If you say another word I'll send you to bed without any cake."

At this dire threat Alma withdrew from the conversation till the cake should be passed, and a gloom settled over the room. Hank felt the constraint and made haste to bolt the last of his supper and escape.

Phoebe came down shortly afterward, attired in her everyday garb and looking meekly sensible. Albert protested weakly.

"Say, Phoebe, it's too bad for you to wash dishes on your birthday night. You go back and put on your pretty things, and Alma'll help her ma wash up this time."

"No, she won't, either," broke in Emmeline. "Alma ain't a bit well, and she's not goin' to be made to work at her age unless she likes. Here, honey, you may have this piece of Ma's cake; she don't want it all. It seems to me you're kind of an unnatural father, Albert Deane. I guess it won't hurt Phoebe to wash a few dishes when she's been lyin' around havin' a good time all day, while I've worked my fingers half off doin' her work. We've all had to work on our birthdays, and I guess if Phoebe's goin' to stay here she'll have to put up with what the rest of us gets, unless she's got money to pay for better."

With that Albert looked helplessly about the room and retired to his newspaper in the sitting room, while Phoebe went swiftly about the usual evening work. Emmeline yanked the boys away from the cake plate and marched them and Alma out of the kitchen with her head held high and her chin in the air. She didn't even put away the cake and bread and pickles and jelly but left it all for Phoebe, who was glad for this.

Before the dishes were done, the front door opened, and Hiram Green sauntered into the sitting room. Phoebe heard him and hurried to hang up her dish towels and flee to her own room.

And thus ended the birthday, though the girl lay awake far into the night thinking over all its wonderful happenings—and not allowing her mind to dwell upon the possibilities of trouble in the future.

Chapter 7

When little Rose Spafford was born, her young mother—who had been Marcia Schuyler—found no one so reliable and helpful in the whole town as Miranda Griscom, granddaughter and household drudge of her next-door neighbor, Mrs. Heath. David Spafford "borrowed" her for the first three or four weeks, and Mrs. Heath gave reluctant consent, because the Heaths and the Spaffords had always been intimate friends. But Grandma Heath realized during that time just how many steps the eccentric Miranda saved her, and she began to look forward to her return with more eagerness than she cared to show.

Miranda reveled in doing as she pleased in the large, well-furnished kitchen of the Spafford house, using the best china to send a tray upstairs to Mrs. Spafford. She often looked triumphantly over toward her grandmother's house and wondered if she was missed. One little gleam of appreciation would have started a flame of abounding love in the girl's lonely heart. But the grim grandmother never appreciated anything her unloved grandchild, the daughter of an undesired son-in-law, tried to do.

As the days sped by Miranda began to dread the time when she must go back to her grandmother's house again, and Marcia and David dreaded it also. They set about planning how they might keep her, and presently they had it all arranged.

David suggested it first.

It was while they both hung over little Rose's cradle, watching her wake up, like the opening of the little bud she was.

Miranda had come to the door for a direction and stood there a moment. "I thought I'd find you two a-hoverin'. Just keep right on. I'll see to supper. Don't you give it a thought."

And then a moment later they heard her high, nasal tones voicing something about a "Sweet, sweet rose on a garden wall," and they smiled at the quaint loving soul. Then David spoke.

"Marcia, we must contrive to keep Miranda here," he said. "She's blossomed out in the last month. It would be cruel to send her back to that dismal house again. They don't need her in the least with Hannah's cousin there all the time. I mean to offer her wages to stay with us. You're not strong enough to care for the baby and do the housework, anyway, and I'd feel safer about you if Miranda were here. Wouldn't you like her?"

Marcia's sweet laugh rang out. "Oh, David, you spoil me! I'm sure I'm perfectly able to do the work and look after this tiny child. But of course I'd like to have Miranda here. I think it would be a good thing if she could get away from her surroundings, and she's a comfort to me in many ways."

"Then it's settled, dear," said David, with his most loving smile.

"Oh, but, David, what will Aunt Amelia say? And Aunt Hortense! They'll tell me I'm weak—or proud, which would be worse yet."

"What does it matter what my aunts think? We're certainly free to do as we please in our own home, and I'm sure of one thing—Aunt Clarinda will think it's all right. She'll be quite pleased. Besides, I'll explain to Aunt Hortense that I want to have you more to myself and take you with me often, and therefore it's my own selfishness, not yours, that makes me do this. She'll listen to that argument, I'm sure."

Marcia smiled, half doubtfully.

"And then there's Mrs. Heath. She'll never consent."

"Leave that to me, my little wife, and don't worry about it. First, let's settle it with Miranda."

Just then Miranda presented herself at the door.

"Your supper's spoilin' on the table. Will you two just walk down and eat it while I have my try at that baby? I haven't seen scarcely a wink of her all this blessed day."

"Miranda," said David, not looking at his wife's warning eyes, "would you be willing to stay with us altogether?"

"Hmm!" said Miranda. "Jes' gimme the try and see!" And she stooped over the cradle with such a wistful gaze that the young mother's heart went out to her.

"Very well, Miranda, then we'll consider it a bargain. I'll pay you wages so we'll feel quite comfortable about asking you to do anything, and you shall call this your home from now on."

"What!" gasped the girl, straightening up. "Did you mean what you said? I never knew you to do a mean thing like tease anyone, David Spafford, but you can't mean what you say. It couldn't come around so nice as that fer me. Don't go to talk about wages. I'd work from mornin' to night fer one chance at that blessed baby there in the cradle. But I know it can't be."

The supper grew cold while they persuaded her it was all true and they really wanted her and then talked over the possible trouble with her grandmother. At last, with her sandy eyelashes wet with tears of joy, Miranda went downstairs and heated the supper all over again for them. And the two upstairs, beside the little bud that had bloomed for them, rejoiced that a heart so faithful and true would be watching over her through babyhood.

Perhaps it was a desire to burn his bridges behind him before his maiden aunts heard of the new arrangement that sent David over to see old Mrs. Heath that very evening. Perhaps it was to relieve the excitement of Miranda, who felt heaven had opened before her but counted on being thrust out of her Eden at once.

No one but Marcia ever heard what passed between David and old Mrs. Heath, and no one else quite knew what arguments he used to bring the determined old woman finally to terms. Miranda, with her nose flattened against the windowpane of the dark kitchen chamber, watching the two blurred figures in the candlelight of Grandmother Heath's sitting room, wondered and prayed and hoped and feared—and prayed again.

It was a good thing David went over to see Mrs. Heath that night, if he cared to escape criticism from his relatives. The next afternoon Miss Amelia, on her daily visit to the exalted place of her new grandniece, remarked, "Well, Marcia, has Miranda gone home yet? I'd think her grandmother would need her after all this time, poor old lady. And you're perfectly strong and able now to attend to your own work again."

Marcia's face flushed, and she gathered her baby closer as if to protect her from the chill that would follow.

"Why, Aunt Amelia," she said brightly, "what do you think! Miranda isn't going home at all. David has a foolish idea he wants her to stay with me and help look after the baby. Besides, he wants me to go with him as I've been doing. I told him it wasn't necessary, but he wanted it. So he's arranged it all, and Mrs. Heath has given her consent."

"Miranda stay here!" The words fell like icicles. Then followed more.

"I am *surprised* at you, Marcia. I thought you had more self-respect than that! It's a disgrace to a young strong woman to let her husband hire a girl to do her work while she gads about the country and leaves her house and her young child. If your own mother had lived she'd have taught you better than that. And then, *Miranda,* of *all people to select!* The child of a renegade! A waif dependent, utterly thankless and irresponsible! She's scatterbrained and untrustworthy. If you needed anyone at any time to sit with the child while you were out for a legitimate cause to call or visit occasionally, either Hortense or I'd be glad to come and relieve you. Indeed, you mustn't think of leaving this wild, good-for-nothing Miranda Griscom with my nephew's child!

"I'll speak to Hortense, and we'll make it our business to come down every day, one or the other of us, and do anything you find your strength is unequal to doing. We're still strong enough, I hope, to do anything for the family honor. I'd be ashamed to have it known that David Spafford's wife was such a weakling she had to hire help. The young wives of our family have always been proud of their housekeeping."

Now Miranda Griscom, whatever might be said of her other virtues, had no convictions against eavesdropping. And with this particular caller she felt it especially necessary to serve her mistress in any way she could. She was sharp enough to know Miss Amelia wouldn't be in favor of her being in David Spafford's household, and she felt her mistress would have to bear some persecution on her account. She therefore resolved to be on hand to protect her. Soon after the aunt was seated with Marcia in the large front bedroom where the cradle was established, Miranda approached the door and applied her ear to the generous crack. She could feel the subject turning to her and had already devised a plan.

As Marcia lifted her face, trying to remove the angry flash from her eyes and think of how to reply to the old woman, Miranda burst into the room.

"Oh, Miss Amelia, 'scuse me fer interruptin', but did your nice old gray cat mebbe foller you down here, and could it 'a' ben her out on our front porch fightin' with Bob Sykes's yellow dog? 'Cause ef 'tis, sumpin' ought to be done right off, 'r he'll bake hash outa her. S'pose you come down an' look. I wouldn't like to make a mistake 'bout it."

Miss Amelia placed her hand on her heart and looked helplessly at Marcia for an instant. "Oh, my dear, you don't suppose—" she began in a trembling voice.

Then she gathered up her shawl and hurried down the stairs after the sympathetic Miranda.

"Come right out here softly," Miranda said, opening the front door cautiously. "Why, they must 'a' gone around the house!"

The old woman followed the girl out on the porch, and together they looked on both sides of the house. But they saw no trace of dog or cat.

"Where could they 'a' gone?" inquired Miranda excitedly. "Mebbe I ought 'a' jus' called you and stayed here an' watched, but I was afraid to wake the baby. You don't suppose that cat would 'a' run home, an' he after her? Is that them up the street? Don't you see a whirl o' dust in the road? Would you like me to go an' see? 'Cause I'm most afraid ef she's tried to run home, fer Bob Sykes hes trained thet dog to run races, an' he's a turrible fast runner, an' your cat is gettin' on in years. It might go hard with her."

Miranda's sympathetic tone quite excited the old woman, whose old gray cat was very dear to her, being the last descendant of an ancient line of cats traditional in the family.

"No, Miranda, you just stay right here. Mrs. Spafford might need you after all this excitement. Tell her not to worry until I know the worst. I'll go right home and see if anything has happened to Matthew. It would be very distressing to me and my sister. If he's escaped from that dog he'll need attention. Just tell Mrs. Spafford I'll come down or send Hortense tomorrow as I promised." And the dignified old lady hurried off up the village street, for once unmindful of her dignity.

"Miranda!" called Marcia, when she'd waited a reasonable time for the aunt's return and not even the girl presented herself.

Miranda appeared in a minute, with a meek yet triumphant mien.

Marcia's eyes were laughing, but she tried to look serious.

"Miranda," she began, trying to suppress the merriment in her voice, "did you really see that cat out there?"

Miranda hesitated for a reply. "Well, I heard a dog bark—"

"Miranda, was that quite honest?" protested Marcia. She felt she should try to improve the moral standard of the girl thus under her charge and influence.

"I don't see anythin' wrong with that," asserted Miranda. "I didn't say a word that wasn't true. I'm always careful 'bout that sence I see how much you think of such things. I asked her ef it might 'a' ben her cat, an' how do I know but 'twas? And it would be easy to 'a' ben Bob Sykes's dog, ef it *was* round, fer that dog never lets a cat come on his block. Anyway I heard a dog bark, and I thought it sounded like Bob's dog. I'm pretty good on sounds."

"But you shouldn't frighten Aunt Amelia. She's an old lady, and it isn't good for old people to get frightened. You know she thinks a great deal of her cat."

"Well, it ain't good fer you to be badgered, and Mr. David told me to look after you, an' I'm doin' it the best way I know how. If I don't do it right I s'pose you'll send me back to Grandma's, an' then who'll take care of that blessed baby!"

When Marcia told it all to David he laughed until tears came.

"Good for Miranda! She'll do, and Aunt Amelia'll never know what happened to poor old Matthew, who was probably napping quietly by the hearth. Well, little girl, I'm glad you didn't have to answer Aunt Amelia's questions. Leave her to me. I'll shoulder all the blame and exonerate you. Don't worry."

"But, David," began Marcia, "Miranda shouldn't tell things that aren't exactly true. How can I teach her?"

"Well, Miranda's standards aren't exactly right, and we must try little by little to raise them higher. But I'll miss my guess if she doesn't manage some way to protect you, even if she does have to tell the truth."

And thus it was that Miranda Griscom became a fixture in the Spafford household and did about as she pleased with her master and mistress and the baby, because she usually pleased to do well.

The years went by, and little Rose Spafford grew into a laughing, dimpled child with charming ways that reminded one of her mother, and Miranda was her devoted slave.

On the Sunday after Phoebe Deane's birthday, David, Marcia, Rose and Miranda all sat in church together. Rose, in dainty pantalets and dress, sat between her mother and Miranda and waited for the sugared caraway seeds she knew would be dropped occasionally into her lap if she were good. David sat at the end of his pew, happy and devout, with Marcia beside him, and Miranda alert, one eye on her worship, the other on what might happen about her.

Across the aisle the sweet face of Phoebe Deane attracted her attention. It was clouded with trouble. Miranda's keen eyes saw that at once. Miranda had often noticed that about Phoebe Deane and wondered, but there were so many other people Miranda had to look after. So Phoebe Deane had never before received her undivided attention.

But this particular morning Phoebe looked so pretty in her buff merino that Miranda was all attention at once. Miranda, homely and red-haired and freckled, whose clothes had been made from Hannah Heath's cast-off wardrobe, yet loved beautiful things and beautiful people. Phoebe, with her brown hair and starry eyes, seemed like a lovely picture to her in the buff merino, with her face framed in its neat straw bonnet.

As her eyes traveled over Phoebe's dress they came finally to the face, so grave and sweet and troubled, as if life was too filled with perplexities to have much joy left in it. Then she looked at the sharp lines of Emmeline's sour face with its thin, pursed lips and decided Emmeline was not a pleasant woman to live with. Alma, preening herself in her Sunday clothes, wasn't a pleasant child either, and she wondered if Phoebe could possibly take any pleasure in putting on her little garments for her and planning surprises and plays, the way she did for Rose. It seemed impossible. Miranda looked down tenderly at Rose, then gratefully toward David and Marcia at the end of the pew, and pitied Phoebe, wishing for her the happiness that had come into her own barren life.

The service was about to commence when Judge Bristol, with his daughter Janet and her cousin Nathaniel Graham, walked up the aisle to their pew, just in front of Albert Deane's.

Now Phoebe had debated hard about coming to church that morning, for she couldn't keep her mind off the stranger who had been so kind to her a few days before. It was impossible not to wonder if he'd be there and whether he would see her and speak to her.

And Phoebe would gladly have stayed at home if she wouldn't have had to explain her reasons to Albert.

She rode to church that morning half ashamed of herself for the undeniable wish to see the stranger once more. When she got out of the carryall at church, she didn't look around or even lift her eyes to see who was standing by the door. She resolved not to think about him. If he came up the aisle, she wouldn't know it, and her eyes would be otherwise occupied. No one would dare say she was watching for him.

Nevertheless, as Janet and her cousin came up the aisle, Phoebe knew by the wild beating of her heart that he was coming, and she commanded her eyes not to lift from the hymnbook in her lap. Yet, in spite of her resolve, when the occupants of the Bristol pew had entered it and were about to sit down, and Nathaniel Graham stood so that his head and shoulders were just above the top of the high-back pew, her eyes fluttered up for one glance—and in that instant they were caught and held by the eyes of the young man in pleased recognition.

In a flash Phoebe's eyes were back on her book, and the young man was seated in the pew with only the top of his fine dark head showing. Yet color rushed into the girl's cheeks, and the young man's eyes held a light of satisfaction that lasted through the service. The glance had been too brief for any act of recognition, like a bow or a smile, and neither would have been in place, for the whole audience could have seen them as he was faced about. Moreover the service had begun. Not a soul witnessed the glance, save the keen-eyed Miranda, and instantly she recognized a certain something that put her on the watch. So Miranda, through the whole long service, studied their faces and wove a romance for herself out of the golden fabric of a glance.

Chapter 8

When the service ended, Phoebe made sure her eyes didn't look toward the stranger. Nathaniel Graham was kept busy for the first few moments shaking hands with old friends and talking with the minister, who came down from the pulpit on purpose to greet him. When he turned around at his first opportunity, the pew behind him was empty, and the eyes that had met his when he came in were nowhere to be seen.

He looked over the receding audience toward the open door and caught the glimmer of the buff merino. Hastily excusing himself to Janet, Nathaniel made his way down the aisle, disappointing some kind old ladies who had been friends of his mother and who lay in wait for him at various pew doors.

Miranda saw it all, and her eager eyes watched to see if he would catch Phoebe. The way being open just then, she pressed out into the aisle and, for once leaving Rose to follow after her mother, hurried to the door.

Nathaniel didn't overtake Phoebe until she'd gone down the church steps and was on the path in front of the churchyard. He stepped up beside her, taking off his hat with a cheery "Good morning," and Phoebe's pink cheeks and smiling eyes welcomed him happily.

"I wanted to be quite sure you were all right after your adventure the other day," he said, looking down into the lovely face with real pleasure.

Before she could answer, Hiram Green stepped up airily as if he belonged and looked at Nathaniel questioningly, saying, "Well, here you are, Phoebe. I lost track of you at the church door. We better step along. The carryall is waitin'."

Nathaniel looked up, annoyed, then puzzled, recognized Hiram with astonishment and said, "I beg your pardon. I didn't know I was keeping you from your friends," to Phoebe. Lifting his hat with a courteous "Good morning, Mr. Green," to Hiram, he stepped back among the little throng coming out the church door.

Now Miranda had been close behind, for she was determined to read every chapter of her romance that appeared in sight. She saw the whole maneuver on Hiram Green's part and the color that flamed angrily into Phoebe's cheek when she recognized Hiram's interference. She also saw the dismay in the girl's face as Nathaniel left her and Hiram Green made as if to walk beside her. Phoebe looked wildly about. There seemed no escape from him as a companion without making a deliberate scene, yet her whole soul revolted at having Nathaniel Graham see her walk off with Hiram.

Quick as a flash, Miranda caught the meaning of Phoebe's look and flew to her assistance.

"Phoebe! Phoebe Deane!" she called. "Wait a minute. I want to tell you something!"

She had raised her voice on purpose, for she stood directly behind Nathaniel. As she'd hoped, he turned to see Phoebe respond. She noted the sudden light in his eyes as he saw the girl to whom he'd just been talking respond to the name, but she didn't know it was a light of satisfaction because he'd found out her name without asking anyone.

He stood a moment and looked after them. He saw Phoebe dismiss the sulky Hiram with a word and go off with Miranda. He saw that Hiram didn't even raise his hat on leaving Phoebe but slouched off angrily without a word.

"Say, Phoebe," said Miranda, "my Mrs. Spafford"—this was her common way of speaking of Marcia in the possessive—"she's ben talkin' a long time 'bout you and wishin' you'd come to see her, an' she's ben layin' out to ask you to tea, but things hes prevented. So could you come Tuesday? You better come early and stay all afternoon, so you can play with Rose. She's the sweetest thing!"

"Oh, I'd love to come," said Phoebe, her face aglow with pleasure. "I've always admired Mrs. Spafford so much, and little Rose is beautiful. Yes, tell her I'll come."

Just then came the strident voice of Emmeline.

"Phoebe! Phoebe Deane! Was you intendin' to go home with us, or had you calculated to ride with Hiram Green? If you're comin' with us we can't wait all day."

With angry heart and trembling limbs Phoebe bade Miranda good-bye and climbed into the carriage, not daring to look behind her to see who had heard her sister-in-law's hateful words. Oh, had the stranger heard them? How dreadful if he had! How contemptible, how unforgivable in Emmeline! She didn't even dare lift her eyes as they drove by the church but sat with drooping lashes and burning cheeks—missing Nathaniel Graham's glance as he stood on the sidewalk with his cousin, waiting for another opportunity to lift his hat.

Miranda watched the Deanes drive away and turned with a vindictive look of triumph to see Hiram Green getting into his chaise alone. Then she began to reflect upon what she'd done.

About four o'clock that afternoon, the dinner dishes being well out of the way and the Sunday quiet resting upon the house, Miranda went to Marcia with the guiltiest look on her face that Marcia had ever seen her wear.

"Well, I've up an' done it now, Mrs. Marcia, an' no mistake. I expect I'll have to leave you, an' the thought of it jes' breaks my heart."

"Why, Miranda!" said Marcia, sitting up very suddenly from the couch. "You're not—you're surely not going to get married!"

"Not by a jugful I ain't. Do you s'pose I'd hev enny man that would take up with freckles an' a turn-up nose in a wife? I've gone and done sumpin' you'll think is a heap worse'n gittin' married. But I didn't tell no lie. I was keerful enough 'bout that. I only told her you'd been talkin' 'long back 'bout askin' her, an' you hed all right 'nough, only I oughtn't to 'a' ast her, an' set the day an' all 'thout you knowin'. I knowed it at the time well 'nough, but I hed to do it, 'cause the circumstances wuz sech. You see thet squint-eyed Hiram Green was makin' it out that she was somewhat great to him, a-paradin' down the walk there from the church an' a-driven' off that nice city cousin of Janet Bristol's with his nice, genteel manners an' his tippin' of his hat, an' her a-lookin' like she'd drop from shame, so I called her to wait, an' I runs up an' talks to her, an' course then she tells Hiram Green he needn't trouble to wait fer her, an' we goes off together in full sight of all. My, I was glad I beat that skinflint Hiram Green, but I was that excited I jes' couldn't think of 'nother thing to do 'cept invite her."

"Who in the world are you talking about, Miranda? And what terrible thing have you done?"

Marcia's laughing eyes reassured Miranda, and she went on with her story.

"Why, that pretty little Phoebe Deane," she explained. "I've invited her to tea Tuesday night. I thought that would suit you better than any other time. Monday night things ain't straight from washday yet, and I didn't want to put it off too long, an' I can make everything myself. But if you don't like it I'll go an' tell her the hull truth on't; only she did look so mortal pleased I hate to spoil her fun."

By degrees Marcia drew the whole story from Miranda, even to a lavish description of the buff merino and its owner's drooping expression.

"Well, I don't see why you thought I'd be displeased," said Marcia. "It's only right you should invite company once in a while. I'm glad you invited her, and as you do most of the work and know our plans pretty well, you knew it would likely be convenient. I'm glad you invited her."

And she gave Miranda one of the smiles that had so endeared her to the lonely girl's heart. Then Miranda went back to her kitchen comforted.

The prospect of another tea party made Phoebe forget the annoyances of her home all through the dull Sabbath afternoon and the trials of Monday with its heavy work. After supper Emmeline produced a great basket of mending which she announced was "all to be finished and put away that evening." Phoebe sat beside the candle and sewed with weary fingers, longing to be away from them all where she might think over quietly the pleasant things that had come into her life.

Hiram Green came in, too, and with a purpose, for he was hardly seated in his usual chair when he began: "Say, Albert, did you see the nincompoop of a nephew of Judge Bristol in the church? Does beat all how he takes on airs jest because he's been off to college. I ken remember him fishin' in his bare feet, and here he was bowin' round among the ladies like he'd always been a fine gentleman and never done a stroke of work in his life. His hands are ez white and soft ez a woman's. He strikes me very ladylike, indeed he does. Smirkin' round and takin' off his hat ez if he'd nothin' better to do. Fine feathers don't make fine birds, I say. I don't believe he could cut a swath o' hay now to save his precious little life. He makes me sick with his airs. Seems like Miss Janet better look after him ef she expects to marry him, er he'll lose his head to every girl he meets."

Something uncontrollable seemed to steal the blood out of Phoebe's heart for a moment, and all her strength was slipping from her. Then a mighty anger rolled through her being and surged to her very fingertips; yet she held those fingers steadily as her needle pierced back and forth through the stocking she was darning. She knew these remarks were entirely for her benefit, and she resolved not to let Hiram see she understood or cared.

"Is he going to marry his cousin Janet?" asked Albert. "I never heard that."

"You didn't? Well, where've you ben all these years? It's ben common talk sence they was little tads. Their mothers 'lowed that was the way it was to be, and they was sent away to separate schools on that account. I s'pose they was afraid they'd take a dislike to each other ef they saw each other constant. 'Pon my word, I think Janet could look higher, an' ef I was her I wouldn't be held by no promise of no dead mothers. But they do say she worships the very ground he walks on, an' she'll hold him to all right enough, so it's no sort o' use fer any other girls to go anglin' after him."

"I heard he's real bright," said Albert genially. "They say he's taken honors, a good many of 'em. He was president of the Philomathean Society in Union College, you know, and that's a great honor."

Albert read a good deal and knew more about the world's affairs than Hiram.

"Oh, bah! That's child's play!" sneered Hiram. "Who couldn't be president of a literary society? It don't take much spunk to preside. I ran the town meeting last year 'bout's well 's ef I'd ben a college president. My opinion is Nate Graham would'v' 'mounted to more ef he'd stayed t' home an' learned farmin' er studied law with his uncle an' worked fer his board. A feller thet's all give over to lyin' around makin' nuthin' of himself don't amount to a row o' pins."

"But they say Dr. Nott thinks he's got brains," persisted Albert. "I'm sure I'd like to see him come out on top. I heard he was studying law in New York now. He was always a pleasant-spoken boy when he was here."

"What's pleasant speakin'!" growled Hiram. "It can't sell a load o' wheat." His unsold wheat was bitterly in his thoughts.

"Well, I don't know 'bout that, Hiram." Albert felt pleasantly argumentative. "I don't know but if I was going to buy wheat I'd a little sooner buy off the man that was pleasant-spoken than the man that wasn't."

Hiram sat glumly and pondered this saying for a few minutes.

Phoebe took advantage of the pause in conversation to lay down her work-basket and say determinedly to Emmeline, "I'll finish these stockings tomorrow, Emmeline. I feel tired, and I'm going upstairs."

It was the first time Phoebe had ever dared take a stand against Emmeline's orders. Emmeline was too astonished to speak for a minute, but just as Phoebe reached the door she said, "Well, really! Tired! I was down half an hour before you this mornin', and I'm not tired to speak of, but I suppose ef I was I'd have to keep right on. And who's to do your work tomorrow mornin' while you do this, I'd like to know?"

But Phoebe had escaped out of hearing, and Emmeline relapsed into vexed silence. Hiram, however, narrowed his cruel little eyes and thought he understood why she had gone.

Chapter 9

P hoebe had pondered much on how she should announce her intended absence that afternoon, almost deciding at one time to slip away without saying a word, but her heart wouldn't allow that.

So while the family ate breakfast she said to Emmeline, "I wish you'd tell me what work you want done besides the rest of the ironing. I'm invited out to tea this afternoon, and I want to get everything done this morning."

"Where to?" exploded Alma.

"Indeed!" said Emmeline disdainfully. "Invited out to tea! What airs we're takin' on with our money! Pretty soon you won't have any time to give at home at all. If I was you I'd go and board somewhere; you have so many social engagements. I'm sure I don't feel like askin' a young lady like you to soil her hands washin' my dishes. I'll wash 'em myself after this. Alma, you go get your apern on and help Ma this mornin'. Aunt Phoebe hasn't got time. She'll have to take all mornin' to curl her hair."

"Now, Emmeline!" said Albert, gently reproachful. "Don't tease the child. It's real nice for her to get invited out. She don't get much chance, that's sure."

"Oh, no, two tea parties inside of a week's nothin'. I've heard of New York ladies goin' out as often as every other day," said Emmeline sarcastically.

Albert never could quite understand his wife's sarcasm, so he turned to Phoebe and voiced the question everyone was bursting with curiosity to have answered.

"Who invited you, Phoebe?"

"Mrs. Spafford," said Phoebe, trying not to show how near she was to crying over Emmeline's hateful speeches.

"Well, now, that's real nice," said Albert. "There isn't a finer man in town than David Spafford. His paper's the best edited in the whole state of New York, and he's got a fine little wife. I don't believe she's many days older than you are, Phoebe. She looked real young when he brought her here, and she hasn't grown a day older that I can see."

"Good reason why," sniffed Emmeline. "She's nothin' to do but lie around and be waited on. I'm sure Phoebe's welcome to such friends if they suit her. Fer my part I'd ruther go to see good self-respectin' women that did a woman's work in the world and not let their husbands make babies of them and go ridin' round in a carriage forever lookin' like a June mornin'. I call it lazy, I do. It's nothin' more n' less—and she keepin' that poor good-fer-nothin' Miranda Griscom slavin' from mornin' to night fer her. If Phoebe was my sister I shouldn't choose such friends fer her. Besides, she hasn't got very good manners not to invite your wife, too, Albert Deane. But I suppose you never thought o' that. I shouldn't think Phoebe would care to accept an invitation that was an insult to her relations, even if they wasn't just blood relations— they're all she's got, that's sure."

"Say, look here, Emmeline. Your speech don't hang together. You just said you didn't care to make friends of Mrs. Spafford, and now you're fussing because she didn't invite you too. It looks like a case of sour grapes, eh, Phoebe?"

Hank caught the joke and laughed loudly, though Phoebe looked grave, knowing how bitter it would be to Emmeline to be laughed at. Two red spots flamed out on Emmeline's cheeks, and her eyes snapped.

"Seems to me things has gone pretty far, Albert Deane," she said in a high, excited voice, "when you can insult your wife in public and then laugh! I shan't forget this, Albert Deane!" And with her head well up she shoved her chair back from the table and left the room, slamming the door shut behind her.

Albert's merry laugh came to an abrupt end. He looked after his wife with startled surprise. Never in all their wedded life had Emmeline taken offense like that around others. He looked helplessly, inquiringly, from one to another.

"Well, now," he began, "you don't suppose she thought I meant that."

"'Course!" said Alma. "You've made her dreadful mad, Pa. My! But you're goin' to get it!"

"Looks mighty like it," snickered Hank.

Albert looked at Phoebe for a reply.

"I'm afraid she thought you were in earnest, Albert. You better go and explain," said Phoebe.

"You better not go fer a while, Pa," called out Johnny. "Wait till she gets over it a little. Go hide in the barn. That's the way I do!"

But Albert was going heavily up the stairs after his offended wife and didn't hear his young son's hopeful voice. He wished if possible to explain away the offense before it struck in too deep for healing and had to be lived down.

This state of things was more helpful to Phoebe than otherwise. Hank took himself off, embarrassed by Phoebe's dignified silence. The children slipped away. Phoebe went at her work unhindered and accomplished it quickly while her thoughts dwelled on the afternoon before her. Upstairs the conference was long and uncertain. Phoebe could hear the low rumbling of Albert's conciliatory tones and the angry rasp of Emmeline's tearful charges. He came downstairs looking sad and tired about an hour before dinnertime and hurried out to the barn to his neglected duties.

He paused in the kitchen to say to Phoebe, "You mustn't mind what Emmeline says, child. Her bark's a great deal worse than her bite always. And, after all, she's had it pretty hard with all the children staying in so much. I'm sure she appreciates what you do. I'm sure she does, but it isn't her way to say much about it. You just go out to tea and have a good time and don't think anymore about this. It'll blow over, you know. Most things do."

Phoebe tried to smile and felt a throb of gratitude toward the brother who really wasn't her brother at all.

"You're a good girl, Phoebe," he went on. "You're like your mother. She was little and pretty and liked things nice and had a quiet voice. I sometimes think maybe it isn't as pleasant here for you as it might be. You're made of different kind of stuff. Your mother was too. I've often wondered whether Father understood her. Men don't understand women very well, I guess. Now I don't really always understand Emmeline, and I guess it's pretty hard for her. Father could be rough and blunt, and maybe that was hard for your mother at times. I remember she used to look sad, though I never saw her much, come to think of it. I was off working for myself when they were married, you know.

"Say, Phoebe," he continued, "you didn't for a minute think I meant what I said about sour grapes and Emmeline, did you? I told her you didn't, but I promised her I'd make sure about it. I knew you didn't. Well, I must go out and see if Hank's done everything."

He went out drawing a long breath as if he'd accomplished an unpleasant task and left Phoebe wondering about her own mother from the words Albert had spoken. Those sentences in her birthday letter came back to her: *Unless you can marry a man to whom you can look up and honor next to God, it's better not to marry at all, believe me. I say it lovingly, for I've seen much sorrow and would protect you.*

Had her father been hard to live with? Phoebe put the thought from her and was almost glad she couldn't answer it. But it made her heart throb with a sense of a fuller understanding of her mother's life and warnings.

Emmeline didn't come downstairs until dinnertime, and her manner was freezing. She poured the coffee, drank a cup of it herself and ate a bit of bread but wouldn't touch anything else on the table—food Phoebe had prepared. She wouldn't respond to the solicitations of her anxious husband, who urged this and that upon her. Hank even suggested the hot biscuits were nicer than usual. But that remark had to be lived down by Hank, for Emmeline usually made the biscuits, and Phoebe had made these. She didn't even look at him in response.

Phoebe was glad when the last bit of pumpkin pie and cheese had disappeared and she could rise from her chair and go about the after-dinner work. Glad, too, that Emmeline went away again and left her to herself, for that way she could more quickly finish up.

She was just hanging up her wiping towels when Emmeline came downstairs with the look of a martyr on her face and the quilting frames in her hand. Over her shoulder was thrown her latest achievement in patchwork, a brilliant combination of reds and yellows and white known as the "rising sun" pattern. It was a large quilt and would be quite a job for one person to put on the frames without an assistant.

Phoebe stopped with an exclamation of dismay.

"You're not going to put that on the frames today, Emmeline? I thought you were saving that for next month!"

Emmeline's grim mouth remained shut for several seconds. At last she snapped out, "I don't know that it makes any difference what you thought. This is a free country, and I've surely a right to do what I please in my own house."

"But, Emmeline, I can't help you this afternoon!"

"I don't know that I've asked you!"

"But you can't do it alone!"

"Indeed! What makes you think I can't! Go right along to your tea party. I was brought up to work, thank fortune, and a few burdens more or less can't make much difference. I'm not a lady of leisure and means like you."

Phoebe stood a minute watching Emmeline's stubby, determined fingers as they fitted a wooden peg into its socket like a period to the conversation. It seemed dreadful to go away and leave Emmeline to put up that quilt alone, but what was she to do? No law in the universe would compel her to give up her first invitation to tea so Emmeline might finish that quilt this particular week.

It was plain she brought it down on purpose to hold her at home. Indignation boiled within Phoebe. If she'd slipped stealthily away this wouldn't have happened, but she'd done her duty in telling Emmeline, and she felt perfectly justified in going. It wasn't as if she'd invited herself. It wouldn't be polite, now that she'd accepted the invitation, not to go. So with sudden determination Phoebe left the kitchen and went up to dress.

She fastened on the buff merino, put her hair in order and tied on her locket, but nowhere could she find the little brown velvet bow that belonged to her hair. She hadn't missed it before, for on Sunday she'd worn her bonnet and dressed in a hurry. In perplexity she looked over her neat boxes of scant finery but couldn't find it. She had to hurry away without it.

She went out the other door, for she couldn't bear to see Emmeline putting up that sunrise quilt alone. The thought of it seemed to cloud the sun and spoil anticipation of her precious afternoon.

Once out in the crisp autumn air she drew a long breath of relief. It was so good to get away from the gloomy atmosphere that had cramped her life for so many years. In a lonely place in the road between farmhouses she uttered a soft little scream under her breath. She felt as if she must do something to let out the agony of wrath and longing and hurt and indignity that threatened to burst her soul. Then she walked on to the town with demure dignity, and the people in the passing carryalls and farm wagons never suspected she was anything but a happy maiden filled with life's joys.

The autumn days lingered in sunny deep-blue haze, though the reds were changing into brown and in the fields there gathered huddled groups of corn shocks like old crones, waving skeleton arms in the breeze and whispering weird gossip. A rusty-throated cricket in the thicket piped out his monotonous dirge to the summer now deceased. A flight of birds sprang into sight across the sky, calling and chattering to one another of a warmer climate. An old red cow stood in her well-grazed meadow, snuffed the short grass and, looking at Phoebe as she passed, mooed a gentle protest at the decline of fresh vegetables. Everything spoke of autumn and the winter that was to come. But Phoebe, with every step she took from home, grew lighter and lighter-hearted.

She wasn't thinking of the stranger, for there was no possibility of meeting him. The Bristol place, a fine old Colonial house behind a tall white fence and high hedge, was over near the Presbyterian church. It wasn't near the Spaffords' house. She felt the freer and happier because there was no question of him to trouble her careful conscience.

Miranda had gone to the window that looked up the road toward the Deanes' at least twenty times since the dinner dishes were washed. She was more nervous over the success of this, her first tea party, than over anything she'd ever done. She was beginning to be afraid her guest wouldn't arrive.

Fidgeting from window to door and back again to the kitchen, Miranda came at last to the library where Marcia sat with her work, watching a frolic between Rose and her kitten outside the window.

"Say, Mrs. Marcia," she began, "you'll find out what troubles that poor little thing and see ef you can't help her, won't you? She's your size an' kind, more'n she is mine, an' you ought to be able to give her some help. You needn't think you've got to tell me everything you find out. I shan't ask. I can find out enough fer my own use when I'm needed, but I think she needs you this time. When there's any use fer me I seem always to kind o' feel it in the air."

"Bless your heart, Miranda. I don't believe you care for anyone unless they need helping!" exclaimed Marcia. "What makes you so sure Phoebe Deane needs helping?"

"Oh, I know," said Miranda mysteriously, "an' so will you when you look at her real hard. There she comes now. Don't you go an' tell I said nothin' 'bout her. You jes' make her tell you. She's that sweet an' so are you that you two can't help pourin' out your perfume to each other like two flowers."

"But trouble isn't perfume, Miranda."

"Hmm! Flowers smells all the sweeter when you crush 'em a little, don't they? There, you set right still where you be. I'll go to the door. Don't you stir. I want her to see you lookin' that way with the sun across the top o' your pretty hair. She'll like it—I know she will."

Marcia sat quite still as she was bidden with the peaceful smile on her lips that David loved so well, smiling over Miranda's strange fancies, yet never thinking of herself as a picture against the windowpanes. In a moment more Phoebe Deane stood in the doorway, with Miranda beside her, looking from one to the other of the two sweet girl-faces in deep admiration and noting with delight that Phoebe fully appreciated the loveliness of her "Mrs. Marcia."

Chapter 10

The afternoon was one of bliss to Phoebe. She laid aside her troubles with her bonnet and basked in the sunlight of Marcia's smile. Here was something she had never known, the friendship of another girl not much older than she was. Marcia, though she'd grown in heart and intellect during her five years of beautiful companionship with David Spafford, hadn't lost the years she skipped by her early marriage but kept their memory fresh in her heart. Perhaps it was the girl in her that attracted her to Phoebe Deane.

They fell into conversation at once. They talked about their mothers, these two who had known so little of real mothering. And Marcia, because she'd felt it herself, understood the wistfulness in Phoebe's tone when she spoke of her loneliness and her longing for her mother. Phoebe told of her mother's birthday letter and the buff merino, and Marcia smoothed down the soft folds of the skirt reverently and told Phoebe it was beautiful, like a present from heaven. She made Phoebe come out where little Rose was, and they played until the child was Phoebe's devoted slave. Then they all went back to the big stately parlor, where Miranda had a great fire of logs blazing. There in a deep easy chair Phoebe was ensconced with Rose cuddled in her lap.

Marcia played exquisite music on her pianoforte, which to the ear of the girl, who seldom heard any music in her life save the singing in church or singing school, seemed entrancing. She almost forgot the child in her lap, forgot to look about on the beautiful room so full of interesting things, forgot even to think as she listened. Her very soul responded to the music.

Then suddenly the music ceased, and Marcia sprang up, saying, "Oh, there's David!" and went to the door to let him in.

Phoebe exclaimed in dismay that it was so late and the beautiful afternoon was at an end. But she forgot her disappointment in wonder over Marcia's joy at her husband's arrival. It brought back the subject that had been in her thoughts ever since the night Hiram Green followed her into the orchard.

Somehow she'd grown up with very little halo about the institution of marriage. It had seemed to her a kind of necessary arrangement but never anything that gave great joy. The married people she knew didn't seem to rejoice in one another's presence. Indeed, they often seemed to be a hindrance to each other. She had never cherished bright dreams of marriage for herself, as most girls do. Life had been too dully tinted since her childhood for her to indulge fancies.

Therefore it was a revelation to her to see how much these two souls cared for one another. She saw it in their glance, in a sudden lighting of the eye, the involuntary cadence of the voice, the evident pleasure of yielding each to the other, the constant presence of joy as a guest in that house, because of the presence of each other. One could never feel that way about Hiram Green—it would be impossible! But hadn't that been the very thing his poor crushed little wife possessed? Yet how could she feel it when it wasn't returned?

She began to think over the married households she knew, but she knew so few of them intimately. There was Granny McVane. Did her husband feel that way about her? And did she spring to meet him at the door after all these years of hard life? Something about the sweet face in its ruffled cap made Phoebe think it possible. And there was Albert. Of course Emmeline didn't feel so, for Emmeline wasn't that kind of woman. But mightn't a different woman have felt that for Albert? He was kind and gentle to women. Too slow and easy to gain real respect, yet—yes, she felt that some women might feel real joy in his presence. There lurked a possibility that he felt that way toward Emmeline, to some degree. But Hiram Green, with his hat pulled down over the narrow eyes, above his cruel mouth—never! He was utterly incapable of so beautiful a feeling. If only he might leave her world forever, it would be a great relief.

When he entered the parlor, David Spafford not only filled it with pleasure for his wife and little girl but brought an added cheer for the guest as well. Phoebe found herself talking with this man of literature and politics and science as easily as if she'd known him well all her life. Afterward she wondered at herself. Somehow he took it for granted that she knew as much as he did, and he made her feel at ease at once.

He asked after Albert Deane as though he were an old friend and seemed to know more about him than Phoebe dreamed. "He has a good head," he added in response to Phoebe's timid answer about the farm and some improvements Albert had introduced. "I had a long talk with him the other day and enjoyed it." Somehow that little remark made Phoebe more at home. She knew Albert's shortcomings keenly, and she wasn't deeply attached to him, but he was all she had, and he'd been kind to her.

Miranda had just called them to supper, and they had reached the table and settled on the right places when the knocker sounded through the hall.

Phoebe looked up, startled. Living as she did in the country, a guest who wasn't intimate enough to walk in without knocking was rare, so an occasion for the knocker to sound would bring forth startled exclamations in the Deane family. But Marcia gave the sign to be seated, and Miranda hastened to the door.

"It's just one of the boys from the office, I think, Marcia," said David. "I told him to bring up the mail if anything important came. The coach wasn't in when I left."

But a man's voice was heard conversing with Miranda.

"I won't keep him but a minute! I'm sorry to disturb him," the voice said. A moment more and Miranda appeared with a guileless face.

"A man to see you, Mr. Spafford. I think it's the nevview of Jedge Bristol's. Shall I tell him you're eatin' supper?"

"What! Nathaniel Graham? No, indeed, Miranda. Just put on another plate and bring him in. Come in, Nathaniel, and take tea with us while you tell us your errand. You're just the one we need to complete our company."

Miranda, innocent and cheerful, hurried away to obey orders, while David helped the willing guest off with his overcoat and brought him to the table. She felt there was no need to say anything about a conversation she'd had with Judge Bristol's "nevview" that afternoon. It was while Marcia was playing the pianoforte in the parlor. Miranda had gone into the garden to pick a bunch of parsley for her chicken gravy—and, as was her custom, to keep a good watch upon all outlying territory. She'd sauntered up to the fence for a glance about and saw Nathaniel Graham coming down the road, wistfully. Yet she dared not add another guest to her tea party, though the very one she would have chosen had wandered her way.

He'd tipped his hat to her and smiled. Miranda liked to have hats tipped to her, even though she was freckled and red-haired. This young man had been in the highest grade of village school when she entered the lowest class, yet he remembered her enough to bow. Her heart swelled with pride in him, and she decided he'd do for the part she wished him to play in life.

"Ah, Miss Miranda," he had paused when almost past, "do you happen to know if Mr. Spafford will be at home this evening? I want to see him very much for a few minutes."

Now, though Miranda had dared not invite another guest, she saw no reason why she shouldn't put him in the way of an invitation. So she'd said thoughtfully, "Let me see! Yes, I think he's at home tonight. Thur's one night this week I heerd him say he was goin' out, but I'm pretty sure it ain't this night. But I'll tell you what you better do ef you're real anxious to see him. You better jest stop 'long about six o'clock. He's always home then, 'n' he'll tell you ef he ain't goin' to be in."

The young man's face had lighted gratefully.

"Thank you. That will suit me very well. I don't need to keep him long, and he can tell me if he'll be in later in the evening. I'll be passing here about that time."

Then Miranda had hustled in with satisfaction to see if her biscuits were beginning to brown. If this plan worked well, nothing further was to be desired.

She spent the remainder of the afternoon in stealthy watch between the kitchen and the parlor door, where, unseen, she could inspect the conversation from time to time and keep advised as to any possible developments. She'd set out to see if Phoebe Deane needed any help, and she meant to have no stone unturned to get at the facts.

So it all happened just as Miranda would have planned. Things were mostly happening her way these days, she told herself with a chuckle and a triumphant glance toward the lights in her grandmother's kitchen, as she went to get another sprigged plate for Nathaniel Graham.

Meanwhile Phoebe's heart was in a great flutter over the introduction. The color came into her cheeks, and her eyes shone like stars in the candlelight as David said, "Nathaniel, let me make you acquainted with our friend, Miss Phoebe Deane. I think she's a newcomer since you left us. Miss Deane, this is our friend Mr. Graham."

And then she found herself murmuring an acknowledgment as the young man took her hand and bowed low over it, saying, "Thank you, David, but I'm not so far behind the times as you think. I've met Miss Deane before."

That flustered her quite a bit, so she could hardly manage to seat herself with her chair properly drawn up to the table. She wondered if they all noticed how her cheeks burned. Ah! If they did they were keeping it to themselves, especially Miranda, who was meekly dishing up the chicken. Wily Miranda! She'd called them to supper without serving it, making due allowance for the digression of another guest she'd planned.

The meal moved along smoothly, with the conversation flowing until Phoebe regained her balance and could take her small, shy part in it. She found pleasure in listening to the talk of David and Nathaniel, so different from that of Albert and Hiram. It was all about the great outside world—politics and the possibilities of war; money and banks and failures; the probabilities of the future; the coming election; the trouble with the Indians; the rumblings of trouble about slavery; the annexation of Texas; the extension of the steam railway.

All of it was new and interesting to Phoebe, who'd heard only a stray word now and then of all these wonderful happenings. Who, for instance, was this "Santa Anna" whose name was spoken of so familiarly? Neither a saint nor a woman, apparently. And what had he or she to do with affairs so serious?

And who was this brave Indian chief Osceola, languishing in prison because he and his people couldn't bear to give up their fathers' home? Why had she never heard of it all before? She'd never thought of the Indians before as anything but terrible, bloodthirsty savages, and, lo, they had feelings and loves and homes like others.

Her cheeks glowed, and her eyes were alight with feeling, and when Nathaniel turned to her now and again he thought how beautiful she was and marveled that he hadn't heard her praises sung from every mouth as soon as he reached the town. He'd been home very little during his college life and years of law study.

Then the conversation came nearer home, and David and Nathaniel talked of their college days. Nathaniel spoke a great deal of Eliphalet Nott, the honored president of his college, and told many a little anecdote of his wisdom and wit.

"This chicken," he began laughingly, as he held up a wishbone toward Phoebe, "reminds me of a story that's told of Dr. Nott. It seems a number of students planned a raid on his chicken house. Dr. Nott's family consists of him, his wife and his daughter, Sally. Well, the rumor of this plot against his chicken house reached the good president's ears, and he prepared to circumvent it.

"The students had planned to go to a tree where several favorite fowls roosted, and one was to climb up while the others stood below and took the booty. They waited until it was late and the lights in the doctor's study went out. Then they stole silently into the yard and made for the hen roost. One man climbed carefully into the tree so as not to disturb the sleeping birds, and the others waited in the dark below.

"The first hen made a good deal of cackling and fuss when she was caught, and while this was going on the students below the tree saw someone approaching them from the house. They scattered into the dark and fled, leaving the poor man in the tree alone. Dr. Nott, well muffled about his face, came quietly up and took his stand below the tree, and in a moment the man in the tree handed down a big white rooster.

" 'This is Daddy Nott,' he said in a whisper, and the man below received the bird without a word.

"In a moment more a second fowl was handed down. 'This is Mommy Nott,' whispered the irreverent student. Again the bird was received without comment.

"Then a third hen was handed down with the comment, 'This is Sally Nott.' The doctor received the third bird and disappeared into the darkness, and the student in the tree came down to find his partners fled, with no knowledge of who had taken the fowls.

"They were much troubled about the circumstance but hoped it was only a joke some fellow student had played on them. But the next day they became extremely anxious when each one received an invitation to dine with Dr. Nott that evening. Not daring to refuse, they presented themselves at Dr. Nott's house at the appointed hour and were received courteously as usual. They began to breathe more freely when they were ushered out to dinner, and there, before the doctor's place, lay three large platters, each containing a fine fowl cooked to a turn.

"They dared not look at one another, but their embarrassment came to a climax when Dr. Nott looked up pleasantly at the student on his right, who had been the man to climb the tree, and asked, 'Hastings, will you have a piece of Daddy Nott or Mommy Nott or Sally Nott?' pointing in order to each platter.

"I think if it hadn't been for the twinkle in the doctor's eye those boys would have taken their hats and left without a word, for they say Hastings looked as if you could knock him over with a feather. But that twinkle broke the horror of it, and they all broke down and laughed until they were heartily ashamed of themselves. And every man there was cured forever of robbing chicken roosts. But, do you know, the doctor never said another word to those fellows about it, and they were his most loyal students from that time on."

Amid the laughter over this story they rose from the table. Little Rose, who had fallen asleep at the table, was whisked off to bed by Miranda, and the others went into the parlor where Marcia played the pianoforte. Phoebe, entranced, listened until suddenly she realized it was half past eight o'clock and she was some distance from home.

Now, for a young woman to be out after nine o'clock in those days was little short of a crime. It would be deemed highly improper by every good person. Therefore, as Phoebe noted the time, she started to her feet in a panic and made her adieus with haste. Marcia went after her bonnet and tied it lovingly beneath her chin, saying she hoped to have her come again soon. David made as if he'd take her home, but Nathaniel waved him back and begged for that privilege himself. So with happy good nights the young man and the girl went out into the quiet village street together and hastened along the way, where already many of the lights were out in the houses.

Chapter 11

As she stepped out into the moonlight with the young man, Phoebe's heart fluttered so she could scarcely speak without letting her voice shake. It seemed so wonderful that she, of all the girls in the village, should be going home with this bright, handsome, noble man. There was nothing foolish or vain in her thought about it. He would never be anything more to her than he was on this walk, for his life was set otherwise, and he belonged to others—in all likelihood, to his cousin Janet. Nevertheless, she felt honored he'd take the trouble to see her home, and she knew the memory of this walk, her first alone with a young man, would remain with her for life.

He seemed to enjoy her company as much as he had David's, for he talked on about the things that had interested them in the evening. He told more college stories and even spoke of his literary society. Remembering Albert's words, Phoebe asked if it was true he'd once been president of the Philomatheans. He modestly acknowledged it, as though the office gave him honor, not he the office. She asked him shyly of the meetings and what they did, and he gave her reminiscences of his college days. Their voices rang out now and then in a laugh.

Out in the quiet country road he suddenly asked her, "Tell me, Miss Deane. Suppose I knew of some people who were oppressed, suffering and wanting their freedom; suppose they needed help to set them free. What do you think I should do? Think of myself and my career, or go and help set them free?"

Phoebe raised her eyes to his earnest face in the moonlight and tried to understand.

"I'm not wise," she said, "and perhaps I wouldn't know what you ought to do, but I think I know what you would do. I think you would forget all about yourself and go to set them free."

He looked down into her face and thought what it meant to a man to have a girl like this one believe in him.

"Thank you!" he said gravely. "I'm honored by your opinion of me. You've told me where duty lies. I'll remember your words when the time comes."

In the quiet of her chamber a few minutes later Phoebe remembered the words of the young people that day upon the hillside and wondered if it was the people of Texas he thought needed to be set free.

He had bid her good night with a pleasant ring in his voice, saying he was glad to know her and hoped to see her again before he left for New York in a few days. Then the door closed behind her, and he walked briskly down the frosty way. The night was cold, even for October, and each startled blade of grass was furred with a tiny frost-spike.

Suddenly, out from behind a cluster of tall elder bushes that bordered the roadside stepped a man, and without warning he dealt Nathaniel a blow between the eyes that made him stagger and almost fall.

"Thet's to teach you to let my girl alone!" snarled Hiram Green like an angry dog, the moonlight illuminating his livid face. "Hev yer learned yer lesson, er d'yeh need another? 'Cause there's plenty more where that come from!"

Nathaniel's senses were stunned for an instant, but he was a master at self-defense, and before the bully had finished his threat with a curse he found himself lying in the ditch with Nathaniel towering over him in a righteous wrath.

"Coward!" he said, looking down on him contemptuously. "You've made a mistake, of course, and struck the wrong man, but that makes no difference. A brave man doesn't strike in the dark."

"No, I haven't made no mistake either," snarled Hiram as he got up from the ground. "I seen you myself with my own eyes, Nate Graham. I seen you trail down the hill out o' the woods after her, 'n' I seen you try to get a kiss from her, an' she run away. I was an eyewitness. I seen yeh. Then you tried to get 'longside her after meetin' was out Sunday, tippin' yer hat so polite, as ef that was everythin' a girl want'd. An' I seen yeh takin' her home tonight after decent folks was a-bed, walkin' 'long a country road talkin' so sweet an' low butter would've melt in yer mouth. No, sir! I ain't made no mistake. An' I jest want you to understand after this you're not to meddle with Phoebe Deane, for she belongs to me!"

By this time Nathaniel had recognized Hiram Green, and his astonishment and dismay knew no bounds. Could a girl like that have anything to do with this coarse, ignorant man? Indignation filled him. He longed to pound the insolent wretch and make him take back all he'd said, but he realized this might be a serious matter for the girl, and it was necessary to proceed cautiously.

So he drew himself up and replied, "There has never been anything between me and Miss Deane to which anyone, no matter how close their relationship to her might be, could object. I met her in the woods while nutting with a party of friends and had the good fortune to help her out of a tangle of laurel and show her the shortcut to the road. I merely spoke to her on Sunday as I spoke to my other acquaintances, and this evening I escorted her home from the house of a friend where we both have been taking tea."

"You lie!" snarled Hiram.

"What did you say, Mr. Green?"

"I said *you lie,* an' I'll say it again, too, ef I like. You needn't git off any more o' your fine words, fer they don't go down with me, even ef you have been to college. All I've got to say is *you let my girl alone from now on!* Ef yeh don't I'll take means to make ye!" And Hiram raised his big fist again.

But the next instant Hiram was sprawling in the dust, and this time Nathaniel held something gleaming in his hand as he stood above him.

"I always go armed," said Nathaniel in a cool voice. "You'll oblige me by lying still where you are until I'm out of sight down the road. Then it will be quite safe for you to rise and go home and wash your face. If I see you get up before that, I'll shoot. Another thing. If I hear another word of this ridiculous nonsense from you I'll have you arrested and brought before my uncle on charges of assault and blackmail and several other things perhaps. As for speaking to the young lady or showing her any courtesy that is ordinarily shown between men and women in good society, that shall be as Miss Deane says, and not in any way as you say. You are not fit to speak her name."

Nathaniel stepped back slowly a few paces, and Hiram attempted to rise, pouring forth a stream of vile language. Nathaniel halted and raised the pistol, flashing in the moonlight.

"You will keep entirely still, Mr. Green. Remember that this is loaded."

Hiram subsided, and Nathaniel walked deliberately backward till the man on the ground could see only a dim speck in the gray of the distance, and a nighthawk in the trees mocked him in a clamorous tone.

All this happened not a stone's throw away from Albert Deane's front gate and might have been discerned from Phoebe's window if her room hadn't been set on the other side of the house.

After a little while Hiram crawled stiffly up from the ground, looked furtively about, shook his fist at the distance where Nathaniel had disappeared, and slunk like a shadow close to the fence till he reached his house. Only a bit of white paper ground down with a great heel mark and a few footprints in the frosty dust told where the encounter had been.

The moon spread her white light over all, and Phoebe slept, smiling in her dreams of the happy afternoon and evening. But Nathaniel sat up far into the night till his candle burned low and sputtered out. He was thinking, and his thoughts weren't all of the oppressed Texans. It occurred to him that other people in the world might be harder to set free than the Texans.

If Hiram Green didn't sleep it was because his heart was busy with evil plans for revenge. He was by no means done with Nathaniel Graham. He might submit under necessity, but he was a man in whom a sense of injury dwelt long and smoldered into a great fire that grew far beyond all proportion of the original offense.

But Phoebe slept on and never dreamed that more evil was brewing.

The lights had been out when she came home, all except a candle in Emmeline's room, but the door was left on the latch for her. She knew Emmeline would reprove her for the late hour of her return, and she was fully prepared for the greeting next morning, spoken frigidly.

"Oh, so you did come home last night, after all! Or was it this morning? I'm surprised. I thought you had gone for good."

At breakfast, things were uncomfortable. Albert persisted in asking Phoebe questions about her tea party, in spite of Emmeline's sarcasms. When Emmeline complained that Phoebe had "sneaked" away without giving her a chance to send for anything to the village and that she needed thread for her quilting that very morning, Phoebe rose from her almost untasted breakfast and offered to go for it at once.

She stepped into the crisp morning with a sigh of relief and walked briskly down the road, happy she had escaped her prison for an hour of the early freshness. Then she stopped suddenly, for there before her lay a letter ground into the dust. There was something strangely familiar about the writing, as if she'd seen it before, yet it wasn't anyone's she knew. It wasn't folded so the address could be seen but lay open and rumpled, with the communication uppermost. The words that stood out clearly to her as she stooped to pick it up were these:

> It is most important that you present this letter, or it will do no good to go. BUT BE SURE NO ONE ELSE SEES IT, OR GREAT HARM MAY COME TO YOU!

She turned the paper over, and there on the other side lay the name that had gleamed at her pleasantly just a few days before through the laurel bushes: *Nathaniel Graham, Esq.*

Was this letter an old one, useless now and of no value to its owner? Surely it must be, and he'd dropped it on his way home with her last night. The wind had blown it open, and a passerby had trodden upon it. That must be the explanation, for surely if it were important he wouldn't have laid it down behind the log so carelessly. Yet the words in the letter read, *It is most important that you present this letter, or it will do no good to go.* Well, perhaps he had already "gone," wherever that was, and the letter had seen its usefulness. But then it further stated that great harm might come to the owner if anyone saw it. She could make sure no one saw it by destroying it, but how would she know she wasn't really destroying an important document? And she might not read further because of that caution, *Be sure no one else sees it.* It was a secret communication to which she had no right, and she must respect it.

She saw there was only one thing to do, and that was to go at once to the owner and give it to him, telling him she hadn't read another word than those she saw at first.

Her troubled gaze saw nothing of the morning's beauties, the bejeweled fringes of grass along the road or the silver-coated red and brown leaves lingering on branches. She passed by Hiram Green's farm just as he was coming down to his barn near the road. He was in full view and near enough for recognition. He quickened his pace as he saw her coming, but her eyes looked straight ahead, and she didn't turn her head toward him. He thought she did it to escape speaking. It angered him anew to have her pass him by unseeing, as if he weren't good enough to treat with ordinary politeness as between neighbors at least. If he needed anything more to justify his heart in its evil plot he had it now.

With lowering brow, he raised his voice and called, "Where you goin' this early, Phoebe?"

But with her face set straight ahead and her mind busy with perplexing questions, she went on her way and never even heard him. Hiram Green's blood boiled.

He waited until she'd passed beyond the red schoolhouse that marked the boundary line between the village and the country and then slouched out from the shelter of the barn and followed her. He wouldn't let her see him, but he meant to know where she was going. She held a letter in her hand as she passed —at least it looked like a letter. Was she writing his rival a letter already? The thought brought a throb of hate toward the man who was better than he, toward the girl who had scorned him and toward the whole world.

Phoebe, unsuspecting and thinking only of her duty, not all a pleasant one for her, went on her way. She felt she must get the letter out of her hands before she did anything else, so she turned down the street past the church to the stately house with its white fence and high hedge, and her heart beat fast against her blue print dress. Seeing the great house she suddenly felt she wasn't dressed for such a call, yet she wouldn't turn back or even hesitate, for it was something that must be done at once. She gave herself no time for thought of what would be said but entered the tall gate, which to her relief stood open. She held the letter tight in her trembling hand.

Hiram arrived at the church corner just in time to see her disappear within the white gates, and his jaw dropped down in astonishment. He hadn't dreamed she'd go to his house. Yet after a moment's thought his eyes narrowed and gleamed with the satisfaction they always showed when he'd seen through some possibility. The situation was awkward for the girl, and his being an eyewitness might someday give him power over her. He took his stand behind the trunk of a weeping willow tree in the churchyard to see what might happen.

Phoebe raised the brass knocker held in the mouth of a lion. How hollow it sounded as it reverberated through the great hall, not at all the cheerful thing it had been when Nathaniel knocked at Marcia Spafford's door. A black woman in a large yellow turban and white apron opened the door. Phoebe managed to ask if Mr. Graham were in.

"Missis Gra'm! Dere ain't no Missis Gra'm," said the old woman, looking her over carefully and rather scornfully. The young ladies who came to that house to visit didn't dress as Phoebe was dressed, in working garb. "Dere's only jes' Mis' Brist'l. Mis' Janet, we calls her."

"Mr. Graham. Mr. Nathaniel Graham," corrected Phoebe, her voice trembling. She thought she felt a rebuke in the woman's words that she should call to see a young man. "I have a message for him. I will wait here, please. No, I'd rather not come in."

"I'll call Miss Janet," said the servant and swept away, closing the door with a bang in Phoebe's face.

She waited several minutes before it was opened again, this time by Janet Bristol.

Chapter 12

Y ou wished to see me?" questioned the tall, handsome girl in the doorway, scrutinizing Phoebe haughtily.

"I wished to see Mr. Graham," said Phoebe, trying to look as if it were quite natural for a young woman to call on a young man in the morning.

"I thought you had a message for him," said Janet sharply, wondering what business this very pretty girl could have with her cousin.

"Yes, I have a message for him, but I must give it to him, if you please," Phoebe said with gentle emphasis. She lifted her eyes, and Janet couldn't help noticing the lovely face and smile.

"Well, that will not be possible, for he is not here," Janet said stiffly.

"Oh! He isn't here? What shall I do? He ought to have it at once. When will he come? I could wait for him."

"He will not be at home until evening," said Janet. "You'll have to leave your message."

"I'm sorry," Phoebe said in a troubled tone. "I can't leave it. The one who sends it said it was private."

"That would not mean you could not tell it to his family," said Janet. She was bristling with curiosity.

"I don't know," said Phoebe, turning to go.

"I can't understand how it is that you, a young girl, should be trusted with a message if it's so private that his own people are not to know," Janet said in a vexed tone.

"I know," said Phoebe. "It is strange, and I'm sorry it happened so. But there's nothing wrong about it, really." She looked up wistfully with her clear eyes so that Janet could scarcely think evil of her. "Perhaps Mr. Graham may be able to explain it to you. I would have no right." She turned and went down the steps. "I will come back this evening."

"Wait," said Janet sharply. "Who are you? I've seen you in church, haven't I?"

"Oh, yes," said Phoebe. "I sit just behind you. I'm Phoebe Deane."

"And who sends this message to my cousin?"

Phoebe's face clouded over. "I don't know."

"Well, that is very strange, indeed. If I were you I wouldn't carry messages for strange people. It doesn't look well. Girls can't be too careful what they do."

Phoebe's face was pained.

"I hope Mr. Graham will be able to explain," she said. "I don't like you to think ill of me." Then she went away, while Janet stood perplexed and annoyed. She tucked the letter safely in the bosom of her gown and held her hand over it as she hurried along, not looking up or noticing anymore than when she had come. She passed Miranda on the other side of the street and never saw her, and Miranda wondered where she was going and why she looked so troubled. If she hadn't been hurrying to the store for something that was needed at once, Miranda would have followed her to find out—perhaps even asked her point-blank.

Phoebe made her way through the village and out onto the country road, and in a short time she arrived at the kitchen of her home, where Emmeline had just finished the breakfast dishes.

"Well," she said grimly, looking up as Phoebe entered and noticing her empty hands. "Where's the thread? Didn't they have any?"

"Oh!" said Phoebe. "I forgot it! I'll go right back!" And without waiting for a word from the amazed Emmeline she turned and sped down the road again toward the village.

"Of all things!" muttered Emmeline, as she went to close the door that had blown open. "She needs a nurse! I didn't suppose going out to tea and havin' a little money in the bank could make a girl lose her head like that! She has turned into a regular scatterbrain. The idea of her forgetting to get that thread when she hadn't another earthly thing to do! I'd like to know who 'twas brung her home last night. I don't know how I could hev missed him till he was way out in the road. It didn't look egzactly like David Spafford, an' yet who could it 'a' ben ef 't wasn't? She must 'a' went to Mis' Spafford's again this mornin' 'stead o' goin' to the store, er she never would 'a' forgot. I have to find out when she gits back. It's my duty!"

Emmeline snapped her lips together over the words as if she anticipated that the duty would be a pleasant one.

In her hasty flight down the road Phoebe almost ran into Hiram Green, who was plodding back from his fruitless errand to his belated chores.

"Boy howdy!" he said, as she started back, blurting, "Excuse me, Mr. Green! I'm in such a hurry I didn't see you." She was gone before her sentence was quite finished, and the breeze wafted it back to him from her retreating figure.

"Boy howdy!" he said again, looking after her. "I wonder what's up now?" And he turned doggedly and followed her again. If this kept up, detective business was going to be lively work. Two trips to the village on foot in one morning were wearisome. Yet he was determined to know what all this meant.

Phoebe did her errand swiftly and was so quick in returning with her purchase that she met Hiram face-to-face outside the store before he had time to conceal himself.

Thrown off his guard, he rallied and tried to play the gallant.

"Thought I'd come 'long and see ef I couldn't carry yer bundle fer yeh."

"Oh, thank you, Mr. Green," said Phoebe. "But I can't wait, for Emmeline is in a great hurry for this. I shall have to run most of the way home. Besides, it's very light. I couldn't think of troubling you." She backed away as she spoke, and with the closing words she turned and flew up the street.

"My!" said Hiram under his breath, almost dazed at the rebuff. "My, but she's a slippery one! But I'll catch her yet where she can't squirm out so easy. See ef I don't!" And with scowling brows he started slowly after her again. He didn't intend to allow any move on her part to go unwatched. He hated her for disliking him.

Miranda, from her watchtower in the Spafford kitchen window, saw Phoebe's flying figure and wondered. She didn't know what it meant, but she was sure it meant something. She felt "stirrings" in her soul that usually called for some action on her part. She was ready when the time should arrive, and she felt it arriving fast and sniffed the air like a trained warhorse. In truth she sniffed nothing more than the aroma of mince pies just out of the great brick oven, standing in a row on the shelf to cool.

The remainder of the morning was not pleasant for Phoebe. Her mind was too busy with her perplexity about the letter to spend much time in planning how to excuse her forgetfulness. She merely said, "I was thinking of something else, Emmeline, so I came back without going to the store at all."

Emmeline scolded and sniffed and scoffed to no purpose. Phoebe silently worked on, her eyes faraway, her whole manner showing that she was paying little heed to what her sister-in-law said. This made Emmeline even more angry. But Phoebe's lips were sealed. She answered questions when it was necessary and quietly worked away. When everything else was done she seated herself at the quilt and began to set tiny stitches in a brilliant corner.

"Don't trouble yourself," said Emmeline. "You might ferget to fasten yer thread er tie a knot in it. I wouldn't be s'prised." But Phoebe worked mechanically on and soon was a whole block ahead of Emmeline.

At dinner she was unusually silent, excusing herself to go back to the quilt as soon as she had eaten a few mouthfuls. Emmeline scrutinized her and became silent. It seemed to her there was something strange about Phoebe. She would have given a good deal to know all about her afternoon at the Spaffords', but Phoebe's monosyllabic answers brought forth little information.

Albert looked at her in a troubled way, then glanced at Emmeline's forbidding face and said nothing.

The afternoon wore away in silence. Several times Emmeline opened her lips to ask a question and snapped them shut again. She made up her mind that Phoebe must be thinking about Hiram Green, and if that was so she'd better keep still and let her think. Nevertheless, there was something serene and lofty about Phoebe's look that was hardly in keeping with a thought of Hiram Green, and her sphinxlike manner made Emmeline feel it was useless to ask questions, though of course Emmeline had never heard of the Sphinx.

At five o'clock Phoebe arose from the quilting frame and without a word got the supper. Then, eating little or nothing herself, she cleared it away and went up to her room. Albert took his newspaper, and Emmeline went grimly at her basket of stockings. She wondered whether the girl intended to come down to help her with them. After all, it was rather profitable to have Phoebe work like this—things got done quickly.

"Is Phoebe sick?" Albert asked suddenly, looking up from his paper.

Emmeline started and pricked her finger with the needle.

"I should like to know what makes you think that," she snapped, frowning at the prick. "You seem to think she's made of some kind of perishable stuff that needs more'n ordinary care. You never seem to think I'm sick as I've noticed."

"Now, Emmeline!" he began pleasantly, "You know you aren't ever sick, and this is your home, and you like to stay in it, and you've got your own folks and all. But Phoebe's kind of different. She doesn't seem to quite belong, and I wouldn't want her to miss anything out of her life because she's living with us."

"Bosh!" said Emmeline. "Phoebe's made of no better stuff 'n I am. She ken do more work when the fit's on her than a yoke of oxen. The fit's ben on her today. She's got her spunk up. That's all the matter. She's tryin' to make up fer losin' yesterday afternoon, jes' to spite me fer what I said about her goin' out. I know her. She's done a hull lot on that there quilt this afternoon. At this rate we'll hev it off the frames before the week's out. She ain't et much 'cause she's mad, but she'll come out of it all right. You make me sick the way you fret about her doldrums."

Albert subsided, and the darning needle clicked in and out with the rapid movement of Emmeline's fingers. They could hear Phoebe moving about her chamber quietly, though it wasn't directly over the sitting room, and presently the sounds ceased altogether, and they thought she had gone to bed. A few minutes later Hiram opened the sitting room door and walked in.

"Where's Phoebe?" he asked, looking at the silent group around the candle. "She ain't out to another tea party, is she?"

"She's gone to bed," said Emmeline. "Is it cold out?"

Phoebe, upstairs by her window, arrayed in her plain brown delaine, brown shirred bonnet and brown cape, waited until the accustomed sounds downstairs told her Hiram had come and was seated. Then she softly climbed out of her window to the roof of a shed a few feet below her window, crept out to the back edge of this and dropped like a cat to the ground. She had performed this feat many times as a child, but never since she wore long dresses. She was glad the moon wasn't up yet and hurried around the back of the house and across the side yard to the fence.

Her feet had scarcely left the last rail when she heard the door latch click, and a broad beam of light flashed across the path not far from her. To her horror she saw Hiram Green's tall form coming out, and then the door slammed shut, and she knew he was out in the night with her.

But she was in the road now with nothing to hinder her, and her light feet flew over the ground, treading on the grassy spots at the edge so she would not make a sound. Somehow she felt he was coming nearer with every step she took. Her heart beat wildly, and great tears started to her eyes. She tried to pray as she fled along. Added to her fear of Hiram was her dread of what he would think if he found her out there in the dark alone. She also feared for the secret of the letter she carried, for instinctively she knew that of all people to find out a secret, Hiram Green would be among the most dangerous. She put her hand over the letter, hidden under her cape, and clenched it fast.

When she passed the silent schoolhouse she turned her head as she hurried along and felt sure she heard him coming. The sky was growing luminous. The moon would soon be up, and then she could be seen. Quite distinctly she heard a man's heavy tread running behind her.

Her heart nearly stopped for an instant, and then, bounding up, she leaped ahead, her lips set, her head down. A few more rods. She could not hold out to run like this much farther. But at last she reached the village pavement and could see the friendly lights of the houses all about her.

She hurried on, not daring to run so fast here, for people were coming ahead. She tried to think and to still the wild fluttering of her heart. If Hiram Green were really following her it would not do for her to go to Judge Bristol's at once. She could hardly hope to reach there and hide from him now, for her strength was almost spent, and not for anything must he know where she was going.

She fled past the houses, oblivious to where she was. She could hear the man's steps on the brick pavement now, and his heavy boots rang out distinctly on the frosty air. She felt as if she had been running for years with an evil fate pursuing her. Her limbs grew heavy, and her feet seemed to drag behind. She half closed her eyes to stop the surging of her blood. Her ears rang, her cheeks burned, and perspiration stood on her lips and brow. Her breath came hard and hurt her.

And then, quite naturally, as if it had been planned, Miranda stepped out from behind the lilacs in the Spafford garden by the gate and walked alongside her, fitting her large, easy gait to Phoebe's weary steps.

"I heard yeh comin' an' thought I'd go a piece with yeh!" she explained, as if this were a common occurrence. "D'ye hev to hurry like this, 'r was yeh doin' it fer exercise?"

"Oh, Miranda!" gasped Phoebe, slowing down and putting a plaintive hand out to reach the strong friendly one in the dark. "I am so glad you're here!"

"So'm I," said Miranda, "but you jest wait till you git your breath. Can't you come in and set a spell 'fore you go on?"

"No, Miranda, I must hurry. I had an errand and must get right back—but I'm almost sure someone is following me. I don't dare look behind, but I heard footsteps and—I'm. . .so. . .frightened. . . ." Her voice trailed off, trembling into another gasp for breath.

"Well, all right, we'll fix 'em. You jest keep your breath fer walkin', an' I'll boss this pilgrimage a spell. We'll go down to the village store fer a spool o' cotton Mis' Spafford ast me t' get the fust thing in the mornin' to sew some sprigged calico curtains she's been gettin' up to the spare bed, an' while we're down to the store we'll jest natcherally lose sight o' that man till he don't know where he's at, an' then we'll meander on our happy way. Don't talk 'r he'll hear you. You jest foller me."

Chapter 13

Phoebe, too exhausted to demur, walked silently beside Miranda, and in a moment more they were safely in the store.

"Say, Mr. Peebles, is Mis' Peebles t' home? 'Cause Phoebe Deane wants t' git a drink o' water powerful bad. Ken she jest go right in and get it whilst I get a spool o' cotton?"

"Why, certainly, young ladies, walk right in," said the affable storekeeper, arising from a nail keg.

Miranda had Phoebe into the back room in no time, and she was calmly debating the virtues of different spools of thread when Hiram Green entered, puffing and snorting like a porpoise. He glanced around, then a blank look spread over his face. The one he sought wasn't there? Could he have been mistaken?

Miranda, paying for her thread, eyed him furtively and put two and two together, figuring out her problem with a relish. She said good evening to Mr. Peebles and deliberately went out the door into the street. Hiram watched her suspiciously, but she held her head high as if she were going straight home. Instead she slipped through the dark around to the side door where she walked in on Mrs. Peebles and the astonished Phoebe without ceremony.

"Did yeh get yer drink, Phoebe? Ev'nin', Mis' Peebles. Thank yeh, no, I can't set down. Mis' Spafford needs this thread t' oncet. She jest ast me wouldn't I run down and git it so's she could finish up some pillar slips she's makin'. Come on, Phoebe, ef yer ready. Ken we go right out this door, Mis' Peebles? There's so many men in the store, an' I can't bear 'em to stare at my pretty red hair, you know." And in a moment more she had whisked Phoebe out the side door into the dark yard, where they could slip through the fence to the side street.

"Now which way?" asked Miranda in a low tone as they emerged from the shadow of the store to the sidewalk.

"Oh, Miranda, you're so kind," said Phoebe, hardly knowing what to do, for she dared not tell her errand to her. "I think I can go quite well by myself now. I'm not much afraid, and I'll soon be done and go home."

"See here, Phoebe Deane. D'yeh think I'm going t' leave a little white-faced thing like you with them two star eyes t' go buffetin' round alone in the dark where there's liable to be lopsided nimshies follerin' round? Yeh can say what yeh like, but I'm goin' to foller yeh till I see yeh safe inside yer own door."

"Oh, you dear, good Miranda!" said Phoebe with a teary smile, clasping her arm tight. "If you only knew how glad I was to see you."

"I knowed all right. I cud see you was scared. But come 'long quick er that hound in there'll be trackin' us again. Which way?"

"To Judge Bristol's," said Phoebe in a low whisper.

"That's a good place to go," said Miranda. "I guess you won't need me inside with you. I'm not much on fancy things, an' I'll fit better outside with the fence posts, but I'll be thar to take yeh home. My! But you'd orter 'a' seen Hiram Green's blank look when he got in the store an' seen you wa'n't there. I'm calculatin' he'll search quite a spell 'fore he makes out which way we disappeared."

Phoebe's heart beat wildly at the thought of her escape. She felt as if an evil fate were dogging her every step.

"Oh, Miranda!" she shivered. "What if you hadn't come along just then!"

"Well, there ain't no use cipherin' on that proposition. I was thar, an' I generally calculate to be thar when I'm needed. Jest you rest easy. There ain't no long-legged, good-fer-nothin' bully like Hiram Green goin' to gather you in, not while I'm able to hob round. Here we be. Now I'll wait in the shadder behind this bush while you go in."

Phoebe timidly approached the house while Miranda, as usual, selected her post with discernment and a view of the lighted window of the front room, where the family was assembled.

Janet didn't keep Phoebe waiting long this time but swept into the doorway in a dress of ruby red with a little gold locket hung from a bit of black velvet ribbon about her neck. Her dark hair was arranged in clusters of curls on each side of her face, and the glow on her cheeks seemed reflected from the color of her garments.

"I'm afraid my cousin is too busy to see you," she said in a kind but condescending tone. "He's busy preparing to leave on the early stage in the morning. He found out he must go to New York sooner than he expected."

"I will not keep him long," said Phoebe earnestly, "but I must see him for just a minute. Will you kindly tell him it is Phoebe Deane and that she says she must see him for just a moment?"

"He will want you to send the message by me," said Janet. "It does not do to say 'must' to my cousin Nathaniel."

But contrary to Janet's expectation Nathaniel came down at once, with welcome in his face. Phoebe stood with her hand on the letter over her heart waiting for him. The watching Miranda eyed him through the front windowpane to see if his countenance would light up properly when he saw his visitor—and was fully satisfied. He hastened to meet her and take her hand in greeting, but she only held out the letter to him.

"I found this, Mr. Graham, spread out in the road and read the one sentence which showed it was private. I haven't read anymore, and I shall never breathe even that one, of course. After I had read that sentence I didn't dare give it into any hands but yours. I may have been wrong, but I tried to do right. I hope you can explain it to your cousin, for I can see she thinks it very strange."

He tried to detain her to thank her and introduce her to his cousin, who had by this time entered and watched them coolly. But Phoebe was in haste to leave, and Janet was haughtily irresponsive.

He followed her to the door and said in a low tone, "Miss Deane, you have done me a greater service than I can possibly repay. I've been hunting frantically for this letter all day. It is most important. I know I can trust you not to speak of it to a soul. I'm deeply grateful. You may not know it, but not only my life and safety but that of others as well has been in your hands today with the keeping of that letter."

"Then I'm glad I've brought it safely to you. I've been frightened all day lest something would happen and I couldn't get it to you without its being found out. And if it has been of service I'm more than glad, because then I have repaid your kindness to me in the woods that day."

Now that she was away from Janet's scrutinizing eyes Phoebe could venture a smile.

"What I did that day was a little thing beside your service," he said.

"A kindness is never a little thing," answered Phoebe gently. "Good night, Mr. Graham. Miranda is waiting for me." And she sped down the path without giving him opportunity for a reply.

Miranda had wandered into the shaft of light down by the gate that streamed from the candle Nathaniel held, and Phoebe flew to her. They turned and looked back as they reached the gate. Nathaniel was still standing on the top step with the candle held above his head to give them light, and through the window they could dimly see Janet's slim figure standing by the mantelpiece toying with some ornaments.

Phoebe gave a sigh of relief that the errand was accomplished and grasped Miranda's arm, and so the two walked softly through the village streets and out the country way into the road that was now white with the new risen moon. Meanwhile Hiram Green, baffled, searched vainly through the village for a clue to Phoebe's whereabouts and finally gave up and dragged his weary limbs home.

Nathaniel turned back into the house again, his vision filled with the face of the girl who had just brought his letter back to him. His relief at finding it was almost lost in the thought of Phoebe Deane and a sudden pang of remembrance of Hiram Green. Could it be? Could it possibly be that she was bound in any way to that man?

Janet roused him from his thought by demanding to know what on earth the message was that made the girl so absurdly secretive.

Nathaniel smiled. "It was just a letter of mine she had found. A letter that I have searched everywhere for."

"How did she know it was your letter?" There was something offensive in Janet's tone.

Nathaniel felt his color rising. He wondered why Janet should be so curious.

"Why, it was addressed to me, of course."

"Then why in the world couldn't she give it to me? She was here in the morning, and we had a long argument about it. She said it was a private message and the person who sent it did not wish anyone but you to see it, and yet she professed not to know who the person was who sent it. I told her that was ridiculous, that of course you had no secrets from your family, but she was quite stubborn and went away. Who is she, anyway, and how does she happen to know you?"

Nathaniel could be haughty, too, when he liked, and he drew himself up to his full height.

"Miss Deane is quite a charming girl, Janet, and you would do well to make her acquaintance. She is a friend of Mrs. Spafford and was visiting her last evening when I happened in on business, and they made me stay to tea."

"That's no sign of where she belongs socially," said Janet. "Mrs. Spafford may have had to invite her just because she didn't know enough to go home before supper. Besides, Mrs. Spafford's choice in friends might not be mine at all."

"Janet, Mr. and Mrs. Spafford are unimpeachable socially and every other way. And I happen to know that Miss Deane was there by invitation. I heard her speaking of it as she bid her good night."

"Oh, indeed!" sneered Janet, beside herself with jealousy. "I suppose you were waiting to take her home!"

"Why, certainly," said Nathaniel, looking surprised. "What has come over you, Janet? You're not talking like your usual kind self."

His tone brought angry tears to Janet's eyes.

"I should think it was enough," she said, trying to hide the tears in her lace handkerchief, "having you go off suddenly like this when we've scarcely had you a week, and you busy and absentminded all the time. And then to have this upstart of a girl coming here with secrets you won't tell me about. I want to know who wrote that letter, Nathaniel, and what it is about. I can't stand it to have that girl smirking behind me in church knowing things about my cousin that I don't know. I must know."

"Janet!" said Nathaniel. "You must be ill. I never saw you act this way before. You know very well I'm just as sorry as can be to have to rush off sooner than I had planned, but it can't be helped. I'm sorry if I've been absentminded. I've been trying to decide some matters of my future, and I suppose that has made me somewhat abstracted. As for the letter, I would gladly tell you about it, but it is another's secret, and I could not do so honorably. You need fear no such feeling on Miss Deane's part, I'm sure. Just meet her with your own pleasant, winning way and tell her I've explained to you it was all right. That ought to satisfy both you and her. She asked me to explain it to you."

"Well, you haven't done so at all. I'm sure I can't see what possible harm it could do for you to tell me about it, since that other girl knows all about it too. I should think you would want me to watch and be sure she doesn't tell—unless the secret is between you two."

Something about Janet's tone hinted at an insinuation. Nathaniel grew stern.

"The secret is not between Miss Deane and me," he said, "and she does not know it anymore than you do. She found it open and read only one line, which told her it was absolutely private. She tells me she did not read another word."

"Very likely!" sneered Janet. "Do you think any woman would find it possible to read only one line of a secret? Your absolute faith in this stranger is quite childlike."

"Janet, would you have read further if it had fallen into your hands?"

"Well, I—why, of course, that would be different," she said, coloring and looking disconcerted. "But you needn't compare me—"

"Janet, you have no right to think she has a lower sense of honor than you do. I feel sure she has not read it."

But Janet, with flashing eyes, swept up the stairs and took refuge in her room, where a storm of tears and mortification followed.

Nathaniel, dismayed, after vainly tapping at her door and begging her to come out and explain her strange conduct, went back to his packing, puzzling over the strange ways of girls with one another. Here, for instance, were two well suited to friendship, and yet he could plainly see they would have nothing to do with each other. He loved his cousin. She had been his playmate and companion from childhood, and he couldn't understand why she had suddenly grown so inconsiderate of his wishes. He tried to put it away, deciding he would say another little word about the charming Miss Deane to Janet in the morning before he left. But the next morning Janet forestalled any such attempt by sending down word that she had a headache and would try to sleep a little longer. She called out a cool good-bye to her cousin through the closed door as he hurried down to the stage waiting for him at the door.

Meanwhile, Miranda and Phoebe hurried out past the old red schoolhouse into the country road, white with frosty moonlight. Phoebe kept protesting that Miranda mustn't go with her.

"Why not, in conscience!" said Miranda. "I'll jest enjoy the walk. I was thinkin' of goin' on a lark this very evenin'; only I hadn't pickcd out a companion."

"But you'll have to come all the way back alone, Miranda."

"Well, what's that? You don't s'pose anybody's goin' to chase *me,* do yeh? If they want to, they're welcome. I'd jest turn round an' say, 'Boo! I'm redhaired an' freckled, an' I don't want nothin' of you nor you of me. Git 'long with yeh!' "

Miranda's manner brought a laugh to Phoebe's lips and helped relieve the tension she had been under. She felt like laughing and crying all at once. Miranda seemed to understand and kept her in ripples of laughter till they neared her home. Not until she saw her charge safe inside her own door would the faithful Miranda turn back.

When they were close to the house, Phoebe suddenly turned and said confidentially, "Well, Miranda, I'll have to tell you how I got out. There was a caller—someone I didn't care to see—so I went upstairs, and they thought I'd gone to bed. I just slipped out my window to the low shed roof and dropped down. I'll have to be very still, for I wouldn't care to have them know I slipped away like that. It might make them ask me questions. You see, I found a letter Mr. Graham had dropped, and it needed to go to him at once. If I had asked Albert to take it, there would have been a big fuss, and Emmeline would have wanted to know all about it, and maybe read it, and I didn't think it would be best—"

"I see," said Miranda, "so you tuk it yourself. O' course. Who wouldn't, I'd like to know? All right, we'll jest slip in through the pasture and round to your shed, an' I'll give yeh a boost up. Two's better'n one fer a job like that. I take it yer caller ain't present any longer. Reckon he made out to foller yeh a piece, but we run him into a hole, an' he didn't make much. Hush, now. Don't go to thankin'. 'Taint worthwhile till I git through, fer I've jest begun this job, an' I intend to see it through. Here, put yer hand on my shoulder. Now let me hold this foot. Don't you be 'fraid. I'm good an' strong. There yeh go! Now yer up! Is that your winder up there? Wal, hope to see yeh again soon. Happy dreams!" And she slid around the corner to watch Phoebe till she disappeared into the dark window above.

Miranda made for the road, looking in at the side window of the Deanes' sitting room on the way to make sure she was right about the caller being gone and to see if they had heard Phoebe, for she thought it might be necessary to invent a diversion of some sort. But she only saw Albert asleep in his chair and Emmeline working grimly at her sewing.

About halfway to the red schoolhouse Miranda met Hiram Green. He looked up, frowning. He thought it was Phoebe and wondered if it were possible she was making another trip to the village that night.

"Ev'nin', Hiram," said Miranda nonchalantly. "Seen anythin' of a little white kitten with one blue eye and one green one, an' a black tip to her tail an' a pink nose? I've been up to see if she follered Phoebe Deane home from our house las' night, but she's gone to bed with the toothache, an' I wouldn't disturb her fer the world. I thought I'd mebbe find her round this way. You ain't seen her, have yeh?"

"No," growled Hiram. "I'd 'a' wrung her neck ef I had."

"Oh, thank you, Mr. Green. You're very kind," said Miranda sweetly. "I'll remember that, next little kitten I lose. I'll know jest who t' apply to fer it. Lovely night, ain't it? Don't trouble yerself 'bout the kitten. I reckon it's safe somewheres. 'Taint everyone ez bloodthirsty's you be. Good night." And Miranda ran down the road before Hiram could decide whether she was poking fun at him or not.

At last he roused himself from his weary pondering and went home to bed. He hadn't been able all day to fathom the mystery of Phoebe's vanishings when he had started out with her in plain view. And this new unknown quantity was more perplexing than all the rest. What, for instance, had Miranda Griscom to do with Phoebe Deane? His slow brain remembered she had been in the store where Phoebe disappeared. Had Miranda spirited her away somewhere? Ah! And it was Miranda who had come up to Phoebe after church and interrupted their walk together! Hang Miranda! He'd like to wring her neck too. With such charming meditations he fell asleep.

Chapter 14

Nathaniel sat inside the coach as it rolled through the village streets and out into the country road toward Albany and tried to think. All remembrance of Janet and her foolishness had left his mind. He had a problem to decide, and it was all the more difficult because the advice of his dearest friends was so at variance.

He took out two letters which represented the two sides of the question and began to reread. The first was the letter Phoebe had brought, disfigured by the dust but still legible. It bore a Texas postmark and was brief and businesslike.

Dear Nephew,

If you are as keen as you used to be you have been keeping yourself informed about Texas and know the whole state of the case better than I can put it. Ever since Austin went to ask the admission of Texas as a separate state into the Mexican Republic and was denied and thrown into prison, our people have been gathering together; and now things are coming to a crisis. Something will be done and that right soon, perhaps in a few days. The troops are gathering near Gonzales. Resistance will be made. But we need help. We want young blood and strong arms and hearts with a conviction for right. No one on earth has a right to deprive us of our property and say we shall not own slaves which we have come by honestly. We will fight and win, as the United States has fought and won its right to govern itself.

Now I call upon you, Nathaniel, to rise up and bring honor to your father's name by raising a company of young men to come down here and set Texas free. I know you are busy with your law studies, but they will keep, and Texas will not. Texas must be set free now or never. When you were a little chap you had strong convictions about what was right, and I feel pretty sure my appeal will not come to deaf ears. Your father loved Texas and came down here to make his fortune. If he had lived he would have been here fighting. He would have been a slave owner and asserted his right as a free man in a free country to protect his property. He would have taught his son to do the same. I call upon you for your father's sake to come down here—for it is the place where you were born—and help Texas. Use your utmost influence to get other young men to come with you.

Your uncle the judge will perhaps help you financially. He owns a couple of slaves himself, I remember, house servants, doesn't he? Ask him how he would like the government of the United States to order him to set them free. I feel sure he will sympathize with Texas in her hour of need and help you do this thing I've asked.

I am a man of few words, but I trust you, Nathaniel, and I feel sure I am not pleading in vain. I shall expect something from you at once. We need the help now, or the cause may be lost. If you feel as I think you do, go to the New York address given below. This letter will be sufficient identification for you as I have written to them about you, but it is most important that you present this letter, or it will do no good to go. BUT BE SURE NO ONE ELSE SEES IT, OR GREAT HARM MAY COME TO YOU! There is grave danger in being found out, but if I didn't know your brave spirit I would not be writing you. Come as soon as possible!

Your uncle,
Royal Graham

The other letter was kept waiting a long time while the young man read and reread this one. Then he let his eyes wander to the brown fields and dim hills in the distance. He was going over all he could remember of his boyhood in that faraway Southern home. He could dimly remember his father, who had been to him a great hero and had taken him with him on horseback wherever he went and never been too weary or too busy for his little son. A blur of sadness came over the picture—the death of his beloved father and an interval of emptiness when the gentle mother was too full of sorrow to comprehend how her young son suffered.

Then one day his uncle Royal, so like yet not like his father, had lifted him in his arms and said, "Good-bye, little chap. Someday you'll come back to us and do your father's work and take his place." And he and his mother had ridden away in an endless succession of coaches until one day they arrived at Judge Bristol's great white house set among the green hedges, and there Nathaniel had found a new home. There, first his mother and then Janet's mother had slipped through the mysterious door of death, and he grew up in the home of his mother's brother, with Janet as a sister.

From time to time he received letters from this shadowy uncle in Texas, and once, when he was about twelve, there had been a brief visit from him which cleared the memory and kept him fresh in Nathaniel's mind. Always there was some hint that when Nathaniel was grown and educated he would come back to Texas and help make it great. This had been a hazy undertone in his life, in spite of the fact that his other uncle, Judge Bristol, constantly talked of his future career as a lawyer in New York City, with a possibility of a political career also.

Nathaniel had gone on with his life, working out the daily plan as it came, all the time feeling that these two plans were contending for supremacy.

Sometimes during leisure moments lately he had wondered if the two could ever be combined and, if not, how they were both to work out. Gradually it dawned upon him that a day was coming when he would have to choose. And now, since these two letters had reached him, he knew the time had come. Yet how was he to know how to choose?

His uncle Royal's letter had reached him the afternoon of the nutting party on the hill. Pompey, his uncle's house servant, had brought it to him just as they were starting out. He had glanced at the familiar writing and put it in his pocket for later reading. He always enjoyed his uncle's letters, but they were not of deep importance to him. He had been too long separated from him to have many interests in common with him. And so he hadn't read the letter until after his return from the hillside, which explains how he had carelessly left it behind the log by Phoebe, as an excuse to return and help her out of the laurel.

In the quiet of his own room, after Janet and the others were sleeping, he had remembered the letter and, relighting his candle, read it. He was startled to discover its contents. The talk of the afternoon floated back to him, idle talk about his going down to set Texas free. Talk that grew out of his own keen interest in the questions of the day and his readiness to argue them out. But he'd never had a definite idea of going to Texas to take part in the struggle until the letter brought him face-to-face with a possible duty.

Perhaps he would have had no question about his decision if the very next day he hadn't received another letter which put an entirely different spin on the issue—and made duty seem an uncertain creature with more faces than one.

The coach was halfway to Albany before Nathaniel finally folded away his uncle's letter and put it in his inner pocket. Then he took up the other letter with a perplexed sigh and read:

Dear Nate,

I'm sitting on a high point of white sand, where I can look off at the blue sea. At my right is a great hairy, prickly cactus with a few yellow blossoms in delicate petals and fringed stamens that look as out of place amid the sand as a diamond on a plank. The sun is very warm and bright, and everything around seems to be basking in it.

As I look off to sea the Gulf Stream is distinct today, a brilliant green ribbon in the brilliant blue of the sea. It winds along so independently in the great ocean, keeping its own individuality in spite of storm and wind and tide. I went out in a small boat across it the other day and could look down and see it as distinctly as if there were a glass wall between it and the other water. I can only think that God took pleasure in making this old earth.

I'm having a holiday, for my pupils are gone away on a visit. This is a delightful land to which I've come and a charming family with whom my lot is cast. I'm having an opportunity to study the South in a most ideal manner, and many of my former ideas of it are becoming much modified. For example, there's slavery. I am by no means so sure as I used to be that it was ordained by God. I wish you were here to talk it over with me and study it too. Certain possibilities in the institution make one shudder. Perhaps, after all, Texas is in the wrong. As you have opportunity, drop into an abolition meeting now and then and see what you think. I've been reading the Liberator *lately. I find much in it that is strong and appeals to my sense of right. You know what a disturbance it has made in the country recently. I hear some mails have even been broken into and burned on account of it. I wonder if this question of slavery will ever be an issue in our country. If it should be I can't help wondering what the South will do. From what I've seen I feel sure they will never stand to have their rights interfered with.*

Now I have to confess that much as I rebelled against giving up my work and coming down here, I feel it has already benefitted me. I can take long walks without weariness and can even talk and sing without becoming hoarse. I don't believe my lungs have ever been affected, and I feel I'm going to get well and come back to my work. With that hope in my veins I can go through these sunny days and feel new life creeping into me with every breath of fresh air. We shall yet work shoulder to shoulder, my friend—I feel it. God bless you and keep you and show you the right way.

Yours faithfully,
Martin Van Rensselaer

Nathaniel folded the letter, placed it in his pocket with the other letter and leaned his head back to think.

Van Rensselaer had been his roommate for four years. They had grown into one another's thoughts as two who are much together and love each other often do. Nathaniel could not quite tell why this letter troubled him. Yet he felt through the whole epistle the stirring of a new principle that seemed to antagonize his sympathy with Texas.

So through the long journey he debated the question back and forth. His duty to his uncle demanded that he go to the address given and investigate the matter of helping Texas. And when he looked at it from his uncle's standpoint and thought of his father, his sympathy was with Texas. On the other hand, his love for his friend and his trust in him demanded that he investigate the other side also. He sensed intuitively that the two things could not go together.

Martin Van Rensselaer had been preparing for the ministry. His zeal and earnestness were great, too great for his strength, and before he finished his theological studies he had broken down and been sent South, as it was feared he had serious lung trouble. The separation had been a great trial to both young men. Martin was three years older than Nathaniel and two years ahead of him in his studies, but in mind and spirit they were as one, so the words of his letter had great influence.

The day grew surly as the coach rumbled on. Sullen clouds lowered in the corners of the sky as if meditating mutiny. A hint of snow bit the air that whistled around the cracks of the coach windows. Nature seemed to have suddenly put on a bare, brown look.

Nathaniel shivered and drew his cloak close about him. He wished the journey were over or that he had someone to advise him. Once or twice he had broached the subject with Judge Bristol, but he'd hesitated to show him either of the letters. He felt that his uncle's letter might arouse antagonism in Judge Bristol on account of the claim it put upon him, as his father's son, to come and give himself. Judge Bristol was almost jealously fond of his sister's son and felt that he belonged to the North. Aside from that, his sympathies would probably have been with Texas. Keeping a few slaves himself as house servants and treating them as kindly as if they were his own children, he saw no reason to object to slavery and deemed it a man's right to do as he pleased with his own property.

The judge would likely have looked upon Martin Van Rensselaer's letter as the product of a sentimental fanatic whose judgment was unsound. Nathaniel was certain that if the judge should read those letters he would advise against having anything to do with either cause personally. Yet Nathaniel's conscience would not let him drop the matter so easily.

The coach thumped on over rough roads and smooth. The coachman called to his horses, snapped his whip and wondered why Nathaniel, who was usually so sociable and liked to sit on the box and talk, stayed glumly inside without a word to him. He sat gloomily mile after mile, trying to think what girl of his acquaintance was good enough for Nathaniel.

But Nathaniel sat inside with closed eyes and tried to think, and ever and again there came a vision of a sweet-faced girl with brown hair and a golden dress sitting among the falling yellow leaves with bowed head. And somehow in his thoughts her trouble became tangled, and it seemed as if three instead of two needed setting free, and he must choose between them all.

Chapter 15

The cold weather had come suddenly, and Phoebe felt like a prisoner. Emmeline's tongue became a daily torture, and the little ways in which she contrived to make Phoebe's life a burden were too numerous to count.

Her paltry fortune in the bank was a source of continual trouble. Scarcely a morning passed without its being referred to in some unpleasant way. Every request was prefaced with some such phrase as "If you're not too grand to soil your hands," or "I don't like to ask a rich lady to do such a thing," till Phoebe felt sometimes that she could bear it no longer and longed to take the few dollars and fling them into the lap of her disagreeable sister-in-law, if by doing so she might gain peace. Like the continual dripping that wears away the stone, the unpleasant reference had worn upon a single nerve until the pain was acute.

But there was another source of discomfort still more trying to the girl than all that had gone before, and this was Hiram Green's new role. He had taken it upon himself to act the fine gentleman. It was somewhat surprising considering the fact that Hiram was known in the village as "near," and this new departure demanded an entirely new outfit of clothes. In his selection he aimed to emulate Nathaniel Graham. As he had neither Nathaniel's taste nor his New York tailor the effect was far from perfect, except perhaps in the eyes of Hiram, who felt quite set up in his fine raiment.

On the first Sunday of his proud appearance in church thus arrayed, he waited boldly at the door until the Deanes came out and then took his place beside Phoebe and walked with her to the carryall as though he belonged there.

Phoebe's thoughts were on other things, and for a moment she hadn't noticed. But suddenly she became conscious of measured footsteps beside her own, looked up and found the reconstructed Hiram strutting by her side like a peacock. In spite of her great annoyance her first impulse was to laugh, and that laugh probably did more than any other thing to turn the venom of Hiram Green's hate upon her innocent head. After all the effort he had made to appear well before her and the congregation assembled, she had laughed. She had dared to laugh aloud, and the hateful Miranda Griscom, who seemed to be always in the way whenever he tried to walk with Phoebe, had laughed back. A slow ugly red rolled into his sunburned face, and his eyes narrowed with resolve to pay back all and more than he had received of scorn.

Miranda was holding Rose by the hand and couldn't get much nearer to Phoebe that morning without attracting attention, so the girl could do nothing to get away from her unpleasant suitor except to hurry to the carryall.

And there before the open-eyed congregation Hiram Green helped her into the carryall with a rude imitation of Nathaniel Graham's gallantry. She should see that others besides the New York college dandy could play the fine gentleman. He finished the operation with an exaggerated flourish of his hat, and just because laughter is so near to tears, the tears sprang up in Phoebe's eyes. She could do nothing but drop her head and try as best she could to hide them.

The all-seeing Alma of course discovered them, and just as they were driving by Judge Bristol and his daughter she called out, "Aunt Phoebe's cryin'. What you cryin' 'bout, Aunt Phoebe? Is it 'cause you can't ride with Hiram Green?"

Thereafter Hiram Green was in attendance upon her at every possible public place. She couldn't go to church without finding him at her elbow the minute the service was over, ready to walk down the aisle beside her. She couldn't go to singing school without his stepping out from behind his gate as she passed and joining her, or if she evaded him he would sit beside her and manage to sing out of the same book. She couldn't go to the village on an errand without his appearing in the way and accompanying her. He seemed to have developed a strange intuition as to her every movement.

He was ever vigilant, and the girl began to feel like a hunted creature.

Even if she stayed at home he appeared at the door ten minutes after the family had gone, a triumphant, unpleasant smile on his face, and sauntered into the kitchen without waiting for her to bid him. There, tilted back in a chair in his favorite attitude, he would watch her every movement and drawl out an occasional remark. That happened only once, however; she never dared to stay again, lest it would be repeated.

She had been busy preparing something for dinner and turned suddenly and caught a look on his face that reminded her of a beast of prey. It flashed upon her that he was actually enjoying her annoyance. Without thinking she stepped into the woodshed and from there fled across the backyard and the meadows between and burst into Granny McVane's bright little room.

The dear old lady sat there rocking by the fire, with her open Bible on her knee. Phoebe was relieved to find her alone. In answer to the gentle "Why, dearie, what can be the matter?" she flung herself on the floor at the old lady's feet and, putting her head in her lap, burst into tears.

She lost her self-control only for a moment, but even that moment relieved the heavy strain on her nerves, and she was able to sit up and tell the old lady all about it. She hadn't intended to tell anything, when in her sudden panic she had beaten a hasty retreat from the enemy. But Granny McVane's face showed so much tender sympathy that all at once it seemed good to tell someone of her trouble.

Granny McVane listened, watched her sympathetically, smoothed back the damp tendrils of hair that had blown about her face and then stooped over and kissed her.

"Don't you ever marry him, Phoebe. Don't you ever do it, if you don't love him, child!" she said solemnly, like a warning. "And just you run over here, dearie, whenever he bothers you. I'll take care of you."

Phoebe, with her natural reserve, hadn't drawn her family into the story except to say they favored the suit of the would-be lover. But it comforted her greatly to have someone on her side, even if it were only this quiet old lady who couldn't really help her much.

They watched out the back windows until they saw Hiram emerge from the Deane house and saunter off down the road. Even then Phoebe was afraid to go back until she saw the carryall far down the road. Then she flew across the fields and entered the back door before they had turned in at the great gate. When they got out and came into the house she was demurely paring potatoes, and Emmeline eyed her suspiciously.

"Seems to me you're pretty late with your potatoes," she remarked disagreeably. "I suppose you had a nice easy time all morning."

But Phoebe did not explain. Only she didn't stay at home again when the family would all be away. She never knew whether Emmeline was aware of Hiram's Sunday visit or not.

Phoebe's state of mind after this occurrence was one of constant nervous alarm. She began to hate the thought of the man who seemed to haunt her at every turn.

Before this one of her greatest pleasures had been to walk to the village after the daily mail or for an errand to the store. Now such walks became a dread. One afternoon in early November she had hurried away and gone around by Granny McVane's, hoping thus to escape Hiram Green's vigilance. She managed to get safely to the village and do her errands, but just as she emerged from the post office the long, lank figure of Hiram loomed before her and slouched into his dogged gait beside her.

"Did you get a letter?" he asked, looking suspiciously at the one she held in her hand. Then as she didn't answer he went on, "You must have a whole lot of folks writin' you quite constant. You seem to go to the post office so much."

Phoebe said nothing. She felt too indignant to speak. How could she get away from her tormentor unless she deliberately ran away from him? And how could she do that right here in the village where everyone was watching? She glanced up furtively. Hiram wore a look of triumph as he talked on, knowing he was annoying her.

"I s'pose you get letters from New York," he said, with a disagreeable insinuation in his tone.

Phoebe didn't know what he meant, but something in his tone made the color come into her cheeks. They were nearing the Spafford house. If only Miranda would come out and speak to her! She looked up at the great bully beside her and saw he was trying to calculate just how near the mark he had come. She stopped short on the pavement.

"I do not wish to walk with you," she said, struggling to keep her voice from trembling.

"Oh, you don't," he mocked. "How 'r' ye goin' to help yourself?"

She looked up into the pitiless cruelty of his eyes and shuddered involuntarily.

"I am going in to see Mrs. Spafford," she said with sudden inspiration, and her voice took on a girlish dignity. With that she put wings to her feet and flew to the Spafford front door, wondering if anyone would let her in before Hiram reached her.

Now Miranda was alone in the house that afternoon, and not much went on in the neighborhood that she didn't keep herself informed about. Therefore, when Phoebe, breathless, reached the front stoop the door swung open before her, and she stepped into her refuge with a gasp of relief and heard it close behind her as two strong freckled arms enclosed her.

"Ben waitin' quite a spell fer ye," she declared, as if it were the expected thing for Phoebe to fly into her arms unannounced in that way, "ever sence I see ye comin' down the street with that pleasant friend of yourn. Wonder you could tear yourself away. Take off yer bonnet and set a spell. Mis' Spafford's gone up t' th' aunts' fer tea and took Rose. I'm all alone. You set down, an' we'll have a real nice time, an' then I'll take you home by 'n' by."

"Oh, Miranda," gasped Phoebe, struggling hysterically between laughter and tears and trying to control the trembling that had taken possession of her body, "I'm such a miserable coward. I'm always running away when I get frightened!"

"Hm! I should hope you would!" said Miranda. "Such a snake in the grass as that! Le's see ef he's gone!" She crouched before the window and peered behind the curtain cautiously.

Hiram had watched Phoebe's sudden disappearance within the door with something like awe. It was almost uncanny having that door open and swallow her up. Besides, he hadn't expected Phoebe to dare run away from him. He stood a moment gazing after her and then sauntered on, calling himself a fool for having met her so near the Spafford house. Another time he would choose his meeting place away from her friends. He had lost this move, but he by no means meant to lose the game, and the hate in his heart grew with determination to have this tempting young life in his power and crush out its resistance.

It goaded him to madness for her to tell him she did not wish to walk with him. Why did she say that? Hadn't he always been respected and thought well of? His farm was as good a spot of land as could be found in the whole New York State, and his barn was talked about through the county. He was prosperous, everybody knew. Before he had married Annie, any girl in the vicinity would have thought him a great catch, and he knew well, by all the indescribable signs, that many girls as good as Phoebe would still be glad to accept his attentions. Why did this little nobody, who was after all merely a poor relation of his neighbor, presume to scorn him? He hated her for it, even while his heart was set upon having her. He wanted her at first because he admired her. Now he wanted to conquer and punish her for scorning him.

As he walked on alone his slow brain tried to form a new plan for revenge, and little by little an idea crept out of his thoughts and looked at him with its two snaky eyes until the poison of its fang had stolen into his heart. The post office! Ah! He would watch to see if she had a letter from that fellow, for surely only the knowledge that another man was at her feet could make her scorn his attentions. If that was so he would crush the rival! He ground his teeth at the thought, and his eyes glittered with hate.

Meanwhile, Hiram Green's children and Alma Deane were playing together behind the big barn that had been one of the disappointments of Annie Green's married life, because it hadn't been a house instead of a barn. The children had dug houses in a haystack and chased the few venturesome hens that hadn't learned to be wary when they were around. Now, for the moment weary of their games, they mounted the fence to rest.

"There comes your pa," announced Alma from her perch on the top rail. The young Greens retired precipitately from the fence, and Alma was forced to follow them if she wished company. They hurried around the other side of the barn out of sight.

"Say," said Alma, after they had reached a spot of safety and ensconced themselves on the sunny exposure of a board across two logs, "my aunt Phoebe went to the village a while ago. She'll be 'long pretty soon. Let's make up somethin' an' shout at her when she comes back. It'll make her mad as hops, an' I'd just like to pay her back fer the way she acts sometimes."

"Ain't she good to you?" inquired the youngest Green anxiously.

"Le's make up sumpin' 'bout her 'n' yer pa. There ain't nothin'll make her so mad. She's mad as mad can be when my ma says anythin' 'bout her gettin' married," went on Alma, ignoring the question.

"All right! What'll we make up?" agreed the three Greens.

They were not anxious to have a stepmother who might make life's restrictions more strenuous then they were already. They were prepared to do battle valiantly if they only had a general, and Alma was thoroughly competent in their eyes to fill that position.

"It'll have to be to a song, you know," went on Alma. "Le's sing the doxol'gy an' see how that goes." So they all stood in a row and droned out the doxology, piping shrilly where they knew words and filling in with homemade syllables where they didn't. Alma had practiced that art of rhyming before and was anxious to display her skill.

"Now listen!" she said and lined it out slowly, with many stops and corrections, until at last the doggerel was completed. And so they sang:

There-was-a-man-in-ow-wer-town
    His-name-was-Hi-rum-Gre-ee-een
And-he-did-ma-a-air-ree-a-wife
    Her-name-was-Phe-be-Dee-ee-een.

Alma was no lax general. She drilled her little company again and again until they could shout the words at the top of their voices, to say nothing of the way they murdered Old Hundred. The young scapegraces looked at their leader with wide-eyed admiration and fairly palpitated for the moment when their victim would arrive. Between rehearsals they mounted the fence by the barn and kept a watchout down the road. At last it was announced that she was coming.

"But there's somebuddy with 'er," said a disappointed little Green.

"We won't dast, will we?"

Alma held up her undaunted chin and mounted the observation post to see who it was.

"Aw! That's all right," she presently announced. " 'Taint nobody but the redheaded girl down to Spaffords'. She can't do nothin'. Come on now—le's get ready."

She marshalled her forces behind the wide board fence next to the pigsty, and there they waited for the signal to begin. Alma thought it prudent to wait until Phoebe and Miranda had almost passed before they sang. Then she raised her hand, and they piped out shrilly, making the words more than plain.

Phoebe started at the first line and hurried her steps, but Miranda glanced back and said, "Hm! I thought 'es much. Like father, like child!"

Maddened by such indifference the children ran along inside the fence and continued to yell at the top of their lungs, regardless of time or tune, until they reached the more open fields near the Deane house, where they dared go no further. Then they retired in triumph to the shelter of the pigsty and the haystack to plume themselves on their success and recount the numerous faces they'd made and the times they'd stuck their tongues out. They didn't anticipate any trouble from the incident as they were too far away from the house for Hiram to hear, and they felt sure Phoebe would never tell on them, as it involved her too closely.

Suddenly, in the midst of the congratulations, without the slightest warning, a strong hand seized the sturdy Alma from the rear and pinioned her arms so she couldn't get away. She set up a yell that could have been heard for a half mile and began to kick and squirm. But Miranda's hands held her fast, while she took in the surroundings at a glance, moved her captive toward a convenient seat on a log and, taking her calmly over her knee, administered in full measure the spanking that child deserved. Alma, meanwhile, was yelling like a loon, unable to believe the despised "red-haired girl from Spaffords' " had displayed so much ability and thoroughness in her methods of redress.

The valiant army of little Greens had retired with haste from the scene and were even then virtuously combing their hair and washing their hands and faces with a view to proving an alibi should the avenger seek further retribution. Alma was left to Miranda's mercy, and though she kicked and yelled right lustily Miranda spanked on until she was tired.

"There!" she said, at last letting her go. "That ain't half you need, but I can't spend any more time on yeh today. Ef yeh ever do that er anythin' like it again I'll come in the night when everybody's asleep and give yeh the rest, an' I ken tell you now I won't let yeh off this easy next time. Mind you behave to yer aunt Phoebe, er I'll hant yeh! D'yeh understand? Wherever yeh go in the dark I'll be there to hant yeh. And when red-haired people hants yeh at night their hair's all on fire in the dark an' it burns yeh, so yeh better watch out!"

She shook her fist at the child, who, now thoroughly frightened, began to cry in earnest and ran home as fast as her fat legs could carry her, not daring to look back lest the supernatural creature with the fiery hair and the strong hand should be upon her again. It was the first time in her brief, impertinent life that Alma had ever been thoroughly frightened.

Her first act on reaching the house was to see how the land lay. She found that her mother had gone out to get some eggs and Phoebe was up in her room with the door buttoned. No one else was about, so Alma stole noiselessly up to Phoebe's door, with righteous innocence on her tearstained face, her voice smoother than butter with deceit.

"Aunt Phoebe!" she called lovingly. "I hope you don't think I sung that mean song at you? I was real 'shamed of them Green children. I run after 'em an' tried to make 'em stop, but they jest wouldn't. I think their pa ought to be told, don't you? Say, Aunt Phoebe, you didn't think 'twas me, did you?"

No answer came from the other side of the door, for Phoebe was lying on her bed shaking with suppressed sobs and couldn't control her voice to reply even if she had known what to say. Her heart was filled with pain, too, that this child she had tended and been kind to should be so hateful.

Alma, rather nonplussed at receiving no answer, tried once or twice and then, calling out sweetly, "Well, I just thought I'd let you know 'twasn't me, Aunt Phoebe," stumped off downstairs to reflect upon the way of sinners. Her main fear was that Phoebe would "tell on her" to her father, and then she knew she would receive the other half of her spanking.

But Phoebe, with a face white with suffering and dark rings under her eyes, said not a word when she came downstairs. She went about her work not even seeming to see the naughty child, until Alma gradually grew more confident and resolved to put the "hanting" out of her mind entirely. This was easier said than done, however, for when night came she dreaded to go to bed and made several unsuccessful attempts to help Phoebe with the supper dishes. She thereby called upon herself much undeserved commendation from her gratified mother and father, which helped ease her conscience not a little.

Chapter 16

Hiram Green put his new plan into practice the very next day. He took care to be on hand when the mail coach arrived, and as soon as the mail was distributed he presented himself at the post-office corner of the store.

"Any mail fer th' Deanes?" he inquired carelessly, after he was told there was nothing for him. "I'm goin' up there on business, an' I'll save 'em the trouble o' comin' down."

This question he put in varied forms, until it grew to be a habit with the postmaster to hand over the Deanes' mail to Hiram every day. This was rather expensive business, for Albert frequently received letters from people who didn't prepay the postage, and it went much against Hiram's grain to hand out eighteen cents or more for another man's letter, even though he was sure he'd receive it again. He made prompt collections from Albert, however, and by this means Phoebe became aware of Hiram's daily visits to the post office. Not that it made any difference to her, for she didn't expect a letter from anyone.

This went on for about two weeks, and during that time Hiram had seen very little of Phoebe, for she kept herself well out of his way. Then one day a letter bearing a New York postmark and closed with heavy seals arrived, addressed to Miss Phoebe Deane.

Hiram grasped it as if it were a long-sought fortune, put it hastily in his pocket, looking furtively around lest anyone had seen it, and slouched off toward home. When he reached there he went straight to his own room and fastened the door. Then he took out the letter and read the address again, written in a fine large hand of a man accustomed to handling a pen. He frowned and turned it over. The seals were stamped with a crest on which was a rampant lion that seemed to defy him. He held the letter up to the light but couldn't make out any words.

Then without hesitation he took out his knife and inserted the sharpest blade under the seals one by one, prying them up carefully so they shouldn't be broken more than necessary. The letter lay open before him at last, and he read with rising fury.

New York, December 20th, 1835

My dear Miss Deane,

 Will you pardon my presumption in daring thus to address you without permission? My pleasant memory of our brief acquaintance has led me to wish a continuance of it, and I'm writing to ask you if

*you are free and willing to correspond with me occasionally. It will
be a great source of pleasure to me if you can accede to my request,
and I'm sure I shall be profited by it also.*

*Night before last our city was visited by a great calamity in the
shape of a terrible fire which is still burning, although they hope
they now have it under control. Its course has been along Wall
Street, the line of the East River and returning to William and Wall
Streets. There must be nearly thirteen acres devastated, and I've
heard it estimated there will be a loss of at least eighteen million
dollars. I'm afraid it will be the cause of much suffering and distress.
I was out last evening watching the conflagration for a time and
helping fight the fire. It was a terrible and beautiful sight.*

*I've just had the honor and privilege of meeting a noble and
brave gentleman. His name is William Lloyd Garrison. I feel sure
you would like to know about him and the work he is doing. If I'm to
have the pleasure of writing you again I shall be glad to tell you
more about him, as I hope to meet him again and know him better.*

*Hoping that you are quite well and I shall soon have a favorable
reply from you, I am,*

Yours with esteem,
Nathaniel Graham

Hiram Green wasn't a rapid reader, and in spite of Nathaniel's clear chirography it took him some time to take in all the letter contained. His first thought was that his rival wasn't out of his way yet. He'd dared to write to her and ask if she was free. Ah! That showed he'd taken note of what Hiram had said about her belonging to him, and he was going to find out for himself. Well, he'd never find out by that letter, for Phoebe would never see it. That was easy enough.

Of course it was against the law to open another person's mail and was a state's prison offense, but who was to know he'd opened it? A letter could tell no tales when it was in ashes and the ashes well buried. How else could they prove it? They couldn't. He was perfectly safe and was getting more power over these two he was coming to hate and wished to crush. He congratulated himself on having been keen enough to have watched the mails. He'd outwitted them and was pleased with himself.

"Hm!" he exclaimed under his breath. "He's a-goin' to get up a correspondence with her, is he? Like to see him! I rather think by the time she answers this letter he'll uv give it up. When he gets around again to give her another try—supposin' he ain't stumped at not hearin' from her this time—I reckon she'll be nicely established in my kitchen doin' my work. Yes, she's worth fightin' for, I guess, fer she ken turn off the work faster'n anybody I've seen.

Wal, I guess there ain't any cause to worry 'bout this."

Then he read it over again, jotting down on an old bit of paper the date, a few items about the New York fire and William Lloyd Garrison's name. After that he sent the old woman who was keeping house for him to the attic in search of a coat he knew wasn't there, while he carefully burned the letter on the hearth, gathering every scrap of its ashes and pulverizing them, to make sure not a trace remained to tell the tale.

As he walked toward his barn he felt like a man of consequence, quite satisfied with himself. Hadn't he outwitted a college man? And no thought of the crime he'd just committed troubled his dull conscience.

That evening he went eagerly to Albert Deane's house and prepared to enjoy himself. The sunrise bed quilt was long since finished and rolled away in the chest of drawers in the spare bedroom. The spinning wheel had taken the place of the quilting frames. And on this particular night Emmeline had demanded that Phoebe stay downstairs and spin, declaring that the yarn should have been ready long ago for more winter stockings.

Hiram noted this fact with satisfaction and tilted his chair in anticipation.

"Heard anythin' 'bout the big fire in New York?" he began, watching Phoebe's back narrowly to see if she would start.

But Phoebe worked steadily on. She paid little heed to anything Hiram said, but as they talked of the fire she wondered whether Nathaniel Graham had been near it and hoped in a quiet way that he'd been kept safe from harm.

"Why, no," said Albert, sitting up with interest. "I haven't looked at the paper yet," he added, unfolding it with zest. "How'd you come to know, Hiram? You say you never read the papers."

"Oh, I have better ways o' knowin' than readin' it in the papers," boasted Hiram. "I had a letter from New York straight, an' the fire's goin' on yet, an' mebbe by this time it's all burnt up."

Phoebe stood where he could see her face as he spoke about receiving a letter, but not a muscle moved to show she heard. Hiram was disappointed. He'd expected to catch some flitting expression that would show him she was interested in letters from New York. But Phoebe expected no letters from New York, so why should she start or look troubled?

"Yes," said Albert, bending over his paper, "an area of thirteen acres—693 houses burned!"

"Valued at eighteen million!" remarked Hiram. He was enjoying the unique position of knowing more than Albert about something.

"Nonsense!" said Emmeline sharply. "Thirteen acres! Why, that's not much bigger'n Hiram's ten-acre lot down by the old chestnut tree. Think of gettin' that many houses on that lot! It couldn't be done. That ain't possible. It's ridiculous! They must think we're all fools to put that in the paper."

"Oh, yes, it could, Emmeline," said Albert, looking up earnestly to convince her. "Why, even so long ago as when I stayed in New York for a month they built the houses real close without much dooryard. They could easy get that many into thirteen acres built close."

"I don't believe it!" said Emmeline, flipping her spinning wheel around skillfully. "And anyway, if 'twas so, I think it was real shiftless to let 'em all burn up. Why didn't they put it out? Those New York folks were born lazy."

"Why, Emmeline, the paper says it was so cold the water froze in the hose-pipes and they couldn't put it out."

"Serves 'em right then fer dependin' on such newfangled things as hose-pipes. It's jest some more of their laziness. Why didn't they form a line and hand buckets? A good fire line with the women an' all in it would beat all the new lazy ways invented to save folks from liftin' their fingers to even put out a fire. I'm surprised some of 'em didn't jest sit still and expect some kind of new machine to be made in time to wheel 'em away to safety 'stead of usin' their legs and runnin' out o' harm's way. Haven't they got a river in New York?"

" 'Course," said Hiram, as if he knew at all. "The fire burned the whole line of the East River." He was glad to be reminded of the rest of his newly acquired information.

"There, that just shows it!" exclaimed Emmeline. "That's just what I said. Shiftless lot, they are. Let their houses burn up right in front of a river! Well, I'm thankful to say I don't live in New York!"

The talk hummed on about her, but Phoebe heard no more. Somehow she kept her busy wheel whirring, but her thoughts had wandered off in a sunlit wood, and she was holding sweet converse with a golden day and a stranger hovering on the pleasant horizon. Near the close of the evening her thoughts came back to listen to what was going on. Hiram had brought the front legs of his chair down to the floor with a thud. Phoebe thought he was going home, and she was glad they'd soon be rid of his hated presence.

"Oh, by the way!" said Hiram, with a sway of conceit. "Albert, have you ever heard of a man named Garrison? William Lloyd Garrison, I believe it is."

He rolled the name out fluently, having practiced in the barn during the evening milking.

"Oh, yes," Albert said with interest. "You know who he is, Hiram. He's a smart fellow, though I'd hate to be in his boots!"

"Why?" Hiram's voice was sharp, and his eyes narrowed as they always did when he was reaching out for clues.

"Why, don't you know about Garrison? He's had a price on his head for some time back. He gets mobbed every time he turns around, too, but I guess he's pretty plucky, for he keeps right on."

"What doing?"

"Why, he's the great abolitionist. He publishes that paper, the *Liberator,* don't you know. You remember two years ago those antislavery meetings that were broken up and all the trouble they had? Well, he started it all. I don't know whether he's very wise or not, but he certainly has a lot of courage."

Hiram's eyes were narrowing to a slit now with knowledge and satisfaction.

"Oh, yes, I place him now," he drawled out. "He wouldn't be a very comfortable 'quaintance fer a man t' have, would he?"

"Well," considered Albert thoughtfully, "I wouldn't like to have any of my relations in his place. I'd be afraid of what might happen. I think likely 'twould take a bit of courage to be friend to a man like that. But they say he has friends, a few of them."

"Hm!" said Hiram. "I guess I better be goin'. 'Night." And he shuffled away at last, casting a curious smile at Phoebe as he left.

The next morning while they were working in the kitchen Emmeline remarked to Phoebe that Albert thought Hiram Green was changing for the better. He seemed to be growing real intellectual. Had Phoebe noticed how well he talked about that New York fire?

Phoebe hadn't noticed.

"What a strange girl you are!" exclaimed Emmeline, much vexed. "I should think you'd see he's takin' all this interest in things jest fer you. It ain't like him to care fer such things. He just thinks it will please you, and you're hard as nails not to 'preciate it."

"You're quite mistaken, Emmeline. Hiram Green never did anything to please anyone but himself, I'm sure," answered Phoebe, taking her apron off and going up to her room.

Phoebe was spending much more time in her room these days than pleased Emmeline. Not that her work suffered, for Phoebe's swift fingers performed all the tasks required of her, but as soon as they were done she was off. The fact that the room was cold didn't affect her. Emmeline was in a state of chronic rage for this isolation from the rest of the family, though perhaps the only reason she liked to have her around was so she might make sarcastic remarks about her. Then, too, it seemed like an assumption of superiority on Phoebe's part. Em-meline couldn't bear superiority.

Phoebe hurried to the seclusion of her own room on every possible occasion because a new source of comfort and pleasure had been opened to her through Marcia Spafford's kindness.

Miranda had reported promptly Phoebe's two escapes from Hiram Green, and not only Marcia but David was interested in the girl. Shortly after Alma's unexpected punishment Miranda was sent up to the Deanes to ask Phoebe down for the afternoon a little while, as "Mis' Spafford has a new book she thinks you'll enjoy readin' with her a while." Much to Emmeline's disgust, for she'd planned a far different occupation for Phoebe, the girl accepted with alacrity and was soon seated in the pleasant library poring over one of Whittier's poems that opened up a new world to her. The poem was one David had just secured to publish in his paper, and they discussed its beauties for a few minutes. Then Marcia opened a delightful new book by Cooper.

Phoebe had a naturally bright mind, and during her school days she had studied all that came to her. Always she stood at the head of the classes, sometimes getting up at the first peep of dawn to study a lesson or work over a problem and sticking to her books until the very last minute. This had been a great source of trouble, because Emmeline objected to "taking her education so hard," as she expressed it.

"Some children have measles and whooping cough and chicken pox and mumps real hard," she'd say, "but most of 'em take learnin' easy. But Phoebe's got learnin' hard. She acts like there wasn't any use for anything else in the world but them books. Land! What good'll they do her? They won't make her spin a smoother thread er quilt a straighter row er sew a finer seam. She'll jest forget everything she learnt when she's married. I'm sure I did." And no one ever disputed this convincing fact.

Nevertheless Phoebe had studied on, trying to please Emmeline by doing all the work required of her but still insisting on getting her lessons even if it deprived her of her rest or noon lunch. She devoured every bit of information that came her way, so that in spite of her environment she had a measure of true mental culture. It may have been this that so mystified and annoyed Emmeline.

So the afternoon was one of pure delight to Phoebe. When she insisted she must go home to help get supper, Miranda was sent with her, and the precious book went along to be read in odd moments. Since then Phoebe felt she had something to help her through the trying days.

The afternoons of reading with Marcia Spafford had become quite the settled thing every week or two, and always she had a book to carry home or a new poem or article to think about.

Emmeline had grown angry about this constant going out and asked questions until she had in a measure discovered what was going on. She held her temper in for a while, for when she spoke to Albert he didn't seem to sympathize with her irritation at Phoebe but only asked the girl to let him see the book she'd been reading. He became so delighted with it himself he forgot to bring in the armful of wood Emmeline asked for until she called him the second time.

After that Albert shared in the literary treasures Phoebe brought to the house, and it became his habit to ask when he came in to supper, "Been down to the village this afternoon, Phoebe? Didn't get anything new to read, did you?"

This made Emmeline furious, and she decided to express her mind once more to the girl.

She chose a morning when Phoebe was tied by a task she couldn't leave. "Now look here, Phoebe Deane, I must say you're goin' beyond all bounds. I think it's about time you stopped. I want you to understand I think the way you're actin' is a downright sin. It isn't enough you should scorn a good honest man that's eatin' his heart out fer yeh, an' you payin' no more 'tention to him 'n if he was the dust o' your feet, an' him able to keep you well, too. An' here you're willin' to set round an' live on relations that ain't real relations at all, an' you with money in the bank a-plenty an' never even offerin' to give so much as a little present to your little nephews and nieces that are all you've got in the world. It ain't enough you should do all that an' be a drug on our hands.

"But here you must get up a 'quaintance with a woman I don' like ner respect at all, an' let her send that poor, hardworkin', good fer-nothin', red-headed girl after you every few days a-takin' you away from your home an' your good honest work that you ought to be willin' to do twice over fer all you've had.

"Phoebe Deane, d' you realize we let you go to school clear up to the top grade when other girls hed to stop an' go to work? It was all *his* doin's; I'd never hev allowed it. I think it jest spoils a girl to get so much knowledge. It's jest as I said 'twould be too. Look at you! Spoiled. You want lily-white hands an' nothin' to do. You want to go to everlastin' tea parties an' bring home books to read the rest o' the time. Now I stopped school when I was in the fourth reader 'n' look at me. There ain't a woman round is better fixed 'n what I am. What do I need of more books? Answer that, Phoebe Deane! Answer me! Would it make me darn the children's stockin's er cook his meals er spin er weave better, er would it make me any better anyway? Answer me!"

Emmeline had two bright red spots on her cheeks and was very angry. When she was angry she always screamed her sentences at her opponent in a high key. Phoebe had the impulse to throw the wet dishcloth at her sister-in-law, and it was hard indeed to restrain her indignation at this speech. There was the lovely Mrs. Spafford lending her books and helping her and encouraging her in every way to improve her mind by reading and study, and even Mr. Spafford seemed anxious she should have all the books to read she desired. And here was this woman talking this way! It was beyond speech. She had nothing to say.

Emmeline stepped up close to the girl, grasped her arm and shook it fiercely until the dishcloth came close to doing a rash deed of its own accord.

"Answer me!" she hissed in the girl's face.

"It might—" the exasperated girl began, then hesitated. What good would it do to say it?

"Well, go on," said the woman, gripping the arm painfully. "You've got some wicked word to say. Just speak it out to the one that hes been more than mother to ye, an' then I s'pose you'll feel better."

"I was only going to say, Emmeline, that more study might have made you understand others better."

"Understand! Understand!" screamed Emmeline, now thoroughly roused. "I'd like to know who I don't understand! Don't I understand my husband an' my children an' my neighbors? I s'pose you mean understand you, you good-fer-nothin' hussy! Well, that ain't necessary! You're so different from everybody else on earth that an angel from heaven er a perfesser from college couldn't understand you, an' learnin' won't make you any different, no matter how much you waste on it."

"Emmeline, listen!" said Phoebe, trying to stop this outburst. "I consider that I've worked for my board since I came here—"

"Consider! You consider! Well, really! Worked for your board, when you was scarcely more use 'n a baby when you come, an' think o' all the trouble o' raisin' ye! And you consider thet you've earned all you've got here! Well, I don't consider any such a thing, I ken tell you."

"Please let me finish, Emmeline. I was going to say I've tried to make Albert take the money I have in the bank as payment for any expense and trouble I've been to him. But he says he promised my mother he wouldn't touch a cent of it, and he won't take it."

"Oh, yes, Albert is softhearted. Well, I didn't promise yer ma, by a long sight, an' I ain't bound to no such fool notions."

"Emmeline, I don't feel the money belongs to you. You didn't bring me here or pay for whatever I've had. Albert did. I can't see why I should give you the money. You've done nothing for me but what you've had to do, and I'm sure I've worked for you enough to pay for that, but I'd much rather give the money to you than to have you talk this way—"

"Oh, I wasn't askin' fer yer money. I wouldn't take it es a gift. I was only showin' yeh up to yourself, what a selfish good-fer-nothin' you are, settin' up airs to read books when there's good honest work goin' on."

Albert happened to come in just then, and the discussion was dropped. But Phoebe with determination continued her visits to Mrs. Spafford whenever Miranda came for her—never alone, lest she encounter Hiram Green—and so the winter dragged slowly on its way.

Chapter 17

Meanwhile Hiram Green still kept up his attention to the post office, watching the Deanes so vigilantly that they couldn't receive mail without his knowing it. This never annoyed Albert, as he was too good-natured to suspect anyone of an ill turn, and he thought it exceedingly kind of Hiram to bring his mail up. As for Phoebe, it simply cut out all opportunity for her to go out, except when Miranda came for her.

"Why can't that Mirandy girl stay home an' mind her business an' let you come when you get ready?" asked Emmeline, in a loud tone one day when Miranda was waiting in the sitting room for Phoebe to get ready to go with her. "She ac's if she was your nurse."

But Miranda continued her vigilance, and that without Phoebe's asking, and somehow Marcia always planned it that if Phoebe could stay to tea, then she and David would walk home with her. It was all delightful for Phoebe, but everything merely offended Emmeline more.

Miranda, in these days, was enjoying herself. She lost no opportunity to observe the detestable Hiram and rejoice that she'd foiled his attempts to bother Phoebe. One day, however, she happened to be in the post office when the mail was distributed. She was buying sugar and loitered a moment after the package was handed her, watching Hiram Green who had slouched over to the counter and asked for his mail.

"Nothin' fer the Deanes?" she heard him ask in a low tone. "Nothin' fer Phoebe? She was 'spectin' somethin', I'm sure."

Miranda cast a sharp glance at him as she passed him. She was glad somehow that he received nothing. She wondered if Phoebe knew he was inquiring for her mail. Miranda tucked it in the back of her mind as something that might be of use in the future and left.

That very day the old woman who kept house for Hiram, in sweeping out his room, came across a bit of red sealing wax stamped with a part of a crest bearing a lion's head with the jaws apart. It was lying on a dark stripe in the rag carpet and hadn't been noticed before. She saw at once it was of no value and tossed it toward the open window, where it lodged on the sill next to the frame. When the window was closed it was shut in tight between sash and sill, with the lion's head, erect and fierce, caught in the crack, a tiny thing and hidden, but reminding one of "truth crushed to earth."

The next day Nathaniel Graham made a flying visit to his home to have a serious conference with his uncle the judge. His investigations concerning the two questions troubling him on his journey back to New York had involved him in matters that had now come to a crisis, and he found that some decision must be reached at once. He'd received several more letters from his uncle in Texas, urging him to come down at once and help their cause. It was becoming more dangerous to do, since Congress hadn't sanctioned any such help, and anyone who attempted it might be in serious difficulties. Yet it was being done every day. People who lived near Texas were gathering money and arms and sending men to help, and even as far away as New York many were quietly working. Public sentiment was strongly with Texas.

He'd been offered command of a company of men who were to sail soon, and he must say yes or no at once. The pressure was strong, and sometimes he almost thought he should go. The time had come to speak to Judge Bristol. Nothing could be decided without his final word, for Nathaniel felt too much honor and love for the one who had been his second father to do anything without his sanction.

As was to be expected the judge was troubled at the thought of Nathaniel's going south to join the conflict. He argued for a long time against it, telling his nephew he had no right to consider such questions until he'd made a place for himself in the world. When Nathaniel admitted he'd been attending abolition meetings and was becoming intimate with some of the leaders, the judge was roused to hostility.

"Nathaniel, how could you?" he exclaimed in deep distress. "I thought your judgment was sound, but to be carried away by these fanatics shows anything but sound judgment. Can't you see this is a question you have no business with? If your uncle in Texas chooses to keep slaves, you have no more right to meddle with his choice than if he chose to keep horses or sheep. And as for this bosh about slavery being such a terrible evil, look at Pompey and Caesar and Dianthe and the rest? Do you think they want to be free? Why, what would the poor things do if I didn't care for them as if they were my own children? It's nonsense.

"Of course, there are a few bad masters and probably will be as long as sin is in the world. But to condemn the whole system of slavery because a few men who happen to own slaves mistreat them would be like condemning marriage because a few men abused their wives. It's nonsense for a few hotheaded fanatics to try to run the rest of the country into the molds they've made and call it righteousness. 'Let other men alone, and they'll let you go in peace' is a better motto. Let every man look out to cast the beam from his own eyes before he attempts to find a mote in his brother's."

When his uncle quoted Scripture, Nathaniel was at a loss how to answer him.

"I wish you could hear Mr. Garrison talk, Uncle."

"I wouldn't listen to him for a moment," he answered hotly. "He's a dangerous man! Keep away from all those gatherings. They only breed discontent and uprisings. You'll see that nothing but a lot of mobs will come from this agitation. Slavery can't be overthrown, and all these meetings are mere talk to let a few men get into prominence. No man in his senses would do the things Garrison has done unless he wanted to get notoriety. That's what makes him so foolhardy. Keep away from him, my boy. There's a price on his head, and you'll do yourself and your prospects no good if you have anything to do with him."

They talked far into the night, with Nathaniel trying to defend the man he'd met only once or twice but was compelled to admire. Janet pouted through the evening because Nathaniel didn't come out to talk with her and finally went to bed in a dark mood.

When at last Nathaniel pressed his uncle's hand at parting, they both knew he wouldn't go to Texas. Indeed, as the young man reflected during the night, he felt his purpose in going there was shaken before he came home to ask Judge Bristol's advice. He wasn't altogether sure, however, that his uncle had considered the matter from the correct viewpoint either, but the talk had somehow helped to crystallize his own views. So now he felt free, rather bound, to return and complete his law course. As for the other matter, that must be left to develop in its time. He was by no means sure he was finished with it yet, for his heart had been too deeply touched and his reason stirred.

As Nathaniel climbed into the coach at the big white gate he felt he'd only put off these questions for a time, but he felt a certain relief that a decision had been reached at least for the present.

He had half a mind to ride on top with the driver, though it was a bitterly cold morning. But quite unexpectedly the driver suggested he better sit inside this time because of the weather. Without giving it a passing thought he went inside, waving his hand and smiling at Janet, who stood at the front door with a fur-trimmed scarlet cloak about her shapely shoulders. The door closed, and he sat down.

There was one other passenger, a girl, who sat far back in the shadows of the coach, but her eyes shone out from the heavy wrappings of cloak and bonnet.

"Oh!" she said, catching her breath.

"And is it you?" he asked eagerly, reaching out to grasp her hand.

Then each remembered, the girl that she was alone in the coach with this man, the man that this girl might belong to another. But in spite of it they were glad to see one another.

The coach rolled out into the main street again, and as it lurched over the crossing Hiram Green, who was hurrying to his daily vigilance at the post office, caught a good view of Nathaniel's back through the coach window. The back gave the impression of an animated conversation being carried on in which the owner of the back was deeply interested.

Hiram almost paused in his walk over the crunching snow. "Oh!" he exclaimed in consternation. "Who knowed he was here!"

Then the thought that at least Nathaniel was about to depart calmed his perturbation, and he hurried on to the office.

Hiram didn't know Phoebe was in the coach. She'd managed to conceal it from him, for she felt sure that if he knew she was going that morning he'd have found it possible to have accompanied her, and she'd have found it impossible to get rid of his company. So the day before, when Emmeline suggested that somebody should go out to Miss Ann Jane Bloodgood's and get some dried saffron flowers she'd promised them last fall to dye the carpet rags, Phoebe said nothing until after Hiram had left that night. Then as she was going upstairs with her candle she turned to Emmeline.

"I've been thinking, Emmeline, that I could go over to Bloodgoods' by the morning coach if Albert could drive me down when he takes his corn to the mill. Then perhaps some of them would be coming over to the village, or I could catch a ride back, or if not I could come back by the evening coach."

Emmeline assented grimly. She wanted the dye and didn't relish the long cold ride in the coach. Ann Jane Bloodgood was too condescending to please her, anyway. So, as Albert was going to mill early, Phoebe made her simple preparations that night and was ready bright and early. Moreover, she coaxed Albert to drive around by Granny McVane's that she might leave a bit of poetry for her which she'd told her about. The poem could have waited, but Albert didn't tell her that. And Phoebe didn't explain to Albert that if they went around by Granny's Hiram wouldn't know she was gone and therefore wouldn't try to follow her. It was a pity Phoebe hadn't confided a little now and then in Albert, though he, poor soul, could do little against such odds as Emmeline and Hiram.

The ten-mile coach ride to Bloodgoods' wide farmhouse spun itself away into nothing in such company, and before Phoebe could believe it was half over she saw the distant roof, sagging low with overhanging snow, and the red barns glimmering warmly a little beyond. Nathaniel saw them, too, for she'd told him at once where she was going so he might not think she'd planned to go with him. He felt that the moments were precious.

"Do you remember what we talked of that night we walked to your home?" he asked.

"Oh, yes," she breathed softly. "You were talking of someone who needed setting free. I've been reading some wonderful poems lately that made me think a great deal of what you said."

He looked at her keenly. How could a girl who read poems and talked so well belong to Hiram Green?

"I've been thinking a great deal about it lately," he went on with just the breath of sign. "I may have to decide soon what I'll do. I wonder if I may ask you to pray for me?"

He watched her, this girl with the drooping eyes and rosy cheeks, the girl who had by her silence refused to answer his letter, and wondered if perhaps by his request he'd offended her. The coach lurched up to the wide piazza and stopped, and the driver jumped heavily into the snowy road. They could hear his steps plowing through the drift by the back wheel. His hand was on the coach door. Then quickly, as if she might be too late, her eyes were lifted to his, and he saw her heart would be in those prayers.

"Oh, I will."

Something like a flash of light went through them as they looked for that instant into one another's eyes, lifting them above earth's petty things. It was intangible. Nathaniel couldn't explain, as he sat back alone in the empty coach and went over the facts of the case, why his heart felt light and the day seemed brighter, just because a girl he knew so little had promised in that tone of voice to pray for him. It thrilled him as he thought it over, until he called himself a fool and told himself nothing was changed; Phoebe hadn't replied to his letter and had politely declined the correspondence, as she would certainly have been justified in doing even if she were the promised wife of Hiram Green. Yet his heart refused to be anything but buoyant.

He berated himself that he hadn't spoken frankly of his letter and heard what she had to say. Perhaps in some way it had never reached her, and yet after all that was scarcely possible. Letters clearly addressed were seldom lost. It might only have embarrassed her if he had spoken.

At the next stop he accepted the coach driver's invitation to "come up top a spell. There's a fine sun comin' up now." He let old Michael babble on about the gossip of the town, until at last the sly old man asked him innocently enough, "And what did ye think av the other passenger, Mr. 'Than'el? An' ain't she a bonnie lassie?"

Then he was treated to a list of Phoebe's virtues sounded forth by one who knew very little of her except that as a child on the way home from school one day she had shyly handed him up a bunch of wayside posies as he drove by her on the road. That childish act had won his loyalty, and old Michael wasn't troubled with the truth. He was thoroughly capable of filling in virtues where he knew none. He went on the principle that what ought to be was. And so when Nathaniel arrived in New York his heart was strangely light, and he wondered often if Phoebe Deane would remember to pray for him. The momentous question seemed now to be in better hands than his own.

Meanwhile Hiram Green, finding in the post office a circular letter for Albert about a new kind of plow that was being put on the market, plodded up to the Deanes. He knew Albert had gone to mill that morning and wouldn't be home yet, but he thought the letter would be an excuse to see Phoebe. He wanted to judge whether Phoebe knew about Nathaniel's visit. He thought he could tell by her face whether she'd had a secret meeting with him or not. Yet it puzzled him to know when it could have been, for Phoebe had been quietly sewing carpet rags all evening before, and he was sure she hadn't gone by with Miranda in the afternoon to the Spaffords. Had she gone to the woods again in the winter, or didn't she know he was here? Perhaps his own skillful manipulating of the mail had nipped this miniature courtship in the bud, as it were, and there'd be no further need of his vigilance.

But when Hiram reached the Deanes and looked about for Phoebe she wasn't there.

"Where's Phoebe?" he demanded, frowning.

"She's gone up to Ann Jane Bloodgood's t' get some saffron flowers," said Emmeline. "Won't you come in, Hiram? She'll be mighty sorry to know she missed you." Emmeline thought it was as well to keep up appearances for Phoebe.

"Yes, I'm sure," drawled Hiram. "How'd she go?" he asked her after an ominous silence in which Emmeline was thinking about what was best to say.

"She went on the coach, an' I reckon she'll come back that way by night ef there don't no one come over from Bloodgoods' this way. You might meet the coach ef you was goin' in to the village again. I don't know's Albert'll feel he hes time after losin' so much o' the day t' mill."

Hiram said nothing, but Emmeline saw he was angry.

"I'd 'a' sent you word she was goin' an' given you the chance to go 'long with her; only she didn't say a word till after you was gone home last night—" she began apologetically.

But Hiram didn't seem to heed her. He got up after a minute, his brows still lowering. He was thinking Phoebe had planned to go with Nathaniel Graham.

"I'll be over t' th' village," he said, as he went out. "Albert needn't go."

Emmeline looked after him immediately.

"I shouldn't be a bit s'prised ef he give er up, the way she goes on. It's wonderful how he holds on to her. She's a fool, that's what she is, an' I've no pity fer her. I wish to goodness she was well married an' out o' the way. She does try me beyond all, with her books an' her visitin's an' her locked doors an' notions."

Meanwhile, Phoebe, unconscious of the plot growing around her, accepted an invitation to remain overnight and the next day with Ann Jane Bloodgood and drive in to town in the afternoon when she went to missionary meeting. Ann Jane was interested in Christian missions and fascinated Phoebe with her tales of Eliot, Brainerd, Carey, Whiteman and Robert Moffat. As she looked over Ann Jane's pile of missionary papers, Phoebe wondered how many people of one sort and another in the world needed setting free from something. It all seemed to be part of what she was praying for, the thing Nathaniel Graham was trying to decide, and he was another just like those wonderful men who were giving their lives to save others. Phoebe was glad she had come, though perhaps she might not have been if she could have seen the thought working in Hiram Green's heart.

After some reflection Hiram harnessed his horses and took the long ride over to Bloodgoods' that afternoon, arriving at the house just after Phoebe and Ann Jane were safely established in Ann Jane's second cousin's best room for a visit a mile away. Ann Jane's second cousin was an invalid and liked company, so the bright faces of the two girls cheered what would otherwise have been a lonely afternoon, and Phoebe escaped the unpleasant encounter with Hiram.

Hiram, his suspicions confirmed, met the evening coach, but no Phoebe appeared. He stepped up to Albert Deane's in the evening long enough to make sure she hadn't returned by any private conveyance. The next day he drove over again, but again found the low farmhouse closed and deserted, for Ann Jane had driven with Phoebe by another road to the village missionary meeting.

His temper not much improved with his two fruitless rides, Hiram returned, watched every passenger from the evening coach alight and then drove to the Deanes' again, where he was surprised to find Phoebe had returned.

That evening when the saffron flowers were discussed he remarked that mighty nice saffron flowers were for sale in Albany and watched Phoebe narrowly. But the round cheek didn't flush or the long lashes flutter in any suspicious way. Nevertheless, Hiram's mind never let go an evil thought once it lodged there. He felt he had a new power over Phoebe that he might use if occasion demanded. He could bide his time.

Chapter 18

S pring was coming at last, and Hiram Green, who'd been biding his time and letting his wrath smolder, thought it was time to do something. All winter Phoebe had kept comparatively free from him, except for his company with the family in the evening. He took every opportunity to make it apparent he was "keeping company" with Phoebe, through his nightly visit, and Phoebe made it plain on every occasion that she didn't consider his visit was for her. She got out of the way when she could, but Emmeline contrived to keep her unusually busy every evening, and her own room was so cold that escape was impossible.

Hiram had made several unsuccessful efforts to establish himself beside Phoebe in public, and he was getting desperate. Every Sunday when he tried to walk down the aisle with her he'd find Miranda and Rose on either side of her, or Mrs. Spafford herself, and sometimes all three, and all serenely unconscious of his presence. They accompanied her down to the carryall. She never went to the village anymore that he could discover, unless Miranda came for her or Albert took her back and forth. Once, though, he saw her flying across the fields from Granny McVane's house with a bundle that looked as if it came from the store.

He complained to Emmeline at last, and she agreed to help him. Albert wasn't taken into the scheme. For some reason it was deemed best not to tell Albert about it. He was apt to ask kind, searching questions, and he always took it for granted that one did everything with the best motives. Besides, he wasn't quick at evasion and might let the cat out of the bag.

A barn raising was to be held about ten miles on the other side of the village, and the whole country round about was invited. The Woodburys, whose barn was to be raised, were distant relatives of Emmeline, so of course the Deanes were going.

Emmeline had shown plainly she would be offended if Phoebe didn't go, though the girl would have much preferred remaining at home with the new book Mrs. Spafford had sent up the day before. It was a matter of selfishness with Emmeline. She wanted Phoebe to help with the big dinner and relieve her so she could visit with the other women.

Part of the scheme was for Albert to go in the chaise with Alma and start while Phoebe was still dressing. Emmeline had managed Albert very adroitly, telling him Hiram wanted a chance to "set in the front seat with Phoebe" in the carryall. Albert, always willing to do a good turn, acceded readily, though Alma was a somewhat reluctant passenger.

When Phoebe came downstairs she found Emmeline already seated in the back seat of the carryall with the other children. She gladly got into the front seat, as it was much pleasanter to be there than beside Emmeline, and she seldom had the opportunity of riding beside her brother, who was more congenial than the others. But in a moment Hiram Green appeared from around the corner of the house. He got quickly into the vacant seat beside Phoebe and whipped up the horses.

"Why, where is Albert?" asked Phoebe in dismay, wishing she could get out.

"He had to go on," explained Emmeline blandly. "Drive fast, Hiram. We'll be late." She added this last because she thought she saw a frightened sideways glance from Phoebe as if she might be going to get out.

Phoebe turned her head to the roadside and tried to watch for the chance wildflowers and forget the talk of crops and gossip that was kept up between Emmeline and Hiram. But the whole pleasant day was clouded for her. Her annoyance was doubled when they passed through the village and Janet Bristol in dainty pink dimity stared at them with haughty sweetness from under her white shirred bonnet and pink-lined sunshade. Janet was evidently not going to the barn raising. She had many interests outside the village where she was born and didn't mingle freely with her fellow townspeople. Only a favored few were her friends and had the privileges of the beautiful old house.

Her passing called forth unfavorable comments from Emmeline and Hiram, and Phoebe writhed at her sister-in-law's tone, loud enough for Janet to hear easily, if she'd felt so inclined.

"The idea of wearing such fancy things in the mornin'!" she exclaimed. "I didn't think the judge was such a fool as to let his daughter come up like that, fixed up fit fer a party this early, an' a sunshade, too! What's she think it's for, I wonder! Her complexion's so dark, a little more of this weak sunshine couldn't make much difference. Mebbe she thinks she looks fine, but she's mistaken. A lazy girl all decked out never looks pretty to me."

"That's 'bout right," declared Hiram, as if he knew all about it. "Give me a good worker ev'ry time, I sez, in preference to one with ringlets an' a nosegay on her dress. But you couldn't expec' much of that one. She's goin' to marry that highfalutin' Nate Graham, an' they'll have money 'nough betwixt 'em to keep her in prettys all the rest of her life. Say, did you hear Nate Graham'd turned abolitionist? Well, it's so; I heard it from a r'liable source. Hev a friend in Noo York writes me once in a while, an' I know what I'm talkin' 'bout. Hed it from headquarters like, you know. Er it's so he may git into trouble ennytime now. There's prices on them abolitionists' heads!"

Hiram turned to look straight into Phoebe's startled face, with an ugly leer of a laugh. The girl's cheeks grew pink, and she turned quickly away. Hiram felt he'd scored one against her. It made him good-natured all day.

But Phoebe found herself trembling with a single thought. Did it mean life or death, this that Nathaniel had asked her to pray about? And had her prayers perhaps helped put him in danger? Ah! But if it were true, how grand in him to be willing to brave danger for what he thought was right. Phoebe knew little about the real question at issue, though she'd read a number of Whittier's poems which had stirred her heart deeply. The great thought in her mind was that a man should be brave enough and good enough to stand against the whole world, if need be, to help a weak brother.

The day was full of noise and bustle and, for Phoebe, hard work. By instinct the women laid on her young shoulders the tasks they wished to shirk, knowing they'd be done well. They trusted Phoebe, and the fun and feasting went on, while she labored in the kitchen, gladly taking extra burdens upon herself, just to keep from being troubled by Hiram.

She was washing dishes and thinking about how she could manage not to sit next to Hiram on the return trip when a little Woodbury entered the kitchen.

"Say, Phoebe Deane," she called out, "your brother says you're to go in the chaise with him this time, an' when you get ready you come out to the barn an' get in. He says you needn't hurry, fer he's busy yet a while."

The child was gone back to her play before Phoebe could thank her, and with lightened heart she went on washing the dishes. Perhaps Albert had surmised her dislike for riding with Hiram and planned this for her sake. She made up her mind to confide in Albert during this ride and see if he couldn't help her get rid of the obnoxious man once and for all. Albert was usually slow and undecided, but once in a great while, when he put his foot down about something, things would go as he said.

She wiped the last dish, washed her hands and ran upstairs for her bonnet and mantilla. Everybody else was gone. The long, slanting rays of the setting sun were streaming in at the window and touching the great four-poster bed where only her wraps remained. She put them on quickly, glad everyone else was out of the way and she wouldn't have to wait for a lot of good-byes. The day had been wearying to her, and she was thankful it was over.

Mr. and Mrs. Woodbury stood together by the great stepping-stone in front of the house. They'd said good-bye to Albert and Emmeline an hour before and had just been seeing off the last wagon load of guests. They turned eagerly to thank Phoebe for her assistance. Indeed, the girl had many warm friends among older people who knew her kind heart and willing hands.

"What! Your folks all gone and left you, Phoebe?" exclaimed Mrs. Woodbury in dismay. "Why, they must 'a' forgot you."

"No, they're not all gone, Mrs. Woodbury. Our chaise is out in the barn waiting for me. Albert sent word to me by your Martha that I needn't hurry, so I finished the dishes."

"Oh! Now that's so good of you, Phoebe," said the tired farmer's wife, who expected to have plenty of cleaning to do after her guests departed. "You shouldn't ov done that. I could 'a' cleaned up. I'm 'fraid you're real tired. Wouldn't you like to stay overnight and get rested?"

But Phoebe shook hands happily with them and hurried down to the chaise. Now the Woodbury barn was out near the road, and the chaise stood facing the road. The horse wasn't tied but waited with turned head as if his master wasn't far away.

Phoebe jumped in, calling, "Come on, Albert. I'm here at last. Did I keep you waiting long?"

Then before she had time to look around or know what was happening Hiram Green stepped out from the barn door, sprang into the seat beside her and with swiftness caught up the whip and gave the horse such a cut that it started off at a brisk trot down the road. He had sent the message by little Martha Woodbury, just as it had been given. Emmeline had managed the rest.

"Oh!" gasped Phoebe. "Why, Mr. Green, Albert is here waiting for me somewhere. Please stop the horse and let me find him. He sent word he'd wait for me."

"That's all right," said Hiram nonchalantly. "Albert decided to go in the carryall. Your sister-in-law was in a great stew to get back fer milkin' time an' made him come, so I offered to bring ye back home."

Phoebe's heart froze. She looked wildly about her and didn't know what to do. The horse was going too fast for her to jump. She had no idea Hiram would stop and let her out if she asked him. His talk that last time they had an encounter had shown her she mustn't let him see he had her in his power. Besides, what excuse could she give for stopping except that she didn't wish to go with him? And how otherwise could she get home that night? How she wished she'd accepted Mrs. Woodbury's kind invitation. Couldn't she, perhaps, manage it yet?

"That's very kind of you," she faltered with white lips, as she tried to marshal her wits and contrive some way out. Then she pretended to look about her in the seat.

"I wonder if I remembered to bring my apron," she said faintly. "Would you mind, Mr. Green, just driving me back to see?"

"Oh, I reckon you'll find it," Hiram said easily. "Ef you don't, you got a few more, ain't you? Here, ain't this it?" He fished out a damp roll from under the seat.

Phoebe had hoped for one wild moment that she'd really dropped it when she got into the chaise, for it didn't seem to be about anywhere, but the sight of the damp blue roll dashed all her confidence. She could only accept the situation as bravely as possible and make the best of it. Her impulse was to turn angrily and tell Hiram Green he'd deceived her. But she knew that would do no good, and the safest thing was to act as if it were all right and try to keep the conversation on everyday topics. If he'd only keep on driving at this pace the journey wouldn't be so intolerably long after all, and they might hope to reach home a little before dark. She summoned all her courage and tried to talk pleasantly, although the countenance of the man beside her, as she glanced at his profile, frightened her. It had both triumph and revenge upon it.

"They had a pleasant day for the raising, Mr. Green," she began.

And then to her horror he slowed the horse to a walk and sat back close to her as if he intended to enjoy the tête-à-tête to its full.

It was an awful strain. Phoebe's cheeks blazed out in two red spots. They dragged their way through woods, and Phoebe sat up very straight, very much to her side of the chaise, and laughed and talked as if she were wound up.

Hiram didn't say much. He sat watching her, almost devouring her changing face, fully understanding her horror of him and this ride, yet determined to make her suffer every minute of the time. It made his anger all the greater as he saw her bravely try to keep up a semblance of respect toward him and knew she didn't feel it. Why couldn't she give it freely and not against her will? What was there about him she disliked? Never mind. She'd pay for her dislike. She would see she'd have to treat him as she would treat those she liked, whether she wished to or not.

She suggested they better drive faster, since it was getting late and would be dark. He said that didn't matter, that Emmeline had said they weren't to hurry. She told him she'd be needed, but he told her it was right she should have a little rest once in a while. And he smiled grimly as he said it, knowing the present ride was anything but rest to the poor tired soul beside him. He seemed to delight in torturing her. The farther she edged away from him, the nearer he came to her. Finally, when they emerged from the woods and met a carryall with some people they both knew, he was sitting quite over on her side, and she was almost out of her seat, her face a picture of rage and helplessness.

Emboldened by the expression on the faces of their acquaintances, Hiram threw his arm across the back of the chaise, until it encircled Phoebe's back, or would have if she hadn't sat upon the extreme front edge of the seat.

They'd reached a settlement of three houses, where a tollgate, stretching its white pole out across the way, and a little store and schoolhouse went by the name of The Crossroads. Hiram flung a bit of money out to the tollman and drove on without stopping. Phoebe's heart was beating wildly. She couldn't sit like that on the edge of her seat another instant. Something must be done.

"Mr. Green, would you mind moving over just a little? I haven't quite enough room," she gasped.

"Oh, that's all right," said Hiram, as heartily as if he didn't understand the situation. "Just sit clos'ter. Don't be shy." His arm came around her waist and by brute strength drew her up to him, so that it looked from behind as if they were a pair of lovers. The top of the chaise was thrown back so they could easily be seen.

They'd just passed the last house. It was the home of old Mrs. Duzenberry and her elderly daughter, Susanna. Living so far from the village they made it a point not to miss anything that went by their door, and at this hour in the afternoon, when their simple tea was brewing, they both sat by the front window, ready to bob to the door the minute anything of interest came by. Of course they both bobbed on this occasion, the daughter with folded arms and alert beak like some old bird of prey and the mother just behind with exclamatory interrogations written in every curve of her cap strings.

Phoebe, glancing back wildly, as she felt herself drawn beyond her power to stop it, saw them gaping at her in amazement, and her cheeks grew crimson with shame.

"Stop!" she cried, putting out her hands and pushing against him.

She might as well have tried to push off a mountain in her path. Hiram only laughed and drew her closer, till his ugly, grizzled face was near her own. She could feel his breath on her cheek, and the horse was going faster now. She didn't know just how it happened, whether Hiram had touched him with the whip or spoken a low word. They were down the road out of sight of the Duzenberrys' before she could wrench herself away from the scoundrel. Even then he let go of her for a moment only so that he might settle himself a little closer and more comfortably, and then the strong, cruel arm came back as if it had a right around her waist, and Hiram's face came cheek to cheek with her own.

She uttered one terrible scream and looked around, but no one was in sight. The sun, which had been slowly sinking like a ball of burning opal, suddenly dropped behind a hill and left the world dull and leaden with a heavy gray sky. Dark blue clouds seemed all around, which until now hadn't been noticed, and a quick uncertain wind was springing up. A low rumble behind them seemed to wrap them in a new dread. But the strong man's grasp held her fast, and her screams brought no help.

In the horror of the moment a thought of her mother came, and she wondered if that mother could see her child and whether it didn't give her deep anguish even in the bliss of heaven to know she was in such straits. Then as the sharp stubble of Hiram's upper lip brushed the softness of her cheek fear gave her strength, and with a sudden mighty effort she broke from his grasp.

Reaching out to the only member of the party who seemed at all likely to give any aid, Phoebe caught the reins and pulled back on them with all her might, while her heart was lifted in a swift prayer for help. Then quick, as if in instant answer, while the gray plow horse reared back upon his haunches and plunged wildly in the air, came a brilliant flash of jagged lightning, as if the sky were cloven in wrath and the light of heaven let through. This was followed instantly by a terrible crash of thunder.

With an oath of mingled rage and awe, Hiram pushed Phoebe from him and reached for the reins to try and soothe the frightened horse, who was plunging and snorting and trembling with fear.

The chaise was on the edge of a deep ditch half filled with muddy water. One wheel was almost over the edge. Hiram saw the danger and reached for his whip. He cut the horse a frantic lash which brought his forefeet to the ground again and caused him to start off down the road on a terrific gallop.

But in that instant, while the chaise poised on the edge of the ditch, Phoebe's resolve had crystallized into action. She gave a wild spring, just as the cut from the whip sent the horse tearing headlong down the road. Her dress caught in the arm of the chaise, and for one instant she poised over the ditch. Then the fabric gave way, and she fell heavily, striking her head against the fence, and lay huddled in the muddy depths. Down the hard road echoed the heavy hoofbeats of the horse in frenzied gallop with no abatement, and over all the majestic thunder rolled.

Chapter 19

Her senses swam off into the relief of unconsciousness, but the cold water creeping up through her clothing chilled her back to life again. In a moment more she opened her eyes in wonder that she was lying there alone, free from her tormentor. She imagined she could hear the echo of the horse's feet, or was it the thunder? Then came the awful thought: What would happen if he returned and found her lying here? He'd be terribly angry at her for having frightened the horse and jumped out of the chaise. He'd take it out on her in some way, she felt sure, and she'd be utterly defenseless against him.

Not a soul was in sight, and it was suddenly growing dark. She must be at least six or seven miles away from home. She didn't come that way often enough to be sure of distances. With near fear she sat up and crept out of the water. The mud was deep, and it was difficult to step, but she managed to get away from the oozy soil and into the road again. Then in a panic she sprang across the ditch and crept under the fence. She must fly from here. When Hiram succeeded in stopping the horse he'd undoubtedly come back for her, and she must get away before he found her.

Which way should she go? She looked back on the road but feared to go that way, lest he'd go to those houses and search for her. There was no telling what he'd say. She had no faith in him. He might say she'd given him the right to put his arm around her. She must get away from here at once where he couldn't find her. Out to the right, across the road, it was all open country. There was no place nearby where she could take refuge. But across this field and another was a growth of trees and bushes. Perhaps she could reach there and hide and make her way home after he'd gone.

She fled across the spring-sodden field as fast as her soaked shoes and trembling limbs could carry her, slipping now and then and almost falling, but going on, wildly, blindly, till she reached the fence. Once she thought she heard the distant bellowing of a bull, but she crept to the other side of the fence and kept on her way, breathless. And now the storm broke into wild splashes of rain, pelting on her face and hair, for her bonnet had fallen back and was hanging around her neck by its ribbons. The net had come off from her hair, and the long locks blew about her face and lashed her in the eyes as she ran. It was dark as night, and Phoebe could see only dimly where she was going. Yet this was a comfort to her rather than a source of fear. She felt it would cover her hiding better. Her worst dread was to come under Hiram Green's power again.

She worked her way through the fields, groping for the fences, and at last she reached an open road and stood almost afraid to try it, lest somewhere she'd see Hiram lurking. The lightning blazed and shivered all about her, trailing across the heavens in awful and wonderful display. The thunder shuddered above her until the earth itself seemed to answer and she felt herself in a rocking abyss of horror. And yet the most awful thing in it all was Hiram Green.

She'd heard all her life that the most dangerous place in a thunderstorm was under tall trees, yet so little did she think of it that she made straight for the shelter of the wood. Though the shocks crashed about her and seemed to be cleaving the forest giants, there she stayed until the storm abated and the genuine darkness had succeeded.

She was wet to the skin and trembling like a leaf. Her strongest impulse was to sink to the earth and weep herself into nothingness, but her common sense wouldn't let her even sit down to rest. She knew she must start at once if she hoped to reach home. Yet by this time she had very little idea of where she was or how to get home.

With another prayer for guidance she started out, keeping sharp lookout along the road so Hiram couldn't come upon her unaware. Twice she heard vehicles in the distance and crept into the shelter of some trees until they passed. She heard pleasant voices talking about the storm and longed to cry out to them for help, yet dared not. What would they think of her, a young girl out alone at that time of night and in such a condition? Besides, they were all strangers. She dared not speak.

She wouldn't have spoken to friends either, for they'd have been even more astonished to find her this way. She thought longingly of Mrs. Spafford and Miranda, but she dreaded lest even Mrs. Spafford might think she'd done wrong to ride even a couple of miles with Hiram Green after all the experience she'd had with him. Yet as she plodded along she wondered how she could have done differently, unless indeed she'd dared to pull up the horse and jump out at once. Very likely, though, she wouldn't have escaped from her tormentor as easily earlier in the afternoon as when she leaped into the ditch.

As she looked back upon the experience it seemed as if the storm had been sent by Providence to provide her a shield and a way of escape. If it hadn't been for the storm the horse wouldn't have been easily frightened into running, and Hiram would soon have found her and compelled her to get into the chaise again. What could she have done against his strength? She shuddered, partly with cold and partly with horror.

A slender thread of pale moon had come up, but it gave a sickly light and soon slipped out of sight again, leaving only the kind stars whose lights looked brilliant but so far away tonight. Everywhere was a soft dripping sound and the seething of the earth drinking in a good draught.

Once when it seemed as if she'd been going for hours she sat down on the wet bank to rest, and a horse and rider galloped out of the blackness past her. She hid her white face in her lap so he may have thought her only a stump beside the fence. She was thankful he didn't stop to see. So far nothing had given her a clue to her whereabouts, and she was cold, so terribly cold.

At last she passed a house she didn't know, and then another, and another. Finally she figured out she was in a little settlement, about three miles from the Deanes' farm. She couldn't tell how she'd wandered or how she came to be so far away when she must have walked at least twenty miles. But the knowledge of where she was brought her new courage.

A road led from this settlement straight to Granny McVane's, so she wouldn't need to go back by the road where Hiram would search for her, if indeed he hadn't already given up the search and gone home. The lights were out everywhere in this village, except in one small house at the farthest end, and she stole past that as if she were a wraith. Then she breathed more freely as she came into the open country road again and knew only two or three houses stood between her and home.

It occurred to her to wonder dully if the horse had thrown Hiram out and maybe he was hurt, and whether she might not after all have to send a search party after him. She wondered what he'd do when he couldn't find her, supposing he wasn't hurt. Perhaps he'd been too angry to go back for her and her dread of him was unnecessary. But she thought she knew him well enough to know he wouldn't easily give her up.

She wondered if he'd tell Albert and whether Albert would be worried—she was sure he'd be good, kind Albert—and what would Emmeline say? Emmeline, who had been at the bottom of all this, she was sure—and then her thoughts would trail on ahead of her in the wet, and her feet would lag behind and she'd feel she couldn't catch up. If only a kind coach would appear! Yet she kept on, holding up her heavy head and gripping her wet mantle close with her cold hands, shivering as she went.

Once she caught herself murmuring, "Oh, Mother, Mother!" and then wondered what it meant. So stumbling on, slower and slower, she came at last to Granny McVane's little house, all dark and quiet, but so kind-looking in the night. She longed to crawl to the doorstep and lie down to die, but duty kept her on. No one must know of this if she could help it. That seemed to be the main thought she could grasp with her weary brain.

The fields behind Granny McVane's were miry. Three times she fell and the last time almost lay still, but some stirring of brain and conscience helped her up and on again, across the last hillock, over the last fence, through the garden and up to the back door of her home.

A light was burning inside, but she was too far gone to think about it now. She tried to open the door, but the latch was heavy and wouldn't lift. She fumbled and almost gave it up, but then it was opened sharply by Emmeline with her hair in a hard knot and old lines under her eyes. She wore a wrapper over her night robe and a blanket around her shoulders. Her feet were thrust into an old pair of Albert's carpet slippers. She held a candle high above her head and looked out shrewdly into the night. It was plain she was just awake and fretted at the unusual disturbance.

"Fer pity's sake, Phoebe! Is that you? Where on earth hev you ben? You've hed us all upside down huntin' fer yeh, an' Albert ain't got home yet. I tol' him 'twas no use. You'd mos' likely gone in somewheres out o' the storm, an' you'd be home all right in the mornin'. But it's just like your crazy ways to come home in the middle o' th' night. Fer goodness' sake, what a sight yeh are! You ain't comin' in the house like that! Why, there'll be mud to clean fer a week. Stop there till I get some water an' a broom."

But Phoebe, with deathly white face and unseeing eyes, stumbled past her without a word, the water and mud oozing out of her shoes at every step and dripping from her garments. Her soaked bonnet hung dejectedly on her shoulders, and her hair was one long drenched mantle of darkness. Emmeline, half awed by the sight, stood still in the doorway and watched her go upstairs, realizing the girl didn't know what she was doing. Then she shut the door sharply as she'd opened it and followed Phoebe upstairs.

Phoebe held out until she reached her own door and opened it. Then she sank without a sound upon the floor and lay there as if dead. All breath and consciousness had fluttered out, it seemed, with that last effort.

Emmeline set the candle down with a sudden, startled exclamation and went to her. She felt her hands cold, like ice, and her face like wet marble, and, hard as she was, she was frightened. Her conscience, so long on vacation, leaped into new life. What part had she borne in this that might yet be a tragedy?

She unlaced the clodded shoes, untied the soaked bonnet, pulled off the wet garments one by one and wrapped the girl in thick warm blankets, dragging her light weight to the bed. But still no sign of consciousness had come. She felt her heart and listened for a breath, but she couldn't tell if she were alive or not. Then she went downstairs with hurried steps, flapping over the kitchen floor in the large carpet slippers, and stirred up the fire that had been banked down, putting the kettle over it to heat. In a little while she had plenty of hot water and various remedies applied, but life seemed scarcely yet to have crept back to her, with only a flutter of eyelids now and then or a fleeting breath like a sigh. The dawn was coming on, and Albert's voice in low strained tones could be heard outside.

"No, I'm not going to stop for anything to eat, Hiram. You may if you like, but I won't stop till I find her. It's been a real bad night, an' to think of that little girl out in it—I can't bear it!" There seemed to be something like a sob in Albert's last words.

"Well, suit yerself," answered Hiram gruffly. "I'm pretty well played out. I'll go home an' get a bite, an' then I'll come on an' meet yeh. You'll likely find her back at Woodburys', I reckon. She wanted to go back, I mind now. We'd ought to 'a' gone there in the first place."

The voices were under her window. Phoebe slowly opened her eyes and, shuddering, grasped Emmeline's hands so tightly that it hurt her.

"Oh, don't let him come—don't let him come!" she pleaded and sank away into unconsciousness again.

It was a long time before they could rouse her, and when she finally opened her eyes she didn't know them. A fierce and terrible fever had flamed up in her veins till her face was brilliant with color, and her long dark hair was scorched dry again in its fires.

Granny McVane came quietly over the next day and offered to nurse her. Then the long blank days of fever stretched themselves out for the unconscious girl, and a fight between life and death began.

Now on that very afternoon of the barn raising Mistress Janet Bristol, in her pink and white frills and furbelows, with a bunch of pink moss roses at her breast and in her haughtiest air, drove over to the Deanes to call on Phoebe. It was a long-delayed response to her cousin Nathaniel's most cousinly letter requesting her to do so. She had parleyed long with herself whether she'd go or not. But, at last, curiosity to see what was in this country girl to attract her handsome, brilliant cousin led her to go.

One can scarcely conjecture what Emmeline would have said and thought if she'd seen the grand carriage drive up before her door, with its coachman and footman in livery. But no one was at home to tell the tale except the white lilacs on the great bush near the front gate, who waved a welcome rich with fragrance. Perhaps they sent the essence of the welcome Phoebe would have gladly given this girl she admired.

So half petulant at this reception when she had condescended to come, Janet scanned the house for some trace of the life of this unknown girl and drove away with the memory of lilac fragrance floating about a dull and commonplace house. She left half determined to tell her cousin she'd done her best and wouldn't go again. No sign was left behind to tell this other girl of the lost call. If she had been able to make her call on Phoebe that afternoon, it's doubtful whether either of the two could have found and understood the other at that time.

Janet drove back to her own world again, and the door between the two closed. That very evening's mail brought a brief letter from Nathaniel, saying his dear friend and chum Martin Van Rensselaer would be coming north in a few days, and he wanted Janet to invite him to spend a little time in the old home. He would try to get away from his work and run up for a few days, and they'd all have a good time together. So while this other girl, whose unsheltered life had been so full of sorrow, was plodding her way through the darkness and rain alone in the night with fear, Janet Bristol sat in her stately parlor, where a bright fire cast rosy lights over her white dress, and planned how to charm the young theologue.

Chapter 20

Miranda was out in the flower bed by the side gate. She had gathered a handful of spicy gray-green southernwood and was standing by the fence looking wistfully down the street. The afternoon coach was in, and she was idly watching to see who came in, but not with her usual vim. The specter of the shadow of death was hovering too near Phoebe for Miranda to take much interest in things in general.

Three days after Phoebe's midnight walk Miranda had gone out to see her and bring her down to take tea with Mrs. Spafford. What was her dismay to find she was refused admittance and that too very shortly.

"Phoebe's sick abed!" snapped Emmeline. She'd been tried beyond measure over all the extra work thrown in her hands by Phoebe's illness, and she had no time for buttered words. "No, she can't see you today or next day. She's got a fever, an' she don't know anybody. The doctor says she mus' be kep' quiet. No, I can't tell yeh how she got it. The land only knows it! Ef she ever gits well mebbe she ken tell herself, but I doubt it. She'll uv forgot by that time. What she does know she fergets mostly. No, you can't go an' take care of her. She's got folks 'nough to do that now, more'n she needs. There ain't a livin' thing to do but let her alone till she comes out of it. You don't suppose *you* c'd take care o' her, do yeh? *Hm!* Wal, I ain't got time to talk." And the door was shut in her face.

Miranda, however, wasn't to be turned aside so easily. With real concern in her face she marched around the woodshed to the place under the little window of the kitchen chamber that she knew was Phoebe's room.

"Phoebe!" she called softly. "Phoe-bee!"

And the sick girl tossing on her bed of fever called wildly, "Don't you hear that Phoebe-bird calling, Mother! Oh, Mother! It's calling me from the top of the barn. It says, 'Phoebe, I'm here! Don't be afraid!' " And the voice trailed off into incoherence again.

Granny McVane hobbled to the window, perplexed, for she too had heard the soft sound.

"Oh, is that you, Granny?" whispered Miranda. "Say, what's the matter with Phoebe? Is she bad?"

"Yes, real bad," whispered back Granny. "She don't know a soul, poor little thing. She thinks her mother's here with her. I don't know much about how it happened. There was an accident, and the horse ran away. She was out in that awful storm the other night. She's calling, and I must go back to her."

In much dismay Miranda hurried back to the village. She besieged the doctor's house until he came home but could get only gravity and shakings of the head.

"She may pull through, she may—" the old doctor would say doubtfully. "She's young and strong, and it might be—but there's been a great shock to the system, and she doesn't respond to my medicines. I can't tell."

Every day the story was the same, though David and Marcia had gone themselves. And though Miranda traveled the mile and a half out to the Deane farm every afternoon after her work was done, there'd been no change. The fever raged on. Miranda's faithful heart was as near discouragement as it had ever come in its dauntless life.

And now this afternoon she had just returned from a particularly fruitless journey to the farm. She couldn't get sight or sound of anyone but Emmeline, who slammed the door in her face as usual after telling her she wished she'd mind her own business and let folks alone that weren't troubling her. Miranda felt, as she trudged back to the village with tears in her eyes, as if she must cry out or do something. She had never come to a place before where her wits couldn't plan out some help for those she loved. Death was different. One could not outwit death.

Then, like a slowly dawning hope, she saw Nathaniel Graham coming up the street with his carpetbag in his hand.

Nathaniel had come up for a day to tell his uncle and cousin all about his dear friend he so much desired to have welcomed for a week or two. He'd been made junior partner in a law firm, the senior partner being an old friend of Judge Bristol, and his work would be strenuous. Otherwise he'd probably have planned to be at the old home all summer. As it was, he could hope for only a few days now and then when he could be spared.

Nathaniel came to a halt with his pleasant smile as he recognized Miranda.

"How do you do, Miss Miranda? Are all your folks well? Are Mr. and Mrs. Spafford at home? I must try to run over and see them before I go back. I'm only here on a brief visit and must return tomorrow. How's the place getting on? All the old friends just the same? Do you ever see Miss Deane? She's well, I hope."

Nathaniel was running through these sentences pleasantly, as one will who's been away from a town for a time. He didn't note the replies carefully, as he thought he knew pretty well what they'd be, having heard from home only a day or two before. He was just going on when something deep and different in Miranda's tone and clouded eyes made him pause and listen.

"No, she ain't well. Phoebe Deane ain't. She's way down sick, an' they don't nobody think she's goin' to get well, I'm sure o' that!"

Then the unexpected happened. Two big tears welled up and rolled down the two dauntless, freckled cheeks. Nobody had ever seen Miranda Griscom cry before.

A sudden nameless fear gripped Nathaniel's heart. Phoebe Deane sick! Near to death! All at once the day clouded for him.

"Tell me, Miranda," he said gently. "She is my friend, too, I think. I didn't know—I hadn't heard. Has she been ill long? What was the cause?"

" 'Bout two weeks," said Miranda, mopping her face with the corner of her clean apron, "an' I can't find out what made her sick. But it's my 'pinion she's bein' tormented to death by that long-legged blatherskite of a Hiram Green. He ain't nothing' but a big bully, fer he's really a coward at heart, an' what's more, folks'll find it out someday ef I don't miss my guess. But he ken git up the low-downdest, pin-prickenist, soul-shakenest tormentin's that ever a saint hed to bear. An' ef Phoebe Deane ain't a saint I don't know who is, 'cept my Mis' Spafford. Them two's ez much alike's two peas—sweet peas, I mean, pink an' white ones in bloom."

Nathaniel warmed to Miranda's eloquence and felt that here was something that must be investigated.

"I believe that man is a scoundrel!" said Nathaniel earnestly. "Do you say he really dares to annoy Miss Deane?"

"Well, I rather guess you'd think so! She can't stir without he's at her side, 'tendin' like he b'longs there. She can't bar the sight o' him, an' he struts up to her at the church door like he owned her, an' ef 'twa'n't fer me an Rose an' Mis' Spafford she couldn't get red of 'im. She can't go to the post office anymore 'thout he hants the very road, though she's told him up 'n' down she won't hev a thing to do 'ith him. I hev to go after her an' take her home when she comes to see us, fear he'll dog her steps, an' he's scared her most to death twice now, chasin' after her, once at night when she was comin' down to your house to bring some letter she'd found."

Nathaniel's face grew suddenly alert, and a glow of indignation rolled over it. He set down his carpetbag and came close to the fence to listen.

"Why, w'd you b'lieve it, that feller found she liked to go to th' post office fer a walk, and he jest follered her every time, an' when she quit goin' he hunted up other ways to trouble her. They tell a tale 'bout th' horse runnin' away an' her bein' out in a big storm the night she took sick, but I b'lieve in my soul he's 't th' bottom of it, an' I'd like to see him get his comeuppance right now."

"Miranda, do you happen to know—I don't suppose you ever heard Miss Deane speak of receiving a letter from me."

Miranda's keen eyes were on his face.

"Long 'bout when?" she demanded.

"Why, last December, I think it was. I wrote her a note and never received any reply. I wondered if it might have been lost, or whether she didn't like my writing it, as I'm almost a stranger."

"No, sirree, she never got that letter! I know fer sure, 'cause I happened to speak to her 'bout hearin' Hiram Green askin' pertick'ler fer her mail in the post office one day, an' I found out he gets the Deanes' mail quite often an' carries it out to 'em. I tole her I thought she wouldn't like him meddlin' with her mail, an' she jest laughed an' said he couldn't do her any harm thet way, 'cause she never got a letter in her life 'cept one her mother wrote her 'fore she died. Thet was only a little while back, 'bout a month er so, 'way after January, fer the snow was most gone the day I tol' her. She can't uv got your letter nohow. I'd be willin' to bet a good fat doughnut thet rascally Hiram Green knows what come o' thet letter. My, but I'd like to prove it on him!"

"Oh, Miranda, he would scarcely dare to tamper with another person's mail. He's a well-informed man and must know that's a crime. He could be put in prison for that. It must have been lost if you're sure she never received it."

"Could he?" said Miranda eagerly. "Could he be put in prison? My! But I'd like to help get him lodged there fer a spell 'til he learned a little bit o' politeness toward th' angels thet walks the airth in mortal form. Dast! Hiram Green dast? He's got cheek enough to dast ennythin'. You don't know him. He wouldn't think ennyone would find out! But, say, I'll tell you what you ken do. You jest write that letter over again, ef you ken rem'mber 'bout what you wanted to say b'fore, an' I'll agree to git to her firsthand this time."

Nathaniel's face was alight with the eagerness of a boy. Somehow Miranda's childish proposal was pleasant to him. Her honest face beamed at him expectantly.

"I'll do it, Miranda," he replied with earnestness. "I'll do it this very day and trust it to your kindness to get it to her safely. Thank you for suggesting it."

Then suddenly a cloud came over the freckled face, and the gray eyes filled with tears again.

"But I mightn't ever git it to 'er, after all, yeh know. They say she's jest hangin' 'tween life 'n' death today, an' t'night's the crisis."

A cloud seemed suddenly to have passed before the sun again; a chill almost imperceptible came in the air. What was that icy something gripping Nathaniel's heart? Why did all the forces of life and nature seem to hang upon the well-being of this young girl? He caught his breath.

"We must pray for her, Miranda, you and I," he said gravely. "She once promised to pray for me."

"Did she?" said Miranda, looking up with solemn awe through the tears. "I'm real glad you tole me that. I'll try, but I ain't much on things like that. I could wallup Hiram Green a grea' deal better'n I could pray. But I s'pose that wouldn't be no good, so I'll do my best at the prayin'. Ef it's kind of botched up, mebbe yours'll make up fer it. But, say, you better write that letter right off. I've heard tell there's things like thet'll help when crises comes. I'm goin' t' make it a pint t' git up there t'night, spite o' that ole Mis' Deane, an' ef I see chance I'll give it to her. I kind of think it might please her to have a letter t' git well fer."

"I'll do it, Miranda. I'll do it at once and bring it around to you before dark. But you must be careful not to trouble her with it till she's able. You know it might make her worse to be bothered with any excitement like a letter from a stranger."

"I'll use my bes' jedgment," said Miranda with happy pride. "I ain't runnin' no resks, so you needn't worry."

With a new interest in his face Nathaniel grasped his carpetbag and hurried to his uncle's house. He found Janet ready with a joyful welcome, but he showed more anxiety to get to his room than to talk to her.

"I suppose it was dusty on the road today," she conceded unwillingly, "but hurry back. I've a great deal to ask you and to tell, and I want you all to myself before your friend comes."

But once in his room he forgot dust and sat down immediately to the great mahogany desk where paper and pens were just as he'd left them when he went away. Janet had to call twice before he made his appearance, for he was deep in writing a letter.

> *My dear Miss Deane,*
>
> *They tell me you are lying very ill, and I feel as if I must write a few words to tell you how anxious and sad I am about you. I want you to know I'm praying that you may get well.*
>
> *I wrote you some time ago asking if you were willing to correspond with me, but I have reason now to think you never received my letter, so I have ventured to write again. I know it may be sometime before you're able even to read this, but I'm sending it by a trusty messenger, and I'm sure you will let me know my answer when you are better. It will be a great source of pleasure and profit to me if you will write to me sometimes.*
>
> *Yours faithfully,*
> *Nathaniel Graham*

He folded and addressed it, sealing it with his crest, and then Janet called for the second time.

"Yes, Janet, I'm coming now, really. I had to write a letter. I'm sorry, but it couldn't wait."

"Oh, how poky! Always business, business!" exclaimed Janet. "It's a good thing your friend is coming tonight for it's plain we'll have no good of you. How have you grown old and serious so soon, Nathaniel? I thought you'd stay a boy a long time."

"Just wait until I send my letter, Janet, and I'll be as young as you please for two whole days."

"Let Caesar take it for you then. There's no need for you to go."

"I'd rather take it myself, cousin," he said, and she knew by his look he would have his way.

"Well, then, I'll go with you," she pouted and taking her sunshade from the hall table unfurled its rosy whiteness.

He was dismayed at this but, making the best of it, smiled good-humoredly. Together they went out into the summer street and walked beneath the long arch of maples newly dressed in green.

"But this isn't the way to the post office," she said, when they had walked some distance.

"But this is the way for my letter," he said pleasantly. "Now, Janet, what have you to ask me so insistently?"

"About this Martin friend of yours. Is he nice? That is, will I like him? It isn't enough that you like him, for you like some very stupid people sometimes. I want to know if I'll like him."

"And how should I be able to tell that, Janet? Of one thing I'm sure—he'll have to like you," he said, surveying his handsome cousin with admiration. "That's a very pretty sunshade you have. May I carry it for you?"

"Well, after that pleasant speech perhaps you may," she said, surrendering it. "About this young man, is it really true, Nathaniel, that he's a minister and is to preach for Dr. MacFarlane while the doctor goes to visit his daughter? Father thought you had arranged for that. You see, it's very important that I like him, because if I don't I simply can't go to church and hear him preach. In fact I may stay away anyway. I'd be so afraid he'd break down if I liked him, and if I didn't I'd want to laugh. It'll be so funny to see a minister at home every day and know all his faults and peculiarities, and then see him get up and try to preach. I'm *sure* I'd laugh."

"I'm sure you would dare do nothing of the kind when Martin preaches."

"Oh, is he then so terribly solemn? I shan't like him in the least."

"Wait until he comes, Janet. The evening coach will soon be in."

They had reached the Spafford house now, and Nathaniel's anxiety about delivering his letter was relieved by seeing Miranda hurry out to the flower bed again. She was quite close to the fence as they came up, but she remained unconscious of their presence until Nathaniel spoke.

"Is that you, Miss Miranda?" he said, lifting his hat as though he hadn't seen her before that afternoon. "Will you kindly deliver this letter for me?"

He handed her the letter directly from his pocket, and Janet couldn't see the address. Miranda took it serenely.

"Yes, sir," she said, scrutinizing the address at a safe angle from Janet's vision. "I'll deliver it safe an' sure. Afternoon, Mis' Janet. Like a bunch o' pink columbine to stick in yer dress? Jes' matches them posies on the muslin delaine." And she snapped off a fine whirl of delicate pink columbine. Janet accepted it graciously, and the two turned back home again.

"Now I can't see why Caesar couldn't have done that," grumbled Janet. "He's just as trustworthy as that funny red-haired girl."

"You wouldn't have your columbine," smiled Nathaniel, "and I'm sure it was just what you needed to complete the picture."

"Now for that pretty speech I'll say no more about it," granted Janet, pleased.

And so they walked along the shaded street, where the sunlight was beginning to lie in long slanting rays on the pavement. Nathaniel talked as he knew his cousin liked for him to do, and all the time she never knew his heart had gone with the letter he'd given to Miranda. Perhaps her interest in the stranger who was coming kept her from missing something. Perhaps it was his lighthearted manner, so free from the perplexing problems that had filled his face with gravity on his recent visits. Perhaps it was just Janet's own gladness with life, the summer weather, and the holiday guests.

Yet underneath Nathaniel's cheerful manner two thoughts ran side by side—one, that Miranda had said Phoebe had repulsed Hiram Green; the other, that she was lying at death's door. And his strong heart was going out in a wild, hopeful pleading that her young life might yet be spared for joy. He felt that this mute pleading was her due, for hadn't she lifted her clear eyes and said, "Oh, I will," when he asked her to pray for him? He must return it in full measure.

The evening coach was late, but it rolled in at last, bringing the eagerly awaited guest, bronzed from his months in the South. The dinner was served around a joyous board, with the judge beaming his pleasure on the little company. The evening was prolonged far beyond the usual retiring hour, while laughter and talk floated on around him. And all the time Nathaniel was conscious of that other house only two miles away, where life and death were battling for a victim.

He went upstairs with Martin for another talk after the house was quiet, but at last they separated. Nathaniel was free to sit by the window in his dark room, looking out into the night now grown brilliant with the late rising moon, and kept tryst with one who was hovering on the brink of the other world.

Chapter 21

I 've a notion to go up an' stay there t'night!" announced Miranda, as she cleared off the tea things. "This's the crisis, an' they might need me fer sumthin'. Anyhow I'm a goin' ef you don't mind."

"Will they let you in?" asked Marcia.

"I shan't ask 'em," said Miranda loftily. "There's more ways 'n one o' gettin' in, an' ef I make up my mind to git there you'll see I'll do it."

Marcia laughed.

"I suppose you will, Miranda. Well, go on. You may be needed. Poor Phoebe! I wish there was something I could do for her."

"Wal, thur is," said Miranda, with unexpected vim. "I've took a contrac' thet I don't seem to make much headway on. I'd like to hev you take a little try at it, an' see ef you can't do better. I 'greed t' pray fer Phoebe Deane, but t' save my life I can't think uv any more ways uv sayin' it thun jest to ast, an' after I've done it oncet it don't seem quite p'lite to keep at it, 'z if I didn't b'lieve 'twas heard. The minister preached a while back 'bout the 'fectual prayer uv a righteous man 'vailin' much, but he didn't say nothin' 'bout a redheaded woman. I reckon I ain't much good at prayin', fer I'm all wore out with it. But ef you'd jest spell me a while, an' lemme go see ef thur ain't sumpthin' to do, I think it would be a sight more 'vailin' then fer me to set still an' jest pray. 'Sides, ef you ain't better 'n most any righteous man I ever see, I'll miss my guess."

Thus the responsibility was divided, and Marcia with a smile on her lips and a tear in her eye went away to pray, while Miranda tied on her bonnet, tucked the letter safely in her pocket after examining its seals and address most minutely and went her way into the night.

She didn't go to the front door but stole around to the woodshed where with the help of a milking stool standing there she mounted to the low roof. With her strong limbs and courage she found the climb nothing. She crept softly along the roof till she reached Phoebe's window and crouched to listen. The window was open a little way, though the night was warm and dry.

"Granny, Granny McVane," she called softly, and Granny, startled from her evening drowsiness, stole over to the window. A candle was burning behind the water pitcher and shed a weird, sickly light through the room. Granny looked old and tired as she came to the window, and it struck Miranda she'd been crying.

"Fer the land sake! Is that you, Miranda?" she exclaimed in horror. "Mercy! How'd you get there? Look out! You'll fall."

"Open the winder till I come in," whispered Miranda.

Granny opened the window cautiously.

"Be quick," she said. "I mustn't let the air get to the bed."

"I should think air was jes' what she'd want this night," whispered Miranda, as she emerged into the room and straightened her garments. "How's she seem? Any change?"

"I think she's failing, I surely do," moaned the old lady softly, the tears running down her cheeks in slow uneven rivulets between the wrinkles. "I don't see how she can hold out till morning anyhow. She's jest burnt up with fever, and sometimes she seems to be gasping for breath. But how'd you get up there? Weren't you scairt?"

"I jes' couldn't keep away a minute longer. The doctor said this was the crisis, an' I had to come. My Mrs. Spafford's home prayin', an' I come to see ef I couldn't help answer them prayers. You might need help tonight, an' I'm goin' to stay. Will any of her folks be in again tonight?"

"No, I reckon not. Emmeline's worn out. The baby's teething and hasn't given her a minute's letup for two nights. She had his gums lanced today and hopes to get a wink of sleep, for there's likely to be plenty doing tomorrow."

Miranda set her lips hard at this and turned to the bed, where Phoebe lay under heavy blankets and comfortables, a low moan, almost a gasp, escaping her parched lips now and then.

The fever seemed to have burnt a place for itself in the white cheeks. Her beautiful hair had been cut short by Emmeline the second day because she couldn't be bothered combing it. It was as well, for it wouldn't have withstood the fever, but to Miranda it seemed like a ruthless tampering with the sacred. Her wrath burned hot within her, even while she was considering what was to be done.

"My goodness alive," was her first word. "I should think she would hev a fever. It's hotter'n mustard in here. Why don't you open them winders wide? I should think you'd roast alive yerself. And land sakes! Look at the covers she's got piled on! Poor little thing!"

Miranda reached out a swift hand and swept several layers off to the floor. A sigh of relief followed from Phoebe.

Miranda placed a firm cool hand on the burning forehead, and the sufferer seemed to take note of the touch eagerly.

"Oh, mercy me! Miranda, you mustn't take the covers off. She must be kept warm to try and break the fever. The doctor's orders were very strict. I wouldn't like to disobey him. It might be her death."

"Does he think she's any better?" questioned Miranda fiercely.

"No." The old lady shook her head sadly. "He said this morning there wasn't a thread of hope, poor little thing. Her fever hasn't let up a mite."

"Well, ef he said that, then I'm goin' to hev my try. She can't do more 'n die, an' ef I was goin' to die I'd like to hev a cool comf'table place to do it in, wouldn't you, Granny, an' not a furnace. Let's give her a few minutes' peace 'fore she dies, anyway. Come, you open them winders. Ef anythin' happens I won't tell, an' ef she's goin' to die anyway, I think it's wicked to make her suffer any longer."

"I don't know what they'll say to me," murmured the old lady, yielding to the dominant Miranda. "I don't think mebbe I ought to do it."

"Well, never mind what you think now. It's my try. Ef you didn't open 'em I would, fer I b'lieve in my heart she wants fresh air, an' I'm goin' to give it to her ef I hev to fight every livin' soul in this house an' smash all the winder lights, so there! Now that's better. It'll be somethin' like in here pretty soon. Where's a towel? Is this fresh water? Say, Granny, couldn't you slip down to the spring without wakin' anyone an' bring us a good cold drink? I'm dyin' fer a dipper o' water. I come up here so fast, and it'll taste good to Phoebe, I know."

"Oh, she mustn't have a drop o' water!" exclaimed the old lady. "Fever patients don't get a mite of water."

"Fever fiddlesticks! You git that water, please, an' then you kin lay down on that couch over there an' take a nap while I set by her."

After much whispered persuasion and bullying, Miranda succeeded in getting the old lady to slip downstairs and go for the water, though the springhouse was almost as far as the barn and Granny wasn't used to prowling around alone at night. While she was gone Miranda boldly dipped a towel in the water pitcher and washed the fevered brow and face. The parched lips crept to the wetness eagerly, and Miranda began to feel assurance to her fingertips. She calmly bathed the girl's hot face and hands, until the low moans became sounds of relief and contentment. Then quite unconscious that she was anticipating science she prepared to give her patient a sponge bath. In the midst of the performance she looked up to see Granny standing over her in horror.

"What are you doing, Mirandy Griscom? You'll kill her. The doctor said she mustn't have a drop of water touch her."

"I'm takin' the fever out uv her. Jes' feel her an' see," said Miranda triumphantly. "Put yer lips on her forrid—thet's the way to tell. Ain't she coolin' off nice?"

"You're killing her, Miranda," said Granny in a terrified tone, "and I've cared fer her so carefully all these weeks, and now to have her go like this! It's death coming that makes her cold."

"Death fiddlesticks!" said Miranda wrathfully. "Well, ef 'tis, she'll die happy. Here, give me that water!"

She took the cup from Granny's trembling hand and held it to Phoebe's dry lips. Eagerly the lips opened and drank in the water as Miranda raised her head on her strong young arm. Then the sick girl lay back with a long sigh of contentment and fell asleep.

It was the first natural sleep she'd had since the awful beginning of the fever. She didn't toss or moan, and Granny hovered doubtfully above her, watching and listening to see if she still breathed, wondering at the fading crimson flames on the white cheeks, dismayed at the cooling brow, even troubled at the quiet sleep.

"I fear she'll slip away in this," she said at last, in a sepulchral whisper. "That was an awful daresome thing you did. I wouldn't like them to find it out on you. They might say you caused her death."

"But she ain't dead yet," said Miranda, "an' ef she slips away in this it's a sight pleasanter'n the way she was when I crep' in. Say now, Granny—don't you think so, honest?"

"Oh, I don't know," sighed Granny, turning away sadly. "Mebbe I oughtn't to have let you."

"You couldn't 'a' he'ped yourself, fer I'd come to do it, an' anyway, ef you'd made a fuss I'd hed to put you out on the roof er somethin' till I got done. Now, Granny, you're all tired out. You jes' go over an' lie down on thet couch an' I'll set by an' watch her a spell."

The conversation was carried on close to Granny's ear, for both nurses were anxious lest some of the sleeping household should hear. Granny knew she would be blamed for Miranda's presence in the sickroom, and Miranda knew she would be ousted if discovered.

Granny settled down at last, with many protests, owned she was "jest the least mite tuckered out" and lay down for what she called a "cat nap." Miranda, meanwhile, wide-eyed and sleepless, sat beside Phoebe and watched her every breath, for she felt more anxiety about what she'd done than she cared to admit to Granny. She'd never had much experience in nursing, except in waiting on Marcia, but her common sense told her people weren't likely to get well as long as they were uncomfortable. Therefore without much consideration she did for Phoebe what she'd like to have done for herself if she were ill. It seemed the right thing, and it seemed to be working, but supposing Granny were right, after all!

Then Miranda remembered the two who were praying.

"Hm," she said to herself, as she sat watching the still face on the pillow. "I reckon that's their part. Mine's to do the best I know. Ef the prayers is good fer anything they ought to piece out whar' I fail. An' I guess they will, too, with them two at it."

After that she got the wet towel and went to work again, bathing the brow and hands whenever the heat seemed to be growing in them again. She was bound to bring that fever down. Now and then the sleeper would draw a long contented sigh, and Miranda felt she'd received her thanks. It was enough to know she'd given her friend a little comfort, if nothing else.

The hours throbbed on. The moon went down. The candle sputtered, and Miranda lighted another. Granny slept and actually snored, weary with her long vigil. Miranda had to touch her occasionally to stop the loud noise lest someone should hear and come to see what it was. But the others in the household were weary, too, for it was in the height of the summer's work now, and all slept soundly.

When the early dawn crept into the sky Miranda felt Phoebe's hands and head and found them cool and natural. She stooped and listened, and her breathing came regularly like a tired child's. For just one instant she touched her lips to the white forehead and rejoiced that the parched burning feeling was gone. The awful weakness yet remained to fight, but at least the fever was gone. What had done it she didn't care, but it was done.

She went gently to Granny and wakened her. The old lady started up with a frightened look, guilty that she'd slept so long, but Miranda reassured her. "It's all right. I'm glad you slep', fer you wa'n't needed, an' I guess you'll feel all the better fer it today. She's slep' real quiet all night long, ain't moaned once, an' jes' feel her. Ain't she feelin' all right? I b'lieve the fever's gone."

Granny went over and touched her face and hands wonderingly. "She does feel better," she admitted, "but I don't know. It mayn't last. I've seen 'em rally toward the end. She'll be so powerful weak now; it'll be all we can do to hold her to earth."

"What's she ben eatin'?" inquired Miranda.

"She hasn't eaten anything of any account for some time back."

"Well, she can't live on jest air an' water ferever. Say, Granny, I've got to be goin' soon, er I'll hev to hide in the closet all day fer sure, but 'spose you slip out to the barn now, while I wait, an' get a few drops o' new milk. Hank's out there milkin'. I heard him go down an' git his milk pails an' stool 'fore I woke you up. We'll give her a spoonful o' warm milk. Mebbe that'll hearten her up."

"It might," said Granny doubtfully. She took the cup and hurried away.

Miranda buttoned the door after her lest Emmeline should take a notion to look in.

When Granny got back, Miranda took the cup and, putting a few drops of the sweet warm fluid in a spoon, touched it to Phoebe's lips. A slow sigh followed, and then Phoebe's eyes opened. She looked straight at Miranda and seemed to know her, for a flicker of a smile shone in her face.

"There, Phoebe, take this spoonful. You've been sick, but it'll make you well," crooned Miranda.

Phoebe obediently swallowed the few drops, and Miranda dipped up a few more.

"It's all right, dear," she said. "I'll take care o' you. Jes' you drink this, an' get well, fer I've got somethin' real nice in my pocket fer you when ye take yer milk an' go to sleep."

Thus Miranda fed her two or three spoonfuls. Then the white lids closed over the trusting eyes, and in a moment more she was sleeping again.

Miranda watched her a few minutes and then cautiously stole away from the bed to the astonished Granny who had been watching with a new respect for the domineering young nurse that had usurped her place.

"I guess she'll sleep most o' the day," Miranda whispered. "Ef she wakes up you jes' give her a spoonful o' fresh milk, er a sup o' water, an' tell her I'll be back bime-by. She'll understan', an' that'll keep her quiet. Tell her I said she mus' lie still an' get well. Don't you dast keep them winders shet up all day again, an' don't pile on the clo'es. She may need a light blanket ef she feels cool, but don't fer mercy's sake get her all het up again, er we might not be able to stop it off so easy next time. I'll be back's soon es it's dark. Bye-bye. I mus' go. I may get ketched es 'tis."

Miranda slid out the window and down the sloping roof, dropping over the eaves just in time to escape being seen by Emmeline, who opened the back door with a sharp click and came out to get a broom she'd forgotten the night before. The morning was almost come now, and the long grass was dripping with dew as Miranda swept through it.

"Reckon they'll think there's ben a fox er somethin' prowlin' 'round the house ef they see my tracks," she said to herself, as she hurried through the dewy fields and out to the road.

Victory was written upon her countenance as she sped along, victory tempered with hope. Perhaps she wasn't judge enough of illness, and it might be that her hopes were vain ones, and apparent signs deceitful, but come what might she would always be glad she'd done what she had. That look in Phoebe's eyes before she fell asleep again was reward enough. It made her heart swell with triumph to think of it.

Two hours later she brought a platter of delicately poached eggs on toast to the breakfast table just as Marcia entered the room.

"Good morning, Miranda. How did it go last night? You evidently got in and found something to do."

Miranda set down the platter and stood with hands on her hips and face shining with morning welcome.

"I tell you, Mrs. Marcia, them prayers was all right. They worked fine. When I got mixed and didn't know what was right to do I just remembered them an' cast off all 'sponsibility. Anyhow, she's sleepin', an' the fever's gone."

Marcia smiled.

"I shouldn't wonder if your part was really prayer, too," she said. "We aren't all heard for our much speaking."

It was a glorious day. The sun shown in a perfect heaven without a cloud to blur it. A soft south breeze kept the air from being too warm. Miranda sang all the morning as she went about her belated work.

After dinner Marcia insisted she should go and take a nap. She obediently lay down for half an hour straight off and stiff on her bright neat patchwork quilt, scarcely relaxing a muscle lest she rumple the bed. She didn't close her eyes, however, but lay smiling at the white ceiling and resting herself by gently crackling the letter in her pocket. She smiled to think how Phoebe would look when she showed it to her.

In exactly half an hour she arose, combed her hair neatly, donned her afternoon dress and her little black silk apron that was her pride on ordinary occasions, and descended to her usual observation post with her knitting. Naps weren't in her line, and she was glad hers was over.

A little later the doctor's chaise drove up to the door, and Miranda went out to see what was wanted, a great fear clutching her heart. But she was reassured by the smile on his face and the good will in the expressions of his wife and her sister, who were riding with him.

"Say, Mirandy, I don't know but I'll take you into partnership. Where'd you learn nursing? You did what I wouldn't have dared do, but it seemed to hit the mark. I'd given her up. I've seen her slipping away for a week, but she's taken a turn for the better now, and I believe she's going to get well. If she does it'll be you that'll get the honor."

Miranda's eyes shone with happy tears.

"You don't say, doctor," she said. "Why, I was real scared when Granny told me you said she wasn't to hev a sup o' water, but it seemed like she must be so turrible hot—"

"Well, I wouldn't have dared try it myself, but I believe it did the business," said the doctor heartily.

"Yes, you deserve great credit, Miranda," said the doctor's wife.

"You do, indeed," echoed her sister pleasantly.

"Granny ain't tole Mis' Deane I was there, hes she?" asked Miranda, to cover her embarrassment. She wasn't used to praise except from her own household.

"No, she hasn't told her yet, but I think I'll tell her myself by tomorrow if all goes well. Can you find time to run over tonight again? Granny might not stay wide awake all the time. She's worn out, and I think it's a critical time."

"Oh, I'll be there!" said Miranda. "You couldn't keep me away."

"How'll you get in? Same way you did last night?" asked the doctor, laughing. "Say, that's a good joke! I've laughed and laughed ever since Granny told me, at the thought of you climbing in the window and the family all sleeping calmly. Good for you, Miranda. You're made of the right stuff. Well, good-bye. I'll fix it up with Mrs. Deane tomorrow so you can go in by the door."

The doctor drove on, laughing, and his wife and sister bowing and smiling.

Miranda, with her head high with pride and her heart full of joy, went in to get supper.

Supper was just cleared away when Nathaniel came over. He talked with David in the dusk of the front stoop a few minutes and then asked diffidently if Miranda was going up to see how Miss Deane was again soon.

Because of his love for Marcia, David half understood and, calling Miranda, left the two together for a moment while he went to call Marcia, who was putting Rose to bed.

"She's better," said Miranda, entering without preamble into the subject nearest their hearts. "The doctor told me so this afternoon. But don't you stop prayin' yet, fer we don't want no halfway job, an' she's powerful weak. I kinder rely on them prayers to do a lot. I got Mrs. Spafford to spell me at mine while I went up to help nurse. She opened her eyes oncet last night when I was givin' her some milk, an' I tole her I had somethin' nice fer her if she'd lie still an' go to sleep an' hurry up an' git well. She kinder seemed to understand, I most think. I've got the letter all safe, an' jes' ez soon ez she gits the least mite better, able to talk, I'll give it to her."

"Thank you, Miss Miranda," said Nathaniel, "and won't you take this to her? It will be better than letters for her for a while until she gets well. You needn't bother her telling anything about it now. Just give it to her. It may help her a little. Then later, if you think best, you may tell her I sent it."

He held out a single tea rose, half blown, with delicate petals of pale saffron.

Miranda took it with awe. It wasn't like anything that grew in the gardens she knew.

"It looks like her," she said reverently.

"It makes me think of her as I first saw her," he answered in a low voice. "She wore a dress like that."

"I know," said Miranda with understanding. "I'll give it to her and tell her all about it when she's better."

"Thank you," said Nathaniel.

Then Marcia and David entered, and Miranda went away to wonder over the rose and prepare for her night's vigil.

Chapter 22

Granny greeted Miranda with a smile as she crept in at the window that night. Phoebe, too, opened her eyes in welcome, though she made no other sign that she was awake. Her face was like sunken marble now that the fever was gone from it, and her two great eyes shone from it like lights of another world. It startled Miranda as she came and looked at her. Then at once she perceived that Phoebe's eyes had sought the rose, and a smile was hovering about her lips.

"It was sent to you," she answered the questioning eyes, putting the rose close down to the white cheek. Phoebe really smiled then faintly.

"She better have some milk now," said Granny anxiously. "She's been asleep so long, an' I didn't disturb her."

"Yes, take some milk," whispered Miranda, "an' I'll tell you all 'bout the rose when you're better."

The night crept on in quiet exultation of Miranda's part. While Phoebe slept, Miranda and the rose kept vigil, and Granny sank into the first restful sleep she'd had since she came to nurse Phoebe. The house was quiet. The watcher hadn't much to do but watch. Now and then she drew the coverlet up a little higher when a fresh breeze came through the window or gave another drink of water or spoonful of milk. The candle was shaded by the water pitcher, and the frail sweet rose looked spectral in the weird light. Miranda looked at the flower, and it looked back at her.

As the hours passed slowly, Miranda found her lips murmuring, "Thanks be! Thanks be!"

Suddenly she drew herself up with a new thought.

"Land sakes! That's sounds like prayin'. Wonder ef 'tis. Anyhow it's thanks-givin', an' that's what I feel. Guess it's my turn to give thanks."

The next day the doctor talked with Albert Deane. He told him how Miranda had crept in at the window and cared for Phoebe and how he believed it had been Phoebe's salvation. Albert was deeply affected. He readily agreed it would be a fine thing for Phoebe if Miranda could come and help Granny care for her, now that she seemed to be on the fair road to recovery.

It was all arranged in a few minutes, and Emmeline wasn't told until just before Miranda arrived.

"It's very strange," she said with her nose in the air, "that I wasn't consulted. I'm sure it's my business more'n yours to look after such things, Albert Deane. An' I wouldn't uv had that sassy creature in the house fer a good deal. Hank's sister would 'a' ben a sight better an' could 'a' helped me between times with Phoebe's extry work. I'm sure it's bad enough havin' sickness this way in the midst o' hayin' season, an' me with all them men to feed an' not havin' Phoebe to help. I could 'a' sent fer my own sister, when it comes to that, an' 'twould 'a' ben a sight pleasanter."

But before there was time for a protest or apology from Albert a knock came at the door, and without waiting for ceremony Miranda walked in.

"Ev'nin', Mis' Deane," she said. "Everything goin' well? I'll go right up, shall I?" Her smiling insolence struck Emmeline dumb for the moment.

"Well, I vow!" declared Emmeline. "Will yeh listen to the impedence. 'I'll go right up, shall I?' Es ef she was the Queen o' Sheby er the doctor himself."

But Miranda was marching serenely upstairs, and if she heard she paid no heed.

"She doesn't mean any harm, Emmeline!" pleaded Albert. "She's jest Phoebe's friend, so don't you mind. It'll relieve you a lot, and if you want Hank's sister to come over, too, I guess we can manage it."

Thus was Miranda domiciled in Phoebe's room for a short space, much to Phoebe's comfort and Miranda's satisfaction.

Emmeline was only half mollified when she came upstairs to look around and "give that Griscom girl a settin' down," as she expressed it. But she who attempted to "sit" on Miranda usually arose unexpectedly.

"Where'd that come from?" was Emmeline's first question, as she pointed at the unoffending rose.

"Mirandy brought it," said Granny, proud of her colleague.

"Hm!" said Emmeline with a sniff. "It ain't healthy to hev plants round in a bedroom, I've heard. D' you raise that kind down to Spaffords?"

"We ain't got just to say a-plenty yet," said Miranda cheerfully, "but we might hev sometime. Would yeh like a slip?"

"No, thank yeh," said Emmeline dryly. "I never had time to waste good daylight fussin' over weeds. I s'pose Mis' Spafford don't do much else."

"Oh, 'casionally!" answered Miranda, undisturbed. "This spring she put up a hundred glasses o' blueberry jelly, made peach preserves, spiced pears an' crab-apple jam, crocheted a white bedspread fer the spare bed an' three anti-macassars fer her aunt Hortense's best parlor chairs, did up the second-story curtains, tucked a muslin slip fer Rose, sewed carpet rags enough fer a whole strip in Shorty Briscutt's new rag carpet, made a set o' shirts fer Mr. Spafford, knit nine pair o' stockin's, spun the winter's yarn, cut out an' made Rose's flannel petticoats an' went to missionary meetin'. But o' course that ain't much, nothin' to what you'd do."

(Oh, Miranda, Miranda! Of the short prayers and the long tongue! Telling all that off with a straight face to the sour-faced woman, Emmeline!)

"She must be a smart woman!" said Granny, much impressed.

"She is," said Miranda glibly. "But here all the time I was fergettin' we'd ought not to talk. We'll bring that fever up. Is there anything special yeh wanted me to look after t'night, Mis' Deane? 'Cause ef there is, jes' don' hesitate to say so. I'm here to work an' not to play."

And before she knew it, Emmeline found herself disarmed and walking meekly downstairs without having said any of the things she had meant to say.

From that time forth Phoebe grew steadily better, though she came near to having a serious setback the day Miranda went down to the village on an errand. Emmeline attempted to "clean up" in her absence, finishing the operation by pitching the tea rose out into the yard below the window.

"I never seen such a fuss," complained Emmeline to Miranda, who stood over Phoebe and felt her fluttering pulse, "all over a dead weed. I declare I can't understand folks gettin' 'tached to trash."

Emmeline was somewhat anxious at the upset state of the patient, who was yet too weak to talk much but roused herself to protest vigorously as the rose was hurled through the window and then couldn't keep back the disappointed tears.

But Miranda, mindful of her patient's weak state and wishing to mollify Emmeline as much as possible, tried to pour oil on the troubled waters.

"Never mind, Mis' Deane. No harm done. Phoebe jes' wanted to keep them leaves fer her han'kerchers; they smell real nice. I'll pick 'em up, Phoebe. They won't be hurt a mite. They're right on the green grass."

Miranda stole down and picked up the leaves tenderly, washing them at the spring, and brought them back to Phoebe. Emmeline had gone off sniffing with her chin in the air.

"I was silly to cry," murmured Phoebe, trying feebly to dry her tears, "but I loved that sweet rose. I wanted to keep it just as it was in a box. You haven't told me about it yet, Miranda. How did she come to send it?"

"It ain't hurt a mite, Phoebe, only jest three leaves come off. I'll lay it together in a box fer yeh. Now lemme put my bonnet off, an' you lay quiet an' shet your eyes while I tell you 'bout that rose. First, though, you must take your milk.

"It wa'n't her at all that sent you that rose, Phoebe Deane. You s'picioned 'twas Mrs. Marcia, didn't you? But 'twa'nt 't all. It was a man—"

"Oh, Miranda!" The words came in a moan of pain from the bed. "Not— not—Miranda, you would never have brought it if Hiram Green—"

"Land sake, child, what's took yeh? 'Course not. Why, ef that nimshi'd undertake to send yeh so much ez a blade o' grass I'd fling it in his mean little face. Don't you worry, dearie. You jest listen. 'Twas Nathaniel Graham sent you that rose. He said I wa'n't to say nothin' 'bout it till you got better, an' then I could say 'twas from him ef I wanted to. I didn't say anythin' yet 'cause I hed more to tell, but I ain't sure you're strong 'nough to hear anymore now. Better take a nap first."

"No, Miranda, do tell me now."

"Wal, I reckon I better. I've most busted wantin' to tell yeh sev'ral times. Say, did you ever get a letter from Nathaniel Graham, Phoebe?"

"Why, no, of course not, Miranda. Why would I get a letter from him?"

"Wal, he said he wrote yeh one oncet, an' he ast me did I know ef you'd got it, and I said no, I was sure you didn't, 'cause you said oncet you hadn't ever got a letter 'cept from your mother, an' so he said he'd write it over again fer yeh, an' I've hed it in my pocket fer a long time waitin' till I dared give it to yeh. So here 'tis, but I won't give it to yeh 'thout you promise to go right to sleep 'fore you read it fer you've hed more goin's on now than 's good fer yeh."

Phoebe protested that she must read the letter first, but Miranda was inexorable and wouldn't even show it to her until she promised. So meekly Phoebe promised and went to sleep with the precious missive clasped in her hands, the wonder of it helping her get quiet.

She slept a long time, for the excitement about the rose had taken her strength. When she awoke, before she opened her eyes she felt the letter, pressing the seals with her fingers, to make sure she hadn't been dreaming. She almost feared to open her eyes lest it shouldn't be true. A letter for her all her own! Somehow she almost dreaded to break the seal and have the first wonder of it over. She hadn't thought what it might contain.

Miranda had brought a little pail of chicken broth Marcia had made for Phoebe, and she had some steaming in a china bowl when Phoebe at last opened her eyes. She made her eat it before she opened the letter, and Phoebe smiled and acquiesced.

She lay smiling and quiet a long time after reading the letter, trying to get used to the thought that Nathaniel had remembered her, cared to write to her and cared to have her write to him, too. It wasn't merely passing kindness toward a stranger. He wanted to be friends, real friends. It was good to feel that one had friends.

Phoebe looked over at Miranda's alert figure, sitting bolt upright and watching her charge with anxiety to see if the letter was all it should be. And then she laughed a soft little ripple that sounded like a shadow of her former self.

"Oh, you dear, good Miranda! You don't know how nice it is to have friends and a real letter."

"Is it a good letter?" asked Miranda wistfully.

"Read it," said Phoebe, handing it to her, smiling. "You certainly have a right to read it after all you've done to get it here."

Miranda took it shyly and went over by the window where the setting sun made it a little less embarrassing. She read it slowly and carefully and the look on her face when she returned it showed she was satisfied.

"I seen him the mornin' he went back to New York," she admitted after a minute. "He said he'd look fer that answer soon ez you got better. You're goin' to write, ain't you?" she asked anxiously. " 'Cause he seemed real set up about it."

"How soon may I answer it?" she answered.

"We'll see," said Miranda briskly. "The first business is to get strong."

Those two girls spent happy days together with nothing to worry them. As Phoebe began to get strong and could be propped up with pillows for a little while each day, Miranda at length allowed her to write a few lines in reply to her letter, and this was the message that in a few days thereafter traveled to New York.

My dear Mr. Graham,

It was very pleasant to receive your letter and know you thought of me and prayed that I might get well. I think your prayers are being answered.

It will be good to have a friend to write to me, and I shall be glad to correspond with you. I want to thank you for the beautiful rose. It helped me get well. Its leaves are sweet yet.

I've been a long time in writing this, for I'm very weak and tired yet, and Miranda won't let me write anymore now. But you will understand and excuse me, won't you?

Your friend,
Phoebe Deane

Miranda had to go home soon after that, for it was plain Emmeline was wanting to get rid of her, and Marcia was to have guests for a couple of weeks. Squire Schuyler and his wife were coming to visit for the first time since little Rose's birth, for it was a long journey for an old man to take, and the squire didn't like to go away from home. Miranda felt she must go, much as she hated to leave Phoebe, and so she bid her good-bye, and Phoebe began to take care of herself.

She was able to walk around her room and soon to go downstairs. But somehow when she got down into the old atmosphere something seemed to choke her, and she felt weary and wanted to creep back to bed again. So, much to Emmeline's disgust, she didn't progress as rapidly as she should have.

"You need to git some ambition," said Emmeline, with loathing, the first morning Phoebe came down to breakfast and sat back after one or two mouthfuls. They had fried ham and eggs and fried potatoes. *Anybody ought to be glad to get that,* Emmeline thought.

But they didn't appeal to Phoebe, and she left her plate almost untasted.

"I think ef you'd get some work and do somethin' mebbe you'd get your strength again. I never see anybody hang back like you do. There ain't any sense in it. What's the matter with yeh, anyway?"

"I don't know," said Phoebe, with an effort at cheerfulness. "I try, but somehow I feel so heavy and tired all the time."

"She isn't strong yet, Emmeline," pleaded Albert kindly.

"Wal, don't I know that?" snapped Emmeline. "But how's she ever goin' to get strong ef she don't work it up?"

Such little pinpricks were hard to bear when Phoebe felt well, and now that her strength was only a breath she seemed unable to bear them at all and after a short effort would creep back to her room and lie down.

Miranda discovered her all huddled in a little heap on her bed late one afternoon when she came up to bring Phoebe her second letter, for Nathaniel had arranged for the present to send his correspondence to Phoebe through Miranda. Neither of them said aloud that it was because Hiram Green brought up the Deanes' mail so often, but both understood.

Miranda and the letter succeeded in cheering up Phoebe, but the ex-nurse felt that things weren't going with her charge as prosperously as they should, and she took her trouble back to Marcia.

"Let's bring her down here, Miranda," proposed Marcia. "Father and Mother are going home on Monday, and it will be quiet and nice here. I think she might spend a month with us and get strong before she goes back and tries to work."

Miranda was delighted and took the first opportunity to convey the invitation to Phoebe, whose cheeks grew pink and eyes bright with anticipation. A whole month with Mrs. Spafford and Miranda! It was too good to be true.

Monday morning they came for her with the big old chaise. Emmeline and Hank's sister were out hanging up clothes. Emmeline's mouth was full of clothespins, and her brow was dark, for Hank's sister talked a great deal and worked slowly. Moreover, she made lumpy starch and couldn't be depended upon to keep the potatoes from burning if one went out to feed the chickens. It was hard to have trained up a good worker and then have her trail off in a thunderstorm and get sick and leave the work in someone else's hands without ambition enough to get well. Emmeline was very ungracious to Marcia. She told Albert she didn't see what business Mrs. Spafford had coming round to run their house. She thought Phoebe was better off at home, but Albert felt that Mrs. Spafford had been very kind.

So with little regret Phoebe was carried away from her childhood home into a sweet new world of loving-kindness and joy, where the round cheeks and happiness of health might be coaxed back. Yet to Phoebe it wasn't an undisturbed bliss, for always she carried with her the thought that by and by she must go back to the old life again. She shuddered at the very thought of it and couldn't bear to face it. It was like going to heaven for a little time and having to return to earth's trials again.

The spring had changed into the summer during Phoebe's illness, and it was almost the middle of July when she began her beautiful visit at the Spaffords.

Chapter 23

Hiram Green had been exceedingly quiet since the night of the runaway. The old plowhorse had kicked something loose about the chaise in his final lurch before he started to run, and it goaded his every step. He thought Hiram was striking him with a club. He thought the thunder was pursuing him and the lightning was reaching for him as it darted through the livid sky. Down the road he flew, mile after mile, not slowing up for curves or bumps in the road but taking a shortcut at the turns, rearing and shying at every flash of lightning. The chaise came lurching after, like one tied to a whirlwind, and Hiram, clinging, cursing, lashing out madly with his whip, was finally forced to spend his time in holding on, thinking every minute would be his last.

As the horse saw his own gate at last, however, he gave a final leap into the air and bounded across the ditch, regardless of what was behind him, perhaps hoping to rid himself of it. The chaise lurched into the air, and Hiram was tossed lightly over the fence and landed in the cow pasture. Something snapped, and the horse entered his own dooryard free at last from the thing which had been pursuing him.

The rain was coming down in driving sheets now and brought Hiram to his feet in spite of his dazed condition. He looked about him in the alternate dimness and vivid brightness and perceived that he was close to the Deanes'. A moment's reflection made it plain he must get up some kind of story, so he put on the best face he could and went in.

"We've hed an axident," he explained, limping into the kitchen, where Emmeline was trying to get supper and keep the fretful baby quiet. "The blamed horse got scared at th' lightnin'. I seen what was goin' to happen an' I held him on his haunches fer a second while Phoebe jumped. She's back there a piece now, I reck'n, fer that blamed critter never stopped till he landed to home, an' he placed me in a awkward persition in the cow pasture, with the chaise all broke up. I guess Phoebe's all right, fer I looked back an' thought I saw her tryin' to wave her hand to me, but I 'spect we better go hunt her up soon 's this here storm lets up. She'll likely go in somewheres. We'd just got past old Mis' Duzenberry's."

That was all the explanation the Deanes had ever had of the adventure. Phoebe had been too ill to speak of it at first, and after she got well enough to come downstairs Albert questioned her at the table about it. She had shuddered and turned so white, saying, "Please, don't, Albert. I can't bear to think of it," that he'd never asked her again.

During her illness Hiram had been politely concerned about her welfare, taking the precaution to visit the post office every day and inquire solicitously for any mail for her in a voice loud enough to be heard all over the room and always being ready to tell just how she was when anyone inquired. It never entered Albert's head that Hiram wasn't as anxious as he was during those days and nights when the fever held sway over the sweet young life. As for Emmeline, she made up her mind that where ignorance was bliss 'twas folly to be wise, and she kept her lips sealed, accepting Hiram's explanation, though all the time secretly she thought there might be some deeper reason for Phoebe's terrible appearance than just a runaway. She was relieved Phoebe said nothing about it, if there had been trouble, and hoped it was forgotten.

The day after Phoebe went to visit at the Spaffords', Hiram came up to see Emmeline in the afternoon when he knew Albert was out in the hayfield.

"Say, do you still favor livin' down to the village?" he asked, seating himself without waiting for an invitation.

Emmeline looked up keenly and wondered what was in the air. "I hev said so," she remarked tentatively, not willing to commit herself without further knowledge.

"Wal, you know that lot o' mine down there opposite the Seceder church? It has a big weepin' willer same 's in the churchyard and a couple o' plum trees in bearin'. How'd you like to live on thet lot?"

"Hm!" said Emmeline stolidly. "Much good 'twould do me to like it. Albert'll never buy that lot, Hiram Green. There ain't no use askin' him. You wasn't thinkin' of buildin' there yerself, was yeh?" Emmeline looked up sharply as this new thought entered her mind. Perhaps he wanted her to hold out the bait of a house in the village to Phoebe.

"Naw, I ain't goin' to build in no village at present, Mis' Deane," he remarked dryly. "Too fur from work fer me, thank you. But I was thinkin' I'd heard you say you wanted to live in the village, an' I thought I'd make a bargain with you. Say, Emmeline, 'taint no use mincin' matters. I'm a-goin' to marry Phoebe Deane, an' I want you should help me to it. I'll make you this offer. It's a real generous one, too. The day I marry Phoebe Deane I'll give you a deed to that lot in the village. Now what d'yeh say? Is't a bargain?"

"What to do?" questioned Emmeline. She would be caught in no trap. "I've done all I know now. I'd like my sister Mandy to come here to live, an' there ain't room fer her while Phoebe stays. But I don't see what I kin do, more'n what I've done a'ready. Wouldn't she make up to yeh none the day you come home from the barn raisin'?"

"Wal, I was gettin' on pretty well 'til that blamed horse took an' run," said Hiram, shifting his eyes from her piercing ones.

"Wal, I can't compel her to marry you," snapped Emmeline.

"You don't hev to," said Hiram. "I've got my plans laid, an' all you got to do is stand by me when the time comes. I ain't tellin' my plans jest yet, but you'll see what they be, an' all is, you remember my offer. Ef you want that village lot jest remember to stand by me."

He unfolded his length from the kitchen chair and went out. Emmeline said nothing.

When he reached the door he turned back and said, "I broke ground this mornin' fer a new house on the knoll. Me an' Phoebe'll be livin' there by this time next year."

"Well, I hope to goodness yeh will," responded Emmeline heartily, "fer I've hed trouble 'nough a'ready with this business. I'll do what I ken, o' course, but do fer goodness' sake hurry up!"

The house on the knoll steadily progressed. Hiram came little to the Deane house during Phoebe's absence but spent this time at the new building when his farmwork did not demand his presence. He also came often to the village and hung around the post office. He was determined for nothing to escape his vigilance in that direction.

Seeing him there one day when the mail was being distributed, Miranda took her place in the front ranks and asked in a clear cool voice: "Anythin' fer Phoebe Deane? She's stayin' t' our house fer a spell now, an' I'll take her mail to her."

Miranda knew the only mail Phoebe would likely receive came addressed to her, so she was more than surprised when the postmaster with his spectacles on the end of his nose held up a letter whose address he carefully studied and then handed it to her rather reluctantly. He would have liked a chance to study that letter more closely.

But nothing fazed Miranda. She took the letter as calmly as if there should be two or three more forthcoming and marched off. Hiram Green, however, got down scowling from his seat on the counter and stalked over to the postmaster.

"I sh'd think you'd hev to be keerful who you give letters to," he remarked in a low tone. "Phoebe Deane might not like that harum-scarum girl bringin' her letters. Did you take notice ef that letter was from New York? She was expectin' quite a important letter from there."

The postmaster looked over his spectacles at Hiram patronizingly.

"I sh'd hope I know who to trust," he remarked with dignity. "No, I didn't take notice. I hev too much to do to notice postmarks."

Hiram, however, was greatly shaken up by the sight of that letter in Miranda's hands and took himself to the hayloft to meditate. If he'd known the letter merely contained a clipping about the progress of missions in South Africa, which Ann Jane Bloodgood had sent thinking it might help Phoebe recover from her illness, as she heard she was feeling "poorly" yet and hoped she would soon hear she was better, he'd have rested easy.

But Hiram thought only that the letter was from Nathaniel; therefore his reflections were bitter.

Two days afterward Hiram was one of a group around a New York agent who had come down to sell goods. He was telling the story of a mob, and his swaggering air and flashy clothes attracted Hiram. He thought them far superior to any of Nathaniel Graham's and determined to model himself after this pattern in future.

"Oh, we do things in great shape down in New York," he was saying. "When folks don't please, we *mob* 'em. If their opinions ain't what we like, we *mob* 'em. If they don't pay us what we ask, we *mob* 'em. Heard 'bout the mob down in Chatham Street last summer—er it might have been two years ago? A lot of black men met to hear a preacher in a little chapel down there. We got wind of it, an' we ordered 'em to leave, but they wouldn't budge 'cause they'd paid their rent, so we just *put* 'em out. There was a man named Tappan who lived down in Rose Street, an' he was there. He was an abolitionist, an' we didn't like him. He'd had somethin' to do with this meetin', so we follered him home with hoots and threats and give his house a good stoning. Did him good. Oh, we do things up in great shape in New York. Next night we went down to the Bowery Theatre. Manager there's English, you know, and he'd said some imperlite things about America, we thought, something about our right to own slaves, so we give him a dose. Oh, we're not afraid of anything down in New York."

Hiram was greatly fascinated by this representative New Yorker, and after the crowd had begun to disperse he went to the stranger and buttonholed him.

"Say, look a' here!" he began, holding a five-dollar bill invitingly near the New Yorker's hand. "I know a feller you ought to mob. I could give yeh his name an' address real easy. He's prominent down there, an' I reckon 'twould be worth somethin' to you folks to know his name. Fact is, I've an interest in the matter myself, an' I'd like to see him come to justice, an' I'm willin' to subscribe this here bill to the cause ef you see your way clear to lookin' the matter up fer me."

"Why, certainly, certainly," said the stranger, grasping the bill affably, "I'll do anything I can for you. I'll hand this over to the treasurer of our side. In fact I'm the treasurer myself, and I thank you very much for your interest. Anything I can do I'm sure I'll be glad to. Can you tell me anymore about this?"

Hiram took him to a quiet corner, and before the interview was ended he had entered into a secret plot against Nathaniel Graham and had pledged himself to give the stranger not only one but four more five-dollar bills when the work should be complete and Nathaniel Graham stand revealed to the world as an abolitionist, a man who should be suppressed. It was all arranged before the stranger left on the evening stagecoach that he would write Hiram what day a move would be made in the matter and just how far he felt they could go.

Hiram went home chuckling and felt that revenge was sweet. He'd get the better of Nathaniel Graham now, and Nathaniel would never know who struck the blow.

A few days afterward a letter came from the stranger saying all things were prospering. But it would be impossible to get up a thoroughly organized mob and do the work without a little more money, for their funds were low. Would it be possible for Hiram to forward the twenty dollars now instead of waiting?

After a sleepless night Hiram doled out the twenty dollars. The stranger wrote that the time had been arranged, and he'd let him know all about it soon. They thought they had their man pinned down tight. The night Hiram received the letter he slept soundly.

Meanwhile the world had been moving in an orbit of beauty for Phoebe. She was tended and guarded like a little child. They made her feel that her presence was a joy to them all. Every member of the family down to Rose made it a point to brighten her stay with them. Rose brought her flowers from the garden, David brought the latest books and poems for her to read, Marcia was her constant loving companion, and Miranda cooked the daintiest dishes known to the culinary art for her tempting.

The letters went back and forth to New York every day or two, for as Phoebe was growing better she was able to write longer epistles, and Nathaniel seemed always to have something to say that needed an immediate answer. Phoebe was growing less shy of him and more and more opened her heart to his friendship like a flower turning to a newly risen sun.

Janet Bristol had been away on a visit during Phoebe's illness, but while she was still with the Spaffords Janet returned and one afternoon came to return Mrs. Spafford's call.

Phoebe wore a thin white dress whose dainty frills modestly showed her white throat and arms which were now taking on something of their old roundness. She was sitting in the cool parlor with Marcia when the caller arrived. Her mother's locket was tied about her throat with a bit of velvet ribbon, and her hair, now coming out in soft curls, made a lovely fluffy halo of brown all about her face.

Janet watched her while she talked with Marcia and wondered at the sweet grace of form and feature. Somehow her former prejudice against this girl melted strangely as Phoebe raised her beautiful eyes and smiled at her. Janet felt drawn to her against her will, yet she couldn't tell why she held back, except that Nathaniel had been so strangely stubborn about that letter. To be sure that was long past, and her mind was fully occupied just now with Nathaniel's theological friend, Martin Van Rensselaer. She was attempting to teach him the ways of the world and draw him out of his gravity. He seemed to be a willing subject, if one might judge from the number of visits he made to the Bristol home during the summer.

Then one bright, beautiful day, just a week before Phoebe's visit was to close, Nathaniel came up from New York.

He reached the village on the afternoon coach, and as it happened Hiram Green stood across the road from the tavern where the coach usually stopped, lounging outside the post office and waiting for the mail to be brought. He didn't intend that any Miranda Griscom should stand in his way. Moreover, this night was the one set for Nathaniel Graham's undoing, and there might be a letter for him from his agent in New York. It filled Hiram with a kind of intoxication to be getting letters from New York.

He stood leaning against a post watching the coach as it rolled down the village street drawn by the four great horses, enveloped in a cloud of dust, and drew up at the tavern with a flourish. Then suddenly he noticed there were two passengers, and one was Nathaniel himself.

Hiram felt weak in the knees. If a ghost had suddenly descended from the coach he couldn't have been more dismayed. Here he had just put twenty-five good dollars into Nathaniel's discomfiture, only to have him appear in his own town smiling and serene as if nothing had been about to happen. It made Hiram sick. He watched him and the other young man who had been his fellow passenger, as they walked down the street toward the Bristol house.

He had sat down when the coach stopped, feeling inadequate to hold himself upright in the midst of his unusual emotions. Now he got up slowly and walked away heavily toward his home, as if he'd been stricken. With head bent down he studied the ground as he walked. He forgot the mail, forgot everything, except that he had put twenty-five dollars into the fruitless enterprise.

Midway between the post office and his home he stopped and wheeled around with an exclamation of dismay. Then after a pause he let forth a series of oaths. Hiram was stirred to the depths of his evil nature. He had just remembered that Phoebe was down in the village at the Spaffords and would likely see Nathaniel. His ugly face contracted in a spasm of anger that gradually died into a settled expression of vengeance. The time had come, and he would wait no longer. If he'd been more impulsive and less of a coward he would have shot his victim then and there, but such was not Hiram's way. Stealthily, with deadly surety he laid his plans, with the patience and fatality that could only come from the father of liars himself.

Three whole days Nathaniel stayed in the village, and much of that time he spent at the Spafford house, walking and talking and reading with Phoebe. Three whole days Hiram spied upon him at every turn, with evil countenance and indifferent mien, lounging by the house or happening in the way. He'd written an angry letter to the man in New York, who later excused himself for not having performed his mission because of Nathaniel's absence but, promising it should yet be done, demanded more money.

Janet and Martin Van Rensselaer came down to the Spafford house the last evening and made a merry party. Hiram hid himself among the lilac bushes at the side of the house, like the serpent of old, and watched the affair all evening, his heart filled with all the evil his nature could conceive.

Phoebe made a beautiful picture in her simple white dress, with her lovely head crowned with the short curling hair and her exquisite face gleaming with the light and mirth of youth, which she was tasting for almost the first time. Miranda saw this as she brought in the sugary seed cakes and a great frosted pitcher of cool drink, made from raspberry and currant jelly, mixed with water from the spring. If Miranda could have known of the watcher outside, the evening might have ended in comedy, for she would certainly have emptied a panful of dishwater from the upper window straight into the lilac bushes. But Miranda's time hadn't come yct, and neither had Hiram's.

So Nathaniel and Phoebe sat by the open window and said a few last pleasant words and looked a good-bye into one another's eyes, the depth and meaning of which neither had as yet fathomed. They didn't know that not two feet away was the evil face of the man who hated them both. He was so near that his viperous breath could almost have touched their cheeks, and his wicked heart, burning with the passionate fires of jealousy and hatred, gathered and devoured their glances as a raging fire will devour fuel. He watched them, and he gloated over them, as a monster will gloat over the victims he intends to destroy.

Chapter 24

The next morning on the early coach Nathaniel and Martin went away. Hiram was there to see that they were really gone and to send word at once to New York.

That afternoon Phoebe went back to her brother's house, with the light of health and happiness beginning to glow in her face. It was hard to go back, but Phoebe was happy in the thought that these friends were true and would continue even in the midst of daily trials.

Everybody had urged her to stay longer, but Phoebe felt she'd already stayed longer than she should have and insisted she must begin life again, that it wasn't right to lie idle.

The truth was, Phoebe had in mind a little plan she wanted to think about and talk over with Albert. This stay with the Spaffords had brought to a climax a great longing she'd had in her heart to go to school somewhere for a little while. She had a great thirst for knowledge and thought perhaps it might be possible to gratify it, for there was that money of hers lying idle in the bank. She might take some of it and go away for a year to a good school if Albert thought so, and she almost believed he would if only he could be persuaded before Emmeline heard of it.

Phoebe had felt her own deficiencies because of her delightful correspondence with Nathaniel Graham. She wished to make herself more his equal, that she might really be able to write letters worthy of his perusal. She little dreamed of the trouble that was swiftly descending.

In modern war we sow our harbors and coasts thick with hidden mines ready to explode should the enemy venture within our borders. In much the same fashion that morning Hiram Green started out to lay his mines in readiness for the sweet young life that was unwarily drifting his way.

He had dressed himself soberly, as befitted the part he was to play. He harnessed his horse and chaise and, taking a wide berth of country in his circuit for the day, drove first to the home of an old aunt he'd never been bound to by many loving ties, yet who served his purpose, for she had a wagging tongue that reached far.

After the greetings were exchanged Hiram sat down with a funereal air in the big chair his relative had brought out of the parlor in honor of his coming and prepared to bring forth his errand.

"Aunt Keziah," he began, in a voice which indicated momentous things to come. "I'm in deep trouble!"

"You don't say, Hiram! What's up now? Any of the children dead or sick?"

"No, I ain't afflicted in that manner this time," said Hiram, "It's somethin' deeper than that, deeper than sickness er death. It's fear o' disgrace."

"What! Hiram! You ain't ben stealin' er forgin' anybody's name, surely?" The old lady sat up as if she'd been shot and fixed her eyes—little eyes like Hiram's with the glitter of steel beads—on her downcast nephew's face.

"No, Aunt, I'm thankful to say I've been kep' from pussonel disgrace," murmured Hiram piously, with a roll of his eyes indicating that his trust was in a power beyond his own.

"Well, you see it's this way, Aunt. You must uv heard I was takin' notice again."

"That was to be expected, Hiram, you so young an' with children to look after. I hope you picked out a good worker."

"Yes," admitted Hiram with satisfaction, "she's a right smart worker, an' I thought she was 'bout as near perfect all through as you could find 'em, an' I kinder got my heart sot on her. I've done everythin' she wanted that I knowed, even to buildin' a new house down on the knoll fer her, which wa'n't necessary 'tall, bein' as the old house is much better'n the one she's ben brung up in. Yet I done it fer her, an' I ben courtin' her fer quite a spell back now; ben to see her every night reg'lar, an' home from meetin' an' singin' school whenever she took notion she wanted to go."

Hiram drew a long sigh, got out a big red and white cotton handkerchief and blew his nose resoundingly. The old lady eyed him suspiciously to gauge his emotion with exactness.

"Long 'bout six or eight weeks ago"—Hiram's voice grew husky now— "she took sick. 'Twas this 'ere way. We was comin' home from a barn raisin' over to Woodburys', an' it was gettin' near dark, an' she took a notion she wanted to pick some vi'lets 'long the road. I seen a storm was comin' up, an' I argued with her agin it, but she would hev her way, an' so I let her out an' tole her to hurry up.

"She got out an' run back o' the kerridge a piece an' begun pickin', an' in a minute all on a suddent somethin' hit the horse's hind leg. I can't tell what it was, mebbe a stone er it might 'a' ben a stick, but I never took no thought at the time. I grabbed fer them reins, an' jest as the horse started to run there come a big clap o' thunder that scared the horse worse'n ever. I hung on to them reins, an' lookin' back I seen her standin' kind o' scared like an' white in the road a-lookin' after me, an' I hollered back, 'You go to the Widder Duzenberry's till I come back fer yeh. It's goin' to rain.' Then I hed to tend to that horse, fer he was runnin' like the very old scratch. Well, 'course I got him stopped and turned him round an' went back, but there wasn't a sign of her anywhere to be seen.

"The Widder Duzenberry said she hedn't seen her sence we druv by fust. I went back fer her brother, an' we searched everywhere but couldn't find her no place, an' will you b'lieve it, we couldn't find a sign of her all night. But the next mornin' she come sailin' in lookin' white an' scared and fainted away an' went right to bed real sick. We couldn't make it all out, an' I never said much 'bout it, 'cause I didn't 'spicion nothin' at the time, but it all looked kinder odd afterward. An' what I'd like to know is, who threw that ar stone thet hit the horse?

"You see, it's all come out now thet she's been cuttin' round the country with a strange young man from New York. She's met him off in the woods an' round. They say they used ter meet not far from here—right down on the timber lot back o' your barn was one place they used to meet. There's a holler tree where they'd hide their letters. You 'member that big tree taller than the rest, a big white oak, 't is, that has a squirrel harbor in it? Well, that's the one. They used to meet there. And once she started off on some errand fer her sister-in-law in the coach, an' he es bold es life went 'long. Nobody knows whar they went—some sez Albany, some sez Schenectady—but anyhow she never come back till late the next day, an' no countin' fer where she'd been.

"Her sister-in-law is a nice respectable woman, and they all come of a good family. They'll feel turrible 'bout this, fer they've never 'spicioned her anymore'n I done. She's got a sweet purty face like she was a saint—"

"Them is always the very kind that goes to the dogs," said Aunt Keziah, shaking her head and laying down her knitting.

"Well, Aunt Keziah," said Hiram, getting out his handkerchief again, "I come to ask your advice in this matter. What be I to do?"

"Do?" snapped Aunt Keziah. "Do, Hiram Green? Why be thankful you found out 'fore you got married. It's hard on you, 'course, but 'tain't near so hard es 'twould 'a' ben ef you'd 'a' found out after you was tied to 'er. An' you just havin' had such a hard time an' all with a sickly wife dyin'. I declare, Hiram Green, you suttin'ly hev been preserved!"

"But don't you think, mebbe, Aunt Keziah, I ought to stick to her? She's such a purty little thing, an' everybody's down on her now, an' she's begged me so hard not to give her up when she's in disgrace. She's promised she'll never hev nothin' more to do with these other fellers—"

Some hypocritical tears were actually being squeezed out of Hiram's little pig eyes and rolling down in stinted quantities upon the ample kerchief. It wouldn't do to wipe them away when they were so hard to manufacture, so Hiram waited till they were almost evaporated and then mopped his eyes vigorously.

"Well, Hiram Green, are you that softhearted? I declare to goodness, but you do need advice! Don't you trust in no sech promises. They ain't wuth the breath they're spoken in. Jest you hev nothin' more to do with the hussy. Thank goodness there's plenty more good workers in the world—healthy ones, too, that won't up 'n' die on ye jest in harves'!"

"Well, Aunt Keziah!" Hiram arose and cleared his throat as if a funeral ceremony had just been concluded. "I thank yeh fer yer good advice. I may see my way clear to foller it. Jest now I'm in doubt. I wanted to know what you thought, an' then I'll consider the matter. It ain't as though I hedn't been goin' with her pretty steady fer a year back. Yeh see what I'll do'll likely tell on how it goes with her from now on."

"Well, don't you go to be sentimental-like, Hiram. That wouldn't set on you at your time o' life. Jest you stand by your rights an' be rid of her. It's what your ma would 'a' said ef she was alive. Now you remember what I say. Don't you be softhearted."

"I'll remember, Aunt," said Hiram dutifully and went out to his chaise.

He took his slow and doleful way winding up the road, and as soon as he was out of sight beyond the turn the alert old lady put on her sunbonnet and slipped up to her cousin's house half a mile away. She was out of breath with the tremendous news she had to tell and marvelling all the way that Hiram had forgotten to tell her not to speak of it. Of course he intended to do so, but then of course he wouldn't object to having Lucy Drake know. Lucy was his own cousin once removed, and it was a family affair in a way.

Hiram's next visit was at the Widow Duzenberry's.

Now the Widow Duzenberry had often thought her good daughter would make a wise choice for Hiram Green and could rule well over the wild little Greens and be an ornament to the Green house and farm. Therefore it seemed a special dispensation of Providence that Susanna had that afternoon donned her best sprigged chintz and done her hair up with her grandmother's high-backed comb. She looked proudly over at her daughter as Hiram sat down in the chair Susanna had primly placed for him near her mother.

When the few preliminary remarks were concluded, and the atmosphere had become somewhat breathless with the excitement of wondering why he'd come, Hiram cleared his throat ominously and began.

"Mrs. Duzenberry," he said, and his countenance took on a deep sadness, "I called today on a very sad errand." The audience was attentive in the extreme. "I want to ask, did you take notice of me an' Phoebe Deane a-ridin' by, the day of Woodburys' barn raisin'?"

"Wal, yes," admitted old Mrs. Duzenberry reluctantly. "Now 't you mention it, I b'lieve I did see you drivin' by, fer there was black clouds comin' up, an' I says to Susanna, says I, 'Susanna, we mebbe ought to bring in that web o' cloth that's out to bleach. It mebbe might blow away.'"

"Well, I thought p'raps you did, Mis' Duzenberry, an' I want to ask, did you take notice of how we was sittin' clost to one 'nother, she with her head restin' on my shoulder like? I hate to speak of it, but, Mis' Duzenberry, wouldn't you 'a' thought Phoebe Deane was real fond o' me!"

Mrs. Duzenberry's face darkened. What had the man come for?

"I certain should," she answered severely. "I don't approve of sech doin's on an open road."

"Well, Mis' Duzenberry, mebbe 'twas a little too sightly a place, but what I wanted to know from you, Mis' Duzenberry, was this. You saw what you saw. Now won't you tell me when a man has gone that fur, in your 'pinion is there anything that would justify him in turnin' back?"

"There might be," said the old lady, somewhat mollified.

"Well, what, fur instance?"

"Wal, he might 'a' found he thought more o' someone else." Her eyes wandered toward her daughter, who was modestly looking out the window.

"Anything else?" Hiram's voice had the husky note now as if he were deeply affected.

"Wal, I might think of somethin' else. Gimme time."

"What ef he found out she wa'n't all he thought she was?"

Mrs. Duzenberry's face brightened.

" 'Course that might 'fect him some," she admitted.

"I see you don't understand me," sighed Hiram. "I take it you ain't heard the bad news 'bout Phoebe Deane."

"She ain't dead, is she? I heard she was better," said Susanna, turning her sharp thin profile toward Hiram.

"No, my good friend," sighed Hiram, "it's worse'n death. It certainly is fer that poor girl. She's to be greatly pitied, however much she may have aired."

The two women were leaning forward now, eager for the news.

"I came to you in my trouble," said Hiram, mopping his face vigorously, "hopin' you would sympathize with me in my extremity an' help me to jedge what to do. I wouldn't like to do the girl no wrong, but still, considerin' all that's come out the last two days—say, Mis' Duzenberry, you didn't see no man hangin' round here that day a little before we druv by, did you? No stranger, ner nuthin'."

"Why, yes, Ma," said Susanna excitedly. "There was a wagon come by a-goin' toward the village, and there was two men, an' one of 'em jumped out an' took somethin' from the other, looked like a bundle er sumthin', an' he walked off toward the woods. He had butternut-colored trousers."

"That's him," said Hiram, frowning. "They say he always wore them trousers when anybody's seen him with her. You know the day they went off in the stage to Albany he was dressed thata way!"

"Did they go off in the stage together in broad daylight? That's scandalous!" exclaimed the mother.

"You know, most o' their goin's on happened over near Fundy Road. Aunt Keziah knows all 'bout it. Poor ole lady. She's all broke up. She always set a good store by me, her only livin' nephew. She'll be wantin' me to give up havin' anythin' more to do with Phoebe now, since all this is come out 'bout her goin's on, but I can't rightly make up my mind whether it's right fer me to desert her er not in her time o' trouble."

"I should think you was fully justified," said Mrs. Duzenberry heartily. "There's other deservin' girls, an' it's puttin' a premium on badness to 'ncourage it that way."

"Good afternoon, Mis' Duzenberry." Hiram rose sadly. "I'm much 'bliged to yeh fer yer advice. I ain't sure what I shall do. 'Course I'll be 'bliged to yeh ef you'll jest keep people from talkin' much as yeh ken. I knowed you knowed the fac's, an' I thought 'twould be best to come straight to you. Good afternoon, Miss Susanna. Perhaps we may meet again under pleasanter circumstances."

"Land alive!" exclaimed Susanna, as they watched him drive sadly away. "Don't he look broke up! Poor feller!"

"Serves him right fer makin' up to a little pink-cheeked critter like that," said the mother. "Say, Susanna, I ain't sure but you better put on yer bonnet an' run up to Keziah Dart's house an' find out 'bout this. We've got to be real keerful not to get mixed up in it, nohow, but I'd like to know jest what she's done. Ef Keziah ain't home, run on to Page's. They'll mebbe know. He said they'd ben seen round there. But speak real cautious. It won't do to tell everything you know. I'll mebbe jest step over to the tollgate. They'll be wantin' to know what Hiram Green was here for. It won't do no harm to mention he was callin' on you. It might take their 'tention off'n him, so's they wouldn't speak 'bout him goin' so much with Phoebe. My! Ain't it a pity! But that's what comes o' havin' good looks. You know I allus told you so, Susanna."

Susanna tossed her head, drew her sunbonnet down over her plain face and went off, while her mother fastened the door and went up to the tollgate.

Hiram's method, as he pursued his course the rest of the afternoon, was to call ostensibly for some other reason and then speak of the gossip as a matter of which everyone knew and refer to those he'd called on before as being able to give more information concerning the facts than he could. He didn't ask any more advice, but in one case where he was asked what he was going to do about it he shook his head dubiously and went away without replying.

Most of his calls were in the country, but before he went home he stopped at the village dressmaker's home. His excuse for going there was that his oldest girl needed a dress for Sunday, and he thought the old woman who kept house for him had enough to do without making it. He asked when she could come and said he'd let her know if that day would be convenient. Just as he was leaving he told her that, since she was going everywhere to other people's houses, he supposed she'd soon hear the terrible stories going around about Phoebe Deane. But he wished that if she heard anything about his breaking off with Phoebe she'd just say he intended not to do anything rashly but would think it over and do what was right.

The keen-eyed newsmonger asked enough questions to have the facts in hand and looked after Hiram's tall, lanky form with admiration. "I tell you," she said to herself, "it ain't every man would hev the courage to say that! He's a good man! Poor little Phoebe Deane. What a pity! Now her life's ruined, fer of course he'll never marry her."

Then Hiram Green, having wisely scattered his calumnies against the innocent, took himself virtuously to his home and left his thistle seed to take root and spring up.

Phoebe Deane, meanwhile, settled down in her own little chamber beside her candle and prepared to write a letter to Nathaniel Graham, as she had promised him she'd do that very night, and in it she told him her plans of going away to school.

Chapter 25

The tongues Hiram had set wagging were all experts, and before many days had passed the fields of gossip were green with springing slander and disgrace for the fair name of Phoebe Deane. All unconsciously she moved above it, making happy plans and singing her sweet song of hope. She didn't mind work, for it was pleasant to feel strong again. She even hummed a sweet tune she heard Marcia play. Emmeline was puzzled to understand it all.

But the thing that puzzled Emmeline most was that Hiram Green hadn't been near the house since the day he had the talk with her about the village lot and boasted he was going to marry Phoebe before another year.

Steadily every day Hiram's new house was growing. Emmeline could see it from her window and wondered if perhaps he was preparing to break his promise and court another girl instead of Phoebe, or was this part of his plan to stay away until the house was done? It troubled Emmeline every day. Neither could she understand how Phoebe could be happy and settle down so cheerfully, having driven her one suitable lover away.

Phoebe had ventured to discuss the plan of her going away with Albert, who seemed rather disappointed for her to go but was nevertheless willing and said he thought such a plan would have pleased her mother. He broached the subject to Emmeline and thereupon brought down on the family a storm of rage.

Emmeline scoffed at the idea. She said Phoebe was already spoiled for anything in life and if she used up her money getting more spoiling she couldn't see how in the world she expected to support herself. *She* wouldn't be a party to Phoebe's living any longer on them if she spent her money on more schooling. Then Emmeline put on her bonnet and ran across the field to Hiram's farm, where she found him at the knoll superintending the putting up of a great stone chimney.

"Say, look-a-here, Hiram Green," she began excitedly, getting him off a little way from the workmen. "What do you mean by sech actions? Hev you give up Phoebe Deane, er haven't yeh? 'Cause ef yeh ain't yeh better be tendin' to business. She's got it int' her fool head now to go off to school, an' she'll do it, too. I ken see Albert's jest soft enough to let 'er."

Hiram smiled a peculiar smile.

"Don't you worry, Emmeline. I know what I'm 'bout, an' you'll git your corner lot yit. Phoebe Deane won't go off to no boardin' school, not yet a while, er I'll miss my guess. Jest you leave it to me!"

"Oh, very well!" said Emmeline, going off in a huff. She returned by a roundabout route to her home, where she proceeded to make life miserable for Phoebe and Albert in spite of all they could do.

Then one morning, lo, the little town was agog with the gossip about Phoebe Deane. It had grown into enormous proportions, for as it traveled from the circle of country round about into the town it condensed into more tangible form, and the number of people who had seen Phoebe Deane with strange young men at the edge of dark or in lonely places grew with each repetition. Everybody seemed to know it and be talking about it except Phoebe herself and her family and friends. Somehow no one had quite dared to mention it before any of them yet; it was too new and startling.

Sunday morning the Deanes went to church, and the people turned strangely away from them, with much whispering, nodding and nudging as they passed. They hadn't expected Phoebe to appear in church. It was considered brazen in her to do so. It was evidently all and more true.

Hiram Green came to church, but he didn't look toward the Deanes' pew. He sat at the back with pious manner and drooping countenance and after church made his melancholy way out without stopping to talk or attempting to get near Phoebe. This was observed significantly, as well as the fact that Mrs. Spafford walked down the aisle in friendly conversation with Phoebe Deane as if nothing had happened. Evidently she hadn't heard yet. Somebody should tell her. They discussed the matter in groups on the way home.

Old Mrs. Baldwin and her daughter Belinda were quite worried about it. They went so far as to call to the doctor and his wife who were passing their house that afternoon on the way to see a sick patient.

"Doctor," said Mrs. Baldwin, coming out to the sidewalk as the doctor drew up to speak to her, "I ain't a going to bother you a minute, but I just wanted to ask if you knew much about this story that's been going round about Phoebe Deane. It seems as though someone ought to tell Mrs. Spafford. She's been real kind to the girl, and she don't seem to have heard it. I don't know her so well, or I would, but somebody ought to do it. I didn't know but you or your wife would undertake to do it. They walked down the aisle together after church this morning, and it seemed too bad. David Spafford wouldn't like to have his wife so conspicuous, I know. Belinda says he was out of town yesterday, so I s'pose he hasn't heard about it yet, but I think something ought to be done."

"Yes, it's a very sad story," chirped the doctor's wife. "I just heard it myself this morning. The doctor didn't want to believe it, but I tell him it comes very straight."

"Oh, yes, it's straight," said Mrs. Baldwin, with an ominous shake of her head and a righteous roll of her eyes. "It's all too straight. I had it from a friend who had it from Hiram Green's aunt's cousin. She said Hiram was just bowed with grief over it, and they were going to have a real hard time to keep him from marrying her in spite of it."

The doctor frowned. He was fond of Phoebe. He felt that they all had better mind their own business and let Phoebe alone.

"I'd be quite willing to speak to Miss Hortense or Miss Amelia Spafford," said the doctor's wife. "I'm intimate with them, you know, and they could do as they thought best about telling their niece."

"That's a good idea," said Mrs. Baldwin. "That quite relieves my mind. I was real worried over that sweet little Mrs. Spafford, and she with that pretty little Rose to bring up. They wouldn't of course want a scandal to come anywhere near them. They better look out for that Griscom girl. She comes from poor stock. I said long ago she'd never be any good, and she's been with that Phoebe Deane off an' on a good bit."

"Oh, I think that was all kindness," said the doctor's wife. "Mrs. Spafford was very kind during Phoebe Deane's illness. The doctor knew all about that."

"Yes, I s'pose the doctor knows all 'bout things. That's the reason I called you and on Sunday too. But I thought it was a work of necessity and mercy. Well, good afternoon, doctor. I won't keep you any longer."

"There's that pretty Miss Bristol ought to be told, too, Ma," said Belinda.

"That's so, Belinda," said the doctor's wife. "I'll take it upon myself to warn her, too. So sad, isn't it? Well, good-bye." And the doctor's chaise drove on.

The doctor was inclined to prevent his wife from taking part in the scandal business, but his wife had her own plans which she didn't reveal. She shut her thin lips and generally did as she pleased.

The very next day she took her way down the shaded street and called on the Spafford aunts, and before she left she had drooped her eyes and told in sepulchral whispers of the disgrace that had befallen the young protégée of their niece, Mrs. David Spafford.

Aunt Amelia and Aunt Hortense lifted their hands in righteous horror and thanked the doctor's wife for the information, saying they were sure Marcia knew nothing of it, and of course they would tell her at once and she would have nothing further to do with the Deanes.

Then the doctor's wife went on her mission to Janet Bristol.

Janet Bristol was properly scandalized and charmingly grateful to the doctor's wife. She said of course Phoebe was nothing to her, but she'd thought her rather pretty and interesting. She was obviously bored with the rest of the good woman's call, and when it was over she went to her writing desk where she scribbled off a letter to her cousin Nathaniel concerning a party she wished to give and for which she wanted him and his friend Martin Van Rensselaer to come up. At the close she added a hasty postscript.

"The doctor's wife has just called. She tells me I must beware of your paragon, Miss Deane, as there is a terribly scandalous story going around about her and a young man. I didn't pay much attention to the horrid details of it. I never like to get my mind filled with such things. But it's bad enough, and of course I shall have nothing further to do with her. I wonder Mrs. Spafford didn't have the discernment to see she wasn't all right. I suspected it from the first, you know, and you see I was right. My intuitions are usually right. I'm glad I didn't have much to do with her."

Now it happened that Rose wasn't well that Sunday and Miranda had stayed at home with her; otherwise, she would surely have discovered the state of things and revealed it to Marcia. It happened also that Marcia started off with David on a long ride early Monday morning. Therefore when Aunt Hortense came down on her direful errand Marcia wasn't there, and Miranda, seeing her coming, escaped with Rose through the back door for a walk in the woods. So another day passed without the scandal reaching either Miranda or Marcia.

On Monday morning the storm broke upon poor Phoebe's defenseless head.

A neighbor had come over from the next farm a quarter of a mile away to borrow a cup of hop yeast. It was an odd time to borrow yeast, at an hour in the week when every well-regulated family was doing its washing, but that was the neighbor's professed errand. She lingered a moment by the door with the yeast cup in her hand and talked to Emmeline.

Phoebe was in the yard hanging up clothes and singing. The little bird was sitting on the weather vane, calling merrily, "Phoe-bee! Phoe-bee!"

"Are yeh goin' to let her stay here now?" the visitor asked in a whisper fraught with meaning and nodded her head toward the girl in the yard.

"Stay?" said Emmeline, looking up aggressively. "Why shouldn't she? Ain't she been here ever since her mother died? I s'pose she'll stay till she gets married."

Emmeline wasn't fond of this neighbor and therefore didn't care to reveal her family secrets to her. She lived in a red house with windows both ways and knew all that went on for miles about.

"Guess she won't run much chance of that now," said the neighbor with a disagreeable laugh. She was prepared to be sociable if Emmeline opened her heart, but she knew how to scratch back when she was slapped.

"Well, I sh'd like to know what you mean, Mis' Prinn. I'm sure I don't know why our Phoebe shouldn't marry es likely as any other girl, an' more so'n some what ain't got good looks."

(Mrs. Prinn's daughter wasn't spoken of generally as a beauty.)

"Good looks don't count fer much when they ain't got good morals."

"Indeed, Mis' Prinn! You do talk kind of mysterious. Did you mean to insinuate that our Phoebe didn't have good morals?"

"I didn't mean to insinuate anything, Mis' Deane. It's all over town the way she's been goin' on, an' I don't see how you can pertend to hide it any longer. Everybody knows it an' b'lieves it."

"I'd certainly like to know what you mean," demanded Emmeline, facing the woman angrily. "I brung that girl up, an' I guess I know what good morals is. Phoebe may have her weak points, but she's all right morally."

"Fac's is fac's, Mis' Deane," said the neighbor with a relish.

"I deny there is any fac's to the contrary," screamed Emmeline, now thoroughly excited into championing the girl she hated. The family honor was at stake. The Deanes had never done anything dishonorable or disgraceful.

"I s'pose you don't deny she spent the night out all night the time o' the storm, do yeh? How d' ye explain that?"

"I should like to know what that hes to do with morals."

The neighbor proceeded to explain with a story so plausible that Emmeline grew livid with rage.

"Well, 'pon my word, you've got a lot to do runnin' round with sech lies as them. Wher'd you get all that, I'd like to know?"

"It all come straight enough, an' everybody knows it, ef you are stone blind. Folks has seen her round in lonely places with a strange feller. They do say he kissed her right in plain sight of the road near the woods one day. An' you know yerself she went off and stayed all night. She was seen in the stage-coach 'long with a strange man. There's witnesses! You can't deny it. What I want to know is, what are you goin' to do 'bout it? 'Cause ef you keep her here after that, I can't let my dotter come here anymore. When girls is talked about like that, decent girls can't hev nothin' to do with 'em. You think you know a hull lot 'bout that girl out there, singin' songs in this brazen way with the hull town talkin' 'bout her, but she's deceived you, that's what she's done. An' I thought I'd be a good enough neighbor to tell you, ef you didn't know a'ready. But es you don't seem to take it as 'twas meant, in kindness, I'd best be goin'."

"You'd best had," screamed Emmeline, "an' be sure you keep your precious dotter to hum. Hum's the place fer delikit little creatures like that. You might find *she* was deceivin' you ef *you* looked sharp enough."

Then Emmeline turned and faced the wondering Phoebe, who had heard the loud voices and slipped in through the woodshed to escape being drawn into the altercation. She had no idea what it all was about. She had been engaged with her own happy thoughts.

"I'd like to know what all this scandal's about, Phoebe Deane. Jest set down there and explain. What kind of goin's on hev you hed, that all the town's talkin' 'bout you? Mis' Prinn comes an' says she can't let her dotter come over here anymore ef you stay here. I don't know that it's much loss, fer she never come to 'mount to much, but I can't hev folks talkin' that way. No decent girl ought to have her name kicked around in that style. I may not hev hed a great ejjacation like you think you've got to have, but I knowed enough to keep my name off folks' tongues, an' it seems you don't. Now I'd like to know what young man or men you've been kitin' round with. Answer me that? They say you've been seen in the woods alone, walkin' at night with a strange man an' goin' off in the stagecoach. Now what in the world does it all mean?"

Phoebe, turning deathly white, with a sudden return of her recent weakness, sank upon a kitchen chair, her arms full of dried clothes, and tried to understand the angry woman who stormed back and forth across her kitchen, livid with rage, pouring out a perfect torrent of wrath and incriminations.

When a moment's interval came, Phoebe would try to answer her, but Emmeline, roused beyond control, wouldn't listen. She stormed and raged at Phoebe, calling her names and telling her what a trial she'd always been, until suddenly Phoebe's newfound strength gave way entirely and she dropped back in a faint against the wall. She would have fallen if Albert hadn't come in just then unnoticed and caught her. He carried her upstairs tenderly and laid her on her bed. In a moment she opened her sad eyes again and looked up at him.

"What's the matter, Phoebe?" he asked tenderly. "Been working too hard?"

But Phoebe could only answer by a rush of tears.

Albert, troubled as a man always is by a woman's tears, stumbled downstairs to Emmeline to find out and was met by an overwhelming story.

"Who says all that 'bout my sister?" he demanded in a cool voice, rising with a dignity that sat strangely upon his kind figure.

"She ain't your sister," hissed Emmeline. "She ain't any but a half relation to you, an' it's time you told her so an' turned her out of the house. She'll be a disgrace to you an' your decent wife an' children. I can't have my Alma brought up in a house with a girl that's disgraced herself like that."

"You keep still, Emmeline," said Albert gravely. "You don't rightly know what you're saying. You've got excited. I'll attend to this matter. What I want to know is, who said this about my sister? I'll go get Hiram Green to help me, and we'll face the scoundrel, whoever it is, and make him take it back before the whole town."

"What ef it's true!" mocked Emmeline.

"It isn't true. It couldn't be true. You know it couldn't, Emmeline."

"I'm not so sure o' that," raged his wife. "Wait till you hear all." And she proceeded to recount what Mrs. Prinn had told her.

"I'm ashamed of you, Emmeline, that you'll think of such a thing for a minute, no matter who told you. Don't say another word about it. I'm going out to find Hiram."

"Ain't you noticed that Hiram ain't ben comin' here lately?" Emmeline's voice was anything but pleasant.

Albert looked at her in astonishment.

"Well, what o' that? He's a good man, and he's fond o' Phoebe. He'll be sure to go with me and defend her."

Albert went out, and she saw him hurrying down the road toward Hiram's.

Hiram, like an old spider, was waiting for him in the barn. He'd been expecting him for two days, not thinking it would take so long for the news to spread into the victim's home. He looked gloomy and noncommittal as Albert came up, and he greeted him with half-averted eyes.

"I've come to get your help," said Albert with expectant goodwill. "Hiram, have you heard all this fool talk about Phoebe? I can't really believe folks would say that about her, but Emmeline's got it in her head everybody knows it."

"Yes, I heard it," admitted Hiram, reaching out for a straw to chew. "I spent one hull day last week goin' round tryin' to stop it, but 'twa'n't no use. I couldn't even find out who started it. You never ken, them things. But the wust of it is, it's all true."

"What!"

"Yes," said Hiram dismally, " 'tis. I'm sorry t' say it to you, what's ben my friend, 'bout her I hoped to marry someday, but I seen some things myself. I seen thet day they talk 'bout in the edge o' the woods, an' I seen her cut an' run when she heard my wagon comin', an' when she looked up an' see it was me she was deadly pale. That was the fust I knowed she wa'n't true to me."

Hiram closed his lying lips and looked off sorrowfully at the hills in the distance.

"Hiram, you must be mistaken. There is some explanation."

"All right, Albert, glad you ken think so. Wish't I could. It mos' breaks my heart thinkin' 'bout her. I'm all bound up in havin' her. I'd take her now with all her disgrace an' run the resk o' keepin' her straight ef she'd promise to behave herself. She's mighty young, an' it does seem too bad. But, yeh see, Albert, I seen her myself with my own eyes in the stagecoach along with the same man what kissed her in the woods, an' yeh know yerself she didn't come back till next night."

With a groan Albert sank down on a box nearby and covered his face with his hands. He had been well brought up, and disgrace like this was something he'd never dreamed of. His agony amazed the ice-hearted Hiram, and he almost quailed before the sight of such sorrow in a man, sorrow he himself had made. It embarrassed him. He turned away to hide his contempt.

"It comes mighty hard on me to see you suffer thet way, Albert, an' not be able to help you," he whined after a minute. "I'll tell you what I'll do. I'll marry her anyway. I'll marry her an' save her reputation. Nobody'll dast say anythin' 'bout my wife, an' ef I marry her that'll be es much es to say all this ain't so, an' mebbe it'll die down."

Albert looked up with manly tears in his eyes.

"That's real good of you, Hiram. I'll take it as mighty kind of you if you think there isn't any other way to stop it. It seems hard on you, though."

"I ain't thinkin' o' myself," swelled Hiram. "I'm thinkin' o' the girl, an' I don't see no other way. When things is true, you know, there ain't no way o' denyin' them, 'specially when folks hes seen so many things. But just oncet get her good an' respectably married, an' it'll all blow over an' be forgot."

They talked a long time, and Hiram embellished the stories that had been told by many a new incident out of fertile brain, until Albert was thoroughly convinced the only way to save Phoebe's reputation was for her to be married at once to Hiram.

Albert went home at last and entered the kitchen with a chastened air. Emmeline eyed him keenly. Phoebe hadn't come downstairs, and his wife had all the work to do again. She wasn't enjoying the state of things.

Albert sat down and looked at the floor.

"Hiram has been very kind," he said slowly, "most kind. He has offered to marry Phoebe at once and stop all this talk."

A light of understanding began to dawn in Emmeline's eyes.

"Hm!" she said. Then, after a thoughtful pause, she added, "But I guess Miss Phoebe Deane'll hev a word to say 'bout that. She don't like him a bit."

"Poor child!" moaned Albert. "She'll nave to take him, whether she likes him or not. Poor little girl. I blame myself I didn't look after her better. Her mother was a real lady and so good to me when I was home. I promised her I'd keep Phoebe safe. She was such a good woman. It would break her heart to have Phoebe go like this."

"Hm! I don't reckon she was no better than other folks. Only she set up to be!" sniffed Emmeline. "Anyhow, this is just what might 'a' ben expected from the headstrong way that girl went on. I see now why she was set on goin' off to school. She knowed this was a-comin' an' wanted to slip an' run 'fore it got out. But she got caught. Sinners generally does." Emmeline wrung out her dishcloth with satisfaction.

"I'll go up now and talk with Phoebe," said Albert, rising sadly as if he hadn't heard his wife.

"I'm sure I wish you joy on your errand. Ef she ac's to you es she does to me you'll come flyin' down faster'n you went up."

But Albert was tapping at Phoebe's door before Emmeline had finished her sentence.

Chapter 26

Phoebe," said Albert, gently sitting down beside the bed where she lay wide-eyed, in white-faced misery, trying to comprehend what this new calamity might mean, "I'm mighty sorry for you, little girl. I wish you had come to me with things more. I might 'a' helped you better if I hadn't been so stupid. But I've found a way out of it all for you. I've found a good man that's willing to marry you and give you the protection of his name and home, and we'll just have you married right away quietly here at home, and that'll stop all the talk."

Phoebe turned a look of mingled horror and helplessness on her brother. He didn't comprehend it and thought she was grasping for a thread of hope.

"Yes, Phoebe, Hiram Green is willing to marry you right off in spite of everything, and we've fixed it up to have the wedding right away, tomorrow. That'll give you time to straighten out your things, and Hiram to get the minister—"

But Albert stopped suddenly as Phoebe uttered a piercing scream of fear and started up as if she would fly from the room.

Albert caught her and tried to soothe her.

"What's the matter now, little girl? Don't look like that. It'll all come out right. Is it because you don't like Hiram enough? But, child, you'll get to like him more as you know him better. Then you'll be so grateful to think what he saved you from. And besides, Phoebe, there isn't any other way. We couldn't stand the disgrace. What would your mother think? She was always so particular about how you should be brought up. And to have you turn out disgraced would break her heart. Phoebe, don't you see there isn't any other way?"

"Albert, I would rather die than marry that wicked man. He is a bad man. I *know* he is bad. He has been trying to make me marry him for a long time, and now he's just taking advantage of this terrible story. Albert, you know these stories are not true. You don't believe them, Albert, do you?"

She looked at him with piteous pleading in her beautiful eyes, and he had to turn his own eyes away to hide their wavering. He couldn't see how this sweet girl could have gone wrong, and yet—there was the evidence!

"You do," said Phoebe. "Albert, you do! You believe all this awful story about me! I never thought you would believe it. But, Albert, listen! I will never marry Hiram Green! You may kill me or send me away, or anything you like, but you cannot make me marry him!"

Albert turned his eyes away from the pitiful figure of the pleading girl and set his lips firmly.

"I'm sorry, Phoebe, but it's got to be done," he said sorrowfully. "I can't have this talk go on. I'll give you a little more time to get used to it, but you can't have much, for this story has to be stopped. We'll say a week. One week from today you'll have to marry Hiram Green, or I'll be forced to turn you out of my house. And you know what that means. I couldn't allow any respectable person to harbor you. You've disgraced us all. But if you marry Hiram it'll be all right presently. Marriage covers up gossip. Why, Phoebe, think of my little Alma. If this goes on, everybody'll point their fingers at her and say her auntie was a bad girl and brought dishonor on the family, and Alma'll grow up without any friends. I've got to look out for my little girl as well as you, Phoebe, and you must believe me; I'm doing the very best for you I know."

Phoebe sat down weakly on the edge of her bed and stared wildly at him. She couldn't believe Albert would talk to her so. She couldn't think of anything to say in answer. She could only stare blankly at him as if he were a terrible apparition.

Albert thought she was quieting down and going to be reasonable, and with a few kind words he backed out of the room. Phoebe dropped back upon her pillow in a frenzy of horror and grief. Wild plans of running away rushed through her brain, which was after all futile, because her limbs seemed suddenly to have grown too feeble to carry her. Her brain refused to think or take in any facts except the great horror of scandal that had risen about her and was threatening to overwhelm her.

Emmeline declined to take any dinner up to her. She said if Phoebe wanted anything to eat she might come down and get it; she wasn't going to wait on a girl like that any longer. Albert fixed a nice plate of dinner and carried it up, but Phoebe lay motionless with open eyes turned toward the wall and refused to speak. He put the plate on a chair beside her and went sadly down again. Phoebe wondered how long it would take someone to die and why God hadn't let her die when she had the fever. What had there been to live for anyway? One short bright month of happiness!

The memory of it gripped her heart anew with shame and horror. What would they say, all those kind friends? Mrs. Spafford and her husband, Miranda and Nathaniel Graham? Would they believe it, too? Of course they would, if her own household turned against her. She was defenseless in a desolate world. She would never again have friends and smiles and comfort. She couldn't go away to school now, for what good would an education be to her with such a disgrace clinging to her name and following her wherever she went? It would be of no use to run away. She might better stay here and die. They couldn't marry her to Hiram Green if she was dead. Could someone die in a week by just lying still?

So the horror in her brain raged over and over, each time bringing some new phase of grief. Now it was a question of whether her friends would desert her; and now it was the haughty expression on Janet Bristol's face that day she carried the letter to Nathaniel; and now it was the leer on Hiram's face as he put his arm about her on that terrible drive; and now it was the thought that she would have no more of Nathaniel's long, delightful letters.

All day long she lay in this state, and when the darkness fell a half delirious sleep came upon her, which carried the fears and thoughts of the day into its unresting slumber. The morning broke into the sorrow of yesterday, and Phoebe, weak and sick, arose with one thought in her mind, that she must write at once to Nathaniel Graham and tell him all. She mustn't be a disgrace to him.

With trembling hands and eyes filled with tears, she wrote:

Dear Mr. Graham,

I am writing to you for the last time. A terrible thing has happened. Someone has been telling awful stories about me, and I am in disgrace. I want you to know that these things are not true. I don't even know how they started, for there has never been any foundation for them. But everybody believes them, and I won't disgrace you by writing to you anymore. You will probably be told the worst that is said, and perhaps you will believe them as others do. I shall not blame you if you do, for it seems as if even God believed them. I don't know how to prove my innocence or what the end of this is to be. I only know it isn't right to keep you in ignorance of my shame and to let you write any longer to one whose name is held in dishonor. I thank you for all the beautiful times you have put into my life, and I must say good-bye forever.

Gratefully,
Phoebe Deane

The letter was blistered with tears before it was finished. She addressed it and hid it in her dress, for she began to wonder how it would get to the mail. Probably Miranda would never come near her again, and she couldn't be seen in the village. She dared not ask anyone else to mail the letter lest it would never reach its destination.

She spent the rest of the day in quietly putting to rights her little belongings, unpacking and gathering things she would like to have destroyed if anything happened to her. She felt weak and dizzy, and the food Albert continued to bring to her seemed nauseous. She couldn't bring herself to taste a mouthful. It was so useless to eat. One only ate to live, and living had been finished for her, it appeared. It wasn't that she had resolved to make away with herself by starvation. She was too right-minded for that. She was simply stunned by the calamity that had befallen her and was waiting for the outcome.

Sometimes as she stood at the window looking out across the fields that had been familiar to her since her childhood, she had a feeling she was going away from them all soon. She wondered if her mother felt so before she died. Then she wondered why she didn't run away. But always when she thought that, something seemed to hold her back, for how could she run far when she couldn't keep up about her room more than a few minutes at a time for dizziness and faintness! And how could she run fast enough to run away from shame? It couldn't be done. Whenever in her dreams she started to run away she always stumbled and fell and then seemed suddenly struck blind and unable to move further. And the whole village came crowding about her and mocking her like a great company of cawing crows met around a poor dead thing.

Late Tuesday afternoon Miranda came out to see her. Emmeline opened the door, and her countenance darkened when she recognized the visitor.

"Now you ken just turn right around and march home," she commanded. "We don't want no folks around. Phoebe Deane's in turrible disgrace, an' you've hed your part in it ef I don't miss my guess. No, you ain't goin' to see her. She's up in her room and ben shut up there ever since she heard how folks hes found out 'bout her capers. You an' yer Mis' Spafford can keep yer pryin' meddlin' fingers out o' this an' let Phoebe Deane alone from now on. We don't want to see yeh anymore. Yer spoilin' an pettin' has only hastened the disgrace."

The door slammed in Miranda's indignant face, and Emmeline went back to her work.

"She needs a good shakin'," remarked Miranda indignantly to herself, "but it might tire me, an' besides I've got other fish to fry."

Undaunted, she marched to the back shed and mounted to Phoebe's window, entering as if it had always been the common mode of ingress.

"Wal, fer the land, Phoebe Deane, what's ben happenin' now?" she asked mildly, surveying Phoebe, who lay white and weak upon her bed, with her untasted dinner beside her.

"Oh, don't you know all about it, Miranda?" Phoebe began to sob.

"No, I don't know a thing. I ben shut up in the house cookin' for two men Mr. David brung home last night, an' they et an' et till I thought there wouldn't be nothin' left fer the family. They was railroad men er somethin'. No, I guess 'twas bankin' men. I fergit what. But they could eat if they did wear their best clothes every day. But, say, ef I was you, I wouldn't talk very loud fer the lady downstairs wasn't real glad to see me this time, an' she might invite me to leave rather suddint ef she 'spicioned I was up here."

But Phoebe didn't laugh as Miranda had hoped. She only looked at her guest with hungry, hopeless eyes, and it was a long time before Miranda could find out the whole miserable story.

"And, Miranda, I've written Mr. Graham a note telling him about it. Of course I couldn't disgrace him by continuing to write any longer, so I've said good-bye to him. Will you do me one last kindness? Will you mail it for me?"

Phoebe's whisper was tragic. It brought tears to Miranda's well-fortified eyes.

" 'Course I'll mail it fer yeh, child, ef yeh want me to. But 'tain't the last kindness I'll do fer yeh by a long run. Shucks! D'you think I'm goin' to give in this easy an' see you sucked under? Not by a jugful. Now look-a-here, child. Ef the hull fool world goes against yeh, I ain't a-goin', ner my Mrs. Marcia ain't, neither, I'm plumb sure o' that. Bet *ef* she did I'd stick *anyhow,* so there! Cross my heart ef I don't! *Now.* D'yeh b'lieve me? An' I'll find a way out o' this, somehow. I ain't thought it out yet, but don't you worry. You set up 'n' eat fer me. I can't do nothin' ef yeh don't keep yer strength up. Now you do your part, an' we'll get out o' this pickle es good es we did out o' the other one. I ain't goin' to hev all my nursin' wasted. Will yeh be good?"

Phoebe promised meekly. She couldn't smile. She could only press Miranda's hand, while great tears welled through the long lashes on her cheeks.

"So that old serpent thinks he's got you fast, does he? Well, he'll find himself mistaken yet, ef I don't miss my guess. The game ain't all played out by a long shot. Marry you next week, will he? Well, we'll see! I may dance at your weddin' yet, but there won't be no Hiram Green as bridegroom. I'd marry him myself 'fore I'd let him hev you, you poor little white dove." And Miranda pressed Phoebe's trembling hand between her strong ones and stole out of the window.

As she hurried along down the road, the waving grain in the fields on either side reminded her of whispered gossip. She seemed to see a harvest of scandal ripening all about the poor stricken girl she loved, and in her ignorant and original phraseology she murmured to herself the thought of the words of old, "Lo, an enemy hath done this." Miranda felt she knew pretty well who the enemy was.

Chapter 27

I hev a notion I'd like to go to New York," said Miranda, bouncing in on Marcia.

"Well," said Marcia, "I think you'd enjoy the trip sometime. We might keep a lookout for somebody going who would be company. Or perhaps Mr. Spafford will be going again soon and he'd have time to look after you."

" 'Fraid I can't wait that long," said Miranda. "I've took a great notion I'd like to have a balzarine dress, an' ef I'm goin' to hev it I'd best get it straight off an' git more good out of it. I look at it this way. I ain't goin' to be young but once, an' time's gettin' on. Ef you don't get balzarine dresses when you're young you most likely won't git 'em 't all, 'cause you'll think 'taint wuthwhile. I've got a good bit of money laid by, an' ef you've no 'bjections, an' think you ken spare me fer a couple o' days I think I'd like to go down to New York an' git it. I don't need no lookin' after, so you needn't worry 'bout that. Nobody steals me, an' es long es I got a tongue I ken ast my way round New York es well es I can round Fundy er any other place."

"Why, of course I can spare you, Miranda, and I suppose you'd be perfectly safe. Only I thought you'd enjoy it more if you had good company. When did you think you'd like to go?"

"Well, I've been plannin' it all out comin' up the street. I've baked an' washed, an' the sweepin' ain't much to do. Ef you don't mind I think I'll go tomorrer mornin'."

"What in the world makes you want to go in such a hurry?"

"Oh, I've just took the notion," said Miranda, smiling. "Mebbe I'll tell yeh when I get back. I shan't be gone too long."

Marcia was a little worried at this sudden turn of affairs. It wasn't like Miranda to hide things from her. Yet she had such confidence in her that she finally settled down to the thought that it was only a whim and perhaps a good night's sleep would overcome it. But the next morning she found the table fully set for breakfast and the meal prepared and keeping warm. Beside her plate a scrawled note lay.

Mrs. Marcia, deer.
I'll liklie be bak tomorrer nite er next, but donte worrie. I got biznes to tend to an I'll tel you bout it wen i get home.

yours til deth, respectfuly,
Miranda Griscom

P.S. you mite pray ef your a mind. Tak keer uf Feby ef I dont git bak.

Before Marcia could get time to run up and see Phoebe, for she somehow felt that Miranda's sudden departure to New York had to do with her visit to Phoebe the day before, Miss Hortense arrived with her most commanding air.

"Marcia, I came on a very special errand," she began primly. "I was down on Monday, but you were away." There was reproach in the tone.

"Yes, I went with David," responded Marcia brightly, but Miss Hortense would brook no interruption.

"It's of no consequence now. I would have come yesterday, but we had company all day, the Pattersons from above Schenectady. I couldn't leave. But I hurried down this morning. It's about the Deane girl, Marcia. I suppose you haven't heard the dreadful reports that are going around. It really is disgraceful in a decent town. I'm only glad she got out of your house before it became town talk. It all shows what ingratitude there is in human nature, to think she should repay your kindness by allowing herself to be talked about in this shameful way."

Marcia exclaimed in dismay, but Miss Hortense went straight on to the precise and bitter end, giving every detail in the scandal that had come to her ears, details at which even Hiram Green would have opened his eyes wide in surprise and would never have believed they grew out of his own story.

Marcia listened in rising indignation.

"I'm sorry such a dreadful story is going around, Aunt Hortense," she answered earnestly. "But really, if you knew the girl, you'd understand how impossible it is for this to be true. She's as sweet and pure and innocent as my little Rose."

"I should be sorry to have David's child compared to that miserable girl, Marcia," said Miss Hortense severely, rising as she spoke. "And I'm sure that after my warning if you don't shut that wretched creature forever out of your acquaintance I shall feel it my duty to appeal to David and tell him the whole story, though I should dislike to have to mention anything so indelicate before him. David is very particular about the character of women. He was brought up to be, and Amelia and I both agree he must be told."

"I shall tell him myself, of course, and he'll see if anything can be done to stop this ridiculous gossip," said Marcia indignantly. "David is as fond of Phoebe as I am."

"You'll find David will look on it in a very different way, my dear. You're young and a woman. You don't know the evil world. David is a man. Men know. Good-bye, my dear. I've warned you!" And Aunt Hortense went pensively down the street, having done her duty.

Marcia put her bonnet on, took little Rose and walked straight out to Albert Deane's house, but when she reached there she was denied admission.

Alma opened the door but didn't ask the caller in. In a moment she came back from consulting her mother and said, "Ma says Aunt Phoebe's up in her room an' don't wish to see no one."

The door was shut unceremoniously by the stolid little girl, who was embarrassed before the beautiful, smiling Rose in her dainty attire. Marcia turned away, dismayed and hurt at the reception she had received, and walked slowly homeward.

"Wasn't that a funny little girl?" said Rose. "She wasn't very polite, was she, Mother?"

Then Marcia went home to wait until she could consult with David.

When Nathaniel Graham received his cousin Janet's letter his anger rose to white heat. Every throb of his heart told him the stories about Phoebe were false. Like Miranda, he felt at once that an enemy had done this, and he felt like searching out the enemy at once and throttling him into repentance. He read the postscript through twice and then sat for a few minutes in deep thought, his face shaded by his hand. The office work went on about him, but his thoughts were far away in a sunlit autumn wood. After a little while he got up suddenly and, going into the inner office where he could be alone, sat down quickly and wrote:

> *My dear Phoebe* (he had never called her that before; it was always "Miss Deane"),
>
> *I have loved you for a long time, ever since that afternoon I found you among the autumn leaves in the woods. I have been trying to wait to tell you until I could be sure you loved me, but now I can wait no longer. I am lonely without you. I want you to be here with me. I love you, darling, and will love you forever and guard you tenderly, if you will give me the right. Will you forgive this abrupt letter and write immediately, giving me the right to come up and tell you all the rest?*
>
> Yours in faithful love,
Nathaniel Graham

After he had sent it off enclosed to Miranda, he scribbled another, to Janet.

> *Dear Janet,*
>
> *Wherever did you get those ridiculous stories about Phoebe Deane? They are as false as they are foolish. Everybody who knows her at all knows they could not be true. I insist that you deny them whenever you have the opportunity and for my sake that you go and call upon her. I may as well tell you I am going to marry her if she will have me, and I want you, Janet, to be like a sister to her, as you have always been to me. Any breath against her name I shall consider as against mine also, so please, Janet, stand up for her for my sake.*
>
> Your loving cousin,
Nathaniel

After these two letters had been dispatched Nathaniel put in the best day's work he had ever done.

Miranda had reached Albany in time to catch the evening boat down the Hudson. She was more tired than she'd ever been in all the years of her hard-working life. The bouncing of the stagecoach, the constant change of scenery and fellow passengers, and the breathlessness of going into a strange region had worn on her nerves. She hadn't let a single thing pass unnoticed, and the result was that even her iron nerves had reached their limit at last. Besides, she was more worried about Phoebe Deane than she had ever been about anything in her life. The girl's ethereal look as she bid her good-bye the night before had gone to her heart. She half feared Phoebe might fall asleep and never awaken while she was gone on her desperate errand of mercy.

"Land sake alive," she murmured to herself, as she crept into her bunk in the tiny stateroom and lay down without putting off any of her garments except her bonnet and cape. "Land sake alive! I feel as ef I'd ben threshin'. No, I feel as ef I'd ben *threshed!*" she corrected. "I didn't know I hed so many bones."

Nevertheless she slept little, having too much to attend to. She awakened at every stop in the night, and she heard all the bells and calls of the crew. Half the time she thought the boat was sinking and wondered if she could swim when she struck the water. Anyhow she meant to try. She had heard it "came natural" to some people.

When morning broke over the heights above the river she watched them grow into splendor and majesty, and long before the city was in sight she was on deck sniffing the air like a veteran warhorse. Her eyes were dilated with excitement, and she made a curious and noticeable figure as she gripped her small bag of modest belongings and sat strained up and ready for her first experience of city life. She felt a passing regret that she couldn't pause to take in more of this wonderful trip, but she promised herself to come that way again someday and hurried over the gangplank with the others when the boat finally landed.

Tucked safely away in her pocket was Phoebe's letter to Nathaniel and safe in her memory was its address. Every passenger she had talked with on the voyage—and she had entered into conversation with all except a man who reminded her of Hiram Green—had given her detailed directions on how to get to that address, and the directions had all been different. Some had told her to walk one way and take a cab, some another way. Some had suggested she take a cab at the wharf.

She did none of these things. She gripped her bag firmly and marched past all the officials, through the buildings out onto the street. There she stood a moment bewildered by the noise and confusion, a marked figure even in that hurrying throng of busy people. Small boys and drivers immediately beset her. She looked each over carefully and then calmly walked straight ahead. So far

New York didn't look very promising to her, but she meant to get into a quieter place before she made any inquiries.

At last after she had walked several blocks and was beginning to feel there was no quiet place and no end to the confusion, she met a benevolent old gentleman walking with a sweet-faced girl who looked as she imagined little Rose would look in a few years. These she hailed and demanded directions and ended by being put into a Broadway coach under the care of the driver, who was to put her out at her destination.

Nathaniel was in the inner office attending to some special business when the office boy tapped at the door.

"There's a strange client out here," he whispered. "We told her you were busy and couldn't be bothered, but she says she's come a long distance and must see you at once. Shall I tell her to come again?"

Nathaniel glanced through the door, and there, close behind the careful office boy, stood the wily Miranda. She had run no risks of not seeing Nathaniel. She had followed the boy, strictly against orders.

Her homely face was aglow with the light of her mission, but in spite of freckles and red hair and her dishevelled appearance, Nathaniel put out an eager hand to welcome her. His first thought was that she had brought an answer to his letter to Phoebe, and his heart leaped up in sudden eagerness. Then at once he knew it was too soon for that, for he had only sent his own letter in the evening mail.

"Come right in, Miranda," he said eagerly. "I'm glad to see you. Are you all alone?" Then something in her face caused a twinge of apprehension.

"Is everyone all well?"

Miranda sat down and waited until the door was shut. Then she broke forth.

"No, everythin' ain't all well. Everythin' 's all wrong. Phoebe Deane's in turrible trouble, an' she's wrote a letter sayin' good-bye to you an' ast me to mail it. I said I would, an' I brung it along. I reckon it didn't make no diff'rence whether it traveled in my pocket er in the mailbag, so it got here."

She held out the letter, and Nathaniel's hand shook as he took it. Miranda noticed what he feared.

"Oh, it's that ole snake-in-th'-grass," said Miranda. "I'd be willin' to stake my life on that. No knowin' how he done it, but it's done. There's plenty to help in a business like gossip, when it comes to that. There's ben awful lies told about her, and she's bein' crushed by it. Wal, I hed to come down to New York to get me a new balzarine dress an' I jest thought I'd drop in an' tell yeh the news. Yeh don't know of a good store where I won't get cheated, do yeh?" she asked, making a pretense of rising.

"Sit down, Miranda," commanded Nathaniel. "You're not going away to leave me like this. You must tell me about it. Miranda, you know, don't you, that Phoebe is my dear friend. You know I must hear all about it."

"Well, ain't she told you in the letter? I reckon you'll go back on her like her own folks hev done, won't you? An' let that scoundrel git her next week like he's planned."

"What do you mean, Miranda? Tell me at once all about it. You know Phoebe Deane is very dear to me."

Miranda's eyes shone, but she meant to have things in black and white.

"How dear?" she asked, looking up in a businesslike way. "Be you goin' to b'lieve what they all say 'bout her an' let them folks go on talkin', 'til she's all wilted down an' dead? 'Cause ef you be, you don't git a single word out o' me. No, sir!"

"Listen, Miranda. Yesterday I wrote to Phoebe asking her to marry me!"

Satisfaction began to dawn upon the face of the self-appointed envoy.

"Well, that ain't no sign you'd do it again today," said Miranda dryly. "You didn't know nothin' 'bout her bein' in trouble then."

"Yesterday morning, Miranda, I received a letter from my cousin telling me about it, and I sat down at once and asked Phoebe to marry me."

"You sure you didn't do it out o' pity?" asked Miranda, lifting sharp eyes to search his face. "I shouldn't want to hev nobody marry her out o' pity, the way Hiram Green's going to do, the old nimshi!"

"Miranda, I love her with all my heart, and I will never believe a word against her. I shall make it the object of my life to protect her and make her happy if she will give me the precious treasure of her love in return. Now are you satisfied, you cruel girl, and will you tell me the whole story? For the little I heard from my cousin has only filled me with apprehension."

Then the freckles beamed out and were lost in smiles as Miranda reached a strong hand and grasped Nathaniel's firm one with a hearty shake.

"You're the right stuff. I knowed you was. That's why I come. I didn't darst tell Mis' Spafford what was up, 'cause she wouldn't 'a' let me come, an' she'd 'a' tried to work it out in some other way. But I hed it all figgered out, an' there wasn't time for any fiddlin' business. It hed to be done 'twoncet ef 'twas to be done 't all, so I told her I wanted a pleasure trip an' a new balzarine, an' I come. Now I'm goin' to tell you all 'bout it, an' then ef there's time fer the balzarine 'fore the evenin' boat starts I'll get it; otherwise it'll hev to git the go-by this time, fer I've got to git right back to Phoebe Deane. She looked jest awful 'fore I left, an' there's no tellin' what they'll do to her while I'm gone."

Nathaniel, with loving apprehension in his eyes, listened to the story, told in Miranda's inimitable style, his face darkening with anger over the mention of Hiram's part.

"The scoundrel!" he murmured, clenching his fingers as if he could hardly refrain from going after him and giving him what he deserved.

"He's all that," said Miranda, "an' a heap more. He's made that poor stupid Albert Deane think all these things is true, an' he's come whinin' round with his 'sorry this' an' 'sorry that,' an' offered to marry Phoebe Deane to save her reputation. Es ef he was fit fer that angel to wipe her feet on! Oh, I'd like to see him strung up, I would. There's only one man I ever heard tell of that was so mean, and he lived here in New York. His name was Temple, Harry Temple. Ef you ever come acrost him jest give him a dig fer my sake. He an' Hiram Green ought to be tied up in a bag together an' sent off the earth to stay. One o' them big, hot-lookin' stars would be a fine place, I often think at night. Albert, he's awful taken back by disgrace, an' he's told Phoebe she hez to git married in jest a week, er he'll hev to turn her out o' the house. Monday mornin' 's the time set fer the marriage, an' Albert 'lows he won't wait 'nother day. He's promised his wife he'll keep to that."

Nathaniel's face grew stern as he listened and then asked questions. At last he said, "Miranda, do you think Phoebe Deane cares for me? Will she be willing to marry me?"

"Wal, I sh'd think, ef I know anythin' 't all 'bout Phoebe Deane, she'd give her two eyes to, but she'll be turrible set 'gainst marryin' you with her in disgrace. She'll think it'll bring shame on you."

"Bless her dear heart," murmured Nathaniel. "I suppose she will." And he touched her letter tenderly as if it had been a living thing.

Miranda's eyes glistened with jubilation, but she said nothing.

"But we'll persuade her out of that," added Nathaniel, with a light of joy in his eyes.

"If you're quite sure it will make her happy," he added, looking at Miranda keenly. "I wouldn't want to have her marry me just to get out of trouble. There might be other ways of helping her, though this way is best."

"Well, I guess you needn't worry 'bout love. She'll love you all right, er my name ain't M'randy!"

"Well, then, we'll just have a substitute bridegroom. I wonder if we'll have trouble with Hiram. I suppose very likely we will, but I guess we can manage that. Let me see. This is Thursday. I can arrange my business by tomorrow night so I can leave it for a few days. If you can stay over till then, I'll take you to my landlady, who is very kind and will make your stay pleasant. Then we can go back together and plan the arrangements. You'll have to help me, you know, for you're the only means of communication."

"No, I can't stay a minute longer 'n t'night," said Miranda, rising in a panic and glancing out the window at the sun as if she feared it were already too late to catch the boat. "I've got to get back to Phoebe Deane. She won't eat, an' she's just fadin' away. There might not be any bride by the time you got there. 'Sides, she can't git your letter till I get back nohow. I'll hev to go home on the boat tonight, an' you come tomorrow. You see, ef there's goin' to be a weddin' I'd like real well to git my balzarine made 'n time to wear it. That'll give me plenty time, with Mis' Spafford to he'p cut 't out. Do you s'pose there's time fer me to go to the store? It took a long time to git up here from the river."

Nathaniel stood up.

"You have plenty of time, and if you'll wait ten minutes I'll go with you. We can get some dinner and go to the store, and we can arrange things on the way."

Miranda settled down in the great office chair and watched Nathaniel's fingers as they wrote on the legal paper. When it was finished and folded he took another piece of paper and wrote:

My darling,

I've just received your letter, and I'm coming to you as quickly as I can arrange my business to get away. Miranda will bring you this and will tell you all I've said. I will be there in time for the wedding morning, and if you will have me instead of Hiram Green I shall face the whole world by your side and tell them they are liars. Then I'll bring you back with me to stay with me always. My heart is longing to see you and comfort you, but I mustn't write anymore for I have a great deal to do before I go. Only this I must say, if you don't feel you love me and don't want to marry me, I will help you some other way to get free from this trouble and to have it all explained before the world. I am resolved upon one thing, and that is that you shall be guarded and loved by me, whether you will marry me or not. You are too precious to suffer.

Yours with more love than you can fathom,
Nathaniel

He sealed and addressed it and handed it to Miranda, who took it with a gleam of satisfaction in her honest eyes. She was almost willing to run home without her balzarine now that she had that letter. She didn't know what he had written, of course, but she knew it was the right thing and would bring the light of hope again to Phoebe's eyes.

Then they went out into the bustling, strange streets of the city.

Miranda was too excited to eat much, though Nathaniel took her to his own boarding place and tried to make her feel at home. She kept asking if it wasn't almost time for the boat to leave, until he had to explain to her just how much time there was and how quickly they could get to the wharf.

They went to a store, and Miranda didn't take long to pick out her dress. It seemed as if the very one she had always longed for lay draped on the counter, and with quick decision she bought it. It had great stripes of soft colors in a palm-leaf pattern, blended into harmony in an oriental manner in the exquisite fabric. It seemed to her almost too fine to go with red hair, but she bought it with joyous abandon. The touch of rich blue and orange and crimson with the darker greens and browns stood out against the delicate whiteness of the background and delighted her. She bought a dainty ruffled muslin shoulder cape to wear with it, and a great shovel bonnet with a white veil tossed hilariously back from its cumbersome shirred depths.

Then Nathaniel added a parasol with a pearl handle that would unhinge and fold up, and Miranda climbed into the coach and rode off to the evening boat feeling she'd had the greatest day of her life. She looked about her on the interesting sights of the city with a kind of pity they had to stay there and not go with her to the wedding.

Chapter 28

Miranda reached home on the afternoon coach and bounced into the house with a face full of importance.

"Wal, I'm glad to git back. Did you find the blueberry pies? I put 'em out the pantry winder to cool an' fergot 'em. I thought of 'em when I was on the boat, but 'twas mos' too late to come back then, so I kep' on.

"Here's my balzarine. Do yeh like it?" And she tossed the bundle into Marcia's lap. "I'm going right at it when I git the work done in the mornin' fer I want to hev it t' wear at Phoebe Deane's weddin'. Did yeh know she was goin' to marry Nathaniel Graham? Say, where's that Rose? I'm most starved for a sight o' her little sweet face. Yer lookin' real good yerself. All's well?"

Marcia listened smilingly to Miranda's torrent of words and gradually drew the whole story from the girl, laughing heartily over the various episodes of Miranda's journey and gravely tender over what Nathaniel had said. Then Miranda heard about Marcia's call on Phoebe and how she'd written Phoebe a letter asking what she could do to help her, inviting her to come at once to them, but had received no answer.

"An' yeh won't, neither," said Miranda decidedly. "She'll never git no letter, I'm sure o' that. Ef that ol' skunk of a Hiram Green don't git it fust, Mis' Deane'll ferret it out an' keep it from her. She's the meanest thing in the shape of a woman I've seen yit, an' I've hed some experience."

Then Miranda rapidly sketched out her plan, and Marcia added some suggestions. Together they prepared the supper, with the single object of getting Miranda off to Phoebe as soon as darkness should come.

It was quite dark, and Phoebe was lying in a still white heap on her bed when Miranda stole softly in. By her side lay a long white package she had taken from her little trunk in the closet, and on it was pinned a note: "Dear Miranda, if I die, please take this, from Phoebe."

She hadn't lighted her candle nor eaten a mouthful all day. The terrible faintness and weakness were becoming constant now. She could only lie on her bed and wait. She couldn't even think anymore. The enemies all about her with their terrible darts had pierced her soul, and her life seemed ebbing away. She felt it going and had no desire to stop it. It was good to be at rest.

Miranda stole in softly and began to move quietly about the room, finding the candle and softly striking the flint and tinder. Phoebe became gradually conscious of her presence, as out of the midst of a misty dream. Then Miranda came and looked down tenderly into her face.

"Raise yer head up, you poor little thing, an' drink this," whispered Miranda, putting a spoonful of strong broth to her lips, that she had taken the precaution to bring with her. "I've got two o' the nicest letters fer yeh that ever was writ, an' another one from my Mrs. Marcia, an' ef yeh don't git some color into them cheeks an' some brightness into them eyes now, my name ain't Mirandy."

Miranda handed out the letters one at a time in their order.

She brought the candle, and Phoebe with her trembling hands opened the first, recognizing the handwriting, and then sat up and read with bated breath.

"Oh, Miranda," she said, looking up with a faint color in her cheeks, "he's asked me to marry him. Wouldn't it be beautiful! But he didn't know when he wrote it—" And the brown head went down as if it were stricken like a lily before a fierce blast.

"Shucks!" said Miranda, dabbing away the mistiness from her eyes. "Yes, he did know, too. His cousin wrote him. Here, you read the other one."

Again Phoebe sat up and read, while Miranda held her candle and tried not to seem to look over her shoulder at the words she could feel in her soul if she couldn't see with her eyes.

"Oh, it can't be true!" said Phoebe, with face aglow with something that almost seemed to be the light of another world. "And I mustn't let him, of course. It wouldn't be right for him to have a wife like this—"

"Shucks!" said Miranda again. "Yes, 'tis true, too, and right an' all the rest, an' you've got to set up and get spry, fer there's a sight to do, an' I can't stay much longer. That weddin' 's comin' off on Monday mornin—time set fer it. 'Taint good luck to put off weddin's, an' this one 's goin' to go through all right.

"Mr. Nathaniel, he's goin' to bring his cousin an' the jedge, an' my Mr. David an' Mrs. Marcia's comin' wether they're ast er not, 'cause they knew 'twa'n't no use fer um to wait fer an invite from that sister-in-law of yourn, so they're comin' anyway. Mr. Nathaniel said as how you weren't to worry. He'll git here Saturday night sure, en' ef there was any other 'rangement you'd like to make he was ready, an' you could send your word by me. But he 'greed with me 'twould make less talk ef the weddin' come off at your home where 'twas to be in the fust place, an' then you could go right away from here an' never come back no more. Say, hev ye got anythin' thet's fit to wear? 'Cause ef yeh ain't I'll let yeh have my new balzarine to wear. I'll hev it all done by Sat'day night. Mrs. Marcia's goin' to help me."

Between tears and smiles Phoebe came to herself. Miranda fed her with more of the strong broth she had brought along. Then together in the dim candlelight the two girls opened the great white box that lay on the floor beside the bed.

"It's my wedding dress, Miranda. Mother made it for me long ago, before she died, and put it in my trunk to keep for me. It was marked, 'For my little girl when she is going to be married.'

"I opened it and found the letter on top, for I thought I was going to die and I wanted to read Mother's last letter, but I didn't take the dress out because I thought I would never wear it, and it made me feel so bad that I left it in its wrappings. I thought if I died I'd like you to have it, because it's the most precious thing I have and you've done more for me than anybody else ever did, but Mother."

Miranda gulped a sudden unexpected sob at this tribute, and it was some time before she could recover her equanimity, though she said "Shucks!" several times.

They took the white bridal garment out of its wrappings, and Phoebe tried it on, there in the dimness of the room. It was thin white book muslin, all daintily embroidered about the neck and sleeves by the dead mother's hand. It fell in soft sheer folds about the white-faced girl and made her look as if she were just going to take her flight to another world.

In another paper was the veil of fine thread lace, simple and beautiful, and a pair of white gloves that had been the mother's, both yellow with age and breathing a perfume of lavender. A pair of dainty little white slippers lay in the bottom of the box, wrapped in tissue paper also. Miranda's eyes shone.

"Now you look like the right kind of bride," she said, standing back and surveying her charge. "That's better 'n all the balzarines in New York."

"You shall wear the balzarine and stand up with me, Miranda," whispered Phoebe, smiling.

"No, sir! We ain't goin't hev this here weddin' spoiled by no red hair an' freckles, even if 't has got a balzarine. Janet Bristol's got to stan' up. She'll make a picter fer folks to talk 'bout. Mr. Nathaniel said he'd manage his cousin all right, an' 'twould quiet the talk down ef his folks took sides along of you. No, sir, I ain't goin' to do no standin' in this show. I'm goin' to set an' take it all in. Come now, you get into bed, an' I'll blow out the light an' go home. I reckon I'll be back tomorrer night to take any messages you want took. Ther'll be plenty o' chance fer you to rest 'fore Monday. Don't say nothin' to yer folks. Let 'em go on with their plans, an' then kinder s'prise 'em."

The next morning Phoebe arose and feeling much refreshed dressed herself carefully and went downstairs. She had a quiet, grave look upon her face, but in her eyes there was a strange light she couldn't keep back. Emmeline looked up in surprise when Phoebe came and took hold with the work. She began to say something slighting, but the look in Phoebe's face somehow stopped her. It was a look of joyful exaltation. And Emmeline, firmly believing the girl was justly talked about, couldn't understand and thought it hypocrisy.

Albert came in in a few minutes and looked relieved.

"Well, Phoebe, I'm glad you've made up your mind to act sensibly and come downstairs. It wasn't right to fight against what had to be and every one of us knew was for the best," he said.

Phoebe didn't answer. In spite of the help that was coming to her it hurt her that Albert believed the slander against her, and the tears came into her eyes as he spoke.

Emmeline saw them and spoke up in a sermonizing tone. "It's right she should feel her shame and repent, Albert. Don't go an' soft-soap it over es ef she hadn't done nothin' to feel sorry fer."

Then Phoebe spoke.

"I have done nothing to feel sorry for, Emmeline. I have not sinned. I'm only sorry you have been willing to believe all this against me."

Then she went quietly on with her work and said no more, though Emmeline's speech was unsealed and she gave Phoebe much good advice during the course of the day.

The next morning near church time Emmeline told Phoebe that Hiram was coming over to see her that morning, and she might open the front parlor to receive him.

"I don't wish to see Hiram, Emmeline," she answered calmly. "I have nothing whatever to say to him."

"Well, upon my word, Phoebe Deane," said Emmeline, getting red in the face with indignation toward the girl. "Goin' to get married tomorrow mornin' an' not wantin' to see Hiram Green! I should think you'd want to talk over 'rangements."

"Yes, I'm going to be married tomorrow morning," said Phoebe with a triumphant ring to her voice, "but I do not want to see Hiram Green. I have no arrangements to talk over with him. My arrangements are all made."

Phoebe went away to her room and remained there for the rest of the day. Nathaniel had arrived. She knew that by special messenger coming and going over the woodshed roof. He had sent sweet messages of cheer and promised to come for her in the morning. Everything was arranged. She could possess her soul in peace and quietness and wait. Her enemies would soon be put to flight. Nathaniel had promised her that, and although she could not in the least see how, she trusted him perfectly.

She had sent her love to him and the locket with her mother's picture. It was all she had to give him, and he understood. It was the one she had worn the first time he ever saw her.

The balzarine dress was finished. The last hook was set in place before supper Saturday night, and Marcia had pronounced it very becoming. It was finished in spite of the fact that Miranda had made several secret excursions into the region of Hiram Green's house and farm. She had made discoveries she told no one, but over which she chuckled when quite alone in the kitchen working.

On her first trip she had seen him go out to his milking and had passed close to the house, where his window was open. She had glanced in, and there on the sill her sharp eyes discovered the bit of red seal with the lion's head on it. She'd carried too many letters with that seal not to know it at once, and she gleefully seized it and carried it to Nathaniel. She had evidence at last that would give her power over the enemy.

She also discovered that Hiram Green attended to his milking himself and had a habit—if one might judge from two mornings as samples—of going to the springhouse with the milk and placing the pans on the great stone shelf. This she had seen by judicious hiding behind shrubbery and trees and the springhouse itself and spying on him. Birds and squirrels tell no tales, and the dewy grass soon dried off and left no trace of her footsteps. During one of these excursions she had examined the fastening of the springhouse carefully and knew the possibilities of button, hasp, staple and peg.

The Spaffords and Miranda went to church as usual, and so did the Bristols. The advent of Nathaniel and his friend Mr. Van Rensselaer in the Bristol pew diverted attention from the empty seat behind them, for this morning the Deanes were conspicuous by their absence.

The day passed quietly. Miranda made her usual visit in the early evening. Phoebe had asked her to stay with her, but Miranda said she had some things to do and departed sooner than usual. The night settled into stillness, and Phoebe slept in joyous assurance that it was her last night in the room where she had seen so much sorrow.

In the morning she went down to breakfast as usual. She didn't eat much but drank some milk and then washed the breakfast dishes as calmly as if she expected to keep on washing them all the rest of her life in this same kitchen.

"Hiram'll be over 'bout half past nine, I reckon," said Albert. He had been instructed by Emmeline to say this. "The minister won't come till ten. If you need to talk to Hiram you'll have plenty of time between. You better be all ready."

"I shall not need to talk to Hiram," said Phoebe, as she hung up the dish towels.

Something in her voice as she said it made Albert look at her wonderingly.

"She's the oddest girl I ever see!" grumbled Emmeline. "One would think by her looks that she expected a chariot of fire to come down an' take her straight up to heaven like 'Lijah. It's kind of dreadful the way she ac's! 'F I was Hiram I'd be 'fraid to marry her."

Miranda arrived over the shed roof soon after Phoebe went upstairs. She wore her old calico, and if those who knew had observed closely, they would have said it was a calico Miranda never used anymore, for it was very old. Her hair was combed with precision, and on her head was an elaborate New York bonnet with a white barege veil, but her balzarine was in a bundle under her arm. It wasn't calculated for roof travel. It worked well for their plans that the shed roof was back and hidden from the kitchen door; otherwise Miranda might have been discovered.

"There! Emmeline can hev that fer a floor cloth," said Miranda, as she flung her old calico in the corner. "I don't mean to return fer it."

She fastened her balzarine with satisfaction, adjusted her muslin shoulder pe, her bonnet and mantilla, the latter a gift from Mrs. Spafford, laid her new sunshade on a chair and pronounced herself ready.

"Has Hiram Green come yet?" asked Phoebe anxiously. She was dreading a scene with Hiram.

"Wal, no, not 'zactly," said Miranda. "An what's more, I don't think he will. Fact is, I've got him fixed fer a spell, but I ain't goin' to say nothin' more 'bout it at present, 'cept that he's detained by bus'ness elsewhar. It's best you shouldn't know nothin' 'bout it ef there's questions ast, but you don't need to worry. 'Less sompin' quite unusual happens he ain't likely to turn up till after the ceremony. Now what's to do to you yet? Them hooks all fastened? My, but you do look han'some!"

"Oh, Miranda, you haven't done anything dreadful, have you?"

"No, I ain't," laughed Miranda. "You'd jest split your sides laughin' ef you could see him 'bout now. But there! Don't say 'nother word. I hear voices. The Bristols hev come an' the minister, too. I reckon your sister-in-law'll hev her hands full slammin' the door in all them faces."

Phoebe, aghast, pulled the curtain aside and peered out.

There in the yard were several carriages and more driving in the gate. She could hear a great many voices all at once. She saw Mrs. Duzenberry and Susanna getting out of their chaise, and Lemuel Skinner and his wife, Hannah. And she thought she heard the village dressmaker's voice high above all, sharp and rasping, the way it always was when she said, "That seam needs pressin'. It does hike up a mite, but it'll be all right when it's pressed."

Phoebe retreated in dismay from the window.

"Oh, Miranda! How did all those people get down there! Emmeline will be so angry. She's still in her room dressing. It doesn't seem as if I dared go down."

"Fer the land sake, how should I know? I s'pose Providence sent 'em, fer they can't say a single word after the ceremony's over. Their mouths'll be all nicely stopped. Don't you worry."

Miranda answered innocently, but for one instant as she looked at Phoebe's frightened face her guilty heart misgave her. Perhaps she had gone a step too far. For it was Miranda who had slipped here and there after church on Sunday and whispered a brief invitation to those who had gossiped the hardest, wording it in such a way that they all thought it was a personal invitation from Phoebe. In every case she added, "Don't say nothin' till after it's over."

Each thinking himself especially favored had arrived in conscious pride, and as they passed Hiram Green's new house they had remarked to themselves what a fine man he was for sticking to Phoebe in spite of all the talk.

But Miranda never told her part in this, and Emmeline never got over wondering who invited all those people.

Miranda's momentary confusion was covered by a gentle tap on the door, and Phoebe in a flutter rushed to hide her friend.

"I'm afraid it's Emmeline," she whispered. "She may not let you go down

"Like to see her keep me up," said Miranda boldly. "My folks hes come. I ain't 'fraid now." She boldly swept the trembling bride out of the way and threw the door open.

Janet Bristol in a silken gown of palest pink entered and walked straight up to Phoebe.

"You dear little thing!" she exclaimed. "How sweet you look. That dress is beautiful, and the veil makes you perfect. Nathaniel asked me to bring you this and make you wear it. It was his mother's."

She fastened a rope of pearls around Phoebe's neck and kissed her as a sister might have done.

Miranda stood back and gazed with satisfaction on the scene. All was set as it should be. She saw nothing further to be desired. Her compunctions were gone.

"Nathaniel is waiting for you at the foot of the stairs," whispered Janet. "He has his mother's ring for you. He wanted me to tell you. Come, they're ready. You must go ahead."

Down the stairs went the trembling bride, followed by her bridesmaid. Miranda grasped her precious parasol and tiptoed down behind.

Nathaniel stood at the foot of the stairs, waiting for her. Emmeline, with a red and angry face, was waiting on her most unexpected guests and hadn't time to notice what was going on about her. The original wedding guests, consisting of a row of little Greens and the old housekeeper, were submerged in the Sunday gowns of the new arrivals.

"Where's Hiram?" whispered Albert in Emmeline's ear, just as she was giving Hiram's aunt Keziah Dart a seat at the best end of the room.

"Goodness! Ain't he come yet? I s'posed he was upstairs talkin' to Phoebe. I heard voices."

She wheeled around, and there stood the wedding party.

Nathaniel, tall and handsome, with his shy, pale bride on his arm; Janet, sparkling in her pink gown and enjoying the discomfiture of guests and hostess alike and smiling over at Martin Van Rensselaer, who stood supporting the bridegroom on the other side—it all bewildered Emmeline.

The little assemblage reached out into the front dooryard and peeped curiously in at the doors and windows as if loathe to lose the choice scene that was passing. The old minister was talking now, and a hush fell over the company.

Anger and amazement held Emmeline still as the ceremony progressed.

"Dearly beloved, we are gathered together—" said the minister, and Emmeline looked around for Hiram. Surely the ceremony wasn't beginning without him! And who was that girl in white under the veil! Not Phoebe! It couldn't be Phoebe Deane, who only a few short minutes before had been hanging up her dish towels. Where did she get the veil and dress? What had happened? How did all these people get here? Had Phoebe invited them? And why didn't somebody stop it?

"Let him speak now or forever after hold his peace," came the words, and Emmeline gave a great gasp and thought of the corner lot opposite the Seceder church.

Then Emmeline became conscious of Miranda in her balzarine and New York bonnet, the very impersonation of mischief, standing in the doorway just behind the bride and watching the scene with a face of triumph.

An impulse came to her to charge across the room at the offending girl and put her out. Here surely was one who had no right in her house and knew it too. Then all at once she caught the eye of Judge Bristol fixed sternly on her face, and she became aware of her own countenance and restrained her feelings. For after all it was no mean thing to be allied to the house of Bristol and know the cloud of dishonor that had threatened them was lifted forever. She looked at Judge Bristol's fine face and heavy white hair and began to swell with conscious pride.

The last "I will" was spoken, the benediction was pronounced, and the hush that followed was broken by Nathaniel's voice.

"I want to say a few words," he said, "about a terrible mistake that has been made by the people of this village regarding my wife's character. I have made a thorough investigation of the matter during the last two days, and I find that the whole thing originated in an infamous lie told with intention to harm one who is entirely innocent. I simply wish to say that whoever has spoken against my wife will have to answer to me for his words in a court of justice. And if any of you who are my friends wish to question any of her past actions, be kind enough to come directly to me and they will be fully explained, for there is not a thing in her past that will not bear the searching light of purity and truth."

As soon as he stopped speaking, David and Marcia stepped up with congratulations.

There was a little stir among the guests. The guilty ones melted away faster than they had gathered, each one anxious to get out without being noticed.

The Bristol coach, drawn by two white horses, with coachman and footman in livery, drew up before the door. Nathaniel handed Phoebe in, and they were driven away in triumph, with the guests they passed shrinking out of sight into their vehicles as far as possible.

Albert and Emmeline looked into each other's dazed faces, then turned to the old housekeeper and the row of little Greens, their faces abnormally shining from unusual contact with soap and water, and asked in concert, "But where is Hiram?"

Miranda, as she rode guilelessly in the carryall with Mrs. Spafford, answered the same question from that lady, with "Whar d' you s'pose? I shet him in the springhouse airly this mornin'!"

Then David Spafford laid down the reins of the old gray horse on his knee and laughed, loud and long. He couldn't stop laughing, and all day long it kept breaking out, as he remembered Miranda's innocent look and thought of Hiram

Green, wrathful and helpless, shut in his own springhouse while his wedding went on without him.

An elaborate and merry wedding breakfast was given at Judge Bristol's, presided over by Janet, who seemed as happy as though she'd planned the match herself and whose smiling wishes were carried out immediately by Martin Van Rensselaer.

Nathaniel had one more duty to perform before he took his bride away to a happier home. He must find and face Hiram Green.

So, leaving Phoebe in the care of Mrs. Spafford and his cousin Janet, and accompanied by his uncle, Martin Van Rensselaer and Lemuel Skinner in the capacity of village constable, he got into the family carryall and drove out to Hiram's farm.

Now Nathaniel hadn't been idle during the Sabbath which intervened between his coming back to the village and his marriage. Aside from the time he spent at the morning church service, he had been doing a Sabbath day's work which he felt would stand well to his account.

He had carefully questioned several of the best-known gossips in the village regarding the story about Phoebe. He had asked keen questions that gave him a plain clue to the whole diabolical plot.

His first act had been to mount his horse and ride out to Ann Jane Bloodgood's, where he had a full account of Phoebe's visit together with a number of missionary items which would have met with more of his attention at another time. With several valuable facts he went pretty straight to most of the houses Hiram visited on the first afternoon when he scattered the seed of scandal. Facing the embarrassed scandalmongers, Nathaniel made them tell just who the first was to speak to them of this. In every case after a careful sifting down each owned that Hiram himself had told them the first word. If Nathaniel hadn't been a lawyer and keen at his calling, he might not have followed the story to its source as well or as quickly as he did. Possibly his former encounter with Hiram Green and his knowledge of many of his deeds helped unravel the mystery.

The old housekeeper and the little Greens hadn't been at home long when the carryall drew up in front of the door and the four men got out.

"I ben everywhar but to the springhouse," said the housekeeper, shaking her head dolefully, "an' I can't find trace of him nowhar. 'Taint likely he'd be in the springhouse, fer the door is shet an' fastened. I ken see the button from the buttery winder. It's the way I allus tell when he's comin' in to breakfast. It's my 'pinion he's clared out 'cause he don't want to marry that gal, that's what I think."

"When did you last see Mr. Green?" questioned the judge sternly.

"Why, I seen him take the milk pails an' go down toward the barn to milk, an' I ain't seen him sence. I thought 'twar odd he didn't come eat his breakfast, but he's kinder oncertain thet way, so I hurried up an' got off to he'p Mis' Deane."

"Have the cows been milked?" The judge ignored the old woman's elaborate explanations.

"The hired man, he says so. I ain't ben down to look myself."

"Where are the milk pails?"

"Well, now, I ain't thought to look."

"What does he usually do with the milk? He surely hasn't taken that with him. Did he bring it in? That ought to give us a clue."

"He most gen'rally takes it straight to the springhouse—" began the old woman.

"Let's go to the springhouse," said Nathaniel.

"I don't see what business 'tis o' yourn," complained the old woman, but they were already on the way. So after a moment's hesitation she threw her apron around her shoulders and went after them.

The row of little Greens followed, a curious and perplexed little procession, ready for any scene of interest that might be about to open before them, even though it involved their unloving father.

It was Lemuel Skinner, with his cherry lips pursed importantly, who stepped forward by virtue of his office, turned the wooden button, drew out the peg, pulled off the hasp and threw the heavy door open.

Out stumbled Hiram Green, half blinded by the light and rubbing his eyes.

"Mr. Green, we have called to see you on a matter of importance," began Lemuel apologetically, quite as if it were the custom to meet householders on the threshold of their springhouse.

"Sorry I can't wait to hear it," swaggered Hiram, blinking and trying to make out who these men were. "I got 'n engagement. Fact is, I'm goin' to be married, an' I'm late a'ready. I'll hev to be excused, Lem!"

"It's quite unnecessary, Mr. Green," said Lemuel, putting out a detaining hand excitedly. "Quite unnecessary, I assure you. The wedding is all over. You're not expected anymore."

Hiram stood back and surveyed Lemuel with contempt.

"How could that be when I wa'n't thar? he sneered. "I guess you didn't know I was goin' to marry Phoebe Deane. I'm right sure no one else'd marry her."

Nathaniel stepped forward, his face white with indignation.

"You are speaking of my wife, Mr. Green," he said, and his voice was enough to arrest the attention of even the self-complacency of a Hiram Green. "Let me never hear you speak of her in that way again. She did not at any moment in her life intend to marry you. You know that well, though you've tried to weave a web of falsehood about her that would put her in your power. The whole thing is known to me from beginning to end, and I do not intend to let it pass lightly. My wife's good name is everything to me—though it seems you were willing to marry one whom you had yourself defamed.

"I've come here this morning, Mr. Green, to give you your choice between going to jail or going with me at once and taking back all the falsehoods you have told about my wife."

Hiram, in sudden comprehension and fear, glanced around the group. He took in Judge Bristol's presence, remembered Nathaniel's threat of the year before about bringing him up before his uncle, remembered that Lemuel Skinner was constable, and was filled with consternation.

With the instinct of a coward and a bully he made a sudden lunge forward toward Nathaniel, his fists clenched and his whole face expressing the fury of a wild animal brought to bay.

"You lie!" he hissed.

But the next instant he lay sprawling at Nathaniel's feet, with Lemuel bustling over him like an excited old hen.

It was Martin Van Rensselaer who had tripped him up just in time.

"Now, gentlemen, gentlemen, don't let's get excited," cackled Lemuel, laying an ineffective hand on the prostrate Hiram.

"Step aside, Mr. Skinner," said Nathaniel, towering over Hiram. "Let me settle this matter first. Now, sir, you may take your choice. Will you go to jail and await your trial for slander, or will you come with us to the people you scattered this outrageous scandal to and take it all back?"

"You've made a big mistake," blustered Hiram. "I never told no stories 'bout Phoebe Deane. It's somebody else 's done it ef 'tain't true—I was goin' to marry her to save her reputation."

"How did you think that would save her reputation?" questioned Judge Bristol, and somehow his voice made cold chills creep down Hiram's spine.

"Why, I- I was goin' to deny everythin' after we was married."

"Your stories don't hang together very well," remarked the judge dryly.

"You will be obliged to deny them now," said Nathaniel wrathfully. "Take your choice at once. I'm not sure after all but the best way would be to house you in jail without further delay. It's almost a crime to let such a low-lived scoundrel as you walk at large. No one's reputation will be safe in the hands of a villain like you. Take your choice at once. I will give you two minutes to decide."

Nathaniel took out his watch.

Silence hung over the meadow behind the springhouse, but a little bird from the tree up the road called, "Phoe-bee! Phoe-bee!" insistently, and a strange tender light came into Nathaniel's eyes.

"The time is up," said Nathaniel.

"What do you want me to do?" asked the captive sullenly.

"I want you to go with me to every house you visited the day you started this mischief and take it all back. Tell them it was untrue and that you got it up out of whole cloth for your own evil purposes."

"But I can't tell a lie," said Hiram piously.

"Can't you? Well, it won't be necessary. Come, which will you choose? Do you prefer to go to jail?"

"Gentlemen, I'm in your hands," whined the coward. "Remember I have little children."

"You should have remembered that yourself and not brought shame upon them and other innocent beings." It was the judge who spoke these words, like a sentence in court.

"Where hev I got to go?"

Nathaniel named the places.

Hiram looked dark and swallowed his mortification.

"Well, I s'pose I've got to go. I'm sure I don't want to lose my good name by goin' to jail."

They set him upon his feet, and the little posse moved slowly up the slope to the house and then to the carryall.

After they were seated in the carryall, with Hiram in the backseat with Lemuel and Martin on either side of him, Nathaniel turned to Hiram.

"Now, Mr. Green, we are going first to your aunt's house and then around to the other places in order. You are to make the following statement and nothing else. You are to say: 'I have come to take back the lies I told about Miss Phoebe Deane and to tell you that they are not true, not one of them. I originated them for my own purposes.' "

Hiram's face darkened. He looked as if he would like to kill Nathaniel. He reached out a long arm again as if to strike him, but Lemuel clutched him convulsively, while Martin threw his weight on the other side and he subsided.

"You can have from now until we reach the jail to think about it, Mr. Green. If you prefer to go to jail instead, you will not be hindered. Mr. Skinner is here to arrest you on my charge if you will not comply with these conditions."

Sullen and silent sat Hiram. He didn't raise his eyes to see the curious passersby as he rode through town.

They looked at Nathaniel and the judge, driving with solemn mien as if on some portentous errand. They noted the stranger and the constable on either side of the lowering Hiram. And they drew their own conclusions, for the news of the wedding had spread like wildfire through the village. Then they stood and watched the carryall out of sight and even followed it to see if it stopped at the jail.

As they drew near the jail Nathaniel turned around once more to Hiram.

"Shall we stop and let you out here, or are you willing to comply with the conditions?"

Hiram raised his eyelashes and gave a sideways glance at the locality, then lowered them quickly as he encountered the impudent gaze of a small boy and muttered, "Drive on."

Hiram went through the distasteful ordeal sullenly. He repeated the words Nathaniel insisted upon, after one or two vain attempts to modify them in his own favor, which only made it worse for him in the eyes of his listeners.

" 'Pon my word," said Aunt Keziah Dart in a mortified tone. " 'F I'd uv told fibs like that I'd 'a' stuck to 'em an' never give in, no matter what. I'm 'shamed to own I'm kin to sech a sneak, Hiram Green. Wan't there gals 'nough 'round the country 'thout all that to do?"

At the Duzenberrys' Susanna rendered Hiram the sympathy of silently weeping in the background, while the Widow Duzenberry stood coldly in the foreground acting as if the whole performance were a personal affront. She closed the interview by calling after Hiram from her front door.

"I'm sorry to see yeh in trouble, Mr. Green. Remember you'll always find a friend here."

Hiram brightened up some. Nevertheless, very little of his old conceit remained when he had gone over the whole ground and was finally set free to go his way to his own home.

Then Nathaniel and Phoebe hastened away in the family coach toward Albany to begin their long life journey together.

Late that afternoon Hank Williams coming up from the village brought with him a letter for Hiram Green which he stopped to leave, hoping to find out from Hiram what had happened during the afternoon. The old housekeeper took the letter saying, "Hiram wa'n't well," and Hank went onward crestfallen.

A few minutes later Hiram tore open his letter. It read:

Mistur Grene,
You hev ben fond out. We want no mor lyres an crimnles in our toun. We hev fond the seels off'n Phebe Denes leter in yor poseshun an we hev uther good evedens thet you open unitd stats male we will giv yo 1 wek to sel ot an lev toun. Ef yo ever sho yer hed agin hear or in Noo York yo wil be tard an fethured an punisht cordin to law.
Yors fer reveng,
A Feller Tounsman

That night while his household slept Hiram Green went forth from his home to parts unknown, leaving his little children to the tender mercies of Aunt Keziah Dart or whoever might be touched with a feeling of pity for them.

And Miranda, who, without the counsel or knowledge of anyone, had written the remarkable epistle which sent him out, lay down serenely and slept the sleep of the just.

And that same night the moon shone brightly over the Hudson River, like a path of silver for the two who sat long on deck, talking of how they loved Miranda, with laughter that was nigh to tears.

Diverse Women

A Collection
of Short Stories
by
Isabella Alden
and
Mrs. C. M. Livingston

Vida

A rustle was heard in the large congregation of St. Paul's Church, well-bred people though they were, as their young minister walked up the aisle with his bride and seated her in the minister's pew. They not only turned their heads, glancing slightly and seeing all without seeming to, as some people know how to do, but they broke the rules in their code of good manners by a succession of neck twistings. It wasn't easy to settle down contented after one short look at the beautiful creature who glided in at the minister's side. If he'd seated an angel in that pew, the sensation couldn't have been greater.

Her beauty was of that rare blonde type—spun gold hair, sapphire eyes and delicate complexion. She was youthful and richly dressed; her dark green velvet suit, white plumes and fine laces set off her striking appearance. Her eyes dropped before the undisguised admiration expressed on many faces.

The minister himself saw nothing of it at all. He was annoyed at finding himself late and was intent on getting to his place in the pulpit at once. It wasn't his ambition to be conspicuous; he was accustomed to slipping quietly into his place from the chapel door. His apparently triumphal march into his church on the first Sunday of his return, after all the people had assembled, wasn't in accord with his taste or planning. It was almost as if he were saying, "Behold us now!" All this threw his thoughts into a tumult, unsettling him in part for his pastoral duties that morning.

At the close of the service that day, the congregation didn't discuss the minister's sermon. They were absorbed in another subject: the minister's wife. The opinions were various. Solemn old deacons looked askance at her in her regal beauty, as they passed by, shook their heads and repeated to each other the familiar saying that wise men often make fools of themselves when they select a wife. One lady said she was "perfectly lovely"; another, that she had "a great deal of style"; and another, that "her dress must have cost a penny," and she didn't see for her part "how a Christian could find it in her conscience to dress like that."

"One would have thought," Mrs. Graves said, "that a man like Mr. Eldred would have chosen a modest, sensible woman for his wife, who'd be useful in the church. But that's the way, isn't it? A minister is like any other man—money and a pretty face will cover up a good many failings."

Mrs. Graves was the mother of three sensible, modest girls, who would have made capital ministers' wives. Why will ministers be so shortsighted?

"But, Mother," Tom Graves asked, "aren't you being pretty fast? How do you know she isn't sensible and modest? You never heard her speak a word."

"Anybody with half an eye doesn't need to hear her speak to know all about her."

"The idea of a minister's wife," said Mrs. Meggs, "with her hair frizzed and such a long trail for church!"

Those who didn't say anything, who made it a rule never to speak uncharitably of anyone, seemed satisfied to let others do it for them. But they looked and sighed their holy horror that their minister had shown so little discretion in choosing a wife. Just think of her leading the women's prayer meeting and being president of the missionary society!

All that was needed was one dear "mother in Israel," with love enough to bear this young thing in the arms of faith to the mercy seat and with courage enough to try to win her to a consecrated life. Everything might have been different then.

When Thane Eldred first met Vida Irving, he was captivated at once. So fair a vision never crossed his path before; whatever of enchantment might have been wanting in golden curls and blue eyes was completed by a rare voice, rich, sweet and fine. If she'd been poor, it might have brought her a fortune. When he heard her sing the sweet hymns he loved in such angelic strains, he took it for granted that the words of fervent devotion expressed her own heart. So fair a bit of clay, he reasoned, must contain a soul of corresponding beauty, and he immediately invested her with all the charms of an angel.

A slight misgiving, it's true, sometimes crossed his mind as to whether she could adapt herself easily to the difficult position of being a pastor's wife. She had the air of an empress, and her manner was often so haughty as to gain enemies. Yet the deluded man with blind eyes reasoned, "I can mold her to what I will when she's mine. It's the fault of a false education. I'm quite sure her heart's all right."

And why did the spoiled beauty condescend to smile upon one, who by his very profession, if closely following in the footsteps of his humble Master, would renounce this world's vanities and enticements and live a life of self-denying work? Not a thought of that ever entered her pretty head. In her estimation a minister was an orator, the idol of a wealthy people and a gentleman of elegant ease. She found the dark-eyed young minister fascinating, and his gracious dignity and impassioned eloquence pleased her. So the sudden attachment was mutual.

Vida's mother, Mrs. Irving, was left a widow with a large fortune as a young woman. She thus devoted herself to her idol, her only child, with unremitting attention. Nothing that would add to her happiness was neglected. Now with her education completed, the fond mother looked about her, seeking a brilliant alliance for this rare daughter. Behold, she found the matter settled. Vida's own sweet will had been the ruling power ever since she came into the world, and the mother was obliged to submit to the inevitable with as good grace as she could command under the circumstances.

A poor minister! Who'd have dreamed the daughter would have made such a choice? With this mother's views of life, and life eternal, it's no wonder she felt bitter disappointment. The prospect, though, wasn't wholly dark, for he was handsome and talented, and that went far toward consoling her. Then, too, he'd probably be called in time to a large, important church and have D.D. at the end of his name. It would sound comforting to say "My son-in-law, Rev. Dr. Eldred, of Boston, or New York City" and talk about his brilliant preaching, his wealthy parishioners, the calls he'd declined and so on.

St. Paul's Church was situated in a small city of large manufacturing interests. While many families of wealth and position were in the church, many were also obliged to work hard and practice the utmost economy in order to have anything left for paying their subscription. Some of these looked without kind eyes on the magnificent changes of outfits Mrs. Eldred brought out Sunday after Sunday: a sealskin sacque, then an Indian shawl and countless suits of rich silks in all possible tints for all possible occasions.

"It makes a body feel as if they hadn't a thing fit to wear, the way Mrs. Eldred comes out in her silks and velvets," remarked Mrs. Jenks, a mechanic's wife, to her neighbor. "I wonder what she'd say to wearing a black alpaca dress seven years running, for her best dress! I declare it made me feel there wa'n't any sort of use scrimping and saving as we do to pay fifteen dollars a year to support the minister. I told John we better pay only five next year, and I'd put the other ten on my back. He's got a rich wife; he don't need much salary now. Just think of her fur sacque and great handsome shawl, and here I haven't had a new wrap this ten years and have to wear my blanket shawl to church."

"Yes, I think as much," answered Mrs. Myers emphatically. "She's as proud as Lucifer, too. Mr. Eldred shook hands with me real friendlylike last Sunday and asked, 'How's the little one?' as he always calls my Tommy. Then he introduced me to her.

"She turned her head toward me and looked me over from head to foot, exactly as if she was figuring to herself, 'Dress, twenty-five cents a yard; shawl, five dollars; hat, two dollars.' Then she gave me what she may call a bow; she swept her eyelashes down and tilted her head back, instead of forward, and I thought I saw the least mite of a curl on her lip. (She's got a dreadful proud mouth, anyway.) She didn't offer to put out her hand, not her! She was afraid I'd soil her white kids, with something less than a dozen buttons on them."

"Well, it's too bad," Mrs. Jenks said, "with him such a good Christian man as he is. Wonder why he wanted to go and marry such a wife, anyhow. I don't believe he more than half approves of her himself, now he sees how she goes on. But, poor man, he's got to make the best of it now. I'll always think good of him though. He was so kind to us when Peter was sick."

Mrs. Eldred wasn't entirely ignorant of the duties expected of a minister's wife. But she'd resolved, as far as she was concerned, to ignore them. Because she married a minister was no sign she was to be subject to the whims of a whole parish; she couldn't consider herself bound by rules that didn't apply equally as well to every other member of the church. Her mother had fore-warned her and advised her to this course.

"A minister's wife, my dear," said the worldly wise mother, "is usually a slave. So just put your foot down in the beginning, and don't wear yourself out. Enjoy yourself all you can. Poor child! You've chosen a dismal life at best for yourself, I fear."

Mrs. Eldred didn't state her peculiar views to her husband. She would just quietly carry out her plans, and he'd learn to submit in time. Mother said that was the way to manage a husband.

It was Thursday night. The first bell for prayer meeting was ringing when Mr. Eldred came down from his study. His young wife sat under the droplight in a large easy chair, absorbed in a book. She was dressed in a white flannel wrapper, and her long, fair hair was unbound, lying in bright waves about her shoulders.

Mr. Eldred contemplated the pretty picture a moment. Then he said, "You look comfortable, my dear. But do you know that's the first bell for prayer meeting?"

"Oh, I'm not going to meeting. I'm perfectly delighted to have an evening to myself once more, when your people are engaged. I'm actually worn out from receiving calls."

Mr. Eldred was disappointed. He'd thought more than once that day how he'd enjoy having his dream realized, with Vida walking with him to his own meeting and sitting nearby, singing as only she could sing. A spice of vanity mingled with it too. How the people would listen and admire her! He felt annoyed and was about to protest, but she looked like such an angel in her soft white dress that he hadn't the heart to find fault. So he kissed her good-bye and went his way alone.

She accompanied him the next week, though it turned out to be a disappointment. Her voice didn't join in the hymns of praise.

She remarked at the close of the meeting, "Do you think I could sing in all that discord? It's horrible; it sets every nerve in my body on edge. People always sing that way in prayer meeting. Everyone tries to sing, even though they don't know one note from another. One old man near me sang five notes below the key, a woman on the other side screamed out as many above, and a girl in front of me had a strong nasal twang. I'd think it would distract you. By the way, what a quantity of common people attend your church!"

Mr. Eldred looked into the fire and repeated half aloud, "The common people heard Him gladly."

As the weeks went on, he realized he must abandon his pleasant plans for companionship in his work. He attended meetings alone made calls alone and grew weary of apologizing for Vida.

She was willing to attire herself royally and make a round of fashionable calls with him on the first families. But when it came to calling on the humbler of the flock she cheerfully remarked that she didn't intend turning city missionary. When ladies called upon her, she'd return their calls—that is, if she wished to continue the acquaintance. But as for running all about town hunting out obscure people, that was out of the question.

A lively clique in the church eagerly welcomed the pastor's wife to their circle. They organized a literary society and gave Shakespearean entertainments.

Mrs. Eldred's fine literary taste and musical abilities made her a valuable acquisition. She soon became the center of the group. If a difficult part needed to be rendered or a queen of beauty represented, Mrs. Eldred was sure to be chosen, and she gave herself with enthusiasm to the activity.

Mr. Eldred joined them in the beginning. But when he discovered the society members were more interested in getting up costumes than in their own mental improvement and the whole thing was degenerating into private theatricals, he withdrew and urged his wife to do the same. But no amount of persuasion could move her in the least; her own will had been her law too long. And this was the person he'd thought to mold! It was so different from the picture he had sketched of these first months of their married life—a picture of sunny, happy days flowing on with scarcely a ripple. Instead, they held long heated discussions that only widened the distance between them.

"I beg your pardon," Vida said in sarcastic tones during one of these skirmishes, "but I think it would be more profitable to you to attend our society meetings than to find fault with me. If you'd study Shakespeare more, it might freshen up your sermons somewhat and lift them out of the ordinary. I can only think you're degenerating. The first discourse I heard you preach was filled with literary allusions, and the language was flowery and beautiful. Your preaching seems to have changed lately. Last Sunday, for example, it was merely talk without rhetoric or eloquence. The words were nearly all of one syllable; the most ignorant in the church could have understood them. I thought you'd receive a call soon to a wealthy church in a large city, but you never will make a reputation if you preach in this style."

Mrs. Eldred's angry passions were raised to a high pitch, or she wouldn't have spoken so bluntly.

The man's sorely tried spirit couldn't repress a groan at the conclusion of this long tirade. He didn't trust himself to speak but went to his study with a slow, heavy step, like one who'd received a mortal wound. The irritation he might otherwise have felt at such words was lost in sorrow at her utter lack of sympathy and apparent ignorance of the spirit and aims of the gospel.

He had been drawing nearer to Christ the last few months and received a new baptism and with it a new view of preaching the gospel. He had doubtless spoken in an unknown tongue to scores of his hearers. Now he put away his elegant essays and, asking the Lord for a message, was trying to tell it with no "great swelling words" but in humility and plain speech, lifting up Christ and hiding himself, intent only on saving souls.

Satan had told him before that the world and some Christians would count his preaching "not deep." Now his own wife had repeated the thought. He'd been so happy in his work and longed to throw himself into it with nothing to come between him and "this one thing I do." But daily trials because of one who should have been his greatest helper saddened him so that much of his labor was mechanical, and he carried a heavy burden. The anxiety continued, for he was well aware that many busy tongues were censuring her, while kinder critics were grieved at her course.

At rare intervals she attended the ladies' meetings, but no amount of persuasion could induce her to take any part in them. She visited those she wanted to and persistently refused to visit others. Thus he labored under constant embarrassment and was in a chronic state of apology for her.

And yet Mrs. Eldred could make herself a most fascinating person. Some evenings she chose to shine at home. Then she would with artistic skill brighten the room and charm her husband from his books, and the time would go on wings, as they read and discussed a new book and sang together their old and new songs. At such times the careworn minister forgot that any clouds obscured his sky.

One evening Mrs. Eldred entered her husband's study, resplendent in white satin and diamonds, saying, "Thane, it's quite time you too were dressed."

"Dressed for what?" he asked with astonishment.

"Why, have you forgotten we have an invitation to Mrs. Grantley's tonight?"

"I recall the invitation now, but I never gave it a second thought, nor did I suppose you had. Didn't you notice from the wording that it was to be a dancing party? I think there must be some mistake about it as I never was invited before our marriage to these parties, nor have we been since. I can't understand why they'd ask us now."

"Why, pray, shouldn't we be invited? It isn't necessary for you to dance, of course. We'll be obliged to go, for I've accepted the invitation," Mrs. Eldred replied, with a nothing-further-to-be-said air.

"I'm sorry you accepted an invitation for me without consulting me, but I can't go," her husband answered seriously.

"Oh, fie! How old and straitlaced you are for a young man. Why, Dr. Henry often went and looked on, and his daughter danced, and people liked him all the better for it. You'll be immensely unpopular if you pursue that course. Don't you think," she continued, encouraged by his silence, "that it savors a little of bigotry and egotism to set oneself up to condemn an amusement many other Christians approve? What's your basis for objection? One would suppose you'd received a direct revelation on the subject."

"I have," he said, and his clear eyes looked full into hers. "Don't you know that a person who's absorbed in Christian work, a consecrated Christian, isn't absorbed in all these amusements, and one who is, has no room in his heart for Christ? A law of natural philosophy states, you know, that 'two bodies cannot occupy the same place at the same time.' There's a somewhat similar law in regard to a soul, stated by the Lord Himself: 'Ye cannot serve two masters.' It's the world or Christ with every soul, and I've chosen Christ."

"I know this much," she said coldly, "that fanatics are the most intolerable of all people. I've danced all my life, and since I became a church member, and it's never been hinted to me before that I wasn't a Christian because I loved it. You don't need to go. John can take me and call for me, and I'll make excuses for you."

"My dear wife! Would you do that? Surely you didn't intend to dance. Even the most liberal would be shocked, I think, if a minister's wife were to dance."

"And why? I'm not the minister. I recognize no restraints that don't apply as well to every Christian woman. You told me yourself that Mrs. Graham is an excellent lady. She's a member of your church and dances, I'm told. Why shouldn't one who professes religion have the same privileges as another?"

"Vida," he said, in a tone of mingled pain and tenderness, "it's only a short time since we were pronounced 'no more twain but one.' You said then the thought made you glad. How can you separate your interests from mine now? Will you do what would dishonor my calling if I were to do it? The world counts us one. Your action is mine. Just or unjust, they don't give you the right to wade quite so far into the sea of worldly pleasures as they themselves feel privileged to do. They'd point the finger of ridicule at both of us and charge us with inconsistency. We won't stop to argue the right and wrong of the subject now. If your conscience doesn't shut you out from the dance, let worldly prudence and a desire to keep our names from common gossip influence you, I pray you, if indeed my wishes and opinion are of no value."

But the young wife was in no frame of mind for recollecting tender vows or listening to reason. She threw off his arm with an impatient gesture and, glancing at her watch, said, "I have not only accepted an invitation to this party but promised to dance. It's getting late, and I must go."

Mr. Eldred controlled his agitation with a mighty effort and in a low, calm tone said, "Then I must save you from disgracing us both. I insist—I *command* you not to go."

Had he struck her, she wouldn't have been more astonished. She stood as if stunned for a moment. Then with a stately air she swept by him and ascended the stairs to her room. What was his consternation presently, as he stood gazing out into the moonlight, to see her pass down the walk, step into a carriage and drive away!

Turning from the window, he paced the floor with as sharp anguish as if she'd gone from him forever. What obstinacy, what unreasoning willfulness— and what would come of it? He spent the long night brooding over his great sorrow, the root of which was the fear that his dear wife did not belong to Christ, for he loved her through all her unloveliness. "Husbands, love your wives even as Christ loved the church." His love had something in it of the divine pity and patience our blessed Lord must feel for His sinning, stumbling children.

Mrs. Eldred wasn't that type of woman who spends her wrath in tears and reproaches. When she was angry, she was unapproachably so, as frigid as an iceberg. The crisis had come. Her husband had dared to command.

The next morning no turn of an eyelid could be construed into penitence. A brawling woman is only a little less endurable than a silent one. You may almost as well "flee to the housetop" from one as the other. What few words Mr. Eldred spoke at the breakfast table received no replies.

In the course of the morning he went to fulfill an engagement a few miles out in the country where he was detained till late in the day. He sat in his study in the gathering twilight, longing for, but not expecting, a word from his wife of contrition and conciliation. He was summoned to tea, but no wife appeared. After a little while he went in search of her. She wasn't in the house. It was growing dark. He was perplexed and anxious.

Again he went to their room, hoping to find some explanation of the strange absence. On the mantel lay a note addressed to him. As he read, he gazed about to assure himself it wasn't a horrible dream and half expected his wife to spring into his arms from some hiding place. But all was silent except his own moans of pain.

Vida had gone! "Fled to Mother for protection from a tyrant," so the letter ran. It was in her own graceful hand with her name at the end. It was no cruel joke. She said, moreover, that it was evident their tastes weren't congenial. It was out of the question for her to be tied down to the sort of life he expected of her. She'd borne reflections on her conduct that she hadn't tolerated from any other being! Tyranny was of all things most hateful to her. The climax was reached when he ventured "to *command*." She recognized no such right and never would. She wouldn't be called to account every time she stepped over a forbidden imaginary line.

It was plain they'd been mistaken in each other and disappointed. They didn't add to each other's happiness, as appeared from the gloom enveloping him day and night. The last months were months of discord. She felt neglected. He was "poring over books or seeking other society in an interminable round of calls." Plainly what he needed in a wife was a sort of copastor. It wasn't too late to secure such a person, "since the law granted divorce for willful desertion."

With this last sentence the letter closed. Not a word betrayed the faintest regret at severing such a solemn bond. He searched it over and over to see if in some corner he couldn't find one tender word for him, a word that would reveal down deep in her heart the light of her great love for him, even such love as he had for her—a faint glimmer through the clouds of anger and recrimination. Not one syllable showed that the writer's heart hadn't turned to ice. Yes, there was another sentence, more cruel and hopeless still: "Don't try to change my resolution, as if it were made in a fit; it is final—*unalterable*."

It couldn't be true. He looked wildly about him as though to have the terrible truth dispelled. He opened the closet door and her bureau drawers, but the pretty, festive dresses were all gone; the dainty garments weren't in their places. A small pair of half-worn slippers and the blue ribbon that had tied her hair were all he found. He seized them convulsively, as a part of Vida when she was sweet and simple—as she could be.

He sat for long hours with the letter in his hand, as one who holds his death warrant. Then falling on his face he cried to his Helper. And He who is of great tender mercies heard and drew near in the darkness and comforted him, even "as one whom his mother comforteth."

When morning dawned, he arose and took up the burden of life again, where he was, before Vida Irving stole into his heart. No, for it could never be the same again. When the lightning sends its lurid bolt down a noble tree, it may not wave green and fair as it once did. Dead branches and the gnarled seam will tell the story that "fire hath scathed the forest oak."

The solemn man who went out into life again carried the marks of the conflict in his sad eyes and pale cheeks. Not the least of this great trial was to meet and answer the looks and questions of the curious. For the present he could truthfully say, "Mrs. Eldred has unexpectedly gone to her mother."

Meanwhile he resigned his charge, much to the sorrow and dismay of all. He disposed of all the elegant furnishings of the parsonage and with haste left the spot that had been the scene of an exquisite torture. No definite plans lay before him, except to get far away from any who could have had the least knowledge of him previously. No fugitive from justice ever felt more nervous haste. He pushed on, never pausing till he reached the verge of civilization in the far Southwest. Not that he'd be a hermit or misanthrope, but perchance he might find a people destitute of the gospel. He'd bring it to them. He must preach Christ till death. This would be his joy and comfort; from now on no other love would come between his soul and his dear Master.

And he found his work, as if an unerring path had been marked out straight to the little log church in the woods.

While Vida sat in a lofty temple of arches and massive pillars, with the sunlight toned to the appropriate dimness as it stole through the stained windows, the same hour her husband stood in the log church of the wilderness, with its arches and pillars outside and the old trees locking arms overhead. Nature softened the fierce rays in this temple as well, for they filtered through thick green boughs. Flecks of light fell here and there, and a stray one rested halolike on the minister's head, transfiguring him in the eyes of the hungry souls whose upturned faces drank in the words of life.

This unlearned, simple people with whom he'd cast his lot had their faults, but they had no distractions to steal their souls from Christ after the manner of more cultured Christians. The church was the apple of their eye. They sacrificed for it and traveled weary miles in the worst of weather, rather than lose a "meeting."

The young gifted pastor of St. Paul's Church was never more appreciated than now by these hardworking, warmhearted pioneers. It was their daily wonder and thanksgiving that such a man had ever been sent to them. Nothing they could do for him was too much, and their loving devotion was like balm to his weary soul. His people were scattered for miles away, but the pastoral calls were as faithfully made as when they fell within the limits of a few squares.

The mild winter climate of that region was like one long autumn of the Eastern states. Mounted on his faithful pony, he spent a large part of every day riding over the prairies. The blue skies and the bright sunshine were tonics to the heart as well as to the body. Sometimes his route lay for miles through the woods, where perfect solitude reigned except for the chatter of birds circling around him. In these long rides his heart went back over the past, reviving the memory of those first precious days with Vida. They seemed far away and their recollection, like the perfume of wilted flowers, plucked from the grave of a dear one. If he couldn't have prayed for her then, hourly, his heart would have broken.

Meanwhile, Mrs. Irving changed her residence, putting hundreds of miles between her new and old homes, so that Vida might begin life anew, as she phrased it, without embarrassment. In a large hotel in the great city, with seaside and mountain trips, parties and operas were much more to Vida's taste than dull life in a quiet parsonage where she was expected to play the role of a pastor's wife.

With her mother as chaperone, she led a lively life, going, coming, reveling at will in her freedom. As before her marriage she attracted much attention. Admired and courted, countless suitors paid her homage. But a positive nature and strong will asserted themselves here. Only such attentions as befitted a wife were tolerated. She knew the law did not count her free.

And if she had analyzed her secret heart, she would find no true reason why she cared to be free. No face she met had power to quicken her pulses or extract from her a second thought. The inner heart had long ago been preempted, but the blind willful creature didn't know it. The face most often seen in her dreams, the voice that whispered in her ear and the sad, dark eyes that seemed to follow her reproachfully belonged to none of the men about her. Since her previous history was unknown, she was a problem in that circle.

There came a change. Mrs. Irving's health began to fail. The eminent physicians far and near were consulted in vain. And since the symptoms became more defined and alarming, Vida couldn't shut her eyes to the fact that her mother was in a most critical state. She was a devoted daughter, though the weeds of selfishness, fostered by the mother's hand at times, almost overwhelmed filial affection. Now she shut herself in from society and devoted herself to her mother with unremitting care. The invalid's every whim was gratified.

One day, after weary months of suffering, she said, "Oh, Vida, dear, I would pray to die, if I weren't afraid."

"Why afraid, Mother? You've been a member of a church these many years and a faithful attendant of its services, and you've been kind to the poor and such a dear mother," said Vida. "I don't think you need to be afraid."

"Oh, child, that won't stand in the great day. Don't mention anything I've done or been, I beg you," moaned the poor mother. "I have been nothing but a miserable worldling. Now I'm almost through with it all, and I have no peace or comfort. It's all dark, dark. Oh, what shall I do?"

"Let me send for Dr. Hines," said Vida.

"Oh, I can't talk to him. He's a stranger, and I'm so weak. What must I do?"

Vida had been a member of the same church. But now she sat wrapped in gloom, feeling powerless to help, yet longing to comfort her dying mother. In the midst of her sad thoughts as she sat watching, gentle slumber stole for a moment over the mother. She remembered the words of a text she'd heard her husband preach from: "What must I do to be saved?" The sermon was gone from her memory.

If it asks that question in the Bible, it must answer it, she thought. So finding a Bible, she sat down to search for the old answer to the old question.

"Reading the Bible, dear?" said her mother, opening her eyes.

"Oh, Mother! I've found the answer!"

The plain, short direction was read. The mother repeated it feebly. " 'Believe on the Lord Jesus Christ, and thou shalt be saved.' "

"Read about Him—oh, do," she said and seemed to summon soul and body to listen as Vida, led no doubt by the Spirit, read here and there of Him who died for us.

Day after day the reading continued. While the mother slept, the daughter pondered the wonderful words she read—preached to her for years and apprehended by her only just now. Her heart was filled with horror and fear at her treatment of such a Savior and at her daring to number herself among His people. Then that heart melted as she read of His love and pity and, casting away her robe of self-righteousness for the first time in her life, she knelt before Him a heartbroken, contrite sinner. He took the burden from her heart and gave her peace.

While she still bowed at the bedside, praying her whispered prayer that her dear mother might "see Jesus," that mother put out her thin hand and laid it on the golden head murmuring, "Dear daughter, I believe in the Lord Jesus Christ. He has forgiven me. It's all peace, peace. Thank Him."

And Vida's clear, low tones of thanksgiving came to her dying mother, sweet as the voice of angels, whose song soon burst upon her ear.

How clear an evidence of Christianity is this—a soul exchanging pride, haughtiness and rebellion for humility and submission. Vida meekly bowed to the storm that burst over her head and was filled with joy and peace that hadn't been hers in the brightest hour of worldly pleasure. It wasn't as hard with this newborn love and trust to see the grave close over that dear mother. It was gilded with the light of that day when "we shall rise again."

In the bereavement hours Vida's heart went out with a longing cry for her husband. The love she had stifled and called dead was there, deeper and purer. Now that she'd been brought by this divine mystery into full sympathy with him, he was the one soul on earth whose love she craved.

Perverse human heart! Here she was, no one to control her actions, possessed of wealth, youth, beauty, freedom to journey to other lands and revel in the grand and beautiful of nature and art. Yet the only thing she desired, or that would satisfy, was to creep back into the niche she had filled in that other heart, that large, pure soul she'd thrust from her in her foolishness and blindness. Now she would devote her life to searching for him, if indeed he were still living, and the doubt brought a sharp pang. Or had he, too, thrust her out and barred the door, so she might never enter? Or—worse to her than death—had he given the place to another, as she had bid him do? It was a weary search, with this terrible uncertainty shrouding it. She advertised in mystical language so only he could understand it. She examined the church records of the denomination with which he was connected but found no clue there.

She attended conventions with large companies of ministers in session and eagerly looked them over, hoping and praying her eyes might fall on that one her heart sought. This strange search was growing exciting and absorbing. She frequently visited towns where a popular preacher or lecturer was announced and became one of the vast throng that passed about him. Then, taking a favorable position, she scanned the upturned faces. At the same time she wondered what that strange, subtle something is by which we recognize each other, so that, if we could view ten thousand faces one by one, we know at a glance the one we seek isn't there. We don't stop, doubt and compare, for we can't be deceived; we know.

She humbled herself and wrote letters far and near to his ministerial friends but received only sorrowful replies. Then she remembered he'd often spoken of the West as a wide and promising field for labor and that sometime he'd like to go there and build up a church. He might have gone there now. So, with this forlorn hope, she started westward, spending the summer journeying, stopping over the Sabbath at straggling villages and visiting different churches. Worn out at length, she recalled an uncle had moved with his family to the Southwest several years before.

She searched out their location and hurried there, intending to spend only a brief season. But yielding to their earnest entreaties she remained through the autumn. It was now drawing near Christmas, and still she lingered. She was growing hopeless, and that pleasant home filled with boys and girls was a diversion from her grief.

"Do, cousin Vida, go with me today, won't you?" asked Harry, a bright boy of fourteen. "I know a splendid place about ten miles from here, where we can get some evergreens. I want to trim up the house for Christmas just as we used to in New York. I'll take the spring wagon and the ponies, and we can bring home lots of greens, cut off in short branches."

"You forget," his mother said, "that your cousin isn't used to riding in spring wagons over rough roads, and ten miles will be a long drive for her."

"Some red berries are there, too," went on Harry, as if he hadn't heard the objections, "and moss and long vines that the frost hasn't found yet. Besides it's a grand day to ride."

"You dear boy," said Vida, "I'll go for half the inducements you offer." She was only too glad to fall in with any plan that distracted her sad thoughts.

The drive lay for a long distance through the lovely open country. The grass in many parts was still as green as in midsummer, and over all shone the perpetual sunshine of that region. The soft golden light that even in midwinter glorifies the commonest object, the bright skies, the balmy air and her lively companion cheered Vida's spirits.

After arriving in the woods, Harry ran here and there eagerly, climbing a tree like a squirrel, then darting into a thicket for mosses. They loaded the wagon with green boughs and filled their baskets with moss and lichens, and the brightly plumed birds flitted about with lively chirping.

As the cousins became more intent on adding to their supply, they became separated. Vida was a little distance behind a low, thick growth of trees, disentangling a long vine of bittersweet, when she heard a voice. There was just one voice like that in all the world. Trembling she bent her head and peeped through the branches. One swift glance and she knew him—her husband!

A strong self-control prevented her from swooning or crying out in her great joy. Shaking like a leaf yet holding firmly to a tree trunk, she gazed into the dear face. It was paler and thinner, with dark rings under the eyes, but the finely curved mouth had the same calm, sweet expression that told of peace within.

How like a king among men he looked, as he stood there, his hands filled too with mosses and lichens, looking with kindness on the boy and talking earnestly. She never realized her utter foolishness so sharply as at that moment. How she longed to fly to him and fall at his feet in sorrowful confession. Two things held her back: no eyes must witness their first meeting, and the dreadful thought that it might be too late. What if he had taken her at her word and loved another?

She hadn't been a woman of the world so long for nothing. She was quite adept in hiding her heart. So when Harry returned, she calmly asked him about the person he'd found in that out-of-the-way place.

"Why, don't you think!" said Harry. "Among all the other things in these woods I found a minister. Wish we could put him right on top of our boughs and things and carry him home, too, for Christmas. Wouldn't Mother be glad to see him though! He preaches every Sunday in a log church down this way, and people come from all around to hear him. He looks as if he could preach, too. And he has such eyes that look you through. Say, let's you and me go to hear him next Sunday, will you?"

"Yes, I will!" Vida said, with such energy that Harry glanced at her and wondered why she had a bright red spot in each cheek. He wondered more before they reached home, for his cousin laughed and sang in childlike joy and was sad and silent by turns. Her restlessness couldn't wait until Sunday. The excitement and suspense were unendurable.

Confiding in her aunt, the two arranged for Moses to accompany her to Cedar Vale the next afternoon. Just what she would do when she reached there wasn't clear to her, but she couldn't stay away.

After the children were off to school again after the nooning, Vida mounted a fleet pony and, attended by her guide, rode quietly away. Her heart beat wildly when they drew near the settlement. They came at last upon the church, standing in a lovely grove of maples. The door stood slightly ajar. At a little distance from it Vida dismounted and directed Moses to wait there for her. She had a consuming desire to look into the church where her husband preached, to stand a moment in the spot where he stood Sunday after Sunday.

She stepped in softly, and there, kneeling by the little pulpit with his head bowed on the desk, was her husband!

Timidly, as one who has no right, she silently drew near and knelt beside him. Stranger eyes may not look upon a scene so sacred, but the two souls bowed together before that altar came nearer to heaven than mortals often come.

Had the waning light not warned them that they were still upon the earth, they might never have tired of looking into one another's eyes. And they told each other the experiences of that lifetime they had lived since their separation and tried to put into words the depths of joy that crowned this blessed hour.

Before leaving the church they knelt again in that sacred spot, and each in low, fervent words gave thanks, longing for a blessing on their reunited lives. And by a mutual and irresistible impulse, both spoke again their marriage vows before the Lord in His temple.

When they rode away that Christmas Eve on their second bridal trip, the setting sun, smiling through the trees and slanting across their pathway, fell on them like a benediction. Slowly and dreamily they went, willing that this ride over crackling twigs and rustling leaves, with the soft light of the dying day closing about them, should go on forever. The husband's earnest admiring gaze brought blushes to the bride's face. He was drawing contrasts. The sweet face and simple dress of the one who rode beside him made a fairer picture than the queenly lady of haughty airs and magnificent attire, who seemed to exist no more.

Never was Christmas more delightful than this one in that merry household. Those memorable evergreens festooned it as a bower—a romance, lived out, not written. No costly gifts were given, and yet the gifts were the most precious— two souls given back to each other. If the joy bells in their hearts had only had voice, their silvery ringing would have filled all the land.

"Vida, can you be happy here until spring?" Thane Eldred asked a few days after Christmas. "My work would suffer, I think, if I were to leave it now."

"Why leave it in the spring, dear? Let's stay here always, in this beautiful, quiet place, where the people love you so. And—I didn't tell you yet," Vida said, half shyly, "but my money isn't mine anymore. I gave it all to the dear Lord. I'd like to build a pretty church with some of it, and we can stay here and work, you and I together. I can help you now, Thane—a little. Don't you like my plan?" she said anxiously, when he didn't speak.

"My darling, you've made me so happy I couldn't speak," he said in a moment. "I wish above all things to go on with my work here, and a new church is needed so much. How strange that you'd be willing to stay and we can work together! Oh, Vida! I prayed—with faith, I thought—but I never dreamed of an hour like this. Surely, 'it has not entered into the hearts to conceive the things which God has prepared for them that love Him'— in this life."

Another sensation passed through an audience when the pastor of the log church brought in his wife, for no one so fair and sweet had ever delighted their rustic eyes. The singing that day was mostly solo or, at least, duets. Her pure, birdlike voice filled the church. And what could they do but listen and wonder whether it might be a lark or an angel come down for a time?

When a teeming, busy town covered the prairie and the heel of agriculture and commerce crushed out the wildflowers, the log church was preserved as a memorial. And the spire of the handsome new one was eagerly pointed out, while its story was treasured and handed down to the children's children.

These two spent their happy lives ministering to this simple people, and their hearts and hands were so filled with work that they had no time to sigh for the privileges of more cultivated surroundings. The pastor's wife was the warm friend and sympathizer of the common people, and her name was singularly appropriate—Vida, well-beloved.

Hildy

"Yes, I s'pose Enos'll bring Hildy home here 'fore long."

Mrs. Blake had slipped on her sunbonnet and stepped up to Turners' to borrow their patty pans. At least that's the reason she gave to Mrs. Turner for her unusually early call; she had another one, though, that she didn't tell.

The two women stood in the springhouse, where rows of milk pans filled the shelves. Some were fresh from the milk pail, with the white foam not settled yet, while others had taken on that golden color that delights a good butter maker.

"I can't say as I'll be sorry on some accounts," said Mrs. Turner. "Hildy's a smart stirring girl and can lend a hand at the work. I'm gettin' pretty old to work as I'm doin', and my rheumatiz gits the better of me some days so't I can't hardly hobble. I'll be glad of a little rest." Mrs. Turner gave several satisfied pats to the roll of butter she was working.

"Do tell!" said Mrs. Blake in surprise, gratified beyond measure at being taken into the other woman's confidence.

Even that farming community had levels, and Mrs. Blake, in her own estimation, was on a lower level than Mrs. Turner and so aspired to intimacy with her wealthier neighbor.

"Do tell! I heard they was keepin' company, but I didn't know it had got along that far. Hildy Adams is a likely kind of a girl, but—" Mrs. Blake stopped short, thinking to feel her way a little more carefully.

"But what?" said Mrs. Turner, looking up sharply. "If you know anything agin Hildy Adams, speak out!"

"Oh, I was only going to say I allus thought the Adamses was just a leetle mite stuck up and tried to hold their heads higher'n the rest of us. D'ye b'lieve you'll git much work out of Hildy after all?"

"The girl that marries Enos has got to work," the old lady said, thumping her butter vigorously. "I guess Hildy has sense enough to know that. She's been fetched up on a farm. Why wouldn't she expect to work? As for their feelin' themselves above folks, they never show that side to me, you know, fur I recken the Turners can hold their own by the side of the Adamses any day. There ain't a girl in the hull country but what 'ud jump at the chance ov marryin' Enos, if I do say it as shouldn't. You talk, Mrs. Blake, as if you thought Hildy was sort of a-condescendin' to marry Enos at all."

"Oh, no," Mrs. Blake hastened to say, "I was only thinkin' that Mrs. Adams has always been so full of ideas and thinks so much of books and newspapers. And then she's independent like, and Hildy's a good deal like her—thinks she knows it all. And then I heerd say—I don't know whether it's so or not—that she reads novels and is always a hurryin' through her work to pore over 'em. So different from my Mary Jane now—she's such a contented creetur. Work right along from sunrise to sunset stiddy as a clock, go to bed at sundown, git up, first one in the house, and work right along—don't waste her time a-readin' nor gaddin' about.

"I was only wonderin' whether Hildy'd settle down to hard work and make a real good farmer's wife, bein' as she's pretty young too. I don't b'leve she's a day over eighteen, if she's that." (Mary Jane was twenty-five.) "I don't mean a word agin the girl now. But I jus' thought I'd put in a word of warnin', bein's I was an old neighbor, cause you seemed so chirk at geetin' rid of some of your work, for fear you might be expectin' what you never'd git."

Mrs. Blake waxed still bolder and cast prudence to the winds. She'd do what she could for Mary Jane yet. Who knew what would come of it?

"There are wus things than rheumatiz," she continued. "You're such a pertikeler housekeeper, Mrs. Turner. How do you s'pose you'll stand it to have a young thing full of ideas and notions come in here and turn things topsy-turvy, fix 'em accordin' to her own notion and put down her foot about havin' her own way about things." Mrs. Blake cast a furtive glance under Mrs. Turner's cap border, fearing she'd gone beyond the mark this time.

"Mrs. Blake," said Mrs. Turner, looking over her spectacles and pausing a moment to give more force to her speech, "I'd think anybody that had lived neighbor to me going on forty years would know I wouldn't allow anyone to walk over me in my own house."

Mrs. Turner looked so severely dignified that poor Mrs. Blake was quite quenched.

"I know what you mean by notions," continued Mrs. Turner. "Mrs. Adams and I have had many a talk and ended up by both bein' of the same opinion still. They think it ain't hulsome to eat pork, and they take cream and butter instead of lard to shorten their piecrust and biskit, and they don't believe in washing their butter. But, you see, if Hildy Adams come here to live, she'll wash the butter, and she'll git rid of some o' them notions her mother put into her head, or I'll miss my guess."

Mrs. Turner energetically pounded and squeezed the yellow mass before her as if she had poor Hilda Adams herself in the butter bowl, molding her into the very shape she wished.

"Jus' so," said Mrs. Blake, "I hope 'twon't be too much for you. I'm glad I ain't in your shoes, though."

Nevertheless Mrs. Blake, as she went home through the smiling meadows and velvet-green wheat fields, felt she'd give her little finger if Mary Jane were only in Hilda Adams's shoes. Not much happiness was conferred upon anybody by that call, for Mrs. Blake had accomplished her object: to find out if possible how matters stood with regard to Hildy and Enos. The truth had been told, thus destroying a castle that had reared itself in the air on the Blake farm, concerning Mary Jane and Enos.

And Mrs. Turner no longer possessed the same contentment Mrs. Blake had found her in. She emptied the sour milk into the cream jug and the cream into the pig trough and was out of sorts with herself, Mrs. Blake, Hildy and Enos.

The object of this talk, Hilda Adams, sat unaware on the side porch of her home, picking over strawberries for tea. The June roses blushed beside her, the sweet breath of lilacs and syringas filled the air, the maples in tender luxuriant green waved above her, and the fresh, springing grass spread its soft carpet at her feet. The surroundings and the girl fit each other; sweet, bright and fresh described them all. As she worked she sang snatches of songs that kept time with the robin's notes in the old elm.

Suddenly a bright tint, not unlike the rosy hue that stained her fingertips, stole into her face, bringing forth a smile. A wagon piled with freshly cut grass passed along the narrow lane, and on it sat a young man in farm attire, his face nearly hidden by his broad-brimmed straw hat.

Enos Turner was a favorite with the young ladies of Willow Vale—not alone because he and his widowed mother owned one of the best farms in the country, but also because he was considered "a real handsome fellow." He had a ruddy color, a shock of straight black hair and a pair of black eyes that were much admired. Tastes differ. Those same eyes might have been made of black-and-white paint as far as soul was concerned, for clear, intelligent and penetrating weren't adjectives that could be applied to them. They were simply eyes.

Hilda and Enos had attended the same school. He liked to sit next to her in the parsing class, for her quick wits could unravel the most intricate sentences and state the case or tense of the most obscure noun or verb. It was like an unknown tongue to Enos. But, thanks to Hilda, he came off passably well. Not even the teacher surmised that in reality Enos knew little more of grammar than did old Browse, one of the oxen on the farm. He declared, at the end of his school days, that "grammar" was a study he "never could see no kind o' use in anyhow" and managed to dispense with its rules in almost all his communications.

Still, Enos was "good at figgers" and said to be "sharp at a bargain" like his father before him. *Selfish* would have been a better word than *sharp*. Extreme selfishness appears to serve one at times almost as well as keen wit, and Enos had grown up feeling that all things in this world must revolve around one center—him.

For a long time he'd seen Hilda home from parsing bees, singing school and the like. It was whispered they were "keeping company" long before matters took serious shape in their own minds. Perhaps they might have been content to go on that way for years if Enos's mother hadn't jogged his self-interest with a reminder.

"There ain't another piece of land in the country like that east lot of the Adamses that joins our farm. And if you don't stir yourself about pretty lively, that Simmons fellow'll get the start of you. Hildy's good-lookin', and I daresay more'n one fellow has his eye on her."

Those words had the desired effect. Not long afterward Enos, in true orthodox fashion, leaning on the gate, in the moonlight under the apple blossoms, spoke words to which Hilda returned a shy, embarrassed, half-confident yes. It was a surprise to her after all, for no tender confidences had ever passed between them. But probably she'd marry sometime, and, y-e-e-s, she was sure she liked Enos better than anybody else she knew of.

When their engagement was spoken of in the hamlet as settled and the neighbors for miles around had weighed all the pros and cons, it was decided to be a good match. Except here and there a wise one declared that "Hildy Adams had forgotten more than Enos Turner ever knew" and "her little finger was worth more than the whole of him."

Hilda's father, like Mrs. Turner, had an eye to the business part of the arrangement and thought of Enos simply as a young man who eventually would fall heir to a fine property. Besides he was industrious and had good habits. Why shouldn't he make Hilda a good husband?

Mrs. Adams was made of finer clay than her husband, and her aspirations and views of life differed totally from his. While the prospect of Hilda's settling so near her was pleasant, her intuitions wouldn't let her give a hearty consent to the engagement. Even while she reasoned with herself, "Why, if the child loves him, it's all right, I suppose," she found it hard to overcome a certain reluctance. Somehow she'd expected different things for her Hilda—what, she'd hardly defined.

She talked cheerfully with Hilda about her marriage, yet her heart often faltered and rebelled. She probed her daughter deeply to make sure she wasn't deceived, but Hilda always answered, "Yes, Mother, I'm sure I care for Enos more than anybody else."

She had hoped Hilda would somehow get out into the world and have opportunities that had been denied her. But now this neighbor's son was claiming her, and Hilda was to go just down the road a mile or two and enter into the toilsome life of a farmer's wife.

If Enos Turner had only been a grand man that approached her high standard of manhood, if she could only feel he possessed noble qualities, so that as the years passed Hilda wouldn't find a vast gulf between her and her husband and mourn over her sad mistake, it wouldn't be so hard to give her up.

It wasn't just a mother's partiality that made her, in spite of herself, compare the two—one to her moss-rose bush, fine and sweet; the other to the mullein stalk that grew just over the fence. The mullein would always be mullein, though so near the lovely rose. If only Enos could be likened even to that strong, rough apple tree down the road. She knew such men who didn't speak better English than Enos did, but they possessed that fine subtle something that goes to make a royal character, fragrant with thoughts and words and deeds of truth and beauty. Even the gnarled tree was covered yearly with green leaves, fair blossoms and golden fruit.

If only some would-be wives might heed Paul's admonition to "see that she reverence her husband" and, indeed, "see" before it's too late that there is something in the would-be husband to reverence, certain problems might be avoided. Some wives are to be pitied in their effort to obey this precept. When the glamor of youthful love has passed and colors are seen by daylight, it isn't always an easy command to keep. Reverence a sour, selfish nature, a clod, a beast of burden, a cloud of tobacco smoke, a cask of beer!

Mrs. Adams had one unfailing resource in every trouble. She carried it to the Lord. If He didn't interfere and remove it, her cheerful faith led her to submit and feel that, since it was His will, it must somehow be the right thing. And now that she had reasoned with her daughter and her husband and could really offer no tangible reason why the affair shouldn't go on, and since it was none of her planning, it must be the will of Providence.

So preparations for the marriage continued. The mystic number of tucked, frilled and embroidered garments lay in snowy piles in bureau drawers, beside ample supplies of housekeeping linen, scented with lavender and rosemary. Mrs. Adams spared no pains to prepare her daughter an outfit compatible with the family's high standing. Everything was finished now, except dressmaking.

"We'll can the fruit and get the housecleaning done first, Mother, and then we'll go to the city and buy the dresses. I think I'd like a soft silvery gray dress for my—my wedding dress," Hilda said with a little flush. To her the future wore a soft silvery haze, but it was rose-tinted instead of gray.

In the midst of the August heat, a young lady came to Willow Vale from the city to get a breath of fresh country air and visit Mary Jane Blake.

Miss Kittie Brown was a tall slender girl with a small waist and a pale, rather pretty face. She was dressed according to the latest fashion in trails and high heels, bows and frizzes, putts and jewelry, and a stylish little hat with a long plume. She had a sky-blue silk dress with ruffles, pleats and ribbons innumerable, a white Swiss muslin and a pink muslin that floated about her like soft clouds, transfiguring her in the eyes of the unsophisticated country youth into something scarcely of earth.

She'd stayed up nights to make these dresses, for she had no other time. She worked as a clerk in a dry-goods store in the city and had barely a minute to call her own. More of Kittie's salary was represented by her clothes, and she thought of little else than what to wear and how to make it. She had a good deal of taste and skill in this direction and dressed herself so well that one must look closely to detect the difference between the clerk and the wealthy woman who tossed over the fine laces at Kittie's counter. Inasmuch as Willow Vale people weren't well versed in detecting flimsy silk from fine or imitation lace from real, her outfits in their eyes were simply magnificent.

Picnics, berry excursions and moonlight gatherings were held in the neighborhood for her benefit. Instead of taking part, Hilda often helped her mother in canning fruit, since she was skilled at it and this year they needed an extra amount. So she sat through the long afternoons, peeling pears and peaches or cooking both them and herself in the fierce heat of the stove, while other young people were off on some expedition. The burden was double this year. Wasn't Hilda to set up housekeeping in a few weeks?

Among the young men paying court to Miss Kittie none was looked upon with such favor as Enos Turner. He wasn't slow to perceive it and feel immensely flattered by such distinction. And it was mutual.

"Enos ought to be ashamed of himself," the girls said, "and he's engaged, too."

He managed in some way, though it was the farmers' busiest season, to be present at all the teas and picnics and pay marked attention to Kittie, who plied her arts industriously. No spider ever spun its web more adroitly. She was delighted with farm life and the country in general. She told him such nothings he could appreciate and sang lackadaisical songs for him. When she wore her Swiss muslin with blue ribbons floating here and there and danced and chattered about, Enos was beside himself and stepped further and further into the web.

Weary of standing in one place in that store, where she had stood for five years, Kittie longed for a house on a green hill, like the Turners'. She wanted to ride in a carriage behind Enos's handsome black colts—into the city to the store where she'd been a clerk and purchase a large bill of goods and hear the other clerks whisper, "Kittie is Mrs. Turner now. She married a rich farmer and lives in Willow Vale." Oh, she could just see herself doing it. Then she might even come into the city to board through the winter, like any other lady who owned a country seat. That Enos was engaged didn't trouble her conscience; rather, it added zest to her plans for trapping him.

Hilda labored on, wondering sometimes why Enos didn't come up more often. But it was harvesttime, and he was busy and got very tired by night, she presumed. Strange as it may seem, no gossip had yet carried her a hint of things in the last few weeks while she was working. Now at the close of this warm September day Hilda sat in the door watching the last pink rays die out of the sky. The pantry shelves were filled with cans of tempting fruit.

"Well, Mother, the fruit's all done—now for housecleaning. And by the last of next week we can go to the city and shop," Hilda said in a satisfied tone.

Just then she heard the clear tones of the church bell in the evening air. "I'm going to prayer meeting!" she exclaimed, jumping up. "I haven't been in three weeks. When did I ever stay away like that before?"

"My feet ache so they'd hardly carry me there tonight," said her mother.

"But I don't like for you to go alone. How do you know you'll have company home either?"

"Why, Enos will be there and will wonder where I am," Hilda answered confidently.

Truth to tell, the hope of meeting Enos was a strong inducement for going at all, tired out as she was. She'd begun to feel not a little nettled at his apparent indifference, excuse him as she might to her father and mother.

Many of the Willow Vale young people attended prayer meeting, not so much because they were religiously inclined, but because they enjoyed being together somewhere, and the meeting furnished an opportunity. They were out in full force tonight, including Enos, who sat nearly opposite Hilda.

But when she turned her eyes toward him to telegraph a joyous greeting, he looked another way. That was an accident, probably; she tried again but received no answering look. Slowly it dawned upon her that Enos didn't wish to look at her; he was evidently offended. The thought of connecting his strange behavior with "that girl visiting at Blakes'," who sat quite near him and sang at the top of her voice, never entered Hilda's mind.

The meeting was neither profitable nor comforting to Hilda, with her thoughts in such a turmoil, and she was glad when it was over. Now she and Enos would have it all explained on the way home. Perhaps he was vexed at her for staying away from everything lately. She passed through the door and, as was her custom, lingered a bit for Enos to come out.

At last he came, but Miss Kittie Brown was talking to him very fast. Presently she slipped her hand through his arm, and they walked off together.

Hilda stood there dazed. Was that Enos? Mary Jane Blake was just behind her, but she didn't want to talk to her. She walked quickly through the village street, out into the quiet and loneliness. She felt no fear, for her heart was too sore to think of that, even though she'd never been on that road alone in the evening. She was thankful to be alone tonight. How could Enos treat her that way? What had she done? Grief and anger ruled her by turns, and in her excitement she sped up the long hill and was soon at home in the sitting room. She'd lit her lamp and fled to her own room before her father or mother could remark upon her excited manner and flushed face. Most of the night she reviewed every possible cause she could have given Enos to act this way.

The days passed, and nothing was seen of Enos in Hilda's home. She thought at first he was only teasing her and the next night he'd surely come. So she dressed herself with care and waited on the porch or strolled to the gate and peered down the road, but he didn't come.

At church and prayer meeting he ignored her, and Hilda had no heart to go elsewhere.

Hilda's mother, meanwhile, was secretly relieved and glad at this sudden turn of events. Yet she saw how the brightness had vanished from the house, and the rosy girl with a spring in her step and a song on her lips had become a pale, silent, suffering girl. Then her mother heart came to the rescue, and in spite of her prejudices against the marriage she begged her husband to go and see if Enos had any explanation to offer. Mr. Adams, although an indulgent father, was too proud a man to do this.

"I won't ask any young man to marry my daughter for a farm," he said. "She has a good home. Let him go. She's a good deal better off, according to my way of thinking, than if she were to marry such a sneaking villain as he's turned out."

As for Enos, he was either too infatuated to think or care about consequences or knew that both Hilda and her parents were too proud to seek redress at the hands of the law. However it was, he rushed on. His crops suffered while he journeyed back and forth to the city visiting the siren who had charmed him. His poor old mother fretted and scolded, but it was no use. He'd always had his way ever since he first toddled about. Was he to be ruled now?

When these reports came to Hilda's ears, she didn't lie down and die or institute proceedings against her treacherous beloved. Instead, she dried her eyes and turned the key in the trunk that held the housekeeping linen, hiding it away with the silvery and rose-colored dreams. Then she plunged into house-cleaning as if it were a sovereign remedy for a broken heart. And who hasn't felt the relief hard labor brings to a wounded spirit? She rubbed and polished and scrubbed, as if she'd expend some of the wrath burning inside her on those inanimate doors and windows. She had left the tearful state and entered one of vehement indignation at such a cruel betrayal of trust—to be cast off without a word of explanation.

If he had appealed to her generosity and with manly frankness said, "I was mistaken; I thought I loved you but I don't," she might have had some respect left for him. As it was, the tender feelings had changed to contempt. If something didn't interpose, Hilda was in danger of becoming one of those unhappy, vindictive women who look upon all mankind with hate and distrust.

Mrs. Adams never found it easier to rejoice in her favorite doctrine.

There's a divinity that shapes our ends,
    Rough-hew them how we will.

"It's real hard just now. I know it is, poor child," she said to console her daughter. "But, dear, someday you'll see it was all right. The dear Lord knows what His plans for you are, and it seems this wasn't His plan. I don't think you'd want to follow any other, would you? I believe the day'll come when you'll not only think it was right, but you'll thank Him for leading you in a different path. He may even mean to let you do something for Him that you couldn't do if everything went on now just as you'd like to have it."

This prudent mother didn't say, "I'm heartily glad at the turn things have taken. I always knew you were superior to him and not intended for each other."

Poor Hilda! She was a weak Christian at best, and now in this time of trial she couldn't rise on wings of faith and imagine how she'd ever rejoice at this deep sorrow. The light in her mother's face, as she talked of the blessedness of His service and her great delight in His will, was beyond her comprehension.

If anyone had told Hilda, when she sat that summer day on the porch hulling her strawberries and dreaming her pleasant dreams, that when the leaves left the branches bare and brown she would be a student in a female college in a distant state and that a person she hadn't then seen would be Enos's wife, she would have laughed in scorn. But so it was. Instead of baking and churning in the Turner homestead, she was knitting her brows over French verbs, profound propositions and puzzling statements in mental science. Meanwhile, Kittie Brown had attained the height of her ambition and gloried in possessing a farm, a span of horses and a husband, and daily taxed her ingenuity to discover how much of said baking and churning she could shirk out of.

Hilda had expended her unwonted energies on extra work until it was all done and life settled down into the old regular routine. It began to be unbearable and monotonous, varied only by going to church and the like, where she was obliged to see Enos and his wife in their wedding finery. That was the bitterest of all. She even chanced to sit with them in prayer meeting and look over the same book with Mrs. Enos Turner.

Mrs. Adams was overjoyed when Hilda suddenly said one day, "Mother, let me go away—let me go to school."

Here at last was what she'd wanted for her daughter. She'd kept a pleasant dream of this in her thoughts throughout Hilda's girlhood, purposing when the right time came to aim at carrying her plan into execution. Then "that fellow" had spoiled it all. (When Mrs. Adams talked to herself, she'd always called her prospective son-in-law "that fellow.") And now to think that Hilda wished this very thing and asked for it; surely things were working "together for good."

A new delightful world opened to Hilda. She had enjoyed no educational advantages except those the rural town afforded. She was always a bright scholar, but here her mind grew like a plant in the sunshine. Study became a delight—a passion. She grasped new truths eagerly, hungrily. She carried off her class honors. To her studies she brought the same energy she had given to scrubbing paint and polishing windows. How inane and petty her former life seemed now. Her chief interests were then: "What shall I get for dinner? What shall I have for a new dress? How shall it be made? When is the next sleigh ride or picnic?"

Other changes went on as well. Mingling with young ladies of culture and refinement, Hilda lost the manners of a shy country girl and took on the ease and grace that fit her so well.

Up till now she hadn't been required to write that schoolgirl's horror, a composition. The demands along that line weren't small in this institution, and here Hilda found a fascination she'd never dreamed of. If she could have, she would have employed her whole time in writing for the literary society, now that she'd tried her wings and found how delightful it was to soar into the realms of imagination. She didn't dread the time when her course of study would close and she'd go back to the old life at home. She never could return to the old life. Books were her friends. She would gather them about her and, shut in from the world, read and study to her heart's content.

But where was the sorrow that was to stay with her, as she once thought, throughout her life? Gone, she knew not where—and she awoke to the fact that she'd been a blind simpleton. In one of her recent visits home, she attended the sewing society. She'd hardly realized, until then, the great change that had come over her. How irksome and vapid the talk seemed, and she used to enjoy it.

When she saw Enos, the blood rushed into her face, and her tongue refused to utter a word. The absurdity of supposing she'd ever loved him came over her, with intense mortification at remembering she'd become nearly distracted when he proved faithless. How could she ever have had one thought in common with him? What did he know of science or philosophy? He was a person without common intelligence and spoke poor English every time he opened his mouth. Then she wondered why she'd never noticed how foolish his conversation was with his coarse jokes and how disagreeable his face without the least trace of refinement. And yet he had the same eyes she once thought handsome. Why, the eyes of Maje, the family watchdog, were better than his; they were true and earnest. She shuddered as she thought how she might have been bound to him for life, and the awakening would have come someday. He hadn't changed; she had. She could scarcely refrain from expressing the contempt she felt for him.

If Hilda had only known that Mrs. Blake said she "shouldn't wonder if Hildy Adams was going into a decline, for she don't git over her disappointment one bit. I watched her when Enos and she shook hands, and she got jist as red as a piny, and then she was kin o' whitelike and still, all the balance of the evening."

Others knew she was changed, too, though they couldn't exactly define it. This cultured, self-possessed young woman, with grace and dignity befitting a princess, was surely not the Hilda Adams they were acquainted with.

But she hadn't seen all the silvery lining of the cloud that once overshadowed her. Sometimes a soul develops like a hothouse plant; the change from tiny leaf to bud and flower is rapid and wonderful. Other souls, transplanted from rocky soil, grow more slowly, though just as surely. Hilda for the last five years had professed to knowing God, but as yet she hadn't progressed in her intimacy with Him. Christian duties were irksome to her, and like many another young professor, her chief enquiry had been, not "Lord, what will You have me do?"

but "Lord, what is the very least amount of service You'll accept from me?" and "How much may I enjoy the world and yet be Your child and gain heaven at last? Can I get along without doing this, and must I give up that?"

And so the battle raged between inclination and conscience. God was to her a hard master, an inexorable tyrant; yet fear compelled her to serve Him. That was her religion. Whatever it did for her, it didn't make her happy. One day something changed. One of those breezes from the heavenly shore that we call a revival passed over the college at B. Many came to Christ, and others who were nominal in their faith became new creatures indeed in Christ Jesus.

This same wonderful blessing came to Hilda's heart. She had never dreamed of such richness and power in the love of Christ, such sweet peace, such glorious promises—all hers by faith. The Savior was no longer to her a dim, misty presence, far away and vague. But He was one to whom her heart went out exultantly, whose name thrilled her as never did a beloved's name.

"Her heart found its master," novelists say. She, like Thomas, could now respond, "My Lord and my God." Oh, the bliss when one turns joyfully and for the first time sees Him, the chief among ten thousand, one's Master, King, Redeemer, living, loving, personal Friend! Weeping Mary quietly wiped her eyes when she "turned herself" and saw Him and said, "Rabboni." That is rest and peace no mere earthly passion possesses.

This call came to Hilda, and she answered with swift step to meet her Bridegroom, laying her heart with abandon on the altar to be His forever. Now indeed life seemed tenfold more beautiful and desirable. She wasn't simply Mary sitting at Jesus' feet. She was a soldier, equipped, loyal, eager, watching her Commander for a glance of His eye, a wave of His hand or the sound of His voice. Yet in all gentleness and humility she sought to know His will for her. She'd gladly leave all and serve Him as a missionary in some faraway land. But that wasn't His will.

Just off from Hilda's room at home was another smaller room, with a south window. It had been used only for storage. One day Hilda's mother had an idea for this room. The dear girl was coming home soon to stay. Mrs. Adams would surprise her by making the room into a study.

So this plain woman proceeded to gratify her aesthetic tastes in its furnishings. She had spent her life on a farm, doing its homely duties, but her soul was filled with poetry and art. She journeyed to the city by herself, taking a whole week for her purchases. She resolved that the room should be delicate and fine in its appointments. She was hard to please, weary clerks decided that day. They judged taste and length of purse by dress and, because of her homespun dress, showed her the least desirable carpet patterns—those with huge bouquets in crude colors.

Mrs. Adams, too much a student of nature, knew the red, green, yellow, blue and purple masses were out of taste. "They're too gaudy," she said in despair, after rejecting piece after piece. "I want something that looks sort of cool and yet bright."

The clerk took the hint. He brought out a body brussels, a light gray ground, with small bunches of pink moss roses and lilies of the valley, lying among soft, shadowy green leaves.

"This is it!" exclaimed Mrs. Adams.

She hadn't meant to pay so much for a carpet. But her conscience was comforted with the economical suggestion that it would outwear two of a cheaper sort.

A week later she sat down in the little room and looked about her with satisfaction. The walls had the same soft gray tint of the carpet and held some choice engravings and a bracket with a vase of flowers. A white muslin curtain adorned the window, and a small bookcase next to it was filled with a few well-chosen books. A writing desk stood in one corner, with a gray couch and an easy chair nearby. A couple of small window chairs and some ivy, climbing over the wall and down the curtains, added the finishing touch to the room.

"There!" said Mrs. Adams. "I don't see anything more to do. Some might think me extravagant, but I had to do it."

Most people write a poem once in their lives. Although their thoughts may not be expressed in silvery words, flowing out in musical chimes, they're poetry all the same. This room was Mrs. Adams's poem.

Here Hilda could begin her life's work, with the tree blossoms and the birds outside. She would write out "the old story" in different themes and ways, but always the same story. She would live a quiet life, cheering and ministering to her father and mother, now growing old but glad and content with Hilda at home again, sitting up in that room writing books.

Mrs. Adams, especially, felt that her cup was running over. All she longed for had come to pass. The Lord had done it for her. While she knit or while she trained her roses that clambered up to Hilda's window, she softly sang over and over,

> In each event of life how clear
>   Thy ruling hand I see.

Hilda didn't spend all her time in quiet. This new gift—this love that filled her heart—had to seek out more active forms of service. She gathered other girls and organized a meeting for prayer and Bible study. Sunday afternoons she went two miles beyond Willow Vale to the mills where many poor people lived. No one had seemed to care for their souls, but Hilda gathered the children and was for a time their teacher. She arranged to meet the mothers an afternoon each week. In that meeting weary mothers found a sympathizing Savior. She continued to do her Lord's work joyfully, wherever the door opened.

Old Mrs. Turner was growing feeble, for she'd let her son's wife fret her almost into the grave. She'd never quite forgiven Enos for choosing this sickly, ignorant, inefficient thing for daughter-in-law instead of Hilda. She had sent numerous messages lately inviting Hilda to visit her.

Contempt and indignation had long since ceased to trouble Hilda. So one bright morning she turned her steps in that direction. She carried a basket of delicious Antwerps to tempt the old woman's appetite and a few of what she took everyone—flowers.

The Turners never had "set much store" by flowers and fruit. Wheat, corn and hogs were the staple products on their farm.

It promised to be a warm day, so she left early and arrived before the Turners had finished breakfast. The family sitting around the table made a glum picture: The old mother looked worn and sad; the husband's shirt was soiled and wrinkled; the wife's dark dress looked grimy and had no collar, and her hair was falling about her face; and the two children were unwashed and uncombed. Dishes were set in disarray on the uninviting table.

Hilda used to come to the side door in the past, and so she did today, for it stood open. Framed in the doorway the girl made a pretty picture. Her light print dress fit her well, and her collar, cuffs, ribbon and gloves spoke of a refined nature. And the glowing face with calm, sweet eyes from under the broad-brimmed hat spoke of rest.

"I declare," said Mother Turner, "if it isn't Hildy Adams."

And the old woman stood up and bustled about. "I do say for it, if you don't git younger and handsomer every year," she continued, willing to plant a thorn in the faded daughter-in-law's heart.

A man with one sensitive fiber in his makeup, with the past fresh in his memory, would have felt abashed, in the presence of the graceful, cultured woman, who seemed to bring an indefinable sweetness into that close, fried-pork-scented room. And it couldn't be due to the aroma of the scarlet berries and the fragrance of the flowers in her basket. But Enos had no tender memories or sense of honor to trouble him.

He aimed to put himself on the old familiar footing and said in answer to his mother's remark, as he tilted back in his chair and surveyed the visitor, " 'Course, Hildy's all right. Ain't ye, Hildy? Just keep up good grit. The right feller'll be along someday. Then there'll be a weddin' down to the old place after all, hey, Hildy?"

Who can describe the mingled emotions that rushed over Hilda, sending a bright scarlet tinge to her cheeks and a look to her eye under which Enos quailed? Wounded pride and anger threatened to overwhelm her, but only for a moment. Then her face cleared, and her voice was calm.

"Did you say your rheumatism was troubling you again, Mrs. Turner?"

Then the old woman led the way into her own room and sat down and told

Hilda about her aches and pains. She said it was hard to sit and see things go to ruin and not be able to lift a finger. "She" tried her (Enos's wife was always "she" to Mrs. Turner) with her laziness and neglect of duties. "She" hadn't a knack at anything except spending money. The butter didn't bring as much by many cents a pound as it used to. And she herself worried and fretted from morning till night and would be glad when she was in her grave.

Mrs. Turner seemed to think the grave would right every wrong. She looked to it as a resting place where she could lie down to pleasant slumber and forget her past sad life. She didn't realize a Christless grave would be a far greater horror of darkness.

Then Hilda told the woman, whose body and soul had thus far been given up to this world, of Jesus and His love and of the blessed rest, not in the grave, but beyond. The dull ear listened, and the dim eye brightened, as the truth found its way through the rubbish of years. Eagerly Hilda told "the old story," the glad tidings of good things.

"Oh, dear," said the old woman, as Hilda rose to go, "why couldn't things have worked right? Enos would 'a' made a different man if you'd 'a' been his wife."

Hilda shuddered inwardly to think if she *had* been his wife—if it were her duty to sit opposite that coarse, illiterate, ill-kept man at that breakfast table and call him *husband!* How could she ever have been attracted? She blushed to remember how he was once a model of manliness in her eyes and his rude jokes considered keen wit. How blind she'd been! If only she'd heeded the advice of her wise-hearted mother, she might have been spared this mortification.

She moved swiftly over the little path on her way home, not stooping to pick the wildflowers at her feet or watch the squirrels at play. She went to her room and knelt before the Lord and thanked Him from the depths of her heart for spoiling her plans and turning, as she thought then, her joy into ashes. And what hadn't He given her in return? Wouldn't she trust Him more easily after this, though the way might look dark? Not the least of His mercy is that often He doesn't let us have our way.

She leaned from her window and buried her face in the honeysuckle blossoms that clambered around it. A sweet contentment filled her heart. How full and rich her life seemed; how thankful and happy she was. She could hear her mother's voice, tremulous with age, from the cool porch below, where she sat knitting and rocking. Mrs. Adams was singing her favorite hymn.

> Judge not the Lord by feeble sense,
>   But trust Him for His grace;
> Behind a frowning providence
>   He hides a smiling face.

At the next verse Hilda joined in.

> His purposes will ripen fast,
>> Unfolding every hour;
> The bud may have a bitter taste,
>> But sweet will be the flower.

"Why, Hilda," said her mother, looking up, "I thought you were hard at work."

"So I am hard at work, Mother," Hilda responded, as she tripped downstairs and out on the porch, kneeling beside her mother. "I'm going back over my life and tracing the 'smiling face' He hid behind that 'frowning providence' I thought would kill me that dreadful summer, when I gave you so much sorrow. It had a 'bitter taste,' sure enough, but, oh, how sweet the flower is! Mother, dear, I wouldn't change my life for anyone's. I'm so happy and love my work and my home so much. How rebellious I was that summer and thought He was hard with me. Then it mortifies me so that I didn't know my own heart better. How I must have tried you, Mother. I don't see how you were so patient with me, and I was so self-willed. How could I have been so deceived?"

"Remember those words, 'God is his own interpreter, and he will make it plain'? He has made it plain, hasn't He, dear child?" said her mother. "His will was for you to sit in your pretty room and write books that refresh the souls of His saints. And you fretted because He wouldn't let you make butter and cheese instead and drudge from morning till night to get a little more money to buy a little more land—and be bound to a man who would have been to you like a clod. Your life would have been hard and bitter. He does make all things work together for good to those who love Him."

The next five years brought changes. Both the father and mother slept in the old churchyard. No, they went to be with Christ. How could Hilda have lived through those desolate days when she first sat alone in the old church pew, if she believed they slept in those two narrow graves she could see from the window and if her faith couldn't hear their voices joining the chorus of the grand old hymn they loved so well?

> Hallelujah to the Lamb who has purchased our pardon.

Week after week Hilda lingered in the old home trying to convince herself to let it pass into other hands and leave it forever. But how could she give up that little room where she had been so happy, that seemed fragrant with her mother's memory?

The thing seemed to settle itself. Faithful John and Hannah, the couple who had grown gray in serving the family, went on with their work, and the machinery of house and farm moved in its accustomed grooves. Then Hilda wondered why she needed to leave. Where could she find a better place for her work than her dear old home? And why shouldn't a woman carry on a farm as well as a man?

Once she decided to stay, life settled down into calm again, and she took up the dropped stitches to continue weaving her life's web patiently and bravely. But it wasn't as desolate as one might imagine, for a kingly guest, unseen by mortals, abode at her house.

New mounds appeared, too, in the Turner cemetery lot. Enos's wife and mother had both been laid under the snows that very winter.

Now Enos, after a brief season of being a widower, was looking about for a successor. He sat on his fence one evening in early spring and whittled a large stick down to a small point. While he whittled he thought, and thinking was new business to him. He seemed to arrive at conclusions, however, for he presently dismounted and went into the house. Not long afterward he emerged clad in his Sunday suit, with his hair oiled and plastered to his head and with other extras he wasn't accustomed to bestowing on himself on a weekday.

"I'll bet a cookie," said old Mrs. Peters, peeping through her syringa bush at him, "that Enos Turner is goin' a-courtin', and his wife's only been dead three months."

Hilda was standing in the twilight at her front gate when Enos sauntered up and paused, remarking about the weather and crops. Hilda could only return civil replies, while considering how she could excuse herself and get away. She found it hard to stand there and suffer another consequence of her early foolishness, with this coarse man feeling privileged to call her "Hildy" and presuming to inquire familiarly into her affairs. She lingered a moment, thinking he intended to offer to buy the coveted east lot or a horse or cow. How amazed she was to hear his offer included not only the whole farm, but its mistress!

Enos had planned it out as he sat on the fence and lost no time in laying it before her. To push his suit he argued that her farm would "go to ruin without a man to manage it." The two farms "jined" would make them the biggest property holders in the town. And finally he was disposed to "do the fair thing, bein' as you waited for me so many years."

Hilda said nothing but turned and walked quickly toward the house.

"Oh! Come now, Hildy," Enos called after her coaxingly. "Didn't think ye'd hold grit agin me more'n ten years."

Undaunted, he confided to some of his friends at the corner grocery his intent "to git hold of the Adams farm 'fore long. Hildy'd come round, if she was kind o' offish now. Never saw a woman yet that wouldn't git married—jes' give her a chance."

One of the most obtuse, presuming, conceited creatures with breath is a coarse-grained, ignorant man. Nothing, however precious and unattainable, is to be despaired of if he wants it.

But the day arrived when Hilda decked the house with her mother's flowers and wore the dress of silvery gray she'd set her heart on years before. She left the old home leaning on the arm of a tall man, not Enos, to fill a large place as wife of a pastor in a distant city. All her experiences had fitted her to become a choice worker in the white fields to which the Master sent her.

When Hilda's husband, the Reverend Lee Winthrop, had paid a flying visit a few months earlier to his old friend, Hilda's pastor, he wasn't searching for an "estimable woman" to preside over his parish or fill the place of his deceased mother. He'd never had a wife, though not a few would have gladly assumed that relationship to this fine man. He was past thirty-five, but his mother had as yet filled the place in his heart and amply met the parish requirements regarding the claims they're supposed to have on a minister's wife. So this turning of the last page in Hilda's girl life was no mere business transaction. It came suddenly to both of them.

One evening Hilda was tying up the sweet peas, because her mother loved them so much. She wasn't looking for her destiny at all. And when Mr. Winthrop passed through the gate and up the narrow path among the roses, he had no thought of searching for a wife—certainly not in this little out-of-the-way place.

Perhaps the good man who brought him to call and left him while he visited a sick parishioner had a wise idea in his head. The two people conversed about flowers, art, books and kindred subjects, discovering a whole mine of thought in common. And by the time they had touched upon the one great theme dear to both, their Master and His work, they knew then as well as they ever did afterward that it would be blessed to spend their lives together. When the visit extended from days into weeks, each felt they'd known the other a whole lifetime. And Hilda, with gladness in her heart, took on this new joy that crowned her days.

Where He Spent Christmas

O h, Mother, I'll get back before it snows much, and I won't mind if a few snowflakes fall on me. Please don't object to my going. A walk is just what I need."

Edna Winters drew on her gloves and stepped from the door of her home, a low-roofed farmhouse on the hill, which, in its gray old age, seemed a part of the hill itself.

It wasn't the beauty of the afternoon that tempted Edna out, for the leaden sky almost met the gray hills. All wore the same sober hue—sky, hills, house, and leafless trees. The wind howled fiercely through the pine trees in the yard, seeming but deep shadows on the general grayness, and occasional snowflakes were already flying about.

Mr. Winters looked through the front window after his daughter and shook his head. "Mother, there's a big storm brewing, if I'm not mistaken. The child shouldn't have gone."

The mother came to inspect the sky.

"Oh, well, she's young and doesn't mind the weather like us old folks. I was only twenty years old, and I remember just how tired I used to get cooped up in the house so much. Besides, she wanted to go to the post office. Tomorrow's Christmas, and the post office will be open only an hour or two."

Mr. Winters was growing old, and rheumatism was keeping him a prisoner just now, so he returned to the fire and his newspaper.

The town with the post office lay a little over two miles away, and Edna often walked in and out for the mere pleasure of it. Even on this dismal day she tripped lightly along, humming a tune and stopping at the edge of the pine woods to gather a few squawberries and a bit of moss. Then, glancing at the threatening sky, she hurried along. Before she reached town, snow was falling thick and fast, and the wind was swirling it into little mounds almost as soon as it came down. She was all but blown inside the door of the post office, with feathery flakes covering her from head to foot.

Moments earlier, Mr. Hugh Monteith had stepped across the street from his banking house and stood waiting for the afternoon mail to be distributed. He turned his head as the door opened to admit Edna.

Removing the veil that protected her head, she shook and brushed herself and walked over to the stove.

Mr. Monteith sensed at once that here was the face he had been in search of for years. Contrary to his own code of etiquette, he stared, though retreating behind a pillar to do so. He took in the whole picture: the face of a pure, clear tint that belongs to a certain type of brown eyes and hair; the hair gathered into a coil at the back of the head, except for one or two loose curls straying from it; the eyes sweet and serious. Although the banker dealt many hours of the day with dollars and cents, notes and bills, he still recognized poetry when he saw it, and that golden brown curl was to him a bit of a poem.

Then her dress was peculiar, and his taste pronounced it perfect for the occasion: a walking dress of soft, dark brown, glinted by a lighter shade of the same color; a brown jacket of substantial cloth; a little brown hat with a brown and white wing perched on one side of it. Her only color was a soft pink the cold air had placed on her cheeks with delicate skill. His quick eye noted the neat glove and the slender boot poised on the hearth of the stove. She looked like a brown thrush about to spread its wings. But she didn't fly; she walked over to the delivery and received a package of letters and papers, asking in low, clear tones, "Is the Eastern mail in?" The voice, refined and pure, was in keeping with eyes, hair and dress.

Securing his mail, Mr. Monteith resolved at once to follow Edna. He thought he knew all the young ladies in town, but this lovely revelation he'd never seen and wondered who she could be. He turned corner after corner as she did, not caring where he went, only that he kept her in view. To his astonishment he soon found himself in the open country. It wasn't a day he'd have chosen for a pleasure walk in the country; the snow eddied and whirled and almost blinded him. But if he lost that face, his ideal realized, would he ever find it again? He had no choice, so on he strode, congratulating himself for having on an overcoat and heavy boots.

The little brown-clad figure ahead of him sped briskly on, and faster and faster came the snow. The wind roared and howled through the pine woods, drifting the snow along the road. Mr. Monteith had a new motive for his journey now. He must protect this young girl and couldn't leave her in such a desolate place with a storm raging. He quickened his steps.

Despair was creeping over Edna. What if she sank down in this lonely place and couldn't go on? She'd left the main road a few minutes before, and this one by the pine woods was seldom traveled. No one would likely find her. In dismay she turned and looked behind her. But no sooner did she see a man coming toward her than fear took hold of her. With new impetus, she ran on as fleetly as a deer.

Mr. Monteith ran too as fast as he could, wondering if she really were of the earth and if she hadn't some means of traveling he didn't possess. He must reach her anyway.

Edna at last stopped before an immense drift that lay directly across the road. She would have plunged in, but Mr. Monteith had reached her by then.

"If you'll allow me to go on first, I think I can make a path for you," he said.

Edna looked up quickly, somewhat reassured by the strong, pleasant tones and the true, gray eyes that looked into hers.

"Let me introduce myself," Mr. Monteith said, pulling a card out of his inner coat pocket and handing it to Edna.

The girl's fear left as she read "Hugh Monteith & Co., Bankers." The name of Monteith had long been familiar to her. She remembered hearing her father speak of having some business with that bank.

"Well, I'm Edna Winters. My father is Samuel Winters, and we live a little more than half a mile from here."

"Then we're acquainted, I'm sure, for your father is one of our depositors. Now let me try to break a road through this barricade," he said and dashed into it.

But as far as he could see through the blinding storm, he could tell the drift reached a long distance ahead. It would take too much time to tread it down, and the cold wind cut like a knife.

He returned to Edna's side. "It's almost impossible to do it. We'll have to hurry now—or die in this storm. Excuse me—this is the best way."

And the tall form stooped and picked up Edna before she knew what he was doing. Then with long strides he waded into the sea of snow. Silence covered them.

But the girl being carried along in the storm was thinking, despite the danger and her protector's gallantry. She felt a little provoked at being snatched up that way without her permission, as if she were a bale of cotton, and provoked, too, at herself for getting into such a predicament. If only she'd stayed at home as her mother advised! Her mother always feared something would happen to her going through those woods by herself, and here it was.

Suddenly she saw humor in the situation and wanted to laugh but was afraid to. She stole a glance at the face beside hers—a finely cut face—but the eyes held no smile, only earnest intent.

When they reached the ground where the snow was level, Mr. Monteith set Edna on her feet and drew her hand through his arm. The two plodded on in silence through the blinding snow and wind that yanked their breath away. Wherever the drifts had built up a barrier Mr. Monteith picked up the girl again and carried her. But he didn't set her down again, for he'd discovered she was almost overcome by fatigue, try as she might to hide it.

"Let me—walk now—if you will," she said between gusts of icy wind.

"Miss Winters—you're my prisoner—until I place you at your—father's door," he said, turning his head toward her so she could hear but not averting his eyes from the way ahead.

She yielded with grace and began to feel some gratitude toward her deliverer.

At home, meanwhile, Mr. Winters had been pacing back and forth from the fire to the window. "Why doesn't the child come?" he said. "I'm sure something has happened to her. If I could only go out and see, I would. But I'd make poor headway in those drifts."

"Why, Father, I think she wouldn't start back in this storm," Mrs. Winters said for the tenth time. Nevertheless, she placed her rocking chair by the window and looked down the road more than she sewed.

And Mr. Winters did the only thing he could. He fled to his unfailing refuge, asking the God who rules the storms to protect his daughter.

Suddenly they saw a strange man bearing their daughter up the hill in his arms. The door was opened long before the two reached it.

"I'm all right, Mother," Edna called out from the porch.

"Why, it's Mr. Monteith, as sure as I live," said Edna's father.

"Yes, Mr. Winters," said Mr. Monteith, "I found a stray lamb of yours on the highway and brought her home."

"May God reward you," said Mrs. Winters, clasping his hand warmly. "I've been very anxious. I didn't see what was to become of her if she was coming in this terrible storm. How providential you happened to be going her way."

Mr. Monteith winced a little at this.

"You'll stay with us tonight, of course," Mr. Winters said.

"Oh, no, indeed! Thank you! I must get back before dark. I'll rest a few minutes, though."

The Storm King was out in full force that day. During those few minutes huge banks piled themselves against windows and doors, and the wind shrieked and moaned like a demon, shaking the house to its foundations.

"Now," said Mr. Winters, as his guest rose to go, "it's madness for you to think of going home tonight, and I must insist you stay. I'm disabled just now, or I'd harness old Prince and get you through."

"Do stay," Edna added, with a pleading tone in her voice. "It isn't safe for you to go."

Mrs. Winters entreated also with motherly words.

How could he resist such urging, especially when it was what he desired? So he agreed and was soon comfortably established in the large old rocker by the fire.

He knew all about fashionable houses, but this old house that looked small and yet stretched itself out into many cozy rooms was a new experience for him. It was quaint and unique, and so was the little household. It was like stepping into a book. What was the charm of the low-ceilinged room he sat in? Was it the broad fireplace, with the logs blazing and snapping? Mr. Winters had stoves to warm the house, but he insisted on keeping this fire to look at.

When they gathered about the tea table, his critical eye noticed many details a less refined man wouldn't have: fine white table linen, delicate old-fashioned china, a piece or two of highly polished silver, and the table not overloaded with too great variety, yet everything delicious and abundant.

Mr. and Mrs. Winters, too, though unpretentious, were persons of refinement and intelligence. Mr. Monteith was puzzled to understand how a young girl, reared in so much seclusion, should possess such grace and culture as Edn did. After tea, when she played and sang, his mystification increased, for the birdlike voice and delicate touch were superior to most he had heard among his city friends. He discovered in conversation, however, that Edna had spent the last six years in one of the finest schools in Boston, staying with her aunt's family. Now she'd returned to gladden the eyes of those two, who almost set her up as an idol. And she had returned unspoiled, taking up her daily home duties again with real zest.

Mr. Monteith found Mr. Winters congenial company. He'd read extensively and was keen in argument, throwing in a bit of literature or a witty story, as the case required. Edna brought her crocheting and made herself into a picture beside the fireplace, her changing expressions and piquant remarks lending interest to the dullest subject.

"It's my opinion, Mr. Monteith," said Mr. Winters, as a fierce blast dashed sheets of snow against the windows, "that, in all probability, you'll be obliged to spend your Christmas with us. If this storm continues at this rate you'll be imprisoned here."

"For which I'll be most thankful," he answered.

"Well, our turkey is all ready, and we'll thank kind Providence for sending you to us, snowbound as we are."

Mr. Winters took down the old Bible and read "a portion with judicious care." After having a hymn and prayer and exchanging good nights, Mr. Monteith was in the guest chamber—a little white room under the eaves, cold-looking in its simplicity except for the firelight glow.

"The name of that chamber was Peace," thought Mr. Monteith, as he surveyed it. And with Bunyan's Pilgrim he felt he'd reached "already the next door to heaven."

It surely must be the "chamber of peace," because "the window opened toward sunrising," and in the morning a glorious panorama spread itself before him. Fences and all unsightly objects had disappeared. Just one broad expanse of whiteness spread out as far as the eye could reach. The rough old hills, from foot to summit, wore a robe of unsullied whiteness; the soft white garment rested lightly on roof and tree, and over all the rising sun shed rays of rosy light. It accorded well with Mr. Monteith's spirit when he heard Mr. Winters singing,

> The New Jerusalem comes down,
> Adorned with shining grace.

The host and his visitor launched into a lively conversation immediately after breakfast, finding countless interests in common. So occupied was Mr. Monteith with the father that he seemed to bestow little attention on the daughter; yet no word or look of hers escaped him.

At one time the previous day's perilous walk was mentioned, and Mr. Winters again expressed his gratitude.

"So strange," he remarked, "that you were coming this way. How did you happen to start out in such a storm?"

Mr. Monteith murmured something about "business," while a slight flush tinged his cheeks. At once he asked Mr. Winters, "What effect do you suppose the resumption of specie payment will have on the state of the country?"

And the unsuspecting old gentleman was ready to enter with avidity into a discussion of that subject.

With Christmas dinner duly disposed of, Edna opened the piano, and Mr. Monteith delighted the older people by joining his exquisite tenor to Edna's voice in some old hymns. Mr. Winters called for some of his favorites—St. Martin's "Golden Hill" and "Exhortation"—and listened with the tears in his eyes at their faithful rendering, even putting in a few notes of bass himself among the quavers of old St. Martin's.

Not until the shadows stole into the room did Mr. Monteith depart, much to his own regret as well as his hosts', with many promises of future visits.

A few days after Christmas the stage driver left at the door a small box marked "Samuel Winters." The old gentleman put on his glasses and opened it with curiosity. A lovely bouquet of roses, carnations and violets lay there. He lifted it out carefully, and a card marked "Hugh Monteith" fell from it.

"That's odd," he said, glancing at Edna, "sending these things to me. They're pretty, though, of course." He buried his face in a rose, then hummed,

> How sweet the breath beneath the hill
> Of Sharon's dewy rose.

After taking in more of the rose's fragrance, he called, "Mother, come here and smell this pink. It's the one my mother used to border her flower beds with when I was a boy."

Then he handed the bouquet into Edna's care while he imagined himself once again in his mother's garden, tying up the sweet peas and training the morning glories. How each flower, like a dear human face, stood before him gazing into his eyes: damask roses, Johnny-jump-ups, larkspur, bachelor's buttons, ragged ladies, marigolds, hollyhocks and a host of others that are out of fashion now. That bouquet furnished him with a pleasant reverie for an hour. It brought no less pleasure to Edna. Their new friend hadn't forgotten them, and her intuition told her for whom the lovely blossoms were intended.

After that it grew to be quite a thing for Mr. Samuel Winters to receive a box of flowers. He always pretended to appropriate them to himself, much to Edna's pleasure, as he also did Mr. Monteith's not infrequent visits to the Pines.

"That's an uncommon young man," he often remarked after a pleasant evening's discussion, "coming so far to chat with me. He's one among a thousand

Most of them haven't time nowadays to speak a civil word to an old man."

He had a deeper purpose in this than might have been supposed. Most things he thought over as he sat looking into the fire. What if this young man unwittingly stole his darling's heart and then flitted away to some other flower, leaving this, his own treasure, with the soul gone out of her life. He believed Mr. Monteith to be an honorable man, but then he'd hedge his blossom about and guard it carefully. There'd be no opportunity for tender speech that meant nothing.

One day Edna was in town walking on a busy street. A prancing span of grays before a light sleigh caught her attention instantly. Among the furs and heavy robes sat Mr. Monteith and a young lady, as beautiful to Edna as a dream. Even in a hurried glance she noticed the pink and white complexion and the blue eyes, peeping through golden frizzes set off by a dark-blue velvet hat with a long white plume. Mr. Monteith raised his hat and bowed to Edna in pleased surprise.

Edna walked on with a little pang at her heart. It might have been less, if she'd known how Miss Paulina Percival had secured an invitation to ride.

Emerging from a store, at no coincidence, just as Mr. Monteith left the bank and was about to step into his sleigh, she engaged him in conversation. Then she exclaimed, "Oh, Mr. Monteith! What a lovely span of grays! They match perfectly. Naughty man, you never asked me to try them," she added with a pretty pout.

"Suppose I ask you now," he said. As he spoke those words, he said to himself, *Miss Winters would never have done that.*

Miss Percival needed no urging and was soon seated in triumph by Mr. Monteith's side, the envy of other young women in the city.

That night Edna stood at the window of her little room, gazing out on the earth that glittered like diamonds in the moonlight. She didn't often find herself in this restless, gloomy mood, with no heart for anything, and began chiding herself for it. Why had the light suddenly gone out of everything and life seemed so flat and dull? Was it simply because she'd seen that bewitching-looking girl riding with Mr. Monteith? And what of it? Was she foolish enough to believe he cared for her, a simple country girl, just because he'd given her a few flowers and called there. He probably considered these common attentions and offered them to many others.

Her cheeks burned at remembering the delight she had felt in his company. The last few weeks had been the happiest she'd ever known. Nothing he might say would justify her, either. She was vexed at herself. Here she'd turned out to be just like any other silly girl, holding her heart in her hand, ready to bestow it unasked. In her self-accusing attitude she forgot that looks and tones may speak volumes in the absence of words.

"Now, Edna Winters," she told herself, staring out at the white hills, "you might as well look things in the face tonight and have it done with. You'll probably spend a great part of your life on this very hill, living on in just the way you did before you knew him. Why not? That's how Samantha Moore and Jane Williams have been doing for many years. They keep right on and on and on. Nothing happens to them. There's no change in their lives. Why should there be in mine? They clean house spring and fall, can fruit, go to town, have the sewing society and so on."

Edna shuddered a little at the picture she'd sketched of her own future. Those women were two neighbors, whose homes nestled peacefully among the hills in front of her. Then, from the sitting room, she heard her father's voice with a tremble in the tones. She walked over to the stovepipe that came up from below to warm her room and bent her head to hear the words.

Oh, God, our help in ages past,
    Our strength in years to come,
Our refuge from the stormy blast,
    And our eternal home.

Sure enough! God would be her "strength in years to come," even though they may be wearisome years. A little "stormy blast" had swept over her. She would fly to her refuge and then the "eternal home." What if this life wasn't just as we'd have it? *The next one will be,* she thought, and so she lay down in peace and slept.

"Well, look!" said Mr. Winters one bright day. "Whom have we here?"

The jingling bells suddenly stopped, and two gray horses and a handsome sleigh stood in front of the gate. "Mr. Monteith, eh? He's most likely come to take me out riding," he said, with a twinkle in his eyes.

"Miss Edna, will you go for a ride?" Mr. Monteith asked when the greetings were over.

Edna's eyes sought her mother's for reply. Not every gentleman, no matter how great and rich, would this primitive, independent father and mother entrust with their treasure. Yes, Edna might go, but he'd be sure to bring her home before dark?

"Trust me. Didn't I bring her home before dark once?" he laughingly asked.

The two were soon tucked among the robes, skimming briskly over the smooth, hard surface, surely the next thing to flying. They flew about the streets of the town a little while and even happened upon Miss Paulina, who stared at Edna.

"Whoever can that be with Mr. Monteith?" she asked the young lady beside her.

Then their route stretched many miles out into the quiet country. The journey was long, but not tedious. In time with the slow, silvery chime of the bells, words were spoken low—the old musical, mysterious words that established a covenant between those two and needed only a word from the father and mother and minister to make binding and never-ending.

Mr. Monteith was said, by young women of the town, to be without heart—at least all their arts had failed to find it. Even skillful Miss Percival hadn't succeeded, much to her sorrow. To be sure, the heart was of small account to her—only so she might be mistress of the stately Monteith mansion, might possess those gray ponies and glitter in the silks and jewels and laces his money would buy. She had no heart herself; her shallow nature allowed no room for one.

Though Paulina had failed thus far, she wasn't discouraged. Mr. Monteith's mother was old and feeble; she would die someday. "We shall see what we shall see," she would say to herself. Then, of course, he would need someone to preside over his home. And who was so well suited to adorn it as she, the town's acknowledged beauty?

When the time of birds and blossoms had arrived again, and picnics and excursions were revived, Paulina said to her dearest friend, "What do you think that delightful man has gotten up now? Mr. Monteith, I mean. He's to have a little breakfast party in the country—just a few of us. We're to go in carriages. I daresay you'll be invited, too. Isn't it a charming novelty? I presume it's to an old uncle and aunt of his." And the butterfly girl tripped on without waiting for replies.

Accordingly, one balmy June morning a merry company alighted at the Pines and was ushered into a fairylike room.

Green vines crept and twined along the white walls, trailing over doors and windows and down the muslin curtains as if they grew there. The flowers weren't made into stiff bouquets, but here and there a handful of roses or sweet-scented violets adorned the room. The old fireplace lost itself in callas, fern and ivy, while the mantel blossomed out into tube roses and mosses. One of the recesses formed by the large chimney was turned into a leafy bower, with the bells of white lilies fringing the green archway.

"Beautiful!" murmured a guest.

"Exquisite!" said another. "I do believe we've come to a wedding."

In another moment Mr. Monteith and his bride stood in the niche under the lilies, and the minister spoke the mystic words that declared them "no more twain, but one."

Edna wasn't glittering in satin and jewels. Her dress was like a soft white cloud floating about her, looped here and there with a cluster of lilies of the valley. A wreath of the same flowers fastened her veil, and the sweet face and luminous eyes shining through its folds seemed like another rare flower.

When the formalities and congratulations were over, Mr. and Mrs. Monteith passed down the walk under the spreading branches to their carriage. The apple blossoms showered fragrant blessings on them as they went their way.

And the bridegroom whispered, "Do you remember the first time you and I came up this hill together?"

Buckwheat Cakes

I t was a little house and a new little family of two—and only six months since they became a family and set up housekeeping. As a matter of course everything in the house was new. One may prate of antiquities and the associations clinging to them that render them beautiful, but, after all, most couples will look back with delight to the time when their surroundings were fresh and pretty. A new pine table or a bright new tin pan has its own charm. This house was a little gem, from the delicately appointed guest chamber to the cement-line cellar.

Mr. and Mrs. Philip Thorne sat at their breakfast table, sparkling with new china and silver, in a dining room cheerful with pretty carpet, plants, a singing bird, warmth and sunshine. The poor girl who peeped in at the window might well wonder "if heaven were nicer than that." The coffee urn sent up a fragrant little cloud, as Mrs. Thorne poured it into delicate cups, with just the right quantity of cream and coffee. The steak was tender and juicy, and the baked potatoes were done to a turn. Yet a slight cloud hung over that table that didn't come from the coffee urn.

"Joanna doesn't understand how to make buckwheat cakes very well, I guess," said Mr. Thorne, eyeing the doubtful-looking pile she'd just deposited on the table.

"Joanna didn't make these. I made them with my own hands," responded Mrs. Thorne.

Those hands were delicate and small, but, truth to tell, they weren't much more skilled than Joanna's.

"Then it must be the baking that spoils them," Mr. Thorne said.

"Why, Philip, how do you know they're spoiled? I'm sure they look all right," said his wife.

"That's just where you and I don't agree, my dear. They're white-looking. They should be a rich brown."

"Whoever heard of brown buckwheat cakes? They are always very light-colored."

"I beg your pardon, but they are not, as far as my observation goes," said her husband. "Besides, these are thick. They should be thin and delicate-looking."

"You're thinking of something else, Philip," said Mrs. Thorne patronizingly. "Buckwheat cakes never look different from these. I've seen them many places."

"You never ate them at my mother's, or you couldn't say so, my dear."

Mrs. Thorne stirred her coffee vigorously. Was Philip going to turn out to be one of those detestable men who always go about telling how "my mother" used to do—"my mother," as if no other mother in the world amounted to anything.

"I've always noticed," she said, "that a person imagines, after being away from home a few years, that there's nothing quite as good as he used to get at home. Even the same things never taste the way they used to. The reason is clear—tastes change as a person grows older."

This sage remark was just a little annoying to Mr. Thorne; he was ten years his wife's senior and didn't like allusions to "growing older."

"No one need try to convince me," he answered quite warmly, "that I'll ever stop enjoying the dishes my mother used to fix if I live to be as old as Methuselah! She's the best cook I ever knew, and she never made cakes like these."

"My mother is a pattern housekeeper," said Mrs. Thorne, with a little flash of her blue eye, "and her cakes look precisely like these."

" 'The proof of the pudding is in the eating,' you'll admit, I suppose. Joanna doesn't need to bring in more cakes for me. They have a sour, bitter taste that's decidedly unpalatable."

And he rose from the table, went into the hall and passed through the front door without his usual parting.

Satan once worked immense mischief by means of an apple. Now he must needs come into that pretty dining room and hide in a plate of buckwheat cakes. It was the first approach to a quarrel in this household and the first buckwheat cakes of the season!

When Mr. Thorne had said the day before, "What if we have some buckwheat cakes," Ruey didn't at all feel the confidence in her ability that her answer implied. But then there was her recipe book. They couldn't be difficult, she reasoned. The recipe said, "Mix warm water, flour and yeast, and let it rise until morning." She had followed these instructions faithfully, and here was the result.

Ruey Thorne, unlike some young wives, didn't think it interesting to profess utter ignorance of domestic matters. On the contrary, she had an ambition to excel as a housekeeper. She had a general knowledge of many things, but every housekeeper knows that practice only brings perfection. It's one thing to watch Bridget make bread a few times and another thing entirely to make it oneself. So much of Ruey's knowledge was theory, not yet reduced to practice, that she imagined herself much more skillful than she really was. Consequently she didn't claim her husband's forbearance because of inexperience. Philip wasn't rich, and she desired to be an economical wife; so she didn't employ an experienced cook and chambermaid but tried to accomplish it all with the aid of an untrained German girl.

"Of course I'll want to direct all my work," she'd remarked with housewifely pride.

If Philip had only understood a little better, he needn't have brought out his mother's veteran cakes in such cruel comparison with these very young ones.

That day wasn't comfortable for either of them. The blue eyes flashed out a tear occasionally, and Ruey told herself, "Who would've thought Philip cared so much for eating! His mother's cakes, indeed! As if anybody could equal my dear precious mother in anything!"

And he told himself he "wouldn't have thought Ruey would have flashed up in that way for such a small thing, and to me, too. Humph! I'd just like for her to taste my mother's cakes. It would open her eyes a little."

Later in the day they told the same parties, "I'm just ashamed of myself for getting spunky about such a little thing. I wish Philip would come. I'll have muffins for tea just to please him. I know I can make muffins," and, "Poor little Ruey, I went off like a bear this morning. I must hurry home. I'll just step in at Barnard's and get that little panel of lilies for her."

So the muffins and the lilies were laid, peace offerings on the domestic altar, and the skies were clear again.

The next morning Ruey went into her neat little kitchen to reconstruct those cakes. She'd see if it weren't possible to suit her husband in this.

"Let me see. He said they were too thick. I'll thin them then. He said they were sour and bitter. Sugar is sweet and should remedy that." So in went the water to thin them and the sugar to sweeten them.

"He said they should be brown, and brown they shall be, if fire will do it." So she proceeded to make a furious fire to heat the griddle. "Now," she said to Joanna, "carry in the coffee and chops; then come and bake the cakes."

The husband and wife were chatting cheerfully when the first installment of cakes arrived—a few crumpled, burnt scraps of something.

"Why, what's this?" said Mr. Thorne.

"Cakes!" said Joanna triumphantly. "And she fixed 'em," she added, pointing to Mrs. Thorne.

The two looked at the cakes, then at each other, and broke into peals of laughter.

"The griddle must be too hot," Mrs. Thorne said and vanished into the kitchen.

She scraped the smoking griddle, washed it and greased it. Next she stirred the gray liquid and placed two or three spoonfuls on the griddle. Then she tried to turn them; sticking plaster never stuck tighter than those cakes adhered to that griddle. She worked carefully, slipping her knife just under the outer edge of the cake, then gradually approaching the center. But when the final flop came, they went into little sticky hopeless heaps.

"They're too thin," she said.

Joanna brought flour.

"Now we'll have it all right."

Then another set took their places on the griddle. These held together and turned—triumph at last! But they didn't look inviting. Mrs. Thorne tasted one. Then she made a wry face.

"Joanna," she said, with forced calmness, "you can throw this batter away."

Then she went back to the dining room, looking very hot and red, and said meekly to Philip, "The cakes are failures this morning. We'll try again tomorrow."

Philip, who'd lost himself in the morning paper, roused up to say, "Don't trouble about them anymore. We have enough else that's nice."

"The cakes will be all right another time, Philip. A mistake was made. They were too thin this morning. Mother never makes them thin."

Philip looked as if he'd like to say, "I don't care what your mother does. My mother's cakes are nice and thin and can't be beaten," but he didn't.

Mrs. Thorne had no intention of abandoning buckwheat cakes as a failure, not she. It wasn't her way to give up easily and yield to discouragement. Difficulties only strengthened her determination to conquer.

"I'll see if I'm to be vanquished by a buckwheat cake," she said, studying her recipe book that same evening. "I shouldn't wonder if there wasn't enough yeast in those others," she said, as she mixed some fresh batter and added an extra quantity of yeast. "Keep them warm while rising," the recipe read. She placed them near the register in the dining room and retired with a complacent feeling that now all the conditions had been surely met.

"The total depravity of inanimate things." Mrs. Thorne had reason to believe in that doctrine the next morning when she entered her dining room and found a small sea of batter on her carpet, surrounding the pail and widening in all directions. This stuff could hardly be called "inanimate," for it oozed from under the pail cover in a most animated manner.

"It's light, at least. That's one consolation," said Mrs. Thorne, trying to be philosophical as she ruefully surveyed her carpet. Then she hastily called Joanna to clean it up. "Philip shouldn't see that."

When the cakes were brought in that morning, Ruey cast a little triumphant look at Philip. By dint of a hot griddle and much grease they had a streak of brown here and there.

"Horrible!" exclaimed Mrs. Thorne, after her first mouthful. "These cakes are sourer than vinegar." Philip shouldn't be the first to speak of any lack, as if she weren't supposed to know more about such matters than he. "What does ail them? I'm sure I made them exactly right this time. I must tell Joanna to put some sugar in them."

"My dear wife, if you'll allow me, I'd suggest soda instead of sugar."

"Really!" responded Ruey, her pride touched in an instant. There it was—he actually thought he knew more about cooking than she did. "And, pray, how do you happen to be so wise? You must have assisted your mother in the kitchen," she said, with a slight curl of her pretty lip. "Up there in the country, boys do those things, I suppose."

Philip was nettled. Ruey had cast little slurs on his country home before, when she got her spirit up. He controlled himself, however, saying only, "I don't profess to understand the science of cookery, but I do know a little chemistry and understand that an acid requires an alkali to neutralize it."

Mrs. Thorne went straight to the kitchen—shutting the door after her with the least perceptible bang—and sprinkled a liberal allowance of soda into the batter. Then she returned to the dining room to await developments. These cakes were yellow and spotted and smelled of hot lye.

Mr. Thorne went bravely through a few mouthfuls until he encountered a lump of soda; the wry face that followed was wholly involuntary.

"I declare they're horrid!" exclaimed Ruey, bursting into tears. "I knew soda would spoil them—bitter stuff!"

Mr. Thorne didn't then attempt to show why soda wouldn't spoil them, if properly used. Grieved at his wife's distress and becoming hygienic, he said, "Don't have anything more to do with these wretched things. They're unwholesome anyway, and we're better off without them. Give them up."

"Never!" said Ruey.

When Ruey spoke that way, Philip knew she meant it. He sighed at the prospect of discordant breakfasts through a series of experiments. A text about "a dinner of herbs" floated through his mind as he walked abstractedly toward his store.

After Mrs. Thorne had dried her tears, she walked to the kitchen and with her own hands scraped that acid, alkaline mess into the drain.

"Buckwheat cakes are mysterious, trying things," she remarked to herself, "but I'll never give up till I can make them like Philip's mother's."

"Tomorrow morning," said Mr. Thorne that evening, "I must start for New York and will need a very early breakfast. Let Joanna just make me a cup of coffee. No cakes, remember," he laughingly added. "You may have a whole week to experiment on them in my absence."

Ruey watched him down the street in the gray dawn of the next morning as he hurried to the depot, and a bright idea came into her head.

Why not take a little trip of her own? She might run up to Father Thorne's. Why not be visiting instead of moping here alone? She wished she'd thought of it and mentioned it to Philip, but it was better not. He'd probably have thought she couldn't go so far alone. But what was a day's journey when it could all be accomplished before dark? Then it was going to be a bright day. She could see that by the rosy flush in the east—just the day for a journey. Besides, Philip couldn't visit them this winter, and how delighted they'd be for her to come and break up the monotony of their lives.

She glanced at the clock—only six o'clock. She'd have ample time to get ready for the eight o'clock train. The dress she had on would do to travel in— just slip her black cashmere into her satchel, and she was ready. Yes, she'd go.

Artful Ruey! Down in her heart she had a secret reason for this visit that didn't come up to the surface with the others. She wanted to know how Philip's mother made those cakes. She couldn't be happy until she succeeded. Here appeared an old trait of the girl Ruey, almost a fault—settled persistency in accomplishing her ends, a determination to walk over all obstacles, however large.

It took much lively stirring about to accomplish it, but the house was put in order, and Mrs. Thorne reached the depot in time for the eight o'clock train. The happy Joanna was dismissed to her home for a week, after carrying he mistress's satchel to the depot. Mrs. Thorne had visited the old homestead with her husband at the time of their marriage and looked forward with real pleasure at the prospect before her.

"Won't they be surprised, though, to see me coming without Philip?"

And then she smiled to think how she was whizzing along in one direction and Philip in another, while he thought her snug at home. This going off by herself held a spice of adventure she enjoyed exceedingly.

There's no more delightful place to step into than the home of two old people, who are young and love you. They have "hearts at leisure," can take time to adore you and are interested in the smallest details of your life. Philip's father and mother belonged to this type; their vitality hadn't diminished.

They received Ruey with open arms and followed her about with their eyes, apparently fearing she would vanish as unexpectedly as she'd appeared— "Philip's wife," caring enough about them to come so far to see them in the middle of winter, all alone too—not many daughters-in-law like that. They hung upon her words and brought out the choicest of everything and urged it upon her.

At bedtime Mother Thorne came up to tuck her in, "just as I did Philip twenty years ago," she said. Then the sweet old face bent over Ruey's for a moment and left a good-night kiss. "The Lord bless and keep you, dear child."

Ruey's heart went out to her and from that hour Philip's mother was her mother.

Breakfast was ready the next morning when she came down, and she sat in Philip's old seat. The sun looked in at the east window, and a stray ray fell upon her and burnished the gold of her hair, so that she looked more like an angel than ever to those dear old eyes. How happy they were—Philip's other self in that vacant chair.

Moreover she ate those famous cakes. It was all true. They were brown; they were thin and delicate, light and sweet and tender—the most delicious morsels, with the amber maple syrup, she'd ever tasted. She must confess it to herself—they were better than her mother's. City people couldn't concoct such amazing cakes as these. Then there was the fragrant golden butter. How she wished poor Philip were there to get some of all these good things.

She hadn't proposed to let her mother-in-law know she was ignorant of anything in the line of housekeeping. But now she resolved to lay down her pride and learn whatever she could, so she followed Mother Thorne as she trotted in and out from pantry to kitchen, initiating herself into the mysteries of this and that dish and storing up many a lesson of housewifely skill. It all came out after a little—the struggle she'd been through with those "horrible cakes."

Father Thorne laughed until the tears came, to hear his pretty daughter-in-law naively narrate her many grievous failures in that line, enlarging not a little on Philip's wry faces when he tried to eat her cakes to save her feelings. She confessed it all. Now she felt free to watch the process of "setting the cakes" and ask all the questions she pleased.

"What made mine so horribly bitter once?" she asked.

"Why, you put too much yeast in, I suppose."

"I only put in a teacupful," said Ruey.

Then Mother Thorne shook with laughter. "Why, child, that ought to make cakes enough for two dozen people. You only need about two tablespoonfuls for the amount you'd make."

"What made them run all over creation when I left them by the fire to rise?"

"Why, maybe you didn't have room enough for them to rise, and they must go somewhere, you know."

"What made them sour?"

"They stood too long after they got light, before they were baked. Very likely they'd have raised in time, if you'd left them on the table, for instance."

"What do you do when they're sour?" asked Ruey.

"Put in a little soda."

"I did. I put soda in, and you never saw such things as they were, yellow and spotted. Ugh! How they tasted! Philip nearly choked himself on one of the lumps of soda in his cake."

"Don't you know," asked Mother Thorne, laughing again, "that you must put in only a little, and you must dissolve that in a spoonful of warm water and then stir it in?"

Ruey studied those cakes as thoroughly as she ever did a problem or a French verb. She insisted on setting them at night and baking them every morning during her stay, and she was finally pronounced adept in the work.

This wasn't all she did. She put new life in the silent old house, sang all her songs, read the newspapers aloud, made a cap for Mother Thorne and a marvelous tidy for the best chair, and told them all about Philip, as if she could tell them anything new. But the pleasant visit had to end; it was almost time for Philip's return.

"Daughter, I'm really afraid for you to set out this morning," Mr. Thorne said on the day Ruey had fixed for her return. "It's been snowing hard all night, and if it keeps on at this rate the railroads will be blocked up."

"Oh, Father! I must start. Philip will be home tonight. What will he think if he doesn't find me there?" Ruey said eagerly.

"Better," said the wise old father, "better stay and telegraph to Ralph."

"Oh, no, indeed. That would spoil all the fun. You know I'll get home at four and Philip at seven. I'll have tea all ready and sit there demurely waiting for him, and he'll never imagine I've been off on a fun trip until I tell him."

And so she started, with many misgivings, however, on the part of the old people.

"She's such a bright little thing," Father Thorne said to his wife when they were toasting their feet at the fire that night before going to bed.

"It's like seeing the crocuses and daffodils coming up or getting a sniff at the hyacinth to have her light down here like a pretty bird and sing and chatter to us. Philip always did know just the right thing to do. He couldn't have found a better wife if he'd searched through the whole land."

The train that carried Ruey thundered on its way, as though it disdained the thought that the snowflakes that filled the air could have anything to do with its progress. The first tiny white feather came and laid itself down on the iron rails. Did it secretly exult that it was one of a myriad that would rear a gigantic barrier before which this puffing fiery monster would stand powerless and acknowledge the soft bits of down to be master of the situation? The storm raged through the day, increasing each hour in strength and fury.

The long train began to plod in a labored way after the manner of mortals stopping often, while snowplows cleared the track ahead. Darkness fell, and still the fearful mass of whiteness piled itself in huge billows about them. The snowplows were futile; as fast as they cleared a space the wind surged down and filled it up in an instant. The mighty engine struggled in vain to press forward, but it only crept at a snail's pace and finally came to a dead halt. There they were fast shut out from the world. They could do nothing but wait for morning.

Most of the passengers might not have resigned themselves to sleep so contentedly had they known they were in the midst of woods many miles from any town of much size, not even near one of the straggling hamlets that dotted the country.

When the morning dawned they found themselves literally enclosed in snow—snow above, beneath, to the right, to the left, behind, before. Those who understood the situation looked appalled.

The world was well represented there in that restless company that stared from their windows into snow. How strange that one particular class didn't set out on this journey. But each class had its type, as if someone had gone about and, gathering up handfuls of every sort of people, stowed them on this train. They were all there, including the woman with five children and the one with a lapdog, and all acted out their individual natures more fully than they might have done under other circumstances.

Many lost that reticence that is supposed to belong to well-bred people on a journey and told their private affairs. The man of business knit his brows and said he "must reach C by a certain time, or the consequences will be disastrous." The fashionable lady wrapped herself in her furs and bestowed withering looks on the crying baby. The grumbler grumbled and was sure somebody was to blame somewhere. The funny man bubbled and sparkled as usual and sent rays like sunshine over lugubrious faces. The profane man opened his mouth and out came toads and scorpions, and the tobacco chewers made dark pools on the floor to vex the souls of clean people. By the close of the day they were a forlorn, hungry people.

One among them, though, seemed untroubled—a plain-looking woman with an unfashionable bonnet and a peaceful face. She drew a little worn Bible from her satchel and read it a while by the dim light. Ruey wondered if she didn't get something from that book that made her patient when others were not—that sent her to relieve the tired mother by caring for the fretful baby a long time. And when another, a sad mother, unable to control her grief any longer, moaned out, "My child will die before I can get to her," this woman went to her with words of comfort.

Ruey's poor perturbed heart envied that calm face. She felt well-nigh distracted, not so much because she was cold and hungry. But what would Philip think when he returned and found her gone? No one knew where she went; not even a neighbor had the least intimation. What a night of horrors he must have had! Oh, to be obliged to sit there and wait when she felt like flying!

She heard the woman with the Bible whisper to the poor mother, "Pray—that will surely help you."

Perhaps it would help me, thought Ruey. She wasn't used to praying, but she needed help. So she put her tired head down and whispered a request for deliverance.

What had Philip done on arriving home? He tried to walk into his house. The door was locked, and there was no response to his repeated rings. He tried other doors with no better success. Then he visited his neighbors. They could give him no clue. He came back and stood in a dazed way on his own steps, looking up and down the street. He went down into the town and peered in the stores, but no Ruey. He called on her most intimate friends; they didn't know she was absent. He racked his brain. Was she out to tea? But she expected him home that very day.

As the evening advanced, he began to be thoroughly alarmed. Perhaps she'd met with some horrible fate in her own home. He forced the door and entered. The pretty rooms were in exquisite order. He searched wildly about for some scrap of paper that might explain the mystery. Wherever she was, she'd evidently been gone some time; the fires were dead and cold. He rushed down into the town again and consulted detectives, who suggested elopement as an explanation. Whereupon his anger rose to a white heat, and he left them.

Another idea struck him. Joanna must know something about this strange matter. She lived in the country. The polar wave had, by this time, reached that region. In the face of a blinding storm Mr. Thorne drove as rapidly as he could to Joanna's home. The sleepy girl, when roused, could at first give only an exasperating "no" to his eager questions. Finally from her broken English he gathered that her mistress had gone away on the cars and had directed her to come back to her duties that very afternoon. She did so, only to find the house closed.

Here was a little light, but it didn't relieve his perplexity. Ruey's father's home was in a distant state. She certainly wouldn't go so far away in the dead of winter. He could recall no acquaintances living near. Had she become insane and wandered away? But she evidently meant to return that day. Why didn't she come? Where was she? The cold sweat stood on his face when he remembered stories of abductions.

He went to the depot and remained the whole night, watching the trains coming in from anywhere. Morning dawned; she hadn't come. As a last resort, he would telegraph to his own home. But why would she go there and without him? It seemed useless, but he did it.

After waiting a long time he finally received an answer: "Ruey left here for home yesterday morning on the seven o'clock train."

Philip soon learned the train was snowbound a hundred miles away. His anxiety now assumed a new phase. Would she starve or freeze before he could reach her? There was no time to lose. Supplying himself with blankets and other provisions, he took the first northerly train, traveled as far as he could by rail, then hired conveyances to carry him to where men and snowplows were cutting a road to the imprisoned cars. Mr. Thorne joined them in their work. His strength seemed superhuman. Burly, muscular men were amazed at his swift, dexterous movements. All day they labored. The following night was terrible for the heartsick passengers. The fires were out and not a morsel of food to eat.

Ruey, chilled and weak, could find no relief in sleep. Her fortitude nearly deserted her, and the tears had their way. She lay curled in her seat, a wretched disconsolate little heap, when a brown-bearded man, muffled in furs, entered, flashing his lantern light here and there, eagerly scrutinizing the faces. He paused at Ruey's seat; an indefinable something attracted him, though the face was covered by two hands.

Suddenly she looked up and saw Philip's dear eyes gazing into hers. No questions were asked or answered just then. He gathered her in his arms for an instant. Then he wrapped her in blankets, brought food and nursed the color back to her pale cheeks.

Long stories were told on both sides, and Ruey laughed and cried by turns. All the passengers were in lively sympathy with the little lady who had found her husband, or rather whose husband had found her.

When Mr. and Mrs. Thorne next sat at their breakfast table, it was graced by a plate of cakes that might have come straight from Mother Thorne's kitchen. And some of the home butter was there, sweet as roses, and some of the golden maple syrup, too, from the trees Philip had played under.

And Ruey sat triumphant, with a little air that said, "Didn't I tell you I'd do it?"

"Ruey," said Philip, "I do believe that 'elopement' of yours paid off, notwithstanding the expense of doubts and fears, money and tears, to say nothing of the muscle I put into that huge drift."

Ruey knew why it "paid off," though she didn't tell her husband just then. She would never forget that night or the plain woman with the old bonnet who carried the untroubled face and the worn book. Deep in her heart a new purpose had taken root—an ambition not only to make cakes like Philip's mother, but to gain that blessed something, which made this other woman so different from those about her.

In a Dream

The poor women and girls are so taken up with cleaning their houses and dishes and preparing their daily meals that they don't give themselves up to thinking in the least. So writes Miss Blunt concerning the women of India. Something similar prevented Mrs. John Williams from giving herself up to thinking, or from thinking about anything but her own private affairs. Not that Mrs. Williams gave herself up to scrubbing doors and windows and cleaning pots and pans with her own hands, but she was "taken up" all the same.

Mrs. Williams still thought, of course. She superintended all her work and did much of her own sewing. Since her family wasn't small or her income large and she kept only one servant, it took a vast deal of thinking and worrying to keep the Williams family up to the standard, which wasn't simply one of neatness and comfort. Indeed, she'd determined she should live in the same style as her friends whose incomes were possibly twice as large as her own; her children's clothes should be as fine and fashionably made as theirs; and she herself should be able to make as good an appearance as the best when she went into society. Furthermore, her parlor should be furnished as well as possible, with all the elegance and taste that the law of the fashionable world required. This was the grand plan to which she aimed all her energies.

Mrs. Williams was a member in good and regular standing of an orthodox church. She regularly occupied her pew in the sanctuary and, when she had no other engagement, attended the weekly prayer meeting. But the most persistent and zealous member of the Ladies' Foreign Missionary Society had succeeded in inducing her to attend their monthly meetings only once. She took pains to explain carefully to her conscience that she believed in foreign missions. But that didn't prove she must spend a whole afternoon each month hearing dry reports about countries with outlandish names. What good did that do anyway?

It was mysterious how ladies could do justice to their families and spend so much time out. She could scarcely keep up with her own calls. But, then, those women who were always on a committee for something and running off to meetings neglected their families. Very likely, too, it just suited some women to get up on a platform before an audience and read a paper or a report. It was just a little leaning to woman's rights. She believed in a woman staying in her own sphere, and for her part she craved no such notoriety.

She always noticed, too, that the women who gave themselves up to those things seemed to lose all regard for their appearance. Now one owed a duty to friends to dress well, and some of those missionary women were wearing their last year's bonnets and dressing in the styles of three or four years back—perfect frights!

She didn't see why women needed a society by themselves either. Probably they raised just as much money before the ladies made such a fuss about it; it all came out of their husbands' pockets anyway. Her husband always contributed to foreign missions and always would probably (it's true he did—a dollar a year!), and wasn't that just as well as her bothering about it?

"There!" said Mrs. Williams one bright April afternoon as she glanced from her window. "There comes that Mrs. Brown. I know what she's after. She wants me to go to that stupid missionary meeting. I suppose this is the afternoon for it. I promised her I'd go again sometime—sorry I did too. To think someone can drop everything and go to a missionary meeting—in the spring of the year, too, when there's so much sewing to be done." And she hastily instructed Bridget to tell Mrs. Brown she was "engaged."

So Mrs. Williams worked diligently on an elaborate dress for her young daughter, with frills and lace and embroidery and many weary stitches. At the close of the day she congratulated herself for accomplishing a fine afternoon's work.

She had to wade through whole seas of sewing, Mrs. Williams said, before she could have any spare afternoons. She had to remodel all her own dresses according to the present style and make new ones. (When Mrs. Williams had a dressmaker in the house—to use her own words—"I almost work myself to death.") Then all the other sewing—the ruffling and tucking and side-pleating and puffing—must be done before the summer wardrobes for her and her little daughters would be completed. Then she had the housecleaning, the smallest detail of which required her personal supervision; all her housekeeping was squared up to certain fine lines.

If she ever had a morsel of time from these things, stern necessity compelled her to spend it in fancy work, for tidies, soft pillows, bracket covers, stand covers and mats were indispensable. When Mrs. Williams was asked to subscribe to *Woman's Work for Woman,* she assured them she already knew all she desired to about woman's work.

At last, the spring sewing and the housecleaning were completed, and the summer heat had come. The day was warm, and Mrs. Williams, in a cool white wrapper, had established herself on the parlor sofa with a book. She'd neglected to tell Bridget she wasn't at home. And just as she reached the most absorbing part of one of George Eliot's novels, a caller was ushered in.

Mrs. Brown! That missionary woman again! Was anyone ever so persecuted before? she wondered to herself.

Here she had just come to a breathing spell, where she had hoped to get a little rest and comfort, and now she must be annoyed. To go was out of the question. It was too hot, and, besides, she didn't feel like going to any meeting. She wanted to finish her book. So she told Mrs. Brown she was worn out with overexertion, and the day was so warm she wouldn't venture out. She would probably fall asleep in the meeting if she went.

Even when work didn't fill Mrs. Williams's heart, it seemed Satan was on alert to keep her from all Christian activity. How he must rejoice at each new band he fastens over the heart he covets. Here was a largehearted, energetic, skillful woman; consecrated, she'd be a power for Christ. Mrs. Williams wasn't hard-hearted. But she found no time to listen to the story of those who don't know God. She knew very little of it at all and, like those women in a far-away land, was so "taken up" that she couldn't give herself to thinking.

When the rage for decorating and pottery seized the female mind, it dawned upon Mrs. Williams's perceptions that all her belongings were exceedingly plain; she must have two large vases for the parlor at least. She lay awake thinking about it a good part of the night. Something must be done. The expensive imported ware was out of the question—beyond the limits of her purse at present.

Mrs. Williams was a woman of resources, who seldom failed to rise to the necessity of the occasion, and thus evolved a delightful plan. As a young girl at school, she'd taken lessons in oil colors and possessed not a little artistic ability. Why not manufacture her own pottery and decorate her own china? She could scarcely wait for morning to appear to execute her plans. She would go into the city, get a few instructions and some materials, and see what she could do.

The next day was a harbinger for a hot day, but what of that? What wouldn't one undergo when pottery was in question? So she spent the sultry summer days examining all the different styles of vases with the same eager minuteness that an amateur milliner studies hats on "opening day." Her vases should be precisely like that elegant pair of Copenhagen ware that cost fifty dollars.

Then this ambitious, energetic, deluded woman went home, shut herself in her room and dabbled in paint from morning till night. Her enthusiasm rose to such a pitch that she neglected her sewing and her calls. After she produced a really creditable pair of vases, she was motivated to go on. She painted lovely little bouquets on her tea set and decorated everything in the house from china to coal-scuttle.

About this time Mrs. Williams received an invitation to a party—not unusual, but this was a select affair and the highest stratum of society. She was holding counsel with herself and doing some very close thinking on the all-important subject of her wardrobe, and finally she came to the usual feminine conclusion that she had "absolutely nothing to wear."

Suddenly she was interrupted by a call from the faithful, punctual members of the missionary society, whose visits were as sure as the sun and the dews. Mrs. Williams had decided self-defense required her to become a member of that society, afford it she must in some way. Her bills for the pottery had amounted to a considerable sum, home industry notwithstanding, and the fact stared her in the face that she must have a new silk for that party. But she'd dodged those people as long as she could.

What a relief it was to learn that only ten cents a month made one a society member. She answered graciously that she'd be most happy to throw in her mite. If Mrs. Williams could have peeped into the collectors' books, she would have seen that others subscribed fifty cents or one dollar a month, and some s copied and followed were benevolent to two or three dollars a month. Then Mrs. Williams would have compassed sea and land to procure the money, before she'd allow her name to be among those with that small amount set after it.

She suggested she pay the whole sum at once. What was the use of troubling them to call every month? When they said they preferred to have it in monthly payments, she thought within herself, *Now that is just like women. They have no business ability. Most of them travel up and down, wasting their time and making twelve trips for what they might accomplish in one.*

After disposing of them, Mrs. Williams sallied forth on a shopping expedition, in high spirits at having come off so easily, yet with a placid feeling in her conscience that now she'd contributed to "foreign missions." She spent the morning in weighing the merits of this piece of silk and that and finally purchased an expensive dress and some soft filmy laces of marvelous beauty at a marvelous price. If her weak conscience made a feeble protest, it was silenced by "I must have it." Who shall say the heathen are all in Africa or China or the islands of the sea?

And so the busy days went on with dressmaking, housecleaning, calling, canning, pickling, parties, pottery and fancy work—time for it all. How could one think much about such faraway interests as heathen women when her hands and heart were so full?

Sometimes we call such "Marthas" and make light of the fact we've loaded ourselves down with such heavy burdens, taking comfort in the thought that one of the women Jesus loved was in the same situation.

One morning Mrs. Williams wasn't bustling about with her usual activity. She sat in her own room with a serious, troubled face. She was in deep thought, but the subject wasn't some scheme for adding to her wardrobe or the furnishings of her house. Perhaps the days aren't past when the Lord speaks to a soul "in a dream, in a vision of the night, when deep sleep falleth upon men." Mrs. Williams wasn't a nervous woman, full of strange notions, and her dreams before this had been ignored as idle fantasies of the brain. But the remarkable and solemn one of the previous night couldn't be dismissed, and, like one of old, her "spirit was troubled."

In her dream the day had come for her to die and leave her busywork forever. She could recall it all vividly—the flash of surprise, the anguish, the feeling she wasn't ready, the swift searching of her heart to find her hope, the despairing cry of "Oh, Christ, forgive me!" And she could hear the weeping friends, not heeded in the all-absorbing thoughts, "What is this? Where am I going?" Then she saw the sinking away, the last gasp, and eternity opened!

In the distance there dawned upon her vision the glorious city, the golden gates, the crowns, the harps, the white-robed throng, the wonderful music thrilling her soul. Trembling, she approached the gate, and her heart leaped, for that kingly one could be no other than Christ the Lord, the one she loved years before the world got hold of her. Surely He'd recognize her. But when she timidly ventured nearer and spoke His name, she saw no smile of welcome, no "Come, ye blessed." The look was cold, the face averted. In tears and agony she begged an angel to open the gates and let her in. When he asked her from what place she came and by what right she hoped to enter, she murmured that she belonged to Christ's church when she was on the earth.

Then he bade her come with him. He lifted a veil and said, "Look!"

Rooms filled with beauty opened into each other and stretched off into the distance. Rich furniture stood in the rooms; carpets of soft velvet covered the floors; mirrors and paintings filled the walls. Exquisite vases of delicate tints and graceful forms enhanced the furnishings, with finest statuary and countless accessories. Costly silks, glittering satins and rare laces lay about in rich profusion. Jewelry flashed out here and there—diamonds, pearls and all precious gems in beautiful settings. Novels in costly binding stood in heavy, dark-grained bookcases, while an abundance of delicate food tempted with its variety.

"It was for such as these," the sad voice of the angel said, "that you bartered your soul. These are the things you coveted and worked for in your earth life."

How empty and unsatisfying it all looked to her now, with that glorious city in full view and the shining ones gathered about their King, with their hallelujahs rising in grand chorus to "Him who loved them and washed them in His blood." In deep distress she begged to be allowed to go in where the Savior was. Then the angel lifted another veil.

Dark places of the earth spread out before her—millions upon millions of human beings bowing before idols, little children cast into cruel flames and a whole world full of sad, wretched women. Besides those were the poor, degraded, ignorant ones of her own city.

"Did you ever read in your Bible," asked the angel, " 'Inasmuch as ye did it not to one of the least of these, ye did it not to Me'?"

Deep horror seized her, for memory brought before her, as in letters of fire, that other world in her own Bible—that awful word "depart."

Mrs. Williams needed no Daniel to interpret her dream. Unlike the king of Babylon's dream, it brought her in brokenness of spirit at the feet of her Savior. And He who said, "A new heart will I give you, and a new spirit will I put within you," was faithful to His promise.

The woman who left her room after hours of soul-searching and confession before God came out with "the new spirit"—a consecrated soul, from then on to obey the Master's slightest wish. The whole aim of her life was changed, with her pursuits and her lifestyle. She found ample time to do the Lord's work, too, and to "look well to the ways of her household." The Lord gave her sweet work for Him.

Doesn't He wait to give any of us who have been halfhearted laggard Christians this "new spirit," this anointing, whenever we give our whole hearts to Him? Then it will be joy, not duty, and we'll say, "Here is my tongue, dear Lord, to speak for You. Here are my hands to minister to You, my feet to r Your errands."

Faith and Gasoline

Mrs. Faith Vincent was crying. There was no denying it. Veritable tears stood in her eyes and rolled down her cheeks all the time she was bathing the plump limbs of her baby and robing her in dainty garments of flannel and embroidery. Then she struggled through the notes of a sad lullaby, and now the long lashes lay quietly on the pretty cheek, and the fair young mama was free to lay her head on the side of the crib and indulge in a good cry.

The clue to all this trouble was condensed in a sentence the young husband let fall as he left for his business a few moments earlier. "I see no other way, my dear. You'll be obliged to take the baby and go to Uncle Joshua's for the summer. The extreme heat will come on now very soon, and you and Daisy won't be able to endure it in this room."

Now that wouldn't be an appalling statement to make to most wives—that they must pack up and get out of the hot, dusty city to a farmhouse in the country, even though they did leave their husbands sweltering behind. But several points were to be taken into consideration in this case.

In the first place Mr. and Mrs. Vincent hadn't yet learned how to maintain a separate existence. Life apart from each other was a tame, spiritless thing, simply to be endured, not enjoyed.

Then, too, Uncle Joshua's home wasn't a paradise, although he and Aunt Patty were kind and pleasant. Faith had vivid memories of a few weeks spent there soon after her marriage. These two old people lived on their farm, spending the evening of their lives in quiet happiness.

But the place was dreary and remote from any town or neighbors. She found it pleasant when her husband was with her and the two took long rambles or spent the day under the trees, reading and talking. But how could she endure it alone—rising with the birds to an early breakfast, then an interminable day stretching before her, with the long afternoon of silence broken only by the click of Aunt Patty's knitting needles, the ticking of the old clock and the hum of the bees. These old people had lived too long in quiet on these silent hills to make much conversation. She couldn't see herself going through the same monotonous round as each long day dragged its slow length, while miles stretched between her and her beloved, laboring on in the distant city. The dreary separation—that was the hard part of it, after all.

It had been just two years since Frank Vincent brought home his bride. He'd succeeded in securing rooms in a pleasant boardinghouse on one of the city's wide, airy streets. He felt justified in using the utmost of his means to provide an attractive home. His Faith had been delicately reared by a wealthy uncle who had frowned upon the attentions of the young bookkeeper, handsome, intelligent and with unblemished reputation though he was, and holding a good position in one of the largest and oldest firms in the city. The uncle had more ambitious plans for his favorite niece. He didn't forbid the marriage but gave Faith to understand that if she persisted in marrying a poor man, when a good half million awaited her acceptance, she did it at her own peril. Not a penny of his would go to eke out a poor clerk's scanty living.

The end of it all was a quiet wedding one morning in her uncle's parlor and a hasty flitting away of the young couple—away from ominous looks and cold politeness, out into their own bright world, where no dark shadows in the shape of grim mercenary uncles should ever cross their path.

It wasn't without many misgivings that the young husband conducted his wife to her apartment. Neat and pretty though it was, it stood in marked contrast with the roomy, elegant mansion where she'd spent her life, and so did the noisy, dusty city with the beautiful, quiet old town where trees and flowers and birds and pure air and room to breathe in made existence doubly delightful. The anxiety was needless; never was a child more pleased with a playhouse than the young bride with her new home.

Life glided peacefully on for many months. Then the clouds gathered in the sky of the financial world. Businessmen became anxious, and retrenchment was the order of the day. Among others to draw in sail was the well-established firm Frank Vincent had served for many years. The salaries of their employees were cut down, in some instances to a mere pittance.

Upon none did the blow fall more heavily than these two inexperienced ones who had made no provision for any such change in their affairs. They were dismayed. Mr. Vincent tried in vain to secure some more lucrative position, but he soon began to feel he was most fortunate in such times to have any assured income. The outgo was greater than the income, and it was plain they must seek a less expensive home.

They made many trips to the suburbs in the hope of obtaining board at a price within their means in some pleasant rural home, but no such home opened its doors. Evidently the suburban dwellers, when they did take boarders, meant to make it "pay."

Then they searched the papers and read all the advertisements under the heading of "Boarding" within the city. They climbed long flights of stairs, interviewed landladies and looked at rooms with the customary faded carpets, shabby wallpaper and musty smell, in narrow streets, that seemed to Faith like prisons. In vain they tried to make their tastes and their purse agree.

They finally came to a third-story room, faded carpet, shabby paper and hard bed. It was a great change, especially when they descended three dark stairways into a comfortless basement dining room and were served sour bread and strong butter, muddy coffee and tough steak. It tried their fortitude sometimes severely, but they were young and brave. They had each other and dear little Daisy, and that was almost enough for this world.

One can't have everything, so Faith stirred the fire and put a bright spread on the bare table and another bit of bright color on the wooden rocking chair. If they hadn't been forced to live by eating, things wouldn't have been so bad after all.

Spring, though, brought troubles. The sun shone squarely on them through the winter and served to brighten up things and save coal. But now he became an enemy, pouring his fierce rays almost the entire long day into the two windows, with old paper shades filled with pinholes and the only protection against him. Large companies of flies, too, arrived daily and evidently came to stay. The butter turned to oil. The food became unpalatable. The whole house seemed stuffy and unendurable.

On one of those warm spring mornings when vital energies flag, Mr. and Mrs. Vincent labored up the third flight of stairs. The halls were filled with execrable odors of fried ham and cheap coffee. They were busy with their own thoughts, possibly of green fields, apple blossoms, spring violets, tables with damask and silver, a cook, inviting rooms and other equally tantalizing suggestions.

Faith, at the top, panting and pale as a lily, drew from her husband the statement, "My dear, you can't endure it any longer. Something must be done."

That something seemed all the more imperative, since Daisy was beginning to droop and have feverish days over the advent of each little white tooth. Many perplexed conferences followed.

"You see," said Mr. Vincent, trying to speak cheerfully, "one of us orphans should have married someone who had a father and mother and an old homestead to go to in an emergency like this. As it is, I don't see any other way except for you to take the baby and go to my uncle Joshua's for the summer. You'll be made welcome, at least, and have good food and good air."

"What if we go to housekeeping in a small way?" Faith suggested.

"It would have to be in a very small way indeed," laughed Frank. "Why, the birds have more to set up housekeeping with than we do. They have furnished rooms, rent free. Think of rent, furniture and all the pots and kettles and pans housekeeping requires, besides wages to a girl. Never do, wifie—my salary wouldn't cover. I've often heard people say it was much cheaper to board than to keep house."

"But we might take a small house in the suburbs and furnish it in stages, and I could do my own work," persisted Faith.

"My poor little white lily," said Frank, "you don't know what you're talking about. Think of a hot little house, you broiling over a cookstove and the baby crying for your care. Besides, my dear, you're not accustomed to work. I shouldn't wonder now if I knew just about as much as you do about cooking. I think I can see you with blistered fingers and aching head, studying cookbooks. No, Faith, we'll be obliged to live in two places this summer, I fear. I know it will be lonely for you at Uncle Joshua's, but for your own sake and the dear baby's we must do it. Let's be cheerful and perhaps by fall business will revive and my salary be increased, or I can get a better position. Now, good-bye, my blossoms. I must be gone." And he hurried down the stairs, lest Faith should see his courage was more than half assumed, for the prospect before him was dismal.

What Mrs. Vincent did when her husband left her we already know. Yet she wasn't one to sit down in weeping despair before a difficulty until she'd put forth every energy to remove it. She sat long and pondered the question. No light came, although she turned her brows into a deep frown in perplexed thought.

"If I could only keep house," she mused. "Frank thinks I know nothing of cooking. I'd just like to have him eat some of my bread and puffy biscuits. I'm so glad I never told him I took lessons from Dinah all one winter before we were married. I'll surprise that boy someday with my knowledge. If it weren't for the horrid heat of the cookstove, I know I could keep house nicely and save money, too, I daresay. But my head would never endure a hot kitchen, I suppose."

Just here the clock chimed out ten, reminding Faith of an engagement at the dressmaker's. Leaving Daisy with her young nurse, Faith was soon on her way, not to Madame Aubrey's, but to plain Mrs. Macpherson's, who lived up two flights of stairs and was nevertheless "a good fitter" and kept her rooms and herself as neat as wax.

While Faith waited, and the busy shears slipped and snipped her wrapper, she had time to look about her. The rooms wore such a pleasant, homelike air. They were cool and comfortable-looking and not a fly to be seen. Faith, reared in the finest and best of everything, now looked with almost covetous eyes on this poor, plain home.

"What a cozy place you have here, Mrs. Macpherson," she said, wearily leaning her head back in the old rocking chair, newly covered with chintz. "It's so nice I'd like to stay."

Mrs. Macpherson glanced up in surprise, for the tones were such tired, sad ones. She noticed for the first time the dark rings under Faith's eyes and the eyes themselves suspiciously red. Her motherly heart went out to the poor young thing.

"Something troubles you, child," she said, "or you don't feel well. Can't I help you?"

The tender tones almost made the tears come anew. And Faith, contrary to her reticent nature, found herself telling kindhearted Mrs. Macpherson just what troubled her.

"Poor dear!" Mrs. Macpherson said. "That's hard, to be sure. But if I can't help you, I know One who can. Why don't you go straight to the dear Lord and tell Him all about it? You see, everything's at His disposal anyway. You know the way to Him, don't you?"

Faith nodded assent and then said despairingly, "It never seemed to me God would condescend to think about the small matters of our everyday lives."

"Why, child, He numbers the hairs of our heads and says that, if He gives thought to such little things as lilies and grass, He'll surely look after us. Doesn't a shepherd care when the sheep are worried? Indeed he does. Would you stay upstairs when you heard your dear baby crying? Oh, but you'd run fast to her. He says He's our Father, and we're His children. So is He going to stay up in heaven and not care about our everyday troubles? No, you just tell Him and believe He'll help you in some way, and He surely will. But here I am, going on like a clock. I beg your pardon, Mrs. Vincent."

"Go on, Mrs. Macpherson," said Faith. "I love to hear you talk. Tell me how you came to feel so sure about things. I need to know. I'm wrongly named 'Faith,' for I have scarcely any."

"Why, when I was left alone in the world with no home and not a penny of my own, I didn't know which way to turn. I had no trade and wasn't strong enough to do housework. I fretted and worried over it a spell. Then it came to me all of a sudden one day that the Lord could help me if He would. I recalled the verses that tell how kind He is, and I just went and told Him about it, feeling as sure He'd help me in some way as if I'd heard Him say it.

"Sure enough He did! The very next day a lady advertised for an apprentice to learn the dressmaker's trade. I went, and she took me, and I got just in my right place. I learned fast, and in a year from that time I could fit as well as she could. She offered me good wages to stay and sew with her, but I was tired of shop life and wanted a bit of a home of my own. So I rented these rooms, and I have all I can do and more too.

"It's a nice pleasant place, I think. It's cool and comfortable, even if it is two flights. You see, I have a north and south window, and if there isn't a good breeze from one way there is from the other. Here's my bedroom (opening the door into a good-sized room with a large window), with blinds too. I can make it as dark as a pocket. And my dining room and kitchen are here all in one. Here the lake water comes in. Oh, I lack for nothing."

"But don't your rooms get all heated up when you cook?" Faith asked.

"Not a bit! See here." And she called Faith's attention to what appeared to be a small light table made of iron. "This is a gasoline stove, and the man who invented it should have every woman who owns one blessing him as long as he lives, for it's a jewel."

Mrs. Macpherson turned a screw, and the flame flickered and glowed in one of the burners like a bright star. "Here's my fire all made. Pretty soon I'll cook my dinner. Over this burner I'll put my oven and bake a potato or two nice and brown in twenty minutes or so. Over the other burner I'll boil my teakettle and make my tea. Then I'll clap on the gridiron and cook a bit of steak—nicest way in the world to cook steak. It's so quick. You know that makes steak juicy—the quicker you can cook it, the better it is."

"Will it bake bread nicely?" Faith asked, growing deeply interested.

"To be sure," Mrs. Macpherson said and produced a plump brown loaf. "You can see it's beautifully done. The least bit over half an hour bakes my loaves. Oh, there isn't a thing the creature won't do. I can tuck a chicken in the oven, and it comes out done to a turn, or put a joint of meat on to boil and go on with my sewing. It cooks itself, you know. I can roast a turkey. Last Christmas I roasted one—invited in a neighbor or two. You'd have thought it came out of my mother's old-fashioned brick oven—it was done so beautifully. I can wash and iron on it too—heats the irons as fast as you can use them.

"It's my opinion that women wouldn't get so used up at their work if they'd have these stoves. It's the heat that takes all the life and soul out of someone. It's pleasant to work if you know how and can keep cool. This stove is a real saving of tempers, for if you ever noticed it, folks begin to get cross just as soon as they get heated up over a cookstove. No, it doesn't give out any heat, and it doesn't have any ashes or smoke or soot or dirt of any kind about it. And it's cheaper than burning coal."

"But haven't I heard gasoline is explosive?" Faith asked.

"It isn't. It'll catch fire if you bring it near a flame, just as alcohol will, but it can't explode. There might be a little danger of its catching fire if you filled it when burning, but nobody would be foolish enough to do that.

"I meant to tell you how this little stove is another proof to me our Father pities us in our troubles and helps us. I used to have an iron cookstove, and even with my little work it would heat up everything so. Just as I got all tuckered out with it, I heard of the gasoline stove, but I couldn't afford to get one, for work was rather scarce then. I expected Him to send me one before long, though, and sure enough He did. It wasn't many days, don't you believe, till a lady came and asked me if I wanted to sew for her and take a gasoline stove for pay. Her husband was a dealer in them. You can be sure I said yes pretty quick! So I got it, and it's been a great comfort to me these three years. No, we don't plod along here with nobody to care how we get along. He cares. I believe He thought about me and sent me the stove, and I always will."

"Well, I'm truly obliged to you, Mrs. Macpherson," said Faith. "You've cheered me up and helped me. I think I'll have more trust after this. And who knows? I may set up housekeeping with a gasoline stove," she added, laughing.

Faith Vincent walked home with an idea in her head and a light in her eye that weren't there when she started. Trust a woman for doing what she wants. It didn't take her long to lay a plan, and by the time she reached home a plan lay fair and clear before her.

Once in her room she sat down and mentally inventoried her possessions She went to her trunk and brought out her jewelry. All the birthday and holida gifts of many years made a goodly array, and several were quite costly. She hesitated a little over a beautiful watch and chain but finally laid them with the others—a fair offering at the shrine of love. She kept only a plain gold pin and the rings her husband gave her. When the baby took her afternoon nap, Faith gathered up the rings, pins, earrings, bracelets, chains and all the other "tinkling ornaments" and wrapped them in a package. Then, leaving the baby in her nurse's care, she went with a resolute look in her eyes to Mr. Seymour's, one of the largest jewelry stores in the city. Mr. Seymour was a member of the same church and took a fatherly interest in the young couple. With inward trepidation Faith unfolded her plans to him. After careful examination he named a price for each article that made her heart leap with joy.

"As a matter of course," he explained, "we never give full value for goods bought in this way. But when a woman sacrifices her jewelry for such a goal, I want to bid her success, so I'll give you what I think I can dispose of them for."

He counted out the fresh bills to Faith. She could have hugged him, but she only said in low, excited tones, "Mr. Seymour, I can't tell you how much I thank you."

She almost flew home and then, dismissing the nurse, acted in an extraordinary manner for her. She danced about the room with the baby, nearly squeezing the breath out of her, and laughed and cried by turns. Then she did some serious thinking. How the clouds of the morning had turned into sunshine! She recognized the Lord's hand in it all. He had given her these suggestions and plans. His loving-kindness was over her; she would never doubt it again.

When her husband returned in the evening, she tried to banish from her tell-tale face all traces of exultation. This was her secret; he couldn't know it yet. So poorly did she succeed that he was happily surprised by finding her cheerful, instead of sad. Yet, inconsistent mortal that he was, he began to feel slightly annoyed that she seemed to be taking the prospective separation so coolly.

"How soon can you be ready to go?" he asked, in the course of the evening.

That roll of bills in Faith's pocket made her eyes dance with joy. "Oh, in about a fortnight. But let's not talk about that tonight. Let me read you this exquisite little bit I found today."

"Women are strange," soliloquized Frank. "I don't believe Faith is going to feel our first separation as much as I will."

Faith studied the daily newspapers diligently for a few days. "To Rent" was always the subject.

"I do believe I've found the right thing at last," she announced to the baby one day.

Then she read aloud: "To rent at Maplewood, a cottage of four rooms, convenient to street and steam cars, pleasantly located, rent low."

Another hurried consultation with the paper disclosed the fact that a train for Maplewood left in an hour. The baby was put to sleep to a hurried tune and left with the nurse. Faith had just enough time to reach the train.

Maplewood proved to be a pretty little suburb four miles out. It was rather new, so it seemed like being in the country. Green fields and hills stretched away on either side, and the one broad, quiet avenue was shaded with maples, grand old forest trees. It looked like paradise to Faith. She soon found the cottage, a lovely nest of white and green glimmering through the trees, the smooth lawn bright with daffodils and crocuses. Vines clambered over the porch, and the sweet breath of lilies and violets distilled subtle perfume on the spring air. She stood on the porch almost afraid to ring, lest she'd hear the house was rented yesterday. But, no, it was to be had, and the nice old woman who owned it and wanted to rent it and live with her daughter was just as much delighted as Faith. So eager and enthusiastic a tenant wasn't found every day. The four pretty rooms, parlor, bedroom, dining room and kitchen, exactly suited. A bargain was soon concluded, and Faith, on a homeward train, congratulated herself on the success of part of her plan.

Many visits were made during the next few days to furniture, carpet, and china stores. One would have supposed, at the least, that Mrs. Vincent was furnishing a hotel. But it's no easy matter to take fine tastes and a small purse and make both ends meet.

The purchases were made at last—first and foremost, the gasoline stove; then the pretty light carpets, the matting, the neat furniture, some cheap white muslin curtains for the windows and a small supply of china. The young housekeeper bought carefully, with nothing for mere show. But when it was all arranged in the little house, and Faith's pictures hung on the white walls, nothing was to be desired in the way of beauty or comfort—that is, in the estimation of those most nearly concerned.

Meanwhile, Faith had kept her secret well, going to and from the cottage, busy and happy as any other robin in the springtime preparing her nest.

The nest was all finished now. Faith stood one afternoon in her kitchen door, taking a critical view of it all, then turned with satisfaction to survey the kitchen. It was a mite of a room, but Faith was proud of it. This was to be her workshop. Here cooking was to be carried on as a fine art. She took a last peep into the china closet, looked lovingly at a row of new and shiny tin dishes and glanced with admiration at the gasoline stove, the presiding genius of the whole. Then she opened the outside door into an old-fashioned garden, filled with lilacs and roses, pinks and southernwood, and all spicy plants and fragrant herbs.

She sat down to rest a few minutes; she'd accomplished such wonders today. Daisy had been left for the day in the care of a kind old lady, and Faith, hiring a woman to help her a few hours, had been hard at work. A stone jar was filled with golden brown loaves of delicious bread and another jar with cake, light as down. A tempting bit of roast lamb sat in the refrigerator. Everything was ready for tomorrow, when the grand secret would be revealed. Faith fe▮

so happy and satisfied. She'd tried and proved the stove. It was all it was represented to be. Assuredly, now, nothing stood in the way of a home together in the country.

"Won't you come home early, and let's take a little trip on the streetcar out into the country?" Faith asked her husband the next morning.

"Yes, indeed!" he answered, sighing. "I must make the most of my family now—only three days left."

The unsuspecting man had no thought that all his worldly possessions weren't long afterward on the way to Maplewood and that his wife waited impatiently to take him there too.

"Now you're out on my invitation, you and the baby," Faith said, as they alighted from the car at Maplewood. "You're to ask no questions, but do as you're told."

She led the way up the pleasant street. Her husband followed in silent wonder as she went up the walk, turned the key of the cottage door and invited him to come in and be seated. Then she went into the next room. A few moments later the door swung open, revealing that cool, darkened dining room.

And Faith, with ill-concealed triumph in her voice, said, "Please walk out to tea, my dear. I'm sure you must be hungry by this time."

As though looking through a mist he saw the white table arranged with exquisite neatness and care, decked with flowers and spread with angel's fare, he almost thought. He turned to Faith with a bewildered look.

"Where are we? Is this heaven? Tell me quick!"

What a merry tea table it was! How they talked and laughed and almost cried by turns, and even the baby seemed to realize some great event had happened and laughed and crowed appropriately.

After tea, when they talked it all over, Frank said, "Who but you would have thought of all this? We'll be so happy here, and I owe it all to you!"

"You forget Mrs. Macpherson," Faith said.

"Yes, and the gasoline stove. Except for that, it seems this couldn't have been accomplished," said her husband.

"We both forget the dear Father in heaven," Faith said in reverent tones, "that we owe everything to Him alone."

By a mutual impulse they knelt down, and the husband, in a few words of prayer, consecrated this new home to the Lord and himself and his dear family anew to His service. He thereby felt added dignity and joy in his manhood, now that "he was a priest in his own house" indeed.

So the months go on in peace and joy. Faith sings at her work, and the baby plays in the garden, and Frank Vincent thinks only one woman in the whole world knows how to cook. The plan failed in no detail. The gasoline stove has proved itself a most efficient servant, and, moreover, Faith manages to lay aside a snug sum every week.

Benjamin's Wife

A busy, toilsome life this mother had led. She had reared a family, laid some of them down to sleep in the old cemetery and struggled through poverty, sickness, and sorrow—she and Ephraim together, always together. He hadn't brought her to a stately home that day so long ago when she put her hand in his. He had no stocks or bonds or broad acres. Yet Mrs. Kensett had for forty years counted herself a rich woman. She possessed the true, tender, undivided heart of a good man—a love that nothing dimmed, that trials only made stronger, that hedged her life about with thoughtful care. Even when gray hairs crowned both of their heads, this husband and wife rejoiced in the love of their youth. Indeed, that love was purified, tried, as gold is tried in the fire.

In the last few years this good old couple seemed to have reached a Beulah land. They had enough laid by to support them comfortably now that their children had all flown from the home nest, and their quiet, happy life flowed on without a ripple.

"Mother," Mr. Kensett had said, "I'm going to stop work now and rest. I'm getting old, and we've got enough to do us, I guess, as long as we stay. You can tend your flower beds and darn my socks, and I'll make the garden and take care of the chickens. We'll just take comfort a spell. If anybody has earned the right to, we have."

As often as once a week, he remarked, "There's one thing I must see to right away. I must make my will, so that if I go first you'll be sure to have the old place all to yourself. I want you to have every cent of it to do as you please with."

And she always answered, "Now, Father, don't! It won't make much difference how it's fixed. It isn't likely anyway that I'll stay long behind you—we've been together so long."

A morning came when the hale, cheery old man didn't rise with the sun and step briskly about his work. The messenger came for him in the night. And when the first streak of light in the early dawn stole through his chamber window and fell upon his face to waken him, he didn't awaken, for he had gone—in the darkness alone with the messenger. Strange journey! Mysterious messenger!

His gray coat hung over the chair where he laid it. The garden tools stood against the fence. The house had a strange silence, the sunshine a cold glare. He who passed in and out yesterday, and worked and smiled and talked and read the news, today lay in the darkened parlor, white, cold and still. No, not that! Today he walked the golden streets, joined in the everlasting song and looked upon the face of his Lord. The old Bible lay open on the stand, the psalmbook beside it, his glasses shut into the place where he sang at family worship a few hours before, and the psalm he sang—his favorite—was in the words of the quaint old version:

> I will both lay me down in peace,
>   And quiet sleep will take;
> Because Thou only me to dwell
>   In safety, Lord, dost make.

Had he known how quiet the sleep was to be, the calm triumphant faith of the singer wouldn't have wavered, nor would the peace have been less with which he laid himself down.

The will had never been made, so the old homestead must be sold and divided among them all. They met at an early day to arrange affairs. Mr. John Kensett, the eldest son, and Mrs. Maria Sinclair, the eldest daughter, were the self-appointed managers. They were both wealthy but were just as eager to secure the small sum that would fall to them, as was Hannah, another daughter, who had married a poor man and had many mouths to feed. Whatever sentiment or tender feeling these first two might originally have possessed, had been rubbed out by the world. In their catechism the answer to "What is the chief end of man?" read: to make money, to be fashionable, to please ourselves, now and here, always and everywhere.

In Benjamin, the youngest of the family, were condensed all the noble qualities and tender, poetical nature of both father and mother, while the other children brought out the unlovely characters of some distant ancestors.

"Why not give it all up to Mother?" said Benjamin. "It will only be enough to keep her in comfort."

"No doubt you think that would be an excellent arrangement," John answered, "inasmuch as you, being the youngest, would naturally live with her and share the benefits. And in the end you'd hope to fall heir to it all, by skillful management. Pretty sharp, Benny! I see you have an eye for business."

"I'm willing to go to the end of the earth and never set foot in the house again or get a cent," Ben exclaimed indignantly, "if Mother can have a place of her own to live in comfort while she lives."

"Hold on, my dear boy! Who said she wasn't going to live in comfort? I believe we all have comfortable homes, and it will be much more sensible for her to live among us than try to keep house and take care of this place. Women always let property run down. It will only be a trouble."

After much talk and some bickerings, it was arranged that Mother had better not try to keep house but would spend a year or two at a time around among them all.

"A year or two in a place," burst out Benjamin again. "The idea of Mother running about like that, begging to be taken in, no place she can call home—it's too bad! This place is hers, she helped earn it, and Father meant for her to have it all. I heard him say so."

"Really, Benjie!" Mrs. Sinclair said. "You're getting excited. Mother doesn't care for the property. It would only be a trouble to her. She'll live much more easily with us. You should see we propose to be quite generous with Mother. Of course the interest of her share won't pay her board anywhere else. But we'll take turns in keeping her for that, besides making her presents of clothing."

"Keep her!" Ben groaned.

"Perhaps Benny proposes to set up housekeeping on his own soon," said John. "Then Mother will have a royal place to go to—and stay, no doubt."

"By the way, my dear young brother, do you think it quite the thing for you to come around finding fault with us who propose to bear all the burdens ourselves, knowing you haven't a cent to give toward it?"

The young man restrained the bitter answer rising to his lips, for his father's mild eye looked into his from the photograph on the wall. He made a firm resolve, though, as he walked sadly away, that the one purpose of his life would be to make a home for his mother, and he would never say "burden" either.

Dear old Mrs. Kensett was so smitten, so amazed to find her other self had gone—where she couldn't follow—that for days it seemed as if she sat waiting, expecting the summons to go herself.

"Surely Ephraim would send for me," she thought in her sorrow and bewilderment. It mattered little to her, then, how or where she lived. All places were alike, since he wasn't in any of them, and she mechanically assented to any proposal that was made her. She did cry out as one hurt, however, when John proposed an auction for the sale of household effects.

"Oh, I can't," she moaned. "Your father made some of that furniture with his own hands."

But the worldly wise son, who'd outgrown "foolish sentimentality," overruled her. It all went—the cradle in which they rocked, the old clock, the table they surrounded so many years. The rage for the antique hadn't yet shown itself, or John's wife and Maria would have secured some of the old-fashioned furniture. As it was, they couldn't think of having their houses encumbered by it. The other two daughters weren't well-to-do and prized money more than mementos. Benjamin protested most earnestly at this sacrilegious disposal of the dear home things. He could do only little himself, as he was still pursuing his law studies, though he did bid on his father's armchair and a few other cherished articles.

John touched him on the shoulder and said, "Ben, are you crazy? What in the world will you do with a lot of old furniture?"

"You'll see," said Ben quickly.

If John could have seen his brother's next proceeding, he would certainl have pronounced him a hopeless lunatic. He took the sum that fell to him and placed it in the bank to his mother's credit.

"The interest money won't amount to much, Mother," he said as he handed her the certificate of deposit. "But I'll enjoy thinking that if you want some little thing you can get it without asking anybody."

Mrs. Sinclair was a woman who lived for society. She had long ago cast aside as puritanical the wholesome restraints that had governed her girlhood. What with parties, operas and theaters, she was a very busy woman. Her young family was much neglected, and she was only too glad to transfer to her old mother what little care she did give them. The restful days were gone. One would have supposed Mrs. Sinclair had engaged, in her mother, a maid and seamstress.

"It's so nice," she told her friends. "Mother takes the entire charge of them and relieves me. Children are such a responsibility."

It was news to her friends that she was an anxious burdened mother.

It was hard for Mrs. Kensett to take up her life at the beginning again, to be confined day after day in a close room with noisy, fretful children, to go through the round of storytelling, tying shoes, mending tops and dolls, and minister to the thousand small wants and worries of undisciplined childhood. She'd gone through all that; those chapters of her life she had considered finished and sealed up.

No occupation in this world is more trying to soul and body than the care of young children. What patience and wisdom, skill and unlimited love it calls for. God gave the work to mothers and furnished them for it, and they cannot shirk it and be guiltless.

When there was a heavy press of work in the house, calling for all the forces, it wasn't unusual for the baby, too, to be bundled into Grandma's room and left for hours. This worked very well while all were in good humor, for Grandma loved children. But sometimes the baby writhed and fretted with aching teeth and wouldn't be comforted, and Master Freddy resented the least correction by vigorous kicks from his stout little boots, and Miss Maude lisped, "I shan't! You ain't my mama!" What wonder that Grandma, absorbed as she was by sad memories, should lose her patience, too, and speak the sharp word that didn't mend matters, while she sighed in spirit for the days that wouldn't come back again.

The daughter remembered, too, that her mother was cunning with her needle. How convenient it became to send the mending basket to her room, "just for some work to pass the time away." And in time numberless little garments were sent there, too, with aprons and dresses, and she sat and stitched from morning till night when she wasn't tending the baby. Nobody suggested a ride or a walk for her or invited her downstairs to while away an evening when there was company.

"Mother isn't used to it," Maria said. "Besides, she can't hear half of what

456—Grace Livingston Hill, Collection No. 4

is said. She enjoys herself better alone. I suppose all old people do."

This course of reasoning seemed to soothe Mrs. Sinclair's conscience when it proved troublesome. But in truth she wouldn't have enjoyed introducing her plain-looking mother to her fashionable friends. "So old style," she was sure they'd say. The old women she was accustomed to meet wore trails and puffs and dress caps. She might have searched for a long time, though, to find another old face of such sweet placid dignity as her mother's.

Life in the crowded city was so new and strange and dismal. How the mother longed amid its dust and smoke for the sweet air of Hawthorn, for a sprig of lilac or a June rose from the garden. Once in a rare while she succeeded in getting to church. It was a difficult thing to bring about, though. When nothing happened to prevent it, the carriage was driven there. But apparently in that family there were more hindrances to churchgoing than to any other sort of going.

Now that spring had come again, Mrs. Kensett looked forward to a change of her home with pleasure. She wanted to get into the country once more, and Martha, the second daughter, had married a farmer and lived in the country. It was a long distance from Hawthorn, and she hadn't visited her daughter since her marriage.

The pleasant home among trees and flowers and greenness she had pictured wasn't there. Instead, a bare frame house stood on a side hill without a tree or vine. There wasn't time to enjoy them if they had been there. The long hot days were filled up with work—endless milking and baking and churning. And the unselfish mother put in her waning strength, early and late, and did what she could to lighten the burden that was making her daughter prematurely old.

Then the dismal winter settled down upon them, monotonous days of sleet and snow and darkness, when nothing happened from week to week to break the dreary routine, when even the Sabbaths brought no relief.

Mrs. Kensett had always been an untiring churchgoer. Rain or shine, she was in her place. Her son-in-law wasn't a Christian and always had an excellent excuse for remaining at home. In the summer the horses were tired, or it was too hot. In the winter it was too cold or too something. Many a dreary Sabbath the sad mother sat at her chamber window and watched the rain come down in a slow, straight drizzle, repeating to herself rather than singing as she rocked back and forth,

> How lovely is Thy dwelling place,
>   O Lord of hosts, to me!
> The tabernacles of Thy grace.
>   How pleasant, Lord, they be!

My thirsty soul longs vehemently,
    Yea, faints Thy courts to see;
My very heart and flesh cry out,
    O living God, for Thee.

She was longing meanwhile with intense desire to sit once again in the old pew and hear the familiar tones of her pastor's voice in that faraway, pleasant village that used to be her home. Now she had no home, wandering from house to house, and yet she wasn't a murmurer; her faith and love didn't falter.

In due course of time she went on her pilgrim way and tarried for a time at daughter Hannah's, a good-natured soul who loved her mother and welcomed her to such as she had. But she lived in a small house with a large flock of children, undisciplined, rough and noisy. In the full little house there seemed to be no quiet corner for retreat, and Grandma often moaned in the words of one of her dear psalms:

O that I like a dove had wings,
    Said I, then would I flee,
Far hence that I might find a place
    Where I in rest might be.

"After all, I need all this," the old saint would say to herself. "It's part of my dear Lord's schooling. I was having too nice a time, with Ephraim and me all alone. I daresay I got out of the way, and He had to bring me back. He sent me all that peaceful, comfortable time. I was very glad to have His will done when it was according to my notion. This is His will all the same, and won't I be willing to take what He sends? He's only getting me ready," she assured herself, then found comfort in another song.

Soon the delightful day will come,
When my dear Lord will call me home,
    And I shall see His face.

Although the house was small and the children noisy, this persecuted grandmother of many homes found herself dreading to leave it and find a new home with her eldest son. John's wife had always been an uncomfortable sort of person to her. She had dreaded her not frequent visits to their home. Both were glad when they were over. Twenty years had passed since his marriage, and she never seemed to get any closer to his wife. Now that the time had come to go and live with them, she shrank from it and postponed it for weeks. But John was inflexible. He was an upright man and bound to do his part in sharing burden of his mother's maintenance.

Mrs. John Kensett was one of those icy women with thin lips and cold gray eyes, made up from the first without a heart—one of those women who make a cool atmosphere about them even in the heat of summer. She was tall and stylish and handsomely dressed, and when she perched her gold eyeglasses on her nose and severely looked one over through them, she was formidable indeed to such a meek woman as her mother-in-law.

She must have married John Kensett because an establishment is more complete with a man at the head of it. For that was the chief end of her life: to keep all things in perfect running order in that elegantly appointed home and to keep abreast of the times in all new adornments and furnishings under the sun. One Scripture admonition, at least, she gave heed to: she looked well to the ways of her household. One might explore from garret to cellar in that house and find nothing out of place, nothing soiled, nothing left undone that should have been done.

She was, besides, a rigid economist in small things. Everything was kept under lock and key and doled out in very small quantities to the servants. Her table could never merit the charge of being vulgarly loaded. The furnace heat was never allowed to run above a certain mark on the thermometer, no matter who shivered, and she had doubtless walked miles in turning gas jets to just the right point.

In this most elegant, precise, immaculate house, where everything and everybody were controlled by certain unvarying and inflexible rules, the old mother felt almost as straitened as she ever had in the small topsy-turvy one.

Her room was scarcely above shivering point, and the back windows overlooked no cheerful prospect. Here day after day she sat alone. She had food and shelter and clothes. What more could old people possibly want?

At mealtimes her son was silent and abstracted or absorbed in his newspaper. If anybody had told him his old mother's heart was nearly breaking for lack of loving sympathy, he would have been astonished. The faded eyes often grew dim with tears as she looked at him—the frigid, unbending man—and remembered him as he was in those first years of her married life—darling little Johnnie in white garments and long curls, running after butterflies and picking flowers. If only he would kiss her once more or do something to make her sure he was Johnnie—she was hungry for a tender word from him.

Ah! If mothers could see down the years that stretch ahead, it wouldn't always be so hard to lay the little lisping ones under the ground. Was it decreed that most mothers shall be in sympathy with that other one, of whom it is written, "A sword shall pierce thine own heart also?"

We shall never know about the wounds from those dear, self-sacrificing mothers. But they're there, even though they may strive to hide them and find excuses for the cold neglect, the indifference to their comfort, the impatience and the putting them to one side as if to say, "What is all this to you? It's time you were dead."

"John is busy," she'd say, as she mounted the stairs to her lonely room, and he buttoned his coat and hastened away to business without a good-bye or a good night.

Then she'd draw out her knitting and knit on, often through tear-blinded eyes. Sometimes she didn't hear a remark the first time and would ask to have it repeated. But the manifest impatience with which it was done always sent a pang like a sword thrust. And the dear mother would cover the wound and think within herself, "I know it's a great trouble to talk to deaf people. I should keep still."

Strange that these stabs come not only from the lost sheep of the family, but from the son who is the honored citizen, from the daughter who shines in her circle as a woman of many virtues, from grandchildren trained up in the Sabbath school.

"Into each life some sunshine must fall, as well as rain." And Mrs. Kensett had much of hers from Benjie's letters. They were regular as the dew and cheery as the sun, a balm for the wounds in the poor heart. They weren't mere scribbles either. "I'm well, and I hope you are; I haven't time to write more now." But they were good long letters, with accounts of all his comings and goings, the people he met, the books he read, here a dash of fun and there a poetical fancy. And through them all, like a golden thread, ran the dear boy's tender love and reverence for his mother.

Never did a maiden watch for love's missive with more ardor. Sometimes he wrote one day, sometimes another, but always once a week, and Mrs. Kensett kept a sharp lookout for the postman. When the time drew near for him to come, she made many journeys down the stairs to see if she could get a glimpse of him. When the expected letter wasn't forthcoming, she felt somehow as if the postman were to blame.

But when it did come—ah, that was the one bright day of the week! How she read and reread it and put it in her pocket and thought it over, while she went on with her knitting. Then when some little point wasn't quite distinct in her mind, she brought it out and read it again, so that by the time another one came this one was worn out.

John's wife thought to regulate this one small pleasant excitement of her mother-in-law's life by remarking to her husband that "somebody ought to tell Benjamin to write on a particular day—Mother was so fidgety when it was time for the mail."

How small a thing is a letter to make one happy! And yet some of us let the sword pierce the dear mother's heart by withholding that which costs us so little. God pity us when our mothers are gone beyond the reach of voice or pen.

One day her letter contained news of great importance. It was read and pondered long. Benjie was going to be married! The mother didn't like the news. Somehow in all her plans for Benjie the wife hadn't come in. Now this would be the last of her comfort in him. He'd marry and settle down and probably be just like John—given up to business. He pictured out his future bride as good and lovely. Of course he thought so, but poor Mrs. Kensett could get no vision of a daughter-in-law except a tall woman with severe expression. "She's an heiress," Benjie wrote. Well, what of that? John's wife had property, too. She would likely be proud and ashamed of a plain old woman like her.

Benjamin was no fortune hunter. He was hard at work in his profession with no other ambition directly before him but to get together a humble home to which he might take his mother. He intended to surprise her as soon as his income would at all warrant it. But as John Milton fastened his eyes earnestly upon Mary Powell when he met her, knowing he had found "Mistress Milton," so Benjamin, the first Sabbath he took a class in the mission Sabbath school, found himself near neighbor to a sweet-faced young teacher. And he knew that no other face in all the world could so closely resemble the ideal picture he'd sketched of that dim, shadowy far-off person, his wife.

Marian Ledyard, too, wouldn't willingly have confessed with what a thrill of pleasure she noticed the young stranger was in his place again the following Sabbath. Nor would she have admitted how for a time she searched diligently through every assembly for that one face that had such a strange power to attract her. In no place, though, did she happen to meet him except that one, where there was no opportunity for acquaintance.

Benjamin had fully resolved to seek her out. But when he learned she was an orphan who possessed a large fortune in her own right, he was too proud to be counted one of the moths that flutter about a candle. So he made another resolve, to think no more about her. That stoical purpose wasn't easy to carry out, especially since the blue eyes were often meeting his, much to the discomfiture of their owner.

The coveted opportunity came at last. The holidays brought the annual entertainment for the children, and under the friendly boughs of the Christmas tree the acquaintance began and progressed remarkably fast. It wasn't strange either, considering that each had been in the other's thoughts constantly for the last six weeks. They walked home in the moonlight, wondering at the singular beauty that crowned the earth. Each one's telltale eyes must have revealed the secret to the other's heart for the usual preliminaries, formalities, windings and turnings of a modern courtship seemed unnecessary. The two drifted together as naturally as fleecy, white clouds in the blue sky. He forgot she was worth half a million, and what did she care that he possessed nothing but his own precious self! Didn't she have enough for both?

Marian Ledyard's riches weren't in stocks and bonds alone. She had been a mere butterfly of fashion and frivolity, absorbed in worldly pursuits. But the Lord met her, and she fell at His feet, saying, "What will You have me to do?" And as she had eagerly, unreservedly followed the world, so now she gave herself body, soul, time and wealth to the service of the Lord. And she was far more sweet and fascinating in her joyful abandonment to her blessed Master's service than she had ever been in the service of that other master. She was that rare combination of a young, wealthy, consecrated Christian.

"Now, Mother," wrote Benjamin, "just as soon as we're married, which will be very soon, you're to come to us. Marian says she remembers her own dear mother and has been lonely without her these many years."

This was no welcome news to the weary mother. If it had been dear Benjamin alone she was to live with, how she'd have hailed her deliverance—but another son's wife! How could she face her and be dependent on her? It would be her house and her money that provided everything. She'd feel like a beggar, she was sure. She could by no stretch of her imagination conceive of a son's wife to be other than a person to be dreaded. She spent many sleepless nights over it and shed tears in secret. Her triumphant faith was never more tried than now.

In some far-off day, by means of some wonderful instrument yet uncreated, our eyes may look upon our friends, separated from them by long distances, and know their comings and goings, their thoughts and motives. Being not possessed of any such power, Mother Kensett vexed her soul in one city, while in another, two young people, happy as birds, held long consultations as to which should be Mother's room and just how it should be furnished. And they ran here and there with the eagerness of children gathering moss and bits of china and all rare and pretty things for a playhouse under the trees.

Marian's ancestral home had been closed for a long time. It was a stately mansion of wide halls and towers and spacious apartments, surrounded by magnificent grounds. During the last few months it had been thoroughly remodeled and refurnished, and now the young couple, after a brief bridal tour, was fairly established in it.

One might suppose Mrs. Kensett would have felt some rising of pride, as, leaning on the arm of her youngest son, she mounted the marble steps and walked through the spacious halls and beautiful parlors of his home.

But John's home was handsome, too. The carpets were soft and rich, the chairs luxurious, and curtained windows spread their draperies about them in soft fine folds.

What of all that when hearts were frozen? Wealth to this mother meant pride, selfishness and irreligion.

She looked about her, feeling sure that a tall, elegant lady in a stiff silk train would sweep in, extend the tips of her fingers and call a servant to get her off to her room with all possible dispatch.

No one was in the parlors, and Benjamin led his mother on into the dining room, a room full of warmth and light. The tea table was already spread, with a delicate, homelike aroma of toast and tea pervading it.

A slight girlish figure in a simple dress of dark blue, with her bright hair rippling away into a knot behind, was bending over the grate toasting a piece of bread by the coals. So noiselessly had they approached that she heard no sound until they stood in front of her.

Mrs. Kensett was still looking for Benjamin's wife to appear in the shape of a cold, grim person of imposing appearance, wearing gold eyeglasses, when suddenly the toasting fork was dropped, and with a low cry of joy Marian sprang into her husband's arms. Then, without waiting for formal words of introduction, she clasped loving arms about the tired mother and nestled a rosy face close to hers and gave her warm clinging kisses, such as are reserved only for our best beloved.

"Dear Mother," she said, "I'm so glad you've come! You're cold. Sit right here." And she wheeled a large chair into the warmest corner and with her own hands removed the wraps and carried them away. "I wanted to have the toast just the right brown, so I was doing it myself," she explained, as she took up her toasting fork and went on with her work.

And the old mother sat and feasted her eyes on the pretty picture—the bright, happy face, the quick, graceful movements—as she put last little touches to the table, chatting pleasantly meanwhile, making tender inquiries about her health and her journey.

Mrs. Kensett began already to feel as if this was a dear daughter separated from her years ago and now restored. "It seemed just as if I'd been away visiting and come home again," she told someone afterward.

After tea and resting, they both went with her in merry procession to her room, carrying shawls and satchel, and waiting with the eager joy of two children to see how she liked everything. She would have been hard to suit if she hadn't liked it. The room was a large, pleasant one, with a sunny bay window, a stand of plants, a case of books and every other thing she could possibly need or desire.

Mrs. Kensett started as her eye fell on familiar objects—the claw-footed mahogany center table with antique carvings, her straight-backed old rocker and "Father's" dear armchair, both newly cushioned and otherwise brightened up. The sofa, too, of ancient pattern, that had stood in her parlor at Hawthorn for forty years, looked like an old friend in a new dress. Benjamin had ransacked all the carpet stores to find a carpet that would resemble as nearly as possible, in color and design, his mother's parlor carpet when he was a boy. He succeeded so well that his mother put on her glasses and bent nearer to make sure it wasn't that identical one.

In an out-of-the-way corner she discovered her little three-legged stand holding a tiny brass candlestick (one of her wedding presents) and the snuffers on the japanned trays. It wasn't just that the old times were brought back so vividly that made the tears come, but this one little thing showed such loving thoughtfulness for her comfort. (John's wife would never have allowed a candle in the house.)

This was Benjamin's hour of triumph and gladness. For this he'd spent years of patient labor, and now it had come in such a strange, unexpected way—and so much more than he had asked or looked for. This princely home, this precious wife and his mother abiding with them all the rest of her days—it was too much, such loving-kindness!

Marian understood. She didn't express surprise when he brought out a little worn psalmbook she had never seen.

"Sing this for me, dear, to some old tune that fits it. I wish I knew what my father sang it to when I was a boy."

"I have a book of old music here. Perhaps I can find the very one," she said. And then the pure voice soared out in the song of praise his father had loved.

> Praise God, for He is kind;
>> His mercy lasts for aye;
> Give thanks with heart and mind
>> To God of Gods always.
> For certainly
>> His mercies dure,
> Most firm and sure,
>> Eternally.

The quaint rendering—new to her—pleased her, and she sang others, closing in low, soft notes with

> The Lord's my Shepherd, I'll not want,
>> He makes me down to lie;
> In pastures green He leadeth me
>> The quiet waters by.

And the dear old mother dreamed, as a strain or two of Lenox and St. Martin's floated up to her room, that she was in the old home and "Father" was conducting family worship.

Little by little, with her coaxing ways, Marian succeeded in effecting a change in her mother-in-law's dress. One day, when everything was finished and she had her arrayed in a fine black cashmere, made according to her own ideas of simplicity, with the white hair crowned with a soft white lace cap and the same soft folds about her neck, her delight was complete.

"You dear, beautiful mother," she said, clasping the lace with a plain jet pin. "It's just delightful to fix you up. Everything sets you out so. It's better than dressing dolls. Won't Benjie be delighted?"

When Maria and John and John's wife came to visit their new sister-in-law, they were astonished beyond measure to find the mother transformed into that handsome old woman who moved about this elegant home with easy dignity as if it were her own.

This rare son and daughter never made their mother feel she was that uncomfortable third person who spoiled delightful confidences for young people. They talked freely together and with her, and she renewed her youth in their lively conversation.

When company was announced she was given to retiring in haste from the room, just as she had at Maria's and John's. But Marian stopped that with "Please do stay, Mother, and help us entertain them. Besides, I want you in that corner with your bright knitting to make our rooms picturesque. You're the greatest ornament they contain."

Then the old woman would say, "Pooh! You don't want an old body like me." And she was pleased that she was wanted and would remain, occasionally throwing in her quaint remark, adding zest to the conversation.

If an old woman could be easily spoiled, Mrs. Kensett was in danger. These two fond children were continually bringing gifts to her—flowers, choice fruit, new books—wherever they went, they remembered her.

It was an altogether new and delightful life she had entered upon. With Marian she visited charitable institutions, dispensed bounties, read the Bible to the sick and poor and ministered comfort to many distressed souls. They attended wonderful meetings and sat in heavenly places, and Marian and she enjoyed each other, quite as much as they did everything else.

The tie that united them wasn't Benjamin alone. Each recognized in the other the lineaments of the Lord they loved, and their sympathies flowed together as if half a century didn't stretch between them. Is there any other influence known that levels all differences and brings souls so near together as this strange personal love for Christ? They talked and read together. They were dear, confidential friends—such conversation is rarely found between mother and daughter.

The following summer, they all took up their abode in Hawthorn, in the old home Marian had purchased and refitted for a summer residence, and Mrs. Kensett trained again the vines in her garden. Her cup was full—especially in the old church when she joined her voice to the great congregation and sang her joy and thanks in the sweet psalm.

O thou my soul, bless God the Lord;
    And all that in me is,
Be stirred up, His holy name
    To magnify and bless.
Bless, O my soul, the Lord thy God,
    And not forgetful be
Of all His gracious benefits.